EINSTEIN
The Life and Times

"A remarkable feat . . . Read the book. It is well worth it."

—C. P. Snow in *Life* Magazine

"A perceptive and painstakingly researched book that captures in great measure and in lucid detail the essence of Einstein as scientist, human being and conscience of the nuclear world which his genius helped bring into being."

—*Publishers' Weekly*

"Achieves the stature of Greek drama."

—*The New York Times*

A NOTE ON THE AUTHOR

RONALD W. CLARK spent three years writing and researching *Einstein: The Life and Times*, traveling across Switzerland, Germany, France, Belgium, the Netherlands, Britain, the United States, and Canada, sifting through the Einstein archives at Princeton, Zurich, and Ulm. His previous books cover a wide range of subjects from eminent Englishmen *(The Huxley's, JBS, Tizard)*, to wartime science *(The Rise of the Boffins, The Birth of the Bomb)*, to mountain climbing *(The Victorian Mountaineers, The Day the Rope Broke)*.

Born in London, Mr. Clark and his wife still make their home there, escaping whenever possible to a remote cottage on the Avebury near the lonely Wiltshire chalk downs.

EINSTEIN
The Life and Times

Ronald W. Clark

AVON
PUBLISHERS OF BARD, CAMELOT, DISCUS, EQUINOX AND FLARE BOOKS

The author and publisher gratefully acknowledge permission to quote from the following works:

The Questioners by Barbara Lovett Cline, copyright © 1965 by Barbara Lovett Cline, reprinted by permission of the publishers, Thomas Y. Crowell Company, New York.

Einstein: His Life and Times, by Philipp Frank, translated by George Rosen, copyright © 1947, 1953 by Alfred A. Knopf, Inc. Reprinted by permission of the publisher.

The Letters of Sigmund Freud, Selected and edited by Ernst L. Freud, Translated by James and Tania Stern, © 1960 by Sigmund Freud Copyrights, Ltd., Basic Books, Inc., Publishers, New York.

"An Interview with Einstein," by I. Bernard Cohen, copyright © 1955 by Scientific American, Inc. All rights reserved. Reprinted by permission.

The Relativity Theory Simplified and the Formative Period of Its Inventor, by Max Talmey, published 1932, used with permission of McGraw-Hill Book Company.

AVON BOOKS
A division of
The Hearst Corporation
959 Eighth Avenue
New York, New York 10019

Published by arrangement with World Publishing Company

First Avon Printing, December, 1972
Fourth Printing

Printed in the U.S.A.

"I have little patience with scientists who take a board of wood, look for its thinnest part, and drill a great number of holes where drilling is easy."

Albert Einstein (quoted by Philipp Frank in "Einstein's Philosophy of Science," **Reviews of Modern Physics,** Vol. 21, No. 3, July 1949)

CONTENTS

Foreword 9

Acknowledgments 13

PART ONE THE MAKING OF A MISSION

Chapter 1. German Boy 19
Chapter 2. Stateless Person 44
Chapter 3. Swiss Civil Servant 72

PART TWO THE VOYAGE OF DISCOVERY

Chapter 4. Einstein's Relativity 101
Chapter 5. Fruits of Success 138
Chapter 6. Moves Up the Ladder 168
Chapter 7. A Jew in Berlin 210
Chapter 8. The Sensorium of God 251
Chapter 9. The Fabric of the Universe 272

PART THREE THE HINGE OF FATE

Chapter 10. The New Messiah 295
Chapter 11. Ambassador-at-Large 330

PART FOUR THE EINSTEIN AGE

Chapter 12. Unter den Linden 377
Chapter 13. The Call of Peace 427
Chapter 14. The Call of Zion 455
Chapter 15. Preparing for the Storm 491
Chapter 16. Good-bye to Berlin 550
Chapter 17. Shopping for Einstein 564
Chapter 18. Of No Address 588

PART FIVE THE ILLUSTRIOUS IMMIGRANT

Chapter 19. Living with the Legend 619
Chapter 20. Einstein, the Bomb, and the Board of Ordnance 659
Chapter 21. The Conscience of the World 711
Chapter 22. Two Stars at the End of the Rocket 735

Sources and Bibliography 765

Notes and Index 785

FOREWORD

The story of Albert Einstein, scientist, philosopher, and contemporary conscience, with all its impact and influence, would fit better within the walls of a library than between the covers of a single book. For Einstein was far more than the scientist who confidently claimed that space and time were not what everybody thought, including the most sophisticated heirs of Newton, and who shrugged it off when he was found to be right. In his technical language, the universe was four-dimensional, while fallible human beings thought they had a right to no more than three. He passionately indulged in pacifism, and as passionately indulged out when Hitler began to show that he really meant what he said about the Jews and the master-race. Throughout it all he stuck to the job in hand, determined to squeeze the next secret from Nature.

The different facets of Einstein's life and work will long continue to be explored. Deeper and deeper theses on ever smaller aspects of his science will continue to be written. The impact of his support for pacifism between the two world wars will one day get the detailed and possibly disillusioning analysis it warrants; so will the result of that honest enthusiasm for Zionism which for long led him to believe that the promised land could be reached without force of arms. In theology he is likely to remain something of an enigma, even among those who do not take his cosmic religion too seriously. As a peg on which to hang an argument on science and government, he is less useful than might be expected; even so, the real relevance of his famous letter to Roosevelt in 1939, and of his lesser-known actions in the winter of 1944, provide the substance of more than one might-have-been which could be explored in detail. Einstein the philosopher is certain to get even more critical study as the deeper implications of his work continue to be investigated. And few can read his correspondence—whose publication is long overdue—without feeling that Einstein's wit is worth a slim volume on its own. All this will come one day.

But something more than these specialist portraits, each with Einstein at the center of a technical argument, emerges from digging hard into the documents, and from a critical appraisal of the myth and reminiscence which have grown around his memory in the last two or three decades. It is the picture of a man who can, without exaggeration, be called one of the great tragic figures of our time. It is the picture of a man who while still young abandoned, with all the passion of the convinced monastic, much of what life had to offer—and who was shot back into the struggle by the unobliging stumble of history. Thus the youth who relinquished his nationality at the age of 17 returned to the fold later; opted out of German nationality a second time in middle life; and even in old age, when reconciliation had become respectable, refused to return to "the land of the mass murderers." The dedicated pacifist, who after his change of stance was reviled for his apostasy, believed himself to be among those who pressed the buttons which destroyed Hiroshima and Nagasaki. The Zionist who put peace with the Arabs as a first essential was forced finally to agree that it was necessary to fight. In science the greatest physicist in three centuries, or possibly of all time, found himself after middle age pushed by the advance of quantum theory into a backwater, "a genuine old museum-piece" as he described himself.

These ironies not only gave Einstein's life a great personal poignancy; they also combined to keep him in the glare of the public limelight, first switched on with such spectacular results in 1919 when, in Whitehead's words, "a great adventure in thought had at length come safe to shore." In this glare, the human figure has tended to be enlarged into the Delphic oracle. The aureole of white hair helped. So did the great luminous eyes. So did the brave stand which Einstein made for civic and academic freedoms. After his death, all this encouraged a biographical molly-coddling which was less than his genius deserved. It also tended to encourage the belief that, as he once put it, all men dance to the tune of an invisible piper. This is not so. "Wherever a system is really complicated, as in the brain or in an organized community," Sir George Thomson has said, "indeterminacy comes in, not necessarily because of *h* [Planck's constant] but because to make a prediction so *many* things must be known that the stray consequences of studying them will disturb the *status quo,* which can never therefore be discovered. History is not and cannot be determinate. The supposed causes only *may* produce the consequences we expect."*

This has rarely been more true than of Albert Einstein, whose thought and action in science and life became interrelated in a way no dramatist would dare to conceive. His extraordinary story has itself some quality of the indeterminacy which in physics he was so reluctant to accept. He would not have liked it. But he would have appreciated the situation. He might even have laughed about it.

RONALD W. CLARK

New York
March 1971

*From a letter to the author from Sir George Thomson, February 16, 1970.

ACKNOWLEDGMENTS

I wish to thank Dr. Otto Nathan, Einstein's literary executor, for permission to quote hitherto unpublished letters and other copyrighted material. I am also especially grateful to Miss Helen Dukas, Einstein's secretary for more than twenty-five years, for her generous and unstinting help in studying the material in the Einstein Archive at Princeton. Neither will agree with all that I have written; indeed, if two devoted colleagues and an impartial biographer were to take the same view all the time, there would be something wrong somewhere. I alone am responsible for the facts put down and the opinions expressed.

I also wish to thank: Dr. Jagdish Mehra of the University of Texas at Austin, Texas, for reading the manuscript; and Professor Norman Bentwich, Josef Fraenkel, Professor N. Kemmer, Professor Sir Bernard Lovell, Dr. R. E. W. Maddison, Professor C. W. McCombie, Dr. David Mitrany, Heinz Norden, Dr. Peter Plesch, Sir George Thomson, and Lancelot Law Whyte for reading portions of the manuscript. A very large number of people in the United States, Europe, and the Middle East have been generous in providing documents and reminiscences. It is unfortunately impossible to name them all, but I would particularly like to thank the following, while reiterating that, throughout the book, any opinions expressed, and the responsibility for the facts given, are entirely my own:

Walter Adams, Director, The London School of Economics and Political Science; Professor Aage Bohr; Dr. Vannevar Bush; Dr. C. H. Collie; Professor A. Vibert Douglas; Eidg. Amt für geistiges Eigentum, Berne; Dr. H. A. Einstein; Churchill Eisenhart; Dr. Elizabeth Eppler, Institute of Jewish Affairs; Professor I. Estermann; Mme. M. Fawtier, UNESCO; Frau Kate Freundlich; Professor

Dennis Gabor; Mrs. Barbara Gamow; Dr. Judith R. Goodstein, California Institute of Technology; Dr. Max Gottschalk; Kurt R. Grossmann; Sir Roy Harrod; Drs. J. van Herwaarden, Rijksuniversiteit te Utrecht, Universiteitsmuseum, Utrecht; Dr. Max J. Herzberger; Richard G. Hewlett, Chief Historian, U. S. Atomic Energy Commission; Professor Banesh Hoffmann; Alvin E. Jaeggli, Eidg. Technische Hochschule Bibliothek, Zurich; Bernard Jaffe; Miss Suzanne Christine Kennedy, Nuffield College, Oxford; Oscar Kocherthaler; Professor C. Lanczos, Dublin Institute for Advanced Studies; Dr. W. Lanzer, Verein für Geschichte der Arbeiterbewegung, Vienna; Colonel Charles A. Lindbergh; Dr. Jacob R. Marcus, American Jewish Archives; Julian L. Meltzer, the Weizmann Archives; Professor Ashley Montagu; Mrs. B. Mulholland; Dr. John N. Nagy; Professor Linus Pauling; Professor J. Pelseneer, Université Libre de Bruxelles; Y. Perotin, League of Nations Archives, Geneva; Dr. Peter Plesch; Professor William Ready, McMaster University, Hamilton, Ontario; Professor Nathan Rosen; Professor Leonora Cohen Rosenfield; Professor J. Rotblat; Dr. Alexander Sachs; Mrs. Esther Salaman; Mrs. Alice Kimball Smith; Drs. P. van der Star, Rijksmuseum voor de Geschiedenis der Natuurwetenschnappen, Leiden; Dr. Gertrud Weiss Szilard; U. S. Department of the Navy; U. S. National Archives and Records Service; E. Vandewoude, Cabinet du Roi, Bruxelles; Dr. Charles Weiner and Mrs. Joan Warnow of the American Institute of Physics, for their help and guidance in the use of materials in the Niels Bohr Library for History and Philosophy of Physics; Jeremy Weston, The Royal Institution; Dr. G. J. Whitrow; Professor Eugene P. Wigner; E. T. Williams, The Rhodes Trust.

Finally, I wish to thank the large number of Jewish organizations in the United States, Britain, Israel, and elsewhere who have helped to resolve specific problems; the numerous German bodies who have supplied information on the question of Einstein's nationality; the librarians and archivists of the university and other sources listed in the section on references who have helped to make my work less arduous; and the following for permission to quote copyrighted material:

Algemeen Rijksarchief, The Hague (H. A. Lorentz correspondence); American Journal of Physics (R. S.

Shankland's "Conversations with Albert Einstein"); His Majesty King Baudouin of the Belgians (letter to Einstein from His Majesty King Albert of the Belgians); Professor Aage Bohr (letters of Professor Niels Bohr); Burndy Library (Ehrenhaft manuscript); The California Institute of Technology Archives, Pasadena (quotations from the Hale and Millikan Papers); Cambridge University Press (Lord Rayleigh's *The Life of Sir J. J. Thomson*; Einstein and Infeld's *The Evolution of Physics*; Hermann Bondi's *Assumption and Myth in Physical Theory*; Sir James Jeans' *The New Background of Science*); Jonathan Cape Ltd. and Alfred Knopf (Phillipp Frank's *Einstein*); Columbia University (1912 correspondence with Einstein); Thomas Y. Crowell Co. (*The Questioners*, by Barbara Lovett Cline); Deutsche Verlags-amstalt Stuttgart, and Dr. H. Tramer (Blumenfeld's *Erlebte Judenfrage*); Miss Margot Einstein (letters of Mrs. Albert Einstein); Eyre & Spottiswoode (Publishers) Ltd. (Anton Reiser's *Albert Einstein: A Biographical Portrait*); Professor Peter Fowler (letter of Ernest Rutherford); Sigmund Freud Copyrights, Basic Books and Hogarth Press Ltd. (*Letters of Sigmund Freud: 1873–1939*); Frau Kate Freundlich (Freundlich correspondence); Victor Gollancz Ltd. (Leopold Infeld's *Quest: The Evolution of a Scientist*); Institute for Advanced Study (letters of Dr. Frank Aydelotte and Dr. Abraham Flexner); Lady Jeans (Sir James Jeans' letter); Martin J. Klein (*Paul Ehrenfest*); Mrs. Henry R. Labouisse (correspondence of Madame Curie); Dr. Wanda Lanzer (Adler correspondence); the executors of the late Lord Cherwell (Lord Cherwell's correspondence); McGraw-Hill Book Company (Max Talmey's *The Relativity Theory Simplified*); Mrs. B. Mulholland (Commander Locker-Lampson's letters); North Holland Publishing Company and Dr. Abraham Pais (*Niels Bohr*, ed. L. Rosenfeld); North Holland Publishing Company (*Niels Bohr: An Essay*, by L. Rosenfeld); Oxford University Press (Robert Oppenheimer's *The Flying Trapeze: Three Crises for Physicists*, the Whidden Lectures, 1962); Dr. Peter Plesch (*Janos*, by John Plesch); *Punch* (for poem, "Einstein and Epstein Are Wonderful Men . . ."); Dr. Nesca Robb (Dr. A. A. Robb's poem); Mme Romain Rolland and Editions Albin Michel (Romain Rolland's *Journal des Années de Guerre 1914–1918*); Professor Peggie Sampson (R. A.

Sampson's letter); The Hon. Godfrey Samuel and The House of Lords (Samuel material); Charles Scribner's Sons (Harlow Shapley's *Through Rugged Ways to the Stars*); *The Scientific American* ("An Interview with Albert Einstein," by I. Bernard Cohen); Raglan Squire (Sir John Squire's answer to Pope's epitaph on Sir Isaac Newton); Staples Press and Miss Joyce Weiner (Carl Seelig's *Albert Einstein*); Dr. Gertrud Weiss Szilard (Dr. Leo Szilard's letters and *Reminiscences*); The Master and Fellows of Trinity College, Cambridge (the writings of Sir Arthur Eddington); United Nations (League of Nations archival material); University Museum, Utrecht (Professor Julius correspondence); Mrs. G. W. Watters (writings of Dr. Leon L. Watters); George Weidenfeld & Nicholson Ltd. (Antonina Vallentin's *Einstein*); the Trustees of the Weizmann Archives (letters written by Chaim Weizmann).

R.W.C.

PART ONE

THE MAKING OF A MISSION

CHAPTER 1

GERMAN BOY

The life of Albert Einstein has a dramatic quality that does not rest exclusively on his theory of relativity. For the extravagant timing of history linked him with three shattering developments of the twentieth century: the rise of modern Germany, the birth of nuclear weapons, and the growth of Zionism. Their impact on his simple genius combined to drive him into a contact with the affairs of the world for which he had little taste. The result would have made him a unique historical figure even had he not radically altered man's ideas of the physical world. Yet Einstein was also something more, something very different from the Delphic, hair-haloed oracle of his later years. To the end he retained a touch of clowning humor as well as a resigned and understanding amusement at the follies of the human race. Behind the great man there lurked a perpetual glint in the eye, a fundamental irreverence for authority, and an unexpected sense of the ridiculous that could unlatch a deep belly laugh that shook the windows; together with decent moral purpose, it combined to make him a character rich in his own nonscientific right.

German by nationality, Jewish by origin, dissenting in spirit, Einstein reacted ambivalently against these three birthday gifts. He threw his German nationality overboard at the age of fifteen but twenty years later, after becoming Swiss, settled in Berlin where he remained throughout the First World War; after Germany's defeat in 1918 he took up German civic rights again, "one of the follies of my life," as he later wrote of it, only to renounce his country a second time when Hitler came to power. His position as a Jew was buttressed by his support of Zionism, yet he offended more than once by insistence that Jews were, more importantly, members of the human species. Moreover his Zionism conflicted at times with his pacifism, and to his old friend, Lord Samuel, he commented that he was, despite anti-Semitic attacks, "pas très Juif." The free thinking ideals of his youth continued into old age; yet these included a belief in the ordered and orderly nature of the universe which was by no means in conflict with the idea of a God—even though what Einstein meant by the word was peculiar to himself and a small number of others. In these and other ways, in his private and his professional life, Einstein became the great contradiction: the German who detested the Germans; the pacifist who encouraged men to arms and played a significant part in the birth of nuclear weapons; the Zionist who wished to placate the Arabs; the physicist who with his "heuristic viewpoint" of 1905 suggested that light could be both wave and particle, and who was ultimately to agree that even matter presented the same enigma. Yet Einstein himself supplied part of the answer to his own riddle. In ordinary life, as well as in the splendid mysteries of physics, absolutes were to be distrusted; events were often relative to circumstance.

He was born in Ulm, an old city on the Danube with narrow winding streets and the great cathedral on which workmen were then building the tallest spire in Europe. Lying in the foothills of the Swabian Alps, where the Blau and the Iller join the Danube, the city had in 1805 been the scene of the Austrian's defeat by Napoleon. Four years later it was ceded to Württemberg under the Treaty of Vienna. In 1842 the old fortifications were restored by German engineers, and with the creation of the new German Empire in the Hall of Mirrors in 1870, Prussian discipline began to reach down from the north German plains towards the free-and-easy Swabians of whom the Einsteins were commonplace examples.

They came from Buchau, a small town between Lake Constance and Ulm, comfortable and complacent on the Federnsee, a minor marsh of prehistoric interest whose story is admirably told in the fine new Federnsee Museum and whose shores are today thronged with weekend tourists. Since 1577 the Jews had formed a distinguished and respectable community in the area. They prospered down the centuries; they hung on, despite the burning of the synagogue in 1938 and all that followed it, until 1968. Only then could the local papers report: "Death of the Last Jew in Buchau." His name was Siegbert Einstein, a relative, many times removed, of the most famous Jew in modern history.

Industrious and mildy prosperous, the Einsteins had lived in Buchau at least since the 1750s according to the six family registers kept by the Jewish authorities. By the middle of the nineteenth century they were numerous, and eleven of that name are shown on the roll of those who subscribed to the new synagogue in 1839. Albert Einstein's great-grandfather had been born in the town in 1759, and the Jewish registers record his marriage to Rebekka Obernauer, the birth of their son Abraham in 1808, and Abraham's marriage to Helene Moos. Their son Hermann, the father of Einstein, was born in Buchau on August 30, 1847. Nineteen years later Abraham and his family moved to Ulm, thirty miles to the north, and in 1876 Hermann married Pauline Koch, born in Cannstadt, only a few miles away, and eleven years his junior.

Like the Einsteins, the Kochs had been part of the Württemberg Jewish community for more than a century, a family with roots rather more to the north—in Goppingen, Jebenhausen, and Cannstadt. Like her husband, Pauline Koch spoke the soft Swabian dialect, hallmark of an ancient duchy that had once spread from Franconia to Switzerland, from Burgundy to Bavaria, and whose inhabitants lacked both the discipline of Prussia and the coarseness of Bavaria.

Although Einstein was not of peasant stock, he came from people almost as close to the earth, and his reactions were often those of the man tied to the hard facts of life by the seasons. His second wife's scathing "My husband mystical!" may not be literally justified, but it illustrates the difference which has grown through the years between the unreservedly philosophical Einstein whom many of his admirers would like him to have been and the more practical man he very often was. Absent-minded scientist, of course; that was real and not sham. Einstein never played to the gallery, although more aware of its existence than is sometimes imagined; but, more than most men, he was absent-minded only about things that didn't matter; or when he knew there was someone to remember for him.

The differences between his parents, a devoted, cheerful couple who faced the results of the husband's happy-go-lucky character with resignation, were largely those of emphasis. The picture of the father that comes through, secondhand, from a grandson he never knew, is of a jovial, hopeful man. This fits the description which Einstein himself presented to his friend Philipp Frank, who wrote of Hermann: "His mode of life and his *Weltanschauung* differed in no respect from those of the average citizen in that locality. When his work was done, he liked to go on outings with his family into the beautiful country round Munich, to the romantic lakes and mountains, and he was fond of stopping at the pleasant, comfortable Bavarian taverns, with their good beer, radishes, and sausages." More than half a century later Albert Einstein remembered those Sunday excursions with enjoyment, the discussions between his father and his mother as to which way they should go, and the husband's careful selection of a route which would end up where his wife wanted. "Exceedingly friendly, mild, and wise," was how he spoke of his father as he approached the age of seventy. Easygoing and unruffleable, a large optimistic man with a thick moustache who looks out from his portraits through a rimmed pince-nez with all the quiet certitude of the nineteenth century, Hermann Einstein would have thought it slightly presumptuous to have fathered a genius.

Pauline Koch, with even features and a mass of dark hair piled high above a broad forehead, brought to the union more than the comparative affluence of a woman whose father was a Stuttgart grain merchant and court purveyor. She brought also a breath of genuine culture, a love of music which was to be inextricably entwined with her son's work and, in the pursuit of her ambition for him, a touch of the ruthlessness with which he followed his star. She appears to have had a wider grasp than her husband of German literature, and while for him Schiller and Heine were an end in themselves, for her they were only a beginning. To Pauline Koch, it might well be thought, Einstein would attribute the imaginative genius which was to make him so much more than a mere scientist. He took a different view. "I have no particular talent, I am merely extremely inquisitive," he replied in later life when asked from whom he had inherited his talents. "So I think we can dispense with this question of heritage."

For a year the young Einsteins lived in Buchau. Then in 1877 they moved back to Ulm where Hermann set up, in a building on the south side of the Cathedral Square which later became the "Englander" wine tavern, a small electrical and engineering workshop financed by his more prosperous in-laws. He and his wife lived a few hundred yards away in an apartment at No. 135, city division B, an undistinguished four-story building renumbered 20 Bahnhofstrasse in 1880 and destroyed in an Allied air raid 64 years later. Below it, one of the tributaries of the river Blau flowed in a cutting beside the street, past the overjutting windows of houses that had not changed much since the fifteenth century, turning before it reached the cathedral and entered the Danube. Here, in the town whose inhabitants proudly claimed that "Ulmense sunt mathematici" (the people of Ulm are mathematicians), Albert Einstein was born on March 14, 1879.

Within a year of the birth, Hermann's small business had collapsed, a victim of his own perpetual good nature and high hopes. He now moved to Munich and with his brother Jakob opened a small electrochemical works. Thus for Einstein Ulm was merely a vestigial memory, a town from whose winding medieval streets the open country could still be seen, a town where the Jews retained their own identity yet lived at ease with the rest of the community; a smallish place through whose squares the cows with their great clanging bells were driven, and into which there drifted, on summer evenings, the scent of the forests and the surrounding hills.

The move to Munich brought the Einstein family from an almost rural environment into the capital of Bavaria, already more than a quarter of a million strong, still fresh from the architectural adornments added to it by the mad King Ludwig I at a cost of 7,000,000 thalers. Overwhelmingly Catholic, its air was heavy with the sound of bells from numerous churches: the cathedral of the archbishopric of Munich-Freising, with its unfinished towers; the Jesuit St. Michael's; the Louis, with Cornelius' fresco of the Last Judgment; and St. Mariahilf with its gorgeous glass and fine woodwork. The city was rich in art galleries, proud of its seven bridges across the Isar, and of the Königsbau built in the style of the Pitti Palace in Florence; a city still epitomizing the baroquerie of southern Germany before it bowed knee to the Prussians from the north. From its narrow alleyways and its fine arcades there was carried on one of the great art trades of Europe; from its breweries there came, each year, no less than 49,000,000 gallons of which 37,000,000 were drunk in the city itself.

In the University of Munich there had begun to work in 1880 a man whose influence on Einstein was to be continuous, critical, and, in the final assessment, enigmatic. This was Max Karl Ernst Ludwig Planck, then aged twenty-two, the latest in a long line of "excellent, reliable, incorruptible, idealistic, and generous men, devoted to the service of Church and State." Born in Kiel while the port was still part of Danish Schleswig-Holstein, aged eight at the time of Prussia's conquest of the province, Max Planck was born into a professional German family which moved south to Munich the following year. Later he studied at the university before going north to Berlin. Then, dedicated to the task of discovering how nature worked, Planck returned to Munich where he served as a *privatdozent* for five years; as he walked daily to the university the young private tutor may have brushed shoulders with a boy whose life was to be intimately linked with his own. For two decades later Einstein was to provide a revolutionary development to Planck's own quantum theory. Another decade on, and Planck was to attract Einstein from the Switzerland he loved to the Germany which he detested. Planck was to encourage him into becoming a German citizen for the second time and, more than once during the 1920s, to dissuade him from leaving the Fatherland. In these, and in other ways, the two men's lives were to be ironically linked in a way which reads like nature aping art.

The first Einstein home in Munich was a small rented house. After five years the family business had prospered sufficiently for a move to be made to a larger home in the suburb of Sendling. This was surrounded by big trees and a rambling garden, usually unkempt, which separated it from the main road. Only a short distance away were buildings soon converted into a small factory for manufacture of electrical equipment. Here Hermann attended to the business while brother Jakob, with more technical knowledge, ran the works.

A year after the family's arrival in Munich, Albert's sister Maja was born. Only two years younger, she was to become constant companion and unfailing confidant. Himself unconcerned with death, he faced the loss of two wives with equanimity; but the death of his sister, at the age of seventy, dented the hard defensive shell he had built round his personal feelings.

In one way the Einsteins failed to fit any of the convenient slots of their history and environment. In a predominantly Catholic community—eighty-four percent in Munich—they were not merely Jews, but Jews who had fallen away. Many deep-grained Jewish characteristics remained, it is true. The tradition of the close-knit intermarrying community is well brought out in the family trees, and Einstein himself was to add to it when, after divorce, he married a double cousin. The deep respect for learning which the Jew shares with the Celt ran in the very marrow of the family. And Einstein was to become but one more witness to the prominent part that Jews have played in the revolutionary developments of science—from Jacques Loeb in physiology to Levi-Civita and Minkowski in mathematics, Paul Ehrenfest in the quantum theory, Haber in chemistry, and Lise Meitner, Leo Szilard, and many others in nuclear physics. Thus he belonged to a group whose loyalties crossed frontiers and oceans, known by its members to be steadfastly self-succoring and claimed by its enemies to operate an international conspiracy.

Despite this, the essential Jewish root of the matter was lacking: the family did not attend the local synagogue. It did not deny itself bacon or ham, nor certain seafoods. It did not demand that animals must be slaughtered according to ritual and did not forbid the eating of meat and dairy products together. All this was to Hermann Einstein but "an ancient superstition" and equally so were the other customs and traditions of the Jewish faith. There was also in the family one particularly hard-bitten agnostic uncle, and Einstein used him as peg for the old Jewish joke. He would always describe with relish how he had surprised him one day in full formal dress preparing to go to the synagogue. The uncle had responded to the nephew's astonishment with the warning: "Ah, but you never know."

Thus Einstein was nourished on a family tradition which had broken with authority; which disagreed, sought independence, had deliberately trodden out of line. This also, as surely as the humanitarian tradition of Jewish self-help, was to pull him the way he went, so that at times he closely resembled J. B. S. Haldane, who came to believe that authority and government itself must be bad—any government and any authority. Sent first to a Catholic elementary school apparently on the grounds that it was convenient, he was there a Jew among Christians; among Jews he was, like the members of his family, an outsider. The pattern was to repeat itself through much of his life.

The bare facts of his early years are well enough known, but an aura of mythology surrounds most of the detail. Neither his sister nor either of his wives contributed significantly to the raw material of biography and with the exception of one chapter in a little-known book written by the man who introduced Einstein to science at the age of thirteen, virtually all of it comes from Einstein himself in middle or old age when he could remember not only "with advantages" but with the hindsight of history to guide him. As he himself has written, "Every reminiscence is colored by today's being what it is, and therefore by a deceptive point of view." This alone would suggest caution; but there is also Einstein's own admission that his evidence could be faulty.

The admission, which is substantiated by Einstein's son, was made in old age after Dr. Janos Plesch, who had known Einstein at least since 1919 when he attended Pauline Einstein on her deathbed, sent him for comment the material he was incorporating in his own autobiography. "It has always struck me as singular," he wrote, "that the marvelous memory of Einstein for scientific matters does not extend to other fields. I don't believe that Einstein could forget anything that interested him scientifically, but matters relating to his childhood, his scientific beginnings, and his development are in a different category, and he rarely talks about them—not because they don't interest him but simply because he doesn't remember them well enough." Einstein agreed, commenting: "You're quite right about my bad memory for personal things. It's really quite astounding. Something for psychoanalysts—if there really are such people." Many of the reported details of Einstein's early years must therefore be believed in more as an act of faith than as the result of reliable evidence—a situation true to a lesser extent of his later life when there grew up round his activities a thick jungle of distortions, misconceptions, inventions, and simple lies. A biography with frontispiece drawing showing "Einstein at the first test of the atomic bomb"—a test of which he knew nothing at the time—is illustration rather than exception.

Nothing in Einstein's early history suggests dormant genius. Quite the contrary. The one feature of his childhood about which there appears no doubt is the lateness with which he learned to speak. Even at the age of nine he was not fluent, while reminiscences of his youth stress hesitancies and the fact that he would reply to questions only after consideration and reflection. His parents feared that he might be subnormal, and it has even been suggested that in his infancy he may have suffered from a form of dyslexia. "Leonardo da Vinci, Hans Christian Andersen, Einstein, and Niels Bohr," it is claimed by the Dyslexic Society—with understandable special pleading—"are supermen who have survived the handicap of dyslexia." Far more plausible is the simpler situation suggested by Einstein's son Hans Albert, who says that his father was withdrawn from the world even as a boy—a pupil for whom teachers held out only poor prospects. This is in line with the family legend that when Hermann Einstein asked his son's headmaster what profession his son should adopt, the answer was simply: "It doesn't matter; he'll never make a success of anything."

As remembered by Einstein in later years, this backwardness had its compensations, since it indirectly helped guide him towards the field he was to make his own. "I sometimes ask myself," he once said, "how did it come that I was the one to develop the theory of relativity. The reason, I think, is that a normal adult never stops to think about problems of space and time. These are things which he has thought of as a child. But my intellectual development was retarded, as a result of which I began to wonder about space and time only when I had already grown up.

Naturally, I could go deeper into the problem than a child with normal abilities."

His boyhood was straightforward enough. From the age of five until the age of ten he attended a Catholic school near his home, and at ten was transferred to the Luitpold Gymnasium, where the children of the middle classes had drummed into them the rudiments of Latin and Greek, of history and geography, as well as of simple mathematics. The choice of a Catholic school was not as curious as it seems. Elementary education in Bavaria was run on a denominational basis. The nearest Jewish school was some distance from the Einstein home and its fees were high. To a family of little religious feeling the dangers of Catholic orientation were outweighed by the sound general instruction which the school gave.

According to some sources he was here confronted for the first time with his Jewishness. For as an object lesson a teacher one day produced a large nail with the words: "The nails with which Christ was nailed to the cross looked like this." Almost sixty years later Einstein gave his seal to the tale: "A true story." But Frank, to whom he appears to have told it, comments that the teacher "did not add, as sometimes happens, that the Crucifixion was the work of the Jews. Nor did the idea enter the minds of the students that because of this they must change their relations with their classmate Albert." It seems likely, despite the highlight sometimes given to the incident, that none of the boys took much notice of the nail from the Crucifixion. And in later life Einstein was to repeat more than once that the fact of his Jewishness was only brought home when he arrived in Berlin a few months before the start of the First World War.

Before he left his Catholic elementary school for the very different Luitpold Gymnasium he received what appears to have been the first genuine shock to his intellectual system. The "appears" is necessary. For this was the famous incident of the pocket compass and while he confirmed that it actually happened he was also to put a gloss on its significance.

The story is simply that when the boy was five, ill in bed, his father showed him a pocket compass. What impressed the child was that since the iron needle always pointed in the same direction, whichever way the case was turned, it must be acted upon by something that existed in space—the space that had always been considered empty. The incident, so redolent of "famous childhoods," is reported persistently in the accounts of Einstein's youth that began to be printed after he achieved popular fame at the end of the First World War. Whether it always had its later significance is another matter. Einstein himself, answering questions in 1953 at the time of his seventy-fourth birthday, gave it perspective by his assessment of how it had—or might have—affected him. Did the compass, and the book on Euclidean geometry which he read a few years later, really influence him, he was asked. "I myself think so, and I believe that these outside influences had a considerable influence on my development," he replied with some caution. "But a man has little insight into what goes on within him. When a young puppy sees a compass for the first time it may have no similar influence, nor on many a child. What does, in fact, determine the particular reaction of an individual? One can postulate more or less plausible theories on this subject, but one never really finds the answer."

Soon afterwards another influence entered Einstein's life. From the age of six he began to learn the violin. The enthusiasm this evoked did not come quickly. He was taught by rote rather than inspiration, and seven years passed before he was aroused by Mozart into an awareness of the mathematical structure of music. Yet his delight in the instrument grew steadily and became a psychological safety valve; it was never quite matched by performance. In later years the violin became the hallmark of the world's most famous scientist; but Einstein's supreme and obvious enjoyment in performance was the thing. Amateur, gifted or not, remained amateur.

Hermann Einstein with his compass and Pauline Einstein with her insistence on music lessons brought two influences to bear on their son. A third was provided by his uncle Jakob, the sound engineer without whom Hermann would have foundered even faster in the sea of good intentions. Jakob Einstein is a relatively shadowy figure, and his memorial is a single anecdote, remembered over more than thirty years and recalled by Einstein to his early biographers. "Algebra is a merry science," Uncle Jakob would say. "We go hunting for a little animal whose name we don't know, so we call it *x*. When we bag our game we pounce on it and give it its right name." Uncle Jakob may or may not have played a significant part in making mathematics appear attractive, but his influence seems to have been long-lasting. In many of Einstein's later attempts to present the theory of relativity to non-mathematicians, there is recourse to something not so very different; to analogies with elevators, trains, and ships that suggest a memory of the stone house at Sendling and Uncle Jakob's "little animal whose name we don't know."

However, the Einstein family included an in-law more important than Father, Mother, or Uncle Jakob. This was Cäsar Koch, Pauline Koch's brother, who lived in Stuttgart and whose visits to the Einstein family were long remembered. "You have always been my best-loved uncle," Einstein wrote to him as a man of forty-five. "You have always been one of the few who have warmed my heart whenever I thought of you, and when I was young your visit was always a great occasion." In January, 1885, Cäsar Koch returned to Germany from Russia, where part of his family was living. With him he brought as a present for Albert a model steam engine, handed over during a visit to Munich that year, and drawn from memory by his nephew thirty years later. Soon afterwards Cäsar married and moved to Antwerp—where the young Albert was subsequently taken on a conducted tour of the Bourse. A well-to-do grain merchant, Cäsar Koch appears to have had few intellectual pretensions. But some confidence was sparked up between uncle and nephew and it was to Cäsar that Einstein was to send, as a boy of sixteen, an outline of the imaginative ideas later developed into the Special Theory of Relativity.

However, nothing so precocious appeared likely when Einstein in 1889 made his first appearance at the Luitpold Gymnasium. Still slightly backward, introspective, keeping to himself the vague stirrings of interest which he felt for the world about him, he had so far given no indication that he was in any way different from the common run of children. The next six years at the Gymnasium were to alter that, although hardly in the way his parents can have hoped.

Within the climate of the time, the Luitpold Gymnasium seems to have been no better and no worse than most establishments of its kind. It is true that it put as great a premium on a thick skin as any British public school but there is no reason to suppose that it was particularly ogreish. Behind what might be regarded as no more than normal discipline it held, in reserve, the ultimate weapon of appeal to the unquestionable Prussian god of authority. Yet boys, and even sensitive boys, have survived as much; some have even survived Eton.

The Gymnasium was to have a critical effect on Einstein in separate ways. The first was that its discipline created in him a deep suspicion of authority in general and of educational authority in particular. This feeling lasted all his life, without qualification. "The teachers in the elementary school appeared to me like sergeants and in the Gymnasium the teachers were like lieutenants," he remembered. More than forty years later, speaking to the seventy-second Convocation of the State University of New York, he noted that to him, "the worst thing seems to be for a school principally to work with methods of fear, force, and artificial authority. Such treatment destroys the healthy feelings, the integrity, and self-confidence of the pupils. All that it produces is a servile helot." And years later, replying to a young girl who had sent him a manuscript, he wrote. "Keep your manuscript for your sons and daughters, in order that they may derive consolation from it and—not give a damn for what their teachers tell them or think of them."

Not giving a damn about accepted beliefs was an attitude which certainly developed at the Gymnasium. The teaching may or may not have justified the principle, but the outcome was singularly fortunate as far as Einstein was concerned. It taught him the virtues of scepticism. It encouraged him to question and to doubt, always valuable qualities in a scientist and particularly so at this period in the history of physics. Here the advance of technology was bringing to light curious new phenomena which, however hard men might try, could not be fitted into the existing order of things. Yet innate conservatism presented a formidable barrier to discussion, let alone acceptance, of new ideas. If Einstein had not been pushed by the Luitpold Gymnasium into the stance of opposition he was to retain all his life, then he might not have questioned so quickly so many assumptions that most men took for granted, nor have arrived at such an early age at the Special Theory of Relativity.

A third effect was of a very different kind. There is no doubt that he despised educational discipline and that this in turn nourished the radical inquiring attitude that is essential to the scientist. Yet it was only years later, as he looked back from middle life to childhood, that he expressed his dislike of the Gymnasium so vehemently. Until then, according to one percipient biographer who came to know him well, "he could not even say that he hated it. According to family legend, this taciturn child, who was not given to complaining, did not even seem very miserable. Only long afterwards did he identify the tone and atmosphere of his schooldays with that of barracks, the negation, in his opinion, of the human being."

Yet by the end of the First World War this school environment had become a symbol in an equation whose validity Einstein never doubted. The Luitpold Gymnasium as he looked back on it equaled ruthless discipline, and the Luitpold Gymnasium was German. Thus the boyhood hardships became transformed into the symbol of all that was worst in the German character—a transformation that was to produce dire and ironic consequences. With the stench of Belsen still in the nostrils after twenty-five years it is easy enough to understand the near paranoia that affected Einstein when in later life he regarded his own countrymen. It is easy enough to understand his reply when, at the age of sixty-nine, he was asked: "Is there any German person towards whom you feel an estimation, and who was your very personal friend among the German-born?" "Respect for Planck," Einstein had replied. "No friendship for any real German. Max von Laue was the closest to me." All this is understandable. Yet Germans were among the first to die in the concentration camps, and it is remarkable to find in Einstein, normally the most compassionate of men, an echo of the cry that the only good German is a dead one. Thus the Luitpold Gymnasium, transmogrified by memory, has a lot to answer for; it convinced Einstein that the Prussians had been handed out a double dose of original sin. Later experiences tended to confirm the belief.

At the Gymnasium there appears to have been, as there frequently is in such schools, one master who stood apart, the odd man out going his nonconformist way. His name was Reuss. He tried to make his pupils think for themselves while most of his colleagues did little more—in Einstein's later opinion—than encourage an academic *Kadavergehorsamkeit* ("the obedience of the corpse") that was required among troops of the Imperial Prussian army. In later life Einstein would recall how Reuss had tried to spark alive a real interest in ancient civilizations and their influences which still could be seen in the contemporary life of southern Germany. There was to be an unexpected footnote to Einstein's memory. For after his first work had begun to pass a disturbing electric shock through the framework of science, he himself visited Munich and called on his old teacher, then living in retirement. But the worn suit and baggy trousers which had already become the Einstein hallmark among his colleagues merely suggested poverty. Reuss had no recollection of Einstein's name and it became clear that he thought his caller was on a begging errand. Einstein left hurriedly.

The influence that initially led Einstein on to his chosen path did not come from the Luitpold Gymnasium but from Max Talmey, a young Jewish medical student who in 1889 matriculated at Munich University. Talmey's elder brother, a practicing doctor, already knew the Einstein family, and quickly introduced him to what Max called "the happy, comfortable, and cheerful Einstein home, where I received the same generous consideration as he did." In later life Talmey was seized with the idea for a universal language, an Esperanto which he felt would be particularly valuable for science. He tried to enlist Einstein's support, became interested in relativity, and then, like so many others, attempted to explain the theory. More important was the inclusion in his little-known book on the subject of his own impressions of Einstein at the age of twelve, the only reliable first-hand account that exists.

"He was a pretty, dark-haired boy . . . a good illustration . . . against the theory of Houston Stewart Chamberlain and others who try to prove that only the blond races produce geniuses," Talmey wrote.

> He showed a particular inclination toward physics and took pleasure in conversing on physical phenomena. I

> gave him therefore as reading matter A. Bernstein's *Popular Books on Physical Science* and L. Buchner's *Force and Matter,* two works that were then quite popular in Germany. The boy was profoundly impressed by them. Bernstein's work especially, which describes physical phenomena lucidly and engagingly, had a great influence on Albert, and enhanced considerably his interest in physical science.

Soon afterwards he began to show keenness for mathematics, and Talmey gave him a copy of Spieker's *Lehrbuch der ebenen Geometrie,* a popular textbook. Thereafter, whenever the young medical student arrived for the midday meal on Thursdays, he would be shown the problems solved by Einstein during the previous week.

> After a short time, a few months, he had worked through the whole book of Spieker. He thereupon devoted himself to higher mathematics, studying all by himself Lubsen's excellent works on the subject. These, too, I had recommended to him if memory serves me right. Soon the flight of his mathematical genius was so high that I could no longer follow. Thereafter philosophy was often a subject of our conversations. I recommended to him the reading of Kant. At that time he was still a child, only thirteen years old, yet Kant's works, incomprehensible to ordinary mortals, seemed to be clear to him. Kant became Albert's favorite philosopher after he had read through his *Critique of Pure Reason* and the works of other philosophers.

He also read Darwin—at least according to the more reliable of his stepsons-in-law. There is no evidence that he was particularly moved. One reason was that the battle for evolution had by this time been fought and won. Yet even in his youth Einstein may have believed, as he was to write years later, that "living matter and clarity are opposites—they run away from one another." The same feeling, that "biological procedures cannot be expressed in mathematical formulas," gave him a lifelong scepticism of medicine according to his friend Gustav Bucky, and it certainly tended to concentrate all his interests on nonbiological subjects. Another side of the same coin was presented to Leo Szilard, a colleague for more than a third of a century who forsook physics for biology: "One can best feel in dealing with living things how primitive physics still is . . ." This attitude, a sense almost of annoyance with the Creator at having produced things which could not be quantified, explains at least something of the invisible barrier which so often rises to separate Einstein the intuitively understanding and kind human being from Einstein ordering his daily life. The bugle calls of science were always sounding and he could rarely devote much time to individual men and women. His reaction to the living world was illustrated one day as he stood with a friend watching flocks of emigrating birds flying overhead: "I think it is easily possible that they follow beams which are so far unknown to us."

Einstein well knew the limitations that this attitude imposed, and to Lord Samuel he once commented of the relation between physics and biology that "it is certainly true that restricting ourselves to concepts and laws of physics, we are unable to get a reasonable view of the total events of life. Perhaps it will be impossible for us ever, as men. But I do not believe that it thence follows that physics principally does not comprehend the processes of life." This was adequate reason; discovering the nature of the physical world was task enough for one man. Nevertheless, it is interesting to speculate on what might have happened to biology in the twentieth century had Einstein decided to turn his genius towards the animate rather than the inanimate world.

The decision appears to have been made soon after the age of twelve. It is not too definite a word although details and date must be inferred rather than demonstrated, deduced from circumstantial evidence rather than illustrated by the hard fact and undeniable statement that form part and parcel of more extrovert and better documented childhoods. By the time he was twelve Einstein had attained, in his own words, "a deep religiosity." His approval of this translation of the German in his autobiographical notes is significant; for religiosity, the "affected or excessive religiousness" of the dictionary, appears to describe accurately the results of what he called "the traditional education-machine." Always sensitive to beauty, abnormally sensitive to music, Einstein had no doubt been deeply impressed by the splendid trappings in which Bavarian Catholicism of those days was decked out. But if his emotions were won over, his mind remained free—with considerable results. "Through the reading of popular scientific books I soon reached the conviction that much of the stories in the Bible could not be true," he wrote.

> The consequence was a positively fanatic [orgy of] free-thinking coupled with the impression that youth is intentionally being deceived by the state through lies; it was a crushing impression. Suspicion against every kind of authority grew out of this experience, a sceptical attitude towards the convictions which were alive in any specific social environment—an attitude which has never again left me, even though later on, because of a better insight into the causal connections, it lost some of its original poignancy.

This is important not because the change of heart itself was unusual but because of Einstein's future history. For centuries young people have abandoned revealed religion at the impressionable age and turned to the laws of nature as a substitute. The process is hardly one for wide-eyed wonder. What was different with Einstein was that the common act should have such uncommon results.

His need of something to fill the void, the desperate need to find order in a chaotic world may possibly have been a particularly Jewish need. Certainly Abba Eban, in 1955 Israeli ambassador to the United States, noted after Einstein's death how "the Hebrew mind has been obsessed for centuries by a concept of order and harmony in the universal design. The search for laws hitherto unknown which govern cosmic forces; the doctrine of a relative harmony in nature; the idea of a calculable relationship between matter and energy—these are all more likely to emerge from a basic Hebrew philosophy and turn of mind than from many others." This may sound like hindsight plus special pleading; yet the long line of Jewish physicists from the nineteenth century, and the even longer list of those who later sought the underlying unifications of the subatomic world, give it a plausibility which cannot easily be contested.

If there were no order or logic in the man-made conceptions of the world based on revealed religion, surely order and logic could be discovered in the huge world which, Einstein wrote, "exists independently of us human beings and which stands before us like a great eternal riddle, at least partially accessible to our inspection and thinking. The contemplation of this world beckoned like a liberation, and I soon noticed that many a man who I had learned to esteem and to admire had found inner freedom and security in devoted occupation with it." The young Einstein, like many a Victorian ecclesiastic who wished "to penetrate into the *arcana* of nature, so as to discern 'the law within the law,' " picked up science where religion appeared to leave off. Later he was to see both as different sides of the same coin, as complementary as the wave and corpuscle conceptions of light, and both just as necessary if one were to see reality in the round. All this, however, developed in the decades after conversion.

Conversion did not come in a day. Common sense, together with what little evidence exists, suggests that Einstein's determination to probe the secrets of the physical world did not appear like a Pauline vision on the Damascus road but crystallized over a period. Nevertheless, it was a conversion which began in early youth, quickly hardened, and set fast for the rest of his life.

Brooding on the "lies" he had been told in the Luitpold Gymnasium, Einstein decided on the work to which he would be willing to devote everything and sacrifice anything with a steely determination which separated him from other men. On two occasions he put down in simple words what that work was. The first came during an hour's meeting—apparently about 1911—with the Jewish philosopher Martin Buber, who pressed him hard "with a concealed question about his faith." Finally, in Buber's words, Einstein "burst forth," revealingly. " 'What we (and by this 'we' he meant we physicists) strive for,' he cried, 'is just to draw His lines after Him.' To draw after—as one retraces a geometrical figure." And a decade later, walking with a young woman physicist to his Berlin University office, Einstein spelled out the same task in more detail. He had no interest in learning a new language, nor in food nor in new clothes. "I'm not much with people," he continued, "and I'm not a family man. I want my peace. I want to know how God created this world. I am not interested in this or that phenomenon, in the spectrum of this or that element. I want to know His thoughts, the rest are details."

This aim was matched by a belief: "God is subtle, but he is not malicious." With these words he was to crystallize his view that complex though the laws of nature might be, difficult though they were to understand, they were yet understandable by human reason. If a man worried away at the law behind the law—if, in Rutherford's words, he knew what questions to ask nature—then the answers could be discovered. God might pose difficult problems but He never broke the rules by posing unanswerable ones. What is more, He never left the answers to blind chance—"God does not play dice with the world."

However, Einstein's God was not the God of most other men. When he wrote of religion, as he often did in middle and later life, he tended to adopt the belief of Alice's Red Queen that "words mean what you want them to mean," and to clothe with different names what to more ordinary mortals—and to most Jews—looked like a variant of simple agnosticism. Replying in 1929 to a cabled inquiry from Rabbi Goldstein of New York, he said that he believed "in Spinoza's God who reveals himself in the harmony of all that exists, not in a God who concerns himself with the fate and actions of men." And it is claimed that years later, asked by Ben-Gurion whether he believed in God, "even he, with his great formula about energy and mass, agreed that there must be something behind the energy." No doubt. But much of Einstein's writing gives the impression of belief in a God even more intangible and impersonal than a celestial machine minder, running the universe with undisputable authority and expert touch. Instead, Einstein's God appears as the physical world itself, with its infinitely marvelous structure operating at atomic level with the beauty of a craftsman's wristwatch, and at stellar level with the majesty of a massive cyclotron. This was belief enough. It grew early and rooted deep. Only later was it dignified by the title of cosmic religion, a phrase which gave plausible respectability to the views of a man who did not believe in a life after death and who felt that if virtue paid off in the earthly one, then this was the result of cause and effect rather than celestial reward. Einstein's God thus stood for an orderly system obeying rules which could be discovered by those who had the courage, the imagination, and the persistence to go on searching for them. And it was to this task which he began to turn his mind soon after the age of twelve. For the rest of his life everything else was to seem almost trivial by comparison.

Einstein had three more years at the Gymnasium, uninterested in the classics, increasingly able at mathematics, precocious in philosophical matters which one can assume he discussed only rarely with his masters and not at all with his fellow pupils. This time in Munich would have been longer still had not the family business failed again. For now the Einsteins decided to cross the Alps to Milan. The reason why is obscure, but it seems that the Kochs came to the rescue once more. A wealthy branch of the family lived in Genoa, and it may well have been their stipulation that the new business enterprise should start where they could keep a watchful eye on the happy-go-lucky optimism of Hermann Einstein.

The family moved from Munich in 1894, taking their daughter Maja with them and leaving Albert in a boardinghouse under the care of a distant relative. It was anticipated that he would in due time finish his course, acquire the diploma which would ensure entry to a university, and would then enter the profession of electrical engineering which his father had vaguely chosen for him. The son had other views and within six months had followed his family across the Alps.

The details of Einstein's departure from the Gymnasium come in various forms, at second remove, from his own comments in middle and old age. What is certain is that he left before acquiring the necessary diploma. It has been stated that he first obtained a doctor's certificate saying that because of a nervous breakdown he should join his parents in Italy, plus a statement from his mathematics master testifying to his ability; before the medical certificate could be presented Einstein was summarily expelled on the grounds that "your presence in the class is disruptive and affects the other students." This should be taken with caution but these general lines of the incident have the ring of truth. For the kindly, gentle Einstein who is remembered today, the friend of all mankind (except the Prussians), a saint insulated from the rest of the world, is largely a figure of his later years; it is a figure very different from the precocious, half-cocksure, almost insolent Swabian of youth and early manhood. Einstein was the boy who knew not merely which monkey wrench to throw in the works, but also how best to throw it. This may well explain why the Gymnasium was glad to send him packing. And the ignominy of being sacked before going could explain much of his later dislike of the place.

He was by now heartily glad to see the last of the Luitpold Gymnasium. The feeling was reciprocated. Yet the years there had left their mark in a way which neither his masters nor even he can fully have appreciated. They had made him detest discipline; but, under his guard, they had taught him the virtues of self-discipline, of concentration, of dedication to an ideal, of an attitude which can be described as firm or as relentless according to taste. Years later, when colleagues were discussing the single-minded determination with which he had followed his star without regard for others, one listener noted: "You must not forget. He was a German."

Little is known about the two years which the young Einstein spent in Italy, but he looked back on them as extremely happy. "I was so surprised, when I crossed the Alps to Italy, to see how the ordinary Italian, the ordinary man and woman, uses words and expressions of a high level of thought and cultural content, so different from the ordinary Germans," he remembered nearly forty years later. "This is due to their long cultural history. The people of northern Italy are the most civilized people I have ever met."

It may not have been literally true that "he went into galleries, and wherever he found a Michelangelo he remained the longest," as claimed by one of his stepsons-in-law in a book which Einstein smartly repudiated. But there is little doubt that he enjoyed the people and the air of freedom, both very different from what he had known in the Munich Gymnasium. When his father's business failed yet again, almost as expected, and was restarted in Pavia, his own travels began to take him farther afield to Padua, Pisa, Siena, and Perugia.

His education appears to have been halted in midstream and the Swiss School in Milan, at which he is sometimes reported to have studied—in those days the International School of the Protestant Families in Milan—has no record of him. His sister Maja and his cousin Robert were on the rolls but Einstein was aged fifteen when he arrived in the city and the Swiss School took children only to the age of thirteen.

However, this freedom could not last, since the continuing precariousness of the family finances made it necessary to prepare for a career. The only record of how he was prodded into this comes secondhand from his son: "At the age of sixteen," he has said, "his father urged him to forget his 'philosophical nonsense,' and apply himself to the 'sensible trade' of electrical engineering." The lack of a necessary Gymnasium certificate at once made itself felt, since entry to a university was barred without it.

There was one possible way out. Conveniently over the Alps from Milan, there existed in Zurich the Swiss Federal Polytechnic School,* outside Germany the best technical school in Central Europe. The Polytechnic demanded no Gymnasium diploma and all a candidate had to do was pass the necessary examination. There was one difficulty however. In the spring of 1895 Einstein was only sixteen, at least two years younger than most scholars when they joined the ETH. However, it was decided that the risk should be taken, and in the autumn he was despatched over the Alps.

Before he went—probably a few weeks or months earlier, although the date is uncertain—he sent to his Uncle Cäsar in Stuttgart a "paper" which was an augury of things to come: "an essay which looks more like a program than a paper" as he described it, and one in which the boy of about sixteen proposed tackling one of the most hotly disputed scientific subjects, the relationship between electricity, magnetism, and the ether, that hypothetical nonmaterial entity which was presumed to fill all space and to transmit electromagnetic waves.

Neither letter nor paper is dated, but in 1950 Einstein recalled that they were written in 1894 or 1895, while the internal reference to the ETH in Zurich suggests that the latter was the more likely date. "My dear Uncle," he began,

*The organization is known variously by its German, French, Italian, and English titles: Eidg. Technische Hochschule (ETH); École Polytechnique Fédérale (EPF); Svizzera Polytecnica Federale (SPF); and Swiss Federal Institute of Technology (FIT).

> I am really very happy that you are still interested in the little things I am doing and working on, even though we could not see each other for a long time, and I am such a terribly lazy correspondent. And yet I always hesitated to send you this [attached] note because it deals with a very special topic; and besides, it is still rather naïve and imperfect, as is to be expected from a young fellow like myself. I shall not mind it at all if you don't read the stuff; but you must recognize it at least as a modest attempt to overcome the laziness in writing which I have inherited from both of my dear parents.
>
> As you probably already know, I am now expected to go to the Polytechnic in Zurich. However, it presents serious difficulties because I ought to be at least two years older for that. We shall let you know in the next letter what happens in this matter. Warmest greetings to dear Aunt and our lovely children.

The accompanying essay, written in sloping and spidery Gothic script on five pages of lined paper, was headed: "Concerning the Investigation State of Aether in Magnetic Fields," and began by outlining the nature of electromagnetic phenomena and stressing the little that was known concerning their relationship with the ether. This could be remedied, it was suggested, by studying the potential states of the aether in magnetic fields of all kinds by comprehensive experimental studies—or, in other words, by measuring "the elastic deformations and the acting deforming forces." This emphasis on experiment was repeated towards the end of the paper where the author said: "I believe that the quantitative researches on the absolute magnitude of the density and the elastic force of the ether can only begin if qualitative results exists that are connected with established ideas."

It was altogether a remarkable paper for a boy of sixteen and if it is straining too far to see in it the seeds of the Special Theory, it gives a firm enough pointer to the subject which was to remain constantly at the back of his mind for a decade. As he wrote in old age, at the age of sixteen Einstein had discovered a paradox by considering what would happen if one could follow a beam of light at the speed of light—the result being "a spatially oscillatory electromagnetic field at rest." He did not put it quite like that to Uncle Cäsar. But it was no doubt still in his mind as he arrived in Zurich, carrying the high hopes of the family and, judging from the odd hint, a firm determination that he would not become an electrical engineer.

CHAPTER 2

STATELESS PERSON

Einstein arrived in Zurich, the bustling mercantile capital of Switzerland, in the autumn of 1895. Set on its long finger of lake among the foothills of the Alps, the city was half cultural remnant from the Middle Ages, half commercial metropolis, a center whose nonconformist devotees were within the next few years to include Lenin, Rosa Luxemburg, and James Joyce. Einstein, for whom the attractions of Zurich never palled, was to be another.

During this first visit as a youth of sixteen and a half he stayed with the family of Gustav Meier, an old friend of his father and a former inhabitant of Ulm. He may have been accompanied by his mother, and it is certain that Mrs. Einstein approached a Zurich councillor on her son's behalf, asking "whether he could use his influence to let Albert jump a class in view of his unusual talent and the fact that, owing to the movement of his family, his schooling had been a little erratic." Einstein did, in fact, take the normal entrance examination for the ETH shortly afterwards. He did not pass. The accepted reason for his failure is that although his knowledge of mathematics was exceptional he did not reach the necessary standard in modern languages or in zoology and botany.

This is less than the whole truth. So is the statement that while the exam was taken at the age of eighteen, Einstein was two years younger. More significantly, his father's decision that he should follow a technical occupation was one which the young Einstein would have found it difficult to evade directly. Subsequently, he admitted that failure in Zurich "was entirely his own fault because he had made no attempt whatever to prepare himself"; and, asked in later life whether he might have been forced into choosing a "profitable profession" rather than becoming a scientist, he bluntly replied, "I was supposed to choose a practical profession, but this was simply unbearable to me." Thus although the horse had now been brought to the water in Zurich nothing could make it drink. But the principal of the ETH, Albin Herzog, had been impressed by Einstein's mathematical ability. Reading between the lines, he had also been impressed by his character. With the support of Meier, it was arranged that the boy should attend the cantonal school at Aarau, twenty miles to the west, where a year's study should enable him to pass the ETH entrance exam.

A small picturesque town on the Aare, from whose banks the vineyards climb the slopes of the Jura, Aarau could justifiably boast of its cantonal school run by Professor Winteler. But wherever Einstein had been sent in Switzerland, he would have been impressed by the contrast with the Munich Gymnasium. For in spite of the Swiss tradition under which every man appears eager to spring to arms, and has his rifle on the wall, the spirit of militarism is singularly absent. Contrariwise, the practice of democracy, about which Einstein early showed what was to be a lifelong enthusiasm, had for centuries been an ingrained feature of the country. Even so, he was lucky with Aarau and with Winteler, with whose family he lived during his stay at the school.

A somewhat casual teacher, as ready to discuss work or politics with his pupils as with his fellow teachers, Winteler was friendly and liberal-minded, an ornithologist never happier than when taking his students and his own children for walks in the nearby mountains. Teaching resembled university lectures rather than high school instruction. There was a room for each subject rather than for each class, and in one of them Einstein was introduced to the outer mysteries of physics by a first-class teacher, August Tuchschmid. More than half a century later he remembered the school as "remaining for me the most pleasing example of such an institution," where teacher and taught were joined in "responsible and happy work such as cannot be achieved by regimentation, however subtle." Instruction was good, authority was exercised with a light hand, and it is clear that in this friendly climate Einstein began to open out, even though the details that have survived are scanty and tantalizing. On a three-day school outing during which pupils climbed the 8,000-foot Santis above Feldkirch, he slipped on a steep slope and was saved from destruction only by the prompt move of a colleague who stretched out his alpenstock for the boy to grasp, a quick action that helped change the course of history. When on another school outing, a master asked him:

"Now Einstein, how do the strata run here? From below upwards or vice versa?" the reply was unexpected: "It is pretty much the same to me whichever way they run, Professor."

The story may well have been embroidered by recollection. But it reflects an attitude that juts out during Einstein's youth from beneath the layers of adulation which increased with the years. The description of "impudent Swabian," given by his fellow pupil Hans Byland, belongs to this period. "Sure of himself, his gray felt hat pushed back on his thick, black hair, he strode energetically up and down in a rapid, I might almost say crazy, tempo of a restless spirit which carries a whole world in itself," Byland has said. "Nothing escaped the sharp gaze of his bright brown eyes. Whoever approached him immediately came under the spell of his superior personality. A sarcastic curl of his rather full mouth with the protruding lower lip did not encourage Philistines to fraternize with him." These rougher corners eventually became smoothed off so that he would bite back the comment he might consider natural and others might consider bitter; but the essential attitude remained, an intellectual disinclination to give a damn for anybody. As a rock never very far below the surface it was as likely to capsize Einstein as anyone else.

This prickly arrogance appears increasingly throughout his student years. The gentle philosopher, benignly asking questions of the universe, was always to be one part of the complete Einstein. But there was another part during youth. He knew not only the clanging existence of metropolitan Munich but the delights of northern Italy. He was, judged by the experience of his contemporaries, a young man of the world, well filled with his own opinions, careless of expressing them without reserve, regarding the passing scene with a sometimes slightly contemptuous smile. Had it not been for his deep underlying sense of the mystery of things, a humility that at this age he was apt to conceal, he would have been the model iconoclast.

Einstein enjoyed Aarau. He enjoyed not only the business of learning, an unexpected revelation after the Munich experience, but also the Swiss with their mixture of serious responsibility and easy-going democracy, their refusal to be drawn into the power game already dividing Europe, their devotion to a neutrality which was personal as well as political. The effect remained. Even in his last decades, dazzled by the American future, Einstein still showed a homesickness for Europe that was epitomized by Zurich or Leiden; in the late 1940s, as the liberal image faded in the United States, the feeling was reinforced, and he tended to look back to a golden age that centered on prewar Switzerland.

Life in Aarau was to have one specific and far-reaching result. For the antagonism to all things German which had been burning away in Einstein for years now came to the surface in what was, for a boy, a remarkable explosion. He refused to continue being German. The usual story is that on arriving in Milan from Munich the youthful Einstein told his father that he no longer wished to be German and at the same time announced that he was severing all formal connection with the Jewish faith. In general it is the second half of the story, which would have caused his religiously happy-go-lucky family little worry, which is given most credence; the first has been considered a later magnification of youthful disenchantment and wishful thinking. In fact, the reverse is true.

As far as the Jewish faith is concerned, the boy had as little to renounce as the grown man. While Einstein the Zionist speaker of adult life had an intense feeling for Jewish culture, a dedication to preservation of the Jewish people, and a deep respect for the Jewish intellectual tradition, his feelings for the faith itself rarely went beyond kindly tolerance and the belief that it did no more harm than other revealed religions. "I am naturally not responsible for what other people have written about me," he has stated when commenting on this alleged youthful renunciation. "At that time I should certainly not have understood how one could have got out of Jewishness."

The question of German nationality was different. At first, the idea of a sixteen-year-old renouncing his country appears slightly bizarre, while in the modern world the mechanics of the operation would be complicated. So much so that the story has been taken rather lightly and André Mercier, head of the department of theoretical physics in the University of Berne, and Secretary General of the International Committee on General Relativity, has gone on record as saying that when Einstein arrived in Switzerland "he was by nationality a German and remained so until he became of age." It has also been pointed out that if the young Einstein did "give up his passport at the age of fifteen," as has been claimed by Dr. Walter Jens of the University of Tübingen, then this act would have been of no legal consequence.

In fact, no passport was involved. On birth, Einstein had become a citizen of the state of Württemberg and, as a result, a German national. According to a letter in the Princeton archives, he had pleaded with his father, even before the latter had crossed the Alps to Milan, to renounce this nationality on his behalf. Nothing appears to have been done. But the boy returned home from Switzerland to Milan to spend the Christmas of 1895 with his parents. And soon after his return to Aarau early in 1896 Hermann Einstein, presumably yielding at last to his son's renewed badgerings, wrote to the Württemberg authorities. They acknowledged the application, and on January 28, 1896, formally ended Einstein's German nationality. Two memoranda sent by them to Ulm on January 30 and February 5 confirmed this with various departments in the city. "Between the ages of fifteen and twenty-one," Einstein wrote, "I was entirely without state papers, which at that time was not a risky thing."* He was in fact nearly seventeen by the time his father's application was acknowledged, but it is true that he completed his education in Switzerland and obtained his degree in Zurich as a stateless person, merely "the son of German parents" as he put it on official forms.

The hatred of Germany revealed by this precocious move may genuinely have sprung from stern discipline and it is quite possible that Einstein was seriously contemplat-

*Einstein usually described himself during this period as "stateless" or "staatenlos," rather than "schrifteblos" ("without papers"). On this occasion he used the phrase "ganz ohne Staatspapiere" ("totally without state papers").

ing his move before his arrival in Milan. His feelings may well have been increased by the contemptuous way in which he was expelled from the school before he could resign. Northern Italy in the mid-1890s provided one contrast with a Germany already flexing its muscles, and the sober Swiss provided another. Whatever the relative importance of these different motivations, the net result was an attitude that later developed into an anti-Germanism that had a trace of paranoia, an emotional fissure which split Einstein's character from end to end like a geological fault.

During those first weeks of 1896 in Aarau none of these dark overtones could be discerned. He was now free of Germany. He would, in due course and with good luck, acquire the Swiss nationality on which he had set his heart. What is more, he had by now succeeded in switching academic horses in midstream: despite the family decision that he should become an electrical engineer, it was now agreed that he should study for a teacher's degree. The details can only be inferred. But it is significant that it was his mother's comparatively well-to-do family which was to underwrite his student days; and it is not difficult to envisage the fond mother being won over by her son's arguments and then persuading her relatives that they would be investing in the future. There is little doubt that in his younger days he had a way with women.

Einstein took his examination at the ETH in the summer of 1896. He passed, returned to his parents in Italy, and in October left them for Switzerland, now dedicated to a four-year course which would, if he were successful, qualify him for a post on the lowest rung of the professional teacher's ladder.

On October 29, 1896, he settled down in Zurich, first in the lodgings of Frau Kagi at 4 Unionstrasse. There he was to remain for two years before moving to Frau Markwalder in 87 Klosbach and then, after twelve months, returning to Frau Kagi at a new address. At the end of each term he visited his family in Milan or, later, Pavia, while in Zurich he was under the watchful but discreet eye of the Karr family, moderately well-to-do people distantly related to Einstein's mother, whose relatives now provided the 100 francs a month on which he lived.

His fellow students came mainly from the families of

minor professional people or small businessmen, typified by Marcel Grossman whose father owned a factory making agricultural machinery at Hongg, a few miles from Zurich. There was Louis Kollros from the watchmaking center of La Chaux-de-Fonds in the Jura, Jakob Ehrat from Schaffhausen with its Rhine falls, and a group of young girls from Hungary of whom one joined the class of '96 with Einstein. This was Mileva Maric, born in 1875 and like the rest of the class a few years older than Einstein, daughter of a Serbian peasant from Titel in southern Hungary who had labored her way to Zurich by dogged determination, handicapped by a limp, anxious to succeed.

Superficially, the picture of Einstein's student days was conventional enough. There was the fairly frequent change of rooms; the frugal diet of restaurants and cafés, supplemented by snacks from the nearby bakery or from kind Swiss landladies. There was the weekend outing to one or more of the minor summits surrounding the Zurichsee, the Swiss version of the reading parties in the Lakes or North Wales which were a feature of the Victorian scene in Britain. And there were frequent visits back to Aarau where his sister Maja was now spending the first of three years in the Aargau teachers seminary.

Einstein was casual of dress, unconventional of habit, with the happy-go-lucky absentmindedness of a man concentrating on other things which he was to retain all his life. "When I was a very young man," he once confided to an old friend, "I visited overnight at the home of friends. In the morning I left, forgetting my valise. My host said to my parents: 'That young man will never amount to anything because he can't remember anything.' " And he would often forget his key and have to wake up his landlady late at night, calling: "It's Einstein—I've forgotten my key again."

He followed the normal student pursuits, picking up on the Zurichsee a passion for sailing that never deserted him, taking occasional walks in the mountains even though, in the later words of his eldest son, "he did not care for large, impressive mountains, but . . . liked surroundings that were gentle and colorful and gave one lightness of spirit." On the water he would invariably have a small notebook. Fräulein Markwalder, who sometimes accompanied him, remembered years later how when the breeze died and the sails dropped, out would come the notebook and he would be scribbling away. "But as soon as there was a breath of wind he was immediately ready to start sailing again."

The picture is almost prosaic. Yet a hint of something to come is suggested by the barely concealed arrogant impatience that showed itself even during the musical evenings to which he was often invited by the parents of his Swiss friends. If attention to his performance was not adequate he would stop, sometimes with a remark that verged on boorishness. To a group of elderly ladies who continued knitting while he played, and who then asked why he was closing his score and putting his violin back in its case, he explained: "We would not dream of disturbing your work." And when, politely asked on one occasion, "Do you count the beat?" he quickly replied, "Heavens, no. It's in my blood." Perhaps there was always something a little risky in questioning Einstein. The "not much with people," as he later put it, was true despite his personality, not because of it. Even as a youth, moodily aloof at times from his companions, he had a quality that attracted as certainly as it could rebuff. As a man, he was the kind who made heads turn when he entered the room, and not merely because the founder of relativity had come in. If the word "charisma" has a modern meaning outside the public relations trade, Einstein had it.

It is noticeable that he appears to have been particularly happy in the company of women. The feelings were often mutual. The well-set-up young man with his shock of jet-black wavy hair, his huge luminous eyes, and his casual air was distinctly attractive. More than one young Zurich girl, more than one Swiss matron, was delighted that the young Herr Einstein was such an excellent performer on the violin and was agreeable to accompany them at evening parties. And he was a frequent visitor to the house of Frau Bachtold where several of the women students lodged, sitting in the living room and attentively listening as Mileva Maric played the piano. At Aarau he had been the confidant of one young woman who played Schubert with him and asked his advice when proposed to by a much older man. At Zurich he appears to have exercised a similar influence. Years later Antonina Vallentin, a great friend of Einstein's second wife, said significantly that "as a young man and even in middle age, Einstein had regular features, plump cheeks, a round chin—masculine good looks of the type that played havoc at the turn of the century."

Einstein's pleasure in the company of women lasted all his life. But there was little more to it than that. Like most famous men he attracted the hangers-on, the adorers, and the semi-charlatans. On at least two occasions women claimed him as the father of their children, but in one instance the claimant was insane while the case of the other appears to have been equally groundless. His doctor-friend, Janos Plesch, suggested in a letter after Einstein's death that he may have formed a liaison during the First World War when he had been left by one wife and had not yet acquired another. Other comparably vague suggestions have been handed down from the early Berlin days. While they cannot be ignored, it would be wrong to give them more weight than unsubstantiated observations deserve—suggestions which tended to be kept afloat by Einstein's own personal attitude. According to Vera Weizmann, wife of the Jewish leader Chaim Weizmann, Einstein's second wife did not mind him flirting with her since "intellectual women did not attract him; out of pity he was attracted to women who did physical work." The same comment has been made in strikingly similar terms by more than one of his friends, who have drawn attention to the fact that he preferred to have women rather than men around him. All this is true. Yet the implications are not the obvious ones. As a young man he tended to keep his women friends at arms length since he wished to devote the maximum energy and resource to the one great game; later on, as youth merged first into middle and later into old age, he still tended to like having women around, but in an almost old-maidish way. He had, after all, resigned himself to the necessary priorities; first research, second Einstein. This was an order of duties which at first makes it easy to be sorry for him—the man who had apparently cut himself off from so many of the things that make life worth living. The feeling is misplaced. Einstein himself was, as he acknowledged to his friend Michelangelo Besso, somewhat cold and something of a tough nut. Monks and nuns, spinsters and dedicated military men, manage to live happily and quite a few live usefully; Einstein, answering a call quite as compelling, enjoyed a satisfaction from his work quite as great as most men enjoy from anything else.

This life-long dedication set him apart in a number of ways. As Bertrand Russell once wrote, "Personal matters never occupied more than odd nooks and crannies in his thoughts." Other men allowed themselves to become implicated in the human predicament, on one level willingly dealing with the trivia of life and on another being swept off course by the normal passions. Einstein avoided such energy-wasting complications at all levels. To this extent his self-imposed task, the determination to keep first things first, forced him into abdicating his human position. He felt an intuitive sympathy with human beings in the mass; but when it came to individuals—and he included himself—he found little time or sympathy or understanding to spare.

Einstein's obsession with exploring and understanding the physical world caught him early. He followed it, as André Mercier has noted, as the result of a double experience, "the experience of the exterior world, revealing material facts, numberless and numerical; and the revelation of an interior or spiritual world which showed him the path he should follow." But there was another dichotomy about the early years. A good deal of his genius lay in the imagination which gave him courage to challenge accepted beliefs. This quality has been rightly stressed, and his old friend Morris Cohen went so far as to claim that "like so many of the very young men who have revolutionized physics in our day [Einstein] has not been embarrassed by too much learning about the past or by what the Germans call the literature of the subject." Yet the "too much" is relative. Einstein's ability to soar up from the nineteenth century basis of physics, and his own dislike of the routine involved in understanding that basis, has tended to undervalue the four-year slog of routine which he went through at the ETH. Yet this routine was demanding enough.

Working to become a teacher in mathematical physics, he had to devote himself to both mathematics and the natural sciences. Under six professors—notably Hermann Minkowski, who was to play such an important part in giving mathematical formality to Special Relativity—he studied mathematical subjects that included the differential and integral calculus, descriptive and analytical geometry, the geometry of numbers, and the theory of the definite integral. Two professors, Weber and Pernet, dealt with physics, while Professor Wolfer lectured on astrophysics and astronomy. The theory of scientific thought and Kantian philosophy was studied under Professor Stadler. To these compulsory subjects Einstein added an odd ragbag of optionals which included not only gnomic projection and exterior ballistics, both of which might have been expected, but also anthropology and the geology of mountains under the famous Albert Heim; banking and stock exchange business; Swiss politics; and, under a *privatdozent*, Goethe's works and philosophy.

Despite the emphasis on mathematics, Einstein himself was more drawn towards the natural sciences. The reason, given in his autobiographical notes, was that he "saw that mathematics was split up into numerous specialties, each of which could easily absorb the short lifetime granted to us. Consequently, I saw myself in the position of Buridan's ass which was unable to decide upon any specific bundle of hay." One result of his choice was the difficulty that faced him when, between 1905 and 1915, he struggled to extend the theory of Special Relativity. As he himself wrote, it dawned on him "only gradually after years of independent scientific work" that "the approach to a more profound knowledge of the basic principles of physics is tied up with the most intricate mathematical methods."

Thus it was physics to which he turned, working "most of the time in the physical laboratory, fascinated by the direct contact with experience." This "contact with experience" was in strange contrast with the period when he would answer a question about his laboratory by pointing to his head and a question about his tools by pointing to his fountain pen. Yet despite this he never ceased to emphasize that the bulk of his work sprang directly and naturally from observed facts; the coordinating theory explaining them might arise from an inspired gleam of intuition, but the need for it arose only after observation.

In June, 1899, Einstein seriously injured a hand in the Zurich laboratories—typically enough after tearing up a chit of paper telling him how to do an experiment one way and then attempting to do it another. And it is significant that a biography by one of his stepsons-in-law, whose facts were described by Einstein himself as "duly accurate," should contain the following sentences:

> He wanted to construct an apparatus which would accurately measure the earth's movement against the ether. ... He wanted to proceed quite empirically, to suit his scientific feeling of the time, and believed that an apparatus such as he sought would lead him to the solution of a problem of far-reaching perspectives of which he already sensed. But there was no chance to build this apparatus. The scepticism of his teachers was too great, the spirit of enterprise too small.

Without Einstein's imprimatur this would sound unlikely. With it, the story provides an interesting gloss.

From the first, however, it was theoretical physics which attracted him, and here he was unlucky. Subsequently he was to write of the "excellent teachers (for example, Hurwitz, Minkowski)" of these Zurich days. But it is significant that he omitted all reference to Heinrich Weber, who gave the physics course. According to Einstein's fellow student Louis Kollros, this course was designed primarily for engineers. "His lectures were outstanding," according to Adolf Fisch—the same youth who had saved Einstein's life on the Santis a few years before—"and a magnificent introduction to theoretical physics, but Weber himself was a typical representative of classical physics. Anything that came after Helmholtz was simply ignored. At the close of our studies we knew all the past of physics but nothing of their present and future." In particular, they knew nothing of Maxwell, whose theory of electromagnetism was already changing not only men's ideas of the physical world, but the practical applications of physics to that world. Of the two sets of notes made by Einstein at Weber's own lectures, one dealt with heat and thermodynamics, the other with technical problems and with electricity from Coulomb's law to induction; yet Maxwell's work was not touched upon. This was not as startling as it sounds. For Maxwell's theory—"the most fascinating subject at the time that I was a student," as Einstein wrote—was symptomatic of the radically new ideas which were about to transform the face of physics.

Only a few years earlier, as the nineteenth century moved towards its close, the empire of the physical sciences had appeared to be on the edge of the millennium. Just as there seemed no possible limit to the industrial development of the United States, to the political advances in Europe over much of which the liberal spirit still reigned, or to the technological progress which could be achieved in the workshops of the world, so did physical science seem to be moving towards a solution of its final problems. Almost a century earlier Laplace had made his great boast: "An intelligence knowing, at a given instance of time, all forces acting in nature, as well as the momentary position of all things of which the universe consists, would be able to comprehend the motions of the largest bodies of the world and those of the lightest atoms in one single formula, provided his intellect were sufficiently powerful to subject all data to analysis; to him nothing would be uncertain, both past and future would be present in his eyes."

This prophecy from the Newton of France had been in some ways an extrapolation from the spectacular success of Newton's own celestial mechanics with whose help the motions of moon, comets, asteroids, and satellites could be computed with splendid accuracy. The confidence appeared to be justified, not only by the advances made throughout the nineteenth century but by the ease with which these could be seen as intelligible parts of one vast but finite corpus of knowledge whose final understanding must be only a few years away. Mechanics, acoustics, and optics were all set on firm foundations during this heroic age of classical physics. Faraday's work on electromagnetism from 1831 onwards produced the dynamo and the first shoots of what was to become the great electrical industry. The first scientific knowledge of electricity led to the electric telegraph. And to crown the fine structure there came Maxwell in the 1860s with the synthesis of his electromagnetic equations, giving the answer to so many natural phenomena and forecasting the radio waves to be discovered by Heinrich Hertz twenty-five years later. "In their various branches the explanations of new discoveries fitted together giving confidence in the whole," says Sir William Dampier, "and it came to be believed that the main lines of scientific theory had been laid down once for all, and that it only remained to carry measurements to the higher degree of accuracy represented by another decimal place, and to frame some reasonably credible theory of the structure of the luminiferous ether."

It was the problem of this luminiferous ether, through which Maxwell's electromagnetic waves appeared to be transmitted like shakings in an invisible jelly, which had during the last decades of the century begun to sap the foundations of classical science, and to reveal the electromagnetic theory as the revolutionary theory it was. Yet this was not the only worm in the apple. The imposing structure which had been built on Newtonian mechanics, the solid edifice of knowledge utilized by so many of the sciences to which it had seemed that man was now putting the finishing touches, had in fact been undermined by a score of experimental physicists tunneling along their own separate routes from a dozen different directions. Their work was continuing and the repercussions from it were beginning to be felt.

In the world of Newtonian physics, an obstinate planet had failed to conform to the calculations, for it had been confirmed that the motion of the perihelion of Mercury's orbit was advancing by a small but regular amount for which the Newtonian hypothesis could provide no explanation. From Vienna there came the heresy of Ernst Mach who was sceptical of the very foundations of Newton's universe, absolute space and absolute time. In the United States Albert Michelson and Edward Morley had performed an experiment which confronted scientists with an appalling choice. Designed to show the existence of the ether, at that time considered essential, it had yielded a null result, leaving science with the alternatives of tossing aside the key which had helped to explain the phenomena of electricity, magnetism, and light or of deciding that the earth was not in fact moving at all. Wien, in Berlin, was investigating discrepancies in the phenomena of heat and radiation which stubbornly refused to be explained by the concepts of classical physics. In Leiden the great Dutch physicist Hendrik Lorentz had formed a new theory of matter in which atoms—still regarded as John Dalton's solid billiard balls of matter when their existence was credited at all—contained electrically charged particles. In the Cavendish Laboratory, Cambridge, J. J. Thomson—

about to be joined by a young New Zealand graduate, Ernest Rutherford—was showing that these extraordinary bits of electricity, or electrons, not only had an existence of their own but a mass and an electric charge which could be measured. If this were not enough to strike at the very vitals of accepted ideas, Becquerel in Paris had found that at least one element, the metal uranium, was giving off streams of radiation and matter, an awkward fact which appeared to make nonsense of contemporary ideas. These were only the more important of a disturbing new group of discoveries made possible as much by technological advance as by exceptionally nimble minds, which were about to destroy the comfortable complacency into which physics had worked itself. It is hardly surprising that in this climate, "Maxwell's theory of the electromagnetic field was . . . not a part of the ordinary syllabus of a provincial German university," as Max Born has pointed out. The reluctance of the more conservative men of science to acknowledge this revolutionary concept—marking a change from Newton's ideas of forces operating at a distance to that of fields of force as fundamental variables—was no more surprising than any other human weakness for things as they are. For the embrace of Newtonian mechanics had continued for so long, and was still so firm, that those who either saw or suspected the fundamental incompatibility of Maxwell's theory with these long-accepted ideas tended to look the other way and, above all, to avoid discussion of such a potentially disturbing subject. "In the beginning (if there was such a thing) God created Newton's laws of motion together with necessary masses and forces. This is all; everything beyond this follows the development of appropriate mathematical methods by means of deduction"—this was the field of physics as presented to Einstein and his fellow students, and accepted by all except the few contemporaries fortunate enough to fall under the influence of a few questioning minds in Berlin, in Leiden, in Paris, or in Cambridge.

Einstein thus comes on to the scene as a student at a moment when physics was about to be revolutionized but when few students were encouraged to be revolutionaries. Without his own basically dissenting spirit he would have got nowhere. With it, the almost inevitable consequence was that he pushed along with his formal work just as much as he had to and found his real education elsewhere, in his own time. Military parallels are naturally obnoxious to civilian minds, but just as insistence on cavalry between the two world wars forced creative military minds such as Liddell Hart, de Gaulle, and Guderian to think for themselves, so the plodding insistence of Weber and his colleagues drove Einstein into reading and studying for himself. The human comparison is distressing, the professional one unavoidable. Einstein would have developed his original mind whatever happened; but the conformity of Weber, the pervasive air of a science learned for examination rather than for probing into the natural world, speeded up the process.

In his autobiographical notes, Einstein remembered how he used his spare time, "in the main in order to study at home the works of Kirchhoff, Helmholtz, Hertz, etc." Maxwell was another of the scientific revolutionaries whose work he studied at home in his lodgings, or on the banks of the Zurichsee while his friend Marcel Grossmann attended lectures on his behalf, took notes, and later passed these on so that when examination questions had to be faced Einstein was adequately briefed.

There was also Henri Poincaré, "the last man to take practically all mathematics, both pure and applied, as his province." Poincaré's influence on Einstein has sometimes been greatly exaggerated. However, it has rarely been noted that the first International Congress of Mathematicians was held in Zurich at the end of Einstein's first year as a student there; that Poincaré was due to attend; and that while he was prevented from doing so, there was read at the conference his famous paper containing the prophecy: "Absolute space, absolute time, even Euclidean geometry, are not conditions to be imposed on mechanics; one can express the facts connecting them in terms of non-Euclidean space." There is no evidence that Einstein attended the conference; but it seems unlikely that news of such an expression, so in tune with the freedom of his own way of thinking, should entirely have passed him by.

Whatever the exact weight of Poincaré's influence on Einstein, at Zurich or after, there is no doubt about the significance of Ernst Mach, that disappointed man who ran a close second to Maxwell himself in Einstein's estimation. The philosopher-scientist whose fortunes slowly sank before his death in 1916, and who is now mainly remembered for the eponymous Mach number of supersonic flight, had been born in 1838 in Turas, Moravia. He was in succession professor of mathematics at Graz and Prague, and professor of physics at Vienna where he expounded his ideas in books, papers, and lectures. He had been strongly influenced by Gustav Fechner, the physicist turned philosopher who had unsuccessfully tried to found the "science of psychophysics," and the basis of Mach's outlook was simple: that all knowledge is a matter of sensations and that what men delude themselves into calling "laws of nature" are merely summaries of experiences provided by their own—fallible—senses. "Colors, space, tones, etc. These are the only realities. Others do not exist," he had written in his daybook.

Einstein's views on the importance of such purely observational factors in discovering the way in which the world is built changed considerably throughout the years. His formulation of the Special Theory of Relativity, he was never tired of emphasizing, "was not speculative in origin; it owes its invention entirely to the desire to make physical theory fit observed facts as well as possible." Yet as the years passed, the value of pure thought, objective and dissociated from exterior circumstance, appeared to increase. In 1930 he wrote to a correspondent who had sent him one of Mach's letters that "his writings had great influence on my development. But how much he influenced my life's work it is impossible for me to fathom."

However, the renunciation of almost all that Mach stood for began only in Einstein's mid-life, the final stage in a long philosophical pilgrimage. During the first or second year of his studies in Zurich there was nothing but awed enthusiasm when his attention was drawn to Mach's *Science of Mechanics* by Michelangelo Besso, an Italian engineering student six years older than Einstein who had come to the ETH from Rome. The book, which shook his dogmatic faith in mechanics as the final basis of all physical thinking, "exercised a profound influence upon me in this regard while I was a student," he said, "I see Mach's greatness in his incorruptible scepticism and independence. . . ."

One expression of this independence was Mach's analysis of Newtonian mechanics and his conclusion that it contained no principle that is self-evident to the human mind. The nub of this criticism was that Newton had used expressions which were impossible of definition in terms of observable quantities or processes—expressions such as "absolute space" and "absolute time," which to Mach were thus quite meaningless. One result was that in Mach's view the Newtonian laws would have to be rewritten in more comprehensible terms, substituting in the law of inertia, for instance, "relative to the fixed stars" for "relative to absolute space." This critical attitude to the whole Newtonian framework as it had been utilized for more than two centuries helped to prepare Einstein's mind for things to come; for if Mach could claim, with at least a measure of plausibility, that men had been misled about the definition of the material world, then a similarly audacious venture was not beyond Einstein. Realization that accepted views could be so readily challenged came as a revelation to the student who intuitively felt that the world of degree courses was at the best incomplete and at the worst wrong. If he were really to discover how God had made the world he could take nothing for granted; not even Newton.

This scepticism was a useful scientific qualification, but one side effect was inevitable: Einstein became, as far as the professorial staff of the ETH was concerned, one of the awkward scholars who might or might not graduate but who in either case was a great deal of trouble. In such a situation it was natural that he should be asked by Professor Pernet, responsible for practical physics, why he did not study medicine, law, or philology rather than physics. It was natural that Pernet, faced with the young man's assertion that he felt he had a natural talent for physics, should reply: "You can do what you like: I only wish to warn you in your own interest." And it was natural that Weber, who disliked the young man addressing him as "Herr Weber" instead of "Herr Professor," should add, after admitting Einstein's cleverness: "But you have one fault: one can't tell you anything." Einstein was not quite as cocky as that. "At nineteen I had not published anything and would have laughed if anyone had suggested such a thing," he wrote in old age.

The situation throughout his four academic years at the ETH from 1896 until 1900 was not improved by his own attitude towards examinations. "The coercion," as he called it in his autobiographical notes, "had such a deterring effect [upon me] that, after I had passed the final examination, I found the consideration of any scientific problems distasteful to me for an entire year." For graduate he did, in August, 1900, receiving an overall mark of 4.91 out of 6.00; celebrating with his particular friends, of whom all except Mileva Maric had been successful; and expecting that he would now be offered, as was the custom of the time, a place on the lowest rung of the academic ladder, an appointment in the physics department of the ETH. However, the laws of human nature worked as rigorously for Albert Einstein as for others. Kollros was given a post under Hurwitz. Marcel Grossmann went to Fiedler, Ehrat to Rudio. Weber the physicist took on two mechanical engineers but overlooked the physicist Einstein. For the difficult fellow, no opening could be found.

The refusal of the ETH to employ him was a blow not only to his prospects but to his pride, and the contrast with his colleagues bit deep. "He, on good terms with the teachers and understanding everything; I, a pariah, discounted and little loved," he wrote to Grossmann's widow years afterwards. ". . . Then the end of our studies. . . . I was suddenly abandoned by everyone, standing at a loss on the threshold of life."

Yet it cannot have been entirely unexpected and it was certainly not unnatural. For the trappings of the grand old man of science have tended to obscure the reality of the self-willed youth from which he developed; the floating aureole of white hair evolved not from the dedicated student but from the rebel. In the autumn of 1900 Albert Einstein was the graduate who denied rather than defied authority, the perverse young man for whom "you must" was the father of "I won't," the keen seeker out of heresies to support; a young man who was written off as virtually unemployable by many self-respecting citizens.

These awkward facts became apparent throughout the next few months. One of the first results of Einstein's failure to gain a post in the ETH was the summary ending of his allowance from the Koch relations in Genoa. Having come of age he would have to stand on his own feet. He crossed the Alps once more to join his parents in

Milan, and from here, in September, 1900, wrote the first of numerous letters asking for work. It went to Adolf Hurwitz, the Zurich professor under whom he had read differential and integral calculus, and asked whether there was "any chance" of becoming his assistant. Shortly afterwards, a further letter followed, revealing the honesty which was to bedevil so many of his efforts. "Since, through lack of time, I was unable to attend the mathematical school there was no chance of practice in practical and theoretical physics, and I have nothing in my favor except the fact that I attended most of the courses which offered me opportunity," this letter admitted. "I think I must mention that in my student years I was mainly occupied with analytical mechanics and theoretical physics." The "mention" was no doubt enough, and the post went elsewhere.

Later that autumn, Einstein was back in Zurich working with Professor Alfred Wolfer under whom he had studied astrophysics and astronomy and who was now a director of the Swiss Federal Observatory. The work, though temporary, served its purpose, as shown in Einstein's first letter to Hurwitz. "I would not have taken the liberty of disturbing you with such a question during the recess had not the granting of my Zurich citizenship, which I have requested, been dependent upon furnishing proof of a fixed job," he said.

Citizenship—in effect, Swiss nationality—had been one of Einstein's objectives since the first weeks of 1896. Almost half a century later he remembered how he had been "happy in Switzerland because there men are left to themselves and privacy is respected," and throughout his student days he had regularly set aside 20 francs a month towards the cost of obtaining Swiss naturalization. Now at last he had the necessary cash, the necessary residential qualifications, and the necessary job. He had made his formal application to the Zurich authorities the previous autumn, on October 19, 1899, enclosing a testimonial of good character and proof of unbroken residence in the city since October 29, 1896. "Meanwhile," he concluded, "I commend my application to your most benevolent consideration, and remain with hope, Albert Einstein, Unionstrasse 4, Zurich-Hottingen." But the wheels of the Zurich authorities ground as slowly as God's, and it was the following summer before the necessary declaration was demanded of his father. It was given on July 4, with Hermann Einstein formally stating that he was "perfectly in agreement with the request of his son, Albert Einstein, regarding immigration to Switzerland and [the granting of] civic rights of the city of Zurich."

Einstein made only passing references to the formalities in later years. But the "duly accurate" biography by his stepson-in-law, written under the pseudonym of Anton Reiser, contained details which can only have come from himself. Even though they came thirty years later they have an interest in that they show Einstein as seen by Einstein. "The process had not been simple," Reiser wrote.

> The Zurich city fathers definitely mistrusted the unworldly dreamy young scholar of German descent who was so bound [sic] to become a citizen of Switzerland. They could not be too sure that he was not engaged in dangerous practices. They decided to examine the young man in person and to question him rigorously. Was he inclined to drink, had his grandfather been syphilitic, did he himself lead a proper life? Young Einstein had to give information on all these questions. He had hardly expected that the acquisition of Swiss naturalization papers was so morally involved a matter. Finally, the authorities observed how harmless and how innocent of the world the young man was. They laughed at him, teased him about his ignorance of the world, and finally honored him by recognizing his right to Swiss citizenship.

The tests do not seem exacting, even for 1900, but they lodged in his memory firmly enough.

On February 21, 1901, Einstein was granted the threefold citizen-rights of the Swiss—of the city, of the canton, and of the Swiss confederation. As such he became due for his three-month military service, like all other young Swiss men. Thirty years later he was to be among those who signed a protest against this system which made "soldiers of every able-bodied citizen from his eighteenth year to the end of his life and provides every household with a gun," claiming that "no more subtle way of preventing disarmament could be found by an enemy of peace." In 1901 he felt differently, dutifully presenting himself to the authorities, who rejected him for military service because of flat feet and varicose veins. According to contemporaries he was shocked and distressed. He certainly kept his *Dienstbuchlein,* or military service book, for many years, at least until the 1930s.

The formality over, Einstein was now a fully fledged Swiss, a status he was to retain all his life and of which he was always proud. There is little doubt that his chances of permanent employment were now greater than they had been as a German Jew. Yet his move had been far from merely utilitarian. He felt a basic attachment to Switzerland and the Swiss which continued throughout the years and grew with self-imposed exile in the United States into reminiscent affection. The reasons for it are revealing.

"I love the Swiss because, by and large, they are more humane than the other people among whom I have lived," he wrote late in life. There was also their pacific political record. For as Einstein's old friend Morris Raphael Cohen has stressed, "Like other opponents of military imperialism, Einstein [was] inclined to look upon the smaller European nations as on the right path"—while tending to ignore the fact that "their present attitude is in part at least due to the fact that the path of military aggrandizement is no longer open to them." Quite apart from this record, which on the political plane gave Switzerland an honorable place among nations, the country had physical and psychological characteristics which helped to make it a national example of all that Einstein felt the world might be if only men behaved sanely. Thus within its frontiers were French- and Italian-speaking peoples as well as German-speaking, and within these boundaries the rough corners of national attitudes tended to be smoothed off by mutual contact. The Swiss therefore tended to be tolerant of national idiosyncrasies and of personal ones as well. In the early years of the century, moreover, before the country had become the home of international agencies, before the reputation of Swiss bank accounts and of Swiss bankers gave it an aura of power, Switzerland existed in a European backwater that was particularly satisfying to Einstein, a man anxious only to be left to his work. Here, safe in the Swiss cocoon, he could carry on with minimum interruption. This was the prospect although it was not to be enjoyed immediately. His expectations of quickly getting a permanent job were still not justified and in March he was back with his parents in Milan.

However, his hopes were rising. In 1901, as much as today, publication produced the rungs of the ladder up which scientists climbed to fame, and in December of the previous year Einstein set up the first rung. This was "Folgerungen aus der Kapillaritätserscheinungen" ("Deductions from the Phenomena of Capillarity"), which appeared on December 13, 1900, in the *Annalen der Physik.* Shortly after the issue appeared he sent a copy to Wilhelm Ostwald, the German physical chemist who was carrying out his pioneer work on the principles of catalysis. The paper had been inspired by Ostwald's own work, and Einstein inquired whether there was a job in Ostwald's laboratory where he would have "the opportunity for further education." He appears to have received no reply, either to this first letter, or to a second which was, unknown to Einstein himself, supported by an appeal from his father. Certainly he got no job.

Before sending the second letter he had also written to Kamerlingh Onnes, the Dutch physicist, who in Leiden was already probing down towards the depths of ultimate cold. "I hear through a student friend," he wrote on a simple reply-paid card, "that there is a post vacant at your university for an assistant, and I take the liberty of applying for this." He outlined his qualifications and added that he was putting in the same post a copy of his treatise published in the *Annalen der Physik.* This card, now in the Leiden Museum for the History of Science, was the first link between Einstein and the Dutch university city, dreaming away among its canals and its great past, most of its honest burghers unaware that Kamerlingh Onnes was founding under their patronage the science of cryogenics and that Lorentz was dramatically introducing atomic ideas into Maxwell's electromagnetic theory. Two decades later Einstein was to become an honored visiting professor to the university. In its great hall he was to give some of his first lectures on the General Theory of Relativity. But his first contact with Leiden was of a different kind. Kamerlingh Onnes did not even answer, and the reply-paid second half of the card, self-addressed to "A. Einstein, via Bigli 21, Milano," remains blank in the museum's archives.

But rescue was at hand. "I have been offered a position in a technical school at Winterthur, to last from May 15 to July 15, to teach mathematics while the regular professor serves a term in the army," he wrote from Milan on May 3 to Professor Alfred Stern of Zurich. Stern taught history in the ETH, and when, years later, he was celebrating his eightieth birthday, Einstein wrote to him saying: "As a student I spent my most harmonious hours in your family circle and I often look back upon those days with pleasure." In 1901 he went on to unburden himself about the pleasure of getting his first job.

> I am beside myself with joy as I have just received confirmation that all is settled. I have no idea who recommended me, because as far as I know not one of my teachers has a good word to say for me, and I did not apply for the post but was invited. There is also a possibility that later on I may be able to find a job with the Swiss Patent Office.
>
> What am I to say now about your kind and fatherly friendship that you have constantly bestowed upon me whenever I had the chance to see you? I know that you are fully aware of my feelings, and do not wish to have them said. But it is true that no one else has ever treated me thus, and often when I came to you in a sad and bitter mood I found peace of mind and happiness in such pleasant company. But before you start laughing at me too much, I am fully aware that I am a curious bird and apart from an upset tummy or something like that, am not really given to melancholia. . . . Within the next few days I will cross the Spluegen on foot, combining duty and pleasure. When I arrive in Zurich, I will certainly visit you.

A few days later he was off, crossing the Alps and walking on down through the valleys of the Grisons to Coire and eastern Switzerland.

Einstein's period as stand-in for Professor Gasser at the Winterthur Technical School was uneventful. But no cause was found for keeping his services after Gasser's return. Once again he found himself back in Zurich, looking for work.

He was now saved by a combination of persistence and personal wire-pulling. In a Zurich newspaper he read that a teacher was required in a boarding school run by a Dr.

Jakob Nuesch of Schaffhausen, the little town on the Swiss frontier, famous alike for its Rhine Falls and its position astride the narrow neck of land joining the main body of Switzerland to its "island" on the right bank of the Rhine. In Schaffhausen there lived Conrad Habicht, a former fellow student from the ETH and a young man able to drop the right word in the right ear. With Habicht's help, Einstein was given the post which turned out to be, for the most part, coaching a young English boy, Louis Cohen. He held it for only a few months.

Just what happened is difficult to discover but easy to imagine. Einstein's detestation of the rigid discipline and the methods of the Gymnasium had in a way been compounded by his experiences in Zurich where he considered the routine teachings of the professors an unmitigated evil and the helpful notes of Marcel Grossmann a satisfactory method of evading them. Schaffhausen was not Munich and the methods of Switzerland were not those of the Fatherland. But Einstein's ideas of minimum routine and minimum discipline were very different from those of his employer, Jakob Nuesch. By the end of the year he was back once more in his old Zurich rooms, out of work again.

By this time, however, there were two gleams of light on the horizon. Before he left Schaffhausen he had completed a thesis on the kinetic theory of gases for his Ph.D. and sent it to the University of Zurich. He had also made formal application for the post in the Swiss Patent Office which was to be his first regular job.

"I, the undersigned, herewith offer myself for the post of engineer Class II at the Federal Patent Office which is announced in the Bundesblatt of 11 December, 1901," this went. He outlined his training at the ETH, mentioned his jobs at Winterthur and Schaffhausen, and then concluded by saying: "The papers which confirm these statements can be found at the present time in the University of Zurich and I hope to be able to forward them within the next few days. I am the son of German parents but I have lived since I was sixteen years of age without a break in Switzerland. I am a citizen of the town of Zurich. With great respect, I sign myself, Albert Einstein, Bahnhofstra., Schaffhausen."

The Swiss Patent Office had been founded only in 1888

and still went its official if individual way under the control of its original director, Herr Friedrich Haller. A large, friendly rough diamond, Haller was an engineer who had won his professional spurs during the 70s and 80s when the Swiss were establishing their reputation for driving railways through mountains, across mountains, and, if really necessary, up the near vertical sides of mountains. Success was the yardstick and if success were attained by a leavening of by-guess-and-by-God to formal scientific work, Haller saw little harm in that. He ran the Patent Office on his own unconventional lines, "with a whip in one hand and a bun in the other" according to a much later Patent Office official, and it was largely his own idiosyncratic rule which appears eventually to have brought Einstein to the Swiss capital as a minor civil servant.

Among Haller's personal friends was Herr Grossmann, father of the Marcel Grossmann of the ETH. Although the Grossmanns' intervention on Einstein's behalf is certain, the details are not clear; yet it seems likely that a casual talk between the two older men brought a generous promise that when a vacancy arose Marcel's friend would be favorably considered. Einstein learned of such an opening in December, 1901, and a few months after applying was among those selected for interview. His friend had earlier sent him an encouraging letter to which he replied:

> Dear Marcel,
> When I found your letter yesterday I was deeply moved by your devotion and compassion which do not let you forget an old, unlucky friend. I could hardly find better friends than you and Ehrat. Needless to say, I would be delighted to get the job. I would spare no effort to live up to your recommendation. I have spent three weeks at my parents' home looking for a position of assistant lecturer at some university. I am sure I would have found one long ago were it not for Weber's intrigues against me. In spite of all this, I don't let a single opportunity pass unheeded, nor have I lost my sense of humor. . . . When God created the ass he gave him a thick skin.

Shortly afterwards, he traveled from Milan to Berne for the all-important personal interview with Haller. The director has left no account of what must have been, for Einstein, a troublesome event. The only evidence that remains consists of a brief paragraph in Reiser. "Albert was examined for two full hours. The director placed before him literature on new patents about which he was required to form an immediate opinion. The examination unfortunately disclosed his obvious lack of technical training." However, this minor detail was no embarrassment to a man such as Haller, intent on helping an old friend. On June 16 Einstein was formally appointed, together with a J. Heinrich Schenk, as Technical Expert, at a salary of 3,500 francs a year. But Haller's goodwill could stretch only so far. The post for which Einstein had applied was Technical Expert (Second Class). He was made Technical Expert (Third Class).

Two legends have grown up about the appointment. One is that Einstein was employed because a knowledge of Maxwell's equations was considered essential and he was the only applicant who had it. The second is that the authorities in Zurich had already marked Einstein as a genius and passed on the good news to Haller, who had seized the chance of bringing on to his staff a young man whose fame and fortune would all come in good time.

The first of these legends is easily disposed of. The vacancy officially advertised in the Swiss *Gazette* listed the qualifications for the Patent Office post merely as follows: "Grundliche Hochschulbildung in mechanisch-technischer oder speziell physikalischer Richtung, Beherrschung der deutschen und Kenntnis der französischen Sprache oder Beherrschung der französischen und Kenntnis der deutschen Sprache, eventuell auch Kenntnis der italienischen Sprache." ("Thorough academic education in technical mechanics, or special leaning towards physics, a mastery of German and knowledge of French, or mastery of French and knowledge of German, and possibly knowledge of Italian.") The "speziell physikalischer Richtung" is the nearest that the requirement comes to a knowledge of Maxwell's laws and it is unlikely that Haller would—as is sometimes suggested—have pulled them into his interviews of candidates to eliminate everyone but Einstein.

It is easy to see the way in which the second legend, of long standing in the Patent Office, quietly grew throughout the years. For in retrospect it must have been maddening for the authorities to reflect that they had taken an ordinary, if not an ugly, duckling under their wing without realizing that he would develop into the most amazing swan of the scientific world. What more natural than that a legend of prescience, of inner awareness of the young man's potential genius, should steadily grow? The picture of Haller, nodding sagely in his retirement whenever the name of Einstein arose, is a picture which one hardly likes to shatter. Yet there appears not the slightest evidence for it. Neither Zurich nor any other Swiss university would have passed Einstein over, and on to others, had they seen in him anything more than an awkward, slightly lazy, and certainly intractable young man who thought he knew more than his elders and betters. He had in fact been set on his path to the future by an act of no more intellectual judgment than a good turn for an old friend.

But it was to be a future very different from what must have been anticipated. The Grossmanns, father and son, no doubt felt that they had shoveled a good companion into a safe job for life. Einstein saw it mainly as a useful base from which he could begin his self-imposed task of exploring the nature of the physical world.

A week after being formally appointed, he took up his post in the Patent Office.

CHAPTER 3

SWISS CIVIL SERVANT

The city to which Einstein moved in the summer of 1902 was very different in character from Zurich. Standing on its high sandstone ridge, three parts encircled by the swift waters of the Aare, looking towards the fine prospect of the Oberland, Berne was less tied to technology and industry, more tuned to the arts, than the city to the east. Embassies and legations occupied many of the fine houses to the south of the river across the Kirchenfeld Bridge. Summer tourists came to gaze at the famous clock tower with its midday procession of model bears which was the pride not only of the city but of all Switzerland. The British had already begun to make the huge main hotel, standing cheek by jowl with the Swiss Parliament house, a base from which they moved into the mountains for the fashionable sport of skiing they had introduced. In Berne the wrappings of the Swiss cocoon, which tended to shelter the country from the buffets of a Europe already being polarized towards either Paris or Berlin, were slightly less protective. Here Einstein was to spend the first creative years of his life, transforming the face of physics from the small back room of an apartment behind the arcades of Kramgasse into which there vibrated the chimes of the city clock tower.

His work as a technical officer in the Swiss Patent Office, then housed in the upper stories of the Federal Telegraph offices in Speichergasse, began on June 23, 1902. The details of his seven-year career there are simple enough. The initial appointment was provisional and it was agreed that when this was confirmed his salary should be "regularized to suit that of his work at the time." Confirmation did not come until September 4, 1904, when

Haller wrote to the Federal Council, noting that Einstein had "proved himself very useful" and proposing that his salary should be raised from 3,500 to 3,900 francs. He should, however, remain Class III rather than be promoted to Class II since "he is not yet fully accustomed to matters of mechanical engineering (he is actually a physicist)."

Upgrading to a higher class followed in 1906 when his salary was increased by another 600 francs. Since the autumn of 1904, Haller then wrote, Einstein had "continued to familiarize himself with the work, so that he now handles very difficult patent applications with the greatest success and is one of the most valued experts in the office." The director went on to note that his young technical officer had "acquired the title of Dr. Phil. from the University of Zurich this winter, and the loss of this man, who is still young, would be much regretted by the administration of the office."

Three points are of interest. The first is that Einstein had won his academic spurs in 1905. They had come after his presentation to the University of Zurich of a twenty-one-page paper on "A New Definition of Molecular Dimensions," dedicated to his friend Marcel Grossmann. Judging by the records, it was touch and go whether he got his doctorate. Professor Alfred Kleiner, director of the Zurich Physics Institute, recommended acceptance of the dissertation. But "as the principal achievement of Einstein's work consists of the treatment of differential equations, it is thus of a mathematical nature and belongs to analytical mechanics . . ." and Kleiner recommended two more opinions. That of Professor Burckhardt appears to have been decisive; despite "crudeness in style and slips of the pen in the formulas which can and must be overlooked," he noted that Einstein's paper showed "thorough mastery of mathematical methods."

Director Haller's remark about his young technical officer not only notes his academic advance but also implies that Einstein was by this time already searching around for another post and had not concealed the fact from his employers. Circumstantial evidence—casual references to teaching posts in Einstein's correspondence of this period—confirms that this was so. Thirdly it is significant that the director of the Patent Office, writing about his employee's progress in the spring of 1906, did not even comment on the three papers that the young man had by this time contributed to a single issue of the *Annalen der Physik*—one important enough to take him into the history books, one which helped to bring him the Nobel Prize sixteen years later, and the third containing the outline of the Special Theory of Relativity.

Einstein's first home in Berne was one small room in Gerechtigkeitsgasse and from this he walked every morning the few hundred yards to the building in whose third-floor office he learned his routine duties. One of his early visitors was the Max Talmey who had introduced him to science a decade earlier and who had recently called on his parents in Milan. They were "rather reticent" about their son, Talmey noted, and in Berne the reason appeared obvious. "I found my friend there and spent a day with him," he wrote. "His environment betrayed a good deal of poverty. He lived in a small, poorly furnished room. I learned that he had a hard life struggle with the scant salary of an official at the Patent Office. His hardships were aggravated through obstacles laid in his way by people who were jealous of him." The "obstacles" should not be taken too seriously. Einstein the potential schoolmaster, with one paper already to his credit in the pages of the *Annalen der Physik,* increasingly sure of himself, was an intellectual cut above his colleagues. He still had the confident brashness that seeps out from some of his early letters, and it is inconceivable that he should not have been put in his place from time to time by more pedestrian companions.

The work of the Patent Office at the turn of the century was strikingly different from what it later became. The difference is illustrated by one fact: until 1908 patents were granted only for inventions which could be represented by a model. The model, it is difficult not to feel, may have been as important as the specification which described, in words which ideally should allow of no dispute, the duties which the device was intended to perform. These inventions, ideas, and proposals which were directed to the office consisted largely of suggestions for practical, utilitarian, basically simple, and often homely applications of technology to the mundane affairs of everyday life. At first glance, all this appears to be singularly unrelated to Einstein's special genius. Yet despite the apparently esoteric quality of the theories on which his fame was founded, these theories sprang, as he was never tired of stressing, from observation of facts and from deductions which would account for these facts. This demanded an intuitive discernment of essentials, and it was just this which was sharpened during his days at the Patent Office. For the work frequently involved rewriting inventors' vague applications to give them legal protection; this in turn required an ability to see, among sometimes tortuous descriptions, the basic idea or ideas on which an application rested. The demand was not so much for the routine application of a routine mind to routine documents, as for perceptive intuition. "It is no exaggeration," says a member of the Patent Office staff, "to say that his activity was, at least in the first few months, literally an apprenticeship in the critical reading of technical specifications and in understanding the drawings that went with them."

Observation and analysis were therefore brought to a sharper edge as from the summer of 1902 onwards Einstein sat in the long narrow room of the government office with his fellow technical officers sorting, reading, and putting into intelligible German the specifications for typewriters and cameras, engineering devices, and the hundred and one curious appliances for which inventors wished to claim legal protection. He himself was in no doubt of what he learned at the Patent Office. "More severe than my father," was how he described the director to his colleague Joseph Sauter. "He taught me to express myself correctly."

But there was more to it than that. Einstein himself subsequently made two comments on his work in Berne. When he took up the post he wrote to his friend Habicht that it would give him "besides eight hours of work . . . eight hours of idleness plus a whole Sunday." And half a century later, on his seventieth birthday, he wrote that the formulation of patent statements had been a blessing. "It gave me," he said, "the opportunity to think about physics. Moreover, a practical profession is a salvation for a man of my type; an academic career compels a young man to scientific production, and only strong characters can resist the temptation of superficial analysis."

It was "the opportunity to think about physics" that

mattered. For while the Patent Office work helped to tickle into first-class condition Einstein's ability to discern the essentials of a scientific statement, it acted also as an undemanding occupation which released his mind for creative work at a different level. The process is not uncommon, and there had been an example in the very city in which he worked—that of Albrecht Haller the scientist, who as secretary of the Berne City Council had in the 1750s kept the Council minutes. Reprimanded one day by the Council chairman for writing a scientific treatise as a meeting proceeded, Haller was able to read out the detailed minutes that he had, simultaneously, been correctly keeping. Many men of genius need an occupation which keeps the wolf from the door while their intellectual work thus continues undisturbed. Trollope working in the Post Office while concentrating on the Barchester novels; Maurice Baring helping Trenchard plan the bombing offensive of 1918 while continuing his work as man of letters; Churchill politicking away through the interwar years while producing *Marlborough*—these are examples of great men immersing part of themselves in a routine that helped to release their creative genius. In Berne, Einstein was another, unobtrusively trotting from Gerechtigkeitsgasse to the Patent Office each morning, usually lunching at his desk, returning to his lodgings each evening with the orthodoxy of the city clerk, then setting himself down in a quiet corner to discover the laws of nature.

His first original papers had no connection with the theory of relativity which was to make him world famous. They concerned, instead, the nature of the forces which hold together the molecules of a liquid. "My major aim . . . ," he has written, "was to find facts which would guarantee as much as possible the existence of atoms of definite finite size." His statement well illustrates the attitude which still permeated scientific thought at the turn of the century. A number of eminent scientists—notably Mach and Ostwald—did not believe in the physical existence of atoms as such. For them, Dalton had lived in vain. They regarded atomic theory "more as a visualizing symbol than as knowledge concerning the factual construction of matter." It was typical that Einstein, still in his early twenties, should set about educating them.

The first five papers in which he started to do this were published between 1901 and 1904.* They were followed by a sixth which came in his *annus mirabilis* of 1905 and which applied several of his earlier results in a dramatically conclusive way. The first two papers, "my two worthless beginner's works" as Einstein himself described them when in December, 1907, he sent offprints of all his other papers to Johannes Stark, dealt with capillarity and potential differences. Neither was particularly successful, but the attraction of their subject for Einstein, dealing as it did with the links between intermolecular and other forces, was made clear in a letter he wrote to Marcel Grossmann in April, 1901. "As regards science," this said,

> I have got a few wonderful ideas in my head which have to be worked out in due course. I am now almost sure that my theory of the power of attraction of atoms can be extended to gases and that the characteristic constants for nearly all elements could be specified without undue difficulty. Then the question of the inner relationship of molecular forces will also take a decisive step forward. Perhaps the researches of others directed to different goals will ultimately prove the theory. In that case I shall then use all I have so far achieved in the field of molecular attraction in my doctor's thesis. It is a magnificent feeling to recognize the unity of a complex of phenomena which appear to be things quite apart from the direct visible truth.

Thus even at this early stage, when dealing with a subject far removed from the new concept of space and time to be embodied in relativity, Einstein revealed two aspects of his approach to science which became the keys to his work: the search for a unity behind disparate phenomena, and the acceptance of a reality "apart from the direct visible truth."

The subject matter of this early work was the immense numbers of particles which made up the liquids or the gases being considered. It is not possible to deal with the movements of individual particles, and therefore statistical methods, which could handle the averaged-out movements

*The part played by thermodynamics in Einstein's search for a unified basis for physics is analyzed by Martin J. Klein in "Thermodynamics in Einstein's Thought," *Science*, Vol. 157 (August 4, 1967), pp. 509-516.

of vast numbers, had to be used. If man had time enough, and equipment sensitive enough, it would be possible to calculate the movement of each molecule and each atom, since these movements were the result of cause and effect. But statistics, as in life insurance, provided a handy short-cut. As yet they provided no more.

His methods in the first two papers were those of thermodynamics. When he had completed them, he turned to the statistical foundations of the subject, attempting in three more papers to derive the laws describing equilibrium and irreversibility from the general equations of mechanics and the theory of probability. He believed his methods to be new, although they had, unknown to him, already been used by the American Josiah Willard Gibbs.*

Between the first of these early papers, written in Zurich, and the last of them, written in Berne, Einstein's circumstances changed. He became the center of a small coterie of young students who were to remain his friends for life; and, soon after this was formed, he married the friend of his Zurich days, Mileva Maric.

The group came into being shortly after Einstein moved to Berne. He had arrived a few weeks before taking up his Patent Office appointment and he was doubtful whether his funds would last until the first pay-day. What he really loved and really understood was physics. Berne was a university city and it was thus the most natural thing in the world that he should set up shop as a private tutor, offering to teach physics at so much an hour.

His first pupil was Maurice Solovine, a young Rumanian studying a ragbag of subjects at Berne University that included literature, philosophy, Greek, mathematics, and geology. "Walking in the streets of Berne one day during the Easter holidays of 1902, and having bought a newspaper, I noticed an advertisement saying that Albert Einstein, former pupil of the École Polytechnique of Zurich, gave lessons in physics at three francs an hour," he has written. Solovine sought out the house, climbed the stairs to the first story, and rang the bell.

"I heard a thunderous *'herein,'* and then Einstein ap-

*Gibbs' main papers were written between 1876 and 1878 and published in the *Transactions of the Connecticut Academy of Sciences*. Only in 1892 were they translated into German.

peared. As the door of his apartment gave on to a dark corridor I was struck by the extraordinary brilliance of his huge eyes," Solovine continues.

> Having entered and taken a chair, I told him that I studied philosophy but that I wanted to study physics a little more thoroughly to gain a real knowledge of nature. He confided in me that he also, when he was younger, had a strong taste for philosophy, but the vagueness and arbitrariness which reigned there had turned him against it, and that he was now concerned solely with physics. We talked for about two hours on all sorts of questions and we found we had similar ideas and were drawn towards one another. As I left he accompanied me downstairs and we talked for about another half hour in the street before an appointment was made for the following day.

The second visit was followed by a third, and on Solovine's suggestion it was agreed that they should read some of the standard works and discuss the problems they presented. Einstein proposed starting with Karl Pearson's *The Grammar of Science,* and this was soon followed by Mill, Hume, Spinoza, Mach, Henri Poincaré, and Riemann, whose non-Euclidean geometry was utilized in Einstein's development of the General Theory of Relativity a decade later.

The two men were soon joined by Conrad Habicht, Einstein's old friend from Zurich who now arrived in Berne to continue his mathematical studies. The faint line between teacher and taught, between the twenty-three-year-old Einstein and his companions of twenty, soon disappeared and the lessons dissolved into discussions that were continued week by week and month by month.

At times they would top off their argument with a long walk. Sometimes a Sunday would be enlivened by an eighteen-mile tramp to the Lake of Thun, by whose side they would camp for the day, before returning to Berne on the evening train. "Very often," Solovine has written,

> I met Einstein at the exist from the Patent Office; sometimes we would take up the discussion we had left off the night before and sometimes we confided to others our hopes and fears. Our material situation was far from being brilliant; but, in spite of that, what enthusiasm we

> had, what fire, what a passion for the things that really mattered! We also made a number of excursions together—walking, sometimes climbing to the top of the Gurten Kulm on Saturday to see the sunrise. The scent of the pines, warmed by the sun during the day, used literally to intoxicate me.

Einstein himself was the natural leader, and not only by virtue of the elder-statesman advantage which a year or two's seniority gave him. Even in his early twenties the force of character which was so to impress observers later on made itself felt. Something of this shows through even in the factual description given by Lucien Chavan, a young electrical engineer in the Federal Post and Telegraph Administration who was an occasional member of what became the self-styled "Olympia Academy." "Einstein is 1.76 meters tall," he wrote beneath a picture of Einstein which was given to the Swiss Postal Library after Chavan's death,

> broad shouldered, with a slight stoop. His short skull seems remarkably broad. His complexion is swarthy. He has a narrow moustache above a large sensitive mouth, an aquiline nose. His brown eyes have a deep benign luster. He has a fine voice, like the vibrant tones of a cello. Einstein speaks a good French with a slight foreign accent.

Discussion was the magnet which held the group together and when it was in full swing little else mattered. Solovine has recorded how shortly before Einstein's birthday he saw caviar displayed in a shop window in the city. Knowing it from his earlier days in Rumania, he decided with Habicht to buy some as an expensive birthday treat. When it was put on the table Einstein was talking about the problems of Galilean inertia. He went on talking, eating the caviar without comment. "It's all the same to me," he said, when told what it was. "You can offer bumpkins the most exquisite things in the world and they don't know how to appreciate them." What mattered was the talk. It went on intermittently until 1905 when Solovine left the country for the University of Lyon and Habicht moved to another part of Switzerland.

The impact of mind on mind, the cut and thrust of

argument, did much to sharpen the intellectual rapier with which Einstein was preparing to attack the body of classical physics. Even so, the Olympia Academy should be viewed in perspective. It was not a group of young men living in the academic stratosphere. The faces which look out from the contemporary photograph above wing collars and bow ties have a smile in the eyes, and if the attitude of Einstein implies a deep earnestness it suggests also an air of half-amused human tolerance which not even seventy years was to remove. During the Academy's nightlong discussions of physics and philosophy, their walks through the solitary Berne streets or on the hills, Einstein certainly clarified his own thoughts and began to see more plainly the special problems to which he must devote himself. But if this was a debating society of a particularly high order it was also something more normal: a group of high-spirited young men, active and contentious, lively legged as well as lively minded and as eager as most others to pursue their discussions in the Café Bollwerk, a few steps from the Patent Office, as they were to pursue them in the quiet of their own rooms. It is history which has isolated the group; to most of the inhabitants of Berne, as well as to its members, the Olympia Academy might have been duplicated in a hundred towns and cities across Europe.

This carefree, almost undergraduate existence, was drastically changed when in January, 1903, Einstein married Mileva Maric. The daughter of a Slav peasant, four years his senior, Mileva was to remain his wife until, early in 1919, a divorce between the couple was agreed on when the prospects of a Nobel Prize, whose 30,000 kroner he promised to pass on to her if he won it, seemed likely to secure her own future and that of their two sons. She had left him in the summer of 1914; but she was wife and companion during the decade which brought him from the anonymity of the Patent Office to a secure position in international science and to the threshhold of world-wide fame. Thus the part that Mileva played in helping him up the ladder of success, or in holding him back, is important in Einstein's own story; it has remained untold partly because of his reluctance to reveal details of his personal affairs—"after 300 years a man's private life should still remain private," he once said of Newton—partly because

Mileva lived on, despite crippling illness, until 1948; partly because legal problems have prevented publication of a long series of letters between the couple. Yet the story, also told in many letters which Einstein wrote to his colleague and confidant Michelangelo Besso, is of incompatibility rather than conflict; of a couple who respected one another as long as they did not have to live together. And it is a story which makes all more remarkable the intellectual accomplishment of a man who, as he wrote on one occasion, would have become mentally and physically exhausted if he had not been able to keep his wife at a distance, out of sight and out of hearing.

This confidence to Besso was made in 1916, when relations between Einstein and Mileva were at their worst, but it illustrates the role of friend and father-confessor which the Italian engineer was to play in Einstein's life. Besso, six years older, had come from Rome to study in the ETH engineering department, but his real link with Einstein was stronger. While Maja Einstein, who had studied at Aarau, was to marry Paul Winteler, the son of the town's schoolmaster, Besso married Paul's sister Anna. In 1904, a year after he married Mileva, Einstein helped Besso into a position as examiner at the Berne Patent Office. The two men walked the same way home. Their confidences were professional—with the result that Besso was to become the only man thanked for help in the famous relativity paper—but they were also personal, and after Einstein moved to Zurich in 1909 his letters to Besso reveal the deteriorating stages of his marriage.

According to some accounts the couple had become engaged while still students, but this was frowned upon by Hermann Einstein who had apparently never met Mileva when he died in Italy in 1902. Certainly Einstein crossed the Alps to be present at his father's deathbed and certainly he married Mileva a few months after his return to Berne. The photographs which survive show her as a not unattractive woman of pleasant features, broadish nose above good sensual mouth, and with an aura of thick dark hair. She had a limp, but this was not serious and judging by the generally unkind descriptions, her deficiencies, such as they were, lay elsewhere. "A modest, unassuming creature" was the best that Fräulein Markwalder, daughter of Einstein's landlady, could muster. Carl Seelig, who like Mileva lived in Zurich for the greater part of his life, comments that

> her dreamy, ponderous nature often curdled her life and her studies. Her contemporaries found Mileva a gloomy, laconic, and distrustful character. Whoever got to know her better began to appreciate her Slav open-mindedness and the simple modesty with which she often followed the liveliest debates from the background.

He notes in addition that she was "hardly the typical Swiss-German house-sprite, the height of whose ambition is a constant war against dust, moths, and dirt." There is more than a touch of race bias in some of this, and it is fair to assume that to many Teutons Mileva had the unpardonable Slav tendency of letting things slip. There was one compensation. Einstein, hearing a friend comment, "I should never have the courage to marry a woman unless she were absolutely sound," replied, "But she has such a lovely voice."

Einstein himself has given various accounts of why he did in fact marry her. One old friend to whom he confided his own account, says, "How it came about he doesn't know himself," and to another he said that he married despite his parents' determined opposition, out of a feeling of duty. In old age he also tried to rationalize his actions, claiming that what he called this tragedy in his life probably explained his immersion in serious work. However, whether the emotional crises of an unhappy marriage are likely to affect the work of the theoretical physicist in the same beneficent way that they can affect the artist is a moot point; certainly Einstein, writing not years later but as the rift with Mileva developed, gave little sign of it.

In many ways, Einstein would in 1903 have been happier with a dedicated housekeeper; instead, he tumbled into marriage, almost by accident, possibly while thinking of more important things. But even in those days, before pacifism, before Zionism, before the antibomb movement, he was a decent man beneath the determination of his scientific exterior. Just as, even then, he felt a responsibility towards the human race, so did he feel a responsibility towards those with whom circumstance had joined him. He hardly had time or inclination to be a family man, but he did his best.

Relations worsened as the years passed, particularly after 1905 when the Theory of Special Relativity began to make him famous. His acquaintances, the men and women against whom he was brushed by the chances of everyday life, were only too ready to admit that relativity was beyond them; his second wife was to say so with an air of relief. With Mileva the situation was different, for was she not a physicist like her husband? Had she not, in fact, got just enough "little learning" to enter the new world he had created, if only he would spare time to explain things? The answer was "No," but she would never believe it.

Another factor was quite as important. When Einstein married, he expected to win more time for work; he expected to shuffle off the domestic detail which hangs round bachelor necks. The physicist who in later life was to discard socks as unnecessary complications and who insisted that washing and shaving with the same soap made life that much simpler, had one basic desire, even in the early 1900s: to transfer to other shoulders the tiresome tasks which diverted time from more important things. Many men have married for worse reasons; and many have found that, failing the grand passion, such mundane considerations have enabled a couple to rub along happily enough.

It is true that Einstein could always isolate himself from surrounding trivia with an enviable ease. In a mob, at a concert, listening to speeches, he could follow the exterior pattern of events while an essential part of his mind worked away at the problem of the moment. But it would, even so, be useful if marriage removed the clutter of workaday duties and diversions. That it failed to do so, that it merely exchanged the preoccupations of bachelordom for those of a family man, is clear from the pictures of his early family life that have survived.

"He was sitting in his study in front of a heap of papers covered with mathematical formulas," says one student who visited him a few years after his marriage. "Writing with his right hand and holding his younger son in his left, he kept replying to questions from his elder son Albert who was playing with his bricks. With the words, 'Wait a minute, I've nearly finished,' he gave me the children to look after for a few moments and went on working." A similar picture is painted by David Reichinstein, one of the Zurich professors. "The door of the apartment was open to allow the floor which had just been scrubbed, as well as the washing hung up in the hall, to dry," he says. "I entered Einstein's room. He was calmly philosophic, with one hand rocking the bassinet in which there was a child. In his mouth Einstein had a bad, a very bad, cigar, and in the other hand an open book. The stove was smoking horribly. How in the world could he bear it?"

The home life of a poorly paid academic in Switzerland in the first decade of the century must be kept in perspective. All the same, a colleague felt it necessary to ask: "How could he bear it?" The answer is that he had to.

Einstein married Mileva Maric in Berne on Tuesday, January 6, 1903. The two witnesses at the quiet wedding were the original members of the Olympia Academy, Maurice Solovine and Conrad Habicht. There was no honeymoon, and after a celebratory meal in a local restaurant the couple returned to their new home, a small apartment in 49 Kramgasse only a hundred yards from Berne's famous clock tower. Here there was a minor incident. Many stories were to arise, or to be invented, of the absent-minded professor; but here, on his wedding day, Einstein did find on arriving back home that he had forgotten the key.

Superficially, he now slipped down into one of the innumerable ruts occupied by minor members of the Swiss civil service. His raise in salary eighteen months after marriage did little more than compensate for the additional expenses of a son, Hans Albert, who was born towards the end of 1903. The distant goal of First-Grade Technical Assistant must have seemed at first glance to be the ultimate end of all human hope and ambition for the aloof young man who walked to work every day from his apartment, its entrance protected by stone arcades supported on stout stone pillars. On one of them, there rests today a plaque: "IN DIESEM HAUS," it records, "SCHUF ALBERT EINSTEIN IN DEN JAHREN 1903–5 SEINE GRUNDLEGENDEABHANDLUNG UBER DIE RELATIVITÄTSTHEORIE" ("In this house between 1903 and 1905 Albert Einstein completed work on the theory of relativity").

In March, 1905, Einstein was twenty-six. Only his papers on intermolecular forces distinguished him from hundreds of other young men serving their time in government offices, and they did not distinguish him all that much. When, early in 1905, he rounded off the series in an inaugural dissertation for the University of Zurich, he had a total of six papers to show for the five years that had passed since his graduation. This work looked more like the result of postgraduate enthusiasm than the start of the most distinguished carrer in physics that Europe had known for centuries. It was a good record for a failed teacher who had ended up in the Patent Office; it was surprisingly little for a man who was about to shake the scientific world.

Up to now, Einstein had no academic status. He had the run of the Patent Office library, strong on engineering but weak on physics, and he read the leading physics journals published in German. But he had access to little else. Neither did he work, nor could he talk and debate even on social occasions, inside a university environment with its incessant point counterpoint of argument, its constant cross-fertilization of ideas, and its stimulating climate of inquiry. The Olympia Academy, lively as it was, was no substitute for this. He corresponded with his former student friends in Zurich and he occasionally visited them. But that was all. Thus from 1902 until 1905 Einstein worked on his own, an outsider of outsiders, scientifically provincial and having few links with the main body of contemporary physics. This isolation accounts for his broad view of specific scientific problems—he ignored the detailed arguments of others because he was unaware of them. It also shows a courage beyond the call of scientific duty, submission to the inner compulsion which was to drive him on throughout life and for which he was willing to sacrifice everything.

Any one of the four main papers which he published in 1905 would have assured him a place in the textbooks. Three were published in the single famous Volume 17 of *Annalen der Physik*—today a bibliographical rarity which changes hands at more than $2,400—and the fourth in Volume 18. All were comparatively short, and all contained the foundations for new theories even though they did not elaborate on them—"blazing rockets which in the dark of the night suddenly cast a brief but powerful illumination over an immense unknown region," as they have been described by Louis de Broglie.

In one way it was the wide variety of the ground illuminated which made this achievement of 1905 so remarkable. It was as if a young explorer had in one dazzling year of travel shown himself to be master navigator, a good man in tropical jungle, and at the same time a first-rate mountaineer. Yet in science there had been one burst of genius strikingly similar to Einstein's. Almost two and a half centuries earlier Newton had been driven by the plague at Cambridge to the quiet of Woolsthorpe and had there produced the calculus, an explanation of the spectral nature of white light, and the law of gravitation.

In the spring of 1905 Einstein gave a résumé of things to come in a letter to his friend Conrad Habicht. "I promise you in return four works, the first one very soon as I am expecting my author's copies," he wrote

> It is on the radiation and energy of light, and it is very revolutionary as you will see for yourself, provided you send me your work first. The second discusses the methods of determining the real dimensions of atoms by investigating the diffusion and internal friction of liquid solutions. The third proves that, according to the molecular theory of heat, bodies of dimensions of the order of 1/1000 mm. suspended in liquid experience apparent random movement due to the thermal motion of molecules. Such movement of suspended bodies has actually been observed by biologists who call it Brownian molecular movement. The fourth work is based on the concepts of electrodynamics of moving bodies and modifies the theory of space and time; the purely kinematic part of this work should interest you. . . .

The promised papers were a peculiar mixture—as though a competently executed watercolor from the local art society had been thrown in with three Rembrandts. For the "second work" was merely Einstein's inaugural dissertation for the University of Zurich which he was having printed in Berne, interesting enough in its own way, but a minnow among the whales of the other three papers. Of these, that dealing with Brownian motion sprang most obviously from earlier work. For his doctoral dissertation had discussed various methods of statistical thermodynamics and it was these tools that he used to predict not only that in certain circumstances the results of molecular movement could actually be seen under the microscope, but also the mass and the numbers of molecules in any particular volume.

This motion had been reported some seventy years earlier by Robert Brown, the Scottish naturalist, and there is some doubt as to how much Einstein knew about it in 1905. Writing forty-five years later, he stated that he had "discovered that, according to atomistic theory, there would have to be a movement of suspended microscopic particles open to observations, without knowing that observations concerning the Brownian motion were already long familiar." However, his letter to Habicht shows that by 1905 he was in fact well aware of Brown's observations even though he may not have known of the further investigations which had followed them.

The Scotsman had discovered that when pollen dust was suspended in water and studied under the microscope the individual particles exhibited a continuous, zigzag, and apparently random motion. "These motions," he wrote, "were such as to satisfy me, after frequently repeated observation, that they arose neither from current in the fluid nor from its gradual evaporation, but belonged to the particle itself." Brown repeated his experiments with pollen from a number of plants. He observed a similar "swarming" motion in all of them and at first believed he had discovered the "primitive molecule." Then he found the same effect when the dusty particles of inorganic matter were treated in the same way. Many men discovered more about the Brownian motion in the years that followed: M. Gouy saw that as the viscosity of the liquid increased, so did the sluggishness of the movements; Franz Exner noted that speed of movement increased with a rise in temperature but decreased if bigger particles were used.

When Einstein later observed this motion through the microscope for himself he was fascinated. "It is an impressive sight," he wrote.

> It seems contradictory to all previous experience. Examination of the position of one suspended particle, say every thirty seconds, reveals the fantastic form of its path. The amazing thing is the apparently eternal charac-

> ter of the motion. A swinging pendulum placed in water soon comes to rest if not impelled by some external force. The existence of a never diminishing motion seems contrary to all experience. This difficulty was splendidly clarified by the kinetic theory of matter.

It was the explanation of this "contrary" experience that Einstein now gave in his paper, "On the Motion of Small Particles Suspended in a Stationary Liquid According to the Molecular Kinetic Theory of Induction." The random motion of the individual particles was due to the kinetic energy of the invisible molecules with which they were constantly colliding. From this point he went on to use his new statistical machinery to predict the mass and number of molecules involved. It was the essence of his theory that the mean kinetic energy of agitation of the particles would be exactly the same as the roughly known energy of agitation in a gas molecule, and this was in fact shown experimentally only a few years later—by Jean Perrin in Paris in 1908 and by Fletcher and Millikan four years later in Chicago.

"To appreciate the importance of this step," Max Born has written of Einstein's successful attempt to quantify the Brownian motion, "one has to remember that at that time [about 1900] atoms and molecules were still far from being as real as they are today—there were still physicists who did not believe in them." The latter included both Mach and "the old fighter against atomistics, Wilhelm Ostwald" who, Arnold Sommerfeld has stated, "told me once that he had been converted to atomistics by the complete explanation of the Brownian motion." Thus Einstein's figures for the invisible molecules had something in common with the Hertzian sparks which showed the existence of the radio waves postulated by Maxwell two decades earlier.

But Einstein's paper was also to have an important consequence for scientific methodology in general. "The accuracy of measurement depends," Max Born has pointed out,

> on the sensitivity of the instruments, and this again on the size and weight of the mobile parts, and the restoring forces acting on them. Before Einstein's work it was tacitly assumed that progress in this direction was limited

> only by experimental technique. Now it became obvious that this was not so. If an indicator, like the needle of a galvanometer, became too small or the suspending fiber too thin, it would never be at rest but perform a kind of Brownian movement. This has in fact been observed. Similar phenomena play a large part in modern electronic technique, where the limit of observation is given by irregular observations which can be heard as a "noise" in a loudspeaker. There is a limit of observability given by the laws of nature themselves.

Einstein's virtual proof of the existence of molecules, invisible to the human eye, postulated by theory rather than produced by experimental evidence, was symptomatic of the line which he was to take throughout the career on which he was now embarking. It was illustrated by his later comments on the difficulties which Mach and Ostwald had felt in accepting the atomic theory as a statement of fact rather than as a convenient hypothesis. "The antipathy of these scholars towards atomistic theory can indubitably be traced back to their positivistic philosophical attitude," he wrote. "This is an interesting example of the fact that even scholars of audacious spirit and fine instinct can be obstructed in the interpretation of facts by philosophical prejudices. The prejudice—which has by no means died out in the meantime—consists in the faith that facts by themselves can and should yield scientific knowledge without free conceptual construction."

Einstein thus believed that theories into which facts were later seen to fit were more likely to stand the test of time than theories constructed entirely from experimental evidence. This was certainly the case with the first paper which he had described in his letter to Habicht, a paper which "fell like a bolt from the blue, so much so that the crisis which it ushered in some fifty years ago is not yet passed today," as Louis de Broglie described it in 1955. It was to help bring Einstein the Nobel Prize for physics sixteen years later, and was to play a key part in the development of modern technology, since the photoelectric effect whose law it propounded was to become a cornerstone of television. It contained Einstein's first implied admission of the duality of nature which was to haunt his life and an early hint of the indeterminacy problem which drove him, as de Broglie has put it, "to end his scientific life in sad isolation and—paradoxically enough—apparently far behind the ideas of his time." Moreover, with the sense of theater which chance was to utilize so often in Einstein's life, it linked his scientific work at the age of twenty-six with two men whose non-scientific beliefs and attitudes were to influence him, and on some occasions to dominate him, for more than forty years—Max Planck, that devoted upholder of the German state who was also the founder of the quantum theory, and Philipp Lenard, composed in almost equal parts of Nobel Prize winner and Jew-baiter.

This famous paper, "On a Heuristic Viewpoint Concerning the Production and Transformation of Light," explained one particular phenomenon, the photoelectric effect, which had been puzzling scientists for years, and it suggested answers to a number of other less important scientific riddles. But it did a great deal more and while it is usually known as Einstein's "photoelectric paper" it did not spring from consideration of this specific problem but from something far more fundamental. For Einstein, mulling over his previous work on thermodynamics and statistical mechanics, noted a discrepancy in current scientific beliefs and wondered how it could be removed: the photoelectric riddle was merely a particularly convenient one which could apparently be resolved by applying a revolutionary explanation of the discrepancy. To understand its importance it is necessary to consider briefly how the nature of light was regarded at the start of the twentieth century.

To the Greeks, the idea that light consisted of minute grains in rapid movement appeared to be borne out by the fact that it traveled in straight lines and bounced off mirrors in the same way that balls bounce off walls. Only in the early 1600s was there made the first of a series of discoveries which culminated, in the last third of the century, in the theory put forward by Huygens: that light was composed of waves propagated through a medium which he called the ether and which permeated all space. Newton, in his *Opticks*, apparently favored the corpuscular theory, although he also outlined a scheme in which corpuscules of light were associated with waves which influenced them—an idea revived some two and a half centuries later in the form of wave mechanics to explain the nature of matter. Not until the nineteenth century did the work first of Fresnel and then of Maxwell provide a wave explanation of light which appeared—at least for a few years—to deal satisfactorily with all the experimental evidence.

It was Hertz who raised one of the first questions which were to bring this comfortable state of affairs to an end. What he found was that when a sheet of glass was put between his wave transmitter and his receiver, the sparks produced in the transmitter failed to produce as large a group of sparks in the receiver. He decided, naturally enough, that the receiving loop must be affected by the sparks' ultraviolet light, which does not penetrate glass, and that in some inexplicable way this light was thus increasing the electrical discharge from his metal receiver. Other scientists discovered that his photoelectric effect, as it came to be known, could be produced by visible as well as by ultraviolet light; that it was produced with some metals more easily than with others; and that the receiving metal acquired a small positive electrical charge.

Now elucidation of the nature of light by Maxwell's electromagnetic equations had been paralleled by another, and apparently contradictory, development. For while it had been found that light was radiated as electromagnetic waves, other physicists—Hendrik Lorentz in Leiden and J. J. Thomson in Cambridge among them—had been discovering that what could only be considered particles, the negatively charged electrons, played an important part in the constitution of electrified matter. It is at this stage that Lenard comes on the scene. A scientist of great skill, Lenard was a German whose desperation at his country's defeat in 1918 quickly led him into the welcoming arms of the Nazi party; in addition, his paranoiac hatred of the Jews brought him, after 1919, into the movement which attempted to discredit both Einstein's honesty and his work. At the turn of the century Lenard put forward a simple explanation of the photoelectric effect; it was that photoelectrons, or negative charges, were knocked out of the metal by the light which hit it. Soon, however, he reported another less easily explicable phenomenon. Since electrons were ejected from the sensitive metal solely as a result of light falling upon it, then it might surely be assumed that an increase in light would produce an increase in the speed at which the electrons were thrown from the metal. However, this was not the case. If the intensity of the light was increased, then a great number of electrons would be ejected from the metal, but they would continue to be ejected at the same speed. But—and this appeared even more inexplicable—if there was a change in the color of the light, or in other words in its frequency, then there would be a change in the speeds at which the electrons were thrown out; and the higher the frequency the higher the speed of ejection.

While Lenard was thus occupied in the familiar scientific operation of answering one riddle and creating another, Max Planck, by this time professor of theoretical physics at the University of Berlin, was grappling with a problem which at first glance seemed to be only indirectly concerned with the photoelectric effect. Planck had taken the chair after the death of Kirchhoff in 1887, and it was from a continuation of Kirchhoff's work that he produced the theory which was to alter man's idea of energy as drastically as Einstein's theory of relativity was to alter ideas of time and space.

Kirchhoff had been interested, like many of his contemporaries, in discovering more about the mechanism by which radiant energy was emitted by electromagnetic waves, already known to include not only the spectrum of visible light but the infrared and ultraviolet rays on either side of them, as well as the newly discovered radio waves. It was known that as a body was heated its maximum energy was produced at shorter and shorter wavelengths, and its color passed from red to yellow and then to bluish white. But all experiments appeared to be affected by the nature of the emitting body, only overcome by Kirchhoff's ingenious method of using "black-body radiation" which utilized a closed container with blackened inner walls and one tiny pinhole. When the container was heated to incandescence, genuinely pure light of all the visible wavelengths could, in theory at least, be observed coming from the pinhole. This primitive equipment was supplemented in 1881 by the bolometer, invented by Samuel Langley, the Harvard professor whose aerodynamic work led on to the Wright brothers and Kitty Hawk. With Langley's bolometer, which depended on the electrical measurement of minute quantities of heat set up in a blackened platinum wire, it was possible to record temperature changes as little as one-millionth of a degree under the impact of specific wavelengths; thus there was now, it appeared, a route to an adequate description of the way that energy was radiated.

During the 1890s, Planck found that this was far from being the case. Despite the efforts of physicists throughout Europe it became clear that while one set of distribution formulas produced by Wilhelm Wien served well enough to explain radiation at low wavelengths, those at high wavelengths demanded the different mathematical explanation produced by Lord Rayleigh—as though nature had changed the rules of the game at half time. No one could explain it. "The discrepancy," Sir Basil Schonland has stated, "suggested that something fundamental had been missed by both. The affair, which was extremely closely examined by the best minds of the time, presented something like a scientific scandal."

It was to this discrepancy that Planck turned during the latter half of the 1890s. In the autumn of 1900 he thought he had solved the problem and on October 14 read a paper to the Berlin Physical Society which proposed a single neat expression to explain how radiation worked. These satisfied the Wien distribution formula at low wavelengths and Rayleigh's distribution formula at high ones; in fact they fitted experimental observations between infrared measurements towards one end of the spectrum and ultraviolet measurements towards the other so well that some men working on ultraviolet found it necessary to repeat their experiments and amend their figures.

For Planck, this was not enough. Intuitively, he felt that something more and something different was required. "After some weeks of the most intense work of my life, clearness began to dawn upon me, and an unexpected view revealed itself in the distance," he later said. To Professor R. W. Wood, he explained in more detail. "Speaking briefly, I can call the whole action a process of despair," he wrote.

> Actually, my nature is peace-loving and I am disinclined towards serious adventure. But for six years (from 1874 on) I had been doing battle with the problem of the

equilibrium between radiation and matter without success. I knew that the problem is of fundamental importance for physics, I knew the formula that reproduced the energy distribution in the normal spectrum; a theoretical interpretation *would have to be* found at any cost, no matter how high. Classical physics was not adequate, that was clear to me. . . .

Some weeks after his October address, Planck found the explanation. Walking in the Grunewald woods in Berlin, he turned to his son. "Today," he said, "I have made a discovery as important as that of Newton."

On December 14, 1900, he appeared again before the Physical Society. This time he announced that his earlier expression could best be derived from an entirely new hypothesis. It was not only new but startling. For Planck now stated that his whole theory was based on one assumption: that energy was emitted not in the continuous flow that everyday commonsense suggested but as discrete bursts for which he used the Latin "How much," or quanta. The size of quanta was, moreover, directly related to the frequency of the electromagnetic wave with which they are associated, violet light, which has twice the frequency of red light, having associated quanta twice as large as those associated with red light. Linking the frequency of the radiation and the size of the quantum there was, in the units current in Planck's time which are still widely but not exclusively used, the magic quantity of $h = 6.6 \times 10^{=27}$, erg. sec., quickly known as Planck's constant and soon recognized as one of the fundamental constants of nature.

At first sight this revolutionary idea appeared to stick a dagger between the ribs of the accepted view that light consisted of waves rather than particles. But not even Planck could go as far as that. His theory, he stressed, was concerned with the relationship between radiation and matter, not with the nature of radiation on its journey between emission and reception; thus he allowed the discontinuous bursts of energy to join up in some inexplicable way and produce waves which dissolved into particulate entities as they were absorbed. The "scientific scandal," as Schonland was later to describe it, had been removed only by creating a fresh one.

In 1903 J. J. Thomson, giving the Silliman Lectures at

Yale University, appears to have been on the verge of dissipating it when he suggested that some form of localized radiant energy might account for a number of unexplained experimental facts, including the manner in which ultraviolet light ejected electrons from a metal surface. But the idea was taken no further. This preserved the wave nature of light; it also left the way open for Einstein. For just as Niels Bohr was later to use the quantum theory to explain the structure of the atom, so did Einstein now use it to justify the idea that light could have characteristics of both wave and particle.

Until 1905 his published papers had dealt almost exclusively with thermodynamics and statistical mechanics; they were essentially studies in which the laws of nature were considered by reference to the random movements of vast numbers of individual particles which obeyed Newton's laws as obediently as the planets. But there were also Einstein's unpublished thoughts; and these were obsessed with the reality of light and its associated electromagnetic waves, a reality conceived not in terms of Newtonian particles but of the field which had been proposed by Faraday and developed by Maxwell. No one had up till now thought of asking the awkward questions which the contradiction begged; or if they had thought of it they had not dared. Einstein both thought and dared.

"There is a profound formal difference between the theoretical ideas that physicists have formed concerning gases and other ponderable bodies, and Maxwell's theory of electromagnetic processes in so-called empty space," began the photoelectric paper. The difference could be resolved, he suggested, if for some purposes light itself could be considered as a collection of independent particles which behaved like the particles of a gas—the heuristic viewpoint of his title. When Einstein began to consider this new concept in the light of his earlier work, he found that it provided some startlingly useful results. The photoelectric explanation was one of them.

For the size of Planck's quanta depended on the frequency of the light concerned, and the small quanta of a low-frequency light would, if they were considered as discrete packages of particulate energy, therefore eject the electrons they hit with a comparatively low speed; the bigger "packets of energy," as the quanta making up the higher-frequency colors could be considered, would of course eject at higher speeds the electrons they hit. This explanation would also account for what happened when the intensity of the light of any specific color was decreased. Each individual quantum which went to make it up would have the same power to eject an electron which it hit. But there would be fewer quanta, fewer "hits," and fewer electrons ejected. As Sir James Jeans said in describing the photochemical law that Einstein produced, his explanation of the photoelectric effect "not only prohibits the killing of two birds by one stone, but also the killing of one bird with two stones."

In his paper Einstein did more than put forward a theory which was, as he said, "in perfect agreement with observation"—and which was later to be confirmed experimentally, by Millikan for visible light, by de Broglie for X rays, and by Jean Thibaud and Ellis for gamma rays. In addition, he calculated the maximum kinetic energy of the electron which was emitted, giving this by the use of the formula $h\nu - e\phi$, where h is Planck's constant, ν is the frequency of the light, and $e\phi$ is the energy lost by the electron in its escape from the metal surface, called the work function. Thus Einstein's conception of light as being formed of light quanta—or photons, as they were later christened—in itself involved a paradoxical contradiction from which a man of lesser mental stature might have edged away. For while light consisting of discrete packets of energy, as indivisible as the atom was still thought to be, conformed—if it conformed to anything—to the corpuscular theory of Newton's day, the idea also utilized frequency, a vital feature of the wave theory. Thus, as Bohr was later to write, physics was "confronted with a novel kind of complementary relationship between the applications of different fundamental concepts of classical physics." Physicists began to study more closely these contradictory ideas which alone seemed to explain verifiable facts, and eventually, in the 1920s, they began to see the limitations of deterministic description. At the level of simple atomic processes, nature could only be described in terms of statistical chance—the case of "God playing dice with the world" that Einstein could never accept. Yet he had pushed the stone that started the avalanche.

This was not clear in 1905. Even so, Einstein had to face the embarrassing contradiction that Planck had tried to avoid: for some purposes, light must be regarded as a stream of particles, as Newton had regarded it; for others, it must be considered in terms of wave motion. But he believed that eventually, if men were only persistent enough, a satisfactory explanation for the contradiction would emerge. This was in fact to be the case some two decades later when de Broglie and Schrödinger, Born and Heisenberg, were to produce a conception of the physical world that could be regarded in terms either of waves or of particles—or as one humorist called it, of "wavicles."

Planck himself was reluctant to accept Einstein's development of his theory, and as late as 1912 was rejecting, in Berlin lectures, the idea that light traveled through space as bunches of localized energy. "I think it is correct to say," writes Robert Millikan, who was to win the Nobel Prize for demonstrating the corpuscular nature of electricity with his work on the electron, "that the Einstein view of light quanta, shooting through space in the form of localized light pulses, or, as we now call them, photons, had practically no convinced adherents prior to about 1915, by which time convincing experimental proof had been found."

Einstein's record was thus an unusual one. He had applied Planck's revolutionary theory with apparent success to a physical phenomenon that classical physics could not explain. He had been more revolutionary than his elders and they would not credit him with what he had done. It needed courage; but this was to be expected from the man who could, in the same issue of the *Annalen der Physik,* explode the bomb which was his new theory of relativity.

PART TWO

THE VOYAGE OF DISCOVERY

CHAPTER 4

EINSTEIN'S RELATIVITY

The Special Theory of Relativity that was to give Einstein his unique position in history was outlined in the third paper which he wrote for the *Annalen der Physik* in the summer of 1905. Entitled simply "On the Electrodynamics of Moving Bodies," it was in many ways one of the most remarkable scientific papers that had ever been written. Even in form and style it was unusual, lacking the notes and references which give weight to most serious expositions and merely noting, in its closing paragraph, that the author was indebted for a number of valuable suggestions to his friend and colleague, M. Besso. Yet this dissertation of some nine thousand words overturned man's accepted ideas of time and space in a way which was, as *The Times* of London once put it, "an affront to common sense," and drastically altered the classical concepts of physics still held by the overwhelming majority of scientists. In addition, it provided such an accurate blueprint for the way in which the physical world was built that within a generation men could no more ignore relativity in the teaching of physics than they could ignore grammar in the teaching of language.

During the sixty-odd years that have passed since Einstein tossed this rock into the pool, an immense literature and exegesis has spread out round the paper, the theory, and its history. This literature does more than describe, explain, and criticize what Einstein wrote, and attempt with varying degrees of success to outline his theory to the layman. It also gives differing assessments of Einstein's debt to his predecessors, and shows scientific historians to be as practiced as their less specialized colleagues in the gentle art of blacking an opponent's eye. This is natural enough. Most revolutionary theories—scientific as well as political—have roots deep in the past; about the exact direction of such roots, historians argue and scholars write theses. As time blurs details, as old men "remember with advantages," as rumor is transformed first into myth and then into fact, the genesis of scientific theory becomes increasingly difficult to describe with more than scholarly plausibility. Darwin's theory of evolution, so long worked over yet springing to the surface almost simultaneously with that of Wallace, is an example from one other field; the conscription of Hertz' radio waves into the utilitarian straitjacket of radar, long possible in many countries and then, within a few months, suddenly crystallizing in Britain, the United States, and Germany, is an example from another.

Relativity is no exception to the rule. Today, two-thirds of a century after Einstein posted the manuscript of his paper to *Annalen der Physik,* the dust is still stirred by discussion of what inspired him. The controversy about how much he owed to his predecessors complicates still further the problem of explaining a complicated subject to the lay public. However, it is not insuperable and is best tackled by outlining briefly the background against which his paper was written; by describing first the daring propositions he put forward and then their implications; and by surveying the sometimes contradictory evidence of the paper's genesis.

In the background of the scientific world as it existed in the first years of the twentieth century there still towered, as central ornament, the bold figure of Sir Isaac Newton. Driven in 1666 from Cambridge to his Lincolnshire home by the plague when only twenty-four, he had been almost of an age with Einstein; and, like Einstein, he had in a single summer delivered three hammer blows at the foundations of contemporary science. The formulation of the law of gravity was the greatest of the three, showing that the fall of the apple and the passage of the moon in its orbit were governed by the same natural laws. For starting with an explanation of the forces which kept the planets on their tracks, Newton constructed the first modern synthesis of the physical world, a logical explanation of the universe. Judged by contemporary standards, his universe was a simple and comforting place through which planets and stars, men and animals, the smallest particles of matter, and even the particles of which light was deemed to consist, moved in accordance with the same mathematical laws. "From the time of Newton up to the end of the last century," J. Robert Oppenheimer has noted

> physicists built, on the basis of these laws, a magnificently precise and beautiful science involving the celestial mechanics of the solar system, involving incredible problems in the Cambridge Tripos, involving the theory of gases, involving the behavior of fluids, of elastic vibrations, of sound—indeed, a comprehensive system so robust and varied and apparently all-powerful that what was in store for it could hardly be imagined.

In the first pages of his *Philosophiae Naturalis Principia Mathematica,* which enshrined these laws, Newton used two words whose definitions formed the basis not only of his whole system but of everything which had been constructed as a by-product of it—two words which between them formed the bottom layer of the house which science had been building for two and a half centuries. One of them was "time," the other was "space." "Absolute, true, and mathematical time," as Newton put it, "of itself and from its own nature, flows equably, without relation to anything external, and by another name is called duration." Space could be "absolute space, in its own nature, without relation to anything external," which "remains always similar and immovable"; or relative space, which was "some movable dimension or measure of the absolute spaces."

From these definitions Newton went on to illustrate the principle of the addition of velocities, a principle so obvious that at first there seems little point in repeating it. Yet it was to be radically amended by Einstein's Special Theory, and it is salutary to consider how Newton expressed it. "Absolute motion," he wrote,

> is the translation of a body from one relative place into another. Thus in a ship under sail the relative place of a body is that part of the ship which the body possesses; or that part of the cavity which the body fills, and which therefore moves together with the ship; and relative rest is the continuance of the body in the same part of that

> immovable space, in which the ship itself, its cavity, and all that it contains, is moved. Wherefore, if the earth is really at rest, the body which relatively rests in the ship, will really and absolutely move with the same velocity which the ship has on the earth. But if the earth also moves, the true and absolute motion of the body will arise, partly from the true motion of the earth, in immovable space, partly from the relative motion of the ship on the earth; and if the body moves also relatively in the ship, its true motion will arise, partly from the true motion of the earth, in immovable space, and partly from the relative motions as well of the ship on the earth, as of the body in the ship; and from these relative motions will arise the relative motion of the body on the earth. As if that part of the earth, where the ship is, was truly moved towards the east, with a velocity of 10,010 parts; while the ship itself, with a fresh gale, and full sails, is carried towards the west, with a velocity expressed by 10 of those parts; but a sailor walks in the ship towards the east, with 1 part of the said velocity; then the sailor will be moved truly in immovable space towards the east, with a velocity of 10,001 parts, and relatively on the earth towards the west, with a velocity of 9 of those parts. . . .

Newton's sailor—pacing 3 miles an hour east on the deck of his ship while the ship sails past the coast at 12 miles an hour in the same direction and therefore moving past the land at 15 miles an hour—has his modern counterpart: the train passenger traveling at 40 miles an hour whose carriage is passed by a second train traveling at 50 miles an hour, to whom a passenger in the faster train is moving at only 10 miles an hour. In both cases it is possible to describe the movement of a person—or a particle—in one frame of reference (the sailor relative to the ship) and then to describe it in a second frame of reference (the sailor relative to the land) by the simple addition of velocities.

Newton's sailor and the train movements of the twentieth century have one other important thing in common. Newton himself gives a clue to it when he writes: "The motions of bodies included in a given space are the same among themselves, whether that space is at rest or moves uniformly forward in a straight line." In other words, the mechanical laws which are applicable in a ship—or a train—when at rest are also applicable when it is moving uniformly. Nature does not give special preference to one situation or the other, and any measurements or experiments made on a vehicle in uniform motion will produce the same results as when it is at rest.

During the second half of the nineteenth century, attacks began to be made on this mechanical view of the universe. From one side came those prepared to strike at its epistemological roots, denying that the apparently sound mechanical structure was anything more than a convenient illusion. Gustav Kirchhoff, whose work prepared the way for the quantum revolution, looked on Newtonian concepts merely as convenient explanations for various unrelated phenomena which had been noted, and which did not demand the creation of a single comprehensive explanation of the physical world. Ernst Mach, the physicist turned philosopher whose influence on Einstein was so great, and who had for the hard currency of observable sensations much the same respect that Soames Forsyte had for property, went further in the same direction. In *The Science of Mechanics: A Critical and Historical Account of Its Development,* Mach boldly challenged Newton's assumptions of absolute space and absolute time, claiming that he had "acted contrary to his expressed intention only to investigate *actual facts.* No one is competent to predicate things about absolute space and absolute motion; they are pure things of thought, pure mental constructs, that cannot be produced in experience." And Henri Poincaré, "the last man to take practically all mathematics, both pure and applied, as his province," went even further, not only throwing overboard in lordly manner absolute time and absolute space but insisting that even the laws of nature, the simple ways of tabulating and ordering the sensations of life which Mach allowed, were merely the free creations of the human mind.

But if such men were able to cast doubt on Newton's absolute space and time, an equally dangerous attack was to come from a different quarter as confusing, and sometimes conflicting, evidence on the nature and behavior of light accumulated during the nineteenth century. To Newton, light was a stream of particles moving according to mechanical laws, although his contemporary, Christiaan Huygens, thought it might be instead a vibration in an unspecified medium, much as sound was a vibration in the air. The problem looked as if it had been solved in midcentury when the French physicist Dominique Arago, followed by Jean Foucault, produced evidence supporting the wave theory. If any doubt remained it appeared to be dispelled during the next few decades. Maxwell's theoretical calculations showed that the vibrations associated with light were due to very rapid oscillations of electric and magnetic fields; twenty years later Hertz, with his demonstration of electromagnetic radio waves, seemed to put this beyond question.

But there was one particular way in which Maxwell's electromagnetism operated in a manner totally different from Newtonian mechanics. Newton had built his law of gravitation on the idea of action at a distance, believing that the pull of gravity between the apple and the ground, the moon and the earth, the earth and the sun, in fact between all the components of the universe, operated as a mysterious and instantaneous force across empty space. Maxwell utilized instead Faraday's idea of "the field," a region of space in which certain physical conditions were created and through which forces were transmitted—somewhat like ripples through an invisible jelly, the electromagnetic waves of light being propagated through the field in straight lines at a finite speed, and the pull of the magnet for iron filings being a property of the field which the magnet had itself created.

Largely due to the concept of the field, it was believed during the last decades of the nineteenth century that electromagnetic waves required a medium through which they could travel, just as sound needs the molecules of air before it can be heard and seismic waves require the medium of the earth before they can be recorded. Scientists decided that this medium was the ether, vaguely postulated since the time of the Greeks. But the presence of the ether had never been confirmed and there was a doubt about its existence, like the pea under the princess' mattress—minute, yet sufficient to prevent peace of mind. It was to resolve this doubt that the famous—indeed, almost legendary—Michelson-Morley experiment was designed in 1887. How much Einstein knew of this before 1905 is questionable, and even more so is the importance to his thinking of what he did know. The awkward results of the experiment permeated the scientific climate of the

1890s and its implications must even have been noted in the Berne Patent Office. Later, moreover, it would be seen as a linchpin of the whole theory of relativity. As Einstein said years later, talking to Sir Herbert Samuel in the grounds of Government House, Jerusalem: "If Michelson-Morley is wrong, then relativity is wrong."

By the time that Einstein came on the scene other experiments had been carried out in an effort to show the existence of the ether by recording the effects of the earth's passage through it. Trouton and Noble had tried to discover experimentally the torque which should, in theory, have been shown by the charging of a condenser hung from a fine filament with its plates inclined to the ether drift. Both Lord Rayleigh and Brace had looked for double refraction in a transparent body produced by the passage of the ether through it. All these experiments had failed to produce any evidence for the existence of the ether. It was, however, the Michelson-Morley experiment which lodged in the scientific gullet, partly because its implications seemed impossible to escape, partly because of its basic simplicity.

What Michelson and Morley set out to discover was the effect of the earth's passage through the postulated ether on the speed of light. Long known to be roughly 186,000 miles per second, this was so great as to present technical problems which would have ruled out the experiment before the last decades of the nineteenth century. On the other hand, the experiment's basic mathematics are quite simple.

To understand them one has merely to consider the case of two oarsmen rowing respectively across a river 400 yards wide, and 400 yards up and down the same stream of water, an analogy which is one of many littering the pages explaining Einstein's work. Both oarsmen have the same speed—which can be arbitrarily given as 500 yards a minute, with the stream running at an equally arbitrary rate of 300 yards a minute. The first oarsman starts from one bank, aiming to arrive at a point on the far bank directly opposite—in other words, 400 yards away. If there were no current he would reach it in four-fifths of a minute. But since there is a current he must point his boat upstream. Now an observer starting at the same point as the oarsman but allowing himself merely to float downstream will see the "aiming point" on the far bank moving "back" at a rate of 300 yards a minute (the rate of the stream's movement), while the oarsman is moving away from him at a rate of 500 yards a minute (the speed at which he is rowing). The construction of a simple right-angled triangle using this information, plus an equally simple use of Pythagoras, will show that the oarsman will have traveled 500 yards before he reaches the far bank and that the time he takes will be one minute for the single journey or two minutes there and back.

Now what of the oarsman given the comparable task of rowing 400 yards upstream and returning to the same point? During the first minute he will have covered 500 minus 300 yards, or 200 yards. So he will take two minutes for the journey against the stream. On his return, his speed of 500 yards a minute will be aided by the 300 yard-a-minute stream so that the 400 yards will take him only half a minute. In other words the time for the double journey measured up and down the stream is more than the double journey measured across the stream and it always will be more except in a currentless river. And by measuring the times both oarsmen take, it is possible to calculate both the speed at which they row and also the speed of the river. Similarly, Michelson and Morley proposed, it should be possible to confirm the existence of the ether.

In their experiment the ether, presumably streaming past the earth at 20 miles a second as the earth moved in its orbit round the sun, would represent the current. A ray of light, split into two, would represent the two oarsmen. These two rays would be directed along two paths identical in length but at right angles to one another; then they would be reflected back to the "test-bed" of the experiment—after having made journeys which would be respectively "across," and "up," and then "down" the presumed flow of the ether. If the "ether flow" had an effect on light comparable to normal mechanical effects, the two returning rays would be out of phase. The result would be interference fringes, or bands of alternately light and dark color, and from these it would be possible to calculate the speed of the ether wind relative to the movement of the earth. Nearly forty years later Edward Appleton used a comparable technique with radio waves to pinpoint the height of the ionosphere from which such waves are reflected back to the earth.

The huge difference between the speed of light and the mere 20 miles per second of the earth's orbit round the sun presented considerable problems, and an earlier experiment carried out in 1881 by Michelson alone had failed. Now these inherent problems had been solved and "pure" science was able to move forward once again on the vehicle provided by technology. This has happened frequently. From the days of William Herschel, whose discovery of infrared rays in 1800 was aided by sensitive thermometers, through the work of Oersted, von Fraunhofer, Wheatstone, and Joule, knowledge of the physical world has marched steadily forward on the achievements of the craftsmen. Maxwell, on arriving at Aberdeen, had stated significantly: "I am happy in the knowledge of a good instrument maker, in addition to a smith, an optician, and a carpenter." In another field, accurate gravimetric analysis was made possible by improvements in the chemical balance. Hermann Bondi has emphasized that "the enormous stream of discoveries at the end of the nineteenth century that gave us such insight as the discovery of X rays, working with radioactivity, and all that, is entirely due to the fact that the technologists developed decent vacuum pumps." Others, commenting on the difference between the science of the twentieth and earlier centuries, have pointed out that we are on a higher level today not because we have more imagination, but because we have better instruments.

The process of pure science moving forward with the packhorses of technology was now illustrated by Michelson and Morley, who set up their apparatus at the Case Institute of Technology in Cleveland, Ohio. The massive stone test-bed, nearly five feet square, was floated in a bowl of mercury to obviate vibrations. The light rays used were ingeniously increased by a system of mirrors. The experiments were carried out at various times of day to lessen the chances of experimental error. Yet the results, however they were considered, told one incontrovertible story: light which traveled back and forth across the ether stream did the journey in exactly the same time as light traveling the same distance up and down the ether stream.

The problem which now faced science was considerable. For there seemed to be only three alternatives. The first was that the earth was standing still, which meant scuttling the whole Copernican theory and was unthinkable. The second was that the ether was carried along by the earth in its passage through space, a possibility which had already been ruled out to the satisfaction of the scientific community by a number of experiments, notably those of the English astronomer James Bradley. The third solution was that the ether simply did not exist, which to many nineteenth century scientists was equivalent to scrapping current views of light, electricity, and magnetism, and starting again.

The only other explanation must surely lie in some perverse feature of the physical world which scientists had not yet suspected, and during the next few years this was sought by three men in particular—George Fitzgerald, professor of natural and experimental philosophy at Trinity College, Dublin; Hendrik Lorentz of Leiden, the kindly humanitarian physicist whose lifetime spanned the closing days of Newtonian cosmology and the splitting of the atom—the man who, wrote Einstein within a few weeks of his own death, "for me personally . . . meant more than all the others I have met on my life's journey"—and the French mathematician Henri Poincaré.

The Fitzgerald explanation came first. To many it must have seemed that he had strained at a gnat and swallowed an elephant. For while Fitzgerald was unwilling to believe that the velocity of light could remain unaffected by the velocity of its source, he suggested instead that all moving objects were shortened along the axis of their movement. A foot rule moving end forwards would be slightly shorter than a stationary foot rule, and the faster it moved the shorter it would be. The speed of the earth's movement was all that was involved, so the contraction would be extremely small, and it would only rise to appreciable amounts as the speed involved rose to a sizable proportion of the speed of light itself. But it was not this alone that made the proposal apparently incapable of proof or disproof. Any test instruments would adjust themselves in the same way, shortening themselves as they were turned into the direction of the earth's movement through the ether. For some years this explanation appeared to be little more than a plausible trick—"I have been rather laughed at for my view over here," Fitzgerald wrote to Lorentz from Dublin in 1894—and it was only transformed into something more when Lorentz turned his mind to the question.*

Lorentz had been among the first to postulate the electron, the negatively charged particle whose existence had finally been proved by J. J. Thomson at Cambridge. It now seemed to him that such a contraction could well be a direct result of electromagnetic forces produced when a body with its electrical charges was moved through the ether. These would disturb the equilibrium of the body, and its particles would assume new relative distances from one another. The result would be a change in the shape of the body, which would become flattened in the direction of its movement. The contraction could thus be explained, as Philipp Frank has put it, as "a logical consequence of several simultaneous hypotheses, namely the validity of the electromagnetic field equations and laws of force and the hypothesis that all bodies are built up of electric charges."

Lorentz' invocation of electromagnetism thus brought a whiff of sanity into the game. Here at least was a credible explanation of how a foot rule in motion could be of a different length from the foot rule at rest. However, if this solved one problem it created others; and it played havoc with the simple transformation which had hitherto been used to describe events taking place in one frame of reference in terms of a different one. This had served well enough throughout the centuries for sailors on ships, for men on horseback, and for the early railways. It serves well enough for flight and even for contemporary space travel. Yet if Lorentz' hypothesis was correct the simple addition of velocities could no longer hold water. For if distances contract with relative speed then the yards paced out on the deck by Newton's sailor will be slightly shorter than the relatively stationary yards on the shore which his

*The history of the Fitzgerald-Lorentz contraction has striking resemblances with the story of Wallace and Darwin's concurrent work on evolution. Fitzgerald was the first to publish the contraction hypothesis, doing so in a letter to *Science;* but not even Fitzgerald himself, let alone Lorentz, knew that the letter had appeared. For details see "The 'Fitzgerald' Contraction" by Alfred M. Bork, *Isis,* No. 57 (1966), pp. 199–207, and "Note on the History of the Fitzgerald-Lorentz Contraction" by Stephen G. Brush, *Isis,* No. 58 (1967), pp. 231–232.

ship has sailed past. The smallness of the difference, so minute that it can be disregarded for practical purposes, can be gauged by even a nonmathematician's comparison of the simple equations, or "transformations," of the Newtonian world with those which Fitzgerald had provided and which were given a fresh significance by Lorentz. In the old Galilean transformation, the new place of the sailor on his deck is given by his old position plus or minus the speed (v) of his walking multiplied by the time (t) he has been on the move—in other words, his old position x, plus or minus vt. But using the new set of equations which Lorentz now developed from Fitzgerald's ideas—and which soon became known as the Lorentz-Fitzgerald transformations—the sailor's new position is represented by this $x \pm vt$ divided by $\sqrt{1} - (v^2/c^2)$. In the case of the sailor walking at 3 miles an hour, v^2 will be 9, and in most examples from everyday life it will be a similarly humble figure; but c is the speed of light in miles per second, and c^2 is many millions of millions miles per hour. Once this is realized, two things become immediately clear: that the sailor need not be worried by the Lorentz transformations and that these will, as Fitzgerald had forecast, begin to have significant applications only when the speeds concerned are a significant percentage of the speed of light.

While Fitzgerald and Lorentz were struggling to produce these explanations for physical experiments, Henri Poincaré was making a different approach. He was concerned not so much with the awkward specific problem of the speed of light as with the conglomeration of problems being presented to physicists at the turn of the century. He was, moreover, tackling them from an angle more philosophical than that of Fitzgerald and Lorentz. "Suppose," he argued, "that in one night all the dimensions of the universe became a thousand times larger. The world will remain *similar* to itself, if we give the word *similitude* the meaning it has in the third book of Euclid. . . . Have we any right, therefore, to say that we know the distance between two points?" Poincaré's answer was "No"—the concept of space being relative to the frame of reference within which its distances were measured.

Poincaré reached the height of his reputation in the 1900s, and in 1904 he was among those invited to a Congress of Arts and Sciences at the Universal Exposition, St. Louis, 1904, held to commemorate the Louisiana Purchase a century earlier. Here he dealt, in a speech which was part of a symposium surveying human thought in the nineteenth century, with the contemporary crisis in physics. "Perhaps," he said, "we should construct a whole new mechanics, of which we only succeed in catching a glimpse, where, inertia increasing with the velocity, the velocity of light would become an impassable limit." The Lorentz transformation would no doubt be included in the new structure and it might well form part of a new principle of relativity which would replace, or supplement, the restricted principle which was epitomized by the Galilean transformation. But Poincaré was, as he stressed, doing his best to fit such new ideas as were required into the existing classical principles—"and as yet," he concluded at St. Louis, "nothing proves that the principles will not come forth from the combat victorious and intact."

His speech was an indication of the scientific unrest and philosophical distrust created not only by the Michelson-Morley experiment but by others made during the preceding two decades in Cambridge and Berlin, Leiden and Paris. But there was no hint of the Special Theory, created by Einstein for different reasons after an approach across different territory.

While Fitzgerald, Lorentz, and Poincaré were trying to rescue physics from the cul-de-sac into which it appeared to have been led by the Michelson-Morley experiment, Einstein was wondering about the world in general, gaining a basic grounding in physics at the ETH, and giving special attention to what he realized, early on, were the revolutionary implications of Maxwell's electromagnetic theory, based on continuous fields. This was a basically new idea of the way in which the world had been made, and it continued to exercise Einstein for a decade, working away like a fermenting yeast in contrast to the boring material with which the Zurich masters tried to fill the stockpot of his mind.

As early as the age of sixteen, he had considered what he would see were he able to follow a beam of light at its own velocity through space. Here is a problem picture as graphic as any of the number with which he was to explain his ideas. What, in fact, would be seen by anyone who could travel as fast as the oscillating electromagnetic waves which by the turn of the century were known to cause the phenomenon of light? The answer, in Einstein's words, was "a spatially oscillatory electromagnetic field at rest." But this was a contradiction in terms of which Maxwell's equations gave no hint. Quite as important, if such a conception were feasible, it would mean that the laws of electromagnetism would be different for observers at rest and for those on the move—at least for those moving at the speed of light. But it seemed soundly established that the mechanical laws of the Newtonian universe were the same for all observers and Einstein saw no reason for thinking that the laws of electromagnetism would be any different. Thus it looked as certain as the Q. E. D. at the end of a theorem that the laws of nature would prevent anyone or anything moving at the speed of light. But this idea, in turn, raised its own problems. For in the mechanical Newtonian world it was always possible to add a little more force and thus make the billiard ball, or the cannonball, go a little faster. What was there to prevent addition plus addition from pushing up speeds above that of light?

This was one of the problems which worried Einstein persistently during his studies at the ETH and during his early years at the Patent Office, a constant background to his other work and a hobbyhorse he could pull down from the shelf of his mind when more pressing work gave him a moment to spare.

Einstein himself has given more than a hint of how he worked away at it. "I must confess," he told Alexander Moszkowski in Berlin in 1915, "that at the very beginning, when the Special Theory of Relativity began to germinate in me, I was visited by all sorts of nervous conflicts. When young, I used to go away for weeks in a state of confusion, as one who at that time had yet to overcome the stage of stupefaction in his first encounter with such questions." To R. S. Shankland, professor at the Case Institute of Technology, Cleveland, Ohio, he said in old age that he had "worked for ten years; first as a student when, of course, he could only spend part time on it, but the problem was always with him. He abandoned many fruitless attempts 'until at last it came to me that time was suspect.'" And to Carl Seelig he wrote on March 11, 1952:

> Between the conception of the idea of this Special Theory of Relativity and the completion of the corresponding publication, there elapsed five or six weeks. But it would hardly be correct to consider this as a birthday, because earlier the arguments and building blocks were being prepared over a period of years, although without bringing about the fundamental decision.

He worked alone, or almost alone. His earlier papers had brought him into the physicists' world—or, more accurately, into contact with it by correspondence. But he had none of the stimulus of university life, he played no part in any scientific group or society. For all practical purposes he was a scientific loner, trying out his ideas not on the sharp minds of professional equals but on the blunt edges of the Swiss civil service. His only two confidants were two colleagues, Josef Sauter and the Michelangelo Besso whom he had eased into the Patent Office the previous year.

Sauter, eight years older than Einstein, was given the young man's notes to criticize after they had walked home from the office one evening and Einstein had outlined his ideas. "I pestered him for a whole month with every possible objection without managing to make him in the least impatient, until I was finally convinced that my objections were no more than the usual judgments of contemporary physics," Sauter has written. "I cannot forget the patience and good temper with which he listened, agreeing or disagreeing with my objections. He went over it again and again until he saw that I had understood his ideas. 'You are the second to whom I have told my discovery,' he said."

Sauter believes that Einstein's confidant was Maurice Solovine. More probably it was Besso, with whom Einstein certainly discussed his ideas and of whom he said: "I could not have found a better sounding board in the whole of Europe." Besso's version of events was: "Einstein the eagle took Besso the sparrow under his wing. Then the sparrow fluttered a little higher." Certainly Besso was the only person given a niche in history in the famous paper outlining the Special Theory.

This was possibly the most important scientific paper that has yet been written in the twentieth century, in some ways the very type of those described by Hermann Bondi. Their aim, he said, "is to leave as disembodied, as impersonalized a piece of writing as anybody might be willing to read, knowing that others have to read it if they wish to know what has been achieved. The paper is very likely to tell the reader almost nothing about how the result was found." Yet if in outlining the Special Theory it thus conformed in one respect, it was an exception in other ways. Supporting evidence was not called upon at all; in fact, the paper which was to set the scientific world on its ears contained not a single footnote or reference, those stigmata of scholarly respectability, and as acknowledgment only a casual reference to Michelangelo Besso, thrown in almost as an afterthought.

Einstein began by doing exactly what he had done when dealing with the photoelectric effect: he noted a contradiction in contemporary scientific beliefs apparent for years but conveniently ignored. In the first case it was the contradiction between the Newtonian world of corpuscles and the Maxwellian world of fields. Here it was something perhaps even more fundamental: the contradiction implicit in Faraday's law of induction. This had for years been one of the accepted facts of life and to raise awkward questions about it was to spit in a sacred place. Yet, Einstein pointed out, the current induced between a magnet and a conductor depends according to observation only on the relative motion of the conducting wire and the magnet "whereas the customary view," in other words, the accepted theory of currents, "draws a sharp distinction between the two cases in which either the one or the other of these bodies is in motion." Faraday had discovered the induction law in 1834 but, as Born has put it, "everybody had known all along that the effect depended only on relative motion, but nobody had taken offense at the theory not accounting for this circumstance." Even had they done so, few would have had the temerity to pass on, in Einstein's grand style, to what he saw as the inevitable consequences.

"Examples of this sort," he continued, "together with

the unsuccessful attempts to discover any motion of the earth relatively to the 'light medium,' suggest that the phenomena of electrodynamics as well as of mechanics possess no properties corresponding to the idea of absolute rest." What they did suggest, he went on, was that "the same laws of electrodynamics and optics will be valid for all frames of reference for which the equations of mechanics hold good."

This linking of electrodynamics and mechanics was the crux of the matter. In the world of electromagnetism, governed by the field laws of Faraday and Maxwell, light was propagated at a constant speed which could not be surpassed; but there seemed to be little connection here with Newtonian mechanics, in which the speed of an object might be indefinitely increased by adding more energy to it. What Einstein now proposed was that the velocity of light was a constant and a maximum in the electromagnetic and the mechanical worlds and that light would thus travel with a constant velocity that was independent of the bodies emitting or receiving it. This would explain the failure to discover the movement of the earth through the ether and it would also answer Einstein's boyhood riddle of how a beam of light would look if you traveled at its own speed. The answer to the riddle was that this would be impossible since only light could reach the speed of light.

Yet the inclusion of Newton's mechanical world within that of Maxwell's electromagnetism is difficult to conceive. For what it says is this: That while a ball thrown forward at *x* miles an hour from a train traveling at *y* miles an hour will apparently be traveling at *x* plus *y* miles an hour, something very different happens with light; whatever the speed of the train from which it is being emitted, light will travel at the same constant speed of some 186,000 miles an hour. Furthermore, it will be received at this same constant speed, whatever the speed of the vehicle that receives it—as though the ball thrown from the speeding train would arrive at the fielder on the ground with the same speed whether he was standing still, running in the direction of the train, or running towards it.

This of course appeared to be ridiculous. As Bertrand Russell has said, "Everybody knows that if you are on an escalator you reach the top sooner if you walk up than if you stand still. But if the escalator moved with the velocity of light you would reach the top at exactly the same moment whether you walked up or stood still." But Einstein went on to link this assumption with his initial idea—that all the laws of nature are identical to all observers moving uniformly relative to one another. It required more than vision and audacity—qualities demanded of Blondin crossing the Falls, of Whymper nonchalantly tackling the unclimbed Matterhorn, of Whittle, confident that the jet would work. It demanded also the quality of intuition, a feel for nature as indefinable as a poet's sense of words or the artist's knowledge of what his last dab of materialistic paint can unlock in the human mind.

Einstein once wrote with his collaborator of "the eternal struggle of the inventive human mind for a fuller understanding of the law governing physical phenomena," and Sir Basil Schonland, writing of Maxwell—whose relaxation was writing verse—has no hesitation in describing him as "fey," a word not commonly used to describe scientific genius. Einstein himself was always ready to agree that inventiveness, imagination, the intuitive approach—the very stuff of which artists rather than scientists are usually thought to be made—played a serious part in his work. And when his friend Janos Plesch commented years later that there seemed to be some connection between mathematics and fiction, a field in which the writer made a world out of invented characters and situations and then compared it with the existing world, Einstein replied: "There may be something in what you say. When I examine myself and my methods of thought I come to the conclusion that the gift of fantasy has meant more to me than my talent for absorbing positive knowledge."

The problems created by linking Einstein's two assumptions—the similarity of all natural laws for all observers and the constancy of the speed of light in both the electromagnetic and the mechanical worlds—become evident when one reconsiders Newton's handy sailor. Consider him standing on the deck as his ship sails parallel to a long jetty. At each end of the jetty there stands a signal lamp and midway between the two lamps there stands an observer. As the sailor passes the observer, flashes of light are sent out by the two lamps. They are sent out, so far as the stationary observer on the jetty is concerned, at exactly the same time. The light rays coming from each end of the jetty have to travel the same distance to reach him, and they will reach him simultaneously. So far, so good. But what about the sailor on the ship—who will have been at an equal distance from both lamps as each sent out its light signal? He knows that both flashes travel with the same speed. Although this speed is very great it is finite, and since he is moving away from one lamp and towards the other he will receive the light signals at different times. As far as he is concerned, they will not have been switched on simultaneously.

Here is the first extraordinary result of linking Einstein's two assumptions. If they are correct—and there is now no doubt about this—the old idea of simultaneity is dethroned; for events which are simultaneous to the observer on the jetty are not simultaneous to the sailor on deck. "So we see," as Einstein put it, "that we cannot attach any *absolute* signification to the concept of simultaneity, but that two events which, viewed from a system of coordinates, are simultaneous, can no longer be looked upon as simultaneous events when envisaged from a system which is in motion relatively to that system."

If the nub of Einstein's Special Relativity can be considered as resting within any one sentence it rests here in the realization that one man's "now" is another man's "then"; that "now" itself is a subjective conception, valid only for an observer within one specific frame of reference.

Yet despite the apparent chaos that this appears to cause, there is one stable factor which it is possible to grasp as thankfully as a rock climber grasps a jug handle hold in a dangerous place. That factor is the constancy of the speed of light, and with its aid all natural phenomena can be described in terms which are correct for all frames of reference in constant relative motion with each other. All that was needed, Einstein went on to demonstrate, were the Lorentz transformation equations. Using these instead of the earlier and simpler Newtonian transformations, it was still possible to connect events in any two frames of reference, whether the difference in their relative speeds was that between a sailor and the deck, between a ship and the coast, or between a physicist in the laboratory and the electrons of atomic experiments which were already known to move at a sizable proportion of the speed of light.

But a price had to be paid for resolving this difference between two conceptions of simultaneity; or, put more accurately, it had to be admitted that if the constancy of the speed of light was allowed to restore order from chaos, then not one but two factors in the equations were different from the simple stable things that man had always imagined. For velocity is provided by distance divided by time, and if velocity was invariant in the Lorentz transformations not only distance but time itself must be variable. If the Newtonian world of mechanics as well as the Maxwellian world of electromagnetism were subject to the invariant velocity of light, both distance—or space—and time were no longer absolute.

It is at this point that the difference between the ideas of Fitzgerald, Lorentz, and even Poincaré, and the ideas of Einstein, begins to appear. For his predecessors, the Lorentz transformation was merely a useful tool for linking objects in relative motion; for Einstein it was not a mathematical tool so much as a revelation about nature itself. As he wrote years later, he had seen "that the bearing of the Lorentz transformation transcends its connection with Maxwell's equations and was concerned with the nature of space and time in general."

The difference between the earlier view and that of Einstein was exemplified by what Max Born, one of the first expositors of relativity, called "the notorious controversy as to whether the contraction is 'real' or only 'apparent.' " Lorentz had one view. "Asked if I consider this contraction as a real one, I should answer 'Yes,' " he said. "It is as real as anything we can observe." Sir Arthur Eddington, the later great exponent of Einstein, held a rather different view. "When a rod is started from rest into uniform motion, nothing whatever happens to the rod," he has written. "We say that it contracts; but length is not a property of the rod; it is a relation between the rod and the observer. *Until the observer is specified the length of the rod is quite indeterminate.*"

But it was not only distance but also time which was now seen to be relative. The idea was not entirely new.

Voigt had suggested in 1887 that it might be mathematically convenient to use a local time in moving reference systems. But just as Einstein transformed earlier ideas of the curious "contraction" by showing that it was space itself which was altered by relative speed, so was his concept of relative time far more than a mathematical convenience. It was, in fact, more than a concept in the proper meaning of the word. For with his Special Theory Einstein was not so much propounding an idea as revealing a truth of nature that had previously been overlooked. And as far as time was concerned the truth was that a clock attached to a system in relative movement ran more slowly than a clock that was stationary. This was not in any sense a mechanical phenomenon; it was not in any way connected with the physical properties of the clock and—as was to be shown less than half a century later—it was as true of clocks operated by atomic vibrations as of those operated by other methods; it was a property of the way in which God had made the world.

Once it is accepted, as it was during the years that followed 1905, that space and time are relatively different in moving and in stationary systems, and that both can be linked by the Lorentz transformations, the position of the velocity of light as the limiting velocity of the universe becomes clear. For the stationary measuring rod which shrinks at an ever faster rate as its speed increases, and reaches half its original length at nine-tenths the speed of light, would shrink to nothing as it reached ten-tenths. Similarly, the recordings on a clock would slow to a standstill as it reached the same speed.

Three questions arise. One is the question of which is the "real" dimension and which the "real" time. Another is the riddle of why the extraordinary characteristic of the universe revealed by the Special Theory had escaped man's notice for so long. The third is the question of what difference the Special Theory could make to the world. The answer to the first is simple. The "real" dimension and the "real" time is that of the observer, and the stationary and the moving observers are each concerned with their own reality. Just as beauty lies in the eye of the beholder, so does each man carry with him his own space and his own time. But there is one rider to this, a restriction put even on relativity. For while the time at which something happens is indeed a relative matter there is a limitation: if two events happen at different places in such a way that a light signal starting at the first event could reach the second before it took place, then no use of the Lorentz transformations will make the first event take place after the second one. In other words, relativity does not claim that if a man is hit by a bullet, then it is possible for an observer somewhere else in the universe to have seen the gun being fired after the bullet landed. This, however, does not invalidate the famous thought-experiment—an experiment possible in theory but ruled out by experimental difficulties—concerning the alleged twin paradox. Here, two twins, one of whom "stays at home" while the other travels through the universe at great speed, age differently—an outcome still disputed by a few who refuse to accept the restrictions on "common sense" that Einstein showed to be necessary.*

The answers to the second question—why have such characteristics of the universe escaped notice for so long?—is that the human physiological apparatus is too insensitive to record the extremely minute changes in space and time which are produced by anything less than exceptionally high speeds. In other and better known ways, the five senses have their limitations. The unreliability of touch is exemplified by the "burn" which cold metal can give.

*Although novelists have often played tricks with time, one of the most extravagant examples was provided, some years before Einstein, by Camille Flammarion, the French astronomer. This was *Lumen,* published in 1873, the story of an adventurer who traveled back through time at 250,000 miles a second to witness, among other things, the end of the Battle of Waterloo before the beginning. "You only comprehend things which you perceive," Lumen told the reader. "And as you persist in regarding your ideas of time and space as *absolute,* although they are only *relative,* and thence form a judgment on truths which are quite beyond your sphere, and which are imperceptible to your terrestrial organism and faculties, I should not do a true service, my friend, in giving you fuller details of my ultraterrestrial observations. . . ."

The weakness was, of course, shown years later by Einstein's revelation that c was the limiting speed in the universe since at the speed of light a body's mass would become infinitely great. Flammarion—in whose honor the 141st of the minor planets was named Lumen—believed in vegetation on the moon and in advanced and intelligent life on Mars, wrote many books of popular astronomy, including *The Plurality of Inhabited Worlds* which went through thirty editions, and late in life turned to psychic research.

Taste is not only notoriously subjective—"One man's meat, another man's poison"—but is also governed, to an extent not yet fully known, by genetic inheritance. So, too, smell is an indicator whose gross incapacity in humans is thrown into relief by insects that can identify members of their species at ranges of up to a mile. Sound is hardly better. The pattern of "reality" heard by the human is different from that heard by the dog—witness the "soundless" dog whistles of trainers; while the "real" world of the near sightless bat is one in which "real" objects are "seen"—and avoided—by ultrasonic waves which play no part in the construction of the external human world.

And sight, a stimulation of the human retina by certain electromagnetic waves, is perhaps the most illusory of all senses. "Seeing is believing," and so it is difficult to appreciate that the light of common day—all that unaided human physiology allows in the visual search for the world around—comes through only a narrow slit in a broad curtain. At one end of this curtain there exist the cosmic rays, a trillionth of a centimeter in wavelength; at the other, the infrared, heat radiations, and the even longer wavelengths used for radar, radio, and television. In between lies the narrow band of the visible spectrum, for long the only source of man's incomplete visual picture, supplemented but slowly as he used instruments to increase his own limited powers. The landscape seen with human eyes is dramatically different, yet no more "real," than the scene captured on the infrared plate and showing a mass of detail beyond human vision; the "real" world of the partially color-blind is the same "real" world seen more colorfully by most human beings and both worlds are composed of the same objects which make up the "real" but again different world of totally color-blind animals.

Thus the human species is unconsciously and inevitably selective in describing the nature of the physical world in which it lives and moves. Once this is appreciated, the implications of Einstein's Special Theory begin to take on a more respectable air. For his achievement showed beyond all reasonable doubt that there existed a further limitation, so far unnoticed, produced by man's lack of experience of speeds comparable to that of light. Until such speeds were reached the variability of space and time which was a product of relative motion was so small as to be unobservable. Thus it was, as Professor Lindemann was later to point out in an article which foreshadowed his power to explain complicated scientific matters to Winston Churchill, "precisely because the old conceptions are so nearly right, because we have no personal experience of their being inaccurate in everyday life, that our so-called common sense revolts when we are asked to give them up, and that we tend to attribute to them a significance infinitely beyond their deserts." In fact, the human concepts of absolute space and time, which Einstein appeared to have violated so brusquely, had been produced simply by the rough-and-ready observation of countless generations of men using a physiological apparatus too coarse-grained to supply any better approximation of reality. As Bertrand Russell once wrote in describing the speeds at which relativity is significant, "Since everyday life does not confront us with such swiftly moving bodies, Nature, always economical, had educated common sense only up to the level of everyday life."

Thus Special Relativity did not so much "overthrow Newton" as show that Newtonian ideas were valid only in circumstances which were restricted even though they did appear to permeate everyday life. As Oppenheimer has written, the apparent paradoxes of relativity

> do not involve any contradictions on the part of nature; what they do involve is a gross change, a rather sharp change, from what learned people and ordinary people thought throughout the past centuries, thought as long as they had thought about things at all. The simple facts, namely that light travels with a velocity that cannot be added to or subtracted from by moving a source of light, the simple fact that objects do contract when they are in motion, the simple fact that processes are slowed down when they take place in motion, and very much so if they move with velocities comparable to the speed of light—these are new elements of the natural world and what the theory of relativity has done is to give coherence and meaning to the connection between them.

But Einstein's revelation was one which only a very few could ever hope to prove by experiment in the laboratory and which would remain forever outside the experience of most people. Thus to the nonscientist—as well as to some physicists—Einstein had really offended against common sense, the limited yardstick with which men measure the exterior world. In addition, the mental effort required before the theory could be fully grasped turned it for the general public, when they were eventually forced to notice it, into a fantasy which further separated the world of science from the world of ordinary men and women. Only Einstein's naïve honesty, and the burning intensity which gave him the quality of the guru down the ages, transformed amused scepticism of the theory into a veneration for its author which no one deplored more than Einstein himself.

Yet even when it is accepted that the theory of Special Relativity is not a metaphysical concept but, as Einstein was never tired of pointing out, an explanation of certain observable features of the universe, even when it is appreciated how this explanation had hitherto slipped through the net of human understanding, the third question remains. For at first glance the Special Theory appears to deal with matters that are outside the range of human experience. Nevertheless there are two answers, one general and the other specific, to the question of what difference the Special Theory was to make to the world.

The general answer has been concisely given by Eddington, the British astronomer who was to play an important role in Einstein's later life. "Distance and duration are the most fundamental terms in physics; velocity, acceleration, force, energy, and so on, all depend on them; and we can scarcely make any statement in physics without direct or indirect reference to them," he has written.

> Surely then we can best indicate the revolutionary consequences of [relativity] by the statement that distance and duration, and all the physical quantities derived from them, do not as hitherto supposed refer to anything absolute in the external world, but are relative quantities which alter when we pass from one observer to another with different motion. The consequence in physics of the discovery that a yard is not an absolute chunk of space, and that what is a yard for one observer may be eighteen inches for another observer, may be compared with the consequence in economics of the discovery that a pound

sterling is not an absolute quantity of wealth, and in certain circumstances may "really" be seven and sixpence.

However, the differences in these varying values of time and space were so small as to become significant only when the speeds involved were far beyond the range of human experience. How, then, could they really affect the world? It is here that one comes to the more specialized answer, and to what, in the light of history, can be considered as either an extraordinary coincidence or as part of the natural evolution of science.

For Einstein's Special Theory was evolved just as the investigations of physicists were reaching into the subatomic world of the nucleus, and as astronomers were for the first time peering out beyond the confines of the galaxy in which the earth is a minute speck towards the immensities of outer space. In the atomic world there were already known to be particles such as the electron which moved at speeds which were a sizable percentage of the speed of light; and in outer space, beyond our own galaxy, it was soon to be discovered that there were others which were moving at similar speeds. Thus in both of the fresh fields which were opening up during the first decades of the twentieth century, the microscopically small and the macroscopically large, the revelations of relativity were to have a significant place.

But there was another, and in some ways more important, result which flowed directly from the acceptance of Einstein's theory which during the next decade was seen as inevitable. For the absolute quality of space and time had not only been generally accepted up to now but have been confirmed by the overwhelming bulk of observational evidence. Now it was realized that the conventional belief, so soundly induced from observation, was gravely lacking, a circumstance with important philosophical implications. For it underlined, more strongly than had previously been the case, that science might really be a search not for absolute truth but for a succession of theories that would progressively approach the truth. It suggested, furthermore, that the best path to be followed might not be that of observation followed by the induction of general laws, but the totally different process of postulating a theory and then discovering whether or not the facts fitted it. Thus a theory should start with more scientific and philosophical assumptions than the facts alone warranted. A decade later the method was to provide the startling results of the General Theory.

How much, it is now necessary to ask, did these revelations owe to Einstein's predecessors? It should be clear by this time that the problem he tackled was different from that faced by Fitzgerald and Lorentz, who were mainly concerned with explaining the awkward result of an important experiment, and different in many ways from that faced by Poincaré, whose problem was largely a philosophical one. Einstein, not overconcerned with specific experiments, or with philosophy, had a grander aim: to penetrate the fog and discern more clearly the principles on which the material world had been built. "The theory of relativity," he once said, "was nothing more than a further consequential development of the field theory." Asked by Hans Reichenbach, later a Berlin colleague and later still a professor of philosophy at the University of California, how the theory of relativity had been arrived at, he "replied that he had discovered it because he was so firmly convinced of the harmony of the universe."

Yet in science as elsewhere, "no man is an Island, entire of itself." Einstein himself spoke repeatedly in later life of his debt to Lorentz—"the four men who laid the foundations of physics on which I have been able to construct my theory are Galileo, Newton, Maxwell, and Lorentz" he said during his visit to the United States in 1921. In more general terms he emphasized that "in science . . . the work of the individual is so bound up with that of his scientific predecessors and contemporaries that it appears almost as an impersonal product of his generation." Thus the problem resolves itself into that of deciding the extent of Einstein's knowledge of specific papers and of the Michelson-Morley experiment.*

*The most detailed analysis of the situation has been given by Gerald Holton in a number of papers. See, in particular, "On the Origins of the Special Theory of Relativity," *American Journal of Physics,* Vol. 28 (1960), pp. 627–636, and "Einstein, Michelson, and the 'Crucial' Experiment," *Isis,* Vol. 60, Part 2, No. 202 (Summer, 1969), pp. 133–197.

Einstein himself made a number of statements on the subject. At first, when he spoke of relativity in Berlin, in the United States, and in London, he was apt to stress, as in London in 1921, merely "that this theory is not speculative in origin; it owes its invention entirely to the desire to make physical theory fit observed fact as well as possible." At Columbia University, the same year, he noted that "to start with, it disturbed me that electrodynamics should pick out *one* state of motion in preference to others, without any experimental justification for this preferential treatment. Thus arose the Special Theory of Relativity. . . ." Both statements tended by implication to sustain the idea that the Michelson-Morley experiment had played a part in his thinking. The point was elaborated in a letter which he wrote from the Institute for Advanced Study at Princeton on March 17, 1942, to one of Michelson's biographers. "It is no doubt that Michelson's experiment was of considerable influence upon my work insofar as it strengthened my conviction concerning the validity of the principle of the Special Theory of Relativity," he said. "On the other side I was pretty much convinced of the validity of the principle before I did know this experiment and its result. In any case, Michelson's experiment removed practically any doubt about the validity of the principle in optics and showed that a profound change of the basic concepts of physics was inevitable."

Later evidence provided by Einstein is contradictory and is probably influenced by the fact that, as Maitland put it, "events now long in the past were once in the future." "When I asked him how he had learned of the Michelson-Morley experiment," says R. S. Shankland, who visited Einstein on February 4, 1950, from the Case Institute of Technology, while preparing a historical account of the experiment, "he told me he had become aware of it through the writings of H. A. Lorentz, but *only after 1905* had it come to his attention. 'Otherwise,' he said, 'I would have mentioned it in my paper.' He continued to say that the experimental results which had influenced him most were the observations of stellar aberration and Fizeau's measurements on the speed of light in moving water. 'They were enough,' he said." Yet when Shankland again visited Princeton on October 24, 1952,

Einstein was not so certain. "This is not so easy," Shankland quotes him as saying.

> "I am not sure when I first heard of the Michelson experiment. I was not conscious that it had influenced me directly during the seven years that relativity had been my life. I guess I just took it for granted that it was true." However, Einstein said that in the years 1905–1909, he thought a great deal about Michelson's result, in his discussions with Lorentz and others in his thinking about general relativity. He then realized (so he told me) that he had also been conscious of Michelson's result before 1905 partly through his reading of the papers of Lorentz and more because he had assumed this result of Michelson to be true.

In 1954, for Michael Polanyi's *The Art of Knowing,* Einstein personally approved the statement that "the Michelson-Morley experiment had a negligible effect on the discovery of relativity." Furthermore, a supplementary note from Dr. N. Balazs, who was working with Einstein in Princeton in the summer of 1953, and who questioned him on the subject for Polanyi, runs as follows:

> The Michelson-Morley experiment had no role in the foundation of the theory. He got acquainted with it while reading Lorentz' paper about the theory of this experiment (he of course does not remember exactly when, though prior to his paper), but it had no further influence on Einstein's consideration and the theory of relativity was not founded to explain its outcome at all.

To David Ben-Gurion, who asked whether the theory of relativity was the result of thought only, Einstein confirmed that this was so but added: "I naturally had before me the experimental works of those preceding me. These served as material for my thoughts and studies." And finally there is the letter from Einstein to Carl Seelig, published after Einstein's death. "There is no doubt, that the Special Theory of Relativity, if we regard its development in retrospect, was ripe for discovery in 1905," he wrote.

> Lorentz had already observed that for the analysis of Maxwell's equations the transformations which later were

known by his name are essential, and Poincaré had even penetrated deeper into these connections. Concerning myself, I knew only Lorentz' important work of 1895, but not Lorentz' later work, nor the consecutive investigations by Poincaré. In this sense my work of 1905 was independent. The new feature of it was the realization of the fact that the bearing of the Lorentz transformation transcended its connections with Maxwell's equations and was concerned with the nature of space and time in general.

From this not entirely satisfactory evidence two general conclusions have been drawn. One is the view of the popular eulogy, in which Einstein is seen as the inspired genius, working in an intellectual vacuum and drawing the Special Theory from his brain like the conjuror producing the rabbit from the hat. The other is typified by the view of Sir Edmund Whittaker, the notable British physicist who in Einstein's biographical memoir for the Royal Society wrote that he had "adopted Poincaré's Principle of Relativity (using Poincaré's name for it) as a new basis of physics."*

The truth appears to be different from both tidy black-and-white versions. It is rather that Einstein, traveling from his own starting point to his own lonely destination, noted Lorentz' work as bearing on his own, different, problems. When light dawned, during that creative fortnight in 1905, what Einstein had already heard of the Michelson-Morley experiment fell into place. But it was no more than an interesting piece of evidence which gave comforting confirmation of the theory which he had already decided could provide a more accurate picture of the material world than that provided by Newtonian mechanics alone. What he had produced was, as he wrote in *The Times* in 1919, "simply a systematic extension of the

*Whittaker took the same point of view in his *History of the Theories of the Aether and Electricity*. Einstein, hearing of this from his friend Born when the second edition was published in 1953, commented as follows: "Everybody does what he considers right, or, in deterministic terms, what he has to do. If he manages to convince others, that is their own affair. I myself have certainly found satisfaction in my efforts, but I would not consider it sensible to defend the results of my own work as being my own 'property,' as some old miser might defend the few coppers he had laboriously scraped together. I do not hold anything against him, nor of course, against you. After all, I do not need to read the thing."

electrodynamics of Clerk Maxwell and Lorentz." Certainly Lorentz himself had no doubt about whose theory it was. "To discuss Einstein's principle of relativity here in Göttingen . . . ," he said when he spoke there in 1910, "appears to be a particularly welcome task."

If there are any missing acknowledgments in Einstein's work, they belong not to Michelson-Morley, to Lorentz, Fitzgerald, or Poincaré but to August Föppl, a German administrator and teacher whose *Introduction to Maxwell's Theory of Electricity* was almost certainly studied by Einstein. The famous relativity paper has similarities in style and argument with Föppl's treatment of "relative and absolute motion in space"; and Föppl himself writes of "a deep-going revision of that conception of space which has been impressed upon human thinking in its previous period of development" as presenting "perhaps the most important problem of science of our time."

Thus Föppl, like the Lorentz equations, can justifiably be considered as another of the useful instruments lying to hand which Einstein was able to utilize. As *The Times* was later to say of Einstein's General Theory, there is no need to defend his originality. "The genius of Einstein consists in taking up the uninterpreted experiments and scattered suggestions of his predecessors, and welding them into a comprehensive scheme that wins universal admiration by its simplicity and beauty."

The "comprehensive scheme" of 1905 had shown that space and time, previously thought to be absolute, in fact depended on relative motion. Yet these are but two of the three yardsticks used to measure the nature of the physical world. The third is mass. Was this, also, linked in some hitherto unexpected way with the speed of light? Einstein considered the question. In view of the apocalyptic consequences, his thoughts, thrown off in a letter to Habicht, apparently in the summer of 1905, have all the casualness of a bomb tossed into the marketplace. After suggesting that Habicht might like to join him in the Patent Office, he adds:

> You don't need to bother about valuable time, there is not always a subtle theme to meditate upon. At least, not an exciting one. There is, of course, the theme of spectral lines, but I do not think that a simple connection of these

phenomena with those already explored exists; so that for the moment the thing does not seem to show very much promise. However, a result of the electrodynamic work has come to my mind. The relativity principle in connection with the Maxwell equations demands that the mass is a direct measure for the energy contained in the bodies; light transfers mass. A remarkable decrease of the mass must result in radium. This thought is amusing and infectious but I cannot possibly know whether the good Lord does not laugh at it and has led me up the garden path.

During the next few weeks Einstein obviously thought more about the amusing and infectious idea. The result was a brief paper which appeared in the *Annalen der Physik* in the autumn of 1905 almost as a footnote to his earlier paper. "The results of the previous investigation lead to a very interesting conclusion, which is here to be deduced," he began. The deduction, carried through little more than a page and a half, went on with the following historic words:

> If a body gives off the energy L in the form of radiation, its mass diminishes by L/c^2. The fact that the energy withdrawn from the body becomes energy of radiation evidently makes no difference, so that we are led to the more general conclusion that
>
> The mass of a body is a measure of its energy content; if the energy changes by L, the mass changes in the same sense by $L/9 \times 10^{20}$, the energy being measured in ergs, and the mass in grams.

Einstein concluded with the comment that the theory might be put to the test by the use of such materials as radium salts whose energy content was very variable, and that radiation appeared to convey inertia between emitting and absorbing bodies. Yet the immediately important conclusion was that mass did in fact increase with relative speed. There had already been laboratory examples of this awkward process. During the last decade of the century, both J. J. Thomson in Cambridge and subsequently W. Kaufmann in Göttingen had investigated the ways in which fast cathode rays, the streams of electrons whose existence had been postulated by Lorentz and confirmed by Thomson, could be electromagnetically deflected; both had found that mass of the particle appeared to depend on velocity. Some years later F. Hasenöhrl had shown that light radiation enclosed in a vessel increased that vessel's resistance to acceleration—and that its mass was altered in the process. Finally, in 1900, Poincaré had suggested that this inertia or resistance to acceleration was a property of all energy and not merely of electromagnetic energy.

Now Einstein had leapfrogged ahead, ignoring the separate experimental results which had been puzzling individual workers and coming up with a simple overall explanation which, almost staring them in the face, had appeared too simple to be true. All mass was merely congealed energy; all energy merely liberated matter. Thus the photons, or light quanta, of the photoelectric effect were just particles which had shed their mass and were traveling with the speed of light in the form of energy; while energy below the speed of light had been transformed by its slowing down, a transformation which had had the effect of congealing it into matter. There had been a whiff of this very idea from Newton, who in his *Opticks* had asked: "Are not gross Bodies and Light convertible into one another, and may not Bodies receive much of their Activity from the Particles of Light which enter their Composition?" The apparent rightness of this was underlined by his comment, a few lines lower, that "the changing of Bodies into Light, and Light into Bodies, is very conformable to the Course of Nature, which seems delighted with Transmutations."

The nub of this revelation—which involved two separate things, the difference between the mass of a body at rest and its mass in motion, and the transformation of a material body into energy—linked the previously separate concepts of conservation of energy and conservation of matter, and was embodied in two equations. One showed that the mass of a body moving at any particular velocity was its mass at rest divided by $\sqrt{1 - v^2/c^2}$. This quickly provides a clue to man's long ignorance of the difference between the mass of a body at rest and in movement; for the difference will be very small indeed until the velocity concerned leaves the speeds of ordinary life and begins to approach the velocity of light. As with space and time, the changes are too small to be noted by man's inadequate senses. The second equation follows on from the fact that the motion whose increase raises the mass of a body is a form of energy. This is the famous $E = mc^2$, which states, in the shorthand of science, that the energy contained in matter is equal in ergs to its mass in grams multiplied by the square of the velocity of light in centimeters per second. Here again, one needed no mathematical expertise to see the essence of the argument: the velocity of light being what it is, a very small amount of mass is equivalent to a vast amount of energy.

Einstein's "follow-through" from his Special Theory of Relativity thus explained how electrons weighed more when moving than when at rest, since this was the natural result of their speed. It helped to explain how materials such as radium, whose radioactivity still puzzled the men experimenting with them, were able to eject particles at great speeds and to go on doing so for long periods, since creation of the comparatively large amounts of energy involved could be attained by the loss of a minute amount of mass. It helped to explain, furthermore, the ability of the sun—and of the stars—to continue radiating a large amount of light and heat by losing only a small amount of mass.

Forty years later, the facts of nature as revealed by Einstein's equation were to be demonstrated in another way. For by then it had been discovered that if the nucleus of a heavy atom could be split into two parts, the mass of its two fragments would be less than that of the original nucleus. The difference in mass would have been transformed into energy; its amount would be minute, but the energy released would be this minute mass multiplied by the square of the speed of light—the energy which, released from vast numbers of nuclei by the fission process, destroyed Hiroshima and Nagasaki.

The chances of splitting the atom appeared insoluble in 1905. But the equation was there. And for writers and cranks, for visionaries and men who lived on the borderland of the mind, a new pipedream became possible. A few scientists thought along similar lines, and in 1921 Hans Thirring commented: ". . . it takes one's breath away to think of what might happen in a town, if the dormant energy of a single brick were to be set free, say in the form of an explosion. It would suffice to raze a city with a million inhabitants to the ground." Most of his professional colleagues did not speculate thus far. Rutherford maintained almost to the end of his life in 1937 that the use of the energy locked within the atom was "moonshine." And when a young man approached Einstein in Prague in 1921, wanting to produce a weapon from nuclear energy based on $E = mc^2$, he was told to calm himself. "You haven't lost anything if I don't discuss your work with you in detail," Einstein said. "It's foolishness is evident at first glance. You cannot learn anything more from a longer discussion."

The demonstration of Einstein's mass-energy equation in the destruction of Hiroshima and Nagasaki has naturally given this by-product of his Special Theory a popular predominance over all others. But it should be emphasized that nuclear fission, whose utilization made nuclear weapons possible, was "discovered" by other men moving along very different paths of research. Fission illustrated—dramatically in the case of the atomic bombs—Einstein's mass-energy equation rather than being based on it.

But the atomic bomb came forty years after Einstein had cut at the foundation of classical physics, and the effects of relativity during these four decades were to be all-pervasive. So much so that while the immense effects of evolution and communism, those two other revolutionary ideas of the last hundred years, are as toughly debated as they are freely admitted, a different attitude exists about relativity. So much has it been assimilated into human knowledge that it is sometimes overlooked altogether.

Yet there are three ways in which man's relationship with his physical world has been changed by relativity. The first, and possibly the least important, is that it has helped him to understand some phenomena which would otherwise have been incomprehensible. The behavior of nuclear particles discovered during the last half-century is only the most obvious example. "We use it," Oppenheimer has said of Special Relativity, "literally in almost every branch of nuclear physics and many branches of atomic physics, and in all branches of physics dealing with the fundamental particles. It has been checked and cross-checked and counter-checked in the most numerous ways and it is a very rich part of our heritage."

In addition to supplying this very practical tool, relativity has enabled man to give more accurate, more descriptive accounts of the world of which he is a part. As Philipp Frank has pointed out, the plain statement that a table is three feet long is not only incomplete but meaningless when compared with the statement that it is three feet long relative to the room in which it stands. "Relativism," he says, "means the introduction of a richer language which allows us to meet adequately the requirements of the enriched experience. We are now able to cover these new facts by plain and direct words and to come one step nearer to what one may call the 'plain truth about the universe.' "

It is this "plain truth about the universe" which suggests the third and most important change that relativity has produced. Its epistemological implications are still hotly debated. Nevertheless, it is indisputable that while the theory has enabled man to describe his position in the universe with greater accuracy it has also thrown into higher relief the limitations of his own personal experiences. "Physical science," Sir James Jeans has emphasized,

> does not of course suggest that we must abandon the intuitive concepts of space and time which we derive from individual experience. These may mean nothing to nature, but they still mean a good deal to us. Whatever conclusions the mathematicians may reach, it is certain that our newspapers, our historians and story-tellers will still place their truths and fictions in a framework of space and time; they will continue to say—this event happened at such an instant in the course of the ever-flowing stream of time, this other event at another instant lower down the stream, and so on.
>
> Such a scheme is perfectly satisfactory for any single individual, or for any group of individuals whose experiences keep them fairly close together in space and time—and, compared with the vast ranges of nature, all the inhabitants of the earth form such a group. The theory of relativity merely suggests that such a scheme is private to single individuals or to small colonies of individuals; it is a parochial method of measuring, and so is not suited for nature as a whole. It can represent all the facts and phenomena of nature, but only by attaching a subjective

> taint to them all; it does not represent nature so much as what the inhabitants of one rocket, or of one planet, or better still an individual pair of human eyes, see of nature. Nothing in our experiences or experiments justifies us in extending either this or any other parochial scheme to the whole of nature, on the supposition that it represents any sort of objective reality.

Relativity has thus helped human beings to appreciate their place in the physical world just as T. H. Huxley's *Man's Place in Nature* gave them a context in the biological world. It is significant that one of the most hardheaded remarks on relativity made after Einstein's death should come from a religious journal. His theory has shown, remarked *The Tablet*, that "space and time for the physicist are defined by the operations used to measure them, and that any theory in which they appear must implicitly take these operations into account. Thus modern science looks at nature from the viewpoint of a man, not from that of an angel."

CHAPTER 5

FRUITS OF SUCCESS

Einstein's papers of 1905 revealed to the small handful of leading European physicists that they had a potential leader in their midst; only the next decade would show whether that potential was to be realized. Other men, in the arts as well as in science, in politics, and in war, had sent up sparks of genius during their early years yet failed to set the world ablaze. And even if Einstein did have the qualities needed to carry through and exploit his early promise, there were still a dozen ways in which chance might circumscribe or cut short his future—the Great War, taking Hasenöhrl on the German side and Moseley on Britain's, was only one pitfall lying ahead.

However, Einstein's statistical work which led to his paper on the Brownian motion, his conception of photons, and his adventurous theory of relativity were all soon seen as more than isolated efforts. Instead, it became clear that they were logically consequential operations, each of which could be further developed to throw fresh light on the current problems of physics. In this development he was to be helped by the climate of the times. From 1905 until 1914 he was able to think and read and move in a truly international scientific society that was shattered with the outbreak of the Great War and was not fully restored for almost half a century. Traveling from Berne or Zurich to Leiden or Salzburg, to Brussels or Vienna, he crossed frontiers that were political but not cultural. Talking with Lorentz in Holland, with Mach in Austria, and in Belgium with Rutherford from England, Madame Curie and Langevin from France, Planck and Nernst from Berlin, he was embraced as a full member of that small truly international group whose work was concentrated on the single task of discovering the nature of the physical world. For a short while, it was a scientific world without politics, an unusual state of affairs to which Einstein always looked back as though it were the norm rather than an exception which occurred as science prepared to tackle the riddles of the atom. Among these colleagues he moved with a calm assurance and a quizzical smile; both came, for all his innate humbleness, from an inner certainty of being right. Thus he looked ahead from 1905, untroubled by the Jewish problem which was later to engage his energies, unworried by thoughts of war in Europe which had surely given up such a recklessly wasteful occupation, totally unaware that his work with brain, pen, and paper would have any impact beyond the circumscribed scientific field in which he moved.

The story of his life for the next decade is therefore first of scientific consolidation and then of scientific exploration, of increasing contact with the men and women who produced the twentieth century's scientific revolution. In it there appear rarely, and as if by accident, the figures of his family and the everyday emotions which move most ordinary men. He was kind, but in a slightly casual way; amiable as long as people allowed him to get on with his work, and totally uninterested in what he regarded as the superficialities of life. "My wife returned yesterday from Serbia, where she has been on holiday with both the children," he wrote to Professor Hurwitz in a typical note. "Do you know what the result is? They've turned Catholic. Well, it's all the same to me."

In the summer of 1905 Einstein himself visited Belgrade with Mileva. They stayed with her relatives and friends, spending a week in the lakeside holiday resort of Kijevo, and then traveling on to Novi Sad where he met his wife's parents for the first time. It was one of numerous holiday journeys to what is now Yugoslavia but was then part of the Austro-Hungarian Empire, holidays which are remembered today by his eldest son Hans as pleasant rambling interludes during which the odd character of a father amiably visits his in-laws from another world, accompanied first by his small son and, later, by a baby second son as well. Einstein never forgot his Serbian hosts and kept up an intermittent correspondence with them for nearly half a century—mentioning only casually, they recounted after his death, that he had been awarded a Nobel Prize.

Other holidays were spent in the nearby Oberland, sometimes in Murren, not yet become overfashionable, quiet holidays of a minor civil servant who superficially seemed likely to spend the rest of his life on much the same local round. He would occasionally visit Cäsar Koch in Antwerp. He kept in touch with his former colleagues of Aarau or Zurich, and to friends and relations he jotted off the postcards with their spidery writing that were later to become collectors' items. It was all rather low key. Yet it was this that still seemed to be the genuine Einstein. Surely the real person was the slightly shabby, poor man's bohemian of the rather broken-down apartment in Marktgasse. Surely the potential genius of which whispers began to come from Planck and the great names in Berlin was merely a dream figure which had stepped down from one of Paul Klee's early landscapes.

The only hint that the potential genius might be the real Einstein came from his ferocious concentration on the task to be done and his determination that nothing should be allowed to divert him from it. A few years earlier it might have been only a hangover from graduate enthusiasm; now it began to look as though it was part and parcel of the mature man. Here there is a similarity—first pointed out by C. P. Snow—between Einstein and Churchill, the "eminently wise man" as Einstein later described him. The comparison is not surprising once the picture-book image of both scientist and statesman is scraped away to reveal the machinery beneath. Of Churchill it has been written that almost obsessional concentration "was one of the keys to his character. It was not always obvious, but he never really thought of anything but the job in hand. He was not a fast worker, especially when dealing with papers, but he was essentially a nonstop worker." Einstein, with the black notebook in his pocket, handy for the moment when the sails began to hang limp, reading while he rocked the cradle in his Berne apartment, was much the same.

He had his music. But this, as he would explain on occasions, was in some ways an extension of his thinking processes, a method of allowing the subconscious to solve particularly tricky problems. "Whenever he felt that he had come to the end of the road or into a difficult situation in his work," his eldest son has said, "he would take refuge in music, and that would usually resolve all his difficulties." Einstein himself once remarked that: "Music has no effect on research work, but both are born of the same source and complement each other through the satisfaction they bestow."

There was also his sailing, and here a remark by his second wife is pertinent: "He is so much on the water that people cannot easily reach him." On the Zurichsee, on the Lake of Thun, or on any of Switzerland's myriad of small lakes, where the hand responded instinctively to the demands of the breeze and an able man could let a boat sail itself, the mind could get on with the job without fear of interruption. What is more, the surroundings helped. "He needed this kind of relaxation from his intense work," says his eldest son. And with relaxation there would often come the solution. For his work needed neither laboratory nor equipment.

During the years that immediately followed 1905 Einstein is thus outwardly the minor Jewish civil servant of slightly radical ideas, the professional odd man out, with a Slav wife and illusions of grandeur that had actually gained him a doctorate of philosophy. But slowly, and as surely as the tide comes in, the other image began to harden, the picture of the man who for some inexplicable reason really was being sought out by those who had made their way in the world. This metamorphosis was nothing to do with the popular acclaim which brought Einstein international renown after the First World War. As far as the outside world was concerned he remained totally unknown until 1912, when some aspects of relativity became headline news in Austria, and almost totally unknown until 1919. But in the academic world the significance of the relativity papers soon began to be appreciated.

First off the mark seems to have been Wilhelm Wien, who as editor of the *Annalen der Physik* had accepted the papers. Immediately after the appearance of the number containing Einstein's first paper, he came into Laub's workroom, which was near his own, at about nine o'clock, as was usual, says Jakob Johann Laub, a former pupil at the ETH who was taking his degree at Leipzig under Wien. He had the copy of the *Annalen* in his hand, and he said that it contained an article by Herr Einstein. He told Laub to refer to it in the next colloguium. This started a lively discussion, from which it appeared that one would not easily become accustomed to the new ideas of time and space.

In Berlin, Planck was equally quick. This is confirmed by Max von Laue, the young son of an army officer whose path was to cross and recross Einstein's for half a century. Von Laue had been born in Koblenz within a few months of Einstein and had gained his doctorate at Strasbourg before starting the work on X rays for which he later won a Nobel Prize. When he came to Berlin in the autumn of 1905 as assistant to Planck, he has written, the first lecture which he heard in the physics colloquium of the university was one by Planck on Einstein's work, "On the Electrodynamics of Moving Bodies," which had appeared in September. It described the beginnings of the theory of relativity which immediately made the greatest impression on him, although he needed years to understand it. But he used the next summer holidays to make a tour through the Swiss mountains in order to visit Albert Einstein in Berne.

Another man who quickly realized the significance of his work was the Pole, Professor Witkowski, who after reading the famous Volume 17 of *Annalen der Physik* exclaimed to his friend Professor Loria in Cracow, "A new Copernicus is born! Read Einstein's paper." But there was a sequel—apparently in 1907—according to Einstein's future collaborator, Leopold Infeld. "Later, when Professor Loria met Professor Max Born at a physics meeting, he told him about Einstein and asked Born if he had read the paper," writes Infeld. "It turned out that neither Born nor anyone else there had heard about Einstein." They went to the library, took from the bookshelves the seventeenth volume of *Annalen der Physik,* and started to read the articles. "Although I was quite familiar with the relativistic idea and the Lorentz transformations," Born has said of the incident, "Einstein's reasoning was a revelation to me." Elsewhere he has said that the paper "had a stronger influence on [his] thinking than any other scientific experience."

It is clear that during the years immediately following 1905 the concept of relativity percolated slowly through accepted ideas like rain through limestone rather than breaking them down like the weight of water cracking a dam. But as water slowly penetrates the myriad channels, so did the Special Theory begin to affect the whole body of physics. There were some setbacks, and one early reaction to the theory was of unqualified rejection. It came as a paper by W. Kaufmann on the constitution of the electron, and it included the following blunt statement: "I anticipate right away the general result of the measurements to be described in the following: *the results are not compatible with the Lorentz-Einsteinian fundamental assumptions.*" The results had been obtained experimentally in Kaufmann's laboratory and were in line with other theories which had given plausible accounts of the electron's characteristics without invoking relativity. But neither Einstein nor anyone else fully realized that the technology of the times was incapable of delivering results accurate enough to support or refute the theory of relativity.

The scientific world awaited Einstein's reply with some interest—much as Central Europe held its breath after Tetzel had committed Luther's theses to the flames. It came the following year in the first of two articles in the *Jahrbuch der Radioaktivität und Elektronik.* Taking the theory of relativity a number of important steps forward, the articles were to be of great importance for other reasons. Here it is only necessary to note the startling way, suggesting assurance or arrogance according to point of view, with which Einstein handled Kaufmann. He agreed that the results could not be faulted; but he added, "it will be possible to decide whether or not the foundations of relativity theory correspond with the facts only if a great variety of observations is at hand." He did not leave it at that. With a statement of revealing certainty he brushed aside the possibility of two other theories cited by Kaufmann being more acceptable. "In my opinion," he went on, "both . . . have rather small probability, because their fundamental assumptions concerning the mass of moving electrons are not explainable in terms of theoretical systems which embrace a greater complex of phenomena." Here was a specific illustration of Einstein's scientific outlook. "A theory," Einstein continued, "is the more impressive the greater the simplicity of its premises is, the more different kinds of things it relates, and the more extended is its area of applicability." A theory which explained a small number of experimental results might or might not be valid, but the mere fact that it did explain them was not, of itself, any particular recommendation. With a theory that mattered, the process was the reverse. It was formulated to explain one of the major blueprints of nature as revealed in general terms; only then was a search made to see whether minor details supported it. Einstein's attitude was not that of "tant pis pour les faits"; but to some sceptics it must have looked dangerously like it.

His attitude was all the more surprising in that it was taken by a young man who lacked academic status. Einstein was still a humble Patent Office employee, even though he was beginning to be sought out, personally or through correspondence, by young scientists who wished to discuss the vital affairs of theoretical physics.

One of the correspondents was von Laue, who in the summer of 1906 called at the Patent Office. The young man who came to meet him made such an unexpected impression that Laue did not believe he could be the father of relativity. He let him go past and only when Einstein returned from the waiting room did they make one another's acquaintance. Their long discussion, continued as the two men walked back to Einstein's home from the office, increased von Laue's understanding of relativity. Recalling the occasion, he remembered that the cigar which he had been offered was so unpleasant that he "accidentally" let it fall from the bridge into the Aare. And he remembered that as they looked at the lovely view of the Bernese Oberland Einstein commented: "I just don't understand how people can run about all over that lot."

The theory of relativity remained the central scientific problem with which he concerned himself. He saw it, rightly most scientists feel today, as one of the vital factors in man's understanding of the natural world, a factor whose omission had distorted ideas across the whole spectrum of physical knowledge. But there was another of equal importance; this was the conception of quanta which Planck had seen as accounting for certain characteristics of radiation and which Einstein with his light quanta, or photons, had adventurously developed. The subject, which seemed to present numerous and almost insuperable problems, continued to exercise him. For while the theory of the photon helped to clarify heat, radiation, and the photoelectric effect, it totally failed to explain interference, the diffraction of light, or other phenomena. There was something, if not wrong, then at least incomplete about the explanations that had so far been put forward, and during these years in Berne Einstein worked hard to lessen this.

One of his confidants was young Laub, who during his degree examination had mentioned relativity. Wien disagreed with certain of his statements and advised him to talk with Einstein. Early in 1907 Laub therefore traveled to Berne and was drawn, like everyone else who met Einstein on a professional basis, into an obsessional discussion that soon rose and swamped everything else. Their interchange of letters gives a good deal of insight into Einstein's preoccupations and into the conditions under which he worked during these years. "He found Einstein kneeling in front of the oven, poking the fire, quite alone in his flat. . . ," says Seelig. "They found so much to discuss that for several weeks at midday, and during the evening, Laub fetched his new sparring partner from the Patent Office, and he visited him again the following year." Their intellectual collaboration produced three joint works dealing with the basic equations of electromagnetism and the pondero-motive force of the electromagnetic field. As the well-trained mathematician, Laub naturally took over the complicated mathematical tasks, while Einstein concentrated on their physical implications.

Einstein did not only outline his work to Laub. He also revealed what the young Patent Office employee of less than thirty thought of the masters of the craft. "I am ceaselessly occupied with the question of the constitution of radiation," he wrote in 1908,

> and am in correspondence on this question with H. A. Lorentz and Planck. The former is an astonishingly profound and at the same time amiable man. Planck is also very pleasant in correspondence. He has, however, one fault: that is that he is clumsy in finding his way about in foreign trains of thought. It is therefore understandable when he makes quite faulty objections to my latest work on radiation. He has not, however, said

> anything against my criticisms. I hope that he has read them and recognized them. This quantum question is so incredibly important and difficult that everyone should busy themselves with it. I have already succeeded in working out something which may be related to it, but I have serious reasons for still thinking that it is rubbish.

Two years later he was still pressing on, writing to Laub in November, 1910: "I now have the greatest hopes of solving the radiation problem, actually without light quanta. I am incredibly curious as to how the thing will turn out. We must renounce the energy principle in its present form." A few days later his curiosity had been satisfied. "Another failure in the solution of the radiation problem," he reported. "The devil played a wicked trick on me."

While much of the gossip in the letters is only of parochial importance, Einstein has some interesting observations on Lenard. After Laub had in 1908 gained an assistantship with Lenard at Heidelberg, Einstein was quick to congratulate him both on the appointment and on the money that went with it. "But I think that the opportunity of working with Lenard is still more important than the assistantship and the income together," he added. "Bear with Lenard's whims. He is a great master and an original mind. Perhaps he can be quite good socially with a man whom he has learned to respect." Two years later, after Laub had apparently been sacked, his opinion had changed. "Lenard really is crazy," he wrote. "Put together entirely with gall and intrigue. However, you can play that game better than he! And you can get away from him whereas he must live with himself until the end. I will do what I can to get you an assistant's place."

The need for "solving the radiation problem actually without light quanta" about which Einstein had written to Laub in 1907 seemed pressing enough, for both Lorentz and Planck continued to stress that the purely corpuscular theory of light which they appeared to postulate failed to account for many observable phenomena. However, Einstein struggled on, as intrigued as his contemporaries at the dual qualities of light which neither he nor any of them could as yet resolve. What he did succeed in doing during this period was to apply Planck's quantum formula to the vibrations of atoms, molecules, and solids, thereby explaining the deviations of the specific heat of solids from the classical laws. The fact that different amounts of heat were needed to raise different solids the same number of degrees had so far been difficult to explain satisfactorily. But in "Plancksche Theorie der Strahlung und die Theorie der spezifischen Warme" ("Planck's Theory of Radiation and the Theory of Specific Heat") Einstein opened the door to a solution. This decisive step led to a good deal of fresh experimental research, to the investigations by Nernst and his followers on specific heat at very low temperatures, and to the solution of subsequent problems by such men as Lindemann, Debye, and Born.

On the face of it, the work had none of the spectacular implications of relativity—or, for that matter, of the "heuristic viewpoint" that light could consist of both waves and particles. But not even Einstein could organize a revolution every year. And if his work on relativity and the photoelectric effect was the addition of a volume to man's knowledge, then his work on specific heat is typical of the way he continued, year after year, adding the odd page or two whenever opportunity offered.

Meanwhile his thoughts were increasingly preoccupied with another subject, linked as closely to philosophy as to physics, more nebulous yet even more fundamental. This was the new questioning of causality, taken for granted in one shape or form for centuries by the majority of scientists who believed that the explanation of every event could be found in its antecedent conditions. The billiard balls on the green baize tables moved along paths that could be predicted once the vectors imposed on them were known; and if the equations involved had for strict accuracy to be those of the Special Theory rather than of Newtonian mechanics, effect yet followed cause in exactly the same way. Surely the motions of the atoms and of their components, infinitely small though they were, could be comparably predicted once it became possible to quantify the forces imposed upon them?

This was not to be so. Doubts had been raised with the discovery of radioactivity and of the way in which the atoms comprising an element disintegrated—apparently without reason and in a pattern which enabled the statistician to forecast the future of a collection of atoms but not of an individual atom. At first it had appeared that this statistical forecast might be similar to the prediction of how a tossed coin would fall—used only because sufficient factors were not known with enough accuracy to allow the use of anything better. Once enough was known, it would surely be possible not merely to predict statistically the outcome of a series of coin tossings but to predict in terms of cause and effect the result of each particular toss. Surely, it was argued, the grand designs of nature operated along similar causal lines, with all that was required being merely sufficient information on the causes.

On this question, which grew steadily in importance as the century advanced, Einstein became increasingly separated from the bulk of his colleagues. While they moved on, he remained faithful to the attitude he had adopted as early as 1907 and which he revealed in a letter of that year to Philipp Frank, a young Austrian who had just taken his doctorate at the University of Vienna. In a paper entitled "Kausalgesetz und Erfahrung" ("Causal Law and Experience"), Frank had set out to show that the law of causality "can be neither confirmed nor disproved by experience; not, however, because it is a truth known *a priori* but because it is a purely conventional definition." Einstein, who developed rich correspondence with any scientist who had similar interests, wrote to Frank. "He approved the logic of my argument," Frank has said,

> but he objected that it demonstrates only that there is a conventional element in the law of causality and not that there is merely a convention or definition. He agreed with me that, whatever may happen in nature, one can never prove that a violation of the law of causality has taken place. One can always introduce by convention a terminology by which this law is saved. But it could happen that in this way our language and terminology might become highly complicated and cumbersome.

What Einstein was saying was this: If all the details of a coin's velocity, mass, moment of inertia, and other relevant factors were known as soon as it was in the air, and if it was still impossible to tell only by statistics which way it would fall, this was due not to a failure of causality. There was simply another causative factor which had not been considered. So with the laws of nature. Current ability to understand events in the atomic world only in statistical terms sprang from the limitations imposed by ignorance. In due course scientists might learn all the necessary facts, and the mysteries would then be removed. In 1907 it was difficult to dispute that this would eventually be so. The arguments were not developed until more than a decade later when the progress of physics slowly revealed that at the atomic level the laws of cause and effect give way to the laws of chance. Einstein remained unmoved, acknowledging that the work of his earlier years had led to the new situation, confident that "God did not play dice with the world."

All this lay two decades away as Einstein the scientist built up his connections with Europe's leading physicists and Einstein the Patent Office employee played the role of minor civil servant. The situation was growing more incongruous. But the reflection was not on Einstein so much as on a system which could apparently find no place for him in the academic world. The first steps to remedy this were taken in 1907—mainly at the instigation of the Professor Kleiner who in 1905 had helped to push through Einstein's Ph.D. in Zurich. Kleiner wanted Einstein on his staff. But during the early years of the century it was impossible for a man to be appointed professor in Switzerland—or in most other continental countries—before serving a spell as *privatdozent*. The holders of such posts, which have no equivalent in Britain or the United States, lecture as much or as little as they like and normally receive only nominal sums from the students whom they serve. In 1907 Kleiner proposed that Einstein should apply for a post as *privatdozent* in the University of Berne, a post in which the looseness of obligation would enable him to combine it easily with his Patent Office job. Einstein applied for entry to the faculty of theoretical physics, submitting as proof of his ability the printed version of the paper which had won him his Zurich doctorate. With his usual mixture of impatience and optimism he did not wait for the outcome before writing to the dean. "Since I am keen that the time I spend on teaching, if my application is accepted, should be profitable," he wrote to Professor Gruner, head of the faculty, "I should like to give a course capable of developing and arousing the interest of certain students. It would perhaps also be profitable if my lectures could be a kind of supplement to your two classes."

However, he was to receive a shock. His application was rejected; partly because it was too short, "an amusing example of academic red tape which is found everywhere," as he later noted; partly because Professor Aimé Forster did not want a *privatdozent* on his staff. There were probably other reasons. The aura of the great man that has surrounded Einstein's name since 1919, when his work on the General Theory suddenly became well known, has overshadowed his position and his nature during the years before the First World War. The Einstein of the early 1900s was not only a scientist of minor academic qualifications who had launched an obscure theory on the world. He was also the man who failed to fit in or to conform, the disrespector of professors, the dropper of conversational bricks, the awkward Jewish customer, the man who although approaching the age of thirty still seemed to prefer the company of students. However, help was at hand. The decision "was revised shortly afterwards, and certainly at the wish of the Zurich University physicist Kleiner, who wanted to appoint me."

Thus Einstein started on his academic career at the age of twenty-nine. His first lectures as a *privatdozent* in Berne were delivered in the winter term of 1908–09. The subject was "The Theory of Radiation." He had only four students and during the following term the number shrank to a single man. Formality was abandoned and the session continued in Einstein's own rooms. The contradictions of his life still obstinately continued. The genius who had at first been rejected by the ETH had been succeeded by the minor Patent Office official who in a single issue of the *Annalen der Physik* had delivered three major blows at the accepted body of physics. Now this picture was succeeded by that of the apparently unsuccessful university part-timer. But once again the situation was on the point of being transformed.

The events which combined to give Einstein a new status were his formulation of the principle of equivalence, the cornerstone of the theory of General Relativity, and the arrival of two papers from Hermann Minkowski, who had left Zurich in 1902 for Göttingen, which gave mathematical form to Special Relativity.

The principle of equivalence, which first saw the light of

day in "The Principle of Relativity and the Inferences to Be Drawn from It," published in two issues of the *Jahrbuch der Radioaktivität und Elektronik* in 1907 and 1908, emerged from a problem that had been worrying Einstein since his formulation of the Special Theory in 1905. This theory had been complete in itself. But it was a characteristic of Einstein's whole scientific life that most of his main achievements sprang directly from their predecessors. Each advance was first consolidated and then used as base for a fresh move into unexplored territory.

In the Special Theory he had shown that there was no place for the word "absolute" when motion was considered. Movement was relative, whether it was the movement of the stars in their courses or of the electrons in the physicist's laboratory. Yet the motion concerned was of a very limited variety—hence the "special" in the description of the theory. For he had dealt only with motion in a straight line at a constant velocity. In the world of everyday life to which he clung with such determination, this was exemplified by the train moving at constant speed, from which it was impossible to discover the existence of motion except by looking out of the window and relating the train to another frame of reference. But this situation altered radically if there was a change in the speed of the train. Then acceleration thrust back a passenger sitting in a forward-facing seat, or deceleration slumped him forward, while the movement of inanimate objects in the train—a glass of water, for instance—would clearly show that a change of movement was taking place. Similarly, if constant motion were maintained in a circular motion—as in a car on a merry-go-round—then the outward pull on the body (or on the glass of water) would once again provide a yardstick for the movement involved. "Because of this," said Einstein in describing how his argument had progressed from Special to General Relativity, "we feel compelled at the present juncture to grant a kind of absolute physical reality to nonuniform motion. . . ."

This discrepancy between the relativity of uniform motion and the apparent nonrelativity of nonuniform motion, between the fact that the first has no meaning unless it is compared to something else, while the second is self-evident within its own frame of reference, greatly worried him. As it has been put by Dr. Sciama, "This was displeasing to Einstein, who felt that the harmony of his theory of relativity required that all motion should be equally relative." He had come to it by considering the empirical equivalence of all inertial systems in regard to light. But he now raised the purely epistemological question: "Why should relativity concern only uniform motion?"

As he sat at his desk on the third floor of the Post and Telegraph Building; walked down towards the Kirchenfeld Bridge in the evening, only half-seeing the splendid vision of the Oberland spread out before him; and as he casually rocked Hans Albert in his cradle, Einstein refused to let the discrepancy remain unexplained. What was it, he wondered, that lay at the heart of inertia, that tendency of a body to resist acceleration?

At first he thought back to Ernst Mach, now in his mid-sixties, still deeply sceptical of the atomic theory, already becoming out of touch, bypassed, and half-forgotten. "I was, of course, familiar with Mach's idea that inertia might not represent a resistance to acceleration as such, so much as a resistance to acceleration relative to the mass of all the other bodies in the world," he has said. "This idea fascinated me; but it did not provide a basis for a new theory." Mach, who attributed the movement of earthly bodies to the influence of the stars—it "savors of astrology and is scientifically incredible," was Bertrand Russell's opinion—was reviving Bishop Berkeley's notion that centrifugal forces were governed by the same thing. Einstein arrived at a somewhat similar conclusion by a very different route. But first he had begun to reflect on one force which had always been taken for granted, the force of gravity. "I made the first step towards the solution of this problem"—that of acceleration—"when I endeavored to include the law of gravity in the framework of the Special Theory of Relativity," he has said.

He began by returning to Newton's conception of inertia which triggers the senses into knowing when the train has jerked forward or a body is being pulled out of a straight line in a swing or on a merry-go-round. First, "every body continues in its state of rest, or of uniform motion in a straight line, unless it is compelled to change that state by forces impressed thereon"; and, secondly, the greater the mass of the body, the greater the force needed to accelerate it or to change its course. These formal statements were the quintessence of everyday experience, the scientists' explanation of the fact that it is easier to throw a tennis ball than a cannonball and less difficult to get a small wheelbarrow on the move than a large one. But there was one exception to this otherwise unfailing rule that different forces were necessary to move objects of different masses. That exception was gravity, the mysterious force which appeared to pervade space and which tended to draw all objects to the ground. More than three centuries earlier Simon Stevenus, quartermaster of the Dutch army, had shown that different weights—reputedly cannonballs of different sizes—fell to the ground at the same speed. Some years later, Galileo repeated and refined the experiment to produce his revolutionary conclusion: that the force of gravity had the same effect on all objects regardless of their size or mass. Air resistance prevented cannonballs and feathers from falling at similar speeds, but if this resistance were eliminated, by the use of a perfect vacuum for instance, then cannonballs and feathers would reach the ground at the same time if dropped from equal heights—a proposition subsequently found to be correct.

The explanation proposed by Newton for this curious exception to his laws of inertia was ingenious; to Einstein it was too ingenious. The explanation was that gravity, reaching up into the heavens to attract material objects down to earth, exercised its power precisely in proportion to the mass concerned. On objects of small mass, the "pull" was relatively small; on those of greater mass, the "pull" was increased—to just the extent needed to bring them all down towards the ground at the accelerating speed of 32 feet per second. Thus the force of gravity operated so that it always counterbalanced inertia—a proposition which Einstein found very hard to take for granted.

There was yet another aspect of Newton's explanation which he found it difficult to accept. For the effect of gravity was in Newtonian terms transmitted through space instantaneously, a proposition which conflicted harshly with Einstein's assumption in the Special Theory that the speed of light is a limiting speed in the universe. The more he contemplated this instantaneous and apparently fortuitous balancing of the effect of gravity and the effect of inertia, the less he liked it. It was an accident of nature that he considered too odd to be truly accidental, a lucky chance which he felt must be the result of something more than luck.

This was a repetition of the situation which had led to the photoelectric paper and to the theory of Special Relativity. In the first, Einstein had started by drawing attention to the contradictions between the corpuscular and the field theories which science had been content to leave rubbing up against one another with little more than an occasional comment. And the famous relativity paper had begun by drawing attention to the discrepancy between the observational and the theoretical aspects of Faraday's law of induction. Now here, once more, was a curious state of affairs which science had either not noticed or had thought it better to leave alone.

Einstein's reaction was typical. He visualized the situation in concrete terms, in the "man in a box" problem which appears in different guises in most discussions of General Relativity. Einstein's illustration was basically simple—although it appears more so now, when men have been shot out of the earth's gravitational field, than it did some half-century ago when space travel was only a theoretical fancy.

In the first place Einstein envisaged a box falling freely down a suitably long shaft. Inside it, an occupant who took his money and keys from his pocket would find that they did not fall to the floor. Man, box, and objects were all falling freely in a gravitational field; but, and this was the important point, their temporary physical situation was identical to what it would have been in space, far beyond any gravitational field. With this in mind, Einstein then mentally transported both box and occupant to such a point in space beyond the pull of gravity. Here, all would have been as before. But he then envisaged the box being accelerated. The means were immaterial, since it was the result that mattered. Money and keys now fell to the bottom of the box. But the same thing would have happened had the box been at rest in a gravitational field. So the effect of gravity on the box at rest was identical with the effect of acceleration beyond the pull of gravity. What is more, it was clearly apparent that if a centrifugal force replaced acceleration the results would be the same. As it was later described by Professor Lindemann, a friend of Einstein for more than forty years, it would be as impossible for the man in the box "to tell whether he was in a gravitational field or subject to uniform acceleration, as it is for an airplane pilot in a cloud to tell whether he is flying straight or executing a properly banked turn."

Thus logical reasoning showed that the effects of gravitation were the equivalent of those of inertia, and that there was no way of distinguishing acceleration of centrifugal force from gravity. At least, this appeared to be so with money and keys and other material objects. But what would happen if one thought, instead, in terms of light? Here it was necessary to change the "thought-experiment." Once again there was the closed box. But this time, instead of dropped keys and money it was necessary to envisage a ray of light crossing the box from one side to the other while the box was being accelerated. The far side of the box would have moved upwards before the ray of light reached it; the wall would be hit by the light ray nearer the floor than the point at which it set out. In other words, to the man in the box there would have apparently been a bend in a horizontal ray of light.

But it was the very substance of Einstein's conception that the two situations—one produced by nonuniform motion and the other produced by gravity—were indistinguishable whether one used merely mechanical tricks or those of electrodynamics. Thus the ray of light, seen as bent by the man in the box when the box was subject to acceleration, would surely be seen in the same way if gravity were involved when the box was at rest. From one point of view this was not as outrageous as it sounded. In 1905 Einstein had given fresh support to the idea that light consisted not of waves but of a stream of minute machine gun bullets, the light quanta which were later christened photons. Why, after all, should not these light quanta be affected by gravity in the same way as everything else?

But even as the idea was contemplated its implications began to grow like the genie from the lamp. For a straight line is the path of a ray of light, while the basis of time measurement is the interval taken by light to pass from one point to another. Thus if light were affected by gravity, time and space would have two different configurations—one when viewed from within the gravitational field and one when viewed from without. In the absence of gravitation the shortest distance between *A* and *B*—the path along which a light ray would travel from *A* to *B*—is a straight line. But when gravitation is present the line traveled by light is not the straight line of ordinary geometry. Nevertheless, there is no way of getting from *A* to *B* faster than light gets along this path. The "light line" then *is* the straight line. This might not matter very much in the mundane affairs of the terrestrial world, where the earth's gravity was for all practical purposes a constant that was a part of life. But for those looking out from the earth to the solar system and the worlds beyond, the principle of equivalence suggested that they might have been looking out through distorting spectacles. Einstein's new idea appeared to have slipped a disk in the backbone of the universe.

Yet he still did not know what gravity was. He still did not know the characteristics of the gravitational field in the way that one could know the characteristics of the electromagnetic field by referring to Maxwell's equations. Only two things seemed clear. One was that gravity did not operate as Newton had said it operated. The second was that it had become "perfectly plain that a reasonable theory of gravitation could only be obtained by an extension of the principle of relativity." Just as "Special" Relativity could produce an accurate account of events in a frame of reference which was moving uniformly in relation to the observer, so could a more general version of the theory do the same thing when the frame of reference was moving at accelerating speeds—and then the theory should automatically be able to describe motion in a gravitational field as well.

Therefore Einstein now began to look out towards the problems beyond the earth just as he had earlier looked in towards the problems of molecules and atoms. The work took time, and another eight years passed before he produced the General Theory, described in 1919 by J. J. Thomson, the president of the Royal Society, as "one of the most momentous pronouncements of human thought" that the world had known. The delay was due not to Einstein's commitment to other research but to the complexity of the problems involved. Their solution came with the aid of other men, among them Hermann Minkowski who in 1909 transformed Einstein's earlier Special Theory into a convenient mathematical tool.

While Einstein had been at work in his Berne apartment, as unaware of his coming influence as Marx in the Reading Room of the British Museum, important events had been taking place in Göttingen. Standing on the outliers of the Harz Mountains, its ancient ramparts planted with lindens, proud of its university and its splendid botanic garden laid out by Albrecht von Haller, the little town still retained a whiff of the Middle Ages. The later memories of Gauss and Riemann were still fresh as there began the "great and brilliant period which mathematics experienced during the first decade of the century . . . , unforgettable to those who lived through it." Among its heroes was Hermann Minkowski, the man who at the ETH had taught Einstein, the "lazy dog" who "never bothered about mathematics at all," as Minkowski described him to Max Born.

Minkowski, Russian by birth, had been in his early thirties when lecturing in Zurich. He had been only a middling teacher but earlier, as a boy of eighteen, had won the Paris Prize for mathematics. It was natural that he should have been drawn to Göttingen in 1902, much as physicists were drawn to the Cavendish at Cambridge during its heyday under Thomson and Rutherford. Minkowski was the most recent of the German Jews who since the early 1800s had been helping to develop mathematics. Karl Jacobi had discovered elliptic functions and been followed by Johann Rosenheim who proved the existence of Jacobi's Abel functions. He in turn had been followed by Georg Cantor, who developed the theory of transfinite numbers.

Minkowski's contribution to the development of Special Relativity was in effect a single paper, "Basic Equations for the Electromagnetic Phenomena in Moving Bodies," published in the *Göttinger Nachrichten* in 1907; and, more far-reaching in its effects, "Space and Time," a popular lecture on the subject which he read to the Gesellschaft Deutscher Naturforscher in Cologne on September 2, 1908. The combined effect of the two was to be immense. For Minkowski not only gave a new mathematical formalism to the Special Theory but also, in the opinion of some, enabled Einstein to solve the problems of gravitation by means of the General Theory—"whether he would ever have done it without the genius of Minkowski we cannot tell," says E. Cunningham. Yet, contrariwise, Minkowski introduced fresh specialized meanings to old familiar words which brought a new confusingly esoteric element to an already difficult subject.

Einstein himself described Minkowski's contribution as the provision of equations in which "the natural laws satisfying the demands of the [special] theory of relativity assume mathematical forms, in which the time coordinate plays exactly the same role as the three space coordinates." To understand the importance of this it is necessary to reconsider exactly what it was that Einstein had already achieved. He had shown that an accurate description of mechanical and optical phenomena is linked with the movement of the observer relative to the phenomena observed. And he had, with his use of the Lorentz equations, been able to demonstrate the mathematical relationship between such observations made by observers moving at different relative speeds. What Minkowski now demonstrated was that a limitless number of different descriptions of the same phenomenon could be provided by a single equation through the introduction, in a certain way, of time as a fourth variable. In this, the three space coordinates were used as in the Lorentz transformation; the time variable, however, was no longer represented by t but by $\sqrt{-1}\,ct$. The result was an equation which dealt with the "real" world, of which the differing descriptions as seen from differently moving bodies were but partial and incomplete expressions; moreover, the curve produced from plotting a series of such equations representing phenomena contiguous in time would represent nothing less than a continuum of the real world—much as to the wolf and the dog of George Lewes, "the external world seems a continuum of scents."

Minkowski thus gave a mathematical formalism to what had been the purely physical conception of Special Relativity. But more important in some ways was the language in which he clothed his work—essential in the mathematical context where it was used, but misleading outside it unless sufficient explanation were given. Thus an event which takes place in three-dimensional space at a specific time is described as a "world-point," while a series of consecutive events—the movement of a rocket, of a man, or of an electron—is described as a "world-line." More significantly, and confusingly, time is described as "the fourth dimension."

Einstein was well aware of the bewilderment which such language created. "The nonmathematician," he wrote, "is seized by a mysterious shuddering when he hears of 'four-dimensional' things, by a feeling not unlike that awakened by thoughts of the occult. And yet there is no more commonplace statement than that the world in which we live is a four-dimensional space-time continumm." Here even Einstein, whose scientific explanations have at times a breathtaking simplicity, does not go quite far enough. For he does not explain that while for the layman the word "dimension" signifies one of the three measurements of a body represented by length, breadth, or thickness, for the mathematician it means a fourth variable which must, naturally enough, be inserted into any equation concerning events, since these occur not only in space but at a certain instant in time.

The change produced by Minkowski was clear enough—"from a 'happening' in three-dimensional, space, physics becomes, as it were, an 'existence' in the four-dimensional 'world,'" as Einstein said. Or, as Jeans had written of Einstein's original paper, "The study of the inner workings of nature passed from the engineer-scientist to the mathematician." Einstein was in no doubt about the difficulties that might ensue in the nonmathematical world. "Since the mathematicians have attacked the relativity theory, I myself no longer understand it any more," he claimed, tongue in cheek. "The people in Göttingen sometimes strike me," he said on another occasion, "not as if they wanted to help one formulate something clearly, but as if they wanted only to show us physicists how much brighter they are than we."

However, all this was merely the ripple of his exterior amusement. He knew, and he was subsequently to stress the fact, that it was Minkowski who not only transformed the Special Theory but who brought it to the attention of men outside the comparatively small world of theoretical physics.

The paper in the *Göttinger Nachrichten* had been important but was of limited influence. Something more significant was involved when in September, 1908, the Deutsche Naturforscher und Artzte, a body used by scientists to help spread the knowledge of their individual disciplines among a wider audience, met in Cologne. Here Minkowski delivered his semipopular lecture on "Space and Time," and after half a century his opening words still have a fine ring:

> Gentlemen! The ideas on space and time which I wish to develop before you grew from the soil of experimental physics. Therein lies their strength. Their tendency is radical. From now on, space by itself and time by itself must sink into the shadows, while only a union of the two preserves independence.

For Minkowski, relativity had become a central fact of life. After he and David Hilbert had visited an art exhibition at Kassel, Hilbert's wife asked what they thought of the pictures. "I do not know," was the reply. "We were so busy discussing relativity that we never really saw the art." Minkowski was among the most austere and dedicated of mathematicians. He was the last man to popularize, to play to the gallery. Yet he had sounded the trumpet for relativity in no uncertain fashion. He was still only forty-four and in the early winter of 1908 it would not have been too outrageous to speculate on the prospects of future long-term collaboration between Minkowski in Göttingen and Einstein in Berne. Then, towards the end of the year he fell ill. He was taken to the hospital and died of peritonitis on January 12, 1909—regretting on his deathbed, according to a legend which has more than a touch of plausibility: "What a pity that I have to die in the age of relativity's development."

The increased fame which Minkowski brought Einstein among a larger circle of German scientists looks less surprising today than it did in 1908. In retrospect it is possible to see Einstein's papers of 1905, the almost equally dramatic paper of 1907, and Minkowski's dénouement of 1908, as parts of a steady increase of reputation which in the end would inevitably be too great to be contained by the four walls of the Patent Office.

The break came the following year. So did Einstein's

first honorary doctorate, his first professional appointment, and his first major invited paper, read to the annual meeting of the same Naturforscherversammlung whose members had twelve months earlier listened to Minkowski. In fact 1909 was the year when the chrysalis opened and the professor of theoretical physics emerged, fully formed, equipped at all points, an independent animal whose eccentricities, once regarded as the irresponsibilities of a too casual youth, were now seen as the stigmata of genius.

The first important event in this year which marked a watershed in Einstein's life was an invitation to Geneva, where the university was celebrating the 350th anniversary of its foundation by Calvin. Einstein, it had been decided, should be awarded an honorary doctorate. Almost forty years afterwards, he recalled that he thought the letter from Geneva was merely a circular and had tossed it into a wastepaper basket; only when Geneva inquired why there had been no reply was the crumpled invitation retrieved and accepted.

Einstein traveled to Geneva early in July and was duly honored, together with Marie Curie, steely and determined, the woman who "felt herself at every moment to be a servant of society"; Ernest Solvay, the Belgian whose chemical profits endowed his eponymous congresses; and Wilhelm Ostwald, who a few months later won the Nobel Prize in chemistry for his work on catalysis.

No firsthand record of Einstein's visit to Geneva appears to have survived, but the secondhand stories are in character if not entirely free from an air of mythology. Certainly he seems to have arrived at the various ceremonies in informal dress, possibly in the straw hat with which legend credits him. And it was in the true Einstein tradition that he should turn to a neighbor at the sumptuous university banquet with the remark: "Do you know what Calvin would have done had he been here? He would have erected an enormous stake and had all of us burnt for sinful extravagance."

Two months after the Geneva visit came something more important. The previous summer Einstein had been visited in Berne by Rudolf Ladenburg, a physicist from Berlin who was also an official of the Naturforscher. The result was an invitation to lecture at the organization's

1909 conference, and in September Einstein left Berne for Salzburg, where this was to be held. The next few days were significant; before he was thirty, he told a colleague of this occasion, he had "never met a real physicist."

At Salzburg Einstein gave his first major "invited paper," thus exhibiting himself before an informed critical audience. He thus came under the close-range scrutiny of the pillars of the scientific establishment. But he in turn was able to scrutinize them. Those he met included Planck, Wien, Rubens, and Sommerfeld. "I am much struck by the last-named," he wrote to Laub on December 31. "He is a splendid chap." And at Salzburg he also met for the first time young Ludwig Hopf, who was to become his assistant in Zurich and Prague, and Max Born from Breslau, the physicist who had listened entranced to Minkowski on "Space and Time" in Cologne and had then joined him in Göttingen.

Judging by what was to follow, it was Planck rather than Sommerfeld whom Einstein might have singled out for special mention; for it was he for whom Einstein was to have a near reverence which Planck noted and turned to Germany's benefit when he could. The two men had been in correspondence, at first desultory, since 1900, but Planck was increasingly impressed by the young man who had boldly taken his quantum theory into fresh fields. In 1908 Planck, an ardent mountaineer—climbing the 12,000-foot Ortler when well into his sixties—had been staying at Axalp in the Bernese Oberland and he and Einstein were to have met there; but the plan fell through. Only now, at Salzburg, did the two men come face to face. Einstein's lasting attitude was illustrated twenty years later. Asked to contribute a preface to Planck's *Where Is Science Going?*, "he said that it would be presumptuous on his part to introduce Max Planck to the public, for the discoverer of the quantum theory did not need the reflected light of any lesser luminary to show him off. That was Einstein's attitude towards Planck, expressed with genuine and naïve emphasis."

At Salzburg, relativity as such was dealt with by Max Born, three years younger than Einstein and still with his name to make. "This seems to be rather amusing," Born wrote subsequently.

Einstein had already proceeded beyond Special Relativity which he left to minor prophets, while he himself pondered about the new riddles arising from the quantum structure of light, and of course about gravitation and General Relativity which at that time was not ripe for general discussion.

Einstein was still only thirty. He had already shaken the scientific world with an esoteric theory about which some of his elders still retained doubts. It would not have been surprising if he had chosen a comparatively "safe" subject on which to discourse before such a high-powered audience. But that was not the Einstein way. His paper was entitled "The development of Our Views on the Nature and Constitution of Radiation," and it was subsequently described by Wolfgang Pauli as "one of the landmarks in the development of theoretical physics." Its challenge came quickly:

> It is undeniable that there is an extensive group of data concerning radiation which show that light has certain fundamental properties that can be understood much more readily from the standpoint of the Newtonian emission theory than from the standpoint of the wave theory. It is my opinion, therefore, that the next phase of the development of theoretical physics will bring us a theory of light that can be interpreted as a kind of fusion of the wave and mission theories. The purpose of the following arguments is to give a foundation for this opinion, and to show that a profound change in our views of the nature and constitution of light is indispensable.

So the young man—still a mere "doctor" with not a professorship to his name—was to make the members of his audience profoundly change their views about light and to suggest that it was both particle and wave as well! Planck, rising first when the discussion was opened, probably spoke for the majority: "That seems to me," he said, "to be a step that, in my opinion, is not yet called for."

Einstein's paper lived up to its promise. For he invoked the $E = mc^2$ of his second relativity paper of 1905 which showed that the emission of energy in the form of light caused a change of mass and therefore supported the corpuscular theory. And he went on to argue that the elementary process of emission took place not as a spherical wave which classical theory demanded but as directed, or needle, radiation. This was grasping Planck's nettle with a vengeance. With the benefit of hindsight, it is clear that only Einstein would have dared to do it.

In the audience was Lise Meitner, a young woman of thirty-one studying under Planck in Berlin. "At that time I certainly did not yet realize the full implications of his theory of relativity," she wrote more than half a century later,

> and the way in which it would contribute to a revolutionary transformation of our concepts of time and space. In the course of this lecture he did, however, take the theory of relativity and from it derive the equation: energy = mass times the square of the velocity of light, and showed that to every radiation must be attributed an inert mass. These two facts were so overwhelmingly new and surprising that, to this day, I remember the lecture very well.

Almost exactly three decades later, walking at Christmas with her nephew Otto Frisch in the Stockholm woods, Lise Meitner hit upon the explanation of what Otto Hahn, one of Planck's successors in Berlin, had just discovered in Berlin: nuclear fission, which with Einstein's mass-energy equation was the key to nuclear weapons.

Einstein left Salzburg after the conference of 1909 for a short holiday in the surrounding country and then returned to Berne. But this time it was a return with a difference. For now, at the age of thirty, he was at last to part company with the Patent Office and to take up his first full-time academic post.

In 1908 it had been decided to establish a chair of theoretical physics in the University of Zurich and Professor Kleiner, who had helped Einstein to become a *privatdozent* in Berne, chose him for the post. However, Kleiner's early enthusiasm had waned, due partly it appears to Einstein's facility for being his own worst enemy. According to Philipp Frank, the professor had attended one of Einstein's lectures in Berne and concluded that it did not seem to be at the right level for students. "I don't demand to be appointed a professor at Zurich," Einstein retorted. Here it may not have been only his brusque honesty coming to the surface. He may have had his sights on something higher than the university. For while this was merely a cantonal institution, the ETH, where Einstein had graduated, and for which he always kept a soft spot in his heart, was a federal organization, standing on the higher educational ground and with the reputation that went with the situation.

Whatever Kleiner's personal feelings, something else was involved. His assistant was Friedrich Adler, the son of Viktor Adler who had founded the Austrian Social Democratic party, and a fellow student with Einstein at the ETH. The father had sent his son to study physics in Switzerland in the hope that he would be kept from politics. Yet it was politics which now stretched out to touch him in the academic world. For the members of the Zurich Board of Education had the final say in the appointment of the newly created chair, and a majority of the board were Social Democrats. In an ideal world this would have been irrelevant; nevertheless, the chair was offered to Adler.

This fact does not appear to have worried Einstein. The affair of the professorship had "ended in smoke, which I am glad of," he wrote to his friend Laub. "There are enough schoolmasters without me." However, it had not yet ended. The young Adler was a man of paranoiac honesty, and of a nature which was to bring him to the door of the execution yard a few years later. Once he learned that Einstein would have accepted the post had it been offered, he reported to the Board of Education in no uncertain words: "If it is possible to obtain a man like Einstein for our university, it would be absurd to appoint me. I must quite frankly say that my ability as a research physicist does not bear even the slightest comparison to Einstein's. Such an opportunity to obtain a man who can benefit us so much by raising the general level of the university should not be lost because of political sympathies."

To his father in Vienna, Adler wrote in much the same style. On November 28 he reported that he had again spoken with Kleiner, urging him to end the protracted argument by making a firm recommendation about Einstein, and adding: "I hope to have achieved this by Christmas."

During this period Einstein himself appears to have been searching around for another nonuniversity appointment. He wrote to Marcel Grossmann, asking whether he should apply for a post in the Technical College at Winterthur; applied to the Gymnasium of the Zurich Kantonsschule for details of a vacancy for a mathematical master; and discusses in more than one letter to Laub the prospects for what appear to be nonuniversity posts. He might have been happy in any of them—according to the hindsight of forty years on. "Teaching is always satisfying if one has an interest in the young," he wrote after the Second World War to one of his wife's young Balkan friends who was starting life as a schoolmistress. "I might have gone in for it myself in earlier years but I could not find a place."

However, while he was still searching around, Adler's honest argument had its effect. Early in the new year Einstein was called to Zurich to see Kleiner who, as he wrote to his friends the Ehrats on February 15, "expressed himself very graciously on the success of the 'exam,' and hinted that something would very soon mature." Only one doubt apparently remained. "If I am not compelled to stay here"—at the Patent Office—"on account of the accursed money," Einstein went on, "my prospects apparently look very rosy for the next autumn." However, the following April he was still waiting. "Would you believe it," Adler wrote to his father on April 16, apparently after a fresh series of appointments had been announced, "Einstein was not mentioned, and I'm glad that I did not wait any longer but began my holiday." But the money problem was finally settled and his appointment was formally announced by the early summer.

On July 6, 1909, he handed in his resignation to the Federal Department of Justice and Police by whom he was formally employed. According to Patent Office legend, Haller at first refused to take the resignation seriously. When forced to realize that Einstein really was intent on leaving, he wrote to the Federal Council, officially making a request for his employee's release. "The departure means a loss for the office," he wrote. "However, Herr Einstein feels that teaching and scientific research are his proper calling, and thus the director of the office has refrained from tempting him to remain by offers of financial betterment."

Einstein, returning to Switzerland from the Salzburg

meeting, first supervised the change of home from Berne to Zurich and then, in October, took up his post in the university. Two days later he realized he had forgotten to report his move to the authorities and wrote to Lucien Chaven, still in Berne: "I send you my *Dienstbüchlein* and the establishment license with the request that you report my departure to the police and the District Command."

CHAPTER 6

MOVES UP THE LADDER

Einstein's appointment in Zurich was that of associate professor, not full professor, and his salary was only the 4,500 francs a year he had been receiving at the Patent Office. It was augmented by lecture fees, and was raised by 1,000 francs in 1910, but these additions did not compensate for the increased expenses of a university professor and the higher cost of living in Zurich. By contrast with his position little more than a decade later, when he could have commanded whatever salary he wished, Einstein still lived and worked among the poorly paid, overworked lower professional classes and, to make ends meet, Mileva took in student lodgers. "In my relativity theory," he once said to Frank, "I set up a clock at every point in space, but in reality I find it difficult to provide even one clock in my room."

Even so, Einstein had at last officially broken through into the academic world and the future seemed plain sailing. The prospect was of a placid life at one or possibly two Swiss universities, of responsibility increasing steadily through the years, life in an ivory tower safe within the citadel. In fact, the future was to be dramatically different. Within five years Einstein was to have served three universities in three countries as well as the Zurich ETH, a more than usually peripatetic record for a scientist of those times. Within a few more years he was to become involved in the battles of pacifism, the struggle of Zionism, and the expanding role of scientists in world affairs. And in 1939 he was to help unleash nuclear weapons on the world. But there was no hint of this in 1909 when he expected, as he was to say after another twenty years, "to spend all his time in more solitary pursuits."

If there was any suggestion of a coming change in his life, it concerned his private affairs. The mutual patience with each other of Einstein and his wife was already wearing thin, and to Besso he wrote, a few weeks after settling into Zurich, that he had not recovered the balance of mind which "M" had made him lose. This situation had a bearing on his movement during the next few years—from Zurich to Prague, back to Zurich, and then on to Berlin. But the restlessness of his wife, who acquiesced in his move to Prague yet whose dislike of the ferment in the Bohemian capital was partly responsible for his return to Switzerland, was only one factor.

There was also his own personal ambition. It is fashionable to think of Einstein as a man insulated from the problems of real life, never worrying about money, scornful of honors and careless of the position which the world accorded him. Later on, as the most famous scientist in the world, he could afford to be casual. But earlier, when he was, as T. H. Huxley once said of his own career, only "at the edge of the crush at the pit-door of this great fools' theater," he had perfectly valid reasons for wishing to press on for recognition. With his ill-organized life, a certain minimum of money was required to cope with the day-to-day routines of life and provide peace and leisure for his work. Apart from this financial need, which justified a circumspect move from one appointment to the next, there was one other, dominating, reason for his shuttlings back and forth across Europe during these years before the First World War. He was, as he often said, the kind of man who did not work well in a team. Furthermore, his mental stature was such that he needed little stimulation from other workers in his own field. At the same time he preferred to work in a congenial intellectual climate. He liked being near the places where, as he once put it in a letter to Janos Plesch, "the future was being brewed."* It is no coincidence that in Prague he was directed by Georg Pick towards the mathematical apparatus which he needed for his General Theory of Relativity, and that he completed this work in a wartime Germany amid a galaxy of talent which included such men as Sommerfeld, von Laue, Planck, and Weyl.

*Compare with Snow's reference to scientists who "feel the future in their bones."

Little of this could have been forecast as he turned to the business of academic life for the first time in the autumn of 1909. With his wife and his son Hans Albert he moved into an apartment in Moussonstrasse at the bottom of the Zurichberg, and here his second son, Eduard, was born in July, 1910.

The Adlers also lived in the same building. "We are on extremely good terms with the Einsteins, who live above us," Friedrich Adler wrote to his parents on October 28,

> and as things turned out I have become closer to him than to any of the other academics. The Einsteins live the same Bohemian life as ourselves. They have a son the same age as Annika who spends a lot of time with us. . . . The more I speak with Einstein, and this happens often, the more convinced do I become that I was right in my opinion of him. Among contemporary physicists he is not only the clearest but the one who has the most independent of brains, and it is true that the majority of physicists don't even understand his approach. Apart from that, he is a pure physicist, which means that he is interested in theoretical problems which unfortunately is not the case with me."

In addition, Einstein was popular as a lecturer. This was due partly to his lack of convention, partly to his humor, partly to memories of the Munich Gymnasium which made it impossible for him to fit into the usual professorial mold. He went to a great deal of trouble over his first lecture, in order to help students, recalled his old friend from Aarau, Dr. Adolf Fisch. "He repeatedly asked the class whether they understood him. In the breaks he was often surrounded by male and female students who wanted to ask questions. In a patient and friendly manner he tried to answer them."

He lectured in Zurich regularly throughout termtime; on an "Introduction to Mechanics," on thermodynamics, the kinetic theory of heat, on electricity and magnetism, and on selected topics from theoretical physics. The number of students was usually in single figures—more the result of the tepid interest in physics than of any lack of ability in the master. Adler neatly sums up the situation after Einstein had taken up his appointment. "My mathematics lecture had an audience of only four, which is as good as can be expected in a small university such as this. But people must go and listen to Einstein, as they have to take their examinations with him, and after seven hours they have had more than enough."

He was precise and clear, he rarely used notes, yet he never floundered as even the best extemporaneous lecturer can. His humor was of the quiet, throwaway kind which illustrated points in his thesis, a sometimes quixotic, frequently irreverent humor which delighted his students. He was, moreover, one of the few lecturers who openly invited his listeners to interrupt him if they failed to understand a point, and it was obviously with the memory of the Luitpold Gymnasium still in his mind that he wrote to Chavan on January 17 saying: "Teaching also gives me great pleasure, chiefly because I see that my boys really enjoy their work."

The flavor of Einstein the teacher is given by Dr. Hans Tanner of Frauenfeld, who attended Einstein's lectures for many months. "During the whole time, as far as I can remember, Einstein only got stuck once," he has said.

> He suddenly stopped in the middle of a lecture and said: "There must be some silly mathematical transformation which I can't find for the moment. Can one of you gentlemen see it?" Naturally none of us could. "Then leave a quarter of a page. We won't lose any time. The answer is as follows."
>
> Some ten minutes later Einstein interrupted himself in the middle of an elucidation. "I've got it." At first we did not know what he meant. During the complicated development of his theme he had still found time to reflect upon the nature of that particular transformation. That was typical of Einstein.

It was also typical that he should cultivate a casual friendship with his students, unusual at that time. Taking them to the Terrasse Café after the weekly physics colloquium, bringing them home to discuss the riddle of the universe over coffee in the manner of the Olympia Academy little more than a decade before, Einstein appeared a happy man, outwardly satisfied with his financial status and content with the fame he had already achieved.

The niche in which circumstance had placed him seemed a satisfactory one. He was sixteen and a half when he arrived in Switzerland. Now he was thirty-one, a whole impressionable lifetime away, a Swiss citizen bound to the country by the strong bonds of all converts, blind to its defects and soberly convinced that in their system of government the Swiss had found the democratic key to the political millennium. He occasionally traveled outside the frontiers and brushed shoulders with other members of the international physicists community—Planck from Berlin, Rutherford from England, Poincaré from Paris—the scientific revolutionaries who were already overturning man's idea of the place he lived in. Yet their more rambustious world—the world of the Berlin laboratories, of the Collège de France, and of the Cavendish, all places against which Zurich had a faintly provincial air—had little attraction for Einstein. He needed no more than pencil, paper, and pipe, peace for relaxation with his violin, a nearby lake to sail on, the opportunity for an occasional not-too-strenuous stroll in pleasant scenery. Switzerland, that happy, happy land, offered it all.

This was outwardly the situation at the end of 1910, when he had been teaching in Zurich for little more than a year. Yet during the first months of 1911 his colleagues heard astounding news: Einstein was about to leave Switzerland for Prague. This was, as his Swiss biographer has noted, "a grievous blow for Swiss science." It would have seemed even more grievous had it been known that Einstein had been considering the move within a few months of coming to the city in October, 1909.

So much, and a good deal more, is clear from the correspondence between Friedrich Adler and Adler's father in Vienna, to whom the son described in blow-by-blow detail the moves which preceded Einstein's next step up the ladder. Although Adler had refused the chair in Zurich eventually taken by Einstein, he had continued to hold a post in the university. "I am still after all a physicist and this has its drawbacks because when Einstein leaves people will look upon it as a tragedy if I am not his successor, which I do not want," he wrote on January 23, 1910. This was no boasting letter from son to father. Adler had in fact been offered the chief editorship of the Social Democrat *Volksrecht* and was at first unable to understand why Einstein was, as he put it on February 15, "so upset that I am not remaining a scientist."

The reason became clear the following month. "Einstein remonstrated most strongly with me about joining the *Volksrecht*," he wrote to his father,

> asking me at least to cancel my holiday for this term. And at last something has come out which *no one* knows; he has received the offer of a post at another university. He has told me this in confidence, so please *do not* repeat it. His argument is that he can then propose me for his post with added confidence, which he wants to do not from feelings of personal friendship but from impartial conviction. This is nice of him but does not alter the situation.

Exactly a month later Einstein revealed to his colleague that the mysterious offer was from the German University in Prague, where the faculty had unanimously put forward his name. "No one knows of this other than myself, and I ask you not to mention it," Adler wrote to his father.

For Einstein there was more than one attraction in an appointment to the capital of Bohemia, third city of Austria-Hungary, a splendid assembly of noble palaces, royal parks, and lavishly decorated churches. The first rector of the university had been Ernst Mach. And at Benetek, a few miles outside Prague, Tycho Brahe, the Dane who had ushered in a great age of astronomy, had employed the young Kepler. These were associations which could not be ignored by a man of Einstein's background. He would not have ignored them even had he been aware of the complex emotional, racial, and political situation which was already beginning to develop in Prague. But in 1910, Einstein was not very aware; he was then even less of a political animal than he became in later life; most of what went on outside his own world he considered irrelevant and much of it he considered unpleasant. Thus he was barely awake to the fact that in Prague the struggle between the indigenous population and their German masters was already bitter if concealed, or that the existence of two universities in the city, German and Czech, created as a compromise solution in 1888, was only one indication of this. In addition, but apparently unknown to him, a large Jewish community had for years added an important religious and racial element to what was essentially a political situation.

As in Zurich two years previously, two main names

were put forward for the Prague appointment. But whereas in Zurich the initial solution had been simple, hacked out by the chopper of political loyalties, the complications in Prague were numerous enough to add an air of farce. On the one hand there was Einstein. On the other there was Gustav Jaumann, professor at the Technical Institute in Brno. The choice between them rested on the recommendation of Anton Lampa, head of the physics faculty, and exercised formally by the Emperor through the Ministry of Education. Lampa favored Einstein, influenced as he himself was by the belief that the latter was still an unequivocal Machist—and no doubt by Planck's words of advice: "If Einstein's theory should prove correct, as I suspect it will, he will be considered the Copernicus of the twentieth century." The Ministry preferred Jaumann not only because he was a Machist; in addition, he had the virtue of Austrian birth.

The situation was further complicated by university regulations, which laid down that the importance of candidates' publications should govern their positions on the entry list. Einstein's papers from 1902 onwards brought him to the top. But this was too much for Jaumann, a self-styled unrecognized genius who now withdrew from the race protesting: "If Einstein has been proposed as first choice because of the belief that he has greater achievements to his credit, then I will have nothing to do with a university that chases after modernity and does not appreciate merit." The move appeared to leave the field open for Einstein.

But now another impediment arose. While the Emperor Franz Joseph had no direct role in the appointment, he could exercise a veto; and it was known that the Emperor would confirm university appointments only of confessing members of a recognized church, a state of grace from which Einstein was self-excluded. This local difficulty became clear soon, and on June 23 Adler wrote to his father telling him that his friend's Prague appointment might not be definite. For although Einstein had never officially renounced his faith, and was therefore technically a Jew, it was well known in Zurich that for all practical purposes he was an "unbeliever."

The position was made clearer in a letter—undated but apparently also written on June 23—which Adler's wife,

Katya, sent to her father-in-law. "On Sunday Einstein came and told us that the offer from Prague was not going to materialize," this went.

> There was a second problem: they did not want "a foreigner." However, [Adler] maintains that the trouble is not that Einstein is a "foreigner" but that he is an unbeliever. The university found this out and this is the inevitable result. . . . Now Einstein is as unpractical as a child in cases like this, and [Adler] finally got out of him the fact that on the application form he put down that he was an unbeliever but did not say that he had not left the Church. As Einstein very much wants the Prague post, and as the first hurdle would be the question of his religion, [Adler] suggested to him at the time that he should pass the whole thing over to Lampa in Prague so that should the question arise in discussion, Lampa would be briefed. Einstein did not do this; and now, following the letter from Lampa, he can hardly do so. Einstein is naturally disappointed that the appointment is rejected since this means that the same thing will happen with any other position for which he applies.

That Einstein's attitude was the result more of muddle than agnostic scruple seems clear from a letter which he wrote less than two years later when Paul Ehrenfest ruled himself out from becoming Einstein's successor by roundly declaring himself an atheist. "I am frankly *annoyed* that you have this caprice of being without religious affiliations," wrote Einstein, already a friend and admirer who would have been overjoyed if Ehrenfest could have taken his chair; "give it up for your children's sake. Besides, once you are professor here you can go back to this curious whim again—and it is only necessary for a little while."

However, in the summer of 1911, when Einstein was an innocent year younger, it seemed too late for him to retrieve his own position by such sleight of mind. But all was not yet lost. "The affair is under way again," Adler wrote to his father on September 23; Einstein had received a request to call on the Minister of Education in Vienna, and was leaving Zurich for the city that morning. "Perhaps," Adler added, "it would be useful for him to see you and discuss things while he is there. . . . In all practical things he is absolutely impractical."

This time there was no hitch. Imperial doubts were circumvented and Einstein's appointment to the chair was at last confirmed. Only, however, after he had reluctantly agreed to take Austro-Hungarian nationality, a necessity since the appointment would make him a civil servant. As a consolation he was allowed to remain a Swiss so that now, for the first but not the last time, he was able to claim the privileges of dual nationality.

According to Katya, Einstein wanted this Prague appointment "very much," and for several reasons. In Prague he would be a full rather than an associate professor; his salary, moreover, would be higher, and friends who later met him in Prague commented on his improved standard of living. In Berne the Einstein home had been lit by oil lamps. In Zurich there had been gas. In Prague it was electricity. This was more than an index of technological advance; in Prague, the Einsteins for the first time had a maid living in.

But the clue to the real attraction of this capital, where the swords of German-Czech animosity were already being sharpened, is to be found in the final words of a letter from Einstein to Lucien Chavan written a few months after his arrival. "I am having a good time here, even though life is not so pleasant as in Switzerland," he wrote.

> Apart from the fact that I am an alien, there is no water here that one can drink without its being boiled. The population for the most part speaks no German and is strongly anti-German. The students, too, are not so intelligent and industrious as in Switzerland, but I have a fine institute with a magnificent library.

In one way Einstein was like many another man—he kept an eye on the main chance. Only in his case the objective was not making a fortune but keeping close to the resources which would stimulate him most. He liked Zurich and the Swiss: but what was that against "a fine institute with a magnificent library?"

The move to Prague took place in March, 1911, and Einstein quickly settled down in his new post, considerably helped by Ludwig Hopf, his young assistant in Zurich who had moved east with him. He was to stay in the city less than eighteen months, yet the experience was to be important. Here he was forced to note, however much he tried to push out of his mind all except his work, the ambiguous position of the Jews in a community already divided against itself. He was forced to notice the emotions aroused in many Jewish friends by the very mention of the Zionist cause, as well as the pan-German feelings which were already moving the Central Powers towards the precipice of the First World War. In Prague he had as pupil Otto Stern, the Silesian physicist who was to follow him to Zurich in 1912, hold a succession of posts in Germany, cross the Atlantic in the great refugee wave of the 1930s, and dramatically reenter Einstein's life during the final months of the Second World War. And in Prague Einstein was introduced to the mathematical machinery which helped him solve the problems of general relativity.

This extension of his powers came through George Pick, once an assistant of Ernst Mach and twenty years older than Einstein. Pick and Einstein had a mutual interest in music. They struck up a strong friendship, and when Einstein spoke of the difficulties he was having, Pick proposed that he consider using the absolute differential calculus of Ricci and Levi-Civita. The two men remained in touch long after Einstein had left Prague, and in June, 1939, with the Germans already in occupation of the city, Pick, then aged eighty, sent a long letter to Einstein in Princeton reminiscently discussing the past. He died, a few years later, in Theresienstadt concentration camp.

Comparatively little is known of Einstein's life in the Bohemian capital, and the fullest account is given by Philipp Frank, the Austrian physicist with whom he had been in correspondence about causality in 1907. Frank had become a leading member of the Vienna Circle, a group including Carnap, Neurath, and Moritz Schlick, which formed the hard core of the logical positivists who stressed "Mach's requirement" that worthwhile statements had to be capable of test by physical experiment. Einstein's Machist beliefs were still strong. Frank was a young physicist of great promise. And when Einstein left Prague in the summer of 1912 Frank, only just twenty-eight, was appointed in his place.

One thing is quite clear both from Frank's account and from the stray reminiscences which Einstein himself passed on to his friends over the years. This is that he responded to "the political air in which the town was steeped" and to the situation in which the Jews of Prague found themselves. For here Czechs and Germans lived in their own closed worlds. The professors of the two universities rarely met and the Germans isolated themselves from the Czech majority within their own cultural ring of concerts and lectures and theaters. "Yet half the Germans were Jews, a fact which tended to drive them towards a mutually supporting alliance. "On the other hand," Frank points out,

> the relation of the Jews to the other Germans had already begun to assume a problematical character. Formerly the German minority in Prague had befriended the Jews as allies against the upward-striving Czechs, but these good relations were breaking down at the time when Einstein was in Prague. When the racial theories and tendencies that later came to be known there as Nazi creed were still almost unknown in Germany itself, they had already an important influence on the Sudeten Germans. Hence a somewhat paradoxical situation existed for the Germans in Prague. They tried to live on good terms with the Jews so as to have an ally against the Czechs. But they also wanted to be regarded as thoroughly German by the Sudeten Germans, and therefore manifested hostility against the Jews. This peculiar situation was characterized outwardly by the fact that the Jews and their worst enemies met in the same cafés and had a common social circle.

All this presented a particularly piquant state of affairs for Einstein—a reneged German, Swiss by choice, who by accepting a post at the German University had been forced to take Austro-Hungarian nationality against his own wishes. It was the first of many nonscientific problems that the pursuit of physics was to pose. He resolved it by openly becoming a member of the Jewish community although tending to ignore his German origin.

The Prague community included Franz Kafka, Hugo Bergmann, and the writer Max Brod. Much of its activity centered on the home of Bertha Fant, an ardent Zionist, and while its sphere of influence was intellectual and artistic rather than political, the ultimate triumph of Zionism was accepted almost as a fact of nature. Einstein could not be troubled with such an idea, and for him these

Jews formed "a small circle . . . of philosophical and Zionist enthusiasts which was loosely grouped round the university." It was one thing to be concerned with the affairs of fellow Jews in a foreign capital; it was quite another to consider Jewry and its problems on a world basis. For, in the words of Philipp Frank, "the problems of nationality and of the relations of the Jews with the rest of the world appeared to him only as a matter of petty significance."

His aloofness from what many fellow Jews regarded as the great cause no doubt affected the interpretation of Einstein which Brod introduced into his novel *The Redemption of Tycho Brahe*. Here the portrait of the young Kepler has many of the characteristics of Einstein. Frank claims that Walther Nernst, professor of physical chemistry in Berlin with whom Einstein was later to be closely associated, told Einstein on reading the book: "You are this man Kepler." This is significant as suggesting how not only Brod in Prague, but Nernst at a later period, considered the Einstein whom they saw at close quarters. For the figure of Kepler-Einstein is that of the scientist at the height of his intellectual powers; fully stretched—in this case on the generalization of relativity; not concerned with the rest of the human race; only distantly aware of the surrounding turmoil; and regarding the responsibility of science as a responsibility confined to the scientific arena.

Some phrases in Brod's book epitomize Albert Einstein at this central period of his life; others give a clue to his failure as from the 1920s onwards he became the supporter of every good cause that could gain his ear. Thus the young Kepler-Einstein begins to inspire the old Tycho Brahe with a feeling of awe.

> The tranquility with which he applied himself to his labors and entirely ignored the warblings of flatterers was to Tycho almost superhuman. There was something incomprehensible in its absence of emotion, like a breath from a distant region of ice. . . . He had no heart and therefore had nothing to fear from the world. He was not capable of emotion or love. And for that reason he was naturally also secure against the aberrations of feelings.

It would have been easy to consider such a man as an intriguer whose continuing success was due to cunning, but it was clear to Brahe "that Kepler was the very opposite of an intriguer; he never pursued a definite aim and in fact transacted all affairs lying outside the bounds of his science in a sort of dream." The picture of a Kepler working with the instinct of genius within his own scientific shell, but all at sea when he left it, is a not too inaccurate picture of Einstein in his later years, of the man with two Achilles heels: a too trusting belief in the goodness of people and a desperately held and innocent belief that the grand investigations of science not only should but could be insulated from the worlds of politics and power. Strangely, the belief survived even Fritz Haber and the First World War. It did not survive his desire to beat the Germans twenty-five years later.

But all this was to come. In Prague there was merely the faintest glimmer of awakening in his Jewish consciousness, an awareness which he himself did not recognize until he arrived in Berlin. This is clear not only from Frank but from the testimony of Dmitri Marianoff, one of Einstein's two stepsons-in-law. Einstein himself protested strongly against Marianoff's biography—as he was to protest against almost any public mention of his private life and tastes—but there is little reason to dispute the nonscientific details of the book, which have obviously come from Einstein in reminiscent family mood, barriers down.

Marianoff makes a point of the way in which Einstein was thrown up against his inner Jewishness by the daily circumstances of Prague life. "Once in his strolls through the city he stumbled on a short alley that led to an old high-walled Jewish cemetery, preserved there since the fifth century," he wrote.

> The story of his race for a thousand years was told before him on the tombstones. On them were inscriptions in Hebrew with symbolic records of a tribe or a name. A fish for Fisher, a stag for Hirsch, two hands for the tribe of Aaron. Here he found the battered, chipped, and crumbling slab of the tomb of Rabbi Loeue, the friend of Tycho Brahe, the sixteenth century astronomer whose statue with the globe and compass in his hands Einstein had just passed in front of the Svato-Tynsky-Chram.

What Einstein also tended to remember from Prague, according to Marianoff, was "the solemn sounds of the organ in Catholic cathedrals, the chorales in Protestant churches, the mournful Jewish melodies, the resonant Hussite hymns, folk music, and the works of Czech, Russian, and German composers." This was the world in which he sought relaxation, moving in "a sort of dream" while his mind concentrated on the work that mattered.

Most important within this work was the continuing riddle of gravity. Throughout the whole of his stay in Prague he worked steadily towards a solution of the problems it presented, returning to the principle of equivalence and the "thought-experiment" with light that he had devised to test its validity. The result was another paper for the *Annalen der Physik*.

"In a memoir published four years ago," it began,

> I tried to answer the question whether the propagation of light is influenced by gravitation. I return to this theme, because my previous presentation of the subject does not satisfy me, and for a stronger reason, because I now see that one of the most important consequences of my former treatment is capable of being tested experimentally. For it follows from the theory here to be brought forward, that rays of light, passing close to the sun, are deflected by its gravitational field, so that the angular distance between the sun and a fixed star appearing near to it is apparently increased by nearly a second of arc.

Here was the essential Einstein, dissatisfied with earlier work and worrying round it until he unearthed the chance of providing experimental evidence.

The "theory here to be brought forward" incorporated his idea of how gravity affected the matter of the physical world. Yet matter, as he had already shown, was really congealed energy, while light quanta, or photons, consisted of particles which had changed their mass in the process of reaching the speed of light. Viewed thus it seemed plausible, even without Einstein's logical structure of argument, that light should be affected by the tug of gravity as certainly as the cannonball. In fact Newton had asked in his *Opticks*: "Do not bodies act upon Light at a distance and by their action bend it's Rays; and is not this action (*cœteris paribus*) strongest at the least distance?" And the German astronomer Soldner had used Newton's corpuscular theory of light for predicting a similar deviation although his figure was only half that demanded by Einstein's theory.

But there was another consequence which Einstein now brought forward for the first time. If light is produced in a star or in the sun, an area of strong gravity, and then streams down on the earth, an area of weak gravity, its energy will not be dissipated by a reduction of speed, since this is impossible, light always having the same constant speed. What would happen, Einstein postulated, was something very different: the wavelength of the light would be changed. This "Einstein shift," the assumption that the spectral lines of sunlight, as compared with the corresponding spectral lines of terrestrial sources of light, must be somewhat displaced toward the red," was spelled out in some detail. However, he was careful to add the qualification that "as other influences (pressure, temperature) affect the position of the centers of the spectral lines, it is difficult to discover whether the inferred influence of the gravitational potential really exists." In fact the Doppler shift, produced by the motion of the stars relative to the solar system, was to provide an additional and even more important complication.

What Einstein concentrated on instead was the deflection of light by the sun, and his paper ended with a prophetic paragraph:

> A ray of light going past the sun would accordingly undergo deflection to the amount of $4.10^{-6}=.83$ seconds of arc. The angular distance of the star from the center of the sun appears to be increased by this amount. As the fixed stars in the parts of the sky near the sun are visible during total eclipses of the sun, this consequence of the theory may be compared with experience. With the planet Jupiter the displacement to be expected reaches to about 1/100 of the amount given. It would be a most desirable thing if astronomers would take up the question here raised. For apart from any theory there is the question whether it is possible with the equipment at present available to detect an influence of gravitational fields on the propagation of light.

The paper of 1911 had one major limitation. For what it considered was one, and only one, special case of the effects of gravity: that in which gravity had the same force and direction throughout the entire space that was being considered. This was a simplification that helped Einstein to move the theory forward, but it worried him, partly because of its artificiality and partly because he realized that its removal—and the consequent creation of a theory more in accord with reality—would demand a mathematical expertise that was still beyond him.

Despite this limitation, which was eventually to lead him deeper into the mathematicians' world, and which was in some ways to blunt the intuitive feel for physics which was his real genius, the paper of 1911 was important for one special reason. In it, Einstein threw down the gauntlet to the experimentalists. Was light bent by gravity as it passed near the sun? Surely this was a question to which it should be possible to provide a clear-cut yes-or-no answer? It was not to be quite as simple as that; but from 1911 onwards he pointed out with increasing persistence that here was one way of proving or disproving experimentally a theory which had been built up logically but which had as its foundation little more than an intuitive hunch.

Meanwhile he worked on in Prague. And meanwhile the new status he was acquiring began to bring lecture invitations in increasing numbers. In January, 1911, he was invited to Leiden by Lorentz, and he and Mileva stayed with the Lorentz family the following month. Shortly afterwards he was formally invited to a major scientific conference, the First Solvay Congress,* held in Brussels between October 30 and November 3, 1911. Einstein, the ex-German Swiss, attended it as an Austro-Hungarian.

The Solvay Congress, the first of many, was organized by the Belgian chemist and industrialist, Ernest Solvay, at the instigation of Walther Nernst, a leading figure in the German scientific hierarchy. Solvay was an able man,

*The Conseil de Physique Solvay is usually translated into English as the Solvay Congress. However, Jean Pelseneer, Professeur Extraordinaire, Université Libre, Brussels, and the author of an unpublished "Historique des Instituts Internationaux de Physique et de Chimie Solvay depuis leur fondation," points out that while a "Congress" involves a large number of scientists or others, Solvay's scheme was almost the reverse—the invitation of a small number of men representing the cream of European physicists. "Council" or "Conference" is suggested—but "Congress" is by this time probably too well used to be changed.

already in his seventies, who had patented his own soda process and whose companies were reported to be making nine-tenths of the world's supply. He had for long been in close contact with Nernst, to whom he proposed the idea of using part of his great wealth for the good of science. Solvay's own hobby was the development of a new physical theory and Nernst pointed out that if he called a conference of Europe's leading physicists he would then be able to outline the theory to them. Subsequently they could discuss among themselves, in a series of invited papers, the crisis in physics which had been introduced during the past decade by the quantum theory, the discovery of radioactivity, and the investigation of the atom. Solvay responded, and in the autumn of 1911 a score of Europe's leading physicists arrived in Brussels. Their fares had been paid, accommodation was provided in the Hotel Metropole, where two rooms had been set aside for the congress, and each was given an honorarium of 1,000 francs for attendance. "The whole undertaking pleases me very much and I scarcely doubt that you are its instigator," said Einstein in accepting Nernst's invitation and agreeing to read a paper.

It was not these lavish trappings but the standing of those who came to Brussels which made the congress more important for Einstein than any other he had attended. Planck, Nernst, and Rubens were among those from Germany; Poincaré, Madame Curie, and Langevin among those from France. James Jeans and Rutherford came from England, while from Austria-Hungary came Einstein and Franz Hasenöhrl, later to be spuriously credited with Einstein's mass-energy equation. Lorentz himself presided over the congress, which was also attended by Kamerlingh Onnes from Leiden. Maurice de Broglie from Paris, Goldschmidt from Brussels, and Frederick Lindemann, then studying under Nernst in Berlin, acted as secretaries. It was very different from the Salzburg meeting. Here Einstein was brought in to an "experts only" conference whose quality can be gauged from the studied photograph which survived in the Metropole through two German occupations. It shows a striking group of men—and one woman—the real revolutionaries of the twentieth century.

In Brussels Einstein met Planck, Nernst, and Lorentz on equal terms for the first time. Here also he met Madame

Curie, then at the height of her fame, and Ernest Rutherford, the epitome of the huge New Zealand farmer looking round for new land to bring into cultivation—but this time the unexplored territory of physics. "Einstein all calculation, Rutherford all experiment," was the verdict of Chaim Weizmann,* the man as close to Rutherford scientifically in the coming war as he was close to Einstein in the postwar Zionist movement. There were other contrasts between the two men, highlighted by the fact that Rutherford never entirely lost a trace of scepticism when dealing with foreigners. Thus when Wien claimed that no Anglo-Saxon could understand relativity, Rutherford had a ready answer: "No. They have too much sense."

In Brussels there also met for the first time the two men who occupied such ironically contrasted positions during the Second World War: Einstein, popularly credited with the most important influence on the creation of nuclear weapons, and Lindemann (later Lord Cherwell), more correctly credited, as Churchill's *eminence grise*, with a comparable influence on Britain's wartime science. Lindemann, only twenty-five at the time of the Solvay Congress, facing a distinguished and disgruntled future, as different from Einstein as man of the world from provincial recluse, was to become firm friend and devoted admirer. "I well remember my co-secretary, M. de Broglie, saying that of all those present Einstein and Poincaré moved in a class by themselves," he wrote almost half a century later. His first reaction was given in a letter to his father.

> I got on very well with Einstein, who made the most impression on me except perhaps Lorentz. He looks rather like Fritz Fleischer "en mal," but has not got a Jewish nose. He asked me to come and stay with him if I came to Prague and I nearly asked him to come and see us at Sidholme.† . . . He says he knows very little mathematics, but he seems to have had a great success with them. . . .

*Einstein, writing some forty years later to Carl Seelig, commented: "I concentrated on speculative theories, whereas Rutherford managed to reach profound conclusions on the basis of almost primitive reflection combined with relatively simple experimental methods."

†The Lindemann home in south Devon.

Lindemann's biographer notes that

> observing this shy genius at close quarters, [he] formed an opinion of Einstein's character which he never revised. He saw there the towering intellect which made him for Lindemann the greatest genius of the century, but he saw also a pathetic naïveté in the ordinary affairs of life. Einstein appeared to him to be living in a universe of his own creation, and almost to need protection when he touched the mundane sphere. In all matters of politics he was a guileless child, and would lend his great name to worthless causes which he did not understand, signing many ridiculous political or other manifestos put before him by designing people.

Yet the two men were united by one thing: the view that human beings counted for little when weighed against the splendid problems of physics. Lindemann, according to one colleague, "had time for a few dukes and a few physicists, but regarded most of the rest of mankind as furry little animals." Substituting "pacifists" for "dukes," much the same was true of Einstein.

The theme of the congress was radiation and quanta, and Einstein contributed a paper, "The Actual State of the Problems of Specific Heats," which dealt with the fundamental arguments he had used to explain the anomalies of specific heat at low temperatures. Madame Curie's reaction was typical. She "appreciated the clearness of his mind, the shrewdness with which he marshaled his facts, and the depth of his knowledge." Most of those attending felt much the same.

While the congress was in progress, Einstein was involved in a typically Einsteinian imbroglio. It arose from his readiness to leave the chair in Prague to which he had been appointed only some eight months previously. Mileva's attitude played a part. Although she had enjoyed life in Switzerland, it is clear from her letters to the Adlers that she approved the move to Prague; thus the readiness to uproot herself again, and so quickly, at first seems surprising. Frank, who was to succeed Einstein in the German University, has given one explanation. To some degree, he has said, it was certainly the wish of his first wife who was accustomed to Zurich. She had found it difficult to adapt herself to the life in Prague. This was strange since she was by birth a Yugoslav woman. But she had come to Switzerland as a student and was not able to perform a second assimilation. Mileva herself, writing from Prague—apparently to Michelangelo Besso's wife—when she knew that she would be leaving, said that she thought she would hardly be homesick for Prague. But, she went on, some nice things had happened. However, Einstein was not a man to be unduly swayed by his wife's feelings; whatever Mileva may have thought about Switzerland, it was to yet another country that his eyes now turned. The reason, as so often with Einstein, can be found in the answer to one question: What would be the effect of the move on his scientific work?

In Prague there was the "fine library"; there was contact with such minds as George Pick. But the enthusiasm of the first few weeks soon evaporated. One reason is supplied by his eldest son, only six at the time but vividly remembering how his father later explained the situation. "He had," he says, "to lecture on experimental physics. And he was always happy when something went right." This was not at all what Einstein had bargained for. He liked contact with young students. He was always happy explaining the excitements of physics. But he liked to do this when he wished, not when he had to, and he liked to keep clear of routine experimental work. In fact he was not really cut out for a normal university chair, and if he had to occupy one he wanted the terms to be more flexible than they were at Prague. "I want my peace," he was to explain a decade later. He wanted it even in 1911; peace in which to think and reach out to touch the stars. At Prague it was difficult to get. Within a few months of arrival, he was preparing to move.

The circumstances are described in a long series of letters between Einstein, Lorentz, and Professor Julius of Utrecht University, the solar physicist who Einstein respected as a "clear-sighted, artistically fine-spirited man." It is not easy to acquit Einstein of some deviousness in the situation which they reveal. However, the evidence is circumstantial and much can be explained by the muddled simplicity with which he handled most affairs outside physics; in this case it was, for him, a singularly fortunate muddle.

On August 20, 1911, some two months before the First

Solvay Congress, Professor Julius informed Einstein that Professor Windt, the university's professor of physics, had died earlier in the month. "Our university and the interests of physics would best be served if it were possible for you to take over the professorship," he wrote. But several members of the faculty would be against the appointment of a foreigner, and his letter should therefore be regarded only as an unofficial feeler. Einstein replied by return, pointing out that he had been in Prague for only four months, had acclimatized himself there, and must ask Julius "to consider another colleague for the vacancy."

However, he was by this time an important enough scientific fish to be worth angling for carefully. The following month Julius tried again after the members of the faculty had met. "It was simply unthinkable at our meeting not to mention your name," he wrote. "Everyone was in full agreement that your reasons for refusing were not decisive and that I should make a further attempt at convincing you." Einstein's reply suggested that perhaps the attractions of Prague were not really so great after all. He recalled his lectures at Leiden the previous spring and noted how everyone there had charmed him, quite apart from the incomparable Lorentz. And he was, he added, "seriously thinking" of accepting the Utrecht offer. But there was one point that Julius might well have taken as a warning. "I must tell you one more thing," Einstein went on. "Before I left my home in Zurich to go to Prague, I promised privately to let the Polytechnic know of any other post that I might take up so that they in turn could tell me if they had knowledge of any vacancy." The implications of this might have been clear to Julius, who had just received a letter from Lorentz saying: "Einstein only prefers Prague because there is little hope of going to the Polytechnic." But he still pressed on, writing on September 27 that he hoped Einstein would be "more impressed with the prospects at Utrecht than at Zurich," and following it up with a further letter on October 11, saying that he was still waiting for Einstein's answer.

Einstein finally replied on October 18. He apologized for the long delay and explained that he had been away for three weeks, first to the Naturforscherversammlung in Karlsruhe. Then he had gone to Zurich "to take part in a vacation course." And at Zurich he had learned that the

Polytechnic might wish to offer him a post, although he added that they were, in fact, "not likely" to press on with the offer. But he asked "for the sake of my fellow citizens" —he was, after all, a burgher of Zurich—for a little more time to make up his mind about Utrecht.

This was the position when he went to Brussels at the end of October for the Solvay Congress. Just what was said there about the Utrecht appointment is not certain. But it is clear that Lorentz, having been asked by his Dutch colleagues to use his influence with Einstein, bungled the mission; also that Einstein backed the choice of Peter Debye, the Dutch physicist who had taken his chair at the University of Zurich the previous year. He also pushed Debye's claims when he went on from Brussels to meet Julius in Utrecht before returning to Prague; and from Prague, on November 15, he wrote to Julius finally turning down the Utrecht post.

In this reply Einstein thanked Julius for his friendly welcome in Utrecht. "These pleasant personal experiences," he went on,

> have made my final decision to stay here more difficult, but I am now finally decided. Look at the situation from my position. Here I have a roomy institute, a beautiful library, and no difficulty with the language which, with my difficulty at learning them, has weighed heavily in the scales. Consider also the personal scruples which we talked about and which I cannot forget. Then you will understand my decision and not hold it against me. However, rest assured that it was extremely difficult to turn down the chance of entering your circle, so pleasant both culturally and physically. The moment I returned I wrote to Debye and have received his reply saying that the opportunity of returning to his fatherland under such pleasant conditions gives him great pleasure. My high opinion of him you already know, so it is unnecessary to repeat it and I need only say that I am very pleased about his acceptance by the university.

Indeed there is no doubt that he was very pleased. For the offer from Zurich, which he had casually mentioned to Julius some weeks earlier, had been hardening. The authorities had already written to Madame Curie and Henri Poincaré about Einstein's suitability for the post, and a letter now arrived in Prague from Marcel Grossmann telling him what was going on. "Naturally, by and large, I am in favor of accepting a chair of theoretical physics in your Polytechnic," he replied. "The prospect of returning to Zurich affords me great delight. This prospect has in the last few days caused me to refuse an offer from Utrecht University." This was not quite the story which he had given to Julius.

Einstein's correspondence with Lorentz hints at a twinge of misgiving. "You have gathered by now, despite my long silence to your last letter, that not the slightest shadow is cast on our relationship through the Utrecht affair," Lorentz wrote to him on December 6.

> I would like to stress once more that there is no question of your having hurt my feelings, and am convinced that you have taken the course that you think right. This does not deny that I am very depressed about the result of your discussion with the Utrecht faculty, but that is not your fault; only that of fate which did not wish to treat us favorably this time. If only I had written to you at the start. But it was not possible as one is very reserved in Utrecht, and rightly so. In the meantime I guessed, but did not know, that you had been contacted. Because I suspected as much, I mentioned to Julius the day before I left for Brussels that you and I would meet (I saw him at the Academy Conference). I had hoped in this way to be able to speak to you about the offer from Utrecht, and immediately received permission to do so, as well as being asked to try to persuade you to accept. If only I had succeeded in expressing myself better or, before it was too late, known about your scruples; I could perhaps have removed any obstacles. But I will not continue with this "if only . . ."; it does not help us. I will console myself with the fact that after all you will be achieving great things in Zurich too.

Lorentz concluded with the best of wishes, hoped that they would meet again soon, noted that if Einstein was able "to open up fresh vistas in physics, that will be one of my greatest joys," and ended with a postscript: "I have caught you out in a mathematical error: Namely, 25 francs = 12 Fl. Dutch, and you sent me Fl. 15.09. I therefore return Fl. 3."

The convoluted negotiations for the Utrecht chair, reminiscent of C. P. Snow at his best, were now followed by a further misunderstanding equally surprising to find among grown men. For two days later Lorentz wrote again, asking whether Einstein's decision to go to Zurich was final. Einstein, not knowing that Lorentz had decided to retire from his chair at Leiden, thought that he still had the Utrecht chair in mind. His ignorance saved him from making an awkward choice. He would have found it difficult to refuse Lorentz, yet he preferred Zurich to Leiden—and was by this time justifiably confident that it would formally be offered to him. He had accepted before Lorentz brought the real situation to his notice.

Einstein had been given outstanding references for what it had now been decided should be a new chair of mathematical physics at the ETH. One was from Madame Curie. "I much admire the work which M. Einstein has published on matters concerning modern theoretical physics," she wrote from Paris on November 17.

> I think, moreover, that mathematical physicists are at one in considering his work as being in the first rank. At Brussels, where I took part in a scientific conference attended by M. Einstein, I was able to appreciate the clearness of his mind, the shrewdness with which he marshaled his facts, and the depth of his knowledge. If one takes into consideration the fact that M. Einstein is still very young, one is justified in basing great hopes on him and in seeing in him one of the leading theoreticians of the future. I think that a scientific institution which gave M. Einstein the means of work which he wants, by appointing him to a chair in the conditions he merits, could only be greatly honored by such a decision and would certainly render a great service to science.

Henri Poincaré wrote in similar vein, stressing Einstein's youth and the vistas which his ideas had opened out. "The role of mathematical physics," he concluded, "is to ask questions; it is only experience that can answer them. The future will show, more and more, the worth of Einstein, and the university which is able to capture this young master is certain of gaining much honor from the operation."

Some news of the situation seems to have seeped through from Zurich to Prague, probably via Marcel Grossmann, and by the end of 1911 Einstein knew that his star was rising rapidly. In addition to the aborted offer from Lorentz, there had come others from Vienna and from the Reichsanstalt in Berlin. Both had been turned down and he now looked hopefully forward to a return to Zurich. By now, moreover, his fame had spread to the United States, and during the first days of 1912 he received an invitation from New York's Columbia University. Would he consider coming for four to six weeks as a special lecturer in physics during the autumn or the spring of 1913? "While I am not authorized to make you any definite proposition, I wish if possible to open the way for one," wrote Geroge Pegram.

> We have in times past been honored by the presence here of such men as Professors Larmor, Planck, Lorentz, and others on the basis of such a lectureship. . . . I can assure you that your coming would be welcomed, not only by the men at Columbia, but by many from neighboring institutions who have been interested in watching, even if not contributing to, the development of the relativity theory. . . .
>
> Personally I have been very much interested in the relativity theory since my attention was first directed to it by Professor Lorentz, and I should be glad to see greater appreciation of it in America, where I confess our physicists have been rather slow to take it up.

Einstein replied on January 29. "Unfortunately," he said, "I am so loaded with different kinds of work that I cannot even think about a trip like that." And with his typical modesty he concluded: "I am convinced that it will be easy for you to find a man who will be more experienced for a task of this nature than I."

His spare time was now filled with thoughts of a return to Zurich, and in February he was able to write happily to Otto Stern: "Two days ago (Halleluja!) I was called to the Zurich Polytechnic and have already handed in my resignation here. Great joy felt by the old people and the two little bears." His feelings were further shown a few weeks later when he ended a letter to Professor Kleiner of the University of Zurich, whom he had been advising on the choice of staff: "With the friendliest of greetings, I remain, Yours A. Einstein, who is tremendously happy that he will soon be setting up his tent once again in Zurich."

Before he left Prague, he had one visitor whose impact was to be considerable. This was Paul Ehrenfest, a man ill-starred for a tragic life whose work in physics was perpetually to hover round the borders of genius. Ehrenfest had been born in Vienna and had studied and graduated there before obtaining a special professorship at the St. Petersburg Polytechnic. But his position as an Austrian barred the way ahead; so did the fact that he was a Jew, even though he declared himself as without religion. In addition, Ehrenfest's gay unconventionality, which so mirrored Einstein's, hardly helped him in the clamber up the academic ladder. He was, it has been written, bored by lectures at which the audience was not expected to interrupt, and especially so if he was the lecturer.

> In contrast to the usual education principles, he infected his students with his own enthusiasm and rushed with them to the outposts of the empire of physics, where the fighting against the great unknowns—relativity and quantum theory—was going on. But at the same time, he did not forget to take them to an occasional tower from which he could show and explain to them in his masterly way the domains already conquered.

In the autumn of 1912 Ehrenfest decided to tour German-speaking Europe in search of a better post, and almost automatically found his way to Einstein in Prague. The two men had been in professional touch a few years earlier, and by 1912 each admired the other's work. "Whatever I can do for you I will certainly do," Einstein wrote in reply to news of Ehrenfest's impending visit: ". . . stay at my house so that we can make good use of the time."

Ehrenfest arrived on February 23 and stayed for a week. The two men talked only a little about the search for a new appointment. As Einstein wrote later, "It was the state of science at the time that took up almost all of our interest. . . . Within a few hours we were true friends, as though our dreams and aspirations were meant for each other."

Martin Klein, whose first volume of Ehrenfest's biography, *The Making of a Theoretical Physicist*, gives such a splendid portrait of the man, has described that first week's encounter in some detail. Its flavor is given by one paragraph:

> Two days of continual scientific dispute (by no means onesided, as Ehrenfest found an error in Einstein's reasoning and supplied a simple intuitive way of seeing the correct result) must have broken down any barriers there might have been between them. By Sunday they were playing Brahms violin and piano sonatas together. "Yes, we will be friends," Ehrenfest wrote in his diary. "Was awfully happy."

He stuck to his nonreligious guns and was not offered the Prague chair. But before the end of the year he had been appointed to Leiden as successor to Lorentz. Soon afterwards Einstein made the first of many journeys to stay with the Ehrenfests, as happy with their children as when he accompanied their parents in playing Bach. "Nature created us for each other," he wrote in 1922. "I find it difficult to find a human contact beneficial to me. I need your friendship perhaps more urgently than you need mine." What he had found was another man to whom physics was the whole of life and who put everything else firmly in its place.

Einstein and his family left Prague for Switzerland in August, 1912. His appointment at the ETH was for ten years, and as he moved into his fifth home in Zurich he may well have looked forward to settling down at last.

In the autumn of 1912 he began holding weekly afternoon colloquia at which new work was discussed. By now his reception was very different from what it had been in the university only three years earlier, and it was not only members of the ETH who attended. Students at the university, and their professors, found ways and means of joining in, and the meetings were usually crowded, Einstein affably discussing the latest developments with anyone who could contrive to be present. He remained unchanged. The meetings over, he would do as he had done years previously, carrying on the discussion outside the building with those who accompanied him to his favorite café. He found it difficult to relinquish his grasp on the problem in hand. Years afterwards his students recalled him standing in a snowstorm under a lamp at the foot of the Zurichberg, handing his umbrella to a companion and jotting down formulas for ten minutes as the snowflakes fell on his notebook.

Von Laue—"the most important of the younger German theorists. His book on the theory of relativity is a little masterpiece," Einstein wrote to Kleiner—now crossed his path again, coming to speak on interference of X rays, an occasion which was followed by Einstein opening the discussion and extemporizing "on the most intricate problems of physics with as much ease as if he were talking about the weather." Many scientists came to Zurich specifically to see him and von Laue recalls one particular visit when he saw Einstein and Ehrenfest striding along in front of a great swarm of physicists as they climbed the Zurichberg, and Ehrenfest bursting out in a jubilant cry: "I have understood it." Von Laue's words echo the same air of nuclear innocence that then permeated the Cavendish Laboratory where Andrade could offer a toast to "the useless electron, and long may it remain so."

Another visitor was Madame Curie, with whom Einstein and his wife stayed in Paris late in March, 1913, when he addressed the Société Française de Physique. It is clear from Madame Curie's correspondence, and from Einstein and Mileva's "thank you" letters, that she had shepherded an unsophisticated pair through the rigors of a hurried and demanding visit. In return, Einstein hoped that she would allow him to worry her "about the small journey into the mountains when term comes to an end." Typically, he ended the invitation with a brief postscript which began "And now a note about physics!"

The Curies—mother and two daughters—arrived in Zurich in July for a fortnight in the Bregaglia Alps and the Engadine with Einstein, his wife, and his eldest son. The holiday was a great success. Years later Hans Einstein remembered how they had crossed the Maloja Pass on foot; how his father and Madame Curie had inspected the glacier mills, Einstein cogitating on the forces which had carved these deep vertical wells; and how Madame Curie, recalling the fact that Einstein was technically a Swiss, demanded that he name every peak on the horizon.

There was ample reason for her to seek out Einstein and to mull over with him, during the informal talks of a walking holiday, the implications of the new ferment in physics in her own specialized field of radioactivity. Fresh radioactive substances were being discovered, and the key to their characteristics and behavior obviously had to be sought within Rutherford's new concept of the atom, now known to consist of a positively charged central nucleus surrounded, at a comparatively great distance, by one, by a few, or by a cloud of orbiting electrons. Einstein, with his instinctive feel for the nature of things, would obviously have worthwhile views—while it was already clear that subnuclear particles moved at speeds fast enough to make relativistic effects important.

However, so far it was only physicists who were brought into intimate day-to-day contact with the implications of relativity. Many other technical men found it difficult to see that "the new physics" formed part of their world, as was evident when Einstein spoke on the subject during a visit to Göttingen.

"I remember watching the engineering professors who were present and who were, of course, horrified by his approach, because to them reality was the wheels in machinery—really solid entities," says Professor Hyman Levy, then a research student at the university.

> And here was this man talking in abstract terms about space-time and the geometry of space-time, not the geometry of a surface which you can think of as a physical surface, but the geometry of space-time, and the curvature of space-time; and showing how you could explain gravitation by the way in which a body moves in space-time along a geodesic—namely the shortest curve in space-time. This was all so abstract that it became unreal to them. I remember seeing one of the professors getting up and walking out in a rage, and as he went out I heard him say, "Das ist absolut Blödsinn" ("That is absolute nonsense").

Whatever arguments there might be among engineers, physicists realized that a new star had risen in the scientific firmament and was still rising fast. Einstein was now among the "European professors distinguished in philosophy and science," and as such he supported in the summer of 1912 the foundation of a scientific association "quite indifferent to metaphysical speculation and so-called critical, transcendental doctrines" and "opposed to all metaphysical undertakings." The idea started in Berlin and foundered with the outbreak of war two years later. But its manifesto was the first such collective statement to be signed by Einstein; and it underlines his frequent statements that Special Relativity was the outcome not of metaphysical speculation but of considering scientifically the results of experimental evidence.

"There has long been felt the need of a philosophy which should grow in a natural manner out of the facts and problems of natural science," begins the manifesto, which was signed by some three dozen professors, including Mach, Einstein, Sigmund Freud, and—perhaps significantly—Föppl. After agreeing that there had evolved "a strictly empirical and positivistic point of view quite indifferent to metaphysical speculation and to so-called critical, transcendental doctrines and systematic relations throughout considerable scientific circles," the manifesto continued:

> On the other hand the particular sciences find themselves forced to consider problems of even greater generality so that they take on of themselves a philosophical character. ... In the theory of relativity [physics] touches the most searching question thus far of epistemology: Is absolute or is only relative knowledge attainable? Indeed: Is absolute knowledge conceivable? It comes here directly upon the question of man's place in the world, the question of the connection of thought with the brain. What is thought? What are concepts? What are laws? In psychological problems, physics and biology come together. And finally, the anthropological sciences, especially history and sociology, find themselves brought into closer and closer connection with biological concepts.
>
> Those who take an interest in these progressive inquiries will find it to their advantage to have a scientific association which shall declare itself opposed to all metaphysical undertakings, and have for its first principle the strictest and most comprehensive ascertainment of facts in all fields of research and in the development or organization and technique. All theories and requirements are to rest exclusively on this ground of facts and find here their ultimate criterion. ...

Einstein signed this document while still trying to generalize his theory of relativity so that it would apply not only to the special case where gravity operated as a force of constant intensity and direction but also in all the multiplicity of special cases which existed throughout the universe. In this he was aided by his old friend Marcel Grossmann, the former colleague of a dozen years before, whose notes during student days had enabled him to skip mathematics and concentrate on physics. This particular chicken was coming home to roost and it was on Grossmann that Einstein now leaned heavily for the mathematical support which he needed. Even so, it was hard going and Einstein, apologizing to Ehrenfest for the delay in writing to him, explained in May, 1913: "My excuse is the actually superhuman exertions with which I have devoted myself to the problem of gravitation. I am now inwardly convinced that I have found the right way, but at the same time I am also sure that a murmur of indignation will travel down the rows of our colleagues when the work appears, which will happen in a few weeks."

There was an ironic outcome of the work. In 1913 Einstein and Grossmann published jointly a paper which came much nearer to the theory of gravity for which Einstein was still groping. This was "Entwurf einer Verallgemeinerten Relativitatstheorie und eine Theorie der Gravitation" ("Outline of a General Theory of Relativity and a Theory of Gravitation"), to which Einstein contributed the physical sections and Grossmann the mathematical. Einstein was dissatisfied with the paper, for its equations appeared to show that instead of a single solution to any particular set of gravitational circumstances there was an infinitude of solutions. He believed "that they were not compatible with experience." This, together with the conclusion that the results would not agree with the principle of causality, led him to believe that the theory was untenable. "These were errors in thinking which caused me two years of hard work before at last, in 1915, I recognized them as such and returned penitently to Riemann curvature, which enabled me to find the relation to the empirical facts of astronomy," he said. Yet the 1913 paper contained the clue to its own apparent discrepancy: what appeared to be an infinitely large number of solutions to one problem was really a single solution applicable to each of an infinitely large number of different frames of reference. Thus the cards of the General Theory of Relativity had been laid face upwards on the table in 1913. They were picked up again by Einstein himself in 1915. But they had lain there unnoticed for two years.

By 1913 Einstein had thus reached a temporary impasse. But his views on the need for generalizing the Special Theory aroused great interest, and in September he put them before the eighty-fifth Deutscher Naturforscherversammlung, held in Vienna. The auditorium was packed with scientists anxious to hear about a theory even more outlandish than Special Relativity. In some ways they were disappointed. Instead of the esoteric explanations they had expected, there came one of Einstein's minor masterpieces of simple statement, an account in which he compared the development of the various theories of gravitation with the development of successive concepts of electricity. As one of his Zionist friends was later to comment, when Einstein wished, he could "speak of basic metaphysical concepts such as time or space as matter-of-factly as others speak of sandwiches or potatoes."

The lecture was remarkable, however, not only for the clear exposition which foreshadowed some of Einstein's later scientific writings, so much more understandable than many of his interpreters, but for an incident which well illustrates his character. In his recent work he had used a generally covariant form of the electromagnetic equation first given the previous year by a young Viennese physicist, Friedrich Kottler. In their paper Einstein and Grossmann had acknowledged their indebtedness, but Einstein had never met Kottler personally. On the spur of the moment he asked whether Kottler was in the audience. A young man rose. Einstein asked him to remain standing—so that all could see the man whose help had been so useful.

Although Special Relativity had by this time become incorporated into the new framework of physics with little more than a disapproving grunt from its more conservative critics, the situation was very different with Einstein's still tentative generalized theory. "It was clear in the discussion that followed that many German-speaking men of science were not yet converted to his ideas," says Robert Lawson, a young English physicist then working in the city's Radium Institute, and the man who later translated into English Einstein's first book on relativity.

"Doubts were expressed on the validity of his views on the equality of inertial and gravitational mass, on the velocity of propagation of gravitational processes, on the possibility of ever being able to detect the deflection of light rays in a gravitational field or the predicted red shift of spectral lines in such a field." At one point the debate grew quite heated, with Felix Ehrenhaft, for long a colleague and later an opponent of Einstein, arguing at length with two of the critics. To relieve the tension, someone pressed the button that automatically shifted the blackboard from one part of the platform to another—calling out as he did so: "Look. The blackboard moves against the lecture hall and not the lecture hall against the blackboard." Einstein remained unperturbed, smiling, and noting only that he was prepared to stand or fall by experimental results.

This lecture propelled him into the news, when a Viennese daily paper produced the headline: "The Minute in Danger, A Sensation of Mathematical Science." Even by 1913, eight years after the publication of the first relativity paper in the *Annalen der Physik,* the subject was still sufficiently unknown to the general public to be presented as a "sensation"—a premonitory hint of what was to happen in 1920 when the implications of General Relativity burst upon an exhausted world.

During this visit to Vienna Einstein heard dramatic news of the theory put forward by the Danish physicist Niels Bohr, which united Rutherford's concept of the nuclear atom with the Planck-Einstein quantum theory. Bohr was still only twenty-eight, but already as deeply concerned as Einstein not only with the upheaval in physics through which they were living, but with its underlying philosophical implications. The two were to be friends for nearly forty years, but the matters on which they agreed were more than balanced by those in which each unsuccessfully struggled to convert the other. Both at first failed to appreciate the practical results which would flow from their work; both, when nuclear weapons arrived, appreciated more quickly than many of their fellow scientists the political and moral implications; both, in many ways epitomizing the stock character of absentminded scientists, were anxious to direct nations into decent ways. These motives united them as much as the argument for and against determinacy divided them, an argument which was to lead Einstein into scientific isolation for the later years of his life.

Bohr had been educated as a physicist in Copenhagen and had come under the special influence of Max Planck. But he had also studied and worked in England, first under J. J. Thomson at the Cavendish and then under Rutherford at Manchester. Long afterwards, reminiscing on his past, he reflected on his good luck that Denmark had been politically free until the German invasion of 1940, thus allowing him to maintain contacts with both German and British schools of thought. One result of these contrasted contacts was the theory, whose confirmation Einstein now heard in 1913, which successfully accounted for some puzzling features of Rutherford's nuclear atom by invoking the idea of Planck's quanta.

According to classical physics, the electrons orbiting the nucleus of Rutherford's atom would lose energy by radiation and inevitably spiral into the nucleus itself, giving out as they did so a continuous spectrum of radiation. But this did not happen; instead, free atoms radiated certain specific and discrete frequencies that were characteristic of the atom concerned. Bohr explained this behavior with two suppositions. The first was that atoms exist only at well-defined stationary states or levels, and that at each of these states the electrons circle the nucleus in specific "allowed" orbits. While this continues the atom emits no radiation. Bohr's second supposition was that when an electron jumped—for whatever reason—from one of its "allowed" orbits to another "allowed" orbit nearer the nucleus, then radiation was emitted; by contrast, when an atom absorbed radiation, one or more of its orbiting electrons jumped from its "allowed" orbit to another farther from the nucleus. Both emission of radiation and its absorption took place in discrete units—the light quanta of the Planck-Einstein quantum theory of 1905. Thus Bohr had vindicated by one stroke of supreme genius both Planck's conception of radiation by discontinuous surges of energy and Rutherford's picture of the atom as a miniature solar system with electrons orbiting a central nucleus.

He had, moreover, gone further than disembodied theory. He had applied this to the hydrogen atom and, "leaning directly on Einstein's treatment of the photoelectric effect," as he himself wrote, had proposed to Rutherford that the theory was now susceptible to spectroscopic proof. Such proof was provided in Cambridge in the autumn of 1913 by Rutherford's son-in-law, Ralph Fowler, then working in the Cavendish. Fowler passed the news to Rutherford and Rutherford passed it on to George de Hevesy, the Hungarian-Danish chemist from the Cavendish who was attending the conference in Vienna. Hevesy in turn told Einstein, and on October 14 wrote to Rutherford describing the occasion.

"Speaking with Einstein on different topics we came to speak on Bohr's theorie [sic]," he wrote from Budapest. "He told me that he had once similar ideas but he did not dare to publish them. 'Should Bohr's theories be right, so it is from [sic] the greatest importance.' When I told him about the Fowler Spectrum the big eyes of Einstein looked still bigger and he told: 'Then it is one of the greatest discoveries.' I felt very happy hearing Einstein saying so." Hevesy's statement that Einstein "had once similar ideas" about this crucial problem was supported years later by Bohr himself, speaking in Moscow at the Institute of Physical Problems. Einstein's reaction, as apparently explained to Bohr himself was: "I could probably have arrived at something like this myself but if all this is true then it means the end of physics."

Einstein recognized the greatness of Bohr's achievement however much he might fear for the future of physics, and in his autobiographical notes of 1949 emphasized how he felt at the time. The work of the previous decade, he said, had undermined the foundation of physics. "That this insecure and contradictory foundation was sufficient to enable a man of Bohr's unique instinct and tact to discover the major laws of the spectral lines and of the electron shells of the atoms together with their significance of chemistry, appeared to me like a miracle—and appears to me as a miracle even today. This is the highest form of musicality in the sphere of thought."

The result of Bohr's work was, as Planck put it in 1920 when he received the Nobel Prize, that "a stream of knowledge poured in a sudden flood, not only over this entire field but into the adjacent territories of physics and chemistry." But there was one other result which increasingly affected Einstein over the years. When the new picture of the atom was outlined—the Rutherford-Bohr model, as it was called—it was appreciated that the causes lying behind the movements of individual subnuclear particles were not known. But causes were nevertheless believed to exist. Only during the next few years did it become more and more apparent that this was not always so: that whatever happened at other levels, individual events at the level of the subatomic world were unpredictable and could only be described statistically. But Einstein would never agree.

This great schism which the apparent indeterminacy of the subnuclear world was to create still lay in the future as Einstein listened to Hevesy in Vienna and lectured to the slightly dubious audience on his latest theory of General Relativity. In the city, he had also met for the first time Ernst Mach, whose writings a decade and a half earlier had buttressed his doubts about Newton's absolute time and absolute space. The meeting took place in 1911, possibly while Einstein was traveling to or from the Solvay Congress, an encounter between the younger man on the crest of the wave and the elderly Mach, crippled in physical health and bypassed intellectually by the swift stream of science. Mach was now in his seventies. Half-paralyzed, he had retired from the University of Vienna a number of years previously and lived in semiseclusion in the suburbs of the city, half-forgotten and seeing few visitors. "On entering his room," says Frank, "one saw a man with a gray, unkempt beard and a half-good-natured, half-cunning expression on his face, who looked like a Slav peasant and said: 'Please speak loudly to me; in addition to my other unpleasant characteristics I am also almost stone-deaf.' "

Einstein had not yet noticeably fallen away from Mach's basic beliefs, even though it seems likely that his acceptance of them was weakening. Similarly Mach, while strongly opposed to what he considered merely the assumptions of relativity, had so far kept the fact to himself. Thus the two men were still openly united on many scientific matters. One of the comparatively few differences was their attitude to atomic theory, Einstein accepting it freely while Mach did so only grudgingly and with considerable philosophical reservation.

Few details of the encounter have survived but Bernard

Cohen, interviewing Einstein shortly before his death, says he recalled one thing:

> Einstein asked Mach what his position would be if it proved possible to predict a property of a gas by assuming the existence of atoms—some property that could not be predicted without the assumption of atoms and yet one that could be observed. Einstein said he had always believed that the invention of scientific concepts and the building of theories upon them was one of the great creative properties of the human mind. His own view was thus opposed to Mach's, because Mach assumed that the laws of science were only an economical way of describing a large collection of facts. Could Mach accept the hypothesis of atoms under the circumstances Einstein had stated, even if it meant very complicated computations? Einstein told me how delighted he was when Mach replied affirmatively. If an atomic hypothesis would make it possible to connect by logic some observable properties which would remain unconnected without this hypothesis, then, Mach said, he would have to accept it. Under these circumstances it would be "economical" to assume that atoms may exist because then one could derive relations between observations. Einstein had been satisfied: indeed more than a little pleased. With a serious expression on his face, he told me the story all over again to be sure that I understood it fully. Wholly apart from the philosophical victory over what Einstein had conceived Mach's philosophy to have been, he had been very gratified because he had admitted that there might, after all, be some use to the atomistic philosophy to which Einstein had been so strongly committed.

The two men parted on the best of terms and when Mach died in 1916 Einstein's tributes were eulogistic and unqualified. "Mach recognized clearly the weak aspects of classical physics," he wrote, "and to that extent was not far from postulating a theory of relativity, and this nearly half a century ago! It is not improbable that Mach would have come to the theory if when he was an alert young spirit the meaning of the constancy of the velocity of light had by that time been raised by the physicists."

Yet before his death Mach had reneged, although Einstein knew nothing of this when he wrote the laudatory obituary notice. In the summer of 1913 Mach signed the Preface to his *The Principles of Physical Optics,* which did not appear until 1921. In this—"what may be my last opportunity," as he put it—he reversed his views on relativity. "I gather from the publications which have reached me, and especially from my correspondence," he wrote,

> that I am gradually becoming regarded as the forerunner of relativity. I am able even now to picture approximately what new expositions and interpretations many of the ideas expressed in my book on mechanics will receive in the future from the point of view of relativity.
>
> It was to be expected that philosophers and physicists should carry on a crusade against me, for, as I have repeatedly observed, I was merely an unprejudiced rambler, endowed with original ideas, in varied fields of knowledge. I must, however, as assuredly disclaim to be a forerunner of the relativists as I withhold from the atomistic doctrine of the present day.
>
> The reason why, and the extent to which, I discredit the present-day relativity theory, which I find to be growing more and more dogmatical, together with the particular reasons which have led me to such a view—the considerations based on the physiology of the senses, the theoretical ideas, and above all the conceptions resulting from my experiments—must remain to be treated in the sequel.

There was no sequel. But the voice from the grave shocked Einstein and deepened the differences which were soon separating his epistemology from that of Mach. Speaking in Paris in 1922, he went on record as describing Mach in terms which would have sounded strange only a short while earlier—"un bon mécanicien" . . . but "deplorable philosophe." And his views on the recantation were specifically given in a letter to a friend who had sent him one of Mach's letters. "There can be no doubt," he said, "that this was a result of his advanced years, and thus a diminished capability for absorbing facts, since the theory's whole line of thought conforms to Mach's who is rightly regarded as the forerunner of the invention of the theory of relativity."

The date at which Mach changed his views is not known. But his Preface was dated, and therefore probably concluded, within a few weeks of his receiving a significant letter which Einstein wrote to him on June 25, 1913. "At the solar eclipse next year," he said, "it will be seen whether the light rays are bent by the sun; in other words whether the basic and fundamental assumption of the equivalence of the acceleration of the reference frame and of the gravitational field really stands up. If so, then your inspired investigations into the foundations of mechanics —despite Planck's unjust criticism—will receive a splendid confirmation."

It would be produced, Einstein hoped, by an expedition to observe the solar eclipse in southern Russia during the late summer of 1914, an expedition under the leadership of Erwin Finlay-Freundlich, an astronomer of mixed German and Scottish descent and then the youngest assistant at the Berlin University Observatory. Einstein's friendship with Freundlich had begun in the summer of 1911 when Professor L. W. Pollak, then a student at Prague University, had visited the Berlin Observatory. He recalled that Einstein had concluded his recent paper by suggesting that the new theory might be tested astronomically, and he mentioned Einstein's passing regret that no one seemed interested.

It is not clear whether Freundlich had actually read Einstein's latest paper. But something in its ideas as he heard them from Pollak sparked his imagination. From then onward he showed a constant, if sometimes critical, interest in the development of relativity, carrying out measurements for Einstein during the next few years, working with him during the war, producing the first book on what became the General Theory of Relativity, and acting as interpreter and shock absorber during Einstein's first visit to Britain in 1921.

Shortly after Pollak's visit, Freundlich wrote to Einstein in Prague, offering to search for any deflection of light near Jupiter, an ambitious idea that must have been doomed from the start. Einstein replied on September 1:

> It would give me great pleasure if you would consider these interesting questions. From past experience I fully realize that the answers will not be easy to obtain. But one thing can be said with certainty: if no such deflection exists, then the idea of the theory is not pertinent. One must remember, you see, that the ideas are very bold. If only we had an orderly planet larger than Jupiter! But mother nature did not see fit to provide us with one that would make things easier for us!

Nothing came of these first efforts, nor of Freundlich's later inspections of old photographic plates which he described in the *Astronomische Nachrichten.* When that failed, he went on to the study of double stars. Einstein still had doubts. "I am very curious about the results of your research. . . ," he wrote to Freundlich in 1913. "If the speed of light is in the least bit affected by the speed of the light source, then my whole theory of relativity and theory of gravity is false."

When the eclipse of 1914 offered a definite chance of providing experimental proof or disproof, the next step was obvious. The Berlin Observatory was unenthusiastic, but willing to let Freundlich visit the Crimea—at his own expense and on his own time. This was the situation in the summer of 1913. Freundlich, who had not yet met Einstein, was preparing to marry and to spend his honeymoon in the Alps and on August 26 he was delighted to receive a letter from Switzerland. "This morning," he wrote to his fiancée, "I had a nice letter from Einstein in Zurich in which he asked me to meet him in Switzerland between September 9 and 15. This is wonderful because it fits in with our plans."

A fortnight later, as the train pulled into Zurich, Freundlich and his bride saw waiting for them the short figure of Fritz Haber, director of the Kaiser Wilhelm Institute for Chemistry which had been opened in Berlin two years earlier. Beside him stood an untidy figure in almost sporting clothes, wearing what Frau Freundlich remembers after half a century as a very conspicuous straw hat: Einstein, the maker of new worlds.

Einstein was delighted to meet his friends, and insisted that they accompany him to Frauenfeld, a few miles from Zurich, where he was to speak to the Swiss Society of Natural Sciences. Then he invited them to lunch with himself and Otto Stern, now working in Zurich as his assistant. Only at the end of the meal did he discover that he had no money. The situation was saved by Stern, who passed him a 100-franc note under the table.

At Frauenfeld, where both he and Grossmann spoke on the new theory, Einstein announced, to the embarrassment of Freundlich, that the company had among them "the man who will be testing the theory next year." From Frauenfeld they all traveled for the Society's outing to

Ermatingen on the shores of Lake Constance, Einstein later insisting that he and the Freundlichs return alone to Zurich. Throughout the entire journey the two men discussed the problems of gravitation while the young bride studied the scenery of a Switzerland she had never before seen.

The Zurich meeting settled details of what Freundlich would do in the Crimea the following summer. Soon afterwards, Einstein invoked the aid of Professor George Ellery Hale of the Mount Wilson Observatory, Pasadena, California, a man whose similarity of outlook with Einstein's is shown by an early passage in his autobiography —"Naturally I do not share the common fallacy of an antagonism between science, literature, and art, which appeals to me in much the same way. Creative imagination is the vital factor in all of them, and I was fortunate to learn this at an early age." Hale passed on Einstein's letter to Professor Campbell of the Lick Observatory. "He writes to me," Hale replied to Einstein on November 8,

> that he has undertaken to secure eclipse photographs of stars near the sun for Dr. Freundlich of the Berlin Observatory, who will measure them in the hope of detecting differential deflections. Doubtless he will send you further particulars, as I requested him to communicate directly with you.
>
> I fear there is no possibility of detecting the effect in full sunlight. . . . The eclipse method, on the contrary, appears to be very promising, as it eliminates all . . . difficulties, and the use of photography would allow a large number of stars to be measured. I therefore strongly recommend that plan.

Einstein also recommended it. So did Freundlich. But the problem of money still remained, as Freundlich pointed out in December. "After receipt of your last letter," Einstein wrote to him on December 7, "I immediately wrote to Planck, who really applied himself seriously to the matter. . . . Should all efforts fail, I shall pay for the thing myself out of my hard-earned savings, at least the first 2,000 marks. So go ahead and, after due consideration, order the plates and don't waste any more time thinking about the money problem." However, Einstein was not to dig into his own pocket. During the first months of 1914 help came from unexpected sources. The money was provided by Krupp von Bohlen und Halbach and by the chemist Emil Fischer.

Thus Einstein, firmly settled in Zurich, would await the results of a German expedition which in the late summer of 1914 would provide proof or disproof of a theory on whose development he was still hard at work. He had at last achieved full professional status in the establishment which had grudgingly accepted him as a student of sixteen, in a country whose atmosphere and environment he enjoyed. His sister Maja had now settled in Lucerne with her husband, Paul Winteler. To the same city, only thirty miles away from Zurich across the intervening hills, there had also come his mother. For Mileva, Switzerland seemed the only country in which it was possible to live and thus family feelings appeared to chime in with professional success. It must have seemed that now, at last, he might finally settle down.

Yet Einstein was not the kind of man for whom family feelings weighed very heavily. And although he felt a compelling need for the intellectual climate of Europe, he did not quickly throw down deep roots. Links provided by sentiment or the emotions were gossamer thick. Thus it is less surprising than it seems that by the autumn of 1913 he was preparing to move to Berlin, capital of a German Empire whose policies he detested and whose inner spirit he deeply distrusted.

CHAPTER 7

A JEW IN BERLIN

Einstein's attendance at the Solvay Congress of 1911 had repercussions which decisively affected the rest of his life. For among those in Brussels most deeply impressed by his ability were Max Planck and Walther Nernst, twin pillars of the Prussian scientific establishment. Following their return to Berlin both men became engaged in a difficult and delicate task which exercised their scientific enthusiasm and their patriotic instincts.

The task was recruitment of staff for the new and ambitious series of research institutes which the Emperor had graciously allowed to be called the Kaiser Wilhelm Gesellschaft zur Förderung der Wissenschaften (the Kaiser Wilhelm Society for the Advancement of the Sciences). These institutes were not only to investigate pure science; they would also, it was intended, help increase Germany's lead in the application of scientific discoveries made during the previous half century. In this field the country was now technologically supreme in Europe, providing much of the continent with dyestuffs, with the tungsten needed for steelmaking, with magnetos for the engines which were revolutionizing land transport and were soon to bring a new dimension to warfare, and providing also the best scientific instruments. Significantly, when war broke out in 1914, the British found much of their artillery using gunsights made exclusively by Goerz of Berlin.

Yet the Germans recognized that applied technology demands a constant diet of pure research. They were aware that in the United States the General Electric Company had invited Charles Steinmetz, the electrophysicist, to head their laboratories and to do what work he pleased. They knew that in Britain Lord Haldane, secretary of state for war until 1912, had seen the country to be "at a profound disadvantage with the Germans, who were building up their Air Service on a foundation of science" and had, as a result, laid the foundations at Farnborough of what was to become the Royal Aircraft Establishment. All this constituted a warning that was heeded by Friedrich Althoff, the permanent secretary in the Prussian Ministry of Education. Althoff "knew the weakness of human beings for decorations and titles, and he exploited it as another man would exploit a gold mine. The 'voluntary subscriptions' he obtained in this way went to further his great plans. Among other things he reorganized the whole system of higher education and brought the main body of scientific research into special research institutes." Then came his crowning achievement, the Kaiser Wilhelm Gesellschaft, the ambitious plans for which were approved by the Emperor himself. They were in the true Althoff tradition. The institutes were to be financed by bankers and industrialists who were to be rewarded not merely by a flush of patriotism but by the title of "Senator," the right to wear handsome gowns, and the honor of an occasional breakfast with the Emperor.

The scheme was announced in the autumn of 1911 and during the following summer work began at Dahlem, on a site near the end of the new underground from Berlin, on buildings for the Institute for Physical Chemistry and Electrochemistry which was to be run by Haber. The Physics Institute was to follow, and as little difficulty was expected in staffing it as there had been in attracting men to work under Haber. Indeed, as far as physics was concerned, the scientific atmosphere of the German capital was almost magnet enough. Only the Cavendish Laboratory at Cambridge, forging ahead into the nuclear world under the command of J.J. Thomson, could compare with the physics faculty of the University of Berlin.

Therefore, it was felt in the Prussian capital, there would be little difficulty in attracting Einstein. It was perhaps strange that a theoretical physicist should be considered the best man to run such an institute; and Einstein himself was the most unlikely of men to grapple successfully with the practical problems of any major organization. However, that was not really the point, since the actual creation of the institute was known to be some way off in the future. What mattered was getting this unconventional Swiss to Berlin for the ideas he might produce.

One possible impediment lay concealed in the word "Swiss," for Einstein had reneged on his German nationality more than a decade and a half previously. And even if the authorities could be induced to accept him, for the sake of German progress if not for the sake of science alone, there was always the chance that Einstein might not accept Berlin. There is little evidence that up to this date he had openly voiced the criticism of the Prussian regime and of the German mentality which later so obsessed him; but such views as he had were almost certainly known, implicitly if not explicitly, to Planck and Nernst. But both were determined men, and in the summer of 1913 they decided to visit Einstein in Zurich.

Some of the preliminaries appear to have been dealt with by this time. While still in Pargue in the spring of 1912, Einstein had written that he would be "going to Berlin to be able to talk shop with different people," and added that he had "appointments with Nernst, Planck, Rubens, Warburg, Haber. . . ." Later, when his German nationality became an issue on his winning the Nobel Prize, he officially wrote that this question of nationality had been discussed with Haber "when my appointment to our Academy was being considered." It seems likely, therefore, that Planck and Nernst, the subject having already been raised, were visiting Zurich to make sure that if a formal offer were made, then it would be accepted.

The high drama of these two major figures in German science traveling south from Berlin to tempt the young Einstein back into the Prussian orbit was equaled by the differences between the men themselves—Planck aloof and superbly professional, always master of the situation, the tall trimmed figure from whom his country could never demand too much; Nernst the businesslike genius, a jolly, plump little man against whom Planck appeared as the epitome of discipline. Both were excellent as fishers for Einstein who had a respect for Planck only just this side idolatry. For Nernst there was even some warmth, shown in the words that Einstein wrote of him years later: "Although sometimes good-naturedly smiling at his childlike vanity and self-complacency, we all had for him not only sincere admiration but also a personal affection. He was neither a nationalist nor a militarist . . . [with] a sense of humor as is very seldom found with men who carry so heavy a load of work."

This appreciation, made after Nernst's death during the Second World War, was as revealing of the writer as of its subject. More than one of Einstein's friends pointed out that whatever "childlike vanity and self-complacency" Nernst might show on the surface, there lay beneath it a keen financial mind that enabled him, almost alone among German scientists, to make a small fortune from his relations with industry.

Planck and Nernst met Einstein in his rooms at the ETH and pleaded their case with him at some length. He was unwilling to give a decision then and there, and the two professors decided to ascend the Rigi, the most famous of nineteenth century Swiss viewpoints, while he was making up his mind. After their excursion by train and funicular railway they would return to Zurich for their answer. Einstein, exhibiting the quirkish humor with which he often tweaked authority's tail, announced that they would know the verdict as soon as they saw him. If he was carrying a white rose the answer would be No; if the rose was red, then he would accept the offer from Berlin if it were formally made.

When the two men later stepped down from their carriage they were relieved to see Einstein trotting up the platform carrying a red rose.

The proposal had been that Einstein should become director of the Kaiser Wilhelm Institute for Physics when it was set up, and would meanwhile give advice on research in the subject carried out in other parts of the organization. However, had this been the sum total of the offer it seems probable that he would have been carrying a white rose rather than red. But the Kaiser Wilhelm appointment was only one part of an attractive package deal.

Almost exactly three years earlier, Jacobus Hendrikus van't Hoff, the originator of the theory of the spatial structure of molecules, had died at the age of fifty-nine. He had been a member of the Prussian Academy of Sciences, the oldest scientific institution in Germany, planned by Leibnitz and established by Frederick the First as the "Society of Sciences," and his chair had remained empty. Planck and Nernst were confident that with the help of their colleagues they could persuade the Prussian Ministry of Education to approve Einstein's appointment to the chair—a necessary move since the Academy existed under the umbrella of the Prussian civil service. Most members occupied only honorary and unpaid positions. A few, however, were endowed from one of various funds, and it was part of the plan that, with such help, Einstein should be offered a salary much in excess of what he was receiving in Zurich. If this were not attraction enough, there was a third item in the offer which Einstein agreed to accept if it were officially made. This was a nominal professorship in the University of Berlin, nominal since under the proposed special arrangements Einstein would be able to lecture as much or as little as he wished and would have none of the normal duties concerned with university administration. To sum up, he would be left free to devote himself, exactly as he wished, to the business of pure research. He would, moreover, be able to do so in the best possible place—to the remark that only a dozen men in the world really understood relativity, Nernst once replied: "Eight of them live in Berlin."

On their return to Berlin, Planck and Nernst, supported by Rubens and Emil Warburg, the founder of modern photochemistry, prepared their draft notice for presentation to the Ministry of Education. The original proposed Einstein "for full membership of the Academy with special personal salary of 6,000 marks," but the figure was subsequently doubled to "12,000," an indication that the Germans were anxious that this particular catch should not slip through their net. The draft—in which the German birth and education of this apparently Swiss professor was inserted almost as an afterthought—described Einstein's early years, and the publication of his first relativity paper.

"This new interpretation of the time concept has had sweeping repercussions on the whole of physics, especially mechanics and even epistemology," it went on. "The mathematician Minkowski subsequently formulated it in terms which unify the whole system of physics inasmuch as time enters the stage as a dimension on completely equal terms with the three conventional dimensions." It then, somewhat surprisingly in the light of later events, turned to what were considered more relevant matters.

"Although this idea of Einstein's has proved itself so fundamental for the development of physical principles, its application still lies for the moment on the frontier of the measurable," it continued.

> Far more important for practical physics is his penetration of other questions on which, for the moment, interest is focused. Thus he was the first man to show the importance of the quantum theory for the energy of atomic and molecular movements, and from this he produced a formula for the specific heat of solids which, although not yet entirely proved in detail, has become a basis for further development of the newer atomic kinetics. He has also linked the quantum hypothesis with photoelectric and photochemical effects by the discovery of interesting new relationships capable of being checked by measurement, and he was one of the first to point out the close relationship between the constant of elasticity and those in the optical vibrations of crystals.
>
> All in all, one can say that among the great problems, so abundant in modern physics, there is hardly one to which Einstein has not brought some outstanding contribution. That he may sometimes have missed the target in his speculations, as, for example in his theory of light quanta, cannot really be held against him. For in the most exact of natural sciences every innovation entails risk. At the moment he is working intensively on a new theory of gravitation, with what success only the future will tell. Apart from his own productivity, Einstein has a special talent for probing peculiar original views and premises, and estimating their interrelationship with uncanny certainty from his own experience.
>
> In this treatment and investigation of classical theory, even in the earliest of his publications, as well as in his demonstration and criticism of new hypotheses, Einstein must rank as a master.

The interest in this account, which was to open the gates to Berlin, lies in the way in which it glosses over Einstein's work on relativity and quickly dismisses the "heuristic viewpoint" of the photoelectric paper for which he was to be awarded the Nobel Prize for Physics nine years later. Nernst and Planck, who presumably drew up the document, took into account not only the conservative views of their colleagues but also the character of the minister. And Planck, reluctant to admit that his quanta did not somehow take on wave characteristics during the journey from here to there, still felt it necessary to insist that when it came to photons Einstein had "missed the target."

Having been approved by the Academy, the proposal was submitted to the government on July 28, 1913. It was nearly four months later before the reply came. On November 20 the minister stated that the Kaiser had approved the appointment, that the Minister of Finance had agreed to grant Dr. Einstein traveling expenses, and that he now wished to be informed if "Professor Einstein actually accepts his new post." Long before this Nernst took the matter as settled. "At Easter, Einstein will move to Berlin," he wrote to Lindemann on August 8, 1913; "Planck and I were in Zurich to see him the other day, and the Academy has already elected him. We have great expectations of him."

Einstein formally accepted on December 7, having by this time asked for his release from the post he had taken up only eighteen months earlier. In his letter to Berlin he stressed his gratitude for the chance of being able to carry on his scientific work free from professional duties. "When I consider that each working day weakens my thinking powers I can accept this high honor only with a certain degree of awe," he went on. "Accepting the post, however, has encouraged me to think that one man cannot ask of another more than that he should devote his whole strength to a good cause, and in this respect I feel myself truly competent."

Einstein's acceptance was significant in a number of ways. The most obvious was later stressed by Sommerfeld who wrote that "we owe the completion of his General Theory of Relativity to his leisure while in Berlin." But there is more to it than that. Had Einstein remained in Zurich until the outbreak of war in August, 1914, it is almost inconceivable that he would have returned to Germany. The anti-Semites in that country would have been deprived, both in the postwar chaos of the early 1920s and in the preparations for the Nazi takeover, of a ready-made target on which to concentrate their fire. It is almost equally unlikely that Einstein would have moved to the United States in 1933—and thus been available on Long Island in the summer of 1939 to prod the Americans into research which gave them nuclear weapons before the end of the war in the Pacific.

For these reasons, if for no other, it is worth considering the pros and cons of what must for Einstein have been a difficult decision. On the credit side there was the enormous attraction of the intellectual climate into which he would be moving. There was also the attraction of the salary. Einstein was never a man to care about money but he was the father of two growing sons and he felt responsible for them if not extravagantly affectionate. There was also the reason which he gave to Ehrenfest for what he called his "Berlinization": "I accepted this peculiar sinecure because giving lectures grates so oddly on my nerves, and I don't have to lecture there at all."

"In addition," says one of his generally more reliable biographers, Philipp Frank, "there were also personal factors that entered into the decision. Einstein had an uncle in Berlin, a fairly successful businessman, whose daughter, Elsa, was now a widow. Einstein remembered that his cousin Elsa as a young girl had often been in Munich and had impressed him as a friendly, happy person. The prospects of being able to enjoy the pleasant company of this cousin in Berlin made him think of the Prussian capital more favorably." This statement must be taken with some caution. Frank, who wrote his book in 1947, more than thirty years later, was an intimate of Einstein, and it is difficult not to believe that the source of the comment was Einstein himself. It is true that he eventually married Elsa Einstein; but when he moved to Berlin in April, 1914, he moved with Mileva and their two sons. The marriage had not yet broken up; and while there are indications that it was almost on the rocks, it seems overharsh to suggest that he accepted the Berlin appointment in the hope that it would eventually bring his marriage to an end. However, that is what happened.

Mileva Einstein's reaction to Berlin, very largely Slav dislike for all things Teuton, which for her contrasted so strongly with the casual happy atmosphere of Switzerland, had a counterpart in Einstein's own feelings. Seventeen years previously he had renounced not only German nationality but what he considered the essential Germanism:

reverence for obedience, regimentation of the body, and a rigidity of the spirit which forced minds narrowly upwards like the pine trunks of the dark German forests. Now, as a man, he would be walking back into the environment from which he had escaped as a boy. Yet throwing down an intellectual gauntlet, taking a calculated risk, were actions which not only had led to Einstein's fame but were typical of his mental makeup; accepting a post in the Kaiser Wilhelm would enable him to do both things. There was also one other factor which mattered more than anything else. Einstein's friend Reichinstein put it clearly after he had talked with him in Berlin about the work that led to the General Theory. "To be able to work when a great idea is at stake," he wrote, "[an idea] which has to be nursed to maturity during a longer period of time, a scientist must be unencumbered by cares, must avoid all disturbing conflicts of life, must bear with all humiliations from his opponents in order to safeguard that precious something which he bears in his soul." In Berlin, under the conditions provided by Planck and Nernst, Einstein would be unencumbered by money worries, would avoid the disturbing conflicts of a teaching routine. More than one friend, more than one colleague, has stressed how he was in some ways more of an artist than a scientist—or at least "an artist in science." And "the true artist will let his wife starve, his children go barefoot, his mother drudge for his living at seventy, sooner than work at anything but his art." Einstein would even put himself in pawn to the Prussians.

The problem of nationality, raised when the question of going to Berlin had first been discussed, at last appeared settled. Haber had pointed out that membership of the Prussian Academy of Sciences would automatically make Einstein a Prussian citizen—and two decades later Professor Ernst Heymann, perpetual secretary of the Academy, wrote of Einstein's "Prussian nationality which he acquired in 1913 simply by becoming a full member of the Academy." Einstein's version was that, "as I attached importance to the fact that there would be no change in my nationality, I made acceptance of a possible appointment dependent on this stipulation, which was agreed to." Exactly what was finally done is not clear even today. But there had been a Professor Haguenin, a Frenchman in the

Academy's Faculty of Letters, who had insisted on remaining French. The position was no doubt different in the case of a German who had renounced his German nationality, but Einstein was left with the impression that in Berlin he would not only retain his Swiss nationality but would avoid becoming a German once again. The government, but not the Academy, later denied that this was so. If the government was right, this did not necessarily mean that Planck and Nernst had failed to keep their promise. The "agreement" may have first been discussed early in the summer. And it was only on July 13, 1913, that a new Nationality Law provided in its Section 14 that state employment in the service of the Reich, or in one of the federal states, automatically gave German citizenship to the respective foreign employee, official, or civil servant.

Certainly for a good deal of his life Einstein believed that he, as a Swiss, had gained professorial status in Berlin only by diplomatic sleight of hand. But it is typical of what his elder son has called his delight in making up good stories for good listeners that he should later give another version. To Dr. Max Gottschalk, a prominent Belgian Jewish scholar and good friend, who asked how a Swiss had become a full German professor, Einstein explained that the Kaiser had visited the university one day. "He asked to be introduced to Professor Einstein and I was brought forward," he said. "After that, as the Kaiser had called me a professor I had to be a full professor."*

Details were settled before the end of 1913, and it was arranged that he should take up his duties in Berlin on April 1, 1914. It had been a remarkable triumph for a man not yet thirty-five, so much so that even Einstein himself, confident as he usually was of Einstein, mentally kept his fingers crossed. In the circumstances this was natural enough. He was still stuck on the General Theory, even with Marcel Grossmann's aid. He was still in the middle of those "errors of thinking which caused me two years of hard work," as he described it, and to Besso he wrote deploring the fact that German theorists were not receptive to general discussion based on fundamental prin-

*His close friend Leon Watters later quotes him as saying: "Though I lived in Germany for many years, I never became a German citizen. I made that a condition of my going there. I never met the Kaiser, probably on that account."

ciples. "I am somewhat uneasy as I see the Berlin adventure approaching," he said. ". . . A free unprejudiced look is generally not characteristic of 'adult' Germans. It's as if they wore blinders."

In Zurich, Louis Kollros, his old colleague of ETH days, organized a farewell supper for him in the Kronenhalle. "We all regretted his departure," Kollros has said. "He himself was delighted at the prospect of being able to devote all his time to research . . . delighted and a little anxious nevertheless; he did not know what the future held in store for him. When I accompanied him home that evening he turned to me and said: 'The gentlemen in Berlin are gambling on me as if I were a prize hen. As for myself I don't even know whether I'm going to lay another egg.' "*

Einstein moved with his family from Zurich to Berlin on April 6, 1914. Haber helped him find and lease a flat in Berlin-Dahlem and here he spent the early part of the summer settling in.

On July 2 he gave his inaugural address to the Academy. "First of all I have to thank you most heartily for conferring on me the greatest boon that could be conferred on a man like myself," he began. "By electing me to your Academy you have freed me from the distractions and cares of a professional life and so made it possible for me to devote myself entirely to scientific studies. I hope that you will continue to believe in my gratitude and industry even when my efforts appear to yield only poor results." He also made it clear what direction these efforts would take, commenting on special relativity, explaining the need to generalize it, and noting that such a generalization could not yet be tested. "We have seen that inductive physics asks questions of deductive and vice versa, and that an answer calls upon the deployment of all our energies. May we soon succeed in making permanent progress by our united efforts!"

While events moved on towards the first item in this

*Einstein was apparently fond of the simile. Talking after dinner in Gottingen one evening with Paul Hertz, who taught theoretical physics there, he compared the whole concept of new ideas to that of a chicken laying an egg: "Kieks—auf einmal ist es da" ("Cheep —suddenly there it is").

permanent progress—Freundlich's expedition to the Crimea—Einstein traveled each morning to his office in the Academy, then housed in the Prussian State Library on Unter den Linden. Here he arranged with his new colleagues from the university how, when, and about what he would lecture during the coming autumn term. And here he was visited by officials of the Kaiser Wilhelm Gesellschaft with whom he arranged details of the new institute. He has denied that when asked to outline his needs he said that these consisted only of pencils and paper which he would supply himself. However, "it is true that I always knew how to arrange things so that I remained unburdened," he has written. "I wanted to have time free for thinking and I had no wish to dictate other people's actions (nothing of the 'Fuehrer')."

In Berlin Einstein was to see for the first time how the ramifications of science spread out not only into philosophy and metaphysics, but into politics and power, and how they penetrated, like the metal rods in a ferroconcrete building, the organizations on which the equilibrium of European peace still rested. At first, he was barely distressed by the new climate. "Life is better here than I anticipated," he wrote to Professor Hurwitz on May 4. "However, a certain discipline as regards clothes, etc., which I have to observe on the commands of a few old gentlemen, in order not to arouse reproaches from the people here, rather disturbs my peace of mind. The Academy in its general ambience is reminiscent of any other faculty. Apparently most of its members confine themselves to a certain peacocklike *grandezza* in their writings. . . ." And there were compensations. His status had been raised not merely in scientific esteem and financial reward, but in the eyes of his relatives, particularly those of his mother. In his youth they had tended to write him off. Now, "they felt honored to receive him in their homes and to be mentioned as his relatives."

There was, above all, the new freedom to devote himself almost entirely to his work. The most urgent thing now was the expedition to southern Russia to observe the eclipse in August, and from April onwards Einstein and his family were in regular and close contact with the Freundlichs. As the date of the expedition's departure approached, Einstein withdrew more and more into his own scientific carapace; more frequently, he became the Einstein of the later newspaper caricatures, insulated from the normal contacts of life by his own interior problems. Thus there was the occasion when he pushed back the plates at the end of a meal with the Freundlichs. Before a word could be said he began to cover a much prized "party" tablecloth with equations as he talked with his host. "Had I kept it unwashed as my husband told me," says Frau Freundlich half a century afterwards, "it would be worth a fortune." But this was typical "I have seen him in his keenness," Lord Samuel once wrote, "when no table was handy, kneel down on the floor and scribble diagrams and equations on a scrap of paper on a chair."

There was also the complementary occasion when the Freundlichs arrived to dine with the Einsteins. After a long wait without their host, Mileva answered the telephone to discover her husband was ringing from Dahlem. He had, he said, been waiting more than an hour at the underground station for Freundlich. As agreed, Freundlich had kept the rendezvous at the Einstein apartment.

By this time Einstein was not only engrossed. He was also confident. Earlier doubts had been swept away and even before coming to Berlin in the spring he had written in high spirits to Besso. "Now I am fully satisfied, and I no longer doubt the correctness of the whole system, whether the observation of the eclipse succeeds or not," went his letter. "The sense of the thing is too evident." This is a revealing phrase. For Einstein was saying that if a man stood fast by his intuition, if he hung on in the face of difficulties, if he really felt from an inner sense of conviction that he were right, then an explanation for discrepancies would arrive; inconsistencies in the evidence would become explicable. It was, although he does not seem to have realized it himself, a final farewell to Mach and his deification of the sensations. It was also indulgence in an act of faith. Only Einstein the philosopher could have convinced Einstein the scientist that if the evidence did not agree with the theory then the evidence must be faulty.

All these hopes were wrecked by Germany's declaration of war on Russia on August 1, 1914, her declaration of war on France two days later, and her invasion of Belgium which brought Britain into the war on August 4; "My dear astronomer Freundlich will become a prisoner of war in Russia instead of being able to observe the eclipse," Einstein wrote to Ehrenfest in Leiden on August 19. "I am worried about him." But Freundlich and the members of his team were luckier than they might have been, although their equipment was impounded and they themselves were arrested and taken to Odessa. By the end of the month their exchange for a number of high-ranking Russian officers had been arranged and by September 2 Freundlich was back in Berlin. Here he spent the rest of the war, mainly at the observatory but giving part-time assistance to Einstein.

Thus the war delayed the testing of the General Theory for five years. But it was to affect Einstein decisively in one other way. For it was the instrument which finally brought his first marriage to an end.

His relations with Mileva had become increasingly fragile. Years later he complained that in Switzerland she had been jealous of all his friends, with the solitary exception of Solovine, and inferred that her disposition had made life together impossible. But he looked back more in sorrow than in pain, accepting with resignation the fact that nothing could have made the marriage work properly and acquitting both his wife and himself of anything worse than bad luck. In 1914 he was far less equable about the matter.

It was at least reasonable that Mileva should return to Zurich with the two sons in the summer of 1914; it was even more reasonable that she should stay with them there when war broke out in August—at least until the immediate prospects had become clearer. But by Christmas it was plain that something more was involved. Mileva remained in Switzerland with the children. Einstein, still a Swiss citizen, remained in Berlin, spending the holiday with Professor and Frau Nernst, a lonely but perhaps not entirely unhappy figure playing his violin to them on Christmas Eve.

Mileva did not return. Einstein did not care. In fact there is a good deal of circumstantial evidence to suggest that he was heartily glad to remain on his own while he got down to the hard work of completing the General Theory. Not all his friends felt this was a satisfactory situation, and Haber in particular began a long series of kindly but unsuccessful attempts to bring the two together again. The slender hope of this is shown by a letter that Einstein wrote to Besso, some months after the famous General Theory paper had been published and after he had experienced a stormy meeting with his wife in Switzerland. If he had not had the strength of mind to keep her at a distance, out of sight and out of mind, he would, he said, have been worn out physically and morally.

Even by Christmas, 1914, one problem was evident—how to provide for Mileva and the two sons, one aged ten, the other four. Einstein had a qualified affection for the boys, as long as it did not take up too much of his time, and he was anxious that they should not suffer from the breakup of their parents' marriage. For the next few years, therefore, money—and the difficulty of getting it without loss from wartime Germany to neutral Switzerland—became one of Einstein's preoccupations.

If the First World War quickly put a temporary spoke in one of Einstein's scientific wheels and brought his private life to a climax, it also did something far more important: it brought him face to face, for the first time, with the interrelationships between science and world affairs. Until now he had looked on science as a vocation to be followed only by men of intelligence and moral integrity, occupying positions not higher than, but usually cut off from, most other people. They were not necessarily better, but they were certainly different. Surely the appalling business of international politics, of war and all that went with it, was something in which they, last of all people, should be involved?

This belief was ingenuous. Newton himself had been an adviser to the British Admiralty. Michael Faraday and Sir Frederick Abel were advisers to the British War Office. Dewar and Abel produced cordite, Nobel invented dynamite, and the studies on the Stassfurt deposits carried out by van't Hoff whose chair Einstein now filled were of great use to Germany's wartime industry. Science had in fact been one of war's handmaidens since bronze replaced stone in prehistoric times. Yet the nature of Einstein's work on the fundamental problems of physics had tended to quarantine him away from this fact and his self-imposed dedication to the task had aided the process. He was therefore shocked at what he witnessed in Berlin. For now his colleagues leaped to arms unbidden, as certain as Rupert Brooke where duty lay. His former assistant, Ludwig Hopf, joined the German Air Ministry and helped to develop military aircraft. Otto Stern was soon serving with the forces on the eastern front, from which he maintained contact with Einstein by a series of brief letters and field postcards. The young Max Born, brought to the University of Berlin from Göttingen when Planck persuaded the Prussian Ministry of Education that he needed help, worked first for the German air force and then for a military board investigating the physics of sound ranging. Schwarzschild the astronomer, whose calculations were to support the first confirmation of Einstein's General Theory, served as a mathematical expert with the German armies on the eastern front. Nernst first became a War Ministry consultant, advising on chemical agents for shells, and subsequently accepted a commission.

Above all there was Fritz Haber, who had at once volunteered for service but been rejected on medical grounds. "His resulting depression," says his biographer, "disappeared when he received a problem from the Ordnance Department. Request was made for gasoline with a low freezing point, since the army expected to fight through a Russian winter." Furthermore it was not long before Haber was in uniform, and telling his wife that a scientist belonged to the world during times of peace but to his country during times of war. It had quickly become clear that his revolutionary method for producing ammonia—for which he was later awarded the Nobel Prize for Chemistry—was essential to the stockpiling of explosives and fertilizer without which the German war effort could hardly have continued. First he was consulted on how this process could best be utilized. Next he was brought in to advise on the practicability of gas warfare, first as a sergeant. "One of [his] great disappointments was lack of a higher military title," says his biographer. "As a full professor at a university, he had the feeling he was equivalent to a general; Academy members had a comparable uniform for court occasions." Later he was commissioned as a captain—but not before he compelled his hesitating colleague Richard Willstatter to join in gas mask research: "I am a sergeant," he said. "I command you to the task." Haber soon joined forces with Nernst, and within a few months was supervising production of enough chlorine for the first German gas attack in the spring of 1915. By the following year he had become the head of Germany's chemical warfare service and, after experimenting with hundreds of substances, achieved a major technological success by introducing mustard gas in 1917. Einstein had no illusions. Reading a report of the Allied use of gas bombs, he remarked to his colleagues: "This is supposed to say that they stunk first, but we know better how to do it."

Even Einstein, critical of his own country since youth, had expected something different from what he now witnessed. "One imagines that at least a few educated Germans had private moments of horror at the slaughter which was about to commence," says Fritz Ringer. "In public, however, German academics of all political persuasions spoke almost exclusively of their optimism and enthusiasm. Indeed, they greeted the war with a sense of relief. Party differences and class antagonisms seemed to evaporate at the call of national duty. Social Democrats marched singing to the front in the company of their betters, and the mandarin intellectuals rejoiced at the apparent rebirth of 'idealism' in Germany."

Reaction from the universities reinforced all Einstein's distaste for what he saw as the exclusively German characteristic of marching to the band. He looked askance at his own colleagues and he later tended to overlook the fact that Lindemann risked his life testing service aircraft, that Madame Curie drove Red Cross ambulances, and that both Rutherford and Langevin worked as scientists on the inter-Allied antisubmarine committee which produced the first Asdic detectors. It might be wrong for Allied scientists to prostitute science; but, by Einstein's implication, it was worse for German scientists to do the same thing since Germany had been the aggressor. It was a plausible argument; but it should have destroyed any vestigial illusion that scientists could remain outside the battle.

The sight of the Berlin scientific establishment devoting itself to war with hardly a murmur of dissent drove Einstein towards a treble commitment to internationalism, pacifism, and socialism. These were all fine ideals and all appealed to the best in him. Yet although there is little evidence that his support of them had any effect on the course of history, that support, the direct result of his wartime experiences in Berlin, led him after the war into waters where he was dangerously out of his depth. By that time, he was a world figure. All his public actions were followed—either with reverence or amusement. The upshot was a worldwide belief that Einstein was fired by an almost saintly honesty of purpose and a less justifiable feeling that scientists almost inevitably lost their way in the corridors of power.

The war thus revolutionized Einstein's attitude to the world about him. He could no longer remain isolated. He had to play his part on the side of the angels. But physics still came first. It held him to Berlin, despite the fact that while he hoped for an Allied victory he was forced to turn a Nelsonian blind eye not only to the work of his colleagues but even to the sources of some of his own money. For this came, at least in part, from Leopold Koppel who in 1916 created the Kaiser Wilhelm Foundation for Military Technical Sciences. The full details of Einstein's links with Koppel are not known, but in a letter to Freundlich in December, 1913, Einstein speaks of Koppel as the man who had "given the money for my salary as a member of the Academy." According to the Max Planck Gesellschaft, into which the Kaiser Wilhelm Institute was transformed in 1946, Einstein's Institute for Physics received regular sums—25,000 marks from October 1, 1917, to March 31, 1918—from the Koppel donation which set up the military foundation. Einstein himself wrote to Born in 1919 referring to another rich man and saying "my academic remuneration does not depend on his purse but on that of Herr Koppel," while Professor Jens of Tübingen University has stated that Einstein "was first given the opportunity for undisturbed research by a Prussian banker who undertook to pay Einstein a supplementary salary of 4,000 Reichsmarks from April 1, 1914, onwards for a period of twelve years," and names the banker as Koppel. "Einstein," he sums up, "knew that the sumptuous bed in which he lay swarmed with bugs."

Whatever the exact figures, it is clear that Einstein at the height of his powers was being supported by the very people he was soon condemning, and exhibiting a surprising ability to prevent his left hand from knowing what his right hand was doing. Yet even had he troubled to think about the matter, there would have been no contradiction in declaiming against the war while using for science the money of those who supported it. Like Major Barbara, Einstein would have reflected that the money was better in his hands than theirs.

Einstein's ingrained distrust of all things military and of all things Prussian was first revealed clearly by his reaction to the "Manifesto to the Civilized World." This was a fulsome and pained expression of surprise that the world should have objected to the German invasion of Belgium. Issued early in October, 1914, it disclaimed Germany's war guilt, justified the violation of Belgium on the grounds that it would have been suicide to have done anything else, spoke of "Russian hordes . . . unleashed against the white race" in the tones of Dr. Goebbels twenty years later, and claimed that "were it not for German militarism, German culture would have been wiped off the face of the earth." The manifesto gained ninety-three supporters from the upper echelons of the intellectual world, where it was circulated. Wilhelm Röntgen, the discoverer of X rays, signed it. So did Ernst Hackel, the evolutionist. So did Paul Ehrlich, the biologist. And so did Max Planck, although he may have been one of those who had, in Einstein's kind words to Lorentz, signed "carelessly, sometimes without having read the text." But, Einstein added, he did not "think that these people can be persuaded to retract."

A reaction to "The Manifesto of the 93," as it became known, came within days from George Nicolai, professor of physiology in the University of Berlin, soon to be the author of *The Biology of War,* and the conscript-turned-pacifist who during the closing months of the war made a sensational escape from Germany by plane. The exact part that Einstein played in the "Manifesto to Europeans" which Nicolai produced is not clear, but Nicolai himself, writing to Einstein on May 18, 1918, gives him credit for being coauthor, and continues: "Indeed, without your participation, it might never have seen the light of day. At least I am inclined to believe, difficult as it is to determine such contingencies, that I should never have done anything alone." Even though the countermanifesto was a joint effort, its wording is extraordinarily reminiscent of the statements, announcements, messages, and exhortations which were to come in a stream from Einstein throughout the next forty years. It was the first of its sort which he wrote or signed, and it is therefore significant enough to be quoted in full:

> Never before has any war so completely disrupted cultural cooperation. It has done so at the very time when progress in technology and communications clearly suggest that we recognize the need for international relations which will necessarily move in the direction of a universal, worldwide civilization. Perhaps we are all the more keenly and painfully aware of the rupture precisely because so many international bonds existed before.
>
> We can scarcely be surprised. Anyone who cares in the least for a common world culture is now doubly committed to fight for the maintenance of the principles on which it must stand. Yet, those from whom such sentiments might have been expected—primarily scientists and artists—have so far responded, almost to a man, as though they had relinquished any further desire for the continuance of international relations. They have spoken in a hostile spirit, and they have failed to speak out for peace.
>
> Nationalist passions cannot excuse this attitude, which is unworthy of what the world has heretofore called culture. It would be a grave misfortune were the spirit to gain general currency among the intellectuals. It would, we are convinced, not only threaten culture as such: it would endanger the very existence of the nations for the protection of which this barbarous war was unleashed.
>
> Technology has shrunk the world. Indeed, today the nations of the great European peninsula seem to jostle one another much as once did the city-states that were crowded into those smaller peninsulas jutting out into the Mediterranean. Travel is so widespread, international supply and demand are so interwoven, that Europe—one could almost say the whole world—is even now a single unit.
>
> Surely, it is the duty of Europeans of education and goodwill at least to try to prevent Europe from succumbing, because of lack of international organization, to the fate that once engulfed ancient Greece! Or will Europe also suffer slow exhaustion and death by fratricidal war?
>
> The struggle raging today can scarcely yield a "victor"; all nations that participate in it will, in all likelihood, pay an exceedingly high price. Hence it appears not only wise but imperative for men of education in all countries to

exert their influence for the kind of peace treaty that will not carry the seeds of future wars, whatever the outcome of the present conflict may be. The unstable and fluid situation in Europe, created by the war, must be utilized to weld the continent into an organic whole. Technically and intellectually, conditions are ripe for such a development.

This is not the place to discuss how this new order in Europe may be brought about. Our sole purpose is to affirm our profound conviction that the time has come when Europe must unite to guard its soil, its people, and its culture. We are stating publicly our faith in European unity, a faith which we believe is shared by many; we hope that this public affirmation of our faith may contribute to the growth of a powerful movement toward such unity.

The first step in this direction would be for all those who truly cherish the culture of Europe to join forces—all those whom Goethe once prophetically called "good Europeans." We must not abandon hope that their voices, speaking in unison, may even today rise above the clash of arms, particularly if they are joined by those who already enjoy renown and authority.

The first step, we repeat, is for Europeans to join forces. If, as we devoutly hope, enough *Europeans* are to be found in Europe—people to whom Europe is a vital cause rather than a geographical term—we shall endeavor to organize a League of Europeans. This league may then raise its voice and take action.

We ourselves seek to make the first move, to issue the challenge. If you are of one mind with us, if you too are determined to create a widespread movement for European unity, we bid you pledge yourself by signing your name.

The manifesto, drawn up in the University of Berlin, was circulated among its professors. It was signed by Nicolai and by Einstein. It was signed by Wilhelm Forster, the eighty-year-old head of the Berlin Observatory who had already signed the Manifesto of the 93, and by Otto Buek. That was all.

Einstein no doubt felt its ineffectiveness a month later and was drawn for the first time into membership of a political party. This was the Bund Neues Vaterland, established on November 16, 1914, and including among its founder members the banker Hugo Simon who in 1919 became Prussian Minister of Finance, and Ernst Reuter who became a famous burgomaster of Berlin after the Second World War. The main object of the group was to bring about an early peace. The second was the creation of an international body that would make future wars impossible. Both were aims with which Einstein wholeheartedly sympathized and he is reported to have been "very active, attending meetings and delivering speeches." The Bund, struggling for existence in a nation not only at war but enthusiastically supporting the war, was obviously doomed to an early death. However, Einstein's support was open, something very different from the support which he was to give, through connections in Holland and Switzerland, to the forces striving for an early end to the war even if this involved Germany's defeat.

It has been said with some justice that "to work in any open way for peace under the Kaiser's regime in 1914 was equivalent to treason," and if Einstein is taken to have been a German some of his actions have more than a touch of it. Had all of them been publicly known in the immediate aftermath of the Armistice, his trials and tribulations during the early 1920s would have been that much greater. For he hoped not only for an end to the war but, more specifically, for German defeat; and he made this hope quite clear to those whom he could trust. The attitude linked him loosely with at least part of the "German resistance" of thirty years later, although with one difference. In Europe of 1914–18 he was not only able to continue his life's work from his privileged position in Berlin; he was also able to carry on his "resistance" work of pleading peace in both Holland and Switzerland with the minimum of personal risk since in any trouble he could always claim the protection of his Swiss passport. There is nothing shameful in the fact that circumstance thus enabled him to have the best of both worlds; yet it tended to widen the gap that already separated him from most other men.

Einstein's first wartime contacts outside Germany—with the exception of personal letters to his wife—were with Ehrenfest and Lorentz in Holland. To the first he revealed his feelings as early as August 19, 1914: "Europe, in her insanity, has started something unbelievable. In such times one realizes to what a sad species of animal one belongs. I quietly pursue my peaceful studies and contemplations and feel only pity and disgust." Writing a few months later, early in December, he elaborated: "The international catastrophe has imposed a heavy burden upon me as an internationlist. In living through this 'great epoch' it is difficult to reconcile oneself to the fact that one belongs to that idiotic, rotten species which boasts of its freedom of will. How I wish that somewhere there existed an island for those who are wise and of goodwill! In such a place even I should be an ardent patriot." Einstein, just emerging from his own closed world, did not yet appreciate how readily good men, and wise ones, can support bad causes; or that his ideal island would have to be defended.

In much the same vein he wrote to Lorentz in the summer of 1915, deploring the national bias which he found "even among men of great stature," noting that frontiers made little difference, and setting down his belief "that men always need some idiotic fiction in the name of which they can face one another. Once it was religion. Now it is the state." In this same letter he also refers to a proposal which Lorentz had rejected. Its details are suggested in a letter from Einstein to Ehrenfest later the same month. In this he admits that the proposal was naïve, and goes on: "Impulse was stronger than judgment. I would so much like to do something to hold together our colleagues in the various 'Fatherlands.' Is not that small group of scholars and intellectuals the only 'Fatherland' which is worthy of serious concern to people like ourselves? Should *their* convictions be determined solely by the accident of frontiers?"

Shortly afterwards, in September, 1915, he left Berlin for Switzerland, intent on the "something" of his letter to Lorentz. With his Swiss passport, his wife still living in Zurich, and his numerous friends in both Zurich and Berne, this was on the face of it an acceptable journey to make. Its main object, however, was to visit Romain Rolland, the famous author and pacifist then living in Vevey on the shores of Lake Geneva.

Einstein had written to Rolland in March. "Through the press and through my association with the stalwart Bund Neues Vaterland," he said,

> I have learned how valiantly you have committed yourself, heart and soul, to the cause of bridging the fateful misunderstandings between the French and German people. I am eager to express to you my deep admiration and respect. May your splendid example inspire other high-minded men to abandon the incomprehensible delusions that, like a malignant plague, have gripped even otherwise intelligent, able, and sensible people.
>
> When posterity recounts the achievements of Europe, shall we let men say that three centuries of painstaking cultural effort carried us no farther than from religious fanaticism to the insanity of nationalism? In both camps today even scholars behave as though eight months ago they suddenly lost their heads.
>
> If you think I could be of any service to you—because of my present domicile or by virtue of my connections with scientists in Germany and abroad—I am at your disposal to the limits of my ability.

It is not quite clear how he thought he could help, but Rolland in neutral Switzerland subsequently received a letter from Berlin saying that there was much good news about their work which could be given by a man close to them—the scholar Einstein who would be visiting Rolland shortly.

Now, in mid-September, Einstein arrived at Vevey from Zurich, accompanied by Dr. Zangger from the ETH who had helped get him back to the Polytechnic in 1912. Rolland's long diary entry of September 16, 1915, is extraordinarily revealing.

"Professor Einstein, the brilliant physicist and mathematician of the University of Berlin, who wrote to me last winter, came to see me from Zurich, where he is staying, with his friend, Professor Dr. Zangger," this reads.

> We spent the whole of the afternoon on the terrace of the Hotel Mooser, at the bottom of the garden, amid swarms of bees who were plundering the ivy, which was in flower. Einstein is still young, not very tall, with an ample figure, great mane of hair a little frizzled and dry, very black but sprinkled with gray, which rises from a high forehead, with nose fleshy and prominent, small mouth, full lips, a small moustache cut short, full cheeks and rounded chin. He speaks French with difficulty and mixes it with German. He is very lively and gay; and he finds no difficulty in giving an amusing twist to the most

serious of subjects. He is Swiss by origin, born in Germany, a naturalized German and then, as far as I can understand, renaturalized Swiss two or three years before the war. I admire the Swiss Germans' brilliant vitality. Two or three small cantons have given Germany her greatest modern painter, Boecklin; her greatest novelist, Keller; her greatest poet, Spitteler; her greatest physicist, Einstein. And what others are there that I fail to mention? And, in all, this common quality as much in Einstein as in Spitteler; absolute independence of the spirit, solitary and happy. Einstein is unbelievably free in his judgments on Germany where he lives. No German has such a liberty. Anyone other than he would suffer by being so isolated in his thoughts during this terrible year. Not he, however. He laughs. And he has even been able, during the war, to write his most important scientific work. I asked him if he expressed his views to his German friends and talked about them. He said no. He contents himself with asking a series of Socratic questions, in order to disturb their complacency. And he says that "people don't like that much." What he says is hardly encouraging; for it shows the impossibility of concluding a peace with Germany before one has crushed her. Einstein says that the situation seems to him far less favorable than it was a few months ago. The victories on the Russian front have revived the pride and the appetite of the Germans. "Hungry" seems to Einstein to be the word which best characterizes the Germans. Above all one sees the will for power, the admiration for force, and their exclusive decision for conquests and annexations. The government is more moderate than the nation. It wishes to evacuate Belgium but is unable to do so. The officers threatened revolt. The big bankers, the industrialists, big business, is all powerful; they expect to be paid for the sacrifices they have made, the Emperor is only a tool in their hands and in those of the officers; he is good, feeble, hopeless about the war that he has never wanted, but into which he was forced because he is so easy to manipulate. All his unpredictable actions of the last few years, and his disconcerting brusquenesses, were carefully prepared by pan-German groups who used him without his knowing it. Tirpitz and Falkenhayn are the protagonists of the most bloody action. Falkenhayn seems the most dangerous; Tirpitz is above all a powerful impersonal machine. As to the intellectuals in the universities, Einstein divides them into two very clear classes; the mathematicians, doctors, and the exact sciences who are tolerant; and the historians and the arts faculties which stir up the nationalist passions. The mass of the nation is immensely submissive, "domesticated" (Einstein approves of this description by Spitteler). Einstein blames above all else the education which is aimed at national pride and blind submission to the state. He does not think that race is responsible since French Huguenots, refugees for two centuries, have the same characteristics. The socialists are the only independent element (to some extent); however, they form only a minority of the party grouped round Bernstein. The Bund Neues Vaterland goes ahead only slowly and does not grow much. Einstein does not expect any salvation of Germany by herself; she has neither the energy nor the audacity to make such an initiative. He hopes for a victory by the Allies which will ruin the power of Prussia and of the dynasty. When I asked whether this would not rally the nation around its unfortunate masters, Einstein the sceptic said that faithfulness was not a part of its nature; for her masters she has the admiration of fear and the respect for force, but no affection; if this force is smashed Germany will become like a country of savages who having adored their idol, throw it into the flames when they realize that they have been defeated. Einstein and Zangger dream of a partitioned Germany; on one hand southern Germany and Austria, on the other Prussia. But such a breakup of the Empire is more than doubtful. In Germany, everyone is convinced of victory; and one hears officially that the war will continue only for another six months or even less. However, Einstein says that those who know realize that the situation is grave and that it will become worse if the war goes on. It is not food which they will feel the most need of but certain chemical products necessary for the war. It is true that the truly admirable ingenuity of the German professors supplies the necessary products in the form of substitutes. All the professors at the universities have been put at the head of military services or commissions. Alone, Einstein has refused to take part. Whatever the outcome of the war the main victim will be France. All Germans know this; and for this reason Germany has a pitying sympathy. When I said that this sympathy from the Germans always has, for us, a disdainful character, Einstein and Zangger strongly protested. The political interest of England grows all the time in their eyes. Zangger, like all the German Swiss, speaks of it with antipathy. He is well informed and gives little-known proofs of British speculation. England has decided that France should hold at Marseilles (as well as at Genoa) goods destined for Switzerland. After that she sells them at double or treble the price to the Swiss. The war is really a battle between two worlds. France and Europe are crushed between them. Einstein, in spite of his lack of sympathy for England, prefers her victory to that of Germany because she will be more able to bring the world back to life.

We speak of the voluntary blindness and the lack of psychology on the part of the Germans. Einstein describes, laughing as he does so, how at each meeting of the Council of the University of Berlin, all the professors meet after the session in a café and there, *each time,* the conversation opens with the same question: "Why does the world hate us?" Then everyone talks, everyone gives his own reply, and everyone takes care not to say the truth. He spoke of one general meeting of the universities which was held in secret last July; there it was discussed whether the German universities should break all their links with the rest of the world's universities and academies. The motion was turned down by the universities of southern Germany, which formed the majority. But the University of Berlin supported it. She is the most official and the most imperialist of them all; her professors are specially chosen with this in mind.

It is clear that Einstein, in the hatred of his fellow countrymen that Rolland's entry indicates, forgot that they, as well as the English, heard "bugles calling for them from sad shires"; for once his humanity escaped him. Another significant point in Rolland's account is the exculpation of the Kaiser. It seems unlikely that Einstein was swayed by personal sympathies, and all accounts of a meeting between the two men appear to be apocryphal. But he clung to the Emperor's good intentions. "The Kaiser meant well," he said in an interview a decade after the end of the war. "He often had the right instinct. His intuitions were frequently more inspired than the labored reasons of his Foreign Office. Unfortunately, the Kaiser was always surrounded by poor advisers." And, asked whether the Kaiser or the Jews were responsible for the debacle of 1918, he replied: "Both are largely guiltless. The German débacle was due to the fact that the German people, especially the upper classes, failed to produce men of character, strong enough to take hold of the reins of government and to tell the truth to the Kaiser."

With Rolland, Einstein laid the blame unequivocally on

what he saw as the essential German spirit, but the intensity of his feeling shocked the Frenchman. The two men exchanged a few more words, standing on the station platform at Vevey as the train prepared to leave for Berne. "In looking at Einstein," wrote Rolland, "I noted how he, one of the very few men whose spirit had remained free among the general servility, had been led, as a reaction, to see the worst side of his own nation and to judge her almost with the severity of her enemies. I know certain men in the French camp who, for the same reason, would shake hands with him. (Incidentally, Einstein is a Jew, which explains his international outlook and the mocking character of his criticism.)" The strength of Einstein's feeling was remarkable; and he must have questioned even the scientific benefits of life in Berlin when he considered that his patrons included the creator and financial supporter of the Kaiser Wilhelm Foundation for Military Technical Sciences.

In neutral Switzerland his views could be declared without fear of serious contradiction. In Germany, he put a slightly different emphasis on reasons for the war. Asked by the Berlin Goethe Association a few months after his return for a short article outlining his feelings, he made no mention of the German guilt he had stressed so strongly to Rolland. "The psychological root of war lies, in my opinion," he wrote "in the biologically based aggressive character of man. We 'lords of creation' are not the only ones who can pride themselves on this; we are considerably surpassed by the bull and the cock. This tendency towards aggression shows itself wherever men are in close proximity, but it shows much more strongly when they are grouped together in narrow closed societies. These almost inevitably anger each other, and this then degenerates into quarrels and mutual homicide unless special precautions are taken." He went on to plead for the outlawing of war and for the European organization he had outlined in the manifesto. "I am also convinced," he concluded, "that in spite of the unspeakably sad conditions of the present time, there should be a political organization in Europe which should outlaw war in the same way that not so long ago the German Reich outlawed war between Bavaria and Württemberg."

Naturally enough, this was all a good deal more cautious than the opinions he had voiced to Rolland. By the end of 1915, prospects of a quick victory had faded and with them went the comparative freedom of the first year of war. Not even Einstein would have survived expression of open hope "for a victory by the Allies which will ruin the power of Prussia and of the dynasty." Indeed, he seems to have compartmentalized his feelings with surprising ease. He remained on the friendliest terms with Haber, the poison gas expert, and with his help was able to squeeze from the German General Staff a travel permit for a colleague. He was also, according to Max Born, one of the Berlin intellectuals who in midwar met high officials in the German Foreign Office to dissuade them from starting unrestricted U-boat warfare "as it would be bound to bring the United States into the war and thus lead to final defeat."

However, Einstein may well have been supporting such humanitarian pleas on moral grounds under the cover of expediency. For as hopes of an early peace faded, any suggestions of limiting operations had a defeatist ring that could no longer be tolerated. The Bund Neues Vaterland was outlawed, and while hints of a negotiated peace might be made privately, they produced in public the same vilification that comparable ideas produced in Britain, France, or, later, the United States. There is little evidence that this tightening of the official attitude had much effect on Einstein's privately expressed views, and his correspondence with Lorentz, largely concerned with scientific work, continued to be sprinkled with the strongest pacifist sentiments which could have been noted by the censor. Luckily he was not involved in work where indiscretion would have been more dangerous to friends than to foes.

There can certainly be no doubt about Einstein's pacifist feelings nor about his more concealed wish for a German defeat. But at the same time he retained the privileged position of a critic whose presence would be tolerated although his views were disliked. This position was the result partly of the renown which the General Theory had brought him in 1915, partly of his legal status as a Swiss. It nevertheless rankled with more than one Allied scientist when the war was over and Einstein's scientific eminence was buttressed by the claim that he had always been an open opponent of the militarists. Certainly as a Swiss he retained advantages, not the least being a freedom to visit neutral countries with less bureaucratic interference than most Germans, and he made use of this at Easter, 1916, to visit his wife in Zurich.

The meeting was disastrous. Einstein, according to his correspondence with Besso, made an "irrevocable" decision not to see Mileva again. Hans stopped writing to his father when Einstein returned to Berlin. And when, Mileva being ill, the question of another visit to Zurich was raised in the summer, Einstein poured out his troubles in a long letter to Besso, who henceforth acted as honest broker between the couple. If he came to Zurich, he said, Mileva would demand to see him and he would have to refuse, partly because of his earlier decision, partly to avoid emotional scenes. The boys would think he was being callous, and he really thought no good would come of it.

He went on to say that Besso had no idea of the tricks which were natural to such a woman as his wife, and explained that he would have been worn out if they had not been apart. It was now two years since she had left him in Berlin and Einstein asked his friend whether, when they had met recently, he had not seen a better man, one who had regained the innocent joy of a real life. If his wife had to go to hospital that would be different. Then he would visit her—and see the children on "neutral ground." Otherwise, "No."

From now onwards Besso—or "Uncle Toby" as Einstein, remembering *Tristram Shandy,* sometimes called him—acted as a regular go-between, helping to arrange schools for the boys, working out expenses, and advising him of the current Mileva situation in Zurich in a long series of letters that were divided between scientific gossip and domestic detail.

With the worsening war situation travel abroad became more complicated. In the autumn of 1916 Einstein visited Holland, but was able to do so only after Lorentz had sent him an official invitation and he had obtained his original Swiss naturalization papers from Zurich.

On the day after arriving at the Ehrenfests' in Leiden, he visited Lorentz in Haarlem, going there with his host.

After dinner, they went up to Lorentz' study where Einstein was ushered into the best and most comfortable chair, which was pulled up to Lorentz' working desk. Einstein was provided with a cigar. Only then did Lorentz begin to question him about the bending of light in a gravitational field. Einstein listened, nodding, puffing happily away at his cigar as he saw how well Lorentz appreciated the tremendous difficulties with which he had had to struggle. Then, as Lorentz continued, Einstein began to puff less frequently. When the older man had finished, Einstein bent over the slip of paper on which Lorentz had been writing mathematical formulas as he spoke. At first he said nothing, merely twisting his finger in the lock of hair over his right ear, an action familiar to those who knew him well.

"Lorentz," wrote Ehrenfest in a note of the visit, "sat smiling at an Einstein completely lost in meditation, exactly the way a father looks at a particularly beloved son—full of secure confidence that the youngster will crack the nut he has given him, but eager to see how. It took quite a while, but suddenly Einstein's head shot up joyfully; he 'had' it. Still a bit of give and take, interrupting one another, a partial disagreement, very quick clarification and a complete mutual understanding, and then both men with beaming eyes skimming over the shining riches of the new theory."

Soon after his return from Leiden to Berlin, Einstein discovered that his old friend Friedrich Adler not only thought along antiwar lines similar to his own but had taken up arms to reinforce them. In 1912 Adler had left Switzerland for Austria and here, desperate at the government's refusal to convene Parliament and thus put its action to the test of public debate, he took what seemed to be the most reasonable logical action. In October, 1916, he walked into the fashionable Hotel Meissel and Schadn and at point-blank range shot dead the Prime Minister, Count Stürgkh.

When Adler was put on trial, Einstein wrote offering to give evidence as a character witness, an offer which Adler, in keeping with his subsequent actions, appears to have loftily declined as being unnecessary. Awaiting trial, he settled down into a succession of prisons and military fortresses to write a long thesis on relativity, *Local Time, System Time, Zone Time.*

On July 14, 1917, Adler wrote to Einstein asking for

advice on his work. Einstein replied cordially, and a typewritten draft of the manuscript soon arrived in Berlin. Meanwhile, other copies were being sent to psychiatrists and physicists who were asked whether Adler was mentally deranged. "The experts, especially the physicists, were placed in a very difficult situation," says Philipp Frank, who himself received a copy. "Adler's father and family desired that this work should be made the basis for the opinion that Adler was mentally deranged. But this would necessarily be highly insulting to the author, since he believed that he had produced an excellent scientific achievement. Moreover, speaking objectively, there was nothing in any way abnormal about it except that his arguments were wrong." Einstein held much the same view, noting that it was based on "very shaky foundations."

Whether or not Adler's critical study of relativity influenced his fate is unclear. But although he was condemned to death, this sentence was commuted to eighteen months, probably the most lenient punishment in history for a Prime Ministerial assasination. The eighteen months do not seem to have been notably rigorous; and a letter to Einstein, written from the military fortress of Stein-an-Donau in July, 1918, reveals a prisoner happily immersed in the problems of science who could end his letter with the comment that in these difficult times conditions were much better inside prison walls than outside them.

Einstein's correspondence with Adler was carried on as he struggled to counteract a serious breakdown that was partly nervous collapse, partly longstanding stomach upset, the latter no doubt exacerbated by the trials of wartime Berlin and a bachelor existence. At first he thought he had cancer and confided the fact to Freundlich, adding that it was unimportant whether or not he died, since his theory of General Relativity had been published and that was what really mattered.* Freundlich induced him to visit a relative of his wife, a Dr. Rosenheim, who quickly diagnosed the stomach trouble which was to worry him for the rest of his life.

The illness was hardly surprising. For years he had been deeply immersed in scientific work which has been de-

*See page 118.

scribed as the greatest intellectual effort of any single human brain. His views on the war were diametrically opposed to those of the men and women around him. In addition, he was living a makeshift existence which gave full rein to the inclination summed up by his doctor friend Janos Plesch. "As his mind knows no limits, so his body follows no set rules," he wrote; "he sleeps until he is wakened; he stays awake until he is told to go to bed; he will go hungry until he is given something to eat; and then he eats until he is stopped." That Einstein, mentally hard-pressed and physically underorganized, should experience a breakdown in wartime Berlin is not to be wondered at; the surprise is that he avoided one so long.

During the first two months of his illness he lost fifty-six pounds in weight. Although he wrote to Lorentz in April that he was getting better, it was summer before he was out and about, and August before he was able to recuperate in Switzerland.

While he was ill Hedwig Born, the young wife of Max Born, became a frequent visitor. "His utter independence and objectivity, and his serene outlook, enabled me to ride up over the awful darkness of those days and to look far beyond the desperate day-to-day conditions," she has said of the war years in the German capital. His "utter independence" was typified by a letter to Ehrenfest in June. "You are complaining about yourself again, and are dissatisfied with yourself," he said. "Just think how little difference it will make in twenty years how one has loitered about on this earth, just so long as one has done nothing base. Whether you write this or that article yourself, or whether someone else writes it, makes very little difference. Stupid you certainly are not, except insofar as you keep thinking about whether or not you are stupid. So away with the hypochondria! Rejoice with your family in the beautiful land of life!"

Isolation from the hopes and fears of ordinary men included isolation from the fear of death itself. "No," Einstein told Frau Born when on one visit during his illness she asked whether he was afraid of dying. "I feel myself so much a part of all life that I am not in the least concerned with the beginning or the end of the concrete existence of any particular person in this unending stream." This, she says, was typical of the unity which he looked for in all nature.

> It is probably not surprising that it was he who helped me to be an objective scientist, and to avoid feeling that the whole thing was impersonal. Modern physics left me standing. Here was only objective truth, which unhappily meant nothing to me, and perhaps the possibility that in the future everything would be expressed scientifically. So I asked Einstein one day, "Do you believe that absolutely everything can be expressed scientifically?" "Yes," he replied, "it would be possible, but it would make no sense. It would be description without meaning—as if you described a Beethoven symphony as a variation of wave pressure." This was a great solace to me.

There was certainly a flaw in Einstein's attempt to regard all human life—even one's own—as merely a bubble on the cosmic stream. To Freundlich, he once confided that there was no one in the world whose death would worry him. "I thought how terrible it was for a man with a wife and two children to believe and say such a thing," says Frau Freundlich. "Then, a year or so afterwards, Einstein's mother died in Berlin, where she had come to spend the last few months of her life with him. In a way I was glad. For Einstein wept, like other men, and I knew that he could really care for someone." And many years later his friend Gustav Bucky wrote: "He believed that nothing really touched him inwardly. But this man who never wanted to show emotion wrote just one sentence to me after my bad illness: 'From now on, I will be thankful every hour of my life that we are left together.' " So often, despite himself, humanity kept breaking in.

Einstein's illness of 1917 had a more important result than stomach trouble. For it at last brought him under the wing, first mothering and eventually matrimonial, of his cousin Elsa. At what point they renewed their youthful acquaintance is vague but it was almost inevitable that he should meet, if only on a family basis, the cousin he remembered from his childhood days in Munich.

Elsa's mother was Pauline Koch's sister, which meant that both Elsa and Albert could claim Cäsar Koch as an uncle, while both were also related rather back along the Einstein family tree. By 1917 Elsa had become Elsa

Lowenthal, a pleasant widow with two daughters, Ilse aged twenty and Margot aged eighteen. In appearance she was comfortable rather than beautiful, and she lacked the curiosity which had at times made Mileva so mentally importunate. "I'm glad my wife doesn't know any science," Einstein later said to a colleague. "My first wife did."

Near-sighted and slightly provincial, Elsa was an easy butt during her husband's triumphal progress through the world for the enemies which her protectiveness made. But she was careful, conscientious, undemanding, and suitably awed by fame—in many ways the ideal wife for the absentminded genius of which Einstein became the epitome. Her character was unconsciously described by Einstein himself when he made a remark to his friend Philipp Frank "based," as Frank says, "on many years of experience." Said Einstein: "When women are in their homes, they are attached to their furniture. They run round it all day long and are always fussing over it. But when I am with a woman on a journey, I am the only piece of furniture that she has available, and she cannot refrain from moving round me all day long and improving something about me."

It is not true that from 1917 onwards Einstein allowed Elsa to make up his mind for him on everything except science, pacifism, and politics. Even outside the three interests of his life, only Einstein made up Einstein's mind. But when he had done so he allowed Elsa to organize details, to implement decisions, to handle the minutiae, and thus allow him to get on with his work. Field Marshal Montgomery once wrote in a privately produced booklet for his troops that "the wise commander . . . will be well advised to withdraw to his tent or caravan after dinner at night and have time for quiet thoughts and reflection." Montgomery had no wish to be worried by unnecessary detail. Neither had Einstein.

During his illness Elsa, not surprisingly, looked after him. In the later stages of his convalescence he joined the Haberlandstrasse ménage. Given the context it was a not unexpected outcome that in 1919, after finally obtaining a divorce from Mileva, he should marry cousin Elsa.

As he slowly recovered in 1917 he decided to finish his recuperation in Switzerland; the Swiss citizen thus exchanged the growing austerity of wartime Berlin for the comparative luxury of a neutral country. He had intended to take the cure at Tarasp in the Lower Engadine but, as he explained to Besso, lack of funds forced him to content himself with a rest at his mother's in Lucerne.

In Switzerland he had hoped to meet Rolland again. When this proved impossible, he wrote instead.

> I am touched by the warm interest you display in a man you have met but once. But for my uncertain health I would not, you may be sure, deny myself the privilege of visiting you. Unfortunately the smallest strain often exacts its toll. The dismal record of mankind has not made me *more* pessimistic than I actually was two years ago. Indeed, I find that the wave of imperialist sentiment that swept over leading circles in Germany has somewhat subsided. Yet, it would still be exceedingly dangerous, I believe, to come to an agreement with the Germany of today.
>
> The victory of 1870 and the subsequent commercial and industrial success in that country have established a religion of power that found in [Heinrich von] Treitschke [German historian] an expression which is not in the least exaggerated. Virtually all men of education have become captivated by this powerful credo which has, in fact, supplanted the ideals of the era of Goethe and Schiller. I know people in Germany whose private lives are guided by utter altruism, yet who awaited the declaration on unrestricted submarine warfare with the utmost impatience. I am firmly convinced that only harsh realities can stem this confusion of minds. These people must be shown that they must respect non-Germans as equals and that, if they are to survive, they must earn the confidence of other countries. Neither by force nor breach of faith will they attain the goals they have set themselves.
>
> I think it is hopeless to struggle against these goals with the weapons of the mind. Those who consider men like Nicolai to be utopians do so with honest conviction. Only facts can cure the misled masses of the delusion that we live for the state, and that the state should, at any price, concentrate all power in its own hands.
>
> To my way of thinking, the best method of resolving this dreary dilemma would be to form an enduring military arbitration pact among America, Britain, France and Russia, with agreements on mutual aid and minimum and maximum limits of military preparedness. Such a treaty should include provisions for most-favored-nation treatment with respect to tariffs. Any nation should be

allowed to join the treaty provided it has a democratically elected parliament in which the chief executive must command a majority. I shall not go beyond this brief outline.

If Germany, which is dependent on foreign markets for the sale of industrial products, were faced with such a stable situation, the view would soon prevail that the path it followed must be abandoned. However, so long as German statesmen are able to hope sooner or later for a shift in the balance of power, there can be no serious expectation that their policy will be changed. As evidence that everything remains as it has always been, I cite the manner in which the recent change in the German chancellorship was staged.

May you find solace in these gloomy times in your inspired creative work.

The vigor of Einstein's anti-German sentiments struck Rolland forcefully. In his diary he pointed out that the policy of crushing Germany had no greater supporters than some prominent Germans. "I note once again," he added, "the extreme injustice, through an excess of justice, to which the most liberal spirits come, vis-à-vis their own country. . . ."

Bearing all this in mind it is at first strange that Einstein should have returned to Berlin as quickly as he did. Zangger wrote to Rolland urging him to induce the visitor to remain in Switzerland. Other friends did the same. But after spending a week with his two sons in Arosa, he returned from the country which he loved to the country he detested.

The unfortunate meeting with Mileva at Easter, 1916, had not been repeated. He had no intention that it should be, and any hint that he was making more than a brief visit to Switzerland might well have brought his wife to his door. He had continued to support her; but now more than ever he had no wish to be brought personally into the negotiations, so far mainly conducted through Besso, the ever-faithful go-between. In a letter written to him on May 15, Einstein confided that he was increasingly hard-pressed financially. Of his total income of about 13,000 marks a year, roughly 7,000 was being sent regularly for the upkeep of his wife and children. Another 600 marks a year went to his mother in Lucerne, and some of his customary additional fees were now disappearing. He had perilously little left to maintain the status of a professor, let alone anything for luxuries or reserves. He had, after all, been obliged to abandon Tarasp for Lucerne.

Soon, however, there was hope of a change. Shortly after his return to Berlin, he told Besso that his address would in future be Haberlandstrasse 5, adding that his move seemed to have taken place already—a turn of phrase which suggests that Elsa was the initiator of the marriage in eighteen months' time.

This marriage was to have little effect on the course of Einstein's purely scientific career, which had reached its climax before 1919. It did, however, affect crucially his impact on the world, as father figure, as oracle, as the man whose support was for years a useful weapon in the hands of any group ingenious enough to win it. For without the care and protecting intervention of this kindly figure—placid and housewifely, of no intellectual pretensions but with a practiced mothering ability which made her the ideal organizer of genius—two things would almost certainly have happened. He would have cracked under the strain of unrelenting publicity and public demands, and withdrawn from pacifism, Zionism, and socialism, into the shell where he carried on his scientific work. He would also have made a fool of himself more often than he did, have issued more statements that he had to retract, signed more documents without reading them properly, and been used more frequently by men of ill will.

From the first, Elsa knew the part that had been cut out for her. "All I can do is to look after his outside affairs, take business matters off his shoulders, and take care that he is not interrupted in his work," she said during his visit to England in 1921. "It is enough to be a means of communication between him and all sorts of human beings." And a decade later, describing her role to Dr. Chaim Tschernowitz, the Jewish scholar who was visiting their house outside Berlin, she said: "When the Americans come to my house they carry away details about Einstein and his life, and about me they say incidentally: he has a good wife, who is very hospitable, and offers a fine table." The point of her remark was not to be missed, says Dr. Tschernowitz. "Einstein might be the lion among thinkers, but this good woman felt, and rightly so, that to a large extent the world owed him to her, who watched over him as one might over a child." Einstein was aware of these possibilities. Thus in the summer of 1917 he willingly became the bohemian setpiece of a bourgeois household.

It was part of his genius that he could isolate himself from his surroundings, and this was never more necessary than in the apartment of No. 5, Haberlandstrasse. On the dark green wallpaper of the main sitting room there hung the expected portrait of Frederick the Great, looking down without a smile on the heavy immobility of the Biedermeier furniture, on the corner cabinets stocked with porcelain, on the huge round central table with the starched white tablecloth edged with crochet, on Schiller and Goethe, the white eyes of their white busts firmly fixed on each other from opposite sides of the room. Beyond lay the library, its walls soon to be ornamented by a large framed picture of Michael Faraday. Into this epitome of all things that were proper came Albert Einstein, unchangeable by the pleas of Elsa, happy to be shepherded by her through the mundane necessities of everyday life, grateful for the protecting shield which she was to interpose between himself and the overcurious world, yet determined to go his own way in the things that mattered.

Before the situation could be regularized, however, Mileva had to agree to a divorce. This she did within less than a year. Negotiations were under way by the early summer of 1918 when Einstein sent through Besso details of how he would be prepared to support her and the children. During these negotiations the question of the Nobel Prize was raised. It is not quite certain who first suggested that the interest from the Prize, then some 30,000 Swedish kroner, would be sufficient to keep Einstein's family in at least modest circumstances, but it appears to have been Mileva. If so, it is a striking tribute to her faith in him.

Early in July, Einstein received the first divorce papers. Then he had to give evidence before a tribunal in Berlin. And after that an ever-growing dossier had to be returned to Zurich. All this he took lightly enough, acknowledging receipt of the first papers with the exclamation "Til Eulenspiegel!" and later noting to Besso that the divorce was entertaining all those in Berlin who were in the know.

As the legal moves continued and as Einstein heard from friends in Holland that the British were planning to carry out a test of his theory during the eclipse of 1919, the war situation began to change dramatically. After the failure of the great German offensive in the spring, the influence of the United States began decisively to affect the balance of forces. On the Western front, preparations continued for the Allied offensive which in August, 1918, ruptured the German front for the first time in four years. In September, the Allied Expeditionary Force at Salonika broke through the Bulgarian lines, and the following month British forces gained a decisive victory over the Turks, those redoubtable German allies in the Middle East. On November 9, the Kaiser abdicated. Karl Ebert, the staunch, imperturbable saddler's son, was handed the chancellorship and at 2 P.M. the Republic was proclaimed from the steps of the Reichstag.

Two days later, as the maroons boomed out the Armistice, Einstein wrote to his mother in Switzerland: "The great event has happened."

For him, as for other Germans of like mind, the Republic and the Armistice were twin trumpets heralding the millennium. Now, they fondly imagined, they would have help in the task of leading their misguided countrymen back into the peaceful ways from which they had been diverted half a century earlier. Perhaps so. But even Einstein, optimistic as ever, might have thought twice as he considered his old friend Planck. A few weeks before the fall of the Kaiser, the Bund Neues Vaterland, which had continued an underground existence since being banned by the authorities in February, 1916, came above ground once more. Einstein sent Planck a copy of the opening declaration and asked for his support. But this would mean a demand for the Kaiser's abdication; Planck replied that his oath to the Emperor made support impossible. No such problems worried Albert Einstein, who threw himself wholeheartedly on the side of the Republic. He was, he wrote to his mother on a second postcard on the day of the Armistice, "very happy at the way things are developing." Shortly afterwards, he himself was to take his part.

With the formation of workers' and soldiers' councils which followed the disintegration of law and order on

November 11, there had come a similar move in the University of Berlin. Here one of the first actions of the student council was to depose and lock up the rector and other members of the staff. The remaining members of the administration knew Einstein's left-wing views and turned to him for help. Would he intervene on their behalf with the students?

Einstein telephoned Max Born and another colleague, the psychologist Max Wertheimer, and the three men made their way to the Reichstag where the student council was meeting.

As soon as Einstein was recognized, all doors were opened, and the trio was escorted to a room where the student council was in session. The chairman, before dealing with their business, asked Einstein what he thought of the new regulations for students. He did not think very much of them, a reaction which caused the council to decide that the problem presented by the three professors was not one for them but, instead, for the new government.

In the Reich Chancellor's Palace, amid a contradiction of Imperial footmen and delegations from the new workers' and soldiers' councils, the three men were received by President Ebert. The fate of the Reich itself still hung in the balance and he could spare them little time. But he wrote for them a few words to the appropriate minister.

A quarter of a century later Einstein recalled: "How naïve we were, even as men forty years old!! I can only laugh when I think about it. Neither of us realized how much more powerful is instinct compared to intelligence."

At the time, November, 1918, Einstein's naïveté mattered little. He was, within the comparatively small world of physicists, a creature of extraordinary power and imagination. Outside it, he was still unknown. This situation was to be dramatically altered within the year.

CHAPTER 8

THE SENSORIUM OF GOD

The autumn of 1918 which brought Germany bitter and apparently irretrievable defeat also brought the Republic. To Einstein this was a gleam of hope in the darkness, the only one which held out a promise for the future as the Empire dissolved between the hammer of the Allied armies on the west and the anvil of emergent communism to the east. Just as he now believed there was political hope for a country he had so long considered beyond hope, so was there at last the prospect of proof or disproof for the General Theory of Relativity over whose difficulties he had triumphed while the war went on.

In Berlin, four years earlier, he had settled down to work in earnest. First he had expectantly looked forward to the results which Freundlich and his party would bring back from the Crimea. Yet even had their efforts not been snuffed out by the war, they would have provided experimental confirmation only for a theory which was incomplete. For while Einstein was now convinced of the revolutionary idea that gravity was not force but a property of space itself, he had not yet been able to construct the mathematical framework within which it could be described. He continued to wrestle with this task as his colleagues went to war, Haber struggled with his poison gas production, and his English friend Lindemann reported at the Royal Aircraft Factory, Farnborough, as a temporary technical assistant at £3 (then $15) a week.

After the failure of the Russian expedition to the Crimea and Freundlich's return to Berlin, he pressed on with the theoretical work for every available minute, letting slide everything that would slide. During this period Freundlich, entering Einstein's study, saw hanging from the ceiling a large meat hook bearing a thick sheaf of letters. These, Einstein explained, he had no time to answer. Freundlich, asking what he did when the hook was filled up, was answered by two words: "Burn them."

The agony continued into the summer of 1915 and into the autumn. "This month," he wrote to Sommerfeld on November 28, 1915, "I have lived through the most exacting period of my life; and it would be true to say that it has also been the most fruitful. Writing letters has been out of the question. I realized that up till now my field equations of gravitation had been entirely devoid of foundation." Then, he went on, he had started again, chosen a fresh line of attack, and had finally triumphed. Sommerfeld was not immediately impressed, a fact which induced Einstein to send him a postcard: "You will become convinced of the General Theory of Relativity as soon as you have studied it. Therefore I will not utter a words in its defense."

Sommerfeld did not have long to wait. There soon appeared Volume 49 of the *Annalen der Physik*. It contained, on pages 769 to 822, "The Foundation of the General Theory of Relativity." "The theory appeared to me then, and it still does," said Born, "the greatest feat of human thinking about nature, the most amazing combination of philosophical penetration, physical intuition, and mathematical skill. But its connections with experience were slender. It appealed to me like a great work of art, to be enjoyed and admired from a distance."

The General Theory, which brought the first realization "that space is not merely a background for events, but possesses an autonomous structure," was to be the starting point for an even larger collection of papers and developments than the Special Theory. Einstein wrote some of them, and for another forty years he was, necessarily, deeply involved in the arguments about the universe that the General Theory unleashed. Yet in some ways he saw this as the cornerstone of the arch he had started to build more than a decade previously and he himself as now free for other things. From this time onwards, according to Wolfgang Pauli—aged only sixteen in 1916 but within five years to be writing one of the classic expositions of the General Theory—Einstein was often to comment: "For the rest of my life I want to reflect on what light is."

Whereas Special Relativity had brought under one set of laws the electromagnetic world of Maxwell and Newtonian mechanics as far as they applied to bodies in uniform relative motion, the General Theory did the same thing for bodies with the accelerated relative motion epitomized in the acceleration of gravity. But first it had been necessary for Einstein to develop the true nature of gravity from his principle of equivalence. Newton had seen it as a force operating instantaneously over limitless distances; Einstein's conception was very different, even though in practice most of his results approximated very closely to those of Newton. Basically, he proposed that gravity was a function of matter itself and that its effects were transmitted between contiguous portions of space-time, rather as the effects of a shunting engine are transmitted down a line of stationary railway cars. Where matter exists, so does energy; the greater the mass of matter involved, the greater the effect of the energy which can be transmitted.

In addition, gravity, as he had postulated as far back as 1911, affected light—the arbiter of straight lines and the wave emanation whose passage over a unit of distance gives a unit of time—exactly as it affected material particles. Thus the universe which Newton had seen, and for which he had constructed his apparently impeccable mechanical laws, was not the real universe but only what he had seen through the misleading spectacles produced by gravity. The law which appeared to have worked out so well had been drawn up for a universe that did not exist, as though a tailor had made a suit for a man he had seen only in a distorting mirror. This was the logical followup from the principle of equivalence and from Einstein's assumption that gravity was basically a field characteristic of matter. That Newton's suit fitted the real man tolerably well was hardly the point.

Einstein's paper gave not only a corrected picture of the universe but also a fresh set of mathematical laws by which its details could be described. These were of two kinds. There were the structural laws, which dealt with the relationships between the mass of a gravitating body and the gravitational field which the very existence of the mass automatically created; and there were the laws of motion, which could be used to describe the paths taken by moving bodies in gravitational fields. These laws utilized Riemannian geometry, the need for which had been the direct result of the assumption that light would be deflected by a gravitational field and that the shortest distance between two points in such a field would not, when viewed from outside it, be coincident with a straight line. For there were certain consequences by assuming that what appeared as a straight line-of-sight to anywhere in the universe, as ramrod true as any sergeant-major could wish, was in fact as curved as the route followed by a ship steaming round the world on the shortest path from *A* to *B* and that the exact curvature would depend on the gravitational field, and therefore the mass of matter, which was involved.

One consequence is evident from the simple consideration of a globe. It is that Euclidean geometry, in which the angles in a triangle always add up to two right angles, is not relevant for a triangle formed by the equator and two lines of longitude. Those running from the equator to the North Pole through Greenwich and New Orleans, for instance, enclose with the equator not two but three right angles—even though equator and lines of longitude follow the shortest routes from point to point. As Einstein allegedly explained to his younger son, Eduard: "When the blind beetle crawls over the surface of a globe, he doesn't notice that the track he has covered is curved. I was lucky enough to have spotted it."

Einstein had seen that his assumption of a curvature of light in a gravitational field meant that Euclidean geometry, satisfactory enough when coping with the small distances of everyday life, had to be replaced by something more sophisticated when dealing with the universe. The geographer and the surveyor have a comparable problem, selecting one projection which is satisfactory for the small areas of topographical maps and another projection for the vastly larger areas of regional or national maps. Einstein searched about for some time before he found what he wanted. In Prague, on George Pick's advice, he had studied the work of Ricci and Levi-Civita. Back in Zurich he had worked with Marcel Grossmann to make the preliminary sketch of the General Theory which appeared in 1913. But it was only when he turned back to Riemann, the young German who had died almost half a century earlier, that he found what he wanted.

Riemann was the mathematician whose masterpiece, *On the Hypotheses Which Determine the Foundations of Geometry (Über die Hypotheseen, welche der Geometrie zu Grunde liegen)*, Einstein had studied a decade earlier with his companions of the Olympia Academy in Berne. Handicapped by a shy character, dogged by bad luck and the bad health which killed him at forty, Riemann had been a brilliant product of nineteenth century Göttingen. At the age of twenty-four he had speculated that "a complete, well-rounded mathematical theory can be established which progresses from the elementary laws for individual points to the processes given to us in the plenum ('continuously filled space') of reality, without distinction between gravitation, electricity, magnetism, or thermostatics." This apparent rejection of "action at a distance" in favor of the field theory was dramatically in advance of its time. Yet it was merely a prelude to the construction of a non-Euclidean geometry which, in the words of the late E. T. Bell, "taught mathematicians to disbelieve in *any* geometry, or in *any* space, as a *necessary* mode of human perception. It was the last nail in the coffin of absolute space, and the first in that of the 'absolutes' of nineteenth century physics."

In Riemann's geometry, parallel lines do not exist, the angles of a triangle do not add up to 180°, and perpendiculars to the same line converge, a conception which is easier to understand in an age of worldwide air travel than when the University of Göttingen was the intellectual pride of the Kingdom of Hanover. In Riemann's world the shortest lines joining any two points are not straight lines but geodesics and, a corollary self-evident even to nonmathematicians, the length of the shortest distance between any two points on such a curved surface is determined by a formula different from that determining the length of a line on a plane surface.

Einstein used Riemannian geometry to create equations by which the movements of the stars in their courses and the structure of the universe itself could be described. But this was followed by the introduction of a phrase well enough understood by mathematicians but almost as confusing to the layman as the definition of time as the fourth "dimension." This was "curvature of space," part of that terminology which Sir Edmund Whittaker later described as "so well established that we can never hope to change it, regrettable though it is, and which has been responsible for a great deal of popular misconception." Mathematicians apply the word "curved" to any space whose geometry was not Euclidean. "It is an unfortunate custom," Whittaker went on,

> because curvature, in the sense of bending, is a meaningless term except when the space is immersed in another space, whereas the property of being non-Euclidean is an intrinsic property which has nothing to do with immersion. However, nothing can be done but to utter a warning that what mathematicians understand by the term "curvature" is not what the word connotes in ordinary speech; what the mathematician means is simply that the relations between the mutual distances of the points are different from the relations which obtain in Euclidean geometry. Curvature (in the mathematical sense) has nothing to do with the *shape* of the space—whether it is bent or not—but is defined solely by the metric, that is to say, the way in which "distance" is defined. It is not the space that is curved, but the geometry of the space.

All this, as pointed out by Max Talmey, the Jewish student who had first introduced the young Einstein to the physical sciences in Munich, could be attributed not only to lack of communication between mathematicians and nonmathematicians, but also to imperfections in translation from the language in which all Einstein's original papers, as well as a great number of others on general relativity, have been written. In German, as Talmey says, one cannot form from the adjective "uneuklidisch" a noun corresponding to the English substantive "non-Euclideanism," formable from the adjective "non-Euclidean." "Nichteuklidisch" is used, but many German authors, in Talmey's words, used the expression "Taum-Krummung," space-curvature, to denote that quality which, in the end, is due to a straight line being interminable in a gravitational field. English writers followed their example although they did not need to do this.

"Space-curvature," the renewed claim that light did not go straight, the idea that the universe could only be viewed from the earth through the distorting spectacles of gravity, would all have combined to create an immediate sensation had Europe been at peace. As it was, only a narrow path led through the minefields of the war from Einstein in the Berlin of 1916 to the shattering first proof of the theory in 1919.

Einstein himself was well aware that proof would not be easy. Two and a half centuries earlier Newton, pressed on the question of whether gravity was or was not exercised instantaneously, admitted that he could see no way of solving the problem experimentally. To do so would require, he commented, "the sensorium of God." Einstein, if challenged, would no doubt have been torn between modesty and a full awareness of what he was accomplishing. For despite the fundamentally different concepts of gravity put forward by Newton and himself, the differences in experimental results would in most cases be slight and thus difficult to detect. As Einstein himself wrote: "The old theory is a special limiting case of the new one. If the gravitational forces are comparatively weak, the old Newtonian law turns out to be a good approximation to the new laws of gravitation. Thus all observations which support the classical theory also support the General Relativity theory. We regain the old theory from the higher level of the new one." Proof, then, would most likely be found in a field where the gravitational force was strong and where some deviation from the Newtonian law had already been noted.

Just such a prospect seemed to be offered by the planet Mercury. In the two hundred years which had followed Newton, the discoveries of science had revealed a succession of facts which had each fallen into place in his grand design. Not only the passage of the moon round the earth and the curving flight of the cricket ball, but the flow of the tides and the fiery trails of the comets were shown to follow the orderly paths which his universal scheme demanded. One feature of this had been the repetition of the planetary circuits round the sun. Venus and Mercury, Mars, Jupiter, and Uranus, together with their orbiting colleagues, followed their same elliptical paths with only insignificant change, tracing out through the heavens circuits that appeared to remain the same throughout the centuries.

The first man to suspect that this might not be so was Dominique Arago, the fiery French republican from whom not even Louis Napoleon could extract an oath of allegiance. In the early 1840s Arago proposed to Urbain Jean Joseph Leverrier, a young French astronomer, that he should carefully analyze the motions of Mercury. The result was surprising. For Leverrier's figures showed clearly that the perihelion of Mercury—the point on its elliptical path which is nearest to the sun—advanced by a specific amount each year. The rate was extremely small, but even after the effects of the other planets had been taken into account the advance still remained some 43 seconds of arc each century. Thus the path of Mercury round the sun was not a static closed ellipse, but a nearly closed circuit, slowly gyrating and coming back to its original position once every 3,000,000 years.

This lack of coincidence with the path planned out for it by Newton in his grand scheme profoundly distressed astronomers, and some desperate expedients were put forward in an effort to correlate fact and theory. Leverrier himself decided that the anomaly would be accounted for if there existed an as yet unseen planet, only 1,000 miles across and circling the sun at a distance of 19,000,000 miles. In the hope of discovery, this was named Vulcan; but despite careful searching of the skies at each subsequent eclipse no such planet could be located. From Asaph Hall, the discoverer of the satellites of Mars, there came an even more ingenious proposal: that in the Newtonian formula concerned, the exponent 2 might be altered to 2.0000001612. The suggested trick had something in common with that of the "scientist," armed with chisel and tape measure, who was found by Flinders Petrie to be "adjusting" a side of the Great Pyramid "which did not quite conform to the length required by his theory." As Einstein was to comment, the discrepancy in Mercury's orbit "could be explained by means of classical mechanics only on the assumption of hypotheses which have little probability, and which were devised solely for this purpose." So much was true even after fullest consideration had been given to the various influences which the planets as a group exercised on each individual in the group, the astronomical problem of "perturbations," as it was called.

The discrepancy had worried Einstein for years. As far

back as 1907 he had written to his colleague Conrad Habicht that he was "busy on a relativistic theory of the gravitation law with which I hope to account for the still unexplained secular changes of the perihelion movement of Mercury." Now with Riemannian geometry the perihelion of a planet moving round a central attracting body in a nearly circular orbit would advance. The amount would not be great, but Mercury's enormous speed, comparatively small size, and closeness to the intense gravitational field of the sun might yield a significant figure. Einstein applied the equations from the General Theory to the motion of Mercury. The results showed that the perihelion should advance about 0.1″ for each complete orbital revolution of the planet. Roughly 420 such revolutions were made in a century. Thus the secular advance of Mercury's perihelion each century as deduced from the General Theory was in fact almost exactly the figure provided by Leverrier's observations. The theory thus, in Einstein's words to the daughter of Simon Newcomb, who spent much of his life in producing more accurate orbital tables for the moon and the planets, "completed the work of the calculus of perturbations and brought about a full agreement between theory and experience."

Einstein announced this result before he had completed his General Theory, reading his paper on it to the Prussian Academy of Sciences in the autumn of 1915. A few weeks later he revealed his feelings to Ehrenfest. "Can you imagine my joy at the feasibility of the general covariance, with the result that the equations of the perihelion movement of Mercury prove correct? I was speechless for several days with excitement." But it was not the excitement of surprise. Asked whether he had been worried about the outcome of the calculations, he replied: "Such questions did not lie in my path. The result could not be otherwise than correct. I was only concerned with putting the answer into a lucid form. I did not for one second doubt that it would agree with observation. There was no sense in getting excited about what was self-evident." However confident he may have been, he was delighted when shortly after the publication of his own Mercury paper the astronomer K. Schwarzschild published a description of how to obtain the same results in a far more elegant manner.

The use of the field equations of the General Theory to supply figures which were unlikely to be coincidental, and which solved one of the most stubborn riddles of astronomy, was cited by Einstein in his paper of 1916. The figures certainly supported his theory but they did not exactly give proof; the Mercury anomaly had been known for years, the General Theory had merely provided one satisfactory explanation and there might be others. The two remaining possibilities for a test put forward by Einstein in 1911 both concerned the behavior of light in a gravitational field and both had one thing in common. They concerned phenomena which had never been either known or suspected; and if they could be shown to exist, they would therefore be in a totally different class. They would in fact be comparable to the prediction of a new planet in the sky just where Neptune was later discovered, or to Mendeleyev's forecast of the undiscovered elements in the Periodic Table. They would by implication give substantial proof that in the General Theory there was to be found a more accurate description of the universe.

The more esoteric of the two tests concerned the effect of gravity on the frequency of light. The mathematical route followed by Einstein led him to assume that an atom radiating in a strong gravitational field would vibrate more slowly than in a weak gravitational field. For if time as well as space was inevitably altered by the deflection of gravity then the vibration of atoms, those impeccable timepieces of the universe, would also be affected. But the frequency of vibration governs the color of light radiated, and an atom radiating in a strong gravitational field would emit light a little closer to the red end of the spectrum than when it was radiating a weaker gravitational field. Such displacements had already been noted by L. F. Jewell in 1897 and by other workers early in the twentieth century, but they had been explained as entirely due to "pressure effects." These did indeed exist, and their presence increased the difficulty of isolating as a separate characteristic "the Einstein shift," as it was soon called. This was extremely small—so small according to Einstein's calculations that it was unlikely to be observed even if the gravitational field of the sun were used as a test bench. However, there are bodies in the universe producing immensely stronger fields than the sun, and a decade after

Einstein's prediction the huge gravitational field of the "white dwarf" star near Sirius—so dense that a cubic inch of it would weigh more than half a ton on earth—was utilized. And almost half a century after Einstein's paper, Robert Oppenheimer was able to write of the Einstein shift: "The most precise and, I think, by far the most beautiful example of this is a recent experiment conducted at Harvard in which light was simply allowed to fall down from the third floor to the basement of the Physics Building. One could see how much bluer it had become; one part in 10^{14}; not very much."

No such possibilities existed in 1916, and readers of Einstein's paper turned naturally to the other proposed method of testing the theory. This was the method which Freundlich had been going to adopt in the Crimea in August, 1914: the observation of light from the stars during an eclipse to discover whether it was deflected when passing through the gravitational field of the sun.

The summer of 1916 was hardly a propitious period for devoting men, money, materials, and thought to any scientific subject unless it seemed likely to help the war effort. Britain and Germany were locked in a struggle whose outcome no one could yet foresee, and American entry into the war was still nearly a year away. All effort was harnessed to the task of winning; in Germany the Kaiser Wilhelm Institutes and the University of Berlin were on national service; and elsewhere the situation was similar. Rutherford from Britain and Langevin from France were deeply engaged on antisubmarine work. Pure science, it seemed, must await the coming of peace.

In these circumstances, one of Einstein's acts was to be of crucial importance. On receiving copies of *Annalen der Physik* containing his paper on the General Theory, he sent one to Willem de Sitter, professor of astronomy in the University of Leiden and a foreign correspondent of the Royal Astronomical Society in London. De Sitter passed on his copy to the Society's secretary, Arthur Eddington, who was now drawn into a developing drama. The long train of events set in motion by de Sitter and continued by Eddington was to have repercussions quite as formidable in their own way as the bloody battles being waged on the Western front.

Arthur Eddington was in 1916 Plumian Professor of Astronomy at Cambridge, and director of the university observatory. A Quaker, with the Friends' typical mixture of bold humanity and mystic faith, he had been a Senior Wrangler, and his *Stellar Movements and the Structure of the Universe,* published in 1914, had created the new subject of stellar dynamics. He was still only thirty-four and it was confidently predicted of him that great promise would be followed by even greater performance. As secretary of the Royal Astronomical Society, Eddington had the task of producing the Society's *Monthly Notices* and this involved close scrutiny of Einstein's paper which arrived from Holland, a scrutiny which soon convinced him of its importance to his own cosmological investigations.

The important factor in 1916 was Eddington's superb mathematical ability, which "enabled him not only to grasp the argument, but very soon to master the absolute differential calculus of Ricci and Levi-Civita, and to use tensors as a tool in developing contributions of his own." One result was that he asked de Sitter to write for the Royal Astronomical Society's *Monthly Notices* three long articles explaining the General Theory. These articles, the second produced after Einstein had held several conversations with de Sitter in Leiden, introduced Einstein's new theory to the non-German-speaking world. Their importance in what was to follow cannot be overestimated. "Even if Einstein has not explained the origin of inertia," concluded the second article,

> his theory represents an enormous progress over the physics of yesterday. Perceiving the irrelevance of the representation by coordinates in which our science is clothed, he has penetrated to the deeper realities which lay hidden behind it and not only has he entirely explained the exception and universal nature of gravitation by the principle of the identity of gravitation and inertia, but he has laid bare intimate connections between branches of science which up to now were considered as entirely independent from each other, and has thus made an important step towards the unity of nature. Finally his theory not only explains all that the old theory of relativity could explain (experiment of Michelson, etc.), but *without any new hypothesis or empirical constant,* it explains the anomalous motion of the perihelion of Mer-

cury, and it predicts a number of phenomena which have not yet been observed. It has thus at once proved to be a very powerful instrument of discovery.

Even in the gloomy concentration of the war, scientists were soon speculating on how to investigate the "number of phenomena which have not yet been observed." Sir Frank Dyson, the Astronomer Royal, ordered a study to be made of photographs taken during the eclipse of 1905 in the hope that something might be discovered from them, but the search was unsuccessful. Lindemann and his father contributed a paper to the *Monthly Notices* on the daylight photography of stars and concluded: "It is suggested that experiments . . . be undertaken by some observatory possessing a suitable instrument, and enjoying a fine climate, with a view to testing Einstein's theory." The possibility had been rejected as impracticable by Hale before the 1914 eclipse, and even if a suitable observatory could have been found and persuaded to do the work it seems unlikely that current technology could have produced useful results. There were other suggestions, but none which seemed likely to be successful.

However, help was at hand. Another solar eclipse would take place on a day when the stellar background would be ideal. If the problem of testing the General Theory "had been put forward at some other period of history," as Eddington later pointed out, "it might have been necessary to wait some thousands of years for a total eclipse of the sun to happen on the lucky date." The wait was only three years.

That this opportunity was seized by the British was due not only to Eddington's personal enthusiasm for relativity but to his influence on Dyson. Sir Frank was to become a firm friend of Einstein, and the latter's portrait by Rothenstein for long hung in a place of honor in Flamsteed House, the Astronomer Royal's official home at Greenwich. Throughout his career he had shown a special interest in solar eclipses, and despite the uncertainties of war he was anxious to make full use of the opportunities provided by 1919. But it was nevertheless largely due to Eddington's influence that Dyson so quickly emphasized the opportunities for testing the General Theory that the eclipse would offer. De Sitter's articles, which had whetted the scientific appetite, had been published largely as a result of Eddington's initiative, and soon afterwards Eddington was commissioned by the Physical Society to prepare his own account of what the General Theory was and signified. The *Report on the Relativity Theory of Gravitation* that followed was published in 1918 and later expanded as *The Mathematical Theory of Relativity*. Long before this, however, Dyson had moved into action.

On May 29, 1919, the sun would be seen in a field of stars of quite exceptional brightness, part of the Hyades group which lies at the head of the constellation Taurus. In a note from Greenwich dated March 2, 1917, and printed in the *Monthly Notices,* Dyson drew attention to "the unique opportunities" which this would offer. "There are an unusual number of bright stars, and with weather conditions as good as those at Sfax in 1905—which were by no means perfect—no less than thirteen stars might be obtained," he wrote, adding that these "should serve for an ample verification, or the contrary," of Einstein's theory. The track of the eclipse would unfortunately cross the Atlantic, but he had been in touch with the secretary of the Royal Geographical Society, who would tell him how many observing stations might be used, and he had "brought the matter forward so that arrangements for observing at as many stations as possible may be made at the earliest possible moment."

These plans were made as the U-boat blockade was tightening on Britain and the Russian front collapsing, as American entry into the war was still problematical, and peace remained below any visible horizon. Yet they typified not so much British isolation from reality as the same sort of lofty confidence seen a quarter of a century later when, with the Germans hammering at the gates of Stalingrad and the Eighth Army with its backs to the Nile, the Allied Ministers of Education in exile met in London to plan what eventually became UNESCO.

During 1917, as British plans for the eclipse expeditions went ahead, Einstein published two more important papers. In one of them he returned to the radiation problem which had occupied him intermittently since 1905; in the other he used the General Theory to give a picture of the universe which was not only important in its own scientific right, but added a spectacular significance to the theory itself.

In the radiation paper, in which he derived Planck's original quantum law from a different starting point, he suggested that as well as spontaneous emission and absorption there could also take place the process of stimulated emission. In 1917 this seemed mainly of theoretical interest; forty years later it was utilized to provide the maser and laser of modern technology. In addition to postulating this fresh process, Einstein also stressed that the momentum transfer which took place with emission was directional. The importance of this, as far as Einstein was concerned, lay in the admission that had to be made at the same time—that the direction was "in the present state of the theory . . . determined only by 'chance.' " It is significant that Einstein put quotation marks round "chance." He still believed that what had to be attributed to chance in the current state of knowledge would one day be explicable on causal grounds. How strongly he continued to feel about this was shown when he wrote to Born seven years later. "I find the idea quite intolerable that an electron exposed to radiation should choose *of its own free will* not only its moment to jump off, but also its direction. In that case, I would rather be a cobbler, or even an employee in a gaming house, than a physicist. . . ." Yet it was his paper of 1917 which provided chapter and verse for just such an idea.

Meanwhile, his development of the General Theory continued. Just how great were the demands made on him is indicated in a letter to Ehrenfest in February. "I have once more broken a little ground in the gravitation theory and by so doing have run the risk of being placed in a madhouse," this went. "I hope you have none in Leiden so that I can pay you a visit without running any risk. What a pity we don't live on Mars so that we could observe the futile activities of human beings only through a telescope. Our Jehovah no longer needs to send down a rain of pitch and sulfur: he has turned modern and automatically devised this activity."

The paper which occasioned this outburst was shorter than the final outline of the General Theory but was in some ways almost as important. For while the details of the General Theory were to remain in dispute over the years, and the first rapture created by the results of the British expeditions was to be qualified by later observations, the importance of Einstein's potentially explosive paper of 1917 was to remain undisputed—even though its suppositions were to be questioned with a brusqueness which has not affected the General Theory itself. The paper was called, quite simply, "Cosmological Considerations on the General Theory of Relativity." What it did was to utilize the equations of the General Theory to speculate on the physical extent of the universe; and in so doing, it is generally accepted, to found the modern study of cosmology. Even for Einstein, this was playing for high stakes.

His reason for starting on this controversial game was a very practical one. The idea that the system of fixed stars should ultimately determine the existence of centrifugal force was an important part of the conceptual background to the General Theory of Relativity. This was not a new idea and had been put forward in general terms by both Berkeley and Mach. However, with his field equations Einstein had given a numerical quantity to account for this action of the surrounding stars. He had linked the distant twinkle of the night sky with the homely gravity of everyday life and one question quickly followed: Were there enough stars in the universe to produce the centrifugal force which could be observed and recorded? The need to answer this question inexorably drew Einstein into thinking about a specific extension of the question to which he was devoting his life. He now needed to know not merely how God had made the world but also about its actual extent. Thus the relativistic cosmology which Einstein now initiated was, as Hubble later described it, a natural offshoot of the General Theory, a "superstructure including other principles." If it was subsequently found to be wanting, it did not necessarily invalidate the General Theory itself.

The comfortable idea of a finite universe with the earth at its center had been suspect from the beginning of the scientific renaissance and had finally been abandoned with the coming of Newton. For with Newton it had seemed clear that a finite material universe would tend to collapse in upon itself much as it had been suspected, before Bohr's prescribed electron orbits, that particles circling an atomic nucleus would inevitably be drawn down towards it. The new universe of Newton's day was something nobler if more impersonal, an infinitude of stars scattered through infinite Euclidean space, an idea that survived against only sporadic objections, usually overcome by special pleading. With the nineteenth century, and the growing interest in astronomy, an alternative was put forward: a finite universe which existed, islandlike, in the immensities of infinite and "empty" space. But all such blueprints had one thing in common: each represented a static universe whose size and contents remained unchanging in quantity throughout the endless passage of time.

As Einstein wrestled with the cosmological implications of the General Theory, the first of these alternatives, the earth-centered universe of the Middle Ages, was effectively ruled out; but both the others were considered. Both were rejected. The reasons for rejecting the Newtonian universe can be simply understood, although in the light of current knowledge about the recession of the galaxies they appear rather dated. For it seemed mathematically clear that the effect of an infinite number of stars would, even at infinite distances, produce an infinitely strong force whose effect would be to give the stars a high velocity through the universe. But observation indicated that compared with the speed of light the velocities of stars were small. Thus it was essential that the stars should be finite in number.

The possibility of a finite "island-universe" in an infinitude of empty space was ruled out for slightly more complex reasons. One was based on a theory of the way in which particles—or stars—would distribute themselves in random movement, and which appeared to make an "island-universe" impossible. Another reason sprang from the fact that since the curvature of space was dependent on the distribution of matter, space would be curved in the vicinity of the island-universe but Euclidean in the empty space of infinity beyond. This in turn meant that bodies beyond the island-universe would move in straight lines, according to Newton's law of inertia, since inertia was itself equivalent to gravitational force, which would not be present.

Einstein was therefore forced to consider whether it was possible to conceive of a universe that would contain a finite number of stars distributed equally through unbounded space. His answer to the apparent contradiction lay in the idea that matter itself produced the curvature of space. For in the "Einstein world," as it soon became known, the curvature produced by matter turned space back on itself so that a ray of light, moving in a straight line in terrestrial terms, would return to its starting point after circling the universe: a universe whose three dimensions contained as finite a number of stars as the number of names on the two-dimensional surface of a globe, but whose surface was itself as unbounded as that of the same globe. These stars were, moreover, distributed equally, as though the names were spread out equally across the surface of a globe. This was an essential if the "Einstein world" was to conform to Einstein's own inner intuition that just as the laws of nature must be the same for all observers, so must the view of the universe. "There must be no favored location in the universe, no center, no boundary; all must see the universe alike," as Hubble put it. "And, in order to ensure this situation, the cosmologist postulates spatial isotropy and spatial homogeneity, which is his way of saying that the universe must be pretty much alike everywhere and in all directions." This universe included local irregularities of curvature, comparable to the hills and valleys on a world globe built in relief; yet it also had an overall curvature, like the overall curvature of the earth itself which produces a terrestrial world with a radius of some four thousand miles.

With the help of the General Theory, two equations could be obtained which included only two unknowns—the curvature of space and the total mass of the particles making up the universe. It was a comparatively simple matter to provide estimates for the mass; thus the universe of the "Cosmological Considerations" of 1917 was a universe to which a size might be given, however rough an estimate this was.

"The whole universe," Einstein said to his friend Alexander Moszkowski in Berlin,

> has a diameter of about 100 million light years, in round numbers. That amounts to about 700 trillion miles [this is the British trillion of 10^{18}]. It follows from the mathematical calculations which I have presented in "Cosmological

> Considerations Arising from the General Theory of Relativity," in which the figure I have just quoted is not given. The exact figure is a minor question. What is important is to recognize that the universe may be regarded as a closed continuum as far as distance measurements are concerned.

Einstein had achieved a plausible result. But he had done so only by a piece of mathematical juggling which was to have an interesting history. This was the introduction of a fresh term into the field equations of the General Theory, the "cosmological constant" which represents a repulsive force which, contrary to ordinary gravitational attraction, increases with the distance between objects. The value given to this term determines the character of the universe which is produced, and from the first it was a matter of controversy. Einstein justified its use when he gave "the theoretical view of the actual universe" at the end of his 1917 paper. "The curvature of space is variable in time and place according to the distribution of matter, but we may roughly approximate to it by means of a spherical space," he wrote.

> At any rate, this view is logically consistent, and from the standpoint of the General Theory of Relativity lies nearest at hand; whether, from the standpoint of present astronomical knowledge, it is tenable, will not here be discussed. In order to arrive at this consistent view, we admittedly had to introduce an extension of the field equations of gravitation which is not justified by our actual knowledge of gravitation. It is to be emphasized, however, that a positive curvature of space is given by our results, even if the supplementary term is not introduced. That term is necessary only for the purpose of making possible a quasi-static distribution of matter, as required by the fact of the small velocities of the stars.

The Einstein world with its "quasi-static distribution of matter," was quickly challenged by de Sitter, who maintained that while the General Theory indicated a curved space, this curvature was continually decreasing. Thus the de Sitter world built on the General Theory was steadily increasing in size; space was constantly straightening itself out, becoming less curved and more Euclidean. This idea of an expanding universe had as yet no observational support, and for some time the ideas of both Einstein and de Sitter on the structure of the universe were considered as equally comparable possibilities between which it was difficult to make a choice. Only in the 1920s, as the work of Hubble and others at Mount Wilson verified the recession of the galaxies and the continual expansion of the universe, was the position drastically altered.* And only in 1930 did Einstein withdraw the "cosmological constant."

Long before this, however, the term had come under attack for totally different reasons from Professor Friedmann, a Russian astronomer who had begun to study Einstein's publications from a purely mathematical standpoint. George Gamow, who was working under Friedmann at the time, has described what happened. "Friedmann noticed that Einstein had made a mistake in his alleged proof that the universe must necessarily be stable and unchangeable in time," he says.

> It is well known to students of high-school algebra that it is permissible to divide both sides of an equation by any quantity, provided that this quantity is not zero. However, in the course of his proof, Einstein had divided both sides of one of his intermediate equations by a complicated expression which, in certain circumstances, could become zero.
>
> In the case, however, when this expression becomes equal to zero, Einstein's proof does not hold, and Friedmann realized that this opened an entire new world of time-dependent universes; expanding, collapsing, and pulsating ones. Thus Einstein's original gravity equation was correct, and changing it was a mistake. Much later, when I was discussing cosmological problems with Einstein, he remarked that the introduction of the cosmological term was the biggest blunder he ever made in his life. But the "blunder," rejected by Einstein, and the cosmological constant, denoted by the Greek letter λ, rears its ugly head again and again and again.

Despite Gamow's well-justified comments, Einstein's entry into the cosmological arena was important both for science and for Einstein. "This suggestion of a finite, but unbounded space is one of the greatest ideas about the

*See page 524.

nature of the world which ever has been conceived," as Max Born put it. "It solved the mysterious fact why the system of stars did not disperse and thin out which it would do if space were infinite; it gave a physical meaning to Mach's principle which postulated that the law of inertia should not be regarded as a property of empty space but as an effect of the total system of stars, and it opened the way to the modern concept of the expanding universe." Furthermore, the idea was put forward at a significant moment, just as observational astronomy was preparing to give practical muscle to the theoretical flesh.

At a different level, Einstein's direct use of the General Theory to present a picture of the universe gave him an almost mystical significance for the layman. A scientist who could give a fresh, and apparently more reliable, explanation for the movements of the stars in their courses was an important enough figure. A physicist who could apparently show that light did not always run straight had at his command an almost conjuring-trick attraction. But a man who could talk in familiar terms of current space, and with a friendly gesture from the blackboard explain how the universe was both finite and boundless, had stretched out to touch untouchable things in a way that made him part magician and part messiah.

That is, if the General Theory were right. As Einstein, Born, and Wertheimer intervened with the students in Berlin in November, 1918, as the Empire went down in defeat, and de Sitter in Holland constructed his own blueprint of the universe, final plans were being made in Britain to discover whether this was so.

CHAPTER 9

THE FABRIC OF THE UNIVERSE

The first turning point in Einstein's life had come with publication of his paper on the electrodynamics of moving bodies, an event whose significance, like the thunder of the guns at Valmy, was recognized at first by only a few. The second was of a totally different order—and not only because the implications of the General Theory were more important. This of itself would have ended his normal life as a Berlin professor, well enough known in his own field but still comparatively obscure outside it. But the circumstances in which the General Theory was tested brought Einstein a worldwide scientific fame which arrived almost literally overnight and swept him away from his scientific moorings into the stream of public events. Between the Armistice of November, 1918, and the end of the following year he became the most famous scientist in the world.

This was not all. Scientific renown came just as events in Germany and elsewhere pushed him into a political activity for which he had little aptitude. He instinctively supported the left-wing movements set free by defeat and became a devoted if muddled supporter both of pacifism and of a world government which could only be maintained by force. He revealed his zealous and perhaps ingenuous belief that Germany's good name would be restored if her war crimes were publicly investigated and, if necessary, admitted. And he became emotionally committed to the cause of Zionism. These actions were enough to make his name disliked by German nationalists while he remained obscure, and detested once he became famous. As a result, his scientific fame became inextricably entangled with political controversies. All this was further complicated at a personal level by his long-sought divorce from Mileva, his marriage to Elsa, and the death of his mother who spent her final days with him in a Berlin threatened equally by starvation, inflation, and revolution.

Within a few months of Germany's defeat Einstein's opinion of his own countrymen had begun to change. Until now he had tended to forget—or to try to forget—that he himself was a German and to submerge what remained of the thought in the reality of his Swiss passport. He had looked upon the majority of his compatriots with almost unqualified distaste, regarding them as the people who supported an aggressive war with only minor protest and condoned barbarous activities which he did not shrink from calling "war crimes." But as the defeat of November, 1918, merged into the starvation of 1919, so the differences between the Germans he had detested and the Allies whom he had so hoped would win tended to disappear. "As for politics, I have become deeply disillusioned," he wrote to Ehrenfest on March 22, 1919. "Those countries whose victory I had considered during the war by far the lesser evil I now consider only slightly less of an evil." And to Lorentz he warned: "We must remember that, on the average, men's moral qualities do not greatly vary from country to country." He held the opinion for little more than a decade between the anti-Prussian hatred of his youth and the more understandable anti-German paranoia of his later years. But during this decade Einstein's native Germanism rose to the surface once again and he was no longer so worried about being what he was.

As early as December 6, 1918, he was writing to Ehrenfest commenting that the Germans, "once having gained some slight understanding of the causes of the war, [had] borne the collapse with calm and dignity." Judgment on German scholars during the war, made from abroad, had been "overly harsh," he noted to Lorentz. It was, he went on, difficult for those who had been outside Germany to appreciate the power of mass suggestion which had been exercised within it. Furthermore, it was "*a priori* incredible that the inhabitants of a whole great country should be branded as morally inferior! The declaration of the 93, foolish as it was, was neither conceived nor signed with any awareness of wrong." And the man who drafted it he described as "a decent and unusually well-meaning man, as long as the red rag of 'politics' is not waved in front of him."

Einstein's attempt to exculpate the German academics, much as the "stab-in-the-back" theory attempted to exculpate the German armed forces, was partly the result of his being knocked off balance during the immediate postwar months. For Einstein and others trustingly expected that they would have Allied cooperation in rebuilding a new and democratic Germany; that they would now be helped in the task of putting their own house in order. The fact that the Reichswehr could boast of a formidable army still in being, that there remained a considerable danger that the Armistice would not easily be enforced, did not damp their hopes. But instead of the hand stretched out in cooperation if not in friendship, they met the rigor of the Allied blockade whose only effect, other than the starvation of civilians, was to make the task of the republican government even more difficult.

All this quickly prodded Einstein into the political activity for which he had little liking and less competence. "I cannot understand how any man can join a political party," he was later to write. But when the Bund Neues Vaterland, illegally revived in September, was formally refounded on November 10, 1918, after an open-air meeting at the foot of Bismarck's statue in front of the Reichstag, Professor Albert Einstein appeared not only as a member but among those who sat on the Working Committee. He was among the one hundred intellectuals from Europe and the United States who in December signed the Pétition du Comité de la Fédération des Peuples, addressed to the heads of state about to meet in Versailles for the Peace Conference and prophetically asking them to "make a peace that does not conceal a future war." And in his letter to Ehrenfest of December 6, 1918, he hoped that he would shortly be visiting Paris "to plead with the Allies to save the famished German population from starvation."

Einstein's changed attitude cannot be accounted for entirely by bitterness at the Allied blockade. With the exception of pacifism—for which he had an honorable blind spot and on whose behalf he would usually sign the most specious of propaganda manifestos—he was not abnormally gullible. His enthusiasms were rarely of the ephemeral sort such as justified the claim that Lloyd George was a pillow, always bearing the imprint of the last head which had rested on it. His changing and sometimes contradictory views on the Germans, and on the need for political action, often sprang from his belief that different situations demanded different attitudes. Circumstances, he felt, really did alter cases, and in fields other than science. Just as there were no absolutes in time and space, so was there nothing immutable about the attitudes that men should take up when dealing with the kaleidoscopic, irrational, and infinitely complicated actions of their fellowmen. The point of view was logical enough. But it gave his enemies useful weapons.

Einstein did not go to Paris at the turn of the year. Instead he went to Zurich, where he had some months earlier been offered a chair to be held jointly at the university and the ETH. He had turned down the offer but had agreed, instead, to visit the city for a month or six weeks, twice a year, and give on each occasion a series of a dozen lectures. Explaining to Besso his reactions to the offer, he said that he lacked the gift to be ubiquitous and that in Berlin he was able to satisfy all his wishes. He would demand from Zurich nothing more than his expenses and would by this sacrifice on the altar of the country, as he called it, free himself of painful feelings while at the same time acting in a correct manner in the eyes of his friends and his Berlin patrons.

The arrangement was convenient for another reason. His divorce was at last in its final stages. The thing would be settled within the first few weeks of 1919 and it would be useful, if not essential, for him to be in Switzerland.

He left Berlin during the last week of January, 1919, arrived in Zurich on January 27, and stayed at the Sternwarte boardinghouse in Hochstrasse. The General Theory of Relativity had in academic circles become as great a subject of discussion as the Special Theory, but it was still a subject for specialists alone and its author was known in Zurich as a former professor rather than as a man about to shake the world. This is illustrated by an incident recalled by Hermann Weyl. Due to the coal shortage which was an aftermath of the European war, the authorities had to "ration" entry to the lectures, which could only be attended by those who bought an invitation card for a few francs. On this occasion Einstein appeared with Professor Weyl and the latter's wife. But Frau Weyl had forgotten her invitation card, and a steward stopped her. Einstein became as angry as Einstein ever could become and said that if Frau Weyl was not allowed in, then there would be no lecture. The steward gave way, under protest. But shortly afterwards Einstein received a letter from the rector in which he was politely but firmly asked not to interfere with the authorities' regulations.

In Zurich Einstein was also asked by the students to lecture on quantum theory. ". . . It is not for me to lecture about quantum theory," he replied. "However hard I tried, I never fully understood it. Besides, I have never gone into the details and tricks on which the quantum theory is at the moment based, so that I cannot give a comprehensive theory. What I have personally accomplished in this subject is easy for you to find out."

His divorce was settled on February 14, 1919. Simultaneously, he awarded to Mileva any money that should come from a Nobel Prize—several years before he was awarded it. When the prize came, three years later, the cash was passed on from Sweden, via Berlin, to Zurich. Some was lost in movement through the foreign exchanges and more by bad management. With what was left Mileva bought a pleasant house on the Zurichberg. The following year she formally obtained permission to retain the name of Einstein; and, as Mileva Einstein, she lived for another quarter of a century, overshadowed by illness and the worry of a schizophrenic younger son.

Einstein did not lose touch with her. Once the final break had been agreed upon, mutual animosities lessened and dislike dissolved, if not into affection at least into mutual understanding. Even before the divorce had gone through Mileva was advising him on his projected marriage to Elsa; what it was can be inferred from his reply—that if he ever wished to leave his second wife, no power on earth would stop him.

As soon as his lecture series in Zurich was completed in the spring of 1919, Einstein returned to Berlin. And here, on June 2, he married Elsa in the registry office at Berlin-Wilmersdorf, traveling back to Zurich shortly afterwards, apparently to discuss the future of his sons with

Mileva. He remained in Zurich until June 25 when he appeared again in Berlin, leaving for Zurich once more on the twenty-eighth and remaining in Switzerland for another three months until, on September 21, he returned to Berlin again.

While thus settling his personal affairs, Einstein was also being swept up by the rising tide of Zionism. Here it is only necessary to note that during his Berlin visits of the spring and summer of 1919 he was approached by the Zionists and won over to their cause. They were gratified. But as they saw it, their "catch" was merely that of a prominent Jewish scientist. Before the year was out their minnow was to grow into a whale.

Espousal of the Zionist cause greatly effected Einstein's position in Germany during the next decade and increased his nonscientific notoriety. This was augmented by the fervor with which he now began to discuss German war crimes. He had first raised the subject with Lorentz in 1915 and he returned to it now in the hope that " ... information about the crimes which were committed by the German High Command in Belgium and France ... would help to create a better understanding among our own people of how the others feel."

It is doubtful whether the crimes that most countries commit in the heat of war can satisfactorily be examined afterwards either by their own nationals or by the victors—let alone on the instigation of someone who had hated his own country from his youth "and ... always felt the dangers that threatened the world from her side." Even among those who believe that the Nuremberg trials were not only necessary but just, many would have preferred to see the work carried out with the visible impartiality of neutrals. In this light, Einstein's revival of the subject was well intentioned but unfortunate. It was doubly so since he was still apparently a renegade German who preferred to travel on a Swiss passport, and whose ignorance of international machinery was equaled by his lack of any personal contact with the machinery of war.

This much was clear to Lorentz, to whom Einstein wrote on April 26, 1919, saying that with five other private citizens he had formed a commission "with the purpose of thoroughly examining those charges concerning Germany's conduct in the war which have become known abroad and are considered as proved." Would Lorentz, Einstein asked, join the commission as one of the neutrals who would help to get documentary evidence?

Lorentz' reply was a cautious masterpiece of tact. He was an internationalist. He was visibly a man of goodwill. More than most, he understood Einstein, and a few months earlier he had written to Ernest Solvay when future congresses were being discussed, noting that "a man such as Einstein, that great physicist, is in no way 'German' in the way that one often uses the word nowadays; his opinion of events in recent years is no different from yours and mine." But Lorentz had also a far clearer idea of the possible, and of the likely, reactions of fallible men. While willing to help Einstein through second parties, he himself deftly sidestepped the invitation to serve on the proposed commission. "You must not deceive yourself that your task will be an easy one," he replied. "The main difficulty, of course, is that this first step has only just been taken; it would have been more successful if it had been taken when Germany was still winning." Moreover, he pointed out, it was extremely urgent that the Germans officially supported the move. "You must be absolutely certain," he went on, "that the government will allow you full discussion and publication and not put obstacles in your way. It seems to me that you must obtain this assurance before you make any contact with the Belgians or the French because if they discover, after they have heard of your intentions, that you are not completely free to speak out, then you will have lost more than you have won." However, Lorentz was about to visit Paris and Brussels. He would make what inquiries he could. And he arranged with a colleague in Holland to pass on news from Einstein while he, Lorentz, was traveling. The results were hardly satisfactory. Lorentz, willing to help, was obliged to inform Einstein of the detestation felt for Germans "good" and "bad" alike, inside the countries which had been occupied.

This was underlined shortly afterwards when he discussed prospects for the next Solvay Congress. "It is clear that at the moment Germans will not be invited (there is difficulty in their coming to Brussels)," he said, "even though there is no mention of their formal exclusion; the door will be held open to you, so that in future it will be possible for everybody to work together again. Unfortunately, however, this will have to wait for many years." There was, in fact, some doubt about whether the door would be held open even for Einstein. M. Tassin, the congress secretary, had to deal in particular with Professor Brillouin, who had attended the 1911 Congress and who on June 1, 1919, wrote from the Collège de France about "the pro-German neutrals, whatever their scientific value," as well about the problem of Germans. "I am thinking, for example," he went on, "of Debye, the Dutchman of great merit, who spent all the war as a professor in Göttingen. Naturally, also of Einstein who, whatever his genius, however great his antimilitarist sentiments, nevertheless spent the whole war in Berlin and is in the same position. It is only afterwards that they have made the necessary political effort to throw light on their German colleagues and dispute the abominable and lying Manifesto of the 93."

Einstein's relations with the congress were to complement his weathercock attitude to his own countrymen. He had attended the Second Congress in 1913, although he read no paper there and, as forecast by Lorentz, he was invited in the summer of 1920 to the Third Congress, to be held the following April. Germans as such were still not to be invited. But as the secretary wrote, "an exception [had] been made for Einstein, of ill-defined nationality, Swiss I believe, who was roundly abused in Berlin during the war because of his pacifist sentiments which have never varied for a moment." Rutherford put it slightly differently. "The only German invited is Einstein who is considered for this purpose to be international," he wrote. Einstein accepted "with great pleasure" and later in the year Lorentz informed Rutherford that he would be speaking at the April, 1921, Congress on "L'Électron et le Magnétisme; effets gyroscopiques." Only in February, two months before the congress was to be held, was he told that Einstein would not be present. The reason was the request for him to speak for the Zionists in the United States in March and April, so that "through [his] personal cooperation the rich American Jews will be persuaded to pay up." Nevertheless, Einstein wished the congress every success.

Two years later, when the Fourth Congress was being

planned for 1924, the situation was different. Once again Einstein was to be invited. But on August 16 he wrote to Lorentz from Lautrach in southern Germany. "This letter is hard for me to write but I have to write it," he began.

> I am here together with Sommerfeld. He is of the opinion that it is not right for me to take part in the Solvay Congress because my German colleagues are excluded. In my opinion it is not right to bring politics into scientific matters, nor should individuals be held responsible for the government of the country to which they happen to belong. If I took part in the congress I would by implication become an accomplice to an action which I consider most strongly to be distressingly unjust. This feeling is all the more strong when I think of the French and Belgians who have recently committed too many crimes to continue to pose as injured innocents.

He was seething over the French invasion of the Ruhr,* and his views of Germany and Germans had been mellowed by the advent of Weimar. But he still looked to a future of international cooperation, and continued: "I should be grateful if you would see to it that I do not even receive an invitation to the congress. I want to be spared the necessity of declining—an act which might hinder the gradual reestablishment of friendly collaboration between physicists of various countries."

To Madame Curie he later admitted that "the disinclination of Belgians and French to meet Germans was not psychologically incomprehensible to me. But when I saw that German scholars were to be excluded on principle merely because of their nationality, I realized that by going to Brussels I should indirectly be supporting such a ruling. That did not tally with my ideas at all. It is unworthy of cultured men to treat one another in that type of superficial way, as though they were members of the common herd being led by mass suggestion."

Only in 1926, after Germany had joined the League of Nations, and the international relations of science were returning to normal, did the position alter. "Now," Lorentz noted on the telegram which told him of the new situation, "I am able to write to Einstein." But in 1926 there was still one more formality to be observed—and in

*See pages 435–436.

view of Einstein's subsequent links with the royal palace in Brussels it has some significance. It was thought proper that the approval of King Albert of the Belgians should be sought, and on April 2, 1926, Lorentz was given an audience at which His Majesty specifically approved the nomination of Einstein to the scientific committee of the coming congress, and the proposal to invite Planck and other former enemy scientists. "His Majesty," Lorentz subsequently reported, "expressed the opinion that, seven years after the war, the feelings which they aroused should be gradually damped down, that a better understanding between peoples was absolutely necessary for the future, and that science could help to bring this about. He also felt it necessary to stress that in view of all that the Germans had done for physics, it would be very difficult to pass them over." This sweet reasonableness was just as well. By 1926 physics was in the ferment of the new quantum mechanics, and the 1927 Congress would have been meaningless without the presence of Heisenberg, Born, Planck, and Einstein from the former enemy countries.

Eight years earlier, as in the summer of 1919 Einstein tried to conscript Lorentz into an investigation of German war crimes, things were not like that. Just what degree of help Lorentz finally gave is not clear, either from the correspondence in the Algemeen Rijksarchief in The Hague or from the complementary letters in the Museum of Science in Leiden. But at the end of the summer the commission on whose behalf Einstein was working produced its first publication. This was a small booklet dealing with alleged atrocities in Lille. It had gone to press while Einstein was in Switzerland, and when he received a copy on his return to Berlin in the second half of September he "was quite startled," as he wrote to Lorentz on the twenty-first. The preface was "tactless" and—partly at Einstein's instigation, one suspects—the whole edition was eventually withdrawn for correction, amendment, and reissue early in 1920.

It is at this point in 1919 that Einstein, facing what seemed to be the Allied condemnation of a whole nation, further qualified his previous rabid anti-Germanism and rejected an extraordinarily tempting offer from Leiden. The reason may have been partly a wish to give "the new

Germany" a chance to pull herself up by her moral bootstraps, partly the fear that a "thirst for power" might be growing up in an "elsewhere" that Einstein—like many other Germans—identified with France.

The offer came from Ehrenfest. He had not yet got the approval of the authorities, but there seemed little doubt that he would get it—even for the terms which he outlined on September 2, 1919. One word which Einstein used to describe them was "fabulous." This was no overstatement. What Ehrenfest suggested—"trial discussions have given me the greatest imaginable hope that it will be possible to arrange everything exactly according to your wishes"—was that Einstein should come to Leiden University. The normal maximum salary of 7,500 guilders, he said, would be Einstein's minimum. There would be no lecturing duties, and the only obligation would be for him to make his base in or near the city. "You can spend as much time as you want in Switzerland, or elsewhere, working, giving lectures, traveling, etc., provided only that one can say 'Einstein is in Leiden—in Leiden is Einstein,' " Ehrenfest added.

To Einstein it was a most tempting offer—one whose acceptance would bring him close to the orbit of Lorentz in Haarlem and of de Sitter, and which would strengthen his ties with Ehrenfest. The terms of his rejection are revealing.

"Your offer is so fabulous and your words are so friendly and so full of affection that you can hardly imagine how confused I have been as a result of your letter," he replied on September 12.

> You know, of course, how happy I am in Leiden. And you know how much I like all of you. But my position is not so simple that I can do the right thing just by following my own inclinations. I am sending you a letter that Planck wrote to me while I was in Zurich. After receiving it I promised him not to turn my back on Berlin unless conditions were such that he would regard such a step as natural and proper. You have hardly any idea of the sacrifices that have been made here, with the general financial situation so difficult so that it is possible for me to stay and also to support my family in Zurich. It would be doubly wrong of me if, just when my political hopes are being realized, I were to walk out unnecessarily, and

perhaps *in part* for my material advantage, on the very people who have surrounded me with love and friendship, and to whom my departure would be doubly painful at this time of supposed humiliation. You have no idea with what affection I am surrounded here; not all of them try only to catch the drops which my brain sweats out.

So you see how things stand with me. I can leave here only if there is a turn of events that makes it impossible for me to remain. Such a turn of events could occur. But unless it does so, my departure would be tantamount to a despicable breach of my word to Planck. I would be breaking faith and would certainly reproach myself later on. (I feel like some relic in an old cathedral—one doesn't quite know what to do with the old bones, but. . . .)

In conclusion he added that he would like to visit Leiden—"if my tyrannical belly permits." He wondered whether he would be able to get a travel permit. He was certainly eager to see his old friends again. He loved Leiden. But as far as any permanent post was concerned, he was staying in Berlin.

Planck, the man of honor who had yet signed the Manifesto of the 93, had in fact for the first but not the last time done as much to keep Einstein in Berlin as he had done to bring him there in 1914. His letter, which, in Einstein's words, had induced him "not to turn his back on Berlin," was written on July 20, 1919, and began by explaining how he, Planck, had contrived to get equipment funds for Freundlich by an ingenious sleight-of-finance.

Then Planck went on to explain his much deeper and more important reason for writing. This was that rumors were circulating that the Zurich authorities were trying to induce Einstein to remain in Switzerland. Planck felt sure, he went on, that Einstein would not make up his mind before he had consulted his friends in Berlin—but the very mention of this was a measure of his worry. He wanted to stress one thing: that a matter as important as Einstein's future both for the Academy and for German science as a whole should not be settled entirely in terms of money. In other words, either the Academy itself, or the State, should put at Einstein's disposal whatever was required to keep him in Berlin—if he wished to remain, that was. Planck concluded with one fervent wish: that

Einstein should let him know if money really was the problem.

Planck was not merely a good German—in both senses of the phrase—but also an imaginative scientist with a keen sense of things to come. And it cannot have been wholly coincidence that his plea for Einstein to remain within the German fold was stressed now. As he must have guessed, a transformation was coming.

A fortnight after Einstein replied to Ehrenfest, turning down the Leiden offer, he received a historic telegram sent by Lorentz from Leiden five days earlier. It was dated September 27, 1919, and ran: "Eddington found star displacement at rim of sun, preliminary measurement between nine-tenths of a second and twice that value." The words were to mark a turning point in the life of Einstein and in the history of science.

In Britain the Royal Astronomical Society had noted of the Special Theory in 1917 that "experimental confirmation has been ample, and no serious doubt of its truth is entertained, criticism being confined to questions of its exact scope and philosophical implications." But confirmation was the result of physicists laboring in their laboratories, almost in the normal course of their work; something on a different scale was required to test the General Theory, and it says much for Sir Frank Dyson that in March, 1917, he had drawn "attention to the unique opportunities afforded by the eclipse of 1919" to test Einstein's theory. "It was not without international significance, for it opportunely put an end to wild talk of boycotting German science," Eddington later wrote of the decision. "By standing foremost in testing, and ultimately verifying, the 'enemy' theory, our national observatory kept alive the finest traditions of science; and the lesson is perhaps still needed in the world today."

In March, 1917, Britain's darkest weeks of the war still lay ahead, and the prospect of sending expeditions to South America and to Africa, where the eclipse could best be seen, could not be viewed without misgiving. Despite this, Dyson was given £1,000 ($5,000) from the government, and a Joint Permanent Eclipse Committee of the Royal Society and the Royal Astronomical Society was set up under his chairmanship. In the spring of 1918, as the Germans broke through to the Marne and once again brought the issue of the war into doubt, plans went steadily ahead for British expeditions to Sobral in northern Brazil and to Principe Island in the Gulf of Guinea.

Early the following year, in January, 1919, a series of test photographs, showing the Hyades against a reference frame of other stars, was taken at Greenwich Observatory. Two months later Eddington and E. T. Cottingham, who were to make the eclipse observations on Principe Island, and A. C. D. Crommelin and C. R. Davidson, who were to do the same at Sobral, met for a final briefing in Flamsteed House, Greenwich. Eddington's enthusiasm for the General Theory was illustrated when Cottingham asked, in Dyson's study: "What will it mean if we get double the Einstein deflection?" "Then," said Dyson, "Eddington will go mad and you will have to come home alone."

Next morning both parties left for Funchal, Crommelin and Davidson traveling on to Brazil while Eddington and Cottingham sailed to Principe, where they arrived on April 23. One month of hard work followed, setting up instruments, taking test photographs, and making final preparations for the great day.

May 29 began with heavy rain, which stopped only about noon. Not until 1:30 P.M., when the eclipse had already begun, did the party get its first glimpse of the sun. "We had to carry out our programme of photographs on faith," wrote Eddington in his diary. "I did not see the eclipse, being too busy changing plates, except for one glance to make sure it had begun and another halfway through to see how much cloud there was. We took sixteen photographs. They are all good of the sun, showing a very remarkable prominence; but the cloud has interfered with the star images. The last six photographs show a few images which I hope will give us what we need. . . ."

It looked as though the effort, so far as the Principe expedition was concerned, might have been abortive. Only on June 3 was the issue settled. "We developed the photographs, two each night for six nights after the eclipse," Eddington wrote, "and I spent the whole day measuring. The cloudy weather upset my plans and I had to treat the measures in a different way from what I intended, consequently I have not been able to make any preliminary announcement of the result. But one plate that I measured gave a result agreeing with Einstein."

This, says Eddington's biographer, "was a moment which Eddington never forgot. On one occasion in later years he referred to it as the greatest moment of his life." Turning to his companion he said, remembering the evening in Dyson's study nearly three months previously: "Cottingham, you won't have to go home alone."

At a dinner of the Royal Astronomical Society following Eddington's return to Britain, he described the trials and tribulations of Principe in a parody of the *Rubaiyat* whose final verses went thus:

The Clock no question makes of Fasts or Slows,
But steadily and with a constant Rate it goes.
And Lo! the clouds are parting and the Sun
A crescent glimmering on the screen—It shows!—
It shows! !

Five minutes, not a moment left to waste,
Five minutes, for the picture to be traced—
The Stars are shining, and coronal light
Streams from the Orb of Darkness—Oh make haste!

For in and out, above, about, below
'Tis nothing but a magic *Shadow* show
Played in a Box, whose Candle is the Sun
Round which we phantom figures come and go.

Oh leave the Wise our measures to collate.
One thing at least is certain, LIGHT has WEIGHT
One thing is certain, and the rest debate—
Light-rays, when near the Sun, DO NOT GO STRAIGHT.

Despite Eddington's moment of drama on Principe, full confirmation did not come all at once. While the Principe photographs had been developed and measured in West Africa, those of the Sobral expedition were brought to Britain before being processed. The first were disappointing. Then came the main set of seven. "They gave a final verdict," wrote Eddington, "definitely confirming Einstein's value of the deflection, in agreement with the results obtained at Principe."

But the news had not yet percolated beyond the small circle of those connected with the expeditions. Einstein knew through his friends in Holland that the expeditions had been in progress, but he had known little more. On September 2 he wrote to Dr. E. Hartmann of Fulda, noting that "so far nothing precise has been published about the expedition's measurements so that even I know nothing about them," and in rejecting Ehrenfest's proposals for a Leiden post ten days later, he asked whether there was news about the British eclipse expedition.

Ehrenfest passed on Einstein's message to Lorentz, who with his more numerous contacts abroad was able to discover what was happening. And on September 27, 1919, there came Lorentz' telegram: "Eddington found star displacement at rim of sun. . . ."

Einstein's first reaction was to write to his mother in Lucerne. "Good news today," he said on a card, "H. A. Lorentz has wired me that the British expeditions have actually proved the light shift near the sun." He would have to stay in Berlin for a few more days, he added; then he would go to Holland on the invitation of Ehrenfest. And in Holland he would be able to get the details he really wanted.

Looking back, both Einstein and his colleagues were apt to harp on his inner certainty. Thus Ilse Rosenthal-Schneider, one of his students, remembers how, as the two of them were discussing a book which raised objections to his theory, Einstein reached for a telegram lying on the windowsill and handed it to her with the words: "Here, this will perhaps interest you." "It was," she has written, "Eddington's cable with the results of measurement of the eclipse expedition. When I was giving expression to my joy that the results coincided with his calculations, he said, quite unmoved, 'But I knew that the theory is correct,' and when I asked, what if there had been no confirmation of his prediction, he countered: 'Then I would have been sorry for the dear Lord—the theory *is* correct.' "

This was not the certainty of hindsight; all along he had believed that the theory would be confirmed. Nevertheless, he was glad enough to begin preparations for a trip to Holland. First he had to obtain the necessary travel documents. On October 5 he wrote to Ehrenfest, explaining that he had been to the Dutch Embassy in Berlin and asking his friends in Holland to help. Kamerlingh Onnes now used his influence as the head of Leiden's world-famous Cryogenic Laboratory to intercede on Einstein's behalf. Within a few days he had a Dutch entry permit.

Before he left Berlin he received further news from Lorentz. "I have not yet written to you about the observation of the rays glancing off the edge of the sun, as I thought that one of the English journals, *Nature,* for instance, would have written fully about it," he explained on October 7.

> This has not yet happened so I do not wish to wait any longer. I have heard of Eddington's results through Mr. Van der Pohl, the conservator of this laboratory. He visited the British Association meeting at Bournemouth and told me on his return what Eddington spoke about. As the plates are still being measured he cannot give exact values, but according to Eddington's opinion the thing is certain and one can say with certainty that the deflection (at the edge of the sun) lies between 0.87″ and 1′74″. Van der Pohl also told me that there was a discussion about it (I wish I had been there) and that Sir Oliver Lodge and Eddington wished you the best of luck with the figures when they came.

He went on to describe some of his own work and then returned to the Eddington results. "They are certainly," he noted, "some of the most beautiful results that science has produced and we should indeed rejoice."

So far, the warnings that a major change in man's ideas of the physical world was at hand had seeped out only gradually. No results had been publicly available when the British expeditions had returned to London. The accounts given at the British Association meeting had stressed that vital measurements and comparisons still had to be completed. Even Lorentz' telegram to Einstein had given a general rather than a specific indication of success. Thus the reports had hardened up slowly, over the weeks, lacking the suddenness which alone could give headline quality in a Europe grappling with the problems of postwar chaos. There was, moreover, to be a last twist before the news finally broke on the world.

This was given in Leiden where Einstein arrived in the latter half of October. The vital results of the British expeditions were known here privately at least by October 23, when he wrote to Planck in Berlin. "This evening," he said, "Hertzsprung showed me a letter from Arthur Eddington according to which the accurate measurements of the plates gave exactly the theoretical value of the light diffraction. It is a gift from Fate that I have been allowed to experience this. . . ."

But even now only a small handful of professors were in the know. Two days later, on the evening of Saturday, October 25, the situation changed dramatically. The Dutch Royal Academy met in Amsterdam. Einstein was there. So was Lorentz and so was Ehrenfest. First the routine business was disposed of. Next, Einstein was formally welcomed. Then, in the words of the Academy's official report, "Mr. H. A. Lorentz communicated the most recent confirmation of Professor Einstein's General Theory of Relativity." But, as the agenda put it, the communication would "not be printed in the report." No press representatives appear to have been present. For another ten days the rest of the world remained in ignorance of the fact that Newton's view of the universe had received an amendment from which it would never totally recover.

It was not until the afternoon of Thursday, November 6, 1919, that the Fellows of the Royal and the Royal Astronomical Societies met in Burlington House to hear the official results of the two eclipse expeditions. Dyson read the reports on behalf of himself, Eddington, and Davidson. He had devoted a good deal of his professional life to the study of solar eclipses and had personally observed no less than three. This time it was different. The aim of the operation had been to test Einstein's theory, and unofficial news of the results had been rumbling round the scientific world for weeks. Here, if nowhere else, men were aware that an age was ending, and the main hall of the Society was crowded. J. J. Thomson, now President of the Royal Society, James Jeans, and Lindemann were present. So were Sir Oliver Lodge and the mathematician and philosopher Alfred Whitehead. All were agitated by the same question. Were the ideas upon which they had relied for so long at last to be found wanting?

"The whole atmosphere of tense interest was exactly that of the Greek drama," wrote Whitehead later.

> We were the chorus commenting on the decree of destiny as disclosed in the development of a supreme incident. There was dramatic quality in the very staging—the traditional ceremonial, and in the background the picture of Newton to remind us that the greatest of scientific generalizations was now, after more than two centuries, to receive its first modification. Nor was the personal interest wanting: a great adventure in thought had at length come safe to shore.

Thomson rose to address the meeting, speaking of Einstein's theory as "one of the greatest achievements in the history of human thought," and then pushing home the full measure of what relativity meant. "It is not the discovery of an outlying island but of a whole continent of new scientific ideas," he said. "It is the greatest discovery in connection with gravitation since Newton enunciated his principles." As *The Times* of London put it, Einstein's theory dealt with the fabric of the universe.

Then Dyson read the body of his report, giving the figures provided by the photographs and describing their significance. "Thus the results of the expeditions to Sobral and Principe," he concluded, "leave little doubt that a deflection of light takes place in the neighborhood of the sun and that it is of the amount demanded by Einstein's generalized theory of relativity as attributable to the sun's gravitational field."

The discussion that followed brought out one thing: that while the results of the eclipse expedition had yielded a convincing key piece of evidence, the new theory was also acceptable on entirely different grounds. Eddington was to emphasize the point nearly twenty years later when there had been further astronomical support. The theory, he said, was primarily concerned with phenomena which, without it, might have seemed mildly puzzling.

> But we do not need to observe an eclipse of the sun to ascertain whether a man is talking coherently or incoher-

ently. The Newtonian framework, as was natural after 250 years, had been found too crude to accommodate the new observational knowledge which was being acquired. In default of a better framework, it was still used, but definitions were strained to purposes for which they were never intended. We were in the position of a librarian whose books were still being arranged according to a subject scheme drawn up a hundred years ago, trying to find the right place for books on Hollywood, the Air Force, and detective novels.

Einstein had altered all that.

PART THREE

THE HINGE OF FATE

CHAPTER 10

THE NEW MESSIAH

Einstein awoke in Berlin on the morning of November 7, 1919, to find himself famous. It was an awkward morning for fame, with the Wilhelmstrasse barricaded, all traffic stopped on the orders of Gustav Noske, the republican Minister of Defense, and warning leaflets from the Citizens Defense Force being handed out to passersby. On the second anniversary of the Russian Revolution it seemed that Berlin was to be torn apart by a struggle between the workers, who believed that the German government had not moved far enough to the left, and the army, who believed that it had moved too far.

He was of course already known to the equivalent of today's science writers. In addition, the esoteric quality of his work had combined with his own individuality to produce a local notoriety. Now, on the morning of November 7, the situation was dramatically changed. Even a month later he could write to Born that the publicity was "so bad that I can hardly breathe, let alone get down to sensible work." Any journalist who felt that the newsworthiness of the British expeditions had ended with their safe return to England learned better as accounts of the previous afternoon's meeting in Burlington House, and the subsequent leading article in *The Times,* arrived in the German capital. Under "The Fabric of the Universe," *The Times* stated that "the scientific conception of the fabric of the Universe must be changed." And after an account of the British expeditions and their purpose, it concluded thus: "But it is confidently believed by the greatest experts that enough has been done to overthrow the certainty of ages, and to require a new philosophy of the universe, a philosophy that will sweep away nearly all that has hitherto been accepted as the axiomatic basis of physical thought."

This was strong meat. Its effect was not lessened by accounts in other papers, which with few exceptions agreed that the world would never be the same again. Attention turned to the man responsible. Little was known about him except that in 1914 he had not signed the notorious Manifesto of the 93. Whether he was Swiss or German was uncertain, but *The Times* described him as an ardent Zionist and added that when the Armistice had been announced the previous year, he "signed an appeal in favor of the German revolution"—probably a reference to his support of the re-formed Bund Neues Vaterland.

Throughout the day Einstein was visited by an almost continuous stream of reporters. He genuinely did not like it. But he soon realized that there is a time for compromise as well as a time for standing firm. There was, moreover, one way in which the distasteful interest could be turned to good use. So there were no free photographs of Einstein; as one reporter later noted, "These, his wife told me, are sold for the benefit of the starving children of Vienna." It was not only photographs which could coax money into the channels through which he thought it should flow. There was also a demand for simple explanations of relativity, for which the newspapers of the world would pay large sums. Einstein never succumbed to the temptation of writing articles galore. But before the end of the month he was in touch with a young correspondent for *Nature* and had agreed to contribute an article to *The Times*.

The *Nature* correspondent was Robert Lawson, the young physicist who had attended his lecture in Vienna six years previously. Interned at the outbreak of war, but nevertheless allowed to continue his scientific work at the Radium Institute, Lawson returned to the University of Sheffield at the end of 1918, and now, as well as writing to Einstein himself, gave Arnold Berliner, the editor of *Naturwissenschaften*, an account of the situation in Britain. "The talk here is of almost nothing but Einstein," he said, "and if he were to come here now I think he would be welcomed like a victorious general. The fact that a theory formulated by a German has been confirmed by observations on the part of Englishmen has brought the possibility of cooperation between these two scientifically minded nations much closer. Quite apart from the great scientific value of his brilliant theory, Einstein has done mankind an incalculable service."

Berliner passed on the letter to Einstein who, in acknowledging Lawson's direct request for material for *Nature,* mentioned the article he was writing for *The Times.* "It cannot do any harm for, thank God, the solar eclipse and the theory of relativity have nothing in common with politics," he said. "In this work, English men of science have behaved splendidly throughout, and to my delight your letter shows me that the feelings of English colleagues have not been influenced as much by the war as one might have feared. Within the last few days I have had also from Eddington a very charming letter, about which I have been extremely pleased. I should like to utilize the favorable circumstances to contribute as much as possible towards the reconciliation of German and English colleagues."

His article appeared on the twenty-eighth, but before this the paper had renewed its efforts to explain to readers how important the confirmation of the General Theory really was. For it was becoming clear that the announcement at the Burlington House meeting was not just a nine-days' wonder. Although some scientists were reluctant to accept all that Einstein had claimed, and although others, like Sir Oliver Lodge, were still gruffly sceptical, the ablest minds in science realized, and publicly acknowledged, that this was not an end but a beginning. On November 15, *The Times* added its weight in a leading article headed "The Revolution in Science." "The ideals of Aristotle and Euclid and Newton which are the basis of all our present conceptions prove in fact not to correspond with what can be observed in the fabric of the universe," it concluded. "Space is merely a relation between two sets of data, and an infinite number of times may coexist. Here and there, past and present, are relative, not absolute, and change according to the ordinates and coordinates selected. Observational science has in fact led back to the purest subjective idealism, if without Berkeley's major premise, itself an abstraction of Aristotelian notions of infinity, to take it out of chaos."

A fortnight later came Einstein's own article. Using the opportunity to deplore the war, he began with a typical flourish by saying: "After the lamentable breach in the former international relations existing among men of science, it is with joy and gratefulness that I accept this opportunity of communication with English astronomers and physicists." He went on to outline the basic principles of relativity, special and general, displaying in what was his first popular exposition all those abilities which still make Einstein on relativity a good deal clearer than most other writers.

At the end of the same article he lightly commented on the status that the English had given him, tossing a joke into the future that was to be thrust back in his face within a decade. "The description of me and my circumstances in *The Times* shows an amusing feat of imagination on the part of the writer," he said. "By an application of the theory of relativity to the taste of readers, today in Germany I am called a German man of science and in England I am represented as a Swiss Jew. If I come to be regarded as a *bête noire* the description will be reversed, and I shall become a Swiss Jew for the Germans and a German man of science for the English." Unwilling to censor the comment, *The Times* was equally unwilling to let it pass unremarked. "We conceded him his little jest," an editorial admitted. "But we note that, in accordance with the general tenor of his theory, Dr. Einstein does not supply an absolute description of himself."

The comment was indicative of an undertow of feeling in some conservative circles, both scientific and lay. Thomson, Eddington, Jeans, and many other bright Fellows of the Royal Society appeared to have accepted the extraordinary ideas of this Jew of whose nationality no one appeared to be certain. But could the thing really be true? Was there not somewhere, in some fashion, a more reasonable explanation to which sane men would wake up one morning? Some distinguished men certainly thought so. Among them was Sir Oliver Lodge, who had left before the end of the famous meeting of November 6, even though expected to speak in the discussion—and who later explained this on the grounds of a previous engagement and the need to catch the six o'clock train. On the twenty-fourth, Lodge, whose *The Ether of Space* well qualified him for leading the sceptics, addressed an impressive if polyglot company which included the Bishop of London, Lord Lytton, Lord Haldane, Sir Francis Younghusband, H. A. L. Fisher, and Sir Martin Conway. Newton, Lodge affirmed, had not understood what gravitation was. "We do not understand it now," he went on. "Einstein's theory would not help us to understand it. If Einstein's third prediction were verified, Einstein's theory would dominate all physics and the next generation of mathematical physicists would have a terrible time." Indeed, they did.

This third prediction, the Einstein shift, still exercised Einstein himself, as he revealed in a letter to Eddington which shows vestigial doubt as well as gratitude, courtesy, and humility. "Above all, I should like to congratulate you on the success of your difficult expedition," he wrote. "Considering the great interest you have taken in the theory of relativity even in earlier days I think I can assume that we are indebted primarily to your initiative for the fact that these expeditions could take place. I am amazed at the interest which my English colleagues have taken in the theory in spite of its difficulty." Then, speaking of the third test, he added: "If it were proved that this effect does not exist in nature, then the whole theory would have to be abandoned."

Einstein was not alone. In addition to the doubters headed by Lodge—and Sir Joseph Larmor, who had been among the first to describe matter as consisting of electrified particles—there were others who feared that relativity might be beyond them, or who had doubts as to whether the results of the eclipse expeditions were, scientifically speaking, a good thing.

The archives reveal some surprising names in both groups. In the first there is Dyson, who wrote to Hale at the Mount Wilson Observatory on December 29. "I was myself a sceptic, and expected a different result," he said. "Now I am trying to understand the principle of relativity and am gradually getting to think I do." Hale was less optimistic. "I congratulate you again on the splendid results you have obtained," he wrote to Dyson on February 9, 1920, "though I confess that the complications of the theory of relativity are altogether too much for my comprehension. If I were a good mathematician I might have some hope of forming a feeble conception of the principle, but as it is I fear it will always remain beyond my grasp. However, this does not decrease my interest in the problem, to which we will try to contribute to the best of our ability." His doubts were repeated to Rutherford to whom he wrote that relativity seemed "to complicate matters a good deal."

Rutherford's own qualifications and doubts were unlike those of Dyson and Hale. He noted that the interest of the general public was very remarkable and almost without precedent, the reason being, he felt, that no one was able to give an intelligent explanation of relativity to the average man. He himself did not have much doubt about the accuracy of Einstein's conclusions and considered it a great bit of work. However, he feared that it might tend to draw scientific men away from experiments toward broad metaphysical conceptions. There were already many like that in Britain, he went on, and no more were needed if science was to continue advancing. This was a typical Rutherfordian attitude, illustrating his built-in belief that the only worthwhile experiments were those whose results he could personally repeat and check. So far as the work of Einstein was relative to Newton, he said in 1923, it was simply "a generalization and broadening of its basis, in fact a typical case of mathematical and physical development." But nine years later the balance had altered. "The theory of relativity by Einstein, quite apart from any question of its validity," he agreed, "cannot but be regarded as a magnificent work of art." His qualifications, however deeply rooted in scientific intuition, may have reflected the slight allergy to Einstein himself which comes out at times in Rutherford's comments. Certainly he showed no wish to have him in Cambridge when the idea was mooted in 1920, or even when Einstein was a refugee from Germany in 1933.

Much the same lukewarm view appears beneath the surface in J. J. Thomson. "[He] accepted these results (1919) and the interpretation put upon them, but he never seemed particularly enthusiastic on the subject nor did he attempt to develop it, either theoretically or by experiment," said his biographer some years later. "I believe, from a conversation which I can recall, that he thought attention was being too much concentrated on it by ordinary scientific workers, with the neglect of other subjects to which they were more likely to be able to make a useful contribution. His attitude to relativity was that of a looker-on. Probably the same was true of nearly all his contemporaries. It was the creation of a younger generation." And when it came to cosmology, Thomson's patience ran out. "We have Einstein's space, de Sitter's space, expanding universes, contracting universes, vibrating universes, mysterious universes," he noted in his memoirs. "In fact the pure mathematician may create universes just by writing down an equation, and indeed if he is an individualist he can have a universe of his own."

The semiquizzical note can be heard in many of the repercussions which followed the November meeting at Burlington House. Eddington, speaking in support of relativity in Trinity College, Cambridge, early in December, said that although 6 feet tall he would, if moving vertically at 161,000 miles a second, shrink to a height of only 3 feet. J. J. Thomson, adopting the same line, remarked that "the tutor who preferred rooms on the ground floor to the attic would hardly be consoled to know that the higher he was up, the more Euclidean his space became because it was further from the effects of gravitation." A good deal of the lightheadedness which took hold of so many serious men when they began to discuss relativity no doubt sprang from Eddington's example. As his biographer has said in writing of *Space, Time and Gravitation,* the relativist could, like the Mad Hatter, experience time standing still. In later books Alice herself moved mystifyingly across his stage, the living embodiment of the Fitzgerald contraction; and the Red Queen, "that ardent relativist," proclaimed the relativity even of nonsense.

The trend was spurred on by the simultaneous fame of Jacob Epstein, and even the sober *Observatory* republished the following verse from *Punch*:

Einstein and Epstein are wonderful men,
  Bringing new miracles into our ken.
Einstein upset the Newtonian rule;
  Epstein demolished the Pheidian School.
Einstein gave fits to the Royal Society
  Epstein delighted in loud notoriety.

Einstein made parallels meet in infinity
Epstein remodelled the form of divinity.

Anti-Germanism, understandably enough after the long haul that victory had demanded, also showed itself in divers reactions, and from Rutherford's Cavendish Laboratory there came a typical poem from A. A. Robb. One of the few English physicists who had given more than passing attention to the Special Theory, Robb had written as early as 1914 that "although generally associated with the names of Einstein and Minkowski, the really essential physical considerations underlying the theories are due to Larmor and Lorentz." His aversion to Einstein was increased by General Relativity and in the introduction to *The Absolute Relations of Time and Space,* he caustically wrote of Einstein's theory of simultaneity that "this seemed to destroy all sense of the reality of the external world and to leave the physical universe no better than a dream, or rather a nightmare."

The acclaim which surged up at the end of 1919 naturally presented too good an opportunity to miss; the result was Robb's "Hymn to Einstein," to be sung to the tune of "Deutschland Über Alles":

Scientists so unbelieving
Have completely changed their ways;
Now they humbly sing to Einstein
Everlasting hymns of praise.
Journalists in search of copy
First request an interview;
Then they boost him, boost him, boost him;
Boost him until all is blue.

He the universe created;
Spoke the word and it was there.
Now he reigns in radiant glory
On his professorial chair.
Editions of daily papers,
Yellow red and every hue
Boost him, boost him, boost him, boost him;
Boost him until all is blue.

Philosophic speculators

Stand in awe around his throne.
University professors
Blow upon his loud trombone.
Praise him on the Riemann symbols
On Christoffel symbols too
They boost him, boost him, boost him;
Boost him until all is blue.

Other scientists neglected
May be feeling somewhat sick;
And imagine that the butter
Is laid on a trifle thick.
Heed not such considerations
Be they false, or be they true;
Boost him, boost him, boost him, boost him;
Boost him until all is blue.

Einstein himself also seems to have been affected. Thus he started, early in December, one hare that was to run through decades of books about relativity, naturally enough ignored by science but enjoyed by many simple souls. Interviewed by the *New York Times*, he was asked how he had come to start work on the General Theory. He had been triggered off, he replied, by seeing a man falling from a Berlin roof. The man had survived with little injury. Einstein had run from his house. The man said that he had not felt the effects of gravity—a pronouncement that had led to a new view of the universe. Here is perhaps a link with Planck's illustration of energy—his story of a workman, carrying bricks to the top of a house and piling up energy which remained there until the bricks slipped and fell on his head weeks later. Here, too, is another illustration of Hans Einstein's statement that his father was always willing to exaggerate in order to explain, and would at times, delight in making up a story to please an audience.

All this, however, was froth on the top of the argument. Beneath the humor, the Alice in Wonderland analogies, and the limericks concerning the young lady called Bright, whose speed was much faster than light,* there lay

*The most respectable is Arthur Butler's: "There was a young lady called Bright/Whose speed was much faster than light/She went out one day/In a relative way/And came back the previous night."

an almost universal agreement that Einstein's view of gravitation was more consistent with the available facts than Newton's. There might be debate over details, the third proof had not yet been obtained, and there were to be several attempts—all either unsuccessful or inconclusive—to show that the outcome of the Michelson-Morley experiment itself could be faulted. But the band of responsible critics was comparatively small, and it was clear that Einstein had in fact cast fresh light not only on the subject of gravitation but on the whole question of how scientific knowledge might be acquired. For Newton's theory had been founded on the most detailed observational evidence; each twinkling pinpoint in the heavens appeared to support the belief that the accumulation of evidence, and the induction from it of general laws, could lead to the ultimate truth. Now it had been shown that by starting with a purely speculative idea, it was possible to construct a theory which would not only be supported by the mass of observational evidence with which Newton had worked, but which would also explain evidence which Newton could not explain. By the opening weeks of 1920 it was clear that Einstein held the field.

But to some people he had yet to live down his presence in Berlin throughout the war, however pacifist his sentiments might be. M. Brouillon had his counterparts in England, as Eddington was forced to make clear early in the New Year. As keen as Einstein himself for the restoration of scientific cooperation between the belligerent countries, Eddington had stressed this point in his first letter when on December 1, 1919, he had written to Einstein from Cambridge saying that since November 6 "all England has been talking about your theory. . . . It is the best possible thing that could have happened for scientific relations between England and Germany," he went on.

> I do not anticipate rapid progress towards official reunion, but there is a big advance towards a more reasonable frame of mind among scientific men, and that is even more important than the renewal of formal associations. . . . Although it seems unfair that Dr. Freundlich, who was first in the field, should not have had the satisfaction of accomplishing the experimental test of

your theory, one feels that things have turned out very fortunately in giving this object lesson of the solidarity of German and British science even in time of war.

So far so good. Eddington's liberal sentiments were held by many men of science, possibly a majority. When, later in December, three names were proposed for the Royal Astronomical Society's Gold Medal, Einstein was approved for the award by an overwhelming majority. He was duly informed and, writing to Born on January 27 about the Peace Treaty, added: "By the way, I am going to England in the spring, to have a medal pressed into my hand and to have a closer look at the other side of this tomfoolery."

A few days later he received an apologetic letter from Eddington, who said that the officials of the Royal Astronomical Society had met to vote on the Gold Medal award, but a purely chauvinistic lobby had mustered at the last minute and had successfully stopped its being made to Einstein. For the first time in thirty years, no Gold Medal would be awarded. "I am sure," wrote Eddington, "that your disappointment will not be in any way personal and that you will share with me the regret that this promising opening of a better international spirit has had a rebuff from reaction. Nevertheless, I am sure the better spirit is making progress."

As with Solvay, Einstein had to wait for a change in the political climate. Then, at last allowed to join in the game, he scooped the pool. In 1925 he was awarded the Royal Society's Copley Medal; and, the following year, the Royal Astronomical Society's Gold Medal.

Whatever the difficulties in making formal British awards to a German, Einstein had by the first months of 1920 gained not only success but notoriety, and his reaction to it was shown in a letter written to Hopf on February 2, 1920. "Saying 'no' has never been a strong point with me, but in my present distress I am at last gradually learning the art," he said. "Since the flood of newspaper articles, I have been so swamped with questions, invitations, challenges, that I dream that I am burning in Hell and that the postman is the Devil eternally roaring at me, throwing new bundles of letters at my head because I have not yet answered the old ones."

The speed with which his fame spread across the world,

down through the intellectual layers to the man in the street, the mixture of semireligious awe and near hysteria which his figure aroused, created a startling phenomenon which has never been fully explained, but is well described by Alexander Moszkowski, a Berlin litterateur and critic who moved on the fringe of the Einstein circle. Moszkowski's book, *Einstein the Searcher,* caused Einstein's friends a great deal of misgiving, and the Borns felt so strongly about it that they persuaded him to try to stop publication. The outcome of a long series of conversations during which Einstein had spoken about his work quite freely and in simple terms, the book was a vulgarization of science more unusual then than it would be today. It also had considerable, and somewhat dramatic, prepublication publicity, and it was this, more than the substance of the book itself, which angered Einstein's would-be protectors. He himself cared very little.

"Everything sank away in the face of this universal theme which had taken possession of humanity," Moszkowski wrote of the huge public interest in relativity.

> The converse of educated people circled about this pole, and could not escape from it, continually reverted to the same theme when pressed aside by necessity or accident. Newspapers entered on a chase for contributors who could furnish them with short or long, technical or nontechnical, notices about Einstein's theory. In all nooks and corners, social evenings of instruction sprang up, and wondering universities appeared with errant professors that led people out of the three-dimensional misery of daily life into the more hospitable Elysian fields of four-dimensionality. Women lost sight of domestic worries and discussed coordinate systems, the principle of simultaneity, and negatively charged electrons. All contemporary questions had gained a fixed center from which threads could be spun to each. Relativity had become the sovereign password.

Exaggerated as it sounds, this account is no more than the truth, even if the truth in fancy dress. The attitude was, moreover, not confined to the uninitiated. "To those who have the vision the world of physics will take on a new and wonderful life," wrote the reviewer in *Nature* of Einstein's own book on relativity. "The commonest phenomena become organic parts of the great plan. The rationality of the universe becomes an exciting romance, not a cold dogma. The thrill of a comprehensive understanding runs through us, and yet we find ourselves on the shores of the unknown. For this new doctrine, after all, is but a touchstone of truth. We must submit all our theories to the test of it; we must allow our deepest thoughts to be gauged by it. The metaphysician and he who speculates over the meaning of life cannot be indifferent."

It was therefore predictable that learned societies should hold many meetings at which the special and the general theories were discussed, that the *Times Educational Supplement* should devote three full-page articles to interpretations of relativity by Professor Lindemann, Dr. Herbert Carr, and Alfred Whitehead, and that an Einstein Sociey should be started in the House of Commons in 1920. "Its formation was due more to the curiosity of those of us who had unexpectedly survived the First World War than to any profound scientific search," says one of its members, Colin Coote.

It was understandable that within a year there should be more than one hundred books on the subject, and that intellectual interest should be shown not only in the world's capitals but in the provinces. "At this time," writes Infeld, later to become one of Einstein's collaborators, "I was a schoolteacher in a small Polish town, and I did what hundreds of others did all over the world. I gave a public lecture on the relativity theory, and the crowd that queued up on a cold winter's night was so great that it could not be accommodated in the largest hall in the town." When Eddington had lectured in Cambridge on a similar night in December, "hundreds were turned away unable to get near the room," in his own words. In Paris the American Eugene Higgins presented $5,000 through the *Scientific American* for the best 3,000-word exposition of relativity. "I am the only one in my entire circle of friends who is not entering," observed Einstein. "I don't believe I could do it." The prize, fittingly enough in view of Einstein's Berne background, was won by Lyndon Bolton, a senior examiner of the British Patent Office.

If all this was explicable in terms of an important new scientific theory which had become the common coin of intelligent conversation, Einstein was also raised to the far less comprehensible position of a popular celebrity. From

London the Palladium music hall asked whether he would appear, virtually at his own figure, for a three-week "performance." The "Einstein cigar" appeared on the market. Children were blessed, or otherwise, with his name. The cartoonists took him to their hearts. In Germany, he was shown in company with the French President Millerand, who was advocating the heaviest possible reparations from that country: "Can't you persuade the simple-minded Bôche that even with an absolute deficit of 67,000,000,000 marks he is still *relatively* well off?" In Britain, a detective shown catching a bank thief with the help of a flashlight whose light rays turned corners, laconically remarked: "Elementary, my dear Einstein." He had in fact been hoisted into position by the same mob which hoists film stars. Reason had little to do with the matter. But in one way the treatment of Einstein was different in its results. Film stars pontificating on the future of the world, boxers dogmatizing on politics, can be good entertainment and few people take them more seriously than this. Einstein was in another category. His theory might not be understandable to most men but it was clear that he had an intellect of unique proportions. Surely his brain could be turned to illuminate, with good effect, some of the problems that worried ordinary mortals? It was easy to answer "Yes."

All this was only a prelude to a long series of invitations to lecture in foreign countries; to the bags of letters and pleas for money which come to famous men and, in Einstein's case, were brought up the stairs by the sackload. It was a prelude to determined appeals from more substantial causes, above all from the Zionists and the pacifists, both quick to realize that in Einstein they might be able to secure a unique totem figure.

The photogenic white-haired messiah to which the world later became accustomed cannot be invoked to explain the extraordinary and worldwide phenomenon. The picture of Einstein as he toured the world in the early 1920s, well booted and accoutered, broad-brimmed hat giving a touch of mystery, is quite the reverse: a picture of the distinguished man of the times, possibly aloof, but certainly established. The sheer audacity of his theory helped. "Light caught bending" was an affront to common sense that few could in their heart of hearts take seriously;

there was, if nothing else, a curiosity value about the man who had apparently shown that it did.

Yet to attribute Einstein's popularity to this alone is to rate too low the inner awareness of the common people. Some weight must be given to Leopold Infeld's view. "It was just after the end of the war," he says.

> People were weary of hatred, of killing and international intrigues. The trenches, bombs, and murder had left a bitter taste. Books about war did not sell. Everyone looked for a new era of peace, and wanted to forget the war. Here was something which captured the imagination; human eyes looking from an earth covered with graves and blood to the heavens covered with the stars. Abstract thought carrying the human mind far away from the sad and disappointing reality. The mystery of the sun's eclipse and of the penetrating power of the human mind. Romantic scenery, a strange glimpse of the eclipsed sun, an imaginary picture of bending light rays, all removed from the oppressive reality of life. One further reason, perhaps even more important; a new event was predicted by a *German* scientist Einstein, and confirmed by *English* astronomers. Scientists belonging to two warring nations had collaborated again! It seemed the beginning of a new era.

Even this was only part of the story. Quite as important was the intuitive realization that the new light cast on the physical world struck at the very vitals of what they had always believed. Few could understand the implications, let alone the complex intellectual structure from which these implications sprang; even so, deep within there lay a sensitive sounding board, developed since the days when man had first stood up on two feet out of four. Erwin Schrödinger, who six years later was to become a standard bearer in the new cause of wave mechanics, hinted at the underlying reason for the Einstein phenomenon in his Tarner Lectures of 1956. "I have sometimes wondered why they made such a great stir both among the general public and among philosophers," he said of the transformations of time and space produced by relativity.

> I suppose it is this, that it meant the dethronement of time as a rigid tyrant imposed on us from outside, a liberation from the unbreakable rule of "before and

> after." For indeed time is our most severe master by ostensibly restricting the existence of each of us to narrow limits—seventy or eighty years, as the Pentateuch has it. To be allowed to play about with such a master's programme believed unassailable until then, to play about with it albeit in a small way, seems to be a great relief, it seems to encourage the thought that the whole "timetable" is probably not quite as serious as it appears at first sight. And this thought is a religious thought, nay I should call it *the* religious thought.

With the "great stir" there started the Einstein mythology, the complex structure of story and half-story, half-truth, quarter-truth, adorned exaggeration, and plain lie, which from now onwards increasingly surrounded his activities. All men caught in the white-hot glare of public interest discover, sometimes with amusement, sometimes with resignation, often with resentment, that their smallest doings are memorialized, embroidered, and explained away in a continuous flow of anecdote whose connection with the truth is frequently marginal. Einstein was to suffer more than most from such attentions and soon learned to regard them with amusement—as must any biographer who meets the same quasi-documented story appearing in different decades, from different continents, and being retailed, in all good faith, to illustrate one or more of Einstein's extraordinary, endearing, or unconventional attitudes.

There were many reasons for the mythology which developed from 1920 onwards. One was that inventions had good ground to grow in. Immersed in his work in Berlin, Einstein did on one occasion use a check as a bookmark; it was therefore pardonable that the story should surface as the account of how he had placed a $1,500 check into a book and then lost the book. His character was kindly and gentle, and he was at least once asked by a neighbor's small girl to help with her sums; after that, small girls all over the world had Einstein doing their homework—despite the fact that he had refused the request on the grounds that it would not be fair. The legends themselves, melting in the harsh light of investigation, show not so much what sort of man he really was as what kind of man the world thought him. Behind his confidence, Einstein was genuinely humble—and legend made him forbear comment when a girl graduate, failing to recognize him, voiced surprise that he should still be studying physics with the words: "I finished physics when I was twenty-five." Only Einstein, out of time with his fellow musicians at an amateur recital, would receive the criticism: "Einstein, can't you count?" Only Einstein, unable to find his glasses and asking the dining-car attendant to read the menu, would be met with the comment: "Sorry, sir, I ain't had education either." And only Einstein, looking like an untidy middle-class nonentity, could go unrecognized by officialdom in a score of stories, pottering his way through the crowd, a Chaplinesque figure somehow embodying all the human virtues of "us" against "them." Thus he became, as the forces of left and right jockeyed for position in the postwar Germany of the Weimar Republic, a new sort of international image, the scientist wth the touch of a saint, a man from whom an awed public expected not only research but revelation.

From outside Germany there came adulation—and in 1921 the much-prized Foreign Fellowship of the Royal Society. Inside, opinion was mixed. Planck and Sommerfeld, von Laue and Rubens, Nernst and Haber were among those who knew what Einstein had accomplished, while some Weimar politicians mentally seized upon him as typifying the new Germany which they hoped could now be presented to the world. Yet there were many others to whom his success was deeply offensive, uniting in one man all that they detested—the success of an intellectual left-wing pacifist Jew.

This feeling counterbalanced the adulation in many ways. In Ulm, for instance, the authorities at first intended to make him a freeman of the city. "But before I approach our collegium," wrote Herr Dr. Schemberger to the Faculty of Philosophy in Tübingen University on behalf of the City Council, "I would like to find out whether it is true that Einstein's work is really of such outstanding merit." The answer was an unqualified "Yes" which concluded: "What Newton did for mechanics, Einstein has done for physics." But when Dr. Schemberger wrote to Einstein on March 22, it was not the freedom of the city which was offered, but merely congratulations and the assurance that the town was glad to have him as one of its sons. Einstein's thanks were read out at the next council meeting. There was to be no freedom. Two years later, when the award of the Nobel Prize for Physics put the seal on his work, the authorities settled for a street to be named after him. Perhaps it was only coincidence that it lay on the outskirts of the city and in a poorish area. More than a quarter of a century later, in 1949, he was asked to become an honorary citizen. Einstein refused.

The honors from outside Germany increased throughout 1920. The first came from Leiden. Lorentz had telegraphed him as soon as he had heard of the Royal Society's meeting in November, 1919, and Einstein's reply, saying how much it had pleased him, although he knew the telegram's contents, is revealing. "It is a proof of your affection which means more to me than all the experimental confirmation in the world," he wrote on November 15. "The day I was allowed to spend with you in Haarlem was one of the most wonderful of my life. You yourself must feel how deep is my love and respect for you." There soon followed the proposal of Kamerlingh Onnes that he be appointed "byzondere Hoogleerarden," or professor extraordinary, for three years at an annual salary of 2,000 guilders. The duties would involve only one or two visits a year, each of a few weeks, and there would be no need to interrupt his Berlin work. Einstein accepted, after receiving a plea to do so from Ehrenfest, and having been told by Lorentz that Kamerlingh Onnes, who just twenty years earlier had ignored Einstein's appeal for work, "would regard it as a high honor if you would discuss with him the researches being carried out in his cryogenic laboratory."

There were numerous delays, and while Einstein visited his friends in Leiden in May, 1920, it was not until five months later that he made his first formal visit as a professor extraordinary. Between these two visits, he met Niels Bohr for the first time. Bohr, who had just started the Institute of Theoretical Physics in Copenhagen, made possible by an endowment from the Carlsberg organization, had been invited by Planck to lecture to the Physikalische Gesellschaft and on his arrival both Planck and Einstein came forward to meet him. So similar in work and outlook, few men were more dissimilar in appearance; Planck formal and precise behind his rimless glasses, immaculately dressed, the German professor down the ages; Einstein still dark-haired, still rather splendid in a leonine way, but already beginning to foreshadow the familiar figure of untidy genius which became the hallmark of his later years.

Something was sparked off between Bohr and Einstein at this meeting, the first of a long series of mental collisions whose succession through the years was to have a quality quite separate from the impact of genius on genius. For it was Einstein who, fifteen years earlier, had first brought an air of unexpected respectability to the idea that light might conceivably consist both of wave and of particle and to the notion that Planck's quantum theory might be applied not only to radiation but to matter itself. It was Bohr who was to bring scientific plausibility to the first of these ideas with his principle of complementarity and substance for the second with his explanation of Rutherford's nuclear atom. Yet these very ideas were to create not a unity between the two men but a chasm. From the early 1920s, as Bohr and those of like mind followed them on to what they saw as inevitable conclusions, Einstein drew back in steadily growing disagreement, withdrawing himself from the mainstream of physics and giving to his later years a tragic air which not even the staunchest of his friends could argue away.

"I am just as keen on him as you are," he wrote of Bohr to Ehrenfest after this first meeting in 1920. "He is an extremely sensitive lad, and goes about the world as if hypnotized." Bohr was quite as impressed with Einstein. "The discussions, to which I have often reverted in my thoughts," he later wrote, "added to all my admiration for Einstein a deep impression of his detached attitude. Certainly his favored use of such picturesque phrases as 'ghost waves [Gespensterfelder] guiding the photons' implied no tendency to mysticism, but illuminated a rather profound humor behind his piercing remarks." And on July 27 he wrote to Rutherford, saying that his visit had been "a very interesting experience, it being the first time I had the opportunity of meeting Planck and Einstein personally, and I spend [sic] the days discussing theoretical problems from morning till night."

Later, he gave some details of these discussions. "What do you hope to achieve?" he had asked, when Einstein had doubted whether it was necessary to give up causality and continuity. "You, the man who introduced the idea of light as particles! If you are so concerned with the situation in physics in which the nature of light allows for a dual interpretation, then ask the German government to ban the use of photoelectric cells if you think that light is waves, or the use of diffraction gratings if light is corpuscular."

Einstein remarked: "There you are: a man like you comes and one would expect that two like-minded persons had met, yet we are unable to find a common language. Maybe we physicists ought to agree on certain general fundamentals, on certain general propositions which we would regard as positive before embarking on discussions."

But Bohr objected: "No. never! I would regard it as the greatest treachery on my part if, in embarking on a new domain of knowledge, I accepted any foregone conclusions." This "certain difference in attitude and outlook" between the two men, as Bohr described it, was clear from the first day. It was sharpened and increased during long discussions over more than three decades. But it was the difference between the sides in a great game in which both men strove "to set the cause beyond renown/ To love the game beyond the prize,/ To honour, while you strike him down,/ The foe that comes with fearless eyes."

Something of their mutual admiration shines out from their first letters. Einstein, thanking Bohr for a gift of food which had arrived from Copenhagen after Bohr's return there, wrote on May 2: "Not often in life has a man given me such happiness by his mere presence as you have done. I now understand why Ehrenfest enjoyed you so much. I am studying your great works and—when I get stuck anywhere—now have the pleasure of seeing your friendly young face before me, smiling and explaining. I have learned much from you, mainly from your sensitive approach to scientific problems." Bohr's reply, written as he learned that Einstein would be visiting Copenhagen, was equally revealing.

> For me, it is one of the greatest experiences of life that I can be near you and talk to you, and I cannot say how grateful I am for all the friendliness which you showed to me on my visit to Berlin, and for your letter which I am ashamed not to have answered before. You do not know

how great a stimulus it was for me to have the long-awaited opportunity of hearing from you personally your views on the very question with which I myself have been busy. I will never forget our conversation on the way from Dahlem to your house, and I very much hope that during your visit here an opportunity will arise of continuing it.

Einstein was by the midsummer of 1920 making numerous lecture visits of the sort that Bohr referred to. After each he returned to Berlin, and after each he found opposition to himself, and to all that he stood for, ominously growing. And now he decided to straighten out the anomalous question of his nationality. He had renounced his German citizenship and as far as he knew was merely a German-born Swiss, an awkward situation which made him a sitting target for his enemies. There was one simple way of coming into the body of the Kirk: he could take up German civic rights again, an action that might underline his support for the Republic and would at least suggest that he was no longer ashamed of his country.

On July 1, 1920, Einstein was sworn into the Weimar constitution and eight and a half months later, on March 15, 1921, into the Prussian constitution. Often unreliable on dates, he gave this account of his resumption of German citizenship to Janos Plesch towards the end of the Second World War: "I accepted it in 1918 after the general disaster, at the urgent representations of my colleagues. It was one of the follies of my life. Politically I hated Germany from my youth and I always felt the dangers that threatened the world from her side."

If Einstein hated Germany, a portion of Germany certainly hated him. The reasons for this, given the situation in the country in July and August, 1920, are simple to explain if difficult to excuse. In countries which had won the war only at desperate cost, Einstein polarized a longing for cooperation and reconstruction, for an end to the anarchy and for the rational use of scientific knowledge for the common good. In Germany it was otherwise. Here patriotic passion, born of defeat, distrusted pacifist leanings and international connections; and if anti-Semitism was a convenient though dishonorable weapon, desperate times demanded desperate measures. Such feelings were epitomized by the new symbol of General von Luttwitz'

Erhardt Brigade, which had marched into Berlin from the Baltic to support the abortive Kapp Putsch a few months earlier. On their helmets they wore a reverse of the swastika, a religious symbol usually associated with the worship of the Aryan sun gods Apollo and Odin.

In the ferment of postwar Germany, where internal divisions were lessened by what appeared to be the vindictive brutality of the Allied blockade, there was more than one group willing to direct rising passions against Einstein, a ready-made target for hatred. There were those scientists who genuinely did not believe in the theories which had brought him a fame unique in their scientific experience. There were others who, whatever they believed, could not bear the thought of such acclaim being lavished on a man who had spent the hard-fought war burrowing away in the University of Berlin. It was bad enough that an unknown professor should have declaimed against the war, held out a welcoming hand to the enemy across the French frontier, and failed even to bend his energies to the commonweal like other scientists such as Haber and Nernst; it was intolerable that the same line should be followed by the man now that he had been jerked to fame overnight. Thus the renown which was to take Einstein round the world in the first half of the 1920s acted as an irritant to the anti-Semitism which burgeoned with the coming of Hitler a decade later. Its roots went deep, it flourished in the postwar period, and as the years passed it became more firmly established, so that it later proved a weapon which the Nazis could wield. They would have utilized something, of course. But the steady growth of anti-Semitism during the interwar years was at least partly due to the ease with which its supporters could concentrate their attacks on Einstein and the "new physics."

The attacks started before the end of 1919. In December, while Einstein was still half-submerged by the first tidal wave of publicity which followed the Royal Society meeting in London, he had written to Ehrenfest noting that "anti-Semitism is strong here [Berlin] and political reaction is violent, at least among the 'intelligentsia.' " A few days later he noted that following an article by Born in the *Frankfurter Zeitung*, both of them would be persecuted by the press and other rabble. It was so bad for him, he went on, that he could scarcely come up for air, let alone work.

Then, in March, Wolfgang Kapp seized Berlin but failed to hold it in the face of a general strike called by the Weimar government. Internal evidence suggests that the same right-wing forces which subsidized the Kapp Putsch—claimed by Kurt Grossman to include "secret groups round Krupp"—played at least some part in the growing anti-Einstein movement. Finally they created the "Study Group of German Natural Philosophers" (Arbeitsgemeinschaft Deutscher Naturforscher), which had at its disposal large sums of money, offered fees to those who would write or speak against Einstein, and advertised its meetings by large posters as though they were announcing public concerts. Leader of this so-called "Study Group" was Paul Weyland, a man entirely unknown in scientific circles and of whom, over the years, nothing was discovered. Much of his support came from assorted riffraff; some of it came from more scientifically respectable sources. The physicist Ernst Gehrcke joined the association and so did a number of other men who could genuinely claim to be classed as *bona fide* even if undistinguished scientists.

Above all there was Philip Lenard, whose work on the photoelectric effect had been the forerunner of Einstein's and whose achievements had been stressed by Einstein in his letters to Laub. Lenard had been considered something of an oddity by many of his colleagues at Heidelberg, but before the war he had not been an anti-Semite. He read the ultrarespectable *Frankfurter Zeitung* and, according to Laub, held a high opinion of Einstein's photoelectric paper. One thing that did rankle was Einstein's implied dismissal of the ether as an unnecessary complication in the universe; this in turn, although rather irrelevantly, led him to denigrate the theory of relativity. His views no doubt hardened during the war. They certainly became fixed by the torrent of praise which poured over Einstein from November, 1919, onwards. And in 1920 Lenard reappears as the Nobel Prize winner enthusiastically providing scientific respectability for the Weyland organization, which described relativity as part of a vast Semitic plot to corrupt the world in general and Germany in particular. Its attacks avoided scientific argument; instead, they concentrated on the "Jewish nature" of relativity, and on the personal character of Einstein. This made them an embarrassment to the scientific community. But to the uninformed public the news that the "Study Group" was supported by a Nobel Prize winner gave the organization a stiffening of pseudo-respectability it would otherwise have lacked.

In August the "Antirelativity Company," as Einstein called it, announced twenty meetings to be held in Germany's biggest towns. Berlin was its headquarters and it hired the Berlin Philharmonic Hall for a setpiece demonstration against both relativity and Einstein, to be held on August 27.

In some ways the packed meeting had an air of farce as much as of high drama. On to the stage came Weyland, apparently the "handsome dark-haired man of about thirty who wore a frockcoat and spoke with enthusiasm about interesting things" later described by Einstein's colleague Leopold Infeld. "He said that uproar about the theory of relativity was hostile to the German spirit. Then there came a university lecturer who had a little beard, was small, who also wore a frockcoat, and who read out his speech from a brochure which had been sold before the lecture. He raised objections about understanding the theory of relativity."

This second spokesman seems to have been Gehrcke, and as he dived into some rudimentary technicalities there was a murmur of "Einstein, Einstein" in the audience. For Einstein had arrived to see what it was all about. There he was, sitting in a box, obviously enjoying himself. As the speakers went on, attacking relativity, omitting, distorting, unbalancing, appealing to the good Aryan common sense of their audience and invoking its members not to take such stuff seriously, the clown that lies not far below genius began to show itself. At the more absurd statements about relativity Einstein could be seen bursting into laughter and clapping his hands in mock applause. When the meeting had ended he greeted his friends: "That was most amusing."

However, the so-called "Study Group" was a symptom of something more sinister than scientific absurdity, and Einstein replied in the columns of the *Berliner Tageblatt*—the first time that he had come down into the marketplace to face his accusers. His statement was headed: "My Answer to the Antirelativity Theory Company Ltd." In many ways it is vintage Einstein. "Under the pretentious name of Study Group of German Natural Philosophers, there has come into existence a variegated society whose provisional aim it is to disparage both the theory of relativity and myself as its author in the eyes of nonphysicists," he began.

> Messrs. Weyland and Gehrcke have recently held their first lecture on this in the Philharmonic. I myself was present. I am very well aware that neither of these speakers are worthy of an answer from my pen, and I have good reasons to believe that motives other than a desire to search for truth are at the bottom of their enterprise. (Were I a German national, with or without swastika, instead of a Jew of liberal, international disposition, then. . . .) I therefore reply only because it has been urged by well-wishers that my views should be made known.
>
> First of all I must point out that there is, to my knowledge, scarcely a scientist who has carried out anything worthwhile in theoretical physics who does not concede that the whole theory of relativity is logically constructed and is in accord with facts which have so far been shown to be incontestable. The most outstanding theoretical physicists—I cite H. A. Lorentz, M. Planck, Sommerfeld, Laue, Born, Larmor, Eddington, Debije, Langevin, Levi-Civita—solidly support the theory and have themselves made worthy contributions to it. As an outspoken opponent of the theory of relativity I can only name Lenard among the physicists of international repute. I admire Lenard as a master of experimental physics; but he has not yet done anything in theoretical physics, and his objections against the General Theory of Relativity are so superficial that until now I have not considered it necessary to answer them in detail. I now propose to rectify that omission.
>
> It is held up against me that it is bad taste for me to speak up for the theory of relativity. I can truly say that all my life I have been a friend of reasonable argument and of the truth. High-falutin' words and phrases bring me out in goose pimples whether they deal with relativity or anything else. I myself have often made fun of such things and this has then been thrown back at me. However, I gladly make a present of this opportunity to the gentlemen of the antirelativity company.

Einstein then turned to the lectures, dealing first with Weyland—"who seems to be no sort of expert (doctor? engineer? politician? I cannot find out)"—and then with Gehrcke. His opponents had relied on such devices as quoting results from one British eclipse station already known to be incorrect due to a technical defect and omitting all reference to the British announcement that the theory had been proved. Thus Einstein's demolition task was easy.

"Finally," he said, referring to the annual meeting of the German Association of Scientists and Doctors which was to be held in Bad Nauheim the coming month, "I notice that at the scientists' gathering at Nauheim there has, at my suggestion, been arranged a discussion on the theory of relativity. Anyone who wants to protest can do so there and put up his ideas to a proper gathering of scientists."

Fifty years ago it was almost unknown for a scientist to use the columns of the daily press in this way. Even Einstein's friends were shocked. Hedwig Born wrote that he must have suffered very much—"for otherwise you would not have allowed yourself to be goaded into that rather unfortunate reply in the newspaper." Ehrenfest was even more condemnatory. "My wife and I absolutely cannot believe that you yourself wrote down at least some of the phrases in this article, 'My Answer,' " he said on August 28. "We don't forget for a minute that you have certainly been provoked in an especially vulgar way, and neither do we forget in what an abnormal moral climate you live there; nevertheless this answer contains certain reactions that are completely non-Einsteinian. We could underline them one by one in pencil. If you really did write them down with your own hand, it proves that these damned pigs have finally succeeded in touching your soul which means so terribly much to us. . . ."

This in fact was what had happened. Einstein felt he had no alternative but to reply to the charges of charlatanism, self-advertisement, and plagiarism. "I had to do it if I wanted to remain in Berlin, where every child recognizes me from the photographs," he replied to Ehrenfest. "If one is a democrat, one has also to acknowledge the claims of publicity."

Second only to the sense of shock that a scientist should

defend himself in this way was astonishment that a member of the scientific fraternity should need to do so. "The incredible thing," von Laue wrote to Sommerfeld, "is that men such as Lenard and Wolf of Heidelberg, who have a reputation as scholars, actually lecture to such an association. Yesterday Gehrcke spoke after Weyland, and although he stoked up the old fires, his quiet manner of speaking was a relief after Weyland, who can compete with the most unscrupulous demagogue. It is a disgrace that such a thing can happen."

Von Laue went on to say that he, Rubens, and Nernst had sent their own short letter of protest against the activities of the association to the leading Berlin newspapers. This, published in the *Berliner Tageblatt,* read as follows:

> We cannot presume in this place to utter our opinion on the profound, exemplary intellectual work which Einstein has brought to his relativity theory. Surprising successes have already been achieved, and further proof must naturally lie in future research. On the other hand, we must stress that apart from Einstein's researches into relativity, his work has assured him a permanent place in the history of science. In this respect his influence on the scientific life not only of Berlin but of the whole of Germany can hardly be overestimated. Whoever is fortunate enough to be close to Einstein knows that he will never be surpassed in his respect for the cultural values of others, in personal modesty and dislike of all publicity.

Sommerfeld himself had been deeply aroused, particularly in view of fresh rumors that Einstein was planning to leave Germany. As president of the German Physics Society he felt it necessary to come to the rescue. "Dear Einstein," he wrote on September 3,

> With real fury I have, as man and as president, followed the Berlin hunt against you. A word of warning to Wolf of Heidelberg was unnecessary. His name, as he has meanwhile written to you, has simply been misused. I feel sure it will be the same with Lenard. A fine type, this Weyland-Gehrcke!
>
> Today I have conferred with Planck about what has to be done about the Association of Scientists [Naturforscher Gesellschaft]. We would like to put to the president, my

> colleague von Müller, a sharp protest against "scientific" demagogy, and a vote of confidence in you. This would not be formally voted upon but would only be raised as an expression of the scientific conscience.
>
> You must not leave Germany! Your whole work is rooted in German (and Dutch) science; nowhere will you find so much understanding as in Germany. It is not in your character to leave Germany now, when she is being so dreadfully misinterpreted by everyone. Just one more point: had you, with your views, lived during the war in France, England, or America, you would certainly have been locked up had you turned your back on the Entente and its false system, as I do not doubt you would have done (as were Jaurès, Russell, Caillaus, etc.).

Sommerfeld went on to explain that a south German magazine group had suggested that Einstein might write an article for them. He was fairly obviously in favor of the idea, particularly as there had been some criticism of the *Berliner Tageblatt* letter. Sommerfeld himself had not read it, but those who had, he said, considered it "not very happy" and rather unlike Einstein. It was, he felt, hardly the right place in which to answer the anti-Semitic attack. And he put in another plea for the south German group.

"I hope that in the meantime you have regained your philosophical laughter and sympathy with the Germany whose trials are everywhere apparent," he concluded. "But no more of desertion."

In emphasizing that Einstein should stand his ground, Sommerfeld was appealing, ironically enough, to Einstein's feelings for Germany, the nation cast off in 1896, whose actions he had bitterly criticized throughout the war. To retire to Holland, or even Switzerland, would be desertion; desertion not only of his scientific colleagues but of that Germany "whose trials are everywhere obvious."

At the end of August, 1920, Einstein was therefore once again being pulled in two directions—away from Berlin by the threat of anti-Semitism and the friendships of Lorentz and Ehrenfest; towards Berlin by his loyalty to university colleagues and his new-found hope for a republican Germany. He knew that a permanent post at Leiden University could be his for the asking and the same was no doubt still true of Zurich. His thoughts were already turning to England, and to a young British visitor who called on him to discuss German requests for periodicals from British universities, he "referred to his lecturing at Oxford and expressed the pleasure that it would be for him to do so some time." Lindemann, recently made head of the Clarendon Laboratory, Oxford, had also called on him in Berlin. They had recalled their last meeting at the Solvay Congress and agreed to exchange future papers, and it is more than likely—especially in the light of future events—that Lindemann put the idea of an Oxford visit into Einstein's head. Something more substantial had already been suggested to Rutherford, who had taken J. J. Thomson's place at the Cavendish the previous year. For on September 1, Jeans had written to him from Zermatt, sending what was probably a report of Einstein's statement in the *Berliner Tageblatt*. "My dear Rutherford," he said,

> You spoke of the need of a first-class applied mathematician or math[ematical] physicist for Cambridge. I have been wondering what you would think of Albert Einstein. From the enclosed it seems quite likely that he will be leaving Berlin very soon—there has been a good deal of disturbance over him there, as you have probably seen, and he would probably consider an English offer I should think.
>
> In my opinion he is just the man needed, in conjunction with yourself, to reestablish a school of mathematical physics in Cambridge. The only serious drawback I think of is that he does not, or did not, speak English, but I imagine he would soon learn. His age is forty-two, nearly forty-three, and I imagine he has still plenty of creative power left.

There is no record of Rutherford's reply, but it seems likely that he was still slightly allergic to Einstein. Nevertheless, for a man of such unique reputation almost all options were open and it would not have been surprising had Einstein now left Germany for a permanent post outside the Reich. But by the time he replied to Sommerfeld on September 6, he had decided otherwise.

"Actually," he wrote,

> I attached too much importance to that attack on me, in that I believed that a great part of our physicists took part in it. So I really thought for two days that I would

> "desert" as you call it. But soon there came reflection, and the knowledge that it would be wrong to leave the circle of my faithful friends. Perhaps I should not have written the article. But I wanted to prevent the feeling that my continuing silence about the protests and the accusations, which were systematically repeated, was due to agreement. It is a bad thing that every utterance of mine is made use of by journalists as a matter of business. I must lock myself up.
>
> I cannot possibly write the article in the *South German Monthly*. In fact, I should be very happy if I could bring myself up to date with my correspondence. Such a declaration at Nauheim would perhaps on the grounds of tidiness be just the thing as far as people abroad are concerned. But I do not on any account want to speak myself, for I am again happy and content and read nothing that depresses me except absolute essentials. . . .

Three days later he wrote to the Borns. "Like the man in the fairy tale who turned everything he touched into gold, so with me everything turns into a fuss in the newspapers," he noted: *"suum cuique."* But he added that "insight and phlegm" had returned and that now he was thinking "only of buying a sailing boat and a country cottage close to water. Somewhere near Berlin."

Yet if he had agreed not to leave Germany, the decision could easily be changed. The agents of the German Republic now acted to prevent such a catastrophe. One was Planck, the other was Haenisch, the German Minister of Education; both were determined that for the sake of German science Einstein should be discouraged from having second thoughts.

Planck wrote to Einstein on September 5, from Gmund am Tegernsee in the South Tyrol. He could scarcely believe reports of the meeting in the Berlin Philharmonic and found it impossible to understand what was going on. But very much more important to him, he continued, was what impression the intrigues were likely to have on Einstein, whom he feared might eventually lose patience and take a step which would punish both German science and his friends for the wrong that had been done by those of a pitiable state of mind. The proper representatives of science should not, indeed dare not, he ended, fail to ensure that Einstein was adequately compensated.

Planck, who could speak not only from his own Olympian height but also from a position of friendship, was supported by the Minister of Education. "Most respected professor," the Minister now wrote to Einstein.

> With sorrow and shame I see by the press that the theory represented by you has become a public object of spiteful attacks which go far beyond the limits of pertinent criticism, and that even your own scientific personality has not been spared from defamation and slanders. It is of special satisfaction to me to know in connection with this affair that scholars of recognized repute, among whom are prominent representatives of the University of Berlin, are supporting you, are denouncing the contemptible attacks upon your person, and are drawing attention to the fact that your scientific work has assured you a unique place in the history of science. Where the best people are defending you, it will be the easier for you to pay no further attention to such ugly actions. Therefore, I may well allow myself to express the definite hope that there is no truth in the rumors that, because of these vicious attacks, you wished to leave Berlin which always was, and always will be, proud to count you, most respected professor, among the first ornaments of the scientific world.

Einstein appears to have delayed his reply, although he no doubt acknowledged the Minister's appeal. He had good reason to be cautious, for it seemed possible that the "Antirelativity Company" might muster considerable support, from rabblerousers if not from scientists. "The first anti-Einstein lecture," the *New York Times* had reported, "had a decided anti-Semitic complexion, which applied equally to the lecture and to a large part of the audience." And in the volatile atmosphere of early Weimar Germany there was a genuine danger of violence at Bad Nauheim, where the meeting of the Gesellschaft Naturforscher was to start on September 25. It seemed likely that there would at the least be a dramatic confrontation comparable to that between Bishop Wilberforce and T. H. Huxley at the British Association in Oxford sixty years earlier.

Bad Nauheim is only some twenty miles from Frankfurt, where Born had recently been appointed professor, and Einstein stayed with the Borns for the duration of the meeting, traveling into the small town each day with his friends. The spa is a leisurely place in the foothills of the

Taunus, lying among the pines, accustomed to conferences and old people, and on the morning of September 25 its inhabitants were surprised to find the Badehaus guarded by armed police with fixed bayonets: an indication both of the extent to which anti-Semitism had already been aroused and of Weimar's wish to avoid trouble. The opposition to Einstein had been fully organized. "I had previously received a letter, signed by Weyland, in which I was guaranteed a very large sum (I forget the details) if I would side with them," Ehrenhaft has written. Instead, he passed on the letter to Einstein.

The Badehalle was packed for the discussion on relativity. "When Lenard began," says Dr. Friedrich Dessauer, who was sitting on Einstein's left, "Einstein wanted to make notes but, as one would expect, he had no pencil. He asked to borrow mine in order to reply clearly and convincingly to Lenard's objections. . . . As a minor joke, Einstein has my pencil to this day. At least, he never returned it to me, so that what has come from it is probably more intelligent than it would have been if I had got it back."

Lenard's style can be judged from his opening words: "I have much pleasure in today taking part in a discussion on the gravitation theory of the ether. But I must say that as soon as one passes from the theory of gravitation to those of the powers of mass proportion, the simple understanding of the scientist must take exception to the theory." One could, he went on, express the result of observations through equations; or one could explain equations in terms of observations. "I would very much favor the second idea whereas Einstein favors the first."

Einstein now rose to reply. No verbatim account appears to have survived. Dr. Dessauer says that the argument was not quite as grim as was feared, and the report in the *Physikalische Zeitschrift* gives the impression of a decorous exchange. However, Born later commented that Einstein "was provoked into making a caustic reply," while Einstein himself later wrote to Born saying: "I . . . will not allow myself to get excited again, as in Nauheim. It is quite inconceivable to me how I could have lost my sense of humor to such an extent through being in bad company." According to Felix Ehrenhaft, he was "interrupted repeatedly by exclamations and uproar. It was obviously an organized interruption. Planck understood this and was pale as death as he raised his voice and told those making the row to be quiet."

When Einstein had finished, Lenard rose to say that he had not heard anything new. "I believe," he added, "that the fields of gravitation which have been spoken of must correspond to examples, and such examples have not yet appeared in practice." Instead of the obvious retort that the British expeditions had provided them, Einstein replied more soothingly: "I would like to say that what seems obvious to people and what does not seem obvious, has changed. Opinions about obviousness are to a certain extent a function of time. I believe that physics is abstract and not obvious, and as an example of the changing views of what is clear, and what is not, I recommend you to consider the clarity with which Galilean mechanics has been interpreted at different times."

The argument was continued at this level. A Professor Rudolph claimed that proof of the General Theory was no argument against the ether. A Professor Palagyi looked on the difference of opinion as merely an example of "the old historical opposition between the experimentalist and the mathematical physicist, such as existed, for example, between Faraday and Maxwell." Max Born weighed in with a brief comment in favor of Einstein, and before much more could be said it was discovered, no doubt to Planck's relief, that time was up. "Since the relativity theory unfortunately has not yet made it possible to extend the absolute time interval that is available for the meeting," he announced, "our session must be adjourned."

The dangerous corner had been turned. Einstein went home to Berlin, comforted. Early in October it was formally announced that he would be remaining there.

If this decision had been made solely on the same grounds as his original decision to join the Kaiser Wilhelm Institute—the wish to remain in closest possible contact with the men who were investigating the nature of the physical world—this would have been understandable enough. But by 1920 it was no longer necessary for Einstein to move towards the center of interest; by now, the mountain would come to Mohammed. Einstein thus stayed on in Berlin for a tangle of motives almost as complex as those which had brought him there six years earlier. According to Frank, his reassuring letter to Haenisch, saying that he would not be leaving, had stated: "Berlin is the place to which I am bound by the closest human and scientific ties." But there was more to it than that. He believed that the Weimar Republic held out a new hope for Europe in general as well as for Germany in particular; and also, according to Frank, he felt that "it was now important for all progressively minded elements to do everything possible to increase the prestige of the German Republic."

His multiple commitments left little time for active work in the revived Bund Neues Vaterland that in 1920 became the German League for Human Rights, but he was a cooperating well-wisher and, says one of its supporters, was "such a celebrity that we took him to one of the large 'no more war' mass demonstrations in the Berlin Lustgarten and presented him to the fifty or sixty thousand people there gathered." It was also significant that early in 1921 he should become a founder member of the Republican League, one of whose principal tasks it was "to enlighten German youth on the causes of the Empire's collapse and to propagate the conviction that Germany's resuscitation is possible solely on the basis of a republican form of government." The Republican League was, for better or for worse, of no particular importance. But Einstein was not lapsing from his wartime socialism into his former contempt for all political action. His founder membership of the League was a straw which showed which way the gale of events was blowing him.

Quite apart from "human and scientific ties" there was another reason for his staying in Berlin. Lenard and his supporters, aiming to discredit all for which Einstein was the symbol, were to have greater effects than they can ever have imagined. For he responded to a challenge with what was at times an almost stubborn pigheadedness. They had provided one.

Basically, he still wanted a quiet life. He still half-believed, as he had hopefully said to Elsa towards the end of December, 1919, that "it will soon all die down." But Lenard and the "Antirelativity Company" had kicked him into full awareness of what anti-Semitism could really be like. Thus there was a compensation for the objectionable limelight that now burned down on him. If he had to live within its glare, he would at least make use of it; he would use the ridiculous acclaim that he was now being given to good, nonridiculous purpose. He would ensure that his fellow Jews were given all possible support in their efforts to preserve their culture, in a homeland of their own if necessary. He would fight the good fight against militarism and nationalism with áll the logic and reason which he still expected other men to appreciate. And Berlin was a better place for that task than Leiden or Cambridge or Zurich.

In almost any other circumstances the Berlin professor of 1918 who had become a world figure by 1920 would have passed by with contempt the door onto the political world which the transformation had swung open for him. Now he passed through, eager to do what he could with his influence in the German capital, sensing that his esoteric work had given him "that power/Which erring men call Chance," but still totally ignorant of the ways in which the machinery of power could be used to produce results.

CHAPTER 11

AMBASSADOR-AT-LARGE

By the time the Berlin church bells were ringing in 1921, it was clear that Einstein had weathered the first of the nationalist, anti-Jewish storms for which he was to act as lightning conductor. It was also clear that his fame was to be neither nine-days' nor nine-months' wonder; the blaze of public interest that had flared up throughout the world showed every sign of continuing into the foreseeable future.

He was therefore faced with a series of foreign engagements and tours which he could hardly avoid. There is no doubt that he hated it all. He always hated excessive recognition, well aware that in spite of what he had done, he was in some ways like the men on Everest who metaphorically stood upon the shoulders of their predecessors. He was never in any doubt about his own worth; he had no reason to be. But he hated the hubbub created around him by those ignorant of the very language of science which he spoke. Nevertheless, there were compensations; for he could dispense his favors much as he had signed photographs during the first flush of fame at the end of 1919. Then the odious publicity had been made bearable by contributions which he exacted for the poor. Now the rigmarole of tours and public lectures was counterbalanced, in the United States by aid to the Zionist cause, in Britain and France by the help he could bring to the forces which wanted to rebuild a new Europe, including Germany, on a basis of mutual trust. In science he had achieved almost transcendental success by paring problems down to their simplest terms. Surely the same process would work in national politics and international affairs? Einstein walked into the lion's den devoutly believing this was so.

The first of his major tours—the "thorns in the side of my colleagues at the Academy," as he called them—was to the United States, in support of the Zionist cause, even though he also lectured at Columbia and Princeton Universities during the same visit. Before this, however, early in 1921, he had gone to both Prague and Vienna, returning to the former city's university as the man who had unexpectedly become its most famous professor.

In Prague he stayed with his old friend Philipp Frank, who has left a vivid account of how Einstein spoke to a crowded audience, explaining relativity in far more homely terms than had been expected. When the clapping and cheering had died down, he said simply: "It will perhaps be pleasanter and more understandable if instead of making a speech I play a piece for you on the violin."

In two curious ways, shadows from the future temporarily darkened this visit to the city where he had first sensed both the undercurrent of European anti-Semitism and the growl that he always believed to be the voice of pan-Germanism. For despite his personal feelings he was now, for those Germans who found it convenient, a German hero; and thus a Sudeten paper could claim, on his arrival in the Czech capital, that "the whole world will now see that a race that has produced a man like Einstein, the Sudeten German race, will never be suppressed." Here in Prague all his fears for the future, all the suspicions that the war had nurtured and that the Weimar government had only partially subdued, rose to the surface once again. To Frank he confided one thing: his fear that he would be forced to leave Germany within ten years. From a man who had so recently sworn allegiance to Weimar and to Prussia, the forecast at first seems puzzling. It was wrong by only two years.

In Prague, also, a young man insisted on speaking to Einstein after his lecture. He had considered Einstein's mass-energy equation, and on its basis concluded it would be possible to use the energy locked within the atom for production of a new and immensely powerful explosive; furthermore, he had invented a machine which he claimed could help make such an explosive. It would be interesting to know more of the youth, and it is tantalizing to speculate on what might have happened had Einstein been other than what he was. All we have is Frank's version of his reaction. "Calm yourself. You haven't lost anything if I don't discuss your work with you in detail. Its foolishness is evident at first glance. You cannot learn more from a longer discussion."

Einstein no doubt meant what he said. But one wonders whether the "foolishness" which he saw was purely technological or whether his mind might not have harked back to the example of John Napier, the discoverer of logarithms, for whose work he had profound respect. During Elizabethan times Napier invented a "tank" and the "burning mirrors" with which he hoped to destroy the Armada; but before his death he burned all records of his allegedly most deadly weapon—a device reputed to have wiped out a flock of Pentland sheep. One wonders also whether, eighteen years later, writing his plea to Roosevelt that the Americans should investigate nuclear weapons, Einstein remembered Prague.

In Vienna, soon afterwards, he spoke in the university Physics Institute and also gave his first big public lecture, being sketched while he was speaking by a young English artist, Edmond Kapp, and refusing to sign one of the sketches "because it makes me look too Chinese." The lecture was given to an audience of 3,000 in one of the city's largest concert halls, and on realizing its size Einstein experienced a minor fit of agoraphobia, insisting that his host Felix Ehrenhaft walk with him to the hall and then sit near him. In 1921 Ehrenhaft held the chair of experimental physics in the University of Vienna, and he and Einstein were still good friends. Later he developed an obsessional idea that Einstein, who was afterwards to describe his old friend as a man "without any self-criticism who has gradually developed into a kind of phony," had plagiarized his work.

"Einstein stayed in my house," Ehrenhaft recalled.

> He came to Vienna with two coats, two pairs of trousers, two white shirts, but only one white collar. When my wife asked him if there was not something that he had left at home he answered "No." However, she found neither slippers nor toilet articles. She supplied everything including the necessary collars. However, when she met him in the hall in the morning he was barefooted, and she asked him if he didn't need slippers. He answered

"No. They are unnecessary ballast." Since his trousers were terribly crumpled, my wife pressed the second pair and put them in order so that he would be neat for the second lecture. When he stepped onto the stage she saw to her horror that he was wearing the unpressed pair.

This was the familiar Einstein *en voyage*, traveling with the minimum of baggage, forgetful of the mechanics of everyday life, and a constant worry to Elsa, who on occasion would pack a suitcase for his journeys only to find on his return that it had not been opened. "How lucky that my husband's head is firmly stuck on: otherwise he would no doubt have left it in Leipzig," she once wrote. "Every time that he travels complications arise. . . . This time he left a new toothbrush and a tube of "Daramad" [toothpaste]. He could not have left anything else behind as he did not have anything else." The trait worried his hosts. It never worried Einstein, with his mind tied to the essentials. If the rest of the world wanted to fuss about such trivia as trousers and ties and toothbrushes, so much for the world.

From Vienna he returned to Germany. And here, during the next few months, he agreed to make a propaganda tour of the United States during which he would speak specifically to raise money for the Hebrew University, already being built in Jerusalem.

Shortly after the trip had been settled, he received a letter from which great consequences were to flow. Dated February 14, 1921, it came from Sir Henry Miers, Vice-Chancellor of Manchester University, and invited Einstein to give the Adamson Lecture there at some date convenient to himself. Professor Sherrington, the President of the Royal Society, and his predecessor J.J. —by this time Sir Joseph—Thomson, had both been Adamson Lecturers, but it was an imaginative stroke of Sir Henry's to invite Einstein so soon after the end of the war, while many Englishmen were still allergic to the idea of meeting Germans either socially or professionally.

Einstein replied on February 23, accepting the invitation, but implying that he would have to speak in German—"my English is practically nonexistent while my French is imperfect"—and noting that he could not settle a date, as he was already irrevocably committed to an

American tour in March. There was no doubt about his reason for acceptance. He looked upon the invitation as evidence of "a genuine wish to reestablish international links among scholars." A month later Sir Henry confirmed acceptance, adding that the lecture should be the first that Einstein delivered in England even though there was little doubt that he would receive other invitations. This was to be the case. Soon after, Lindemann wrote to Sir Henry from Oxford to ask how much Einstein was being paid for the lecture and added: "I should like to arrange one here but there seems to be a difficulty about funds." London University's King's College went further, inviting Einstein to speak after he left Manchester—"what Manchester thinks today London thinks tomorrow."

Einstein left Germany for the United States at the end of March, 1921.* Meanwhile Lindemann was involved in arrangements for the visit to England. He had received a letter from Freundlich and as a result wrote to Sir Henry: "Einstein would like [Freundlich] to be with him in England, if possible, to help him avoid any incidents when traveling. Freundlich's mother was English, in fact he proposes to stay with an aunt in Manchester, so that he should be able to look after the courier part of the visit." A special request to Lord Curzon, then Foreign Secretary, expedited the necessary visa and Freundlich was waiting when the White Star liner *Celtic* docked at Liverpool on June 8. On board was Einstein, with his wife, somewhat exhausted after a marathon three-month tour but quite confident that he had helped Zionism towards a promising future.

In the United States he had learned to be cautious of interviews, and he now refused to comment on relativity, noting that "quite apart from the sensational aspect, there was a deeper scientific aspect, and he had to distinguish between those who really understood the subject and those who did not." In addition he may have wondered what his reception would be in a country where the Gold Medal of a learned society could be given with one hand and snatched back with the other.

The following day he began by addressing the members of the University Jewish Students Society on the needs of

*See page 468.

the Hebrew University, explaining what had made him "an international man," underlining the current anti-Semitism in German universities, and speaking of the Jerusalem plans as "not a question of taste but of necessity."

Later, in the main hall of the university, he came to the subject of relativity. He spoke in German throughout this first public appearance in Britain but, reported the *Manchester Guardian*—in the words of David Mitrany, a young Rumanian political scientist later to become Einstein's colleague and close personal friend at Princeton—"the excellence of his diction, together with the kindly twinkle which never ceased to shine in his eye even through the sternest run of the argument, did not fail to make their impression upon the audience." Subsequently he was created a doctor of science, the first such honor to be bestowed upon a German in England since the outbreak of war seven years previously.

After half a century—and after a war with Germany that was waged almost as much on ideological as on national lines—it is difficult to appreciate the psychological barrier which Einstein, and men like him, had to overcome. But the idiocy which had brought death in Britain to dachshunds on account of their ancestry was still plastering London with warnings that "Every Performance of a German Play Is a Vote for German 'Culture.'" It was not only the Germans who could demonstrate nationalism run mad, and even when the objectivity of Einstein's work and nature is allowed for, his success in Britain is something of an achievement. The *Manchester Guardian* helped in its leading article on June 10 to explain how this came about, and to indicate what it was that raised Einstein to his unique position. "The man in the street, a traveler between life and death, is compact of all elements, and is neither devoid of science nor of poetry," it said.

> He may have few ideas in either, but he probably cherishes what he has, and whatever touches them nearly is of moment to him. Professor Einstein's theory of relativity, however vaguely he may comprehend it, disturbs fundamentally his basic conceptions of the universe and even of his own mind. It challenges somehow the absolute nature of his thought. The very idea that he can

use his mind in a disinterested way is assailed by a conception which gives partiality to every perception. And with his keen thrust at personal things, the idea of relativity stretches out to the very conceptions of the universe, as can be seen from the mere titles of the closing chapters of Professor Einstein's little book on the subject.

From Manchester, Einstein moved south to London, where Sir John Squire had added to Pope's epitaph on Newton, so that it now ran:

> Nature and Nature's law lay hid in night.
> God said "Let Newton be" and all was light.
> It did not last: the Devil howling "Ho!
> Let Einstein be!" restored the status quo.

There had been more than one change of plan in his departure from the United States and in the date of his arrival in London. "I recall . . . I had invitations to meet him in London and Manchester on the same night," Eddington wrote to Lindemann when he was due to see Einstein again a decade later. "This is doubtless explicable by the principle of indeterminacy; still I hope on this occasion you will have a more condensed distribution"—an Eddington remark comparable to his comment that Einstein had "taken Newton's plant, which had outgrown its pot, and transplanted it to a more open field."

In London, the Einsteins' host was Viscount Haldane of Cloan, former Secretary of State for War and former Lord Chancellor. Haldane had a special link both with Germany and with Einstein's philosophical outlook. He had studied at Göttingen before Einstein was born, and had often returned to renew his friendships in the town; he had been sent by the British government on an abortive mission to Germany in 1912 and had subsequently, almost on the outbreak of war, been unwise enough to speak of Germany as his "spiritual home." Not unexpectedly, he had been hounded from office in 1915 after a propaganda campaign which alleged, among other things, that he was an illegitimate brother of the Kaiser, had a German wife—he was in fact a lifelong bachelor—and had delayed the mobilization of the British Expeditionary Force in 1914. In a postwar Britain drained of most things except bitterness, Haldane was therefore in a delicate position vis-à-vis the Germans. It was certainly courageous of Einstein to have come so willingly to London; it was equally courageous of Haldane to be his host.

The former Minister "had much admiration for the power of systematic reflection which distinguished the German people," and his interest in Einstein lay in a genuine and dogged preoccupation with epistemology, a preoccupation which had just produced *The Reign of Relativity*. This dealt only in passing with Einstein's theories, and was more concerned with "Knowledge itself and the relativity of reality to the character of Knowledge"—"Haldane is doing for Einstein what Herbert Spencer did for Darwin," said Sir Oliver Lodge. "To say that he understood [relativity] better than any other British pure philosopher at that time would, I am afraid, be a poor compliment," was Eddington's reaction. "For what it is worth, it is undoubtedly true. . . ." And Asquith's account of Haldane explaining relativity at a dinner party is significant: "Gradually a cloud descended until, at last, even the candles lost their lighting power in the complexities of Haldane's explanations." The First Viscount felt a respect for Einstein verging on veneration, and for years only two pictures hung in the study at Cloan, his Scottish home: one of his mother, the other of Albert Einstein.

In 1921 Haldane also had a less scientific interest in the visit. "Einstein arrives here in the early days of June," he wrote on May 12 to John Murray, his publisher, "and his advent will make a market for us which we must not lose." His foresight was well justified. In mid-June he was able to inform his mother that *The Reign of Relativity*, which was to go into three editions in six weeks, was "being sold with Einstein's books in the bookshops." He had in fact written to Einstein from his home in Queen Anne's Gate as soon as news of the proposed visit to England leaked out. "Will you do me the honor of being my guest at the above address during your London stay," he asked. "I do not know whether you are coming alone or whether your wife will be with you. But it does not matter because the house is large enough." He followed the letter with a telegram, and the small *Absagen* written on it suggests that Einstein had at first declined. If so, he changed his mind—a wise course since there were few men better qualified than Haldane to convoy him through a Britain which was still uncertain whether it much wished to honor any German scientist, relativity or not.

In spite of this, there was, Haldane wrote to his mother in Scotland on May 26, "much interest in the Einstein visit. Lord Stamfordham [private secretary to King George V] talked to me of it last night." Four days later he told her: "The social world is beginning to worry for invitations to meet Einstein, and I am sternly refusing two smart ladies—which I have no doubt they think rather brutal." Two days later he wrote to his sister: "I have repelled Lady Cunard, who wanted to get up a party for Einstein."

It was not only fashionable London that was eager to meet this mystery man who had emerged from the shambles of a defeated Germany. From St. Pancras, where Haldane met the Einsteins at two o'clock on Friday the tenth, the visitors were taken direct to a meeting of the Royal Astronomical Society in Burlington House.

Here Eddington, recently elected president, recalled how the first printed references to the General Theory had been published in England in the Society's *Monthly Notices*. He described the preliminaries to the two eclipse expeditions, and he indicated how one man's imaginative concept had changed the traditional view of the universe. Einstein, modestly smiling, accepted it all with the self-assured charm of a very bright boy.

Then the visitors were taken to Queen Anne's Gate where a dinner party of quite exceptional nature was to be held for them that evening. Earlier, Haldane had planned a reception at which the Prime Minister was to be present. But Lloyd George had failed to follow in President Harding's footsteps and meet Einstein.*

The private dinner party which did duty for the reception was a glittering enough occasion. Heading the list of guests was the Archbishop of Canterbury. His apprehensions about the evening can be judged by a letter written to J. J. Thomson a few weeks earlier by Lord Sanderson, for many years a high Foreign Office official. "The Archbishop . . . can make neither head nor tail of Einstein, and protests that the more he listens to Haldane, and the more

*See page 473.

newspaper articles he reads on the subject, the less he understands," Sanderson confided.

> I am, or believe myself to be, in an intermediate stage, roaming the lawns and meadow leazes halfway down. I therefore offered to write for the Archbishop a short sketch of what I imagined to be the pith of the theory in its more elementary form. I enclose it with his comment. It is of course very inadequate, but I fancy that as far as it goes it is not entirely at variance with Einstein's argument—some of his followers and critics seem to me to go further. But I should have been sorry to have misled the Archbishop. Do you think you could glance through it, or ask some expert to do so, and write a short note of any gross errors?

Thomson obliged, thus helping to brief Archbishop Davidson for what seemed likely to be an intellectual tournament on the heroic scale. For also present in Queen Anne's Gate on the evening of the tenth were Eddington and Alfred Whitehead who had been among the "chorus" at the Burlington House meeting two years earlier. Dr. Inge, the "gloomy Dean" of St. Paul's, was present with his wife. So were Bernard Shaw, Professor Harold Laski of the London School of Economics, and General Sir Ian Hamilton, the ill-starred leader from Gallipoli who had been a close friend of Haldane since the latter's days as Secretary of State for War. Over this formidable brains trust, a regiment which could have laid down an intellectual barrage sufficient to overcome most men, there presided Haldane and his sister Elizabeth, a distinguished woman in her own right and the translator of Descartes and Hegel.

The main outcome of the evening, disappointing to Haldane in some respects, must have been reassuring to the Archbishop. "I have never seen a more typical scientific lion in appearance—he might have been prepared for the role on the stage—" she later wrote percipiently, "a mass of long black hair tossed back, and a general appearance of scientific untidiness, but he was modest and quiet to talk to, and disclaimed a great deal of what is attributed to him." Choosing his moment carefully, Davidson turned to Einstein and queried: "Lord Haldane tells us that your theory ought to make a great difference to our morale." But Einstein merely replied: "Do not believe a word of it. It makes no difference. It is purely abstract—science." This was only a briefer version of Einstein's reply to an interviewer a few years later. "The meaning of relativity has been widely misunderstood," he said. "Philosophers play with the word, like a child with a doll. Relativity, as I see it, merely denotes that certain physical and mechanical facts, which have been regarded as positive and permanent, are relative with regard to certain other facts in the sphere of physics and mechanics." However, he took the Archbishop's interest as natural, and noted later that more clergymen than physicists were interested in relativity. "Because," he explained when asked the reason, "clergymen are interested in the general laws of nature and physicists, very often, are not."

The Archbishop's wife fared little better than her husband. When, after dinner, she explained to Elsa how a friend had been talking about Professor Einstein's theory "especially in its mystical aspect," Frau Einstein broke into laughter with the words: "Mystical! Mystical! My husband mystical!" echoing his own reply to a Dutch lady who in the German embassy in The Hague said that she liked his mysticism. "Mysticism is in fact the only reproach that people cannot level at my theory," he had replied.

Frau Einstein's reply was not what was expected. But it was part of the defense which the Einsteins erected around themselves, Elsa unconsciously no doubt, but her husband after due thought. "I can well understand [him] hastily shearing off the subject," Eddington later noted of the remark to Davidson; "in those days one had to become an expert in dodging persons who mixed up the fourth dimension with spiritualism. But surely the answer need not be preserved as though it were one of Einstein's more perspicacious utterances. The non sequitur is obvious." What might also have been obvious by this time was a certain flagging in the guest of honor who had been spared Lady Cunard but after a long morning's journey from Manchester had been whisked to the Royal Astronomical Society, taken from Burlington House through a quick change into formal clothes, and then presented on a plate as the main dish of a testing evening.

Saturday was a day of comparative rest during which

Einstein, sitting on a simple kitchen chair at the back of Haldane's house, was informally photographed. And, apparently at the same time, "Einstein . . . had one done of myself to hang in his study in Berlin," Haldane proudly informed his mother. The following day the guests were taken to lunch with the Rothschilds, where they met Lord Crewe and Lord Rayleigh who had first seen Einstein at the Solvay Congress a decade earlier. According to Sir Almeric Fitzroy, the clerk of the Privy Council, Rayleigh listened to Einstein's explanation of relativity, then commented: "If your theories are sound, I understand it is open to us to affirm that the events, say, of the Norman Conquest have not yet occurred." Afterwards, Haldane related to his mother in one of the long accounts which he wrote to her almost daily, Lord Rothschild drove the party to a Jewish meeting, through the city to the Tower, and back along the Embankment. "In the evening we dined at the Harmers where Einstein played the violin. . . ."

Then they returned to the row of fashionable but modest town houses where Einstein was introduced to London life. Some of the later second- and third-hand accounts of the visit appear not only to have been overimpressed with Haldane's "Lordship," but also to have confused Queen Anne's Gate with Haldane's Scottish estate which Einstein never visited. Thus in some stories they moved in an atmosphere of deferential butlers, vast Tudor beds, and the exaggerations of a Hollywood spectacular.

Boris Kunetzov is typical. "Their room in his palatial residence was bigger than the whole of their Berlin apartment," he says. "Einstein's embarrassment turned into dismay when he found that a footman had been assigned to him. When he saw the liveried monument he whispered to his wife: 'Elsa, do you think they will let us out if we try to run away?' They slept in a spacious bedroom with heavily curtained windows. Next morning Einstein rose early, as was his custom, and tried in vain to open the curtains. Behind him his wife asked laughingly: 'Albertle, why didn't you call the footman to do it?' 'Oh, no,' he replied, 'he frightens me.'" No doubt they were impressed, after Berlin, with the wealth that still remained in Britain at the end of a long war; but, equally without doubt, they took it in their stride.

On Monday morning Einstein was taken by Haldane to

Westminster Abbey, where he placed a wreath on Newton's grave before being handed over to the Dean. After lunch he prepared for his first public appearance in London. It was to be made at King's College in the Strand, and the Principal, Ernest (later Sir Ernest) Barker, had some misgivings about his guest's reception. "Feeling against Germany was very much stronger after that war of 1914–18 than it has been since the war of 1939–45" he later wrote, "and there were fears that the lecture might be disturbed or even prevented." All the tickets, sold in aid of charity for distressed European students, were taken up well in advance, and when Haldane led Einstein onto the platform even the gangways were filled with students. Among those in the audience were Whitehead, James Jeans, Professor Lindemann—and William Rothenstein, making notes for his remarkable portrait of Einstein who is presented as a Struwwelpeter character, smiling from an aureole of almost electrified hair.

He had insisted on speaking in German—partly because of his almost nonexistent English; partly, it was reported, because "he had complete confidence in English broadmindedness." Thus the hall was filled by those who, as Barker said, "would probably understand nothing, being ignorant alike of German and of relativity, but would nonetheless be eager to listen." There was no applause when the two men had walked onto the platform. The meeting could easily swing either way.

"Einstein had no notes, no hesitations, and no repetitions," wrote the anonymous commentator of the *Nation*, "and the logical order in which he expounded his ideas was masterly beyond praise. One sat wondering how much of this exquisite performance was being wasted upon the audience; to how many was this carefully precise German an unintelligible noise?" As on other occasions, the objectivity of Einstein's demeanor, the otherworldliness of his dreamy eyes, and his shock of flowing hair, disarmed potential critics. He talked for an hour, without interruption, somehow evoking an interest even among those who could understand little more than the occasional phrase. Then he paused and, still speaking in German, announced: "My lecture is already a little long." There was an unexpected storm of encouraging applause. "I shall take that as an invitation," he said. "But my further remarks will not be so easy to follow." Finally, he sat down. Then someone started clapping. The applause grew and whole rows of men stood up, a spontaneous acclamation of courage as much as of relativity.

One interesting point in the lecture was Einstein's statement on the ancestry of relativity. "I am anxious to draw attention to the fact that this theory is not speculative in origin," he said. "It owes its invention entirely to the desire to make physical theory fit observed facts as well as possible. We have here no revolutionary act, but the natural combination of a line that can be traced through centuries. The abandonment of certain notions connected with space, time, and motion, hitherto treated as fundamentals, must not be regarded as arbitrary, but only as conditioned by observed facts." Emphasis on observational experience compared with the flash of intuition was really more true of the General than of the Special Theory. But it was more revealingly true of the earlier, "pro-Machian" philosophy that had so far supported Einstein than of the newer outlook which was already taking its place as his faith in sensation as the real yardstick of the physical world began to falter. When, later in life, he was asked by Hans Reichenbach, professor of philosophy in the University of California, how he had arrived at the theory of relativity, Einstein no longer mentioned observed facts. On that occasion his explanation was of a totally different kind: he had come to it, he said, because he had been "so firmly convinced of the harmony of the universe."

In Britain, men of goodwill were well aware of Einstein's potential influence in bringing a new attitude of reconciliation into the relationship between wartime enemies, and many said as much during his visit. Thus Haldane had introduced the King's College lecture with the statement that Britain was grateful to Germany for giving the world the genius of Einstein just as Germany has been grateful to Britain for giving the world the genius of Newton. That evening, when Einstein was entertained in King's College, Ernest Barker opened his after-dinner speech by comparing two "observers" of the theory of relativity, and then suggested that his listeners should substitute two nations for them. "Each of these two nations had its own way of life, its own space, its own ethics and character. If it were possible to find some means by which these two nations could have the same view of life, then there would be new possibilities, whether by leagues of nations, or other ways, to arrive at better understanding with each other." Then Barker turned to Einstein. "If at your command, the straight lines have been banished from the universe, there is yet one straight line that will always remain—the straight line of right and justice. May both our nations follow this straight line side by side in a parallel movement which, in spite of Euclid, will yet bring them together in friendship with one another and with the other nations of the world."

The words were significant, not only of the attitude of men like Barker in Britain but of others in France, in the United States, and elsewhere. A few months later, when Australian universities invited Einstein to visit their country, *The Times* noted that "it is considered that as Australia is resuming trade with Germany, no better start can be made than by extending an invitation to one of the world's greatest scientists." On this occasion pressure of engagements forced Einstein to refuse. But from the time of this first visit to Britain he was even more eager to play the role of reconciliator.

On the morning following the King's College lecture, Lindemann collected Einstein from Queen Anne's Gate and drove him to Oxford, where the two men spent the day. Two months earlier, when he had first heard of Einstein's coming visit, Lindemann had invited him to stay at his father's home in Sidmouth, Devon. Einstein had declined and Lindemann had to be content with showing him the Clarendon Laboratory where he had recently taken up the chair of experimental philosophy. Before leaving for home the next day, Einstein wrote to Haldane's mother. "One of the most memorable weeks of my life lies behind me," he said. "Visiting this country for the first time I have learned to marvel at its splendid traditions and treasures of knowledge. One of the most beautiful experiences was the intimacy with your two children, the harmonious hospitality of their home, and the wonderful relations which unite them with yourself. For the first time in my life I have heard of a prominent public man who converses by letter every day with his mother. The scientific talk with Lord Haldane has been for me a source of pure stimulation, and so has the personal intimacy with him and his remarkable knowledge." For a man of Einstein's knobbly honesty, this was an outstanding tribute, and a further suggestion that beneath Haldane's formal exterior a great man may have been trying to get out.

There was no doubt about the success of the visit. As the *Nation* noted in an editorial headed "The Entente of the Intellectuals," the reception of the King's College lecture had marked "a definite turning point in the postwar feeling" of Britain; the general welcome given to Einstein had gone "some way to restore the prewar unity of culture for Europe and the civilized world." And, Haldane later wrote to Lindemann: "I think the German ambassador was right when he told me on Monday evening that the reception of Einstein in England would do something towards making the way smoother for the approach to better international relations." Thus a main aim of the visit, a loosening of the pack ice which kept Britain and Germany apart, had been achieved.

As Einstein returned across the North Sea, Haldane wrote in his diary: "Professor Whitehead, the mathematician, dined with me alone, to compare notes." There was much to compare. British scientists had been immensely impressed by Einstein, but some of them still thought that the extraneous metaphysical overtones were part of the man himself and of his theory. This was well illustrated by R. A. Sampson, the Astronomer Royal for Scotland, who was present at the London lecture and who wrote to Lindemann three days later. "I would say at once," he wrote,

> that there is no room for question that Einstein "explained" gravitation, and as it seems to me, said absolutely the last word upon it. Beyond this I prefer to keep reserve on certain points, as thinking them unproved and the attempt to prove them misdirected.
>
> One of them is the retranslation into spatial terms of the formula to which gravitation has been reduced. That formula is so general that it transcends any "meaning," and to give it one is gratuitous.
>
> Next I reject the philosophical implication that all that we know is equally relative and intangible or else unreal.
>
> As regards reality if we admit that our existence is real, though presumably relative to some more compre-

hensive existence, and we can explain neither our own nor the other, then it is evidently not a condition of reality that we should be able to explain what we mean. Hence I have no difficulty in admitting absolute rotation even though I do not know what I mean.

Nor for that matter absolute translation (but Einstein has proved this an uncalled-for idea in gravitation).

It appears to me that Einstein's argument regarding rotation proves that we do not know that the earth rotates. Yet I assert that we do know that it rotates, though the argument is mathematically correct. You ask, with respect to what does it rotate? I have no final answer, but I don't think you will say it is open to a rational man to hold that it does not rotate. . . .

Einstein returned to Berlin as the first postwar German to be lionized in the United States and Britain. The word "German" is important. For whatever his previous feelings, the German defeat of 1918 had induced him to slough off the hard skin of bitter distaste for his compatriots which had first formed in Munich. In this he was illogical. Whatever inner spirit may drive a nation on towards its destiny, for better or worse, it is unlikely to be altered within a few years by the tribulations of defeat or the triumphs of victory. If the Germany of 1921 held high hopes, then these lay within its marrow in 1890; and if the Germany of the Luitpold Gymnasium was more than a local nightmare, then there was little hope for her in 1921. Einstein did not see it that way. Weimar had changed everything, and if he still held reservations about the treatment that the Jews could expect, he yet hoped that Germany was now freely walking back into the European body politic.

Certainly he now had confident hopes for her future. It is not clear whether he believed that his earlier feelings had been unbalanced, or whether the whole German nation had undergone a Pauline conversion on the road to Versailles. But although he was still using a Swiss passport, he now had no inhibitions about traveling as an unofficial German ambassador.

He wanted to prevent any revival of the wartime hatred between Germany and Britain, and he was as discouraging as he could be when, shortly after his return to Berlin, Sommerfeld asked him to help get published in Britain an article he had written on the *Lusitania* Medal. The original had been struck in Germany the day after the torpedoing of the British liner without warning and the loss of 1,198 men and women, including 100 Americans. This was an opportunity too good to miss, and a medal was struck in England—generally being attributed to Lord Northcliffe, later in charge of propaganda in enemy countries. The British medal claimed to be an exact replica of the German, but was dated the day before the sinking and showed a skeleton handing out tickets to passengers.

Sommerfeld's article pointing out the trickery was published in the *Münchner Neuesten Nachrichten* on June 24, and ten days later he sent a copy to Einstein, noting that the London *Athenaeum* had sympathetically reported the King's College lecture and urging that they could hardly ignore a piece of gentle lobbying. "Quite frankly, I regret that you have written it, possibly due to isolation during the war," Einstein replied. "No intelligent Englishman believes stories about the war. When I was in England I got the impression that the scientists there are less prejudiced and more objective than our German scientists. But I must point out that quite a number of well-known English scientists were pacifists and refused war duties; i.e., Eddington and Russell. If you had been there you also would have had the feeling that it was not right to tell people such things. What the public thinks, I do not know, but in our country, too, many lies are printed without any denials." He questioned the point of washing old dirty linen in public and implored Sommerfeld, "in the interests of international understanding," to leave things alone.

Einstein's genuine attempts to create a climate of reconciliation so strikingly in contrast to his attitude after the Second World War—and the power which his position gave him to push forward this cause, were not lost on his compatriots. In Berlin, on July 1, 1921, he was the guest of honor at a party given by Herr von Winterfeldt, President of the German Red Cross, and attended by President Ebert, many members of the German Cabinet, and the chief burgomaster of Berlin. Here, his remarks were to be the subject of criticism. "In America," he told those present,

> there undeniably predominated a markedly unfriendly feeling towards everything German. American public

opinion was so excited that even the use of the German language was suppressed. At present a noticeable change is taking place. I was received heartily by America's learned men and learned corporations. They gladly spoke German, and everywhere were mindful with genuine sympathy of the German scientists and institutes with which they maintained so close a friendship before the war. In England the impression forced itself upon me that the English statesmen and scholars had it in mind again to bring about friendly relations with Germany. The heartiness of the speeches in England could hardly be surpassed. Better times appear to be coming.

That Einstein should not only make such a judgment between the attitudes of his two hosts—strongly in contrast with the general opinion of most other people—but that he should openly announce it, indicates a double lack of judgment. The *New York Times* was quick to jump on his words, noting that "perhaps . . . in spite of his wonderful mind [he] is as much mistaken, and in about the same way, when he says that 'England' is warmly pro-German as he is when he said that 'America' is warmly anti-German."

This was not quite the case. The trouble was that Einstein learned only tardily that the casual statements of famous men, perhaps tossed off rather lightheartedly, can look very different when presented under black headlines. And it was typical that he should conclude a letter to Sommerfeld, protesting against a *Figaro* article by a correspondent with whom he had talked, by saying: "The man had no right to reproduce utterances of mine. Furthermore, whether by intent or not I do not know, he had many things wrongly emphasized, although he has not lied."

Einstein's weakness for making unguarded statements that could easily be used against him was shown in one incident, trivial in itself, which had important repercussions on the way he later allowed himself to be presented to the world. This started with a report from Cyril Brown, a *New York Times* correspondent in Berlin. The report quoted an account of Einstein's views on the United States, given to a "sympathetic-looking Hollander." The statements were distinctly unflattering. After admitting that American men worked hard, Einstein was quoted as saying: "For the rest, they are the toy dogs of the women, who spend the money in a most unmeasurable, illimitable way and wrap themselves in a fog of extravagance." Later, the genesis of the *New York Times* story became known. Einstein had spoken in German to the reporter of the *Nieuwe Rotterdamsche Courant,* which had printed its story in Dutch; the *Berliner Tageblatt* had taken parts of the Dutch story and printed it in German; the *Times* correspondent had then taken parts of the *Berliner Tageblatt* story and cabled this in English to New York. With the best will in the world, excluding any assumption that the Berlin paper would wish to make Einstein look ridiculous, or that the *Times* man overemphasized any anti-Americanism, these choppings, subbings, and translations inevitably did more than alter the balance of the original. Few readers, even in the more sophisticated present, would be expected to allow for all this; half a century ago the "toy dogs" remark—apparently quoted elsewhere as "lapdogs"—had the effect of a match to gunpowder.

It was followed by a leading article in the *New York Times.* After claiming that the report appeared to be correct even though the writer wished it were not, it put forward as possible causes of Einstein's irritation "the failure of himself and his companion to make more than a partial success of the special mission on which they came to the U.S., and the antagonism they aroused where they had expected to win full approval and cooperation." Further criticism followed; so did letters to the editor; and, on the eleventh, a second editorial, presumably written after the paper had been in touch with its Berlin correspondent. "Dr. Einstein," it said, "will not be forgiven and should not be, for his boorish ridicule of hospitable hosts who honored him because they believed the guarantors of his greatness in his own domain. That he is small out of that domain is a matter of no great consequence, however, for it is a peculiarity shared by many other specialists of like eminence, and in no degree reduces their value to the world."

By this time Einstein had been bearded by the correspondent of the *New York World* to whom he said that "the Amsterdam interview in no way expressed my sentiment. I never made the unfavorable comments on the American people and their mode of life." This attempt by a rival to undercut the *Times'* own story failed to impress that paper, which rather loftily replied that it was easy to get the impression that Einstein had now "explained rather than denied the essential part of the *Courant*'s article." However, the *Times* had second thoughts; and after another two and a half weeks it admitted in a long report from Berlin that Einstein's remarks did not, after all, "turn out to be as harsh as they appear in the cabled reports."

The effect of this tempest in a teacup was considerable. Years later Einstein was still refusing interviews on the grounds that he had been misquoted as calling American men lapdogs of their women; and it says much for the tact and tenacity of the *New York Times'* chief correspondent in Berlin that his paper became one of the few to which Einstein was eventually willing to speak freely. Nevertheless, the memory of the incident remained. It had come just as he was on the crest of popularity's wave and it reinforced his natural dislike of sharing his nonscientific thoughts and emotions with a public for whom he had become a compound of guru, film star, oracle, and saint. Thus the dichotomy which marked so much of his life began to appear here as well. For his views on Zionism and pacifism, for his explanations of what the grand structure of science could mean, he needed the large public which only the popular press could provide; he was usually unwilling to pay the price, to subject himself to what even in the best-run world must be a fair percentage of distortions and inventions. When he was willing to take the risk, his innate honesty, his insistence on telling the truth at all cost, combined with a flair for making headlineable statements to gain him the sympathy of all but the most bloody-minded opponents. When he was not being his own enemy, he could get a "good press" that was the despairing envy of experienced publicists. Too often, he mentally muttered "lapdogs" and was content to let his case go by default.

One result of his journey to the United States and Britain was that Einstein now felt there was a genuine hope of reopening scientific relations between these countries and Germany. It could be argued that the German aggression of 1914, and the excesses to which it led, had cleared the disease from a body politic which could now, more mature, more internationally oriented, play its part in creating a new and better Europe. Einstein, the new citizen of the Weimar Republic, sincerely hoped so.

France was a different proposition, as he realized when, early in 1922, he was invited to lecture in Paris. The invitation had first been made in 1913 when those administering the Michonis Fund in the Collège de France asked him to succeed Lorentz as visiting lecturer the following year. Einstein accepted, but the visit had been canceled with the outbreak of war. Now his old friend Langevin revived the idea. One impediment immediately arose. Many French scientists felt that such an invitation would imply that their hatred of the Germans was diminishing. They protested, and their protests might have succeeded had it not been for the support which Langevin obtained from Paul Painlevé. Powerful Minister of War a few years earlier, and now Premier and President of the Chamber of Deputies, Painlevé was a mathematician by profession, an amateur enthusiast of relativity, and he gladly gave unofficial blessing to Langevin's proposal.

In Berlin, Einstein was at first dubious. The idea chimed in with his wish to reforge the links between German scientists and those in other countries, but he had no illusion about the deep and bitter feelings that outside the limited scientific, artistic, and professional circles—and sometimes inside them—still divided the peoples of France and Germany. At first, he tentatively refused the invitation. Then he mentioned it in passing to Walther Rathenau, the German Minister of Reconstruction.

Rathenau was in many ways the antithesis of all that Einstein stood for. A German-Jewish industrialist, he had inherited control of the great Allgemeine Elektrizität-Gesellschaft (A.E.G.) and twice during the war had striven hard to save the Empire: first in 1916 when he had reorganized German economy to counter the effects of the British blockade; secondly in 1918 when, almost alone among responsible officials, he had proposed a *levée en masse* to meet the advancing Allies. With the coming of the Weimar Republic, Rathenau founded the new Democratic party and rose swiftly to ministerial status. He first met Einstein in the house of a mutual friend, and Einstein invited him to the Haberlandstrasse home. The friendship ripened. Einstein was concerned by the effect which

Rathenau's acceptance of a ministry might have on the position of the Jews in Germany; Rathenau, in his turn, was interested in Einstein as a unique unofficial ambassador. There was no doubt about the advice he now gave. "Rathenau has told me that it is my duty to accept, and so I accept," Einstein wrote to Langevin.

In Paris there were fears that the visit would bring protests from French nationalists, and as arrangements for the occasion were completed, Langevin was careful to secure an apartment to which his guest could be taken in secret. "Langevin has got a roof for me and will tell you where it is," Einstein wrote to his old friend Maurice Solovine, who was reading proofs of the French edition of Einstein's book on relativity, *"but keep it strictly secret;* otherwise the days during my stay in Paris are going to be very irksome."

Langevin himself remained uncertain of the reception to be expected and on the afternoon of March 28, 1922, traveled out from Paris to Jeumont on the Belgian frontier. With him went Charles Nordmann, the astronomer of the Paris Observatory whose *Einstein and the Universe,* published in France the previous year, was a minor classic of popular description and interpretation.

Nordmann has left, in the *Revue des Deux Mondes* and *L'Illustration,* two graphic accounts of the visit. At the frontier station they found their guest unassumingly sitting in the corner of a second-class apartment. Nordmann had never met him and it is clear from his account that he was vastly impressed—not so much by the "creator of worlds," which would have been natural enough, as by the physical presence of the man. Einstein's sense of command was later to become so overlaid with the image of the seemingly frail, white-haired saint—"Charlie Chaplin with the brow of Shakespeare," as the *New Statesman* once put it—that it is well to be reminded of what he was like in his prime.

"The first impression that one gets is of astonishing youth," Nordmann wrote.

> Einstein is big (he is about 1 m 76), with large shoulders and the back only very slightly bent. His head, the head where the world of science has been re-created, immedi-

ately attracts and fixes the attention. His skull is clearly, and to an extraordinary degree, brachycephalic, great in breadth and receding towards the nape of the neck without exceeding the vertical. Here is an illustration which brings to nought the old assurances of the phrenologists and of certain biologists, according to which genius is the prerogative of the dolichocephales. The skull of Einstein reminds me, above all else, of that of Renan, who was also a brachycephale. As with Renan the forehead is huge; its breadth exceptional, its spherical form striking one more than its height. A few horizontal folds cross this moving face which is sometimes cut, at moments of concentration or thought, by two deep vertical furrows which raise his eyebrows.

His complexion is smooth, unpolished, of a certain duskiness, bright. A small moustache, dark and very short, decorates a sensual mouth, very red, fairly large, whose corners gradually rise in a smooth and permanent smile. The nose, of simple shape, is slightly acquiline.

Under his eyebrows, whose lines seem to converge towards the middle of his forehead, appear two very deep eyes whose grave and melancholy expression contrast with the smile of this pagan mouth. The expression is usually distant, as though fixed on infinity, at times slightly clouded over. This gives his general expression a touch of inspiration and of sadness which accentuates once again the creases produced by reflection and which, almost linking with his eyelids, lengthen his eyes, as though with a touch of *kohl*. Very black hair, flecked with silver, unkempt, falls in curls towards the nape of his neck and his ears, after having been brought straight up, like a frozen wave, above his forehead.

Above all, the impression is one of disconcerting youth, strongly romantic, and at certain moments evoking in me the irrepressible idea of a young Beethoven, on which meditation had already left its mark, and who had once been beautiful. And then, suddenly, laughter breaks out and one sees a student. Thus appeared to us the man who has plumbed with his mind, deeper than any before him, the astonishing depths of the mysterious universe.

The three men faced a four-hour journey, from which Nordmann remembered some revealing remarks. When they began to talk of quantum problems, Einstein noted, significantly: "That is a wall before which one is stopped. The difficulties are terrible; for me, the theory of relativity was only a sort of respite which I gave myself during their examination." And, remarking that there was something crazy about it, he went on: "But there, physicists are all a bit crazy, aren't they? But it's just the same with race-horses: what one buys, one has to sell!"

When they discussed the worldwide interest that his ideas had aroused, Einstein noted, as he repeatedly did with undisguised amazement: "It's unbelievable." Of the opposition to him and his ideas in Germany he commented, putting his hands on his chest: "So long as they don't get violent, I want to let everyone say what they wish, for I myself have always said exactly what pleased me." And, asked about the left-wing parties, he said, with a broad smile: "I don't know what to say about that since I believe that the left is *'une chose polydimensionelle.'* "

It was midnight by the time they arrived at the Gare du Nord. Here there was a reception party of journalists and photographers. Einstein had no wish to meet them; Langevin was still worried about nationalist protests. Thus one plan suited both men. Together with Nordmann, they left the train by dropping from the coach on the side away from the platform, crossed the railway lines, and disappeared into a side door on the farther platform. Then, unnoticed, they vanished into the Métro. Einstein enjoyed the operation—particularly as the Métro train moved off below the spot where the crowds were still waiting.

On the afternoon of Friday, March 31, he was driven to the Collège de France. Here, in the main hall, where Ernest Renan, Henri Bergson, and other giants of the French establishment had lectured, he explained the conflict between classical relativity and electrodynamics in a slow French to which his slight accent added a touch of mystery. Langevin sat immediately behind, ready to prompt him with the occasional word if he hesitated. Madame Curie was among the audience. So was Bergson. But the room was not packed as some had expected. Tickets had been sent only to a restricted number of scientists and students with a special interest in the subject. Paul Painlevé himself stood by the door, checking the formal invitations.

Einstein spoke to other selected audiences during the next few days, to the Collège's philosophical and mathematical sections and, on April 6, to a session of the

French Philosophical Society at the Sorbonne. Langevin was again present, as well as Bergson and Painlevé. His reception was kind if questioning, an attitude less critical than that of Émile Picard, permanent secretary of the French Academy of Sciences, who was quoted as saying: "On the subject of relativity I see red." Einstein was closely questioned about the philosophical implications of his theory. And here, answering a question from Émile Mayerson, he appeared finally to cut the strings which had held him to Mach. "Mach's system studied the relationships which exist between the data of experience," he said. "For Mach, science is the sum total of these relationships. It is a bad point of view; in short, what Mach created was a catalogue and not a system. To the extent that Mach was a good mechanic he was a deplorable philosopher."

Some gaps in the French welcome were the result of politics as much as science, and the Society of French Physicists, strongly nationalist in outlook, virtually refused to accept his presence in the capital. Opinion was more evenly divided in the Academy, where a number of friends argued strongly that he should address "the immortals." But the fact that Germany was not yet a member of the League of Nations was raised as a barrier. The argument was finally settled when thirty members announced they would leave in a body as soon as Einstein entered the room.

As well as the French people, the French press was in two minds about the problem of how to regard members of the nation they had fought for more than four long years. "If a German were to discover a remedy for cancer or tuberculosis," asked one paper, "would these thirty academicians have to wait for the application of the remedy until Germany joined the League?" Among others which tried to edge their readers towards conciliation was the paper with the large headline: "Einstein in Paris! It Is the Victory of the Archangel over the Demon of the Abyss." Yet the verdict of the Academy, essentially a verdict on Germany, would probably have been endorsed by the majority of Frenchmen. Einstein would have sympathized, even had he not agreed. For there were occasions when his perceptions about the human race equaled his intuitive genius in science. He knew that in France he was suspect three times over. He was the man who had upset the scientific applecart—or at least appeared to have done so—and thus he naturally aroused the resentment of those who believed in things-as-they-are. He was not only a scientific iconoclast but German as well. To compound the crime he was not only German but a German Jew. It is not surprising that he received only a qualified welcome in a country which had recently lost more than 1,350,000 men dead and missing at German hands and which still argued over the rights and wrongs of the Dreyfus case.

However, it was not only in France that Einstein's new popularity was less than wholehearted. England had welcomed him the previous year, but now *The Times,* a fair enough reflection of informed opinion, produced an enigmatic editorial. It began by quoting a remark of Painlevé in Paris: "A sustained effort of the brain is necessary to penetrate the thought of the great German savant and to follow his logic. Thus the craze of society to discuss Einstein between two rubbers of bridge appears to be one of the funniest things in the world." In a mild attempt to cut both Einstein and relativity down to size, the paper then continued: "Relativity is an interesting word in itself and it expresses just what a number of people are always doing, namely thinking of everything in terms of something else." Mathematical theories, it continued, "never make much practical difference, and perhaps it is as well that they should not; for if, owing to the theory of relativity, the apple no longer fell to the ground, a number of other things might happen, some of them dangerous, and Einstein might become as unpopular as he is now popular." This may have been no more than *The Times* on an off morning, but it is easy to see it as a mild reproof to the scientist who was already revealing, now that people were taking notice of him, an interest in public affairs that was unexpected, unwelcome, and slightly irregular.

Before he left France Einstein was to demonstrate this interest in a highly delicate way. During the journey into Paris he had confided to Nordmann that he would like to see the battlefields and on the last day of his visit he was collected from his apartment at 6:30 in the morning by Nordmann, Solovine, and Langevin.

Einstein brought the single small traveling bag that was his entire luggage, and the party drove off northeastwards along the line of the German advance in 1914. They were quickly among the ruins of war, a landscape of flattened villages, moldering trench systems, and entire forests leveled by artillery barrage. Frequently they stopped and dismounted, Einstein visibly shaken, bewildered, and almost uncomprehending that war could really have been like this, even worse than the propagandists claimed. At one point, among devastated farms and beside trees withered by gas, he turned to his friends. "All the students of Germany must be brought here," he said, "all the students of the world, so that they can see how ugly war really is. People often have a wrong idea because it comes from books. Thus most Germans have an image of Frenchmen that is purely literary; and many men have an equally literary idea of war and the ruins that it creates. How necessary it is that they should come and *see*."

They went on through St. Quentin, where the Americans had first gone into action in strength, and then into the ruins of Rheims, Einstein stopping from time to time with the single word "Terrible." In Rheims they had lunch, and here an extraordinary incident occurred.

At a nearby table sat two senior French officers, immaculate in full dress, and a fashionably accoutered woman. Nordmann noticed that they first appeared to recognize Einstein and then confirmed his identity by sending a waiter to Nordmann's chauffeur. As the Einstein party later rose to leave the restaurant, the French officers and their companion stood up, turned to Einstein and, without saying a word, politely bowed.

From Rheims they drove north across fifty miles of devastation and Einstein was put on the train to Cologne. As it prepared to move off, he waved his broad-brimmed hat towards the German frontier: "I will describe all I have seen to the people over there."

He arrived back in Berlin to find that during his absence a showing of the first "relativity film" had taken place. Made by a Professor Nicolai and a Herr Kornbaum, it consisted of four parts. The first showed the familiar experiment of an object falling first from a car in motion and then from a car at rest; the second, the contradictions met with in the accepted theory of light. The third part tried to show how relativity solved these problems in terms of space and time, while the last dealt with the deflection of starlight revealed by the British expedition of 1919. The film was ingenious, but it took for granted that the audience had a working knowledge of physics, and thus failed to achieve complete success in a complicated problem. Strangely enough, it was only after a lapse of almost two months that Einstein wrote to the German papers saying that he had had no hand in the film's production and had in fact asked its makers to use a different title. But it crossed the Atlantic and was reviewed in *Vanity Fair* for a fee of $100 by Morris Raphael Cohen, who had translated Einstein's lectures at the City College of New York.* "It was the only movie I had ever gone to," he later wrote. "I have often expressed a willingness to go to another movie on the same terms but have found no takers."

Einstein's visit to Paris sparked off further invitations, one of which came from the Zurich Student Union. "Tell them," he wrote to Weyl on June 6,

> that I, as an old Zurich boy, had much pleasure from their invitation. But I so desperately need peace and quiet, and what I could say on the subject of physics can, with respect, be whistled from the birds on the rooftops, so that I still find it difficult to open my mouth. Don't hold it against me that I declined your invitation, and don't say: "He could go to Paris but not come to us." To have refused the Paris invitation would have been treachery to international ideals, devotion to which is now more necessary than ever. But there is no need for "reparations" in the case of my own fellow countrymen. They always retain their sobriety, equanimity, and toleration.

International ideals continued to occupy him. Some Frenchmen, it had been clear from his experiences in Paris, were ready to stretch out their hands in a gesture of reconciliation. And it was with this fact very much in mind that on June 11 he addressed a meeting of the German Peace Federation on the floor of the Reichstag. He made a plea for European unity, deplored the differences created by language, and said that in future men of goodwill should ask, not "What can be done for my country?" but rather "What must my country do to make it possible for the greater entity to exist?" And he went on to express the beliefs he was to hold for another decade—

*See page 473.

until the rise of Hitler made him abandon them in despair: I hold it to be of extreme consequence that whenever the possibility arises, men of different languages, of different political and cultural ideas, should get in touch with one another across their frontiers—not with the feeling that something might be squeezed out of the other for their and their country's benefit, but with a spirit of goodwill to bridge the gap between the spiritual groups in comparatively independent spheres."

Perhaps there was at last a chance to build a new world from the postwar chaos. Perhaps there was more than a glimmer of hope for Europe. Einstein thought so, and when he was invited by Sir Eric Drummond, Secretary General of the League of Nations, to join the newly formed International Committee on Intellectual Cooperation, he quickly agreed. The Weimar Republic was still threatened from within, a prickly bitterness still hampered Franco-German relations, and a sense of imminent chaos suffused Berlin itself. Even so, it did appear that the forces which stood for international reconstruction, for the slow painful business of recasting Germany in a less military mold so that she could live with her continental neighbors, were at last gaining strength.

Then, on June 24, 1922, Walter Rathenau was assassinated by right-wing extremists as he left his home in the Berlin Grünewald. The murder was part of a pattern. Earlier in the month two nationalists had only just failed to kill Herr Scheidemann, the former Prime Minister, and a few days after Rathenau's death attackers seriously wounded another prominent Jew, the publicist Maximilian Harden.

Einstein saw Rathenau's murder as symbolic of a rising tide of anti-Semitism which would soon be lapping round his own feet. It pushed him into temporary resignation from the League committee and it drove him to the edge of leaving Germany—for the second time in less than two years. This time, moreover, he took the decision, planned his withdrawal, and was dissuaded only by pleas from the League officials in Geneva to change his mind and remain in Berlin.

Rathenau had become Foreign Minister in February, and had taken the post despite warnings from Einstein. "I regretted the fact that he became a Minister," he wrote.

"In view of the attitude which large numbers of the educated classes in Germany assume towards the Jews, I have always thought that their natural conduct in public should be one of proud reserve." In this case anti-Semitism had quickly been reinforced by something more. By April, Rathenau had successfully concluded the Treaty of Rapallo under which Germany and Russia reestablished diplomatic relations, renounced financial claims on each other, and pledged themselves to economic cooperation. Engineered without the knowledge of America, Britain, or France, it had been an omen of things to come; to many in Germany it had seemed yet another sign that the Weimar Republic in general and Jews in particular were tarred with the same red brush of communism.

Thus Rathenau's murder tended to polarize the two forces already jockeying for influence within the Republic. The day of his burial was proclaimed an official day of mourning, and all schools, universities, and theaters were ordered to close. But in Heidelberg Philipp Lenard ostentatiously gave his lectures as usual. And in Berlin it was rumored that Einstein, the Jewish scientific equivalent of the Jewish Foreign Minister, was next on the assassins' list.

The rumors had some foundation. While Einstein had been in the United States the previous year a young German, Rudolph Leibus, had been charged in Berlin with offering a reward for the murder of Einstein, Professor Foerster, and Harden, on the grounds that "it was a patriotic duty to shoot these leaders of pacifist sentiment." Found guilty, Herr Leibus was fined the equivalent of $16. It seems unlikely that the rate for provocation to murder had risen since then.

Einstein himself was under no illusions. On July 4 he wrote to Geneva resigning from the newly formed commission.* At the same time he explained to Madame Curie, whom he had only recently recommended to accept, that he was doing so "not only because of the tragic death of Rathenau but because on other occasions I have observed a strong feeling of anti-Semitism among the people whom I am supposed to represent; as they seem on the whole to lean that way, I feel that I am no longer the right person for the job."

*See page 431.

However, this was only a beginning, and two days later he wrote to Max Planck from Kiel, canceling a lecture which he had planned to give to the Natural Science Society in Berlin. He had been informed independently by serious persons that it would be dangerous for him in the near future to stay in Berlin or, for that matter, to appear anywhere in public in Germany, for he was supposed to belong to that group of persons whom the people were planning to assassinate, he said.

> Of course, I have no positive proof of this, but in the prevailing situation it seems quite plausible. . . . The trouble is that the newspapers have mentioned my name too often, thus mobilizing the rabble against me. I have no alternative but to be patient—and to leave the city.

Madame Curie now wrote pleading with him to stay on the League commission, saying that this would have been Rathenau's response. Einstein replied on July 11 that she did not understand the situation in Germany and added that it was quite impossible for a Jew to serve both the German and an international intelligentsia. Then he went further.

"I accept the full consequences of this situation *sine ira et studio,*" he said,

> and have decided to relinquish as quietly as possible both my position at the Academy and as director of the Kaiser Wilhelm Institute for Physics, and then to settle down somewhere as a private individual. In any case I cannot stay in Berlin as threats have already been made on my life by the ultranationalists. It is of course difficult to prove whether these threats are real. In any case I shall take this as an excuse to move away from turbulent Berlin to somewhere quiet where I am able to work. Material conditions have made that impossible here.

Five days later he wrote to Solovine: "Here, since the fearful assassination of Rathenau, one lives through exciting days. I, also, am always ready. I have stopped my lectures and I am officially absent, although in fact I am always here. Anti-Semitism is very strong."

By mid-July, 1922, Einstein was therefore yet again resigned to being driven from Germany. He had lived there eight years, longer than he had lived anywhere since his youth. Now, once more, he would be moving on. Just how little this worried him at the time is indicated by a letter written two years earlier to Max Born, who had sought his advice on going to Göttingen. "After all, it is not so important where you live," he had said.

> The best thing is to follow your heart, without thinking much about it. Also, as a man who has no roots anywhere, I don't feel qualified to give advice. My father's ashes lie in Milan. I buried my mother here a few days ago. I myself have been gadding about incessantly—a foreigner everywhere. My children are in Switzerland under conditions that entail a complicated venture for me if I want to see them. Such a man as myself considers it an ideal to be at home somewhere with his dear ones; he has no right to advise you in this matter.

Now, as in 1919 and 1920, he was only dissuaded at the last moment from moving: possibly to Holland, possibly to Switzerland. However, dissuaded he was, by Pierre Comert of the League of Nations, who appealed to him on much the same grounds as Madame Curie: to leave Germany now would be to abandon ship.*

Some grounds for confidence were indeed provided the following month at the centennial meeting of the Gesellschaft Deutscher Naturforscher in Leipzig. Einstein, still anxious not to provide too easy a target for the anti-Semites, had refused to attend as a key speaker. But the authorities had insisted on making relativity an important feature, and lectures on it were planned by von Laue and others. As soon as this became known, the former members of the "Antirelativity Company" went into action, preparing a broadsheet which was sent to the papers and distributed in Leipzig as the conference opened. "The undersigned," it said, "consider it irreconcilable with the seriousness and dignity of German science that a theory, much open to attack, is prematurely and vulgarly broadcast to the lay world and that the Society of German Scientists and Physicists is used to support such attempts." But "the undersigned" was an even less impressive group than had been mustered at Bad Nauheim the previous year. It looked as though the antirelativity plank in the anti-Semites' platform was cracking.

*See page 431.

However, Einstein was by this time alert enough to realize that the situation might change once again, just as significantly and just as quickly. Doubts remained beneath the brave front which he put on affairs—even though in the autumn of 1922 he was given one recognition which many felt he should have received earlier, the Nobel Prize for Physics.

However, it is possibly truer in the case of physics than in the other categories for which the prize is awarded—chemistry, physiology or medicine, literature, and peace that considerable time must pass before achievements can be properly evaluated. Thus only in 1947 did Appleton receive the prize for his investigations of the ionosphere carried out in 1924 and 1925, and it was not until 1951 that Cockcroft and Walton were awarded the prize for their artificial disintegration of the nucleus in 1932. In the case of Einstein, other factors were at work. Whether the argument still raging over General Relativity was one of them is a question whose answer will forever be locked within the bosom of the Swedish Academy of Science. However, there was no need to invoke the General Theory, since Einstein's earlier work was available. But here the members of the Academy were balked by a wording of their mandate which might have worried them even more had they decided to consider the Special Theory as the basis of the award. For when Alfred Nobel laid down the lines on which the physics prize was to be given, he stipulated that it should be for a "discovery"; furthermore, it should be one from which mankind had derived great use. Now it was questionable whether the Special Theory was, strictly speaking, a "discovery" at all; even if it were, it was still difficult to claim that by the early 1920s mankind had derived any great use from it. Relativity was already a commonplace tool in laboratories where subatomic particles were being investigated, but this was not what Nobel had meant. However, during the autumn of 1922 the Academy decided that it could make the award and yet dodge the difficult relativity issues. The prize was awarded "independently of such value as may be ultimately attached to his theories of relativity and gravity, if these are confirmed, for his services to the theory of physics, and especially for his discovery of the law of the photoelectric effect." Here they were on safe ground; for the photoelectric law was not only a discovery revealing the quantitative relationship between light and the emission of electrons, but was even by the early 1920s being utilized in practical ways.

The announcement produced one reaction that was hardly unexpected: Lenard wrote bitterly to the Swedish Academy accusing it of trying to restore Einstein's prestige without committing itself to the support of relativity. But the award also produced something of greater significance. This was an anguished inquiry from the Swiss and German ambassadors in Stockholm, both of whom wanted to claim Einstein as their own. The result was a mixture of pathos and farce which was not without international interest; for on the answer to the question depended the country whose ambassador could appear with Einstein at the elaborate Nobel Prize ceremony and at the state banquet given by the King of Sweden every year in honor of the prize winners.

Einstein was traveling on a Swiss passport, a fact which the German Foreign Office immediately passed on to the German ambassador, Herr Nadolny, but which Nadolny, in the professional nature of things, was reluctant to take at its face value. He appears to have been justified. For when he telegraphed an inquiry to the Berlin Academy of Sciences at the beginning of December, he immediately received the reply: "Einstein ist Reichsdeutscher." "The Swiss ambassador was surprised when I told him this," Nadolny later wrote. "However, when I described the telegram to him he calmed down and accepted the situation with the comment that Einstein was generally looked upon as a German and probably now wished to be considered as a German." Nadolny, on his part, was equally gracious, suggesting to Berlin that Switzerland's part in Einstein's life and work should be stressed in any announcement to the papers and later proposing that the Swiss ambassador might, "as a worthwhile courtesy," be invited to the Nobel Lecture which Einstein was to give in Stockholm. The outcome was in fact a compromise. Einstein himself was unable to accept the award personally, being out of Europe on December 11, the anniversary of Nobel's death on which the prizes are awarded. This lucky chance enabled both the Germans and the Swiss to play parts in the act. For in Stockholm the award was received by the German ambassador on Einstein's behalf, but in Berlin it was handed over to him, at his own request, not by the Swedish ambassador to Germany but by the Swiss. But in the Nobel records Einstein was recorded as "German."

One result of the imbroglio was that the Berlin Academy was instructed by the German Minister of Science, Art, and Popular Education to elucidate once and for all the riddle of Einstein's nationality. Its report, made on January 13, 1923, merely stated that since all civil servants must be Germans and Einstein had in 1914 become a civil servant, "it must be inferred" that he was German, "even if he did not possess it [German nationality] from birth." The earlier Swiss nationality was not involved, it concluded, and the Academy therefore considered their man "chiefly Reichsdeutscher," the "chiefly" being a qualification which may have crept into the argument due either to caution or an inability to find the vital documents.

This, however, was not the end of the matter. When Einstein returned to Germany early in 1923 he was asked by the Academy to put forward his own views. "Referring to your letter of February 15," he replied on March 24, 1923,

> allow me to inform you as follows. When my appointment to the Academy was being considered, my colleague Haber informed me that my appointment would result in my becoming a Prussian citizen. As I attached importance to retaining my [Swiss] nationality, I made acceptance of a possible appointment dependent on this, a stipulation which was agreed to. I do not doubt that this can be confirmed by ministry documents. Furthermore, I know that these facts are well known to my colleagues Haber and Nernst.

However, the German civil service would not easily let go—and it was supported by the German consul general in Barcelona who reported to Berlin after Einstein's visit there early in 1923*: "On the whole the local visit of Einstein, who, however, always appears as German not as Swiss, is reckoned a complete success, as much for himself

*See page 370.

and for German science as for German-Spanish cultural relations."

On May 14, 1923, the Minister wrote to Einstein stating that there was nothing in the records concerning his nationality and advising that if he wished the matter to be finally settled he should get in touch with a senior civil servant, Dr. von Rothenburg. The interview took place six months later. Its result was a statement by Einstein dated February 7, 1924. In it he says that the senior civil servant had represented firmly the view that he, Einstein, acquired the rights of a Prussian citizen with his appointment to the Academy, since no other view could be established from the documents. There the affair rested until, nine years later, Einstein gave up his passport in the German embassy in Brussels and walked off German soil for the last time.

Documents may have been destroyed. The officials of 1923 may have been unduly anxious to claim that Einstein had been a German since 1914. But it seems curious that the swearing in to Weimar in 1920 and to Prussia in 1921, his stelf-styled "folly," should not have been mentioned during this dispute. Yet no one can doubt either Einstein's passionate dislike of becoming a German again in 1914, or his equally passionate change of heart which followed the birth of the Republic.

There is one explanation which fits the known facts. It is conceivable that Planck and Nernst, despite their friendly intentions in 1913, were unable to prevent Einstein's automatic reenrollment as a fully fledged German. He was also a Swiss; he had his Swiss passport. Why should they trouble him by telling him the technical truth that he was also, inevitably under the new law of June, 1913, a son of the Fatherland once again? When, in the euphoria of Weimar, he wished to become a German, Planck and Nernst could hardly dissuade him on the grounds that he already was a German, and in the circumstances it would have been natural for them to encourage the purely formal act which did not alter his status but which he remembered as "one of the follies" of his life. Planck and Nernst could then let their consciences rest happy: if it was not exactly true that two wrongs had in this case produced a right, at least two misunderstandings had combined to bring about the desired result and Einstein could move about the world as an unofficial German ambassador, which appeared to satisfy all parties.

The Nobel Prize money went to Mileva. Even Einstein's closest friends did not know this, and Lorentz wrote happily that, quite apart from the honor, there was "a material side to the Nobel Prize and I trust that this will ease the cares of your daily life." By this time his financial position was more reassuring. Requests to lecture came thick and fast, and it was the acceptance of one of these, arranged by "a cunning publisher of a very well-established periodical" in Japan, which had taken him from the country during the Nobel ceremonies. Acceptance of the Japanese invitation was very much a leap in the dark and both his brief diary notes and the oblique references in several newspaper interviews suggest that in practice it turned out to be a disillusioning experience, even though he liked what he considered to be the simple, gentle Japanese. Little more might have been expected. He had been invited to lecture from one end of the country to the other, all expenses paid; he should not have been surprised if he was to be milked hard in the process.

As might have been forecast, he was shocked by conditions east of Suez. Thus after arrival in Colombo, at the end of October, 1922, he noted: ". . . We rode in small one-man carriages drawn at a trot by men of herculean strength yet delicate build. I was bitterly ashamed to share responsibility for the abominable treatment accorded fellow human beings but was unable to do anything about it." From Ceylon he and Elsa traveled on to Shanghai. Here they were met by the sound of "Deutschland, Deutschland über Alles," sung by the members of the city's German colony and arousing mixed emotions in Einstein's German-Swiss heart.

They arrived in Japan in mid-November. He held a press conference at the Imperial Hotel in Tokyo and then prepared for his first lecture. This was to be given in the main hall of Tokyo University, and by the time that he was due, the *Japan Weekly Chronicle* recorded, "the hall was filled with scholars, teachers, and students. Some women were present, too." There was also Yamamoto Sanehiko, the proprietor of the paper *Kaizosha.* Einstein began speaking at 1:30 P.M. and continued for three hours, a formidable effort even allowing time for translation. After this there was an hour's break, presumably for what might be called light refreshments. At 5:30 he was back at the rostrum once more. He started where he had left off, apparently delighted at having such attentive listeners and continued for another three hours. "The audience," it was reported, "were astonished at his staying power."

It was an auspicious start to what was on the whole an unsatisfactory tour. The Einsteins were introduced to the Emperor and the Empress, a singular honor, and Einstein later recorded how he had spoken with the Empress in French. They attended the Feast of Chrysanthemums in the Imperial Gardens and there were a number of other formal receptions before the start of the month-long tour. The audiences to which he now spoke were less serious than those in Tokyo, being attracted by his name as much as by the almost mystic significance which relativity had assumed for the Japanese. Not everyone welcomed its new status. "The excessive reliance on science and the contempt for faith have made a failure of the last century or so," noted the *Japan Weekly Chronicle*. "It is sad to reflect that the Japanese should nevertheless be so elated over a new scientific theory."

To Einstein, "elated" would have seemed an understatement as he was paraded through Japan, a scientific curiosity to be gazed at as well as listened to. In view of the time taken for translation he cut his original lecture, only to restore its former length after being told he had gravely offended his hosts by giving them less than Tokyo. His reactions can be gauged by a report in the *Japan Weekly Chronicle,* whose correspondent noted that the tour was "weighing on him rather heavily." Einstein had also shown, it went on, "a strong distaste for the popular style of lecture, boosted and crowded with people who are simply curious to pay the fee to see the latest lion. He had expected that his audience would consist only of curious students of physics."

His impact can be estimated not only by the reception but by the levels at which relativity appears to have been discussed. One account, published in the *Mainichi* and reprinted in English in the *Japan Weekly Chronicle,* need not be credited with literal accuracy; but it does indicate the national importance which was accorded in Japan to a theory which only a minute proportion of the population could understand.

The report described a discussion "of quite unusual nature" by the Cabinet Council: "One of the Ministers asked whether ordinary people would understand Professor Einstein's lectures on the theory of relativity," it began.

> Mr. Kamada, Minister of Education, rather rashly said of course they would. Dr. Okano, Minister of Justice, contradicted Mr. Kamada, saying that they would never understand. Mr. Arai, Minister of Agriculture and Commerce, was rather sorry for Mr. Kamada, so he said that they would perhaps understand vaguely. The headstrong Minister of Justice insisted that there could be no midway between understanding and not understanding. If they understood, they understood clearly. If they did not understand, they did not understand at all. A chill fell on the company. Mr. Baba, the tactful director of the Legislation Bureau, said that they could understand if they made efforts. Their efforts would be useless, persisted the Minister of Justice. He had himself ordered a book on the theory of relativity when the theory was first introduced into Japan last year and tried to study it. On the first page he found higher mathematics, and he had to shut the book for the present. When the members of the Imperial Academy were invited to dinner at the Hama detached palace, he had mentioned the problem to Dr. Tanakadate Aikitsu, who was seated next to him. Dr. Fujisawa Rikitaio (an authority on mathematics), overhearing their discussion, said that in America they were collecting popular explanations of the theory, offering an enormous prize. Such being the case, Dr. Fujisawa said, it was wiser not to begin the study at once. He supported Dr. Okano's opinion. Hearing this elaborate explanation, Mr. Baba, director of the Legislation Bureau, decided to eschew Einstein for the time being.

The rest of the population behaved otherwise and by the end of December Einstein was thankful to board ship for Europe. Even so, he had a high opinion of the people themselves; "Japan is wonderful," he wrote to his friend Solovine on his return to Berlin. "Beautiful manners, an interest in everything, an artistic touch and intellectual naïveté coupled with common sense. A refined people in a picturesque country." On the way home he visited

Palestine, formally opening there the Hebrew University whose foundation stone had been laid on Mount Scopus some five years earlier.* Then he and his wife sailed on to Marseilles, traveling from the port of Madrid where, during his absence from Europe, arrangements had been completed for what was to be another triumphal tour.

The lecture which Einstein gave to the Academy of Sciences in Madrid, before being elected a member, was attended by King Alphonso XIII. The rector of Madrid University proposed that not only Professor, but also Frau Einstein should be granted the diploma of Doctor *honoris causa.* And the Spanish Minister of Education offered him a home, in the name of the Spanish nation, should conditions in Germany "impede the tranquil continuation of his intellectual studies." There, opinion continued divided; the anti-Semite lobby continued to make itself heard, but in Ulm the city councillors decided on March 20 that a new street should be named Einsteinstrasse.

In Spain, there was only one hint of trouble. Before reaching Madrid, Einstein lectured in Barcelona and here he attended a meeting of the local Syndicalists, workers dedicated to obtaining control of industry by direct action. Exactly what he said to them is not clear, but *The Times,* not notably inaccurate in such matters, quoted him addressing them with the words: "I also am a revolutionary, though only a scientific one. The persecutions you tell me of seem to have been more stupid than wicked. You see only the bad side of things. There is also a good side." This seems harmless enough, but the left-wing Spanish newspapers may have embroidered their stories, and Einstein was obliged to state that reports of this meeting did "not correctly convey what he said"—an elegant phrase which, as *The Times* reported from Madrid, "thus dissipated a rather painful impression which was made in some circles here by the words attributed to him."

Einstein arrived back in Berlin only a few weeks before an announcement in Washington gave further support to the General Theory. The previous September there had been another total eclipse of the sun, visible throughout a narrow belt stretching from Somaliland across the Indian Ocean to Australia, and a number of expeditions had been

*See page 478.

sent out to gather further evidence for or against the theory. A party from the Greenwich Observatory and a Dutch-German expedition—the German contingent led by Freundlich with special equipment prepared in the Potsdam Observatory—had gone to Christmas Island in the Pacific. From Sydney a phototelescope had been taken to Cunnamulla in Queensland, and the government of New South Wales had sent a party to Cordillo Downs, deep in the Australian interior, to which a dismantled telescope had been carried more than one hundred miles from the railhead on the backs of camels. In addition, Australian, Canadian, and American astronomers had set up their instruments near Broome on the northwest coast of Australia, the American expedition being led by Professor W. W. Campbell of the Lick Observatory.

As in 1919, the observers were at the mercy of the weather. This time, however, one minor source of possible error had been eliminated. In 1919, the light from the sun and its nearby stars had been collected by mirrors whose small distortions complicated the resulting calculations; in most of the instruments now being used, the light was directly collected by the telescopes' object glasses. Other refinements had been incorporated in the equipment and it was generally accepted, as *The Times* wrote on September 21, 1922, that "if the expected verification has been made this morning it will have to be admitted that human observations of the universe can be reconciled with a theory from which absolute space and absolute time have been excluded, although at present they are not reconcilable with a theory based on these Newtonian conceptions."

Seven months later it was revealed that the verification had been made. Some teams had been frustrated by bad weather, but Professor Campbell's party had met with almost perfect conditions. Hundreds of star images were recorded on their four special phototelescopes and some scores of these, shown on ten plates, had been selected for calculation and checking. Now, on April 12, 1923, Campbell reported that the prints taken on September 21 and compared with those taken at Tahiti three months before the eclipse, showed agreement with Einstein's prediction "as close as the most ardent proponent of the relativity theory could hope for." The following evening, Eddington reported the results of the Lick expedition to his fellow astronomers in Burlington House, recalling the two expeditions of 1919 and adding: "I think it was the Bellman in 'The Hunting of the Snark' who laid down the rule: 'When I say it three times, it is right.' [sic] The stars have now said it three times to three separate expeditions, and I am convinced that their answer is right."

Not everyone was pleased. "It is an interesting commentary on the reluctance of many leading men of science to accept the relativity theory," says Eddington's biographer, "that when Campbell was asked what he anticipated from the eclipse plates, he replied: 'I hoped it would not be true.' Undoubtedly some Fellows of the Royal Society and even a few in the Royal Astronomical Society felt the same way."

Even though the Lick expedition provided the third proof "that light does not go straight" when affected by gravity, conservative doubts were to some extent justified by later events. For as technological advance made more accurate results possible, speculation continued about the amount of deflection involved; and thirty years later it could be claimed that this was "still controversial, at least in regard to magnitude."

Back in Germany, Einstein must have felt that his travels were over for the time being. His fears of the previous summer were evaporating and he now looked forward to an untroubled continuation of work in Berlin. He might well have been warned by the extraordinary story of his alleged "trip to Russia." In the *Deutsche Allgemeine Zeitung* of September 15, 1923, there appeared the report that Einstein was expected in Moscow at the end of the month. On October 6 the *Berliner Tageblatt* took up the story with an announcement that he had left for the Russian capital, while on October 27, the nationalist *Berliner Borsenzeitung* quoted Russian reports that Einstein would be "arriving in Petersburg on October 28 and will speak on the relativity theory to a group of trained scientific workers." Not to be outdone, the *Kieler Zeitung* reported on November 2 that: "Einstein is staying in Petersburg for three days." With such a wealth of circumstantial report, his fellow countrymen could be justified in thinking that he had visited Russia, even though dates and details might not be correct. In fact he was never in the country. The story was merely another item in the anti-Jewish, antirelativity campaign, which was always anxious to tar its enemies with the Communist brush.

Yet the canard, damaging to Einstein at a time when many still considered Weimar's resumption of relations with Russia to be a betrayal, was given a plausibility by his own actions. For he was not only on comparatively friendly terms with Georgÿ Tschisherrin, the Russian Peoples' Commissar for Foreign Affairs in Berlin, but was on at least one occasion used as an intermediary by the Zionist leader, Kurt Blumenfeld, in an effort to ease the conditions of the Jews in Russia.

Blumenfeld has himself told the story, revealing how he one day met an East European Jew who had been closely following Zionist activities. "You have won Einstein for the Zionist cause," said this man. "Tschisherrin has the greatest respect for Einstein, with whom he has often spoken. Get him to introduce you to Tschisherrin; if you meet him alone with Einstein then something can come of it." Blumenfeld recalls how he mentioned the matter to Einstein, who immediately went to the telephone, saying: "This conversation can be really interesting." A few days later, the two men visited the Soviet embassy, the ambassador saying a few minutes after their meeting: "I know what is in your mind." The interview was long and inconclusive. Tschisherrin was prepared to admit that the movement of small groups of Russian Jews to Palestine might be allowed but that "mass emigration is out of the question: it conflicts with the Soviet system." Einstein was certainly willing to intervene with the Russians if this were likely to help the cause of Zionism. He would just as willingly have intervened with the devil had he seen any hope of success. But he was not used to supping with long spoons.

Early in November he was suddenly jerked awake again to his position in Germany, and to the dangerous situation of anyone who fraternized with Communists. During the first days of the month he was visited by a prominent Jewish leader who appears to have advised him that his life was in danger. Just how serious the warning was is not known. But on November 7, Einstein wrote to Planck a letter—no copy of which has survived—saying that he was leaving the country for a few days and canceling a dinner date with Planck at Haberlandstrasse for the evening of the ninth.

Planck failed to receive the letter and arrived at the Einstein home on the ninth, only to be received by Elsa with news of her husband's sudden departure for Leiden. Both had good cause for alarm. For between the writing of Einstein's letter on the seventh and Planck's arrival in Haberlandstrasse, the National Socialists, led by Hitler and supported by General Ludendorff, had begun their attempt to take over the Bavarian government in Munich as prelude to a march on Berlin. There had been fighting during the day and what was to happen next was still uncertain.

Einstein's flight was not in fact linked with the Munich putsch. It was, rather, an indication of the anti-Semitic climate of the times, but on the night of the ninth it can hardly have looked fortuitous. The rising was put down and on November 10 Planck wrote to Einstein in Leiden, pleading with him yet again not to accept any of the offers which would no doubt be made to him.

There is no evidence whatever that Einstein suffered from personal fear; rather the reverse. But he wanted to get on with his work, he knew that there would be little chance of that under a National Socialist government, and it was in character that until he learned that the putsch had been crushed he should seek the security of Leiden. It was equally in character that Planck should write to him in the name of German science and implore him to come back. He came.

He did not return entirely in reply to Planck's appeal; much as he respected the older man's scientific genius, Einstein always went his own way. He did not return because of Elsa and the comfort of the Haberlandstrasse home. In 1923, as in 1914, Berlin still provided—as long as Weimar remained—the intellectual climate in which he could best get on with his work.

PART FOUR

THE EINSTEIN AGE

CHAPTER 12

UNTER DEN LINDEN

Einstein returned from Holland to Berlin towards the end of November, 1923. For the next decade the city was his base for a central, consolidating period of his life. But what consolidated was not only the physicist with the international reputation, the man who had shown the universe to be built differently from accepted ideas. This absentminded scientist turning his huge luminous and inquiring eyes on visitors, behaving at times with an almost studied childlike simplicity, more an actor playing Einstein than the man himself, was only one facet. It was matched by another, by the man whom the President of the United States and the Emperor of Japan had been honored to meet, the Nobel Prize winner coaxed into helping the League of Nations, the physicist whose advice was constantly sought by the more formidable of the Jewish leaders. Moreover this Swabian, whose triumphs in the realm of abstract thought had brought him the fame of an oracle and the veneration that goes with it, had during the transformation decided to use the reputation that chance had unexpectedly tossed him. He would campaign with the Zionists for a Jewish homeland in Palestine and he would help build a new Europe—although whether it should be built on unarmed pacifist goodwill or beneath the umbrella of international arms was something which he found it difficult to decide.

With these political ambitions, it would have been natural enough if Einstein had exercised considerable influence outside his specialist field during the decade which began in 1924. Many physicists did so. The British government was apt to consult Rutherford as a matter of course on any question affecting science. There were Madame Curie and Professor Langevin in France, Lorentz in Holland. Edward Appleton, pioneer of the ionosphere, had a finger in innumerable government pies. Lindemann later became, as Lord Cherwell, one of the most influential, and controversial, politicoscientific figures of his time. Yet Einstein operated throughout this period at a very different level and with very different results. His name was invaluable for transferring cash from wealthy Jews into Zionist funds. His name on pacifist manifestos was always a sign of honest intent, and of considerable publicity value until the law of diminishing returns came into action. But during the years between the two world wars the effect of his efforts in these fields was in many ways as counterproductive as his enthusiasm was unlimited. The reasons do not lie entirely in the fact that, operating as a Jew in Germany, he was something of a fish out of water; other Jews in other spheres drove opinion the way they wanted it until the Nazis came to power.

He was handicapped in all his efforts to implement his good intentions by the very qualities that made him the genius he was. First, and of overwhelming importance, was his determination to devote as much time as possible to discovering how the physical world was built. He wanted to aid the Jews and he wanted to help keep the peace of the world. But whenever he was in danger of becoming too deeply involved, there was some new riddle of the universe that demanded attention. Kurt Blumenfeld, who recruited Einstein into the Zionist cause, shrewdly noted of him to Weizmann that "Zionism and Palestine were only peripheral concerns"; and in 1923 Einstein himself revealed his own view of the priorities when he told Weizmann that he would give his name and would talk to people in Berlin but would not "travel around or visit congresses, since in order to preserve my rights as a thinker I have to stay quiet in order to work." His dedication to the pacifist cause was equally unquestioned between 1919 and 1933. But his enthusiasm had perpetually to contend with the fact that there were scientific papers to be written or read, and men like Planck or Sommerfeld or von Laue to discuss them with. Thus he was forced to overlook his homework, to skimp his practice in a game that constantly demanded it.

With this tendency to give less attention to nonscientific matters than enthusiasm required, there went a dislike for the formalities demanded of those who try to influence others, and a contempt for the sleight-of-mind that is often called for. Einstein despised the careful cultivation of men or women for particular ends, the balancing of interest against interest, the bland statement that conceals truth rather than illuminates it, and the ability to judge the right moment for dropping the right hint into the right ear.

Finally there was his sense of the ridiculous. He did not mind what he looked like and he often did not mind what he said. He was, quite simply, too unconcerned to worry about trifles, even when circumstances began to push him more frequently than his scientific colleagues onto the public stage where trifles matter. But they managed to look like figures from the great drama of public affairs; he too often evoked the music-hall. Thus it was inevitable that he should occupy a large place in human hearts and a small one in the corridors of power.

The Berlin into which Einstein settled down in 1924 has a special niche in history. This was the Berlin whose fortunes changed as Germany struggled up from the post-war economic morass and was then pushed back into it by the world depression of 1929, a city which had done with the soldiers' councils of the revolution, and the troops of the Kapp Putsch, but was soon to be beguiled by the presidency of Hindenburg; and, eventually, by Hindenburg's candidate for the chancellorship, Adolf Hitler.

In the capital, Einstein not only occupied a unique position but lived under conditions more favorable than those he had previously been used to. For the first time in his life he had one home for more than a few years. To counteract the undertow of anti-Semitic nationalism, quiescent for a while but never very far below the surface, there was the respect of the university and the Kaiser Wilhelm Institute which he knew was his due. In Leiden, where he delighted to stay with the Ehrenfests on his visits as professor extraordinary, he was enormously popular. Royalties from his book on relativity and his salary from Leiden helped to raise him from the rut of most professors; he had always been careless of money but now he could almost afford to be. He had his music and he had his sailing—on a fine choice of lakes which ringed Berlin with the circlet of watery fingers that were to be marker points for the bombers in the Second World War, whatever the camouflage experts could do. He had, moreover, an entré into the polyglot world of educated industrialists and civilized financiers, of artists and actors and designers who during the first years of Weimar appeared to have taken over the privileged position in the state so long occupied by the military. Thus he was a close friend of Willy Meinhardt, the head of the Osram company, at whose house in the Engadine he began to stay. He was a friend of Slevogt, the painter, of Emil Orlik, the designer. A typical party organized by his doctor friend, Janos Plesch, consisted of Einstein and Haber, Slevogt and Orlik, Fritz Kreisler, Arthur Schnabel, and the German Foreign Minister, Count Rantzau. Just as in his student days Einstein had at times been more than the retiring contemplative physicist, so now, on the crest of the wave, he became for a while almost as human as other men, expanding in the Weimar renaissance.

It was during this period that he walked one evening, as described by Plesch, to a favorite restaurant with the Russian physicist Joffe, with Plesch, and with a third companion. Einstein and Joffe, walking behind the other couple, were talking loudly and Einstein burst out in a roar of enjoyment. When they caught up with their friends, Einstein explained: "Poor old Joffe can't make up his mind through which hole an electron will go if he fires it through a lead obstacle with a number of holes. An electron is indivisible, and therefore it must go through one hole only. But which hole? And the solution"—with a gust of Einstein laughter—"is really very simple; it goes through the fifth dimension." Physics was still, as yet, too important to be taken too seriously.

Einstein's base for operations was of course No. 5, Haberlandstrasse, where his wife quietly helped to organize his life and where his stepdaughter Ilse often acted as secretary. The most important room in the apartment was Einstein's study in a corner turret of the block, reached by a small staircase and with a view only of rooftops and the sky. Here were the expected books, a round table in the small window alcove stacked with papers, notes, references, and an assortment of pamphlets. Here also, almost hidden on top of a bookcase, was the cigar box surreptitiously filled from time to time by Einstein's friends, who knew how Elsa tried to ration him to one a day for the sake of his health. The study was Einstein's absolute preserve. No cleaner was allowed in. Neither was Elsa. "It was here that his work was done and his friends received to discuss problems without interference," Plesch has written. "It was always a matter of regret to his wife (he always referred to her as 'my old lady') that she was unable to look after him and his things in that room as everywhere else, but Einstein was adamant; never mind the dust and disorder; it was the independence that mattered."

Here he spent most of his mornings and many of the afternoons when not engaged on university business or lectures, filling sheet after sheet of paper with calculations; immersed in the implications and development of the General Theory; and, from 1920 onwards, struggling to find the mathematical framework which would include both the phenomena of electromagnetism and those of gravity, the unified field theory which would encompass, as the *New York Times* put it, "the wheeling of the planets, the speeding of light on its course, the attraction of earth for a falling stone, the luster of the diamond, the instability of radium, the lightness of hydrogen and the heaviness of lead, the flow of electricity through a wire, millions of manifestations of matter, energy, time, space."

The academic situation in Germany can be judged from an appeal for money which he made early in April, 1924. Before the war, the income of the Kaiser Wilhelm Institute for Physics had been *75,000* marks, worth $17,750; now it was *22,000* marks, worth $1,125. In real terms the salaries of scholars and teachers, Einstein had estimated in a British journal the previous year, were only a fifth of what they had been before the war; in many cases they were much less. Fewer scientific meetings were taking place, and one reason was that many who would have attended lacked the streetcar fares to take them across Berlin. Einstein himself was in a different category. He wanted to pay for his own assistants, as was then customary. But his rich industrial friends would have none of this in the straitened circumstances of postwar Berlin, and put a lump sum into a special bank account on which he could draw as and when he wished. However much he drew, the account was always made up to the original sum.

That his appeal was not special pleading is borne out by a young Oxford man, Edward Skillings, who some time earlier had visited Berlin and eight other university centers to assess German requests for English books and periodicals. "It is plain to see that large sections of the professors are suffering from grievous privations both physical and mental," he reported. In Halle the wife of one of them explained that her husband would not be able to work without the "fearfully humiliating" help from England. In Göttingen the professor Skillings hoped to see had recently died of undernourishment. These were of course only details in the larger picture of gloom and depression which was already beginning to lower the confidence of the Germans in the ability of their new republican government—a foreseeable result which could be attributed either to a casual lack of Allied interest or to a Machiavellian method of sapping the authority of a left-wing government. Einstein had no doubt about which was the more likely alternative. "Everyone here knows that the financial obligations laid upon the country cannot be fulfilled at their present figure, even with the utmost exertion," he wrote. "All this has bred in us the conviction that there is no hope of working our way by legitimate means out of our present serfdom. This paralyzes economic activities and drives people to evade taxation, and to try to remove their capital from the country."

Against this dull and depressing background, the phenomenon of relativity, embodied in the photogenic figure of Einstein himself, was a colorful exception, an example which the nationalists could have used, had they only wished, to illustrate the genius of German science. Part of the phenomenon was the "relativity industry" which by the early 1920s was flooding the continent, as well as Britain and the United States, with explanations that ranged from the erudite to the simpleminded. "The stream continues," wrote E. Cunningham in *Nature* in June, 1922. "Here are seven more books on relativity." The previous year a bibliography, prepared by the director of the International Catalogue of Scientific Literature, included nearly 650 papers, articles, and books dealing with the subject, and many score more had been added by the time that Dr. Cunningham settled down to his reviewing.

Von Laue in Germany had been the first to write a full-scale book explaining Special Relativity—*Das Relativitätsprinzip*—which appeared in Brunswick in 1911. Five years later Freundlich did much the same for the General Theory with *The Foundations of Einstein's Theory of Gravitation.* "There really is a need for improvement if misunderstandings are to be avoided," Einstein had written to Freundlich on seeing his draft. "I will gladly . . . explain everything conscientiously to you. Should we disagree over certain points, that doesn't matter, but in that case my preface which you ask for will have to be omitted." Apparently there were no disagreements and the book appeared with Einstein's preface. Eddington's *Report on the Relativity Theory of Gravitation* for the Physical Society of London had quickly gone into a second edition, and his *Space, Time, and Gravitation,* which appeared in 1920, had, like the *Report,* "awakened English-speaking physicists and astronomers to the importance of the new theory. They began to bestir themselves for there was 'the sound of a gong in the tops of the mulberry trees'; old ideas were in the melting pot; an exciting spirit of adventure was vaguely felt even by those not mathematically equipped to read the book critically."

Einstein's major paper on the General Theory had been reprinted in book form in Leipzig in 1916, and his *Relativity: The Special and the General Theory* appeared the following year. By 1920 it had run through fourteen German editions totaling 65,000 copies. The English edition, translated by Robert Lawson and published in 1920, ran through seven editions in nineteen months. In addition, the lectures which Einstein gave in Princeton in the spring of 1921 were quickly reprinted and a number of his original papers on relativity, together with others by Lorentz and Minkowski, were reprinted as a book two years later in Germany and Britain.

Lorentz, Planck, Born, and Weyl were among Einstein's colleagues who wrote books on the subject, and even Lenard was represented with his strongly critical *Über Relativitätsprinzip, Aether, Gravitation.* In Paris, Charles Nordmann had written *Einstein and the Universe: A Popular Exposition of the Famous Theory,* in which razor-sharp French logic cut through to reveal the simplicity of Einstein's ideas with an effectiveness that not even Einstein could better. More remarkable than any of these was the massive encyclopedia article which Sommerfeld had commissioned from Wolfgang Pauli for the *Encyklopädie der mathematischen Wissenschaften*. Aged only twenty, Pauli was one of Sommerfeld's students who had attended the famous Bad Nauheim meeting; his account of relativity for the encyclopedia was quickly reprinted in book form, "in view of the apparently insatiable demand . . . for accounts of the theory of relativity," as Sommerfeld said in the preface. Reprinted forty years later, it was then described by Niels Bohr as "still one of the most valuable expositions of the basis and scope of Einstein's original conceptions."

Just over the horizon, and to appear in 1925, was Bertrand Russell's *The ABC of Relativity*, a book almost as important for the friendship which it was to encourage between Einstein and Russell as for its extraordinarily clear presentation of the subject. Russell, who in the columns of the *Athenaeum* had been among the first to describe the implications of the 1919 eclipse expeditions, was in the next third of a century to show remarkable similarities with Einstein. Like Einstein he was basically pacifist. Like Einstein he supported the Second World War as certainly as he opposed the First. Both men were frequently, and unjustifiably, tarred with the Communist brush, and both were concerned with the fundamental problem of the human predicament. But two main differences kept them apart. Einstein was proud of his similarities with his fellowmen. Russell proud of those things which made him different. And while Einstein left his study only against his better judgment, Russell was always up front in the political battle. While Einstein had worked on at the Kaiser Wilhelm Institute between 1914–18 under what he called his patrons, Russell had gone to prison for his pacifist views.

The study did not only see Einstein at work on those problems of the natural world that obsessed all physicists. Here he also dealt as best he could with the torrent of appeals, begging letters, and requests for advice that poured down on him during these years of fame and notoriety. If Einstein could prove that light did not go straight then he could do anything, however impossible it sounded. Such was a common belief.

Rudolf Kayser, who married Einstein's elder stepdaughter, Ilse, has a picture which may not be literally true but at least gives a good impression of what had to be dealt with. "Poor people beg for money, for clothing, and jobs," he has written.

> A young man has taken the notion to become an explorer; won't Einstein help him to go to India or Africa? A woman telegraphs—would the professor please obtain a visa? Actors ask for engagements; young people in small towns who have hardly attended high school would like to come to Berlin and become his disciples. Einstein reads all these requests with kindliness and understanding, and also with a sense of humor. These are obligations of fame which one must bear with a smile, but this fame has consequences, frequently responsible for bitterness. There are letters and magazine articles filled with hatred, malice, envy, and vulgarity. And since Einstein is a Jew and an opponent of all nationalistic pride, all the garbage of political strife is also cast at him. In addition, there come the fools and the prophets, who sprout, like mushrooms, especially in the years of insecurity and anarchy. This one writes that he has finally discovered the essence of sleep. That one writes that he has found the only correct way to lower the price of coal. Another one has invented new senses, since the old five senses are no longer sufficient for man's use. Technicians report on their new inventions. They send blueprints of new contraptions and flying machines. Still another is engaged in overthrowing the traditional astronomy and building up a new one. Still another believes that he has found new mathematical formulas. . . .

He was much tried in other ways. The flat-earthers, the spiritualists, the inveterate believers, all latched on to the apparent enigma of relativity to bolster their own ideas. Sometimes they rolled many of them into one packet like the author of *Spiritism: The Hidden Secret in Einstein's Theory of Relativity,* for whom Hebrew words, the "uranium cubic diatonal," and mystic numbers all contributed to the secret. So, almost inevitably, did another old standby. "This wonderful portrayal of the earth and the heavens as interlocked bodies of darkness and light is involved," readers were informed, "in the dimensions of the Great Pyramid of Egypt whose missing top expresses the space area of the 'time' of the day and of the night, of the universal 'unit space of division.'" Einstein might well have murmured, with some of the internationalists who looked askance at his statements on their affairs, "God save me from my friends."

To those in his own line of country he was always generous of time, money, and effort, a fact which quickly permeated the academic world. Thus the young foreign student who wished to study chemistry in Bonn, had been rejected by the Prussian Ministry of Education, and who knew it was against the law to make a second application, wrote as a matter of course to Einstein. He sent his entire biography, with every detail. "When you are twenty," he wrote years later, "you feel as important as I did. You are certain that the whole world appreciates this importance. Einstein did." For he not only recommended a second, albeit unlawful, application but produced for enclosure a letter from himself supporting the application and denouncing the injustice.

A clear picture of this Einstein, always eager to help lame scientific dogs over bureaucratic stiles, is given by Leopold Infeld, a young Pole studying at the University of Cracow who was later to collaborate with him in the United States. Infeld wished to complete his studies in Berlin but found that Poles were unwelcome there and Polish Jews more so. Finally, in desperation, he telephoned Einstein and was given a time to call.

"Shy, deeply touched, in a holiday spirit of expectation at meeting the greatest living physicist, I pressed the bell of Einstein's flat," he wrote of the occasion.

> I was shown into a waiting room full of heavy furniture and explained to Mrs. Einstein why I had come. She apologized and explained that I would have to wait because a Chinese Minister of Education was just then talking to her husband. I waited, my cheeks burning with excitement. . . . [He] opened the door of his study to let the Chinese gentleman out and me in. Einstein was dressed in a morning coat and striped trousers with one important button missing. It was the familiar face which one saw at that time so often in pictures and magazines. But no picture could reproduce the shining glow of his eyes.

Einstein listened to what Infeld had to say, claimed that his signature did not carry very much weight—"because I have given very many recommendations and they are anti-Semites"—and then wrote a few helpful words to Planck. "Instead of thinking about his genius, about his achievements in physics," Infeld wrote, "I thought then, and later, about his great kindness, about his loud laugh, about the gentle way he talked, about the brilliance of his eyes, about the clumsiness with which he looked about for a piece of paper on a desk full of paper, about the queer mixture of great warmth and great aloofness."

The incident was significant both of Einstein's perpetual kindness and of his Achilles heel; for he wrote, says Infeld, "without knowing whether I had the slightest idea of physics." The practice continued—so much so that refugee scientists, arriving in Oxford in 1933 and proudly showing a testimonial from Einstein, were often advised to keep quiet about it.

The combination of prodigious intellect and human vulnerability which made him such a contradictory human being became more obvious during these early 1920s as the image of the tousle-headed eccentric began to form and harden round the central character of the man. At one level, the physicist who technically headed the Kaiser Wilhelm Institute for Physics, still being developed, was the remote genius who had changed the human picture of the universe, a being so divorced from other men that his *obiter dicta* had the authority of the Delphic oracle. At another level he was the Einstein who delighted in taking control of the elevator in his Haberlandstrasse block and manipulating the buttons so that guests were whisked up, back, then up and down again past the floor at which they wished to alight. This was the Einstein who when nagged about well-worn dress clothes would say: "I will simply fasten a notice to it saying: 'This suit has just been cleaned.' " He retained the mixture of clown and small boy delighted with simple jokes, engrossed by absurdities. He was always ready to respond to the ridiculous challenge, and when a group of eminent friends called for him one evening, he accepted a bet to take off his waistcoat without first removing his coat. He was wearing his only dress suit, but immediately began a series of elaborate contortions. These continued for some while. It seemed he would have to pay up. Then, with a final tortuous twist he did the trick, triumphantly waving his crumpled waistcoat and exploding into his long deep belly laugh. This was not at all the thing for the quieter waters of Berlin academic society. It was not even the thing for some of Einstein's friends, such as Haber with his perfectly run home. Ehrenhaft recalls how on one occasion he and his wife arrived at the Habers together with Einstein and Elsa, both men properly dinner-jacketed. As they sat down in the drawing room Elsa exclaimed: "But Albert, you haven't put your socks on." "Yes, yes," he replied unblinkingly. "I have already disclosed the secret to Frau Ehrenhaft."

But Einstein's idiosyncrasies were accepted. And his friend Willy Meinhardt, president of the Osram concern, helping his guest find his overcoat, could without offense produce it with the words: "This must be Einstein's; it's made by Peek & Kloppenburg"—at that time the cut-price tailors of Berlin.

The stories of Einstein's reluctance to attend formal functions, to play the social lion in the expected way, are still numerous and must have been more so in the Berlin of half a century ago. Many are certainly apocryphal but some ring true, as when he replied to a Berlin hostess who had described her list of guests: "So you would like me to serve as a centerpiece?" His frequent description of the more formal social functions was "feeding time at the zoo," while of academic dinners he confessed to one of his stepsons-in-law: "On occasions like this I retire to the back of my mind and there I am happy."

He genuinely hated it all—announcing to a companion as he joined one dinner party: "Now I go on the trapeze." Antonina Vallentin, who knew him well during the Berlin days, says that it was in vain that

> one would explain to him the customary formalities, and those who had not known him long would explain patiently, as to a backward child. They would repeat: This is done. . . . Why is it done? he would ask. Until you noticed his smile, he seemed like a malicious child. Tails? Why tails? I never had any and never missed them. Once his wife employed all her powers of persuasion, her charm and humor, to make him order an evening suit for a solemn occasion, and after violent resistance from him

a compromise was eventually reached: a dinner jacket instead of tails. Afterwards he merely said, yes, he did have a dinner jacket in his cupboard which he was even ready to exhibit, until the day came when "the fine thing," as he called it, had grown too small and was no longer presentable.

If a streak of bloody-mindedness, a reluctance to be pushed down paths which he did not wish to pursue, tended to buttress such protests, the deep feeling behind them was genuine enough: the feeling that pretentiousness and hypocrisy were among the ingredients of the "dressing-up" on which so much of the world insisted. Behind this gentle charade there was also an urgency which for Einstein had a particular poignancy. All those buttons; all those tails; all that putting on and taking off, wasting valuable minutes and hours while in the distance he could hear, with Marvell, "time's wingéd chariot hurrying near." What a waste it all was. And so with shoes, which could be replaced by sandals, and socks that could be dispensed with altogether. How he would have sympathized with his near-contemporary J.B.S. Haldane, who rejoiced on his emigration to India that he would now be able to go foot-free, and added: "Sixty years in socks is enough." Einstein, for his part, was delighted that he could turn to a companion at a formal dinner where his own merits were being lauded and whisper: "But the man doesn't wear socks!"

These newsworthy stigmata of the *enfant terrible,* like his frequent avowals of humility, sprang from deeply rooted convictions. At times he might deliberately strike a posture, but what often appeared to be awkwardness for awkwardness' sake was the natural action of a natural man. "I am happy because I want nothing from anyone," he once told an American correspondent. "I do not care for money. Decorations, titles, or distinctions mean nothing to me. I do not crave praise. The only thing that gives me pleasure, apart from my work, my violin, and my sailboat, is the appreciation of my fellow workers." Here is a hint of the bridge between the skylarking clown, the eccentric who at times gives the impression of acting with one eye on posterity, and the dedicated scientist. As his elder son says, he was always "a great ham." He enjoyed sending people away with the answers they expected to get. But for most of the time his air of wondering aberration from the normal standards of life was genuine enough. He was just too occupied with more important matters to worry.

It was this fierce dedication, as much as the revelations of the eclipse expeditions, which helped to set him apart from other scientists. At the lower levels, men said that only three physicists understood the riddles of the world—Einstein, Planck, and Lorentz. More to the point was Planck's reply to Freundlich, who one day presented him with a problem and hoped for an answer off the cuff. Freundlich's widow still recalls how her husband repeated to her what Planck had said: "I shall have to think about it and then I will write down the answer. I cannot provide it at once, just like that. Einstein could do so. I cannot." It is unlikely that the exact words are remembered correctly over half a century; but their significance was unforgettable.

The same attitude is shown in an incident recalled by Ehrenfest's widow. This involved Einstein, Nernst, and Lorentz at a meeting of the Berlin Physical Society. After Nernst had made a statement, Einstein said: "You know, I don't think that reference is admissible." Whereupon Nernst replied: "But Herr colleague, it is the very reference which you yourself used in your last publication." To Einstein, this presented no difficulty. "How can I help it if the dear God will not take account of what I said in my last publication?" he asked. This was no more than permitted byplay. Something more was contributed by Lorentz, who did not laugh with the rest of the assembly. Instead, he remained silent for a moment. Then he spoke: "Ah, yes. Anything is allowed to Einstein."*

Einstein was lucky in having at least some support from industry. The prediction that light reaching the earth from the stars would be altered in frequency by the gravitational field through which it passed had interested Freundlich since his first contacts with Einstein. He had close connections with German business, and soon after the war

*Like most Einstein stories, this circulates in a variety of versions. Infeld, recalling it in 1955, has Einstein exclaiming: "Do you really propose that I should start an argument with the Lord because He has not made the world in accord with the opinions I have expressed?"

persuaded a number of industrialists, notably Dr. Bosch, a director of I. G. Farben, to finance an institute which could investigate the phenomenon. This was the Einstein Institute in Potsdam, later to be amalgamated with the observatory there as the Institute for Solar Research. Throughout the 1920s a long series of observations was made from it. The results were inconclusive, a fact which may have played its part in the gradual estrangement between Einstein and Freundlich. Certainly Einstein visited the institute less and less frequently. Certainly Planck took it that there had been a definite rupture in their relations—so much so that he wrote to Freundlich offering to intervene. Memories must be taken with caution; but Freundlich, with his Scottish ancestry, was remarkably British in looks, sympathies, and demeanor. Einstein, in the early 1920s, had great hopes for Germany. "It was almost," says Frau Freundlich, thinking back with a pin-sharp perception that cannot be discounted, "as though my husband was too British, not Jewish enough."

The heart of the institute was a long-focus telescope accommodated in a sixty-foot tower, surrounded by a second tower built of stone, and the sunlight reflected down this was turned through 90 degrees and taken along a forty-foot room, partly sunk in the ground. The demands made on the architect, Erich Mendelsohn, were considerable, and he satisfied them by designing a building in marked contrast to those standing nearby in the grounds of the observatory. They, built at the end of the previous century, were in the sober, traditional Prussian style and utilized the red bricks of the Mark Brandenburg. Mendelsohn's "Einstein Tower," as it was soon known, was a concrete construction, whose flowing white outlines were in some ways symbolic of the artistic renaissance already sweeping the Weimar Republic. It was even suggested that while the older buildings with their separate bricks epitomized the Euclidean concept of mathematics and atomic structure as understood at the turn of the century, Mendelsohn's long, elegant curves epitomized post-Einsteinian physics. Certainly the building became one of the things to be seen in Potsdam, and more than one tourist agency added the Einstein Tower to its tour of the Potsdam palaces.

Not everyone liked the new building. Photographs were

taken to illustrate its slightly bizarre outline, and among the German papers that described it, there was one which called it "a cross between a New York skyscraper and an Egyptian pyramid." The architecture of the institute was in fact to play its own small part in the anti-Einstein campaign which grew with the rise of the National Socialist party in the 1930s. For, it was asked, was it not in keeping that investigation of the absurd relativity theory should be carried out in a grotesque building which had no roots in German traditions? Was it not typical that the theory of the Jew Einstein should be investigated by the half-Jew Freundlich from a building which offended so deeply the decent nationalist traditions? A small point, but one not to be ignored by any competent rabblerouser.

Einstein's observations with Freundlich were fitted into gaps between many other duties. He had an office in the Academy of Sciences and his work for the Kaiser Wilhelm Institute took a good deal of time. Under his agreement with the university he did not have to lecture, but he nevertheless did so fairly frequently. On these occasions, as at most other continental universities, attendance was not restricted to students taking specific courses. Some came more out of curiosity than scientific interest and it was easy even for nonstudents to slip in as long as they did not cause trouble. On more than one occasion a ripple of anticipation passed through the listeners as a prostitute in full war paint came in, sat in one of the back rows to see for herself what the great man was like, and then left as silently as she had come. Einstein would continue unchecked; but it was clear from his quizzical half-smile that he noticed.

Every Thursday afternoon he attended the special-students physics seminar, watching for talent, listening to ideas, quite happy if even the youngest member of the group could suggest a line of thought worth following. "When my turn came to give a talk, I was terribly nervous," says Esther Salaman, then a young student in Berlin.

> Einstein was in the front row, with his pipe; beside him was von Laue. Turning round after I had pointed to my slides, I saw in the semi-darkness Einstein looking at me as if to say "Don't worry." I was talking about some

work on radioactivity done at the Cavendish Laboratory at Cambridge, which raised a difficult problem. A young lecturer got up and suggested a solution in a long statement, but I could not follow. Einstein came to my rescue. "Clever, but not true," he said ("Schlau, aber nicht wahr"), and he restated the problem, and said what we knew and did not know about it so clearly and simply that everyone was satisfied.

There were also the seminars organized by von Laue at which the latest scientific papers would be discussed by Planck, Nernst, Haber, Lise Meitner, or Einstein. These members of the university staff would occupy the front row of the old university building in which the meetings were held. Behind them there often sat physicists from the larger German industrial companies, invited men whose presence in the rarefied upper atmosphere of the academic world was a sign of the cooperation which had strengthened the country's industrial sinews since the start of the century.

Then the talking started. "Sometimes he would step up to the blackboard," says Professor Cornelius Lanczos, who was his assistant for a while. "Then, all at once, what had seemed complicated seemed simple." The transformation was stimulating. In these early 1920s Einstein was at the height of his powers as a creative physicist, confident of his own abilities, still believing that just one more heave on the intellectual rope would bring victory and an explanation of the mysteries which clouded the quantum theory. This position was very comparable to that of the assured company of physicists who half a century earlier believed that the natural world by that time contained few secrets. Before them, only just over the horizon, had lain Rutherford's nuclear atom; before Einstein lay the indeterminacy in physics which would end the world he knew.

Before him there also lay a fresh and daunting experience: investigation of the unified field problem, a problem with which he knew that he was making little or no progress despite the recurrent but illusory signs of success. The reason was not merely that the 1920s were Einstein's forties, and that as they ran out he drew further away from the magic age at which the creative scientist—in contrast to the artist, who utilizes experience as well as logic—is usually admitted to have shot his bolt. Einstein was genius enough to have broken this "finished at forty" convention as he broke many others. But after 1920 something more was involved. As he turned to the unified field, his work became increasingly that of the mathematician rather than the physicist. It was no longer so much the investigation of the natural world which presented difficulties as the presentation of known facts within an adequate mathematical structure. This change of emphasis came at an unfortunate moment. For the mathematical stockpile of the preceding century was now almost exhausted and few mathematicians had been building a new one. Einstein, moving ever more deeply into the subject, was for the first time in his life handicapped by a lack of instruments, of the mathematical tools which he knew to be essential if the job were to be tackled properly. Thus in the specialty to which he increasingly devoted his energies Einstein found himself blocked in a way he had not previously experienced. Yet even this was only half the story. For as he turned to mathematics his old intuitive sense of physics began to fall away. Like an artist turning to sculpture after a lifetime of painting, he began to lose the "feel" of the medium he knew so well. He was still Einstein. He was still head and shoulders above the rest. But it was to be a shorter head and shoulders, and in the battle royal over quantum mechanics that lay only a decade ahead his view was to be that much more restricted.

Something of this shows in the photographs. He had always been the introvert Einstein compared with the extrovert Rutherford. Nevertheless, until he began to tackle the unified field seriously—and until he found himself foxed by the developments of quantum mechanics—he had much the same confidence as Rutherford, accused of being on the crest of the wave and answering: "Well, I made the wave, didn't I—at least to some extent." The transformation was noticeable from the mid-1920s onwards and it was not entirely age or the deepening tones of the international situation that created it. For the first time in his life Einstein was getting out of his depth in scientific waters.

All this was as yet no more than the smallest cloud on the horizon. He was still the supreme master rather than the old master. This comes through clearly in memories of a seminar on statistical mechanics held for graduate students in the winter of 1921–22. "I was finishing my doctor's thesis in mathematics and was probably the only mathematician in the group," says Max Herzburger, later one of the world's greatest instrumental opticians.

> Each student who had to give one of the talks was attached to a professor who helped him prepare his remarks, and I had the great fortune to be attached to Dr. Einstein. I frequently visited him and went with him for walks in the nearby park to discuss the problems of my lecture. The discussions were unforgettable. He took nothing as certain truth merely because it was written in books, and he was always asking questions which led to a deeper understanding of the problem.

The impression on Denis Gabor, then another young student, is as vivid now as half a century ago. "I can still hear his voice," he writes,

> and I could repeat some of his sayings verbatim. On some occasions he took the floor, and one was particularly unforgettable. One doctor, who later became very famous as the theoretician of electrical circuits, but who at that time was a very shy young man, made rather a bad job of Einstein's famous elucidation of Planck's law of radiation. Einstein went to the blackboard and started by saying that the job was to reconcile Wien's law with Rayleigh's so that they would contradict one another as little as possible. By the way, he went on, Wien found his law by noticing how similar the radiation curves are to Maxwell's law. "You see," he continued, "that the saying of Oxenstiern—'with how little wisdom the world is governed'—is true also in science. What the individual contributes to it is very little. The whole is of course admirable." He then went on to give with enormous gusto his dissertation which is found in all books on physics. I have never known anybody who enjoyed science so sensuously as Einstein. Physics melted in his mouth!

Also present on this occasion was the young Hungarian who became the *deus ex machina* of Einstein's later years, an extraordinary character well meriting his sobriquet of "the gray eminence of physics." This was Leo Szilard, the man who on March 12, 1934—more than four years before Otto Hahn split the uranium atom, more than five years before Einstein's famous letter to Roosevelt—applied for a patent covering the laws of nuclear chain reaction and later filed it as a secret Admiralty patent because of his "conviction that if a nuclear chain reaction can be made to work it can be used to set up violent explosions." In 1922 Szilard was only twenty-four. But he was a student in whom Einstein quickly saw "one of those men, rich in ideas, who create intellectual and spiritual life wherever they are." He soon became a regular visitor to the Haberlandstrasse home.

Both Szilard and Einstein were theoreticians; but both had a complementary side to their interests, as though a miniature painter were to take up carpentry as a hobby. Thus Szilard had a practical inventive flair that tied in with Einstein's long experience in the Berne Patent Office. One result was a series of joint patents, lodged in Britain and the United States as well as in Germany, for what was then a revolutionary form of heat-exchange refrigerator. Some recollections claim that Elsa expected Einstein to make a fortune from the patents; others, more plausibly, claim that the hopes were Szilard's. Little came of the scheme although the Einstein-Szilard heat pump, which provides its essential mechanism, has become a feature of many postwar nuclear power stations.

Einstein's self-imposed duties at the university, his collaboration with Freundlich at the Potsdam observatory, and his work at the Kaiser Wilhelm Institute, would have been enough to occupy the mental energies of a normal man; to him, they were the background to more important things. What still concerned him most was any indication that he, or physicists elsewhere in the world, were touching things nearer the heart of nature. Thus he was a familiar figure at conferences, picking out the men he wanted to meet but dodging the social round. He conferred with Bohr in Denmark, and was a frequent visitor to Holland, where he never missed a chance of seeing Lorentz.

In Leiden he usually stayed with the Ehrenfests, writing his name on the huge white wall of the study that did duty for a visitors' book and relaxing as he did in few other places.

In Berlin he would take time off with Max Planck, carrying his violin round on informal social visits—as far as anything could be informal with Planck—and after dinner enjoying duets with his host as pianist. His small circle of artists, industrialists, and literary people could almost be considered cronies. In his own mild way, he enjoyed good food and drink with a peasant heartiness and years later looked in astonishment at a colleague who turned down a glass of wine. "One should not neglect the pleasures that nature provides," was his comment. Yet Berlin, with its undercurrent of anti-Semitism, with its sense of still being the center of a struggle for power between two diametrically opposed forces, had a near-the-brink atmosphere that was lacking in Holland. In Leiden Einstein could not only talk physics as easily as draw breath; here he could still find something of the nonpolitical atmosphere he had known before his Berlin days. Here he could be quite uninhibited, quite relaxed—and when he allowed himself to be, Einstein was a good and total relaxer.

A former colleague, Margarete Uexküll, had married Anton Nieuwenhuis, a Dutch government doctor, and was now a neighbor of the Ehrenfests. She recalls how Einstein—perhaps with a cast back to his days in Berne—enjoyed living in a house where happy-go-lucky Slav hospitality reigned. "He could sleep when he was tired, and eat when he was hungry rather than at set mealtimes," she has said.

> There was always a table in the dining room set with milk, bread, cheese, and fruit. As the Ehrenfest's villa was next to ours and the two gardens were adjoining, we could not avoid watching Einstein's daily habits. More than once a day he would pass our house with his pipe well alight, out along the Rhine and Schie canal, sometimes in lively conversation with a colleague, sometimes with the children. When the sun shone he sunbathed on the terrace, smoking, reading, or just thinking; he could then take off most of his clothes, since no one could see him from the street. He was indifferent to material comforts and I once heard him say: "What more does a human being want? Manuscript, violin, bed, table, and chair, that is enough."

He also wanted the company of children, although it was not in his nature to admit it. Therefore he was a happy man when he took Ehrenfest's small children and their companions down to the seacoast dunes a few miles away and let them bury him up to the neck in the sands without a trace of concern. He was happy when he stood at the open windows of Ehrenfest's study on a summer evening, playing the violin in his shirtsleeves while Ehrenfest accompanied him on the grand piano in the book-lined room. How often he must have thought back a decade to the rejected chance of spending a life in the comparable quiet of Utrecht, only a few miles away. And yet how often did he not congratulate himself on keeping his priorities right, on following his star to Berlin where a combination of free time and intellectual stimulus had enabled him to crack the nut of the General Theory.

Even in Leiden, he could be plucked out of his freedom. Thus Margarete records one uproarious occasion on which Einstein and Ehrenfest were awakened by the telephone from an after-lunch siesta. Queen Wilhelmina, the Prince Regent, and Emma the Queen-Mother were visiting the Marine School in Leiden. They had heard that Einstein was "in residence," and they requested that he and his host should attend the reception being held later that same day.

No question or answer was needed to pose the first problem. Einstein knew that his nearest black suit was five hundred miles away in Berlin. Ehrenfest knew that his solitary specimen was lying in a mothproofed trunk in the attic. Frau Ehrenfest rose to the occasion by telephoning several professors of Einstein's build and begging them to have their suits delivered as soon as possible. A few hours later the two men presented themselves to their Majesties, Einstein in a suit that fitted where it touched, Ehrenfest smelling strongly of mothballs.

This was only the beginning of a difficult evening. After a formal shaking of hands by the Queen, the two men tried to disappear in the crowd, duty done, honor satisfied—and now to get out of those clothes. They had not gone far when they were cut off by the Queen-Mother's adjutant and asked to return. "I noticed that you tried to escape me, but I managed to catch you," she said, according to the story that Einstein and his friend told their neighbor. "Surely you could offer your hand to an old lady too?"

Einstein's regular visits to Leiden, the amiable round of work in Berlin, interest in the affairs of Zionism in general and of the Hebrew University in particular, as well as a steadily increasing involvement in the problem of world peace, were all interrupted in 1925 by a lecture tour to South America. In itself, this was of little importance in his life. Indirectly, it was of great significance since it caused him to turn down an invitation to the California Institute of Technology later in the same year. Had he accepted, it is unlikely that he would have spent the last two decades of his life in Princeton.

There were many reasons why Einstein would have enjoyed a visit to the United States in 1925, not the least being that two quite separate but equally important confirmations of his "heuristic viewpoint" of 1905 had come from American scientists. The first was given by Robert Millikan, who as a professor at the University of Chicago had in 1915 determined the size of the charge on a single electron. But he had also done something more. "I spent ten years of my life testing that 1905 equation of Einstein's," he wrote, "and, contrary to all my expectations, I was compelled in 1915 to assert its unambiguous experimental verification in spite of its unreasonableness, since it seemed to violate everything that we knew about the interference of light."

Eight years later Arthur Compton found that when X rays were scattered by matter the wavelength of some was lengthened; in other words, their energy was decreased. The unequivocal way in which this confirmed Einstein's ideas of two decades previously is made clear in a key paragraph of the paper describing what soon came to be known as the Compton effect. "We find," Compton wrote,

> that the wavelength and the intensity of the scattered rays are what they should be if a quantum of radiation bounced from an electron, just as one billiard ball bounces from another. Not only this, but we actually observe the recoiling billiard ball, or electron, from which the quantum has bounced, and we find that it moves with just the speed it should if a quantum had bumped into it. The obvious conclusion would be that X rays, and so also light, consist of discrete units, proceeding in definite directions, each unit possessing the energy $h\nu$ and the corresponding momentum $h\lambda$. So in a recent letter to me

> Sommerfeld has expressed the opinion that this discovery of the change of wavelength of radiation, due to scattering, sounds the death knell of the wave theory of radiation.

It was not to be quite that. But it was to lead on, easily enough, to the idea that was to develop during the next few years: that not only radiation but matter itself might be both corpuscle and wave.

Millikan had met Einstein briefly during 1921 in Chicago.* Later in the year he moved to California as head of the Troop College of Technology at Pasadena, renamed the California Institute of Technology, and by 1925 he was attracting to it not only a galaxy of brilliant staff but also as many distinguished visitors as could be encouraged into his orbit. There was one particular reason for thinking that Einstein might soon be among them, quite apart from any general desire to discuss physics at firsthand with his American counterparts.

For it was at Mount Wilson Observatory, high in the Sierra above Pasadena, that Dayton Miller had for years been carrying out a complex repetition of the Michelson-Morley experiment whose verdict he still hoped to alter. In the spring of 1921 he announced results which at first glance appeared to do this. They broke down on investigation, but four years later he issued further figures. Einstein's reaction to the second announcement was shown by a letter to Millikan in June in which he reported on his unified field theory. "I believe that I have really found the relationship between gravitation and electricity, assuming that the Miller experiments are based on a fundamental error," he said. "Otherwise the whole relativity theory collapses like a house of cards." Other scientists, to whom Miller announced his results at a special meeting, lacked Einstein's qualifications. "Not one of them thought for a moment of abandoning relativity," Michael Polanyi has commented. "Instead—as Sir Charles Darwin once described it—they sent Miller home to get his results right." Einstein later came round to much the same view, noting to Millikan in September: "Privately I do not believe in the accuracy of Miller's results, although I have no right to say this openly." He would have been further persuaded

*See page 473.

by his friend Max Born, who visited Mount Wilson in the winter of 1925–26, operated Miller's interferometer and found it very shaky and unreliable. A tiny movement of the hand, or a slight cough, made the interference fringes so unstable that no readings were possible.

At Mount Wilson there was also Walter S. Adams, who had shown some years earlier that the companion to Sirius—the star later known as Sirius B—must be of the phenomenal density of about one ton to the cubic inch. At the beginning of the century this would have been considered impossible. But Rutherford, showing that the atom consisted largely of empty space, had thereby opened up the possibility of superdense stars in which subatomic particles were squeezed together in a concentration unknown on earth. Eddington pointed out soon after the success of the 1919 eclipse expeditions that such stars must have extremely intense gravitational fields. If Adams were correct, the "Einstein shift" exercised by Sirius B should be thirty times that exercised by the sun, and this would bring it well within the range of experimental test. Adams took up the challenge, and by the beginning of 1925 was planning experiments wlhich did eventually show a shift towards the red. Results were not precisely those predicted by the General Theory but they were near enough to be considered as additional confirmation. If the presence of Millikan as head of Caltech and of Adams at Mount Wilson was not in itself enough to attract Einstein to Pasadena, there was also Edwin Hubble, now using the observatory's 100-inch telescope to open up the study of the universe beyond the galaxy and raise fresh questions about the "Einstein world" of general relativity.

The new institute thus had a general leaning towards the cosmology that Einstein had forced science to consider. Eddington had been a visitor in 1924, and it was at a dinner held in his honor that Professor W. H. Williams, himself a specialist in relativity, had produced "The Einstein and the Eddington," a parody of "The Walrus and the Carpenter," following a round of golf with Eddington. Recited at a faculty club dinner, it ran as follows:

> The Einstein and the Eddington
>   Were counting up their score;
> The Einstein's card showed ninety-eight

And Eddington's was more,
And both lay bunkered in the trap
And both stood up and swore.

I hate to see, the Einstein said,
Such quantities of sand;
Just why they placed a bunker here
I cannot understand;
If one could smooth this landscape out,
I think it would be grand.

If seven maids with seven mops
Would sweep the fairway clean
I'm sure that I could make this hole
In less than seventeen.
I doubt it, said the Eddington,
Your slice is pretty mean.

. . .

The time has come, said Eddington,
To talk of many things;
Of cubes and clocks and meter-sticks,
And why a pendulum swings,
And how far space is out of plumb,
And whether time has wings.

I learned at school the apple's fall
To gravity was due,
But now you tell me that the cause
Is merely G mu nu.
I cannot bring myself to think
That this is really true.

. . .

And space, it has dimensions four,
Instead of only three.
The square on the hypotenuse
Ain't what it used to be.
It grieves me sore, the things you've done
To plane geometry.

though interesting in themselves, have resulted in my failing to follow very closely the swift march of theoretical physics. On the other hand, they have not progressed to the point where I can be certain of their physical fruitfulness. As for the future, that is only a gamble. So you will probably not lose much by my failure to come."

There were other reasons as well and, as was often the case, they were explained by Elsa, who poured tlhem out in a typical letter to Millikan. "For days my husband hesitated," she wrote on September 18, 1925.

> Your offer was too generous! Now, after long reflection, he has to decline after all. With a heavy heart, on account of other invitations he had received! For instance, Russia and England have both invited him for years in the heartiest manner. Then, if he were in California, there would certainly come urgent invitations from various cities like New York, Chicago, and others. It would be painful to decline them all. On the other hand, it could be unpleasant if he went via the Panama Canal both ways, and avoided New York. Confidentially, my dear professor, it is too much for him to visit these cities. This dilemma is so great that he will have to forgo California. And he would *gladly* have come! His state of health is very good. But he must take good care of himself at all times, as he was very ill last year.

Millikan renewed the invitation in 1927. Again Einstein was forced to decline. He wrote: "I can hardly consider taking such a journey any more. (From an animal I have become a vegetable.)"

Thus the link with Pasadena—and with the work of Hubble and Hale at Mount Wilson which was dramatically to affect Einstein's cosmological outlook—did not begin until 1930, and was to last a mere three years. Then he was swept into the arms of Abraham Flexner and the Institute for Advanced Study at Princeton, a development which would probably not have taken place had his links with Pasadena been more permanent by that time. The result was that throughout the later 1920s Einstein remained in Europe, and for most of the time in Germany, ever more deeply involved in two major dramas. The first concerned postwar Germany's struggle first to pull herself back into European political respectability and then to

You hold that time is badly warped,
That even light is bent;
I think I get the idea there,
If this is what you meant;
The mail the postman brings today,
Tomorrow will be sent.

. . .

The shortest line, Einstein replied,
Is not the one that's straight;
It curves around upon itself,
Much like a figure eight,
And if you go too rapidly
You will arrive too late.

But Easter day is Christmas time
And far away is near,
And two and two is more than four
And over there is here.
You may be right, said Eddington,
It seems a trifle queer.

Pasadena's concern with relativity was certainly strong enough to augment Einstein's general interest in the work of the American physicists, and early in 1925 he tentatively agreed to visit the institute later in the year. However, he had previously arranged to visit South America—partly to lecture at the Argentine State University, partly in the hope of coaxing money into Zionist funds from wealthy Jews. He loved the place—"Nature's Paradise," as he described it on a card to Lord Haldane—but was slightly embarrassed by the fulsome welcome of the German colony which metaphorically clasped him to its Teutonic bosom. "Strange people, these Germans," he wrote in his diary after being greeted by the German ambassador. "I am a foul-smelling flower to them, yet they keep tucking me in their buttonholes."

As usual, he did not spare himself. "The journey made my nerves so bad that the doctor very urgently advises me not to let myself in for so great an undertaking for severa[l] years," he wrote to Millikan on his return to Berlin. "[I] must say that my formal studies during recent yea[rs] hold her position—a struggle closely linked with her attitude to rearmament. It was a drama which for Einstein rose to its climax in 1933 with his decision to remain outside Germany forever and his breathtaking apostasy of pacifism that for many disciples had all the horror of a good man suddenly cutting his own throat.

Yet this story of Germany between the wars was in some ways less important for Einstein than the scientific drama which from now onwards increasingly overshadowed his life. This concerned the riddle of the dual nature of things, by this time being extended from radiation to matter itself, and its solution by a method which led on to the dethronement of causality, up to now a cornerstone of physics. For as the physicists of the postwar world began to explain the duality of nature inherent in Einstein's conception of the photon, it eventually became difficult to fault one uncomfortable conclusion: that in the subatomic world probabilities, rather than events, were all that could be forecast from any particular set of circumstances. This was a conclusion against which Einstein battled with conservative determination, fighting a stubborn rearguard action and then, when all appeared lost, taking up a stance which his friend Max Born described as aloof and sceptical—"a tragedy, for him, as he gropes his way in loneliness, and for us who miss our leader and standard bearer."

The story began during the early 1920s as it became evident that the great advances in physics started in the first decade of the century were losing their head of steam. They had solved individual problems, but they had done nothing to replace the all-embracing pattern of classical physics which they had first questioned, then shattered. Planck's qauntum theory, Einstein's photons, Rutherford's first ground plan of the nuclear atom and Bohr's disturbing explanation of it— had each provided isolated answers to isolated problems. Yet in the process they seemed to have produced more riddles than they had solved. "By the spring of 1925," writes Martin Klein, "the theoretical picture had been elaborated by the work of many physicists into a tantalizingly incomplete and confused tangle of successes and failures, so that Wolfgang Pauli, one of the most acute, and most outspoken, of the young theorists could write to a friend: 'Physics is very muddled again at the moment; it is much too hard for me anyway, and I wish I were a movie comedian or something like that and had never heard anything about physics.' "

Yet within a few years the confusions of this situation had been drastically altered by a fresh picture of the subatomic world. This new conception which came into being during the 1920s has been considerably modified during the last forty years. Yet its fundamentals have stood the test and have tended to show it as a natural evolution from the ideas which started with the electron of Lorentz and J. J. Thomson and were altered and expanded by Planck, Einstein, Rutherford, and Bohr.

A fundamental premise of classical physics was that events followed each other in succession on a basis which could be predicted if only one understood the laws of nature and had sufficient facts. Laplace's belief that the positions and the velocities of all the objects of the universe would provide sufficient data for a prediction of the future might be an extravagant illustration. Yet this was little more than a grand if fantastic extrapolation of the idea that events could be determined, not only in the laboratory but throughout the whole range of human experience. Certain factors in the quantum theory had first cast a ray of doubt upon this comfortable assumption: the electron in the Bohr atom, jumping from one orbit to another without obvious cause, tended to increase this doubt. Was there, perhaps, no real "cause" for such movements? Though they could be "predicted" in one sense of the word, must this forever be merely a statistical prediction, possible only because of the vast numbers involved? And if there were no identifiable "cause," if events at the subatomic level were governed solely by chance, might this not also be true at other levels? Might not the whole conception of causality in the universe be merely an illusion?

This possibility had already gravely disturbed Einstein. It had disturbed not only the remnants of his belief in classical physics, but his sense of rightness in an ordered and orderly world, and as early as January, 1920, he had voiced his doubts to Mac Born.* "The question of causali-

*Einstein's preoccupation with this theme from 1920 until the end of his life is referred to regularly throughout the long series of ty worries me also a lot," he had written on January 27. "Will the quantum absorption and emission of light ever be grasped in the sense of complete causality, or will there remain a statistical residue? I have to confess that I lack the courage of conviction. However, I should be very, very loath to abandon complete causality. . . ."

Thus the new concept of the subatomic world was even by 1920 beginning to produce a gulf. Bohr, Born, and a number of Einstein's other contemporaries, as well as many of the younger men who were in great part responsible for the new idea readily jumped the gap. Einstein stayed where he was. Therefore, the scene in many ways paralleled that into which he had launched his theory of relativity two decades earlier. But then he had been in the iconoclastic vanguard; now he took up station with the small conservative rearguard.

A chronological account of the story shows revealingly how two different groups of thinkers, starting to clear the confusion of the early 1920s from different points of attack, produced two different concepts of nature which were quickly synthesized into one, a process which transformed the newly conceived wave mechanics into the more embracing quantum mechanics.*

The first move came in 1923, and it was more directly linked with Einstein himself than is commonly realized. It was made by Louis de Broglie—younger brother of Maurice de Broglie who had been co-secretary of the First Solvay Congress—a French physicist who had begun by studying medieval history, changed to physics in midstream, and worked on radio during the war. During his early studies before 1914 de Broglie had been captivated by relativity. "When, after a long absence, I returned to my studies with greater maturity at the end of World War

letters published in *Briefwechsel 1916–1956 Albert Einstein/Max Born* (Munich, Nymphenburger, 1969; London, Macmillan, 1970). Some of Einstein's letters to Born have appeared elsewhere in slightly different translations; for clarity references are to the collected letters.

*Twenty-one of the key letters by Einstein, Schröedinger, Planck, and Lorentz which deal with this period, together with an illuminating introduction by Martin J. Klein, are published in *Letters on Wave Mechanics,* K. Przibram, ed. (New York, Philosophical Library, 1967; London, Vision Press, 1967).

I," he has written, "it was again the ideas of Einstein" which guided him. "I had a sudden inspiration," he says. "Einstein's wave particle dualism was an absolutely general phenomenon extending to all physical nature, and, that being the case, the motion of all particles, photons, electrons, protons, or any others, must be associated with the propagation of a wave."

De Broglie outlined this unconventional proposal, "the suggestion made . . . purely on grounds of intellectual beauty, to ascribe wave nature to ponderable particles," as it has been described, in three papers published in the Académie des Sciences' *Comptes Rendus* in 1923. "In the months that followed," he says, "I did my utmost to develop and extend my ideas still further in preparation of my doctoral thesis. Before doing so, I asked Paul Langevin, who was so well versed in the theory of relativity and in quantum theory, to examine my conclusions, and he saw fit to ask me for a second copy which he proposed to send to Einstein. Einstein quickly realized that my generalization of his theory of light quanta was bound to open entirely new horizons to atomic physics, and wrote back to Langevin saying that I had 'lifted a corner of the great veil.' "

What was revealed behind the veil was more startling than the earlier idea that light might be considered as a collection of particles at one moment and as a series of waves at another. De Broglie's idea was not of the either/or variety; instead, he postulated that particles such as electrons were guided by what were soon to be called "de Broglie waves" or "matter waves." These waves produced the interference effects that were familiar to scientists in their studies of light. Where the interference effects added up, they produced the "preferred orbits" which Bohr had already postulated, and within these the movements of the particles were governed by the laws of wave propagation.

While de Broglie was developing this revolutionary idea for his doctoral thesis, Einstein again came into the picture. In the summer of 1924 he received from S. N. Bose, an Indian physicist of Dacca University, a short paper on "Planck's Law and the Hypothesis of Light Quanta," which considered radiation as a form of gas consisting of photons. Einstein was so impressed by the paper that he himself translated it into German and sent it to the editor of the *Zeitschrift für Physik*, who published it in July. The reason for his interest was simple. He had seen immediately that it was possible to extend Bose's statistical methods to ordinary atoms— "Bose-Einstein statistics," as they became known—if it were assumed, as de Broglie was assuming, that material particles had the simultaneous wave and particulate properties he himself had assumed for radiation two decades earlier. "His quick and immediate response . . . proved ultimately to be the turning point in my career as a scientist," says Bose today.

Einstein developed this theme in two papers for the Prussian Academy. Before he read the second he had received from his friend Langevin a draft of de Broglie's doctoral thesis, and he stressed in his paper how useful he had found de Broglie's ideas. "The scientific world of the time hung on every one of Einstein's words," de Broglie has written, "for he was then at the peak of his fame. By stressing the importance of wave mechanics, the illustrious scientist had done a great deal to hasten its development. Without his paper my thesis might not have been appreciated until very much later."

This was indeed so. But Einstein's comment on de Broglie's dissertation had also been noted by Erwin Schrödinger, a thirty-seven-year-old Viennese who was later to show a remarkable facility for riding across the fontiers between science and the humanities without noticing their existence, a man of two cultures who could claim ironically of later cosmic ray studies that they promised "the stepped-up realization of the plan to exterminate mankind which is close to all our hearts." Schrödinger was in no doubt about the debt he owed to Einstein. "The whole thing," he later wrote to Einstein, "would certainly not have originated yet, and perhaps never would have (I mean, not from me), if I had not had the importance of de Broglie's ideas really brought home to me by your second paper on gas degeneracy."

Schrödinger now exhibited one of those brief spurts of concentrated genius which have more than once changed the face of physics. Within four months he erected the basic structure of what became known as wave mechanics. In this, the emphasis of the de Broglie waves on the electron particle was taken a step further. The particle itself now gave way to what was, in effect, a standing electron wave; instead of being a wave-controlled corpuscle it became a corpuscular wave.

What had thus occurred within a very few years was a steady merging of the particle and wave concepts. The electron—and possibly the other particles about which physicists were still comparatively ignorant—had changed from being either a particle or a wave to being one under certain circumstances and the other under different circumstances. Now it appeared that it was both at the same time. Here it seemed that science had run up not only against "common sense," which was already suspect when it began to deal with events in the subatomic world, but against rational logic. For could anything really be one thing and its opposite at one and the same time?

Waiting to provide the answer was Niels Bohr. His answer was an unqualified "Yes." He said so in the "principle of complementarity," which proposed that whether light or electrons were waves or moving particles depended entirely on the specific properties which were being investigated; the subject under study had dual characteristics, and whether it conformed to those we knew as wavelike properties or to those we knew as particulate depended solely on how we studied it. Bohr had his own characteristic way of explaining what he called the poetry of complementarity, and his disciple L. Rosenfeld describes how Bohr used a scene in Japan to illustrate it.

> At sunset the top of Fujiyama disappeared behind a curtain of gold-fringed clouds: the black mass of the mountain, surmounted by this fulgent crown, conveyed an impression of awe and majesty. On the next morning, it offered an entirely different spectacle: the pointed summit alone, covered with shining snow, emerged from the dense mist filling the valley; the landscape was radiating gladness and joy. So, Bohr mused, the two half-mountains together are not simply equal to a mountain: to each belongs a peculiar, individual impression, and the two are complementary.

Schrödinger's wave mechanics, which was quickly seen to provide a plausible explanation for much that had not previously been explicable, was thus credible on the grounds that reality is what you make it. This was disturbing enough to those who believed that all ignorance in science could be removed by an addition of knowledge. But more was to follow.

Even before de Broglie and Schrödinger had begun to explain the inner workings of the atom by what was essentially a physicist's combination of wave and particle ideas, a totally different approach was being made by Werner Heisenberg, a German in his early twenties. Heisenberg started from Mach's assumption that theories should be based on physically verifiable phenomena, and in trying to discover the structure of the atom he seized upon the spectral lines that were the individual fingerprints of each element's atoms. The wavelengths for these could be determined by the use of a mathematical system called matrix mechanics or quantum mechanics. Thus by 1927 the de Broglie-Schrödinger picture of the electron was being matched by a purely mathematical explanation of the atom which used the spectral lines as a starting point but soon abandoned discrete pictorial representation for a discrete set of numbers.

These two advances had in fact been along parallel paths. And they were now brought together by arguments which effectively showed that both explanations were saying the same thing in different languages. Schrödinger made the first move in uniting the two ideas and Born carried it further by providing a statistical interpretation of Schrödinger's wave conception; but he did so only by admitting that he was dealing with large numbers of random events and that his results dealt solely with their probability. The suggestion that a satisfactory picture of the physical world could consist not of a description of events but of their probabilities had already been made in Heisenberg's famous "uncertainty principle." This showed convincingly that at the subatomic level the mere act of observation affected what one was observing, and that the nearer one reached an accurate figure for either the position or the momentum of a particle, the less accurate became the figure for the other. Moreover, the uncertainty in the two factors was found to be linked, as though by a master craftsman, with a figure which had by this time become familiar: Planck's constant of the quantum theory, discovered a quarter of a century earlier.

At this point, a stage in one of the great dramas of

physics was brought to a satisfactory conclusion. De Broglie had played his part with Heisenberg. Schrödinger and Born had contributed in equal measure to the new conception and both, forced to leave Germany a few years later, were to disagree on its implications. Planck with the magician's wand of his universal constant, and Einstein with his power to influence men's minds by example, had played significant parts. Together they had produced "the new physics"; now they had to lie on the bed they had made.

The significant outcome of these events was, as de Broglie put it many years later, that quantum physics now appeared to be

> governed by statistical laws and not by any casual mechanisms, hidden or otherwise. The "wave" of wave mechanics ceased to be a physical reality and became a solution of partial differential equations of the classical type, and thus the means of representing the probability of certain phenomena taking place. The corpuscle, too, was turned into a mere phantom—we can no longer say "at such an instant a corpuscle will be found in such a place with such an energy or momentum," but only "at such an instant there will be such a probability that a corpuscle will be found at such and such a place." In other words, while a given experiment can either localize a corpuscle or ascertain its momentum, it cannot do both.

There were subtle differences in the manner in which the physicists involved regarded this central feature of indeterminacy which occupied a key position in the new picture of the subatomic world. While Born, Heisenberg, and Bohr accepted it without qualification, Einstein and Planck accepted it only with the strongest qualifications. Yet these two were the very men who a quarter of a century earlier had pulled into physics the very ideas which they now thought of as its Trojan horse.

The break with the old world which this new concept epitomizes can be illustrated by two statements. One is by Sir Basil Schonland, who describes the new world in *The Atomists*. "It appeared experimentally proven," he says,

> that at the bottom of all phenomena there were to be discerned laws of chance which made it impossible to

> think of an ordered deterministic world; the basic laws of nature appeared to be fundamentally statistical and indeterminate, governed by the purest chance. On a large scale they could appear exactly the reverse but this was only because they involved such a vast number of events. They had the monumental stability of an enormous life insurance company though, like it, they rested on individual uncertainty.

This was the world now presented, as Max Born put it, to the generation to which Einstein, Bohr, and he belonged. It was a generation which had been

> taught that there exists an objective physical world, which unfolds itself according to immutable laws independent of us; we are watching this process like the audience watch a play in a theater. Einstein still believes that this should be the relation between the scientific observer and his subject. Quantum mechanics, however, interprets the experience gained in atomic physics in a different way. We may compare the observer of a physical phenomenon not with the audience of a theatrical performance, but with that of a football game where the act of watching, accompanied by applauding or hissing, has a marked influence on the speed and concentration of the players, and thus on what is watched. In fact, a better simile is life itself, where audience and actors are the same persons. It is the action of the experimentalist who designs the apparatus which determines essential features of the observations. Hence there is no objectively existing situation, as was supposed to exist in classical physics.

The distressing position in which Einstein now found himself was not unique. J. Robert Oppenheimer has pointed out how "many of the men who have contributed to the great changes in science have really been very unhappy over what they have been forced to do," and cites not only Planck and Einstein but Kepler and de Broglie. The process is not restricted to physics. Lord Conway, bemoaning the *vulgarisation des Alpes* which his own guidebooks had done so much to bring about, has pointed out that "each generation makes of the world more or less the kind of place they dream it should be, and each when its day is done is often in a mood to regret the work of its own hands and to praise the conditions that obtained when it was young."

So with Einstein. At times he was wryly humorous about his inability to accept the new world which his colleagues had created. Philipp Frank visited him in Berlin, apparently in 1932, and they began to talk of the new physics. Then, says Frank,

> Einstein said, partly as a joke, something like this: "A new fashion has now arisen in physics. By means of ingeniously formulated theoretical experiments it is proved that certain physical magnitudes cannot be measured, or, to put it more precisely, that according to accepted natural laws the investigated bodies behave in such a way as to baffle all attempts at measurement. From this the conclusion is drawn that it is completely meaningless to retain these magnitudes in the language of physics. To speak about them is pure metaphysics."

And when Frank pointed out to Einstein that he had invented the fashion in 1905, Einstein answered: "A good joke should not be repeated too often." More cogently, he explained to Infeld—the Pole who had visited him in Berlin and who was later to join him in the United States—"Yes, I may have started it, but I regarded these ideas as temporary, I never thought that others would take them so much more seriously than I did."

His feelings went deep, and were epitomized in the famous phrase—linked with his name as firmly as the equation $E = mc^2$—which he used in a letter to Max Born on December 12, 1926. "Quantum mechanics is certainly imposing. But an inner voice tells me that it is not yet the real thing. The theory says a lot, but does not really bring us any closer to the secret of the Old One. I, at any rate, am convinced that He does not throw dice."

That final remark was altered, repeated, paraphrased, and was to go round the world. But the central meaning was clear and unqualified—that, in its usually repeated form, "God does not play dice with the world." As Einstein put it years later to James Franck: "I can, if the worst comes to the worst, still realize that the Good Lord may have created a world in which there are no natural laws. In short, a chaos. But that there should be statistical laws with definite solutions, *i.e.* laws which compel the

Good Lord to throw the dice in each individual case, I find highly disagreeable."

Thus he regarded the statistical laws necessary to explain the subatomic world as merely second-best; he could not accept them as the fundamental laws of physical reality—these, he believed, should determine events themselves rather than their probabilities. In time, when much more had been learned, it would be possible to throw overboard the current, purely statistical, explanations and replace them with something better. More satisfactory laws would be discovered—eventually men would find out how a non-dice-throwing God had made the world.

This was the stance which he took up in the late 1920s. He retained it, almost unchanged, to the end of his life. He has rarely described it more clearly than in a letter he wrote to Herbert Samuel in October, 1937, after the publication of Samuel's *Belief and Action*. "You have rightly underlined that these [statistical] physicists do not distinguish between observed and objectively existing facts," he said.

> There is no causality regarding the first; to have shown this is one of their greatest merits. Whether the objective facts are subject to causality is a question, the answer to which necessarily depends on the theory from which we start. Therefore, it will never be possible to decide whether the world is causal or not. Up to now we possess for the description of atomic events only a statistical theory. But if we should succeed in constructing a theory of deterministic character, based on less independent suppositions than the present statistical physics, nobody will insist in sustaining the latter as the base of physics. I must confess that I am convinced that this possibility will be realized. It ought also to be noted that the statistical quanta mechanics do cover or explain neither all the recognized partial results of our present theoretical physics nor all recognized empirical facts. It is therefore an uncritical attitude to declare the statistical character of nature to be a fact. It may only be excused by the fact that up to now we do not have any other theory.

The formulation of this new idea of the subatomic world took place between the publication of de Broglie's papers in 1924, and the summer and autumn of 1927 which saw the publication of Heisenberg's uncertainty principle and the exposition of Bohr's complementarity principle. But most physicists still retained qualifications. Most realized that in matters of this sort there is no finality and that the solution of one set of problems usually produces another; most realized that it would be unwise to take up too dogmatic a stance. Then, in October, they were forced out of their corners, compelled to stand up and be counted, to state their loyalties. The occasion was the Fifth Solvay Congress in 1927. Together with the Sixth, which was held three years later in 1930, it marked a notable change in Einstein's position in the scientific world.

The general subject of discussion at the Fifth Congress was "Electrons and Photons," and the list of speakers and papers made it clear that differing views of the wavelike or corpuscular nature of matter would be hammered out energetically; so, it was equally clear, would the underlying riddle of causality versus indeterminacy, that ghost which European physicists had raised and which now looked over their shoulders wherever they went. Lorentz came from Holland, Sir William Bragg with his son Lawrence from England, Arthur Compton from the United States, Born and Heisenberg from Göttingen, Einstein from Berlin, Schrödinger from Stuttgart, and de Broglie from Paris. And from Copenhagen there came Bohr, anxious to explain his complementarity principle, strongly supported by Heisenberg. "At the Solvay meetings," Bohr later wrote, "Einstein had from their beginning been a most prominent figure, and several of us came to the conference with great anticipations to learn his reaction to the latest stage of the development which, to our view, went far in clarifying the problems which he had himself from the outset elicited so ingeniously."

At the start of the conference, Bohr threw down the gauntlet with an account of the epistemological problems presented by the latest developments in physics. He agreed that certainty had been removed from the subatomic world, that there was now, as he put it elsewhere, the impossibility of any sharp separation between the behavior of atomic objects and the interaction with the measuring instruments which serve to define the conditions under which the phenomena appear." This meant that the wave or particle concept was determined by the type of experiment. Yet even when it had been decided to study the wave or the particle characteristics, Heisenberg's uncertainty principle still masked an exact picture of what nature was like. The trapdoor of indeterminacy had been opened and those involved would have to make the best they could of it.

Einstein made very little. Strangely perhaps, he read no paper at the Fifth Congress—in fact, it is usually overlooked that his account of specific heats in 1911 is the only Solvay paper he ever did read. But when those attending the congress met after the sessions in the Fondation Universitaire—the university club founded after the First World War with the residue of the Hoover Fund—Einstein came out into the open. He still disliked uncertainty and Bohr's complementarity, and he bluntly said so.

Then the discussion opened out. Lorentz did his best to give the floor to only one speaker at a time. But everyone felt strongly. Everyone wanted to put his own view. There was the nearest thing to an uproar that could occur in such distinguished company, and in the near confusion Ehrenfest moved up to the blackboard which successive speakers had used and wrote on it: "The Lord did there confound the language of all the earth."

On that and following evenings, Bohr made abortive attempts to convince Einstein of his views. Ingenious experiments were postulated by Einstein, in which it was sought to show that with the right equipment all the characteristics of an electron could theoretically be discovered. Each time Bohr proved that this was not so. Both sides stuck to their guns. Einstein maintained that the statistical nature of the quantum theory and the apparent impossibility of discovering all the characteristics of physical reality that sprang from it was merely the result of ignorance. In due course physicists would be able not merely to estimate the probability of an event happening but to discover whether it would happen. Bohr, and the many who supported him, claimed that indeterminacy was here a part of nature itself.

Strong passions and strong loyalties were aroused even though "a most humorous spirit animated the discussions," according to Bohr.

> On his side, Einstein mockingly asked us whether we could really believe that the providential authorities took recourse to dice playing [. . . ob der liebe Gott würfelt], to which I replied by pointing at the great caution, already called for by ancient thinkers, in ascribing attributes to Providence in everyday language. I remember, also, how at the peak of the discussion Ehrenfest, in his affectionate manner of teasing his friends, jokingly hinted at the apparent similarity between Einstein's attitude and that of the opponents of relativity theory; but instantly Ehrenfest added that he would not be able to find relief in his own mind before concord with Einstein was reached.

Schrödinger attempted to provide a causal interpretation for wave mechanics and de Broglie proposed what he described as a "double solution," which some felt tried to make the best of both worlds. But at the end of the day the field was occupied by Born, Bohr, Heisenberg, Pauli, and Dirac whose statistical interpretations fitted in with the new uncertainty principle and all that went with it.

Throughout all this Einstein remained Einstein. "During a fairly long walk, he made a profound impression on me and fully confirmed my faith in him," writes de Broglie, whose papers had started the avalanche.

> I was particularly won over by his sweet disposition, by his general kindness, by his simplicity, and by his friendliness. Occasionally, gaiety would gain the upper hand and he would strike a more personal note and even disclose some detail of his day-to-day life. Then again, reverting to his characteristic mood of reflection and meditation, he would launch into a profound and original discussion of a variety of scientific and other problems. I shall always remember the enchantment of all those meetings, from which I carried away an indelible impression of Einstein's great human qualities.

To de Broglie, Einstein revealed an instinctive reason for his inability to accept the purely statistical interpretation of wave mechanics. It was a reason which linked him with Rutherford, who used to state that "it should be possible to explain the laws of physics to a barmaid." Einstein, having a final discussion with de Broglie on the platform of the Gare du Nord in Paris, whence they had traveled from Brussels to attend the Fresnel centenary celebrations, said "that all physical theories, their mathematical expressions apart, ought to lend themselves to so simple a description 'that even a child could understand them.'" And what could be less simple than the statistical interpretations of wave mechanics?

None of the protagonists was willing to let go this particular argument and it was taken up with renewed vigor when the next Solvay Congress was held in 1930. The central problem still revolved round the one question: Was it, or was it not, theoretically possible to ascertain the position of a particle and also its momentum at one specific moment?

In 1930 Einstein proposed a "thought-experiment"—one that was theoretically possible even if ruled out by experimental limitations. The proposal was to enclose light within a mirror-lined box which was weighed. One photon would be automatically released by a time-control mechanism within the box, which would then be weighed again. From the change in mass it would be possible, using Einstein's equation, to calculate the energy or momentum of the photon which was released at one specific moment. At first, and even at second glance, Einstein appeared to have an unbreakable case. Only the following day did Bohr realize that Einstein had overlooked one thing: the effect of the weighing on the clock.

There have been many explanations of the results of this exchange but none clearer than that given by Barbara Cline, and it is worth quoting in full. "Bohr's reasoning applied to any method of weighing," she says.

> but to illustrate that reasoning most clearly he chose to imagine that Einstein's box of light was hung on a spring from a rigid scale. Thus when a photon was released the box would move in recoil. Its vertical position in relation to the earth's surface would change and therefore its position within the earth's gravitational field. According to the General Theory of Relativity, this change in spatial position would mean a change in the rate of the clock, preset and attached to the box. The change would be extremely small but in this case crucial. For due to a chain of inevitable uncertainties: the uncertainty of the escaping photon's direction, therefore of the box's recoil, therefore of its position within the earth's gravitational field, the precise time when the photon was released from

the box could *not* be determined. It was indeed indeterminable to the extent given by Heisenberg's law—the cornerstone of the Copenhagen interpretation. This was the way Bohr answered the serious challenge of Einstein, who had forgotten to apply his own General Theory of Relativity.

The argument, which had really started seven years earlier and had changed the face of physics, involved two separate but linked questions: Was matter as well as radiation wavelike and yet corpuscular as well, depending only on how it was considered; and were the laws of the subatomic world the indeterminate laws of statistics? The first of these problems had the greater practical effect on the scientific world, and Sir William Bragg, the director of the Royal Institution who had been present at the 1927 Congress, had once commented: "On Mondays, Wednesdays, and Fridays we teach the wave theory and on Tuesdays, Thursdays, and Saturdays the corpuscular theory." Forty years on, the synthesis had been made. "Everything that has already happened is particles, everything in the future is waves," states Sir Lawrence Bragg, Sir William's son and in turn the director of the same institution. "The advancing sieve of time coagulates waves into particles at the moment 'now.' " On this Einstein had moved in step, seeing the contradiction as one with which he could cope, a contradiction of common sense no less amenable to reason than the apparent contradictions of relativity.

Indeterminacy was a riddle at a different level, more fundamental and, as far as Einstein was concerned, more important. Here his discomfiture—and it cannot be called less, however much his colleagues tried to soften the blow—ended the first series of battles in the long campaign he was to wage. They had altered his status in a small but certain way. His touch was as sure as ever, but it belonged to a previous age.

The gap remained throughout the years. At the height of the initial debate, early in 1927, Einstein showed his feelings at the end of a message to the Newton celebrations in England, concluding with the hope: "May the spirit of Newton's method give us the power to restore unison between physical reality and the profoundest characteristic of Newton's teaching—strict causality." Years afterwards he was just as hopeful. And in 1944, in a letter to Born, he put down what Born has described as "probably the best and most lucid formulation of Einstein's point of view." In this he said:

> You believe in the God who plays dice, and I in complete law and order in a world which objectively exists, and which I, in a wildly speculative way, am trying to capture. I firmly *believe,* but I hope that someone will discover a more realistic way, or rather a more tangible basis than it has been my lot to do. Even the great initial success of the quantum theory does not make me believe in the fundamental dice game, although I am well aware that our younger colleagues interpret this as a consequence of senility.

He hoped on to the end. Just how little his hopes were justified is shown by Max Born, speaking three months after Einstein's death, at the conference held in Berne to celebrate the fiftieth anniversary of the Special Theory.

> A man of Einstein's greatness, who has achieved so much by thinking, has the right to go to the limit of the *a priori* method. Current physics has not followed him; it has continued to accumulate empirical facts, and to interpret them in a way which Einstein thoroughly disliked. For him a potential or a field component was a real natural object which changed according to definite deterministic laws. Modern physics operates with wave functions which, in their mathematical behavior, are very similar to classical potentials, but do not represent real objects. They serve for determining the *probability* of finding real objects, whether these are particles, or electromagnetic potentials, or other physical quantities.

A number of reasons can be adduced for the way which Einstein thus began to slip from the mainstream of physics during the later 1920s. It can be claimed that the gemlike flame burned a little less gemlike as he diverted his energies into pacifism, the needs of the Hebrew University in Jerusalem, or the requirements of the Jewish Agency. Just as tenably, it can be argued that he spent more time in such pursuits because he felt his powers diminishing. More plausibly, it can be attributed to concentration on mathematics, so essential to his work on the unified field theory.

Yet the opposition which he maintained so stubbornly towards the indeterminacy of quantum mechanics was not based entirely on his inability to "see" it as he had "seen" many other innovations in physics. It was based on something more fundamental, upon an interior assumption about the world that had much more resemblance to religious faith than to the ever-questioning scepticism of science. Einstein believed that the universe had been designed so that its workings could be comprehensible; therefore these workings must conform to discoverable laws; thus there was no room for chance and indeterminacy—God, after all, did not play the game that way. At a different level he stressed these beliefs in an interview in October, 1929, when the argument about quantum mechanics was at its height. "I claim credit for nothing," he said, at a mention of his modesty. "Everything is determined, the beginning as well as the end, by forces over which we have no control. It is determined for the insect as well as for the star. Human beings, vegetables, or cosmic dust, we all dance to a mysterious tune, intoned in the distance by an invisible piper."

Although he felt so strongly about the problem which was to cut him off from his colleagues, Einstein still laid the cards fairly on the table, sometimes with an objectivity that tended to mask his feelings. This was shown when, early in 1928, he lectured at Davos in Switzerland. He was very vulnerable to any call from that country and responded to an appeal that was to have important repercussions. The first was a serious breakdown in health. Then, as a result of this, there came employment of Helen Dukas, a young German woman who for the next quarter of a century was to be his secretary, general factotum, and, after the death of Elsa, dedicated watchdog.

The appeal came from the Davoser Hochschule, which was starting university courses for young men and women in the surrounding sanatoria. Treatment in these meant a break from regular studies, usually for months and often for years; but special courses could alter all that, and the Davos authorities appealed for specialist teachers to give their services for a few weeks late in March. Einstein responded readily enough. The opening ceremonies on March 28 were followed by a series of study groups held in the Kurhaus; by discussions; and by a concert of chamber music given for the benefit of the school. He enthusiastically took part in everything, willingly agreeing to play the violin in an *ad hoc* trio with cellist and pianist, and on the night of the concert was one of the star turns. Not least enjoyed by the audience was the sight of Einstein himself, refusing to bow but taking the music score, then bending it forward so that it was Schubert who acknowledged the applause.

His lecture was on "Fundamental Concepts of Physics and Their Most Recent Changes," and there was no doubt as to what he considered these were: "Today faith in unbroken causality is threatened precisely by those whose path it had illumined as their chief and unrestricted leader at the front, namely, by the representatives of physics," he noted. "To understand this drift, which deserves the greatest interest of all thinking men, we must take a bird's-eye view of the development of the fundamental concepts of physics up to the present time." He went on to outline Newtonian mechanics and to describe how relativity had welded together both Newton's ideas and the more recent ideas of the field theory and had shaken the fundamental concepts of time and space. But now doubt had been thrown on the theory of strict causality, which had previously remained untouched. "We reach here," he went on, "a complication of questions with which the modern generation of physicists is struggling in a gigantic display of intellectual power."

Then he tackled the difficult task of putting across to his nonspecialist audience, in simple terms, how the latest theories which explained the structure of the atom succeeded in doing so only at the sacrifice of strict causality. "All natural laws," he admitted, "are therefore claimed to be, 'in principle,' of the statistical variety and our imperfect observation practices alone have cheated us into a belief in strict causality." Finally he noted that the new theory explained not only radiation but matter by a combination of corpuscular and wave ideas. "We stand here before a new property of matter for which the strictly causal theories hitherto in vogue are unable to account," he concluded. But his scientific instinct was against accepting this; as he was to maintain to the end of his life, the theories which invoked indeterminacy were forced to do so only because of man's ignorance.

With the Hochschule course behind him, Einstein accepted an invitation to stay at Zuoz, in the neighboring Lower Engadine, with Willy Meinhardt. During the visit he was called to Leipzig to give evidence as an expert witness in a patent dispute between the Siemens Company and the A.E.G., whose former president had been his friend Walther Rathenau.

He returned from Leipzig to Zuoz unexpectedly. Typically, he refused to let a porter carry his heavy suitcase. The result of the walk over slippery snow was an unexpected collapse which revealed a delicate heart. "The P.T. adepts have declared that it wouldn't have happened if Einstein had kept himself in constant trim by regular exercises," Dr. Plesch has written.

> Up to a point no doubt there is something in what they say. Einstein never took any exercise beyond a short walk when he felt like it (which wasn't often, because he has no sense of direction, and therefore would seldom venture very far afield), and whatever he got sailing his boat, though that was sometimes quite arduous—not the sailing exactly, but the rowing home of a heavy yacht in the evening calm when there wasn't a breath of air to stretch the sails. The Zuoz incident was therefore, as Einstein freely admits, perhaps the last of quite a series of overexertions.

Einstein himself, writing to Plesch, noted that the main cause of the trouble had really been "the oar of a difficult sailing boat in an evening calm."

The results were serious enough. He was moved back to Berlin in easy stages. The details of the heart trouble remained unclear. Numerous remedies were sought. All were unsuccessful. Finally Janos Plesch tried his hand.

Dr. Plesch was four years older than Einstein, a wealthy Hungarian who had built up in Berlin a successful and fashionable medical practice. With a fine town house in Berlin and an equally fine country estate at Gatow, with an intimate circle of acquaintances in the diplomatic and theatrical world, Plesch was in character the complete opposite of Einstein. What united the two men was not only Plesch's diagnostic success, which dented Einstein's built-in scepticism of doctors; there was also his interest in the world of art and letters and his love for splendid living, which had already touched Einstein's innate if usually suppressed love of good food and drink.

Plesch quickly diagnosed inflammation of the walls of the heart, put his patient on a salt-free diet, and eventually packed him off with Elsa and her two daughters, Ilse and Margot, to a small seaside resort on the Baltic coast north of Hamburg. Here he recuperated. But it was a slow business, not helped by the fact that he continued sailing until Plesch put a stop to it.

As a result of the illness he was deprived of his normal secretarial help at the Kaiser Wilhelm Institute and the university, and before he left Berlin to recuperate was obliged to engage a secretary for work at home. Newspaper advertisements were ruled out since they would produce a glut of useless replies. Elsa mentioned the problem to Rosa Dukas, executive secretary of the Jewish Orphan Organization of which she was the honorary president; Miss Dukas proposed her sister Helen, who had recently left a publisher.

Helen Dukas, who presented herself at No. 5, Haberlandstrasse, on Friday, April 13, was competent and diffident in almost equal parts. She had at first rejected her sister's suggestion. She knew nothing of physics; she felt it would all be beyond her; but she was persuaded to give the work a chance. "The professor lay reading in bed," she has said of their first meeting. "When he looked up and saw me he stretched out his hand and said smilingly: 'Here lies an old corpse.' At that moment all my fear fell away from me, although even then I was not sure whether I would be able to work for him." She continued to do so, with increasing duties that eventually turned her into both secretary and housekeeper, until Einstein's death twenty-seven years later.

Her first task was to find a substitute for him at the coming meeting in Geneva of the International Commission on Intellectual Cooperation. For his work on this, like his work for the pacifist causes which he supported, and for the Zionists, was now to suffer a temporary interruption. He had already achieved mixed results in these fields when he began his fiftieth year—and as Germany moved on toward the time, little more than a year away, when rising unemployment, the support of industrialists who feared communism, and the creation of a scapegoat in the shape of the Jews, would together transform Hitler's National Socialists into the second largest party in the country.

CHAPTER 13

THE CALL OF PEACE

Einstein's breakdown of 1928 put a rein on his activities for a time. But he was not a man to spare himself longer than necessary and as soon as possible was working once more in the pacifist cause which he had vigorously supported since 1914. He had long been a staunch upholder of the German League for Human Rights which the Bund Neues Vaterland had become, and from his sickbed was soon sending regular notes to its secretary general, Kurt Grossmann, asking for information or giving advice. And shortly after his recovery he was persuaded to make for the League a gramophone record of "My Credo" in which his soft kindly voice outlined his pacifist beliefs as though they were something that any sensible man must agree with.

Before the war Einstein had taken no part in the pacifist movements centered on Switzerland. His interests were strictly circumscribed by physics in those days and he concerned himself as little with the problems of politics and power as with Zionism until he saw, from Berlin, the convulsions that war produced, the eagerness with which his colleagues leaped to service, and the disruption that war caused to the grand international machinery of science. Then, like thousands of others, he was swept up emotionally, without giving much thought to the practical results of what he was doing. "My pacifism is an instinctive feeling, a feeling that possesses me because the murder of men is disgusting," he once explained to Paul Hutchinson, editor of the *Christian Century*. "My attitude is not derived from any intellectual theory but is based on my deepest antipathy to every kind of cruelty and hatred. . . . I am an absolute pacifist." In an introduction to a handbook on pacifism, *Die Friedensbewegung*, he declared that "a human being who considers spiritual values as supreme must be a pacifist." More poignantly in the light of future events, he later told *Die Wahrheit* of Prague that if another war broke out he would "unconditionally refuse to do war service, direct or indirect, and would try to persuade my friends to take the same stand, regardless of how the cause of the war should be judged." Not long afterwards he was persuading his friends to do the reverse.

During the first postwar years pacifists had stong popular support, not only in Germany, but throughout a continent exhausted by four years of bloodletting. Thus Einstein for once marched with the crowd rather than against it. But national ambitions and strengths returned. As the price of war became blurred by time and by the jollifications of regimental reunions, so did support for the martyrdom of pacifism ebb away. By contrast, Einstein's beliefs, explained whenever he found the opportunity in a plethora of interviews, statements, and articles, remained rock hard throughout the 1920s.

Mingled with these pacifist appeals were calls first for European government and later for world government. Implicit in most of them [illegible] of force or [illegible] threat of [illegible] governments were to survive, but Einstein came only reluctantly and slowly to the point where he would admit that this was the case. In the early 1920s it was a natural enough evolution for those so removed from affairs that they genuinely believed an appeal to international goodwill would work. But the reluctance to admit that to "fight for peace" was in pacifist terms more than a contradiction of words helped to keep the League disarmed and impotent, handed the best cards to the potential aggressor, and paved the way for Hitler. Einstein himself eventually saw as much and in 1936 could admit that "it is no exaggeration to say that the British and, to some extent, French pacifists are largely responsible for the desperate situation today because they prevented energetic measures from being taken at a time when it would have been relatively easy to adopt them." Before 1933 no one was more energetic in the process than Einstein himself.

However, in the immediate postwar years, it was the League on which the hopes of peace rested. Einstein therefore supported the League. Or, more accurately, he supported it until experience rubbed him up against it at close quarters. Then disillusion quickly set in. He was surprised that miracles were not worked overnight and shocked that when human beings began to manage great affairs of state they still behaved like human beings. After that, his support of the League had increasingly to be propped up by his friends.

He had returned to Berlin from France only a few weeks when, on May 17, 1922, he was invited by Sir Eric Drummond, secretary general of the League, to become a member of the International Committee on Intellectual Cooperation* then being formed. The committee was the brainchild of Henri Bergson and was to represent, said Gilbert Murray, a subsequent chairman, "the deeper spirit of the League." In many ways it was an ancestor of UNESCO, which sprang from the United Nations after the Second World War, and its members were appointed, in the words of the undersecretary general, "not as representatives of their respective countries but on account of their personal achievements. At the same time, the council endeavored as far as possible to give representation on the committee to the big cultural groups of the world. In this sense, therefore, each member may be said to represent a certain culture, though he does not sit in the committee as the official representative of any country in particular." This ingenious explanation, given in 1924 in reply to an inquirer who asked whether Einstein represented Germany on the committee, covered a delicate point, since Germany had not then joined the League. Einstein was, in fact, brought onto the committee "as a representative of German science," although it is not clear whether he himself really appreciated the fact.

The invitation to serve was the final move in a long series of negotiations. Some French officials objected to having a German on the committee; the Germans who clung to the periphery of the League claimed brusquely that Einstein was not a German but merely a Swiss Jew.

*The English title was International Committee on Intellectual Cooperation; the French was Commission internationale de cooperation intellectuelle. Both sides often swapped "Committee" and "Commission" as the spirit moved them—and in even official letters dropped the "intellectual."

A subsequent difficulty, Gilbert Murray has stated, was provided by Einstein's own mistrust of the committee as a body formed by the victors. But "a conversation with leading members very soon satisfied him as to our real international and peaceful spirit."

Einstein therefore replied by return to Drummond's invitations of May, 1922. "Although I am not clear at all as to the character of the work to be done by the committee, I consider it my duty to accept your invitation. In my opinion, no one, in times such as these, should refuse to take part in any effort made to bring about international cooperation." Shortly afterwards he wrote to Madame Curie, who had also been asked to serve. "Although it is not clear to me what the commission will be able to achieve, I nevertheless accepted after brief consideration," he said. "Somewhere in the background there must surely be the idea of building up international understanding; whether we can gain any influence depends of course on how we handle things. It would really give me pleasure if you also would accept, as I know there is complete understanding between us." Einstein's acceptance gave the officials of the League much satisfaction. For while Madame Curie, Lorentz, Paul Painlevé, and Gilbert Murray were to be members, Einstein was the keystone of the arch.

However, the League was to pay a price for its acquisition. Einstein's "purity of heart," as Murray described it, the fact that he was so "very reluctant to believe evil," his inability or unwillingness to admit that whatever the fine intentions of the League, it had to operate in the world of fallible men, combined to limit his usefulness. This much is clear from the files. It should not create surprise. One of Einstein's sincerest admirers, the late Morris Raphael Cohen, made the point when he reviewed Einstein's *The World As I See It* in the *Menorah Journal*. "The example of the incomparable Newton, as well as of contemporaries like Millikan and Eddington, should warn us against assuming that those who achieve great things in physical science will necessarily display unusual wisdom in politics and religion," he said. "It is not merely that devotion to science leaves little time to acquire comparable knowledge on these more complicated subjects. When Harvey suggested that Newton pay less attention to his theosophic and theologic speculations, the latter proudly rebuked him: 'Sir, I have given these subjects prolonged study.' But the result of this study, as seen in Newton's commentary on the Book of Daniel and on the Apocalypse, is a striking indication of how highly specialized is human genius." Perhaps, more accurately, how specialized it can be. At least two of the geniuses on the Committee on Intellectual Cooperation, Lorentz and Madame Curie, showed no trace of the vacillations and contradictions with which Einstein was to spread alarm and despondency among his colleagues.

The first of these came less than two months after his acceptance. On July 1, Einstein wrote a brief letter to Pierre Comert, head of the Information Secretariat at the League, brusquely stating that he felt it necessary to resign from the committee, whose first meeting was to be held late in the summer. No reason was given, although in an accompanying note Einstein expressed concern that the situation in Berlin was such that a Jew was well advised to exercise restraint about taking part in politics. In addition, he added, somewhat irrelevantly since his appointment was still on an international rather than a national basis: "I have no desire to represent people who certainly would not choose me as their representative, and with whom I find myself in disagreement on the questions to be dealt with. . . ."

To Madame Curie Einstein wrote in more detail, explaining that he was resigning not only because of the murder of Rathenau* but because of anti-Semitism in Berlin and his feeling that he was "no longer the right person for the job." The reply was both to the point and rather tart. "Dear Mr. Einstein," she said,

> I have received your letter, which has caused me a great disappointment. It seems to me that the reason you give for your abstention is not convincing. It is precisely because dangerous and prejudicial currents of opinion do exist that it is necessary to fight them and you are able to exercise, to this extent, an excellent influence, if only by your personal reputation which enables you to fight for toleration. I think that your friend Rathenau, whom I judge to have been an honest man, would have encouraged you to make at least an effort at peaceful, intellectual

*See page 359.

international collaboration. Surely you can change your mind. Your friends here have kind memories of you.

While Madame Curie was writing to Einstein on a personal basis, the officials of the League had been thrown into despair, and desperate efforts to retrieve the situation were being made by the secretary of the committee. This was Nitobe, a Japanese Samurai, born with the right to wear two swords, whose philosophic journey was to lead him into the ranks of the Quakers. On receiving Einstein's resignation Nitobe had cabled to Murray: "Einstein resigns giving no reasons stop important to have him stop fear his resignation will have bad effect stop grateful if you can use your influence." He also appealed to Bergson, who said that he had no personal contacts with Einstein but made an ingenious suggestion: "It is my belief that since the Committee of Intellectual Cooperation is now properly constituted, the resignation of one of its members cannot become definitive until the committee has accepted it. Therefore, before we meet you can ask Einstein to reconsider his decision." The League officials clutched gratefully at this straw and Comert was dispatched to Berlin, where he met Einstein on July 27 and 28. His account of the interviews is revealing.

"I explained to you," he subsequently wrote to Einstein,

that your sudden and motiveless retreat would gravely prejudice the Committee of Intellectual Cooperation since the public would be able to put a bad interpretation on your sudden decision to withdraw your collaboration.

With great sincerity, and in all confidence, you then told me of the particular distressing reasons which induced you to consider your resignation.

I was very impressed by them. We will ignore entirely these circumstances. I told you that the difficulties of your personal position in Germany appeared to me so considerable that the members of the Council of the League of Nations would never, in my opinion, have dared to appeal to you if they had suspected that this appointment would make your position in Berlin even more critical.

Then we examined together, in complete confidence, if it would be advisable in these conditions—new to me—to confirm your resignation. Although very anxious to assure your collaboration with the Committee of Intellectual

Table of Ancestors of Albert Einstein

Professor Dr. Albert Einstein
Born March 14, 1879 Ulm
Died April 18, 1955 Princeton, N.J.

Hermann Einstein
born 1847
Buchau
died 1902
Milan

Pauline Koch
born 1858
Cannstatt
died 1920
Berlin

Abraham Einstein
born 1808
Buchau
died 1868
Ulm

Helene Moos
born 1814
Buchau
died 1887
München

Julius Koch
born 1816
Jebenhausen
died 1895
Cannstatt

Jette Bernheimer
born 1825
Jebenhausen
died ?

Ruppert Einstein
born 1759
Buchau
died 1834
Buchau

Rebekka Obernauer
born 1770
died 1853

Hayum Moos

Fanny Schmal

Zadok Loeb Doerzbacher Koch
born 1783
Dörzbach
died 1852
Jebenhausen

Blümle Sontheimer
born 1786
Jebenhausen
died 1856
Jebenhausen

Gedalja Chaim Bernheimer
born 1788
Jebenhausen
died 1873
Göppingen

Elcha Weil
born 1789
Jebenhausen
died 1872
Göppingen

Naftali Einstein
born
Buchau

Helene
born
Steppach

Samuel Obernauer

Judith Hilb

Moos

Schmal

Loeb Samuel Dörzbacher

Golies

Loeb Moses Sontheimer
born 1745
Malsch
died 1831
Jebenhausen

Vögele Juda
born 1737
Nordstetten
died 1807
Jebenhausen

Jakob Simon Bernheimer
born 1756
Illereichen
died 1790

Lea Hajm
born 1753
Buchau
died 1833
Freudenthal

Beerle Weil
born 1750
Tettensee
died 1840
Jebenhausen

Roesle Katz
born 1760
Freudenthal
died 1826
Jebenhausen

Einstein, third from right front row, seen with his Munich schoolfellows. Undated photograph believed to have been taken in the early 1890s. (Stadtarchiv, Ulm)

Einstein's mother, Pauline Koch. Photograph of unknown date, probably taken at the turn of the century. (ETH, Zurich)

Einstein in his early twenties. Undated photograph, believed to have been taken in Zurich or Berne, shortly before Einstein joined the Swiss Patent Office. (ETH, Zurich)

Einstein and his first wife, Mileva Maric, taken in 1911 when both were in their early thirties. (ETH, Zurich)

The first Solvay Congress, 1911. A unique photograph, taken in the Hotel Metropole, Brussels, and showing the cream of European physicists in the early years of the century. Seated, left to right: Nernst, Brillouin, Solvay, Lorentz, Warburg, Perrin, Wien, Madame Curie, Poincaré. Standing: Goldschmidt, Planck, Rubens, Sommerfeld, Lindemann, de Broglie, Knudsen, Hasenöhrl, Hostelet, Herzen, Jeans, Rutherford, Kamerlingh Onnes, Einstein, Langevin. (Institut International de Physique, Solvay)

Einstein and Lorentz.
Undated photograph believed to have been taken in Leiden shortly after the end of the First World War. (Rijksmuseum voor de Geschiedenis der Natuurwetenschappen, Leiden)

Einstein and President Harding, taken during Einstein's first visit to the United States in 1921. (UPI)

Einstein and Chaim Weizmann arriving in the United States aboard the *S. S. Rotterdam*, April 2, 1921. Left to right: Menachem Mendel Ussishkin; Professor Chaim Weizmann; unidentified woman; Einstein; unidentified woman—almost certainly Elsa Einstein; Ben Zien Messensohn. (UPI)

Ehrenfest, Ehrenfest's son, and Einstein, taken in Ehrenfest's home in Leiden, June, 1920. (Rijksmuseum voor de Geschiedenis der Natuurwetenschappen, Leiden)

Einstein at the age of 50, shown in his Berlin home with his second wife, Elsa Einstein, and his stepdaughter, Margot. (Ullstein)

Einstein at a reception held by Reich Chancellor Dr. Heinrich Bruning in Berlin, August 1931. Left to right: Max Planck; Ramsay MacDonald; Einstein; Dr. Dietrich, German Finance Minister (foreground); and Geheimrat Schmitz, of I. G. Farben. (Salamon)

Einstein and relatives leaving Europe for the United States December 9, 1930. The photograph includes (extreme left) Frau Dmitri Marianoff, Einstein's stepdaughter; her husband, Dr. Marianoff; Einstein; and, extreme right, Frau Einstein. (UPI)

The blackboard used by Einstein when he lectured at Nottingham University on June 6, 1930. (Nottingham University)

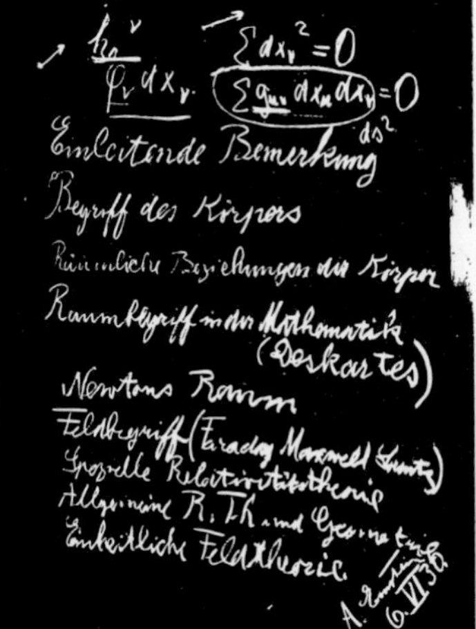

Einstein and his friend Dr. Plesch; taken, probably in the early 1930s, in the grounds of Dr. Plesch's house outside Berlin. (UPI)

Einstein and His Majesty, King Albert of the Belgians, shown in the grounds of the Royal Palace at Laeken, Belgium, in the early 1930s. (Royal Archives, Brussels)

Einstein playing the violin. Undated photograph, stated to have been taken on board ship while traveling to the United States in 1930. (UPI)

Five Nobel Prize winners, showing from left to right, Nernst, Einstein, Planck, Millikan, and von Laue. (Rijksmuseum voor de Geschiedenis der Natuurwetenschappen, Leiden)

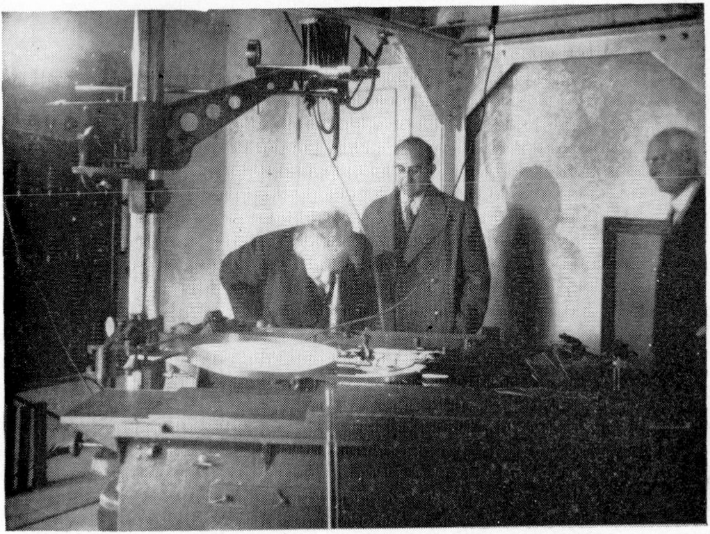

Einstein in the 150-foot solar tower telescope at the Mount Wilson Observatory, Pasadena, California, in 1930. On the extreme right is Dr. St. John of the Mount Wilson Observatory Staff. The figure at center, stated to be Einstein's interpreter, is believed to be his assistant, Dr. Meyer. (Hale Observatories, Pasadena)

Einstein "in hiding" on Roughton Heath, near Cromer, Norfolk, in September, 1933, shortly after the publication of *The Brown Book of the Hitler Terror* and fears for his life. On horseback is his host, Commander Oliver Locker-Lampson. (UPI)

Helen Dukas (Einstein's secretary), Einstein, and his stepdaughter, Margot, being sworn in as U. S. citizens. (UPI)

Einstein at Oxford in 1931 when on May 23 he was made an honorary doctor of science. (UPI)

Einstein with Ben-Gurion on the porch of his home at 112 Mercer Street, Princeton. (King Features)

Einstein in his study at Princeton on July 24, 1943, at the commencement of his work for the U. S. Navy's Bureau of Ordnance. With him are Captain Geoffrey E. Sage, U.S.N., and Lt. Cdr. Frederick L. Douthit, U.S.N.R.

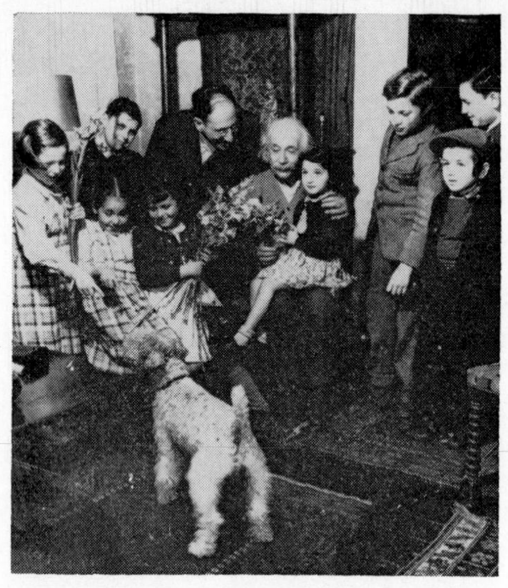

In his Princeton home, Einstein holds Leonora Aragones, 5, on his lap, as he and the dog Chico entertain a group of recently arrived young displaced persons who visited him in honor of his 70th birthday on March 14, 1949. Accompanying the children is William Rosenwald, National Chairman of the United Jewish Appeal. (Acme)

Einstein with Irene Joliot-Curie, daughter of Madame Curie. (UPI)

Einstein in his Princeton study. (Camera Press)

Einstein's desk and chair at the Institute for Advanced Study, Princeton, after his death. (UPI)

Overleaf: Einstein,
a portrait by Robert M. Gottschalk.

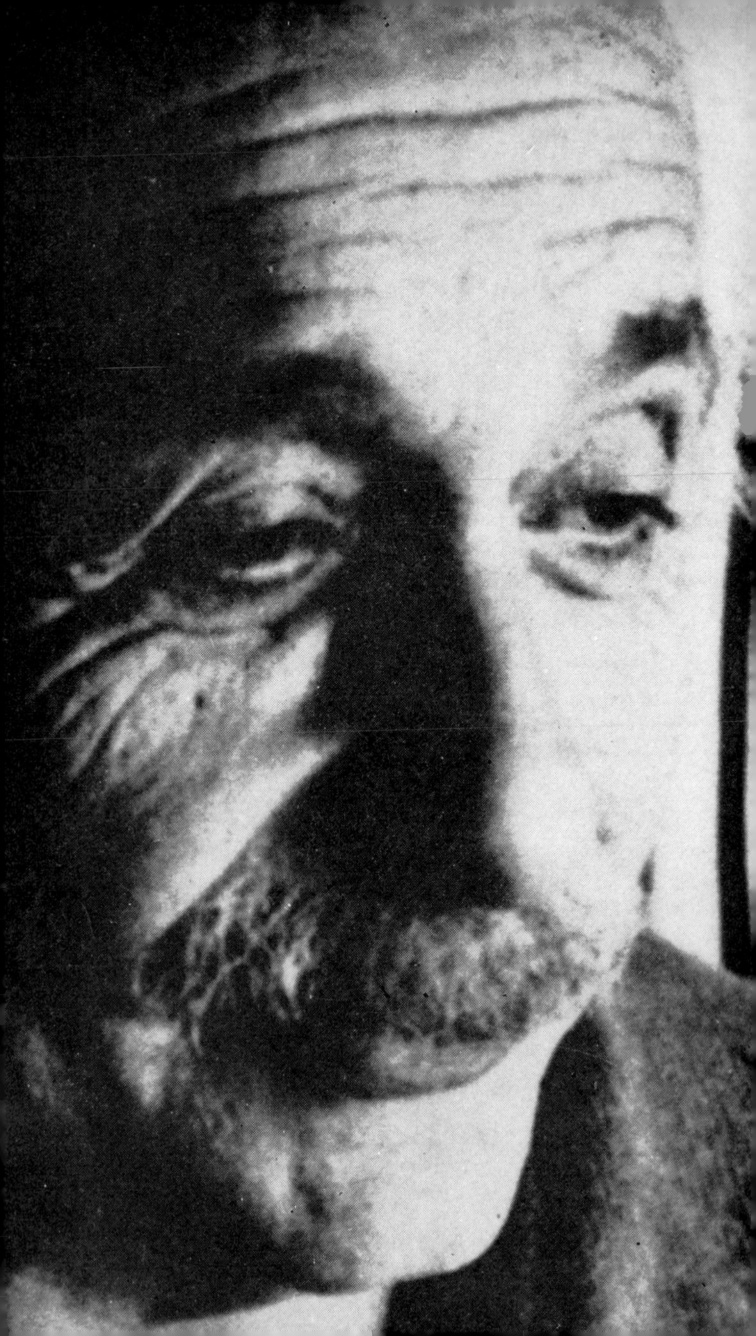

Cooperation, I do not think that I put any excessive insistence on your rejoining us. I understand very well that the committee could not lightly assume the responsibility of hindering the work of a man such as yourself by attracting to him personally serious sources of irritation.

However, before my departure from Berlin, and with a spirit which I sincerely admire, you told me that you were giving up all thought of resignation. The work of the League of Nations, you told me, was so dear to your heart that for it you were ready to accept certain risks rather than compromise, by an inexplicable resignation, the task of the committee. At one point during our interview I recall that concerning this you alluded to the eventuality, on your return from Japan, of a change in your domicile in order to ensure the peace and security of your work.

At the end of our conversations you wrote anew, on July 29, to the secretary general. Your preparations for leaving for Japan prevented you from attending the first meeting of the Committee of Intellectual Cooperation but you declared that upon your return your collaboration would be even more zealous, thus making up, in some fashion, for the loss of time occasioned by your absence. It was with this friendly letter that you left us for the Far East.

The committee held its first session in Geneva in August, and the official report explained that "Professor A. Einstein was prevented from assisting in the work of the committee owing to his absence on a scientific mission to Japan."

In fact Einstein did not leave for Japan until some months later and at the end of August he was writing to Lord Haldane from Berlin in support of a solution to the reparations problem put forward in the *Berliner Tageblatt*. He noted that "from French friends I understand that Poincaré would not be completely opposed to such a plan but that on the English side there would be inherent opposition," and concluded: "Meanwhile I ask you please to ensure that my name is not made public in this affair."

He sailed for Japan with his wife in October, 1922, having failed to obtain a substitute to serve on the committee until his return. To Geneva he explained that one professor had waited until it was too late before accepting and that another had been on holiday. Most professors who could honestly be said to represent German science were obviously reluctant to aid a League from which Germany was still excluded.

Einstein's absence, extended by a visit to Palestine, and a return to Germany by way of Madrid, continued until February, 1923, and it was only late in March that he returned to Berlin. He had not been in touch with the League. But, hearing indirectly that he was on his way home, its officials now expected that he would make preparations as promised for attending the session of the committee due to start in July. They were to be startlingly disappointed.

On his way to Berlin, Einstein broke his journey in Zurich. And here, on March 21, he wrote to the League resigning from the committee yet again. A copy of his letter was, moreover, immediately made available to the *Nouvelle Gazette de Zurich*, in whose columns the League officials were able to read it the following morning—while the letter itself was presumably still passing through their administrative machinery.

"I have recently become convinced that the League of Nations has neither the force nor the goodwill [*la bonne volonté*] necessary for the accomplishment of its task," it said. "As a convinced pacifist it does not seem to me to be a good thing to have any relations whatsoever with it. I ask you to strike my name from the list of committee members."

This was his second resignation from a committee whose meetings he had not yet attended. The reaction in Geneva can be gauged from the letter sent by Comert to Einstein the following month.

> Abruptly, on March 21, without any preliminary notice, you sent us your resignation from Zurich, where we did not even know that you had arrived.
>
> Your letter announces only your resignation from the Committee of Intellectual Cooperation. It is a condemnation, without appeal, of the League of Nations which, you say, possesses neither the force nor the goodwill to carry out its task and with which you refuse, in your capacity as convinced pacifist, to have any connection.
>
> This judgment, my dear Professor Einstein, without having followed the work of your commission, without having attended a single one of its meetings, on your

> return from a voyage during which it was perhaps not easy to follow European affairs.
>
> Before this letter was able to reach Geneva, it was given to the Zurich papers, published, and thus communicated to the whole world.
>
> This sudden *volte-face,* with all its repercussions, strikes an unhappy blow at those who, like us, looking towards a realizable and human ideal, follow humbly and obstinately, in a devastated Europe, the work of international peace which symbolizes for us the League of Nations. They had hoped that your collaboration would help to guide the work of the Committee of Intellectual Cooperation in the most useful way. Knowing that the task of the League of Nations cannot be carried out without the support of all men of goodwill, they were particularly happy at the help of an authority as eminent as yourself. Today their hope is disappointed. But their faith in this great work has been sufficiently hardened by the daily battle to resist the shock without being shattered. They will go on, dear Professor Einstein, with the work they have begun and with the sincere hope, I dare to say the conviction, that the road which separates you from us today will one day lead you back to us.

Einstein's formal resignation was handed in at the second session of the committee which began in July. By this time he had explained his action in more detail to *Die Friedenswarte,* a German pacifist paper. He had resigned, he said,

> because the activities of the League of Nations had convinced me that there appeared to be no action, no matter how brutal, committed by the present power group, against which the League could take a stand. I withdrew because the League, as it functions at present, not only does not embody the ideal of an international organization but actually discredits such an ideal.
>
> I did it, however, with inner reluctance, because the hope had not quite died in me that a better body might yet grow from this shell of a League of Nations. I am comforted by the thought that one of the cleanest and finest of men was elected in my place, Professor Lorentz of Haarlem, and with this nobody could be happier than I. May the League in the future prove my harsh words to have been mistaken.

Einstein's action—produced, he later admitted, "more by a passing mood of despondency than by mature reflection"—had been caused by the French occupation of the Ruhr. Inflation in Germany had become unbearable and at the end of 1922 the Weimar government suspended payment of the German reparations agreed upon in April, 1921. The French, tried beyond endurance, in January, 1923, occupied the small oval heartland of industrial Germany in an effort to squeeze blood from a stone. The result was to bring Einstein in line with the protesting German nationalists, although for reasons very different from theirs. They felt that the League, and all it stood for, was too strong; Einstein's objections were the complete opposite, as he made clear in a letter to Madame Curie, written to her nine months later when the twenty-fifth anniversary of the discovery of radium was being celebrated in Paris.

> I know that, quite rightly, I annoyed you when I left the League of Nations Committee with bitter comments, after I had recommended you only six months earlier to participate in the commission's work. But this was not done from bad motives or from a weakness for Germany, but really because I was convinced that the League of Nations (not the committee to which I was to belong) was a pliant tool of power politics under the cover of objectivity. Thus I wanted nothing to do with the League of Nations. I was also of the opinion that a completely open exchange of opinions could not damage the organization. Perhaps I was wrong, but this was my firm conviction.

Both the British and the Americans condemned the occupation of the Ruhr. So did many Frenchmen. While there was therefore widespread regret within the League at the way in which Einstein had demonstrated his attitude, it was submerged in the belief that he must be encouraged back into the fold once more. There appeared to be a chance of this in the spring of 1924 when, on April 17, the acting secretary of the committee received a confidential note reporting that Einstein had told a friend in Berlin "how he profoundly regretted the precipitate gesture of his resignation." Would it not be possible to tempt him back?

Gilbert Murray was conscripted for the task and on May 16 wrote to Einstein telling him that if he was ready to reconsider his position, then the committee "would unanimously welcome your presence." Einstein's reply was in his usual honest and outspoken fashion. He would like to rejoin the committee because he felt that its work might aid the improvement of Franco-German relations. And he concluded on a typically humble note. "If I should not be elected—which in view of what has passed would be entirely justified—I should be glad to do any work for the committee with which it might care to entrust me."

His return was discussed at the twenty-ninth session of the Council of the League on June 16, and Henri Bergson "could see nothing but advantage in Professor Einstein again taking a seat on the committee." The council agreed. But whereas all members had so far been elected "not as representatives of their respective countries but on account of their personal achievements," it was decided "that Professor Einstein should sit on the committee as representative of German science." The formal offer was now made, and Einstein wrote his acceptance to Sir Eric Drummond on the twenty-fifth. "I accept with the sincerest gratitude my reelection to the Committee on Intellectual Cooperation," he said. "In view of my past attitude this election gives proof of a singular broadmindedness and magnanimity, which I fully appreciate. I will spare no effort to promote the good cause for which the committee is working."

There is one interesting point about his letter of acceptance. Attached to it in the League files there is a note: "Not to be roneographed. The S.G. [secretary general] says that council members should each have a copy sent privately." There is also a note which says: "As the Einstein letter is private, I do not think it should be printed in the *Official Journal*." The League was anxious that no undue attention should be paid to Einstein's "past attitude" and that no one should be led on to disinter the reasons for which he had resigned little more than a year previously.

When Einstein was formally introduced to the committee together with a second new member at the start of the fourth session on Friday, July 25, 1924, the statement by Henri Bergson was equally circumspect, not to say smooth. "The chairman also welcomed M. Einstein, both as an old and a new colleague," says the official report.

"He had been appointed a member of the committee, just as the other members had been, without requesting the appointment. He had returned to the committee at his own request, having wished to become a member of it. He therefore doubly belonged to it." Bergson went on to recapitulate Einstein's achievements and concluded with the assurance that "if by his presence on a committee of the League of Nations he succeeds in attracting to this ideal all those who have been interested in his lofty speculation, he will have rendered a new and very great service to humanity."

Einstein did not succeed in doing as much as this. The results of his somewhat intermittent attendance at the committee's sessions until his final resignation in the spring of 1932 were a good deal less important than he can have expected or many of his colleagues can have hoped. This was not entirely, or perhaps even mainly, the fault of Einstein. The disparate forces brought together in the committee were almost equally suspicious of the France that had become the most powerful force on the continent and had every intention of remaining so, and of the German Republic that was working its passage back into respectability.

These stresses showed in the academic world as clearly as elsewhere—"it must be admitted," Einstein said on January 16, 1926, "that scientists and artists, at least in the countries with which I am familiar, are guided by narrow nationalism to a much greater extent than are public men." This was not true of him. He was handicapped certainly, but rather by his temperamental inability to make the compromises and accommodations demanded by committee work. Furthermore, his earlier resignation in protest against the French occupation of the Ruhr now made it necessary for him to stress that he was no chauvinist; and his international status, German-born, Swiss by adoption, then full German again, made him particularly vulnerable to attack. All this tended to counterbalance the prestige of his name, which the League had been so eager to utilize but which was a somewhat doubtful asset in the work of the next few years.

One of the first developments after Einstein had at last joined the committee was the establishment of the International Institute of Intellectual Cooperation, in effect its executive organ. It was to be financed by the French government and set up in Paris, and there was an unwritten agreement that its head should always be a Frenchman. After initially welcoming the idea, Einstein grew suspicious of possible French domination. He himself was unable to oppose the details due to absence in South America, but he tried to persuade Lorentz to protest in his name. Lorentz declined.

The meetings of the committee continued to be held in Geneva, and here Einstein played his part in discussing the various proposals put forward for cooperation. "We had no funds but we could often help a man whose books or scientific instruments had been destroyed by getting him admitted to a laboratory or a library, and sometimes got men restored to lost positions," Gilbert Murray has written. "I remember one case where we failed, but the man in question wrote me a letter explaining what a comfort it had been to him in his loneliness, to know that scientists like Einstein and Lorentz and Madame Curie had at least been thinking about him."

At a different level, Einstein sat on subcommittees dealing with bibliography and with a proposed international meteorological bureau. He gave personal advice on the allocation among Russian émigré intellectuals of money donated by the Red Cross and he spent much time discussing how the prospects of peace in the future might be increased by means of school education in the present. All were low-key affairs. They had their place on the outer periphery of international relations but even here their prospects depended very much on the extent to which cooperation could be forced through on the more crucial issues of armaments and trade. Thus the straight fact that the committee achieved comparatively little during its existence is largely a measure of the status, or lack of it, which it was accorded. At the level where real decisions were made, no one took culture very seriously.

Gilbert Murray was the committee member brought most intimately into contact with Einstein. "One had the feeling that all of us were capable of understanding what each one said and meant, a feeling by no means always present to international committees," he had written.

> One felt also in the mass of one's colleagues a sense of what I would venture to call by the rather bold name of purity of heart. Einstein was one clear case—immense intellectual power, perfect goodwill, and simplicity. . . . What struck me most about [him], apart from his mathematics and his music, which were both beyond my range, was his gaiety and instinctive kindliness. . . . Bergson once said of him that he had made discoveries at a greater distance from the ordinary organs of human knowledge than any other man in history. . . .

And to Bertrand Russell, Murray wrote, after Einstein's death: "Of course he was perfectly simple and unassuming. But once I saw him sitting by the lake and went up to speak to him and saw that he was lost in thought and didn't see anything. He was very reluctant to believe evil . . . one felt a sort of confidence that he would quite simply take the right view about everything."

Einstein's main interest was the effect of education in removing the misunderstandings and hatreds which help to make war not only possible but popular, an interest closely linked with the pacifist activities which were taking up an increasing amount of his time. "To my mind the main task," he said when addressing the committee informally on one occasion, "is how generally to improve the education of the young. The League can do no greater work than help make better the elementary school system throughout the world." And it is a tribute to the extraordinary weight of his name that this informal and slightly obvious statement, thrown off in a Geneva conference room, should have been worth a leading article in the *New York Times*, which noted this was an Einstein statement which "even the least learned in mathematics and physics can understand."

His attitude was plainly stated in a letter which he wrote to Millikan in Pasadena early in 1925. "In July I again have to attend a meeting for the League of Nations committee," he said. "There one comes back to your idea of fighting the chauvinistic influence in the schools as much as one can." He went on to give his impressions of the committee as it existed at that date. "Honestly, and taking everything into consideration, the efficiency of the committee is not very great," he said.

> Real activity can, it seems to me, come from an individual Jew but not from a corporate body, especially if what is involved is not only a question of exercise of power but the exercise of spiritual and moral force. I am glad to be able to say that the French who are active in the Committee are of a good and honorable disposition. On the other hand, it cannot be denied that French influence is incomparably greater than it should be if rated by their intellect. England and America are very good but are not strong enough in defending their interests. One must try to strengthen and cultivate the germ of international understanding and cooperation. H. A. Lorentz has unfortunately not been successful in Brussels in carrying through the admission of the Germans to the international organizations, which naturally strengthens the chauvinism of present-day scientists. Strange to say, politicians and businessmen in Europe are as liberal in their thought as the scientists; one cannot help regarding this as a sign of decadence. In America this seems quite the reverse, and to be more important.

His general attitude, and a hint of the reason why he failed to influence the committee very much, is given in a letter from Dr. A. Trowbridge, an American observer, reporting to Millikan on the meeting held in Paris on January 14, 1926. "Einstein came in a little late and sat very silent throughout the proceedings," he said. "There was some suggestion of putting him on some standing committee, but he declined on the plea of overwork. His sole communication to the proceedings was a statement that 'in some countries,' where there was a distinctly antagonistic feeling towards the League of Nations, it might be necessary to add some other method than that suitable in countries where there already existed a predisposition in favor of the League of Nations. I am not sure whether Einstein meant under 'some countries' Germany or the United States—I think, however, the former."

Einstein's interest in education led to one of the few concrete results of his cooperation with the League. Soon after its formation, the committee was asked "to encourage an exchange of letters between leaders of thought, on the lines of those which have always taken place at the great epochs of European history; to select subjects best calculated to serve the common interest of the League of Nations and of the intellectual life of mankind; and to publish this correspondence from time to time." The first volume, entitled *A League of Minds*, contained letters from M. Henri Focillon, Señor Salvador de Madariaga, Gilbert Murray, Paul Valéry, and others. And in the autumn of 1931, M. Steinig, a League official, traveled to Berlin with the aim of securing Einstein's cooperation on a second volume. Just what it would deal with was relatively immaterial, although certain possibilities had been discussed in Geneva; what was required was a long original letter from Einstein which could be published under the League's auspices.

The idea strongly attracted Einstein who had, Steinig later reported to M. Bonnet, director of the institute in Paris, "a horror of platonic declarations which did not look forward to an immediately realizable end. After M. Einstein had underlined his interest in education as a means of ensuring peace, we decided," M. Steinig went on,

> that he would accept in principle the idea of writing two letters to two different people on this question: one of these letters would probably be addressed to M. Langevin, and M. Einstein proposed here to deal with an exchange of views between representatives of French and German organizations on the means of influencing the content of history books in the two countries, for instance. One could, M. Einstein considered, progressively correct the historical accuracy of such books by removing "tendentious errors" on the one hand and, on the other, the errors which provoked and nourished the feelings of national hostility.
>
> Another letter, which would be produced in the form of a questionnaire, would be addressed to M. Freud of Vienna. M. Einstein will probably ask him to explain how an education inspired by the new principles of psychoanalysis would be able to contribute in guiding the ideas of children towards peace and in diminishing the aggressive impulses which are the foundation of all war.

The choice of Langevin, an old personal friend across the German frontier, was reasonable enough but at first it seems strange that Freud should have been mentioned. While Einstein had a firm respect for Freud's personal stature and integrity he had at this time little use for his theories and had met him only once. But it seems likely that this idea had been planted earlier, after a meeting of the committee when Einstein and a number of colleagues had dined with Dr. Ernst Jackh, a former director of the Hochschule für Politik in Berlin, at the house of the German undersecretary general of the League in Geneva. "As we were going into dinner," Jackh has written,

> I asked Professor Einstein: "Would you agree that it is no mere chance that your theory of relativity, and Professor Freud's psychoanalysis, the League of Nations and its World Court, and other phenomena of our time, have developed together: that they are all an expression of the same revolutionary phase through which the contemporary world is passing?"
>
> Professor Einstein looked at me, said nothing for a moment, and then: "This synthetic vision is new to me. Let me think it over."
>
> During dinner I watched him, and I noticed that he was eating and drinking nothing, but was staring in front of him and meditating. After dinner, he came up to me and said, "You are quite right: I endorse your Holism."

Einstein proposed to Steinig that he himself should write to Langevin while Steinig made first contact with Freud in Vienna. A subsequent note from Bonnet to Einstein tactfully suggested that as Langevin was already in China on a mission for the committee, and as Bonnet himself would soon be leaving for China, it might be best for Einstein to omit the first personal contact. Here it is not oversuspicious to recall Einstein's original feelings about the French and the siting of the institute in Paris, run by a French director. The Langevin project never matured; the reasons are not clear; but the problem of reconciling the French and the German views of history given in the textbooks never had to be argued out in public.

Meanwhile, Einstein's proposals were discussed in Paris, and in due course Steinig wrote to Freud. "I hasten to answer your letter because you tell me you intend to use my comments when you meet Professor Einstein at the end of this month," Freud replied on June 6, 1932.

> While reading your letter I have indulged in as much enthusiasm as I am able to muster at my age (seventy-six) and in my state of disillusionment. The words in

which you express your hopes and those of Einstein for a future role of psychoanalysis in the life of individuals and nations ring true and of course give me very great pleasure. It has been no little disappointment to me that at a time when we can continue our work only under the greatest social and material difficulties, I haven't seen the slightest sign of interest for our efforts on the part of the League of Nations. Thus practical and idealistic considerations combine to induce me to put myself with all that remains of my energies at the disposal of the Institute for Intellectual Cooperation.

I cannot quite imagine as yet what form my participation is going to take. It will devolve upon Einstein to make suggestions. I would prefer not to hold forth on my own and hope that the character of a discussion can be maintained in such a way, perhaps, that instead of answering one question put to me by Einstein, I respond from the point of view of psychoanalysis to statements in which he expresses his opinions. I would also prefer not to pick out a single topic from among those enumerated in your letter. It is rather a question of a number of problems of which the most important for practical purposes is the influence of psychoanalysis on education. But as I say, in all these practical details I am ready to follow Einstein's suggestions. When you see him you won't be able to tell him anything more about my personal relationship to him than he knows already, although I only once had the long-desired opportunity of talking to him.

As for yourself, please accept my cordial thanks for your interest in psychoanalysis.

Yours very sincerely,
Freud

Subsequently, Steinig met Freud to explain the project in more detail. Freud was not optimistic. "All my life I have had to tell people truths that were difficult to swallow," he said, according to Steinig. "Now that I am old I certainly do not want to fool them." But he would answer Einstein's open letter as best he could.

This letter, dated July 30, 1932, posed one simple question: "Is there any way of delivering mankind from the menace of war?" Having asked the question, Einstein then continued to give his own answer—the creation of an international authority, whose nonexistence he put down simply to the fault of the "governing class," to those "whose aspirations are on purely mercenary, economic lines," and to the additional fact that "the ruling class at present has the schools and press, usually the Church as well, under its thumb." Yet war only appeared to be possible, he admitted, because "man has within him a lust for hatred and destruction." And here, of course, the psychoanalyst might be able to help.

Freud's long discursive answer was in some ways self-contradictory. He wrote of "pacifists like us"; yet while he agreed with Einstein that an international court of authority was essential to peace, he noted the need for "its investment with adequate executive force." He agreed with Einstein on man's instinct for hatred and destruction, and then continued:

> The upshot of these observations, as bearing on the subject in hand, is that there is no likelihood of our being able to suppress humanity's aggressive tendencies. In some happy corners of the earth, they say, where nature brings forth abundantly whatever man desires, there flourish races whose lives go gently by, unknowing of aggression or constraint. This I can hardly credit; I would like further details about these happy folk. The Bolshevists, too, aspire to do away with human aggressiveness by ensuring the satisfaction of material needs and enforcing equality between man and man. To me this hope seems vain. Meanwhile they busily perfect their armaments, and their hatred of outsiders is not the least of the factors of cohesion among themselves.

Freud concluded this depressing prognostication with one faint hope: that it was not too chimerical to believe that war might one day be ended through a combination of two factors. One of these was man's cultural disposition and the other was "a well-founded dread of the form that future wars will take." The idea of peace by the threat of terror was not one which Einstein welcomed. Yet a mere seven years later he was, by signing a letter to Roosevelt, to prod research along the road to the ultimate weapon.

The Einstein-Freud correspondence was published the following year in Paris, after lengthy discussion about what the little booklet should be called. *Law and Violence*, much favored for a while, was finally rejected for *Why War?*. Editions appeared in French and in German—

although *Warum Krieg?* was banned in Germany, where not even advertisements for it were allowed.

Why War?—the one permanent memorial to Einstein's membership of the committee—appeared only after he had finally severed all connection with the League and had made a public and ill-judged protest against the disarmament conference being held under the League's auspices in Geneva.

The reasons for this change of stance were twofold and complementary. First in importance was his increasing involvement in the plethora of pacifist movements which grew up during the 1920s. His own personal attitude to pacifism remained unaltered; nevertheless, the framework within which it could be expressed changed substantially between 1920 and 1930. For the first few years after the Armistice another world war was so unthinkable that no argument against one was necessary. But slowly the situation began to deteriorate. As it did so, there arose the prospect of the League, certainly a potential keeper of the peace but a policeman without even a baton in his hand.

Einstein, like most other men, was at times self-contradictory. But a great deal of the confusion which surrounds his pacifist attitude disappears once it is considered dispassionately and historically and once his somewhat tortuous self-justifications are ignored. The truth is that in 1920 he was an unqualified pacifist; that the logic of events added first one qualification and then another; and that with the coming to power of Hitler even Einstein was forced to realize that pacifism would not work. The evolution took place gradually but unevenly; at times it slipped back, and at times he himself does not seem to be clear what he really wanted to say. Furthermore, he continued to call himself a pacifist even while agreeing that the dictators could only be stopped by force of arms, an attitude which spread alarm and despondency through the pacifist camp.

But as late as 1928 his attitude was still uncomplicated. "It seems to me," he wrote, in refusing an invitation from the Women's International League for Peace and Freedom to a conference in Geneva on the subject of gas warfare, "an utterly futile task to prescribe rules and limitations for the conduct of war. . . . The masses of people can most effectively fight the institution of war by establishing in time of peace an organization for absolute refusal of military service." He further outlined his state of belief in a letter to the British No More War movement later in the year. "I am convinced," he wrote, "that the international movement to refuse participation in any kind of war service is one of the most encouraging developments of our time. Every thoughtful, well-meaning and conscientious human being should assume, in time of peace, the solemn and unconditional obligation not to participate in any war, for any reason, or to lend support of any kind, whether direct or indirect."

The phrase "support of any kind, whether direct or indirect" is plain enough. Yet within little more than a year Einstein was writing to the Finnish Minister of Defense, applauding the fact that his country allowed conscientious objectors to be employed, without penalty, for nonmilitary work under civilian control. "It is evident," says Harold Bing, the British pacifist leader, "that Einstein considered that governments were justified in requiring of conscientious objectors to military service, some kind of civilian alternative. He had not grasped the logical position of the absolutist who refused all service under a system of military conscription." More surprisingly, even after his experiences in wartime Berlin, he had failed to grasp the fact that service in a nation at war is indivisible, that the peaceful plowman plows to feed the civilians who make the guns which serve the forces.

Yet Einstein's apparent ambiguity deeply disturbed pacifists who believed that they had his unequivocal support. "On August 30, 1930," writes Bing,

> I was taken by Martha Steinitz [sometime secretary of the Bund der Kriegsdienstgegener and later joint secretary of the WRI] to meet Einstein at his lakeside summer house near Potsdam *... and, in reply to his questions, explained why I and others had refused alternative service because to accept such service was to recognize the state's right of conscription and to acquiesce in the conscription of others and because any work imposed upon us by the state in wartime would be intended to assist the war effort. At the end of our conversation he declared that he now understood the absolutist position.

*See pages 501–502.

Understood maybe. But only three months later he gave little evidence of this in one of his most famous pacifist speeches. This was made in the Ritz-Carlton Hotel in New York on December 14, after he had broken his journey en route to Pasadena. There was the usual injunction on pacifists to replace words with deeds, and a demand for refusal to be conscripted. "Even if only two percent of those assigned to perform military service should announce their refusal to fight," he said, ". . . governments would be powerless, they would not dare send such a large number of people to jail." However, this phrase, which was to produce a rash of button badges with the words "two percent" on them, was followed by a plea to countries which operate conscription to bring in laws "permitting pacifists in place of military service to do some strenuous or dangerous work, in the interest of their country or of mankind as a whole. . . ." It is possible to claim that Einstein had, in fact, not "understood the absolutist position." It is possible to claim that he did understand it, but rejected it and felt happy about objectors carrying out work which would in fact assist a war effort. A third possibility is that in the press of preparations for his American visit,* amid the work which had to be finished before he left Berlin, he had not thought out to a conclusion the implications of what seemed to him a satisfactory solution to a tough moral problem.

But there is another explanation of his evolving pacifist attitudes. Perhaps in pacifism, as in space, there should be no absolutes, a standpoint which makes more comprehensible his attitude of 1931, evolving from that of the "two percent" of a few months previously. "As he sees the problem, there are two ways of resisting war," said the chairman of War Resisters International, Fenner (now Lord) Brockway, after he had visited Einstein at the head of a WRI delegation, "the legal way and the revolutionary way. The legal way involves the offer of alternative service, not as a privilege for a few, but as a right for all. The revolutionary way involves uncompromising resistance, with a view to breaking the power of militarism in time of peace or the resources of the state in time of war. The general conclusion of Professor Einstein was that

*See page 517.

both tendencies are valuable, and that certain circumstances justify the one and certain circumstances the other." All was as relative here as it was in physics.

His dedication to the pacifist movement tended increasingly to tug Einstein away from the overcozy international atmosphere of the League. Always an instinctive outsider, he felt unhappy in the role of insider automatically conferred by membership of the committee. In addition, there were problems within the organization itself. "National Committees" had been created which by 1930 were acting as liaison groups between the central body in Geneva and the intellectual communities of individual countries. Einstein was a member of the German committee, created after Germany had joined the League in 1926, but his opinions were given only qualified support by fellow members, and their recommendations led him to claim that the whole system of national committees was a "blessing to the policy of cultural oppression of cultural minorities." He felt that his fellow members on the main committee were dragging their feet on education and had failed to support those who had "thrown themselves without reserve into the business of working for an international order and against the military system."

These criticisms were made in a letter to M. Albert Dufour-Feronce, a League undersecretary, in July, 1930. In a typically casual way Einstein thought that a reference here to his "resolve to go no more to Geneva" would be taken as a formal resignation. He put in no appearance in 1931 and in April, 1932, arrived back from the United States to find awaiting him an invitation to a meeting in July. He replied immediately, saying he thought his mandate had expired in 1931. "I was fully convinced, during the early years, that I was not suitable for doing useful work on this committee," he continued. "It would therefore be acceptable, and more just, if another takes my place. This would in any case suit me better, as I will find it difficult to find the time, next summer, to attend the Geneva conference.

"At the same time I would like to mention that I accepted membership at the time, only because owing to the political stance of German academics you would have had great difficulty in finding someone whose political and international views would have been suitable."

The letter, written to M. Montenach, the Swiss secretary of the committee, was quickly followed in the League by an internal note outlining various steps which it was hoped would stave off Einstein's resignation. Gilbert Murray was again asked to intercede. M. Dufour-Feronce, who had once worked in the German Foreign Office and who knew Einstein personally, was to do the same. "You might," Dufour-Feronce was instructed by Montenach, "insist on his making a special effort to come to Geneva for six days to attend the session of the committee beginning on July 18. You could say that the other members of the committee who have been for nearly ten years his colleagues and have much affection and admiration for him would greatly appreciate such a gesture of sympathy and interest which would be made by his attending the session before the expiration of his term of office."

All these blandishments failed. And Einstein, who found it "difficult to find the time" to attend Geneva for the July meeting, arrived there instead in May, and in circumstances which would certainly have made impossible any further connection with the League.

So far, despite his support for the militant pacifists, he had clung to the hope that the League, however greatly its operations might fall below his own standards, offered a genuine promise for the future. Now—and for the next eighteen months—he put more faith in the belief that "if the workers of this world, men and women, decide not to manufacture and transport ammunition, it would stop war for all time." And he also, increasingly, voiced an open distrust of what the League was doing, unconsciously echoing Wells' gibe about "this little corner of Balfourian jobs and gentility."

Einstein's distrust exploded in reaction to the Disarmament Conference which opened in Geneva in February, 1932. It was a reaction which illustrated his bigness of heart but revealed the immense gap which divided the real world of nation-states and politicians from the world which Einstein felt must exist because it should exist. It was a reaction which undermined those who believed he might be a useful ally in a practical struggle to avert war, and it was one which offered a useful weapon to those only waiting to claim that outside his own field Einstein was something between crank and buffoon. In almost every way it was one of his most disastrous interventions in public affairs.

The Disarmament Conference which sat in Geneva between 1932 and 1934 was attended by representatives of sixty nations—including nonmembers of the League such as Russia and the United States—and was an effort to reduce armaments within the framework of the League Covenant. At first Einstein had welcomed the idea of such a conference, even if only as a last hope. "I believe [it] should take place in any event, at the very least, it will help to clarify the situation and focus attention on this important problem," he told the editor of the French journal *Paix Mondiale*. However, it must have been obvious to any knowledgeable observer that if the conference was to have the slightest chance of success, it would involve months of wrangling, a balancing of weapon against weapon, a long delicate series of negotiations in which a choice between comparable evils was taken only after much discussion. The reaction of Einstein, with his simple belief that all countries must abolish arms and subjugate their future to an international organization, was easy enough to forecast. It came in May, 1932, when the conference had been meeting for only three months and its committees were deep in intricate argument.

Earlier in the year he had been asked by the Rev. J. B. Th. Hugenholz, a Dutch delegate to the Joint Peace Council of the International Union of Antimilitarist Ministers and Clergymen, to attend a meeting of the council in Geneva in May. He declined. But towards the end of that month, following a visit to Oxford, he decided to visit Geneva after all—"because," he said, "some friends convinced me that it was my duty to do so." On Sunday, May 22, he left London for Geneva with Lord Ponsonby, not only a leading pacifist but an old friend. Ponsonby was also an intimate of Arthur Henderson, the former British Foreign Mininster now presiding over the Disarmament Conference. Under Henderson, Ponsonby had carried out much of the detailed negotiation which had preceded the trade agreement between Britain and Russia. They were men of somewhat similar outlook and it has even been suggested that Henderson "engineered" Einstein's appearance at Geneva. There is no evidence of this, and if Henderson played any part at all, which seems unlikely, even he must have been surprised at the genie which he had encouraged out of the bottle.

On the morning of Monday, May 23, Einstein visited the League headquarters. As he entered the public gallery, the Japanese and Russian delegates of the Air Commission were arguing that the mobility of aircraft carriers increased the offensiveness of the planes they carried; for the United States Allen Dulles and for Britain Captain J. T. Babington—who had won a hard-earned D.S.O. for the wartime bombing of the Friedrichshafen Airship Factory—were arguing the reverse. The speaker stopped for a moment, then continued, according to Konrad Bercovici, a young Rumanian-American journalist. "That brief second, however, was an acknowledgment, a more marked acknowledgment, of the greatness the man radiated than if all had stopped everything they were doing and applauded him," he wrote. "All eyes were turned towards Einstein. Where he was, the world was."

But Einstein had not come just to watch. That afternoon he held a press conference at the Brègues Hotel attended by about sixty correspondents. What he said, both here and elsewhere in Geneva, has been variously reported. The editors of *Einstein on Peace* print one account, which appears to be a cut version, while noting that the War Resisters International had another transcript which Einstein "rather freely revised . . . insofar as it deals with me." But there is no doubt about the tenor of his statement, whose main points are given in a few key sentences in the "official" version: "One does not make wars less likely to occur by formulating rules of warfare." "War cannot be humanized. It can only be abolished." "People must be persuaded to refuse all military service." These seem reasonable propositions, even if they can be challenged, and at first Romain Rolland's comment quoted in *Einstein on Peace*—that Einstein "tended to become impractical once outside the scientific field"—seems a little harsh.

However, it was not what he said but the context of his opinions which tended to destroy his credibility for all except those who had already been converted to the conspiracy theory of war. This is made clear by Bercovici's account of the Geneva visit and of an interview with Einstein which he succeeded in obtaining before the press conference started. According to the editors of *Einstein on Peace*—naturally anxious to present their subject in the best light—this account, "while possibly exaggerated, suggests, nonetheless, the universal and instinctive appreciation of Einstein's personality." It consists essentially of a long quoted statement, triggered off when Bercovici said that he had come to the city to watch the comedy of peace.

"This is not a comedy," Einstein replied.

> It is a tragedy. The greatest tragedy of modern times, despite the cap and bells and buffoonery. No one has any right to treat this tragedy lightly or to laugh when one should cry. We should be standing on rooftops, all of us, and denouncing this conference as a travesty! . . .
>
> If you want peace in America then you must join us in Europe, and together we shall ask the workers to refuse to manufacture and transport any military weapons, and also to refuse to serve any military organization. Then we will have no more conscriptions; we will have no more war! Governments could go on talking from now to doomsday. The militarists could lay any plans they wish.
>
> If the workers of this world, men and women, decide not to manufacture and transport ammunition, it would end war for all time. We must do that. Dedicate our lives to drying up the source of war: ammunition factories.
>
> I have absolute information that if a war should break out today anywhere in Europe so many conscientious objectors would throw away or refuse to shoulder arms that one-half of every army would be busy putting down the revolt of the other half before going to fight the enemy. The trouble with the delegates here and with most people ruling over nations today is that they don't know what their peoples think and how their peoples feel about war.
>
> The trouble with most of these delegates is that they are unintelligent and insincere and are but puppets moved by strings in the hands of politicians at home—politicians and ammunition manufacturers. Any declaration of war would be followed by world-wide revolutions. We must prevent that, prevent the destruction of Western civilization by the uncivilized governments of the world.

No one would claim that this is necessarily an accurate sentence by sentence verbatim account of what Einstein said. But from all available evidence it would seem to reflect his excited—and, as Bercovici puts it at one point, "almost hysterical"—attitude. Yet Germany had not yet walked out of the conference, and was not to do so for another eighteen months. The French, who were to insist that some system of general security should precede disarmament, were still trying. Hope still existed.

Against this background, Einstein's attitude marks the high tide of his pacifism, which had been rising since the First World War. And with the reflection that within fourteen months he was to be encouraging men to take up arms, the only other nonscientific preoccupation of his life must now be considered: the support of Zionism, for which he showed the same white-hot idealism, a quality often producing results which, here also, counterbalanced the value of his name.

CHAPTER 14

THE CALL OF ZION

It is demonstrably unfair, yet still perfectly true, to claim that the Zionists seized upon Einstein's fame from 1919 onwards and exploited it to their advantage. No movement dedicated to so difficult a mission can let its tactics be too closely controlled by the principles of a gentlefolks' aid society; and with a genius of Weizmann's caliber in control it was inevitable that the magnetism of Einstein, the incorruptible man of science, should be conscripted to the general task of implementing the Balfour Declaration, and to the special one of coaxing money from the pockets of American Jewry. The Zionists should not be criticized for this. If criticism is warranted it springs, rather, from their failure to bring Einstein unconditionally within their fold; to capture him so completely that his statements of support would never contain the irritating qualifications which he saw as essential to honesty but which could be a niggling hindrance to men fighting for their ideals. One should have sympathy for both sides. How difficult it must have been for Einstein to move from the world of physics into the passionate turmoil of creating the new Jerusalem! How tantalizing it must have been for the Zionists to have captured the most famous living Jew for the cause—and then find that he was a bad speaker who often said things out of naïveté which caused trouble!

Einstein himself has stated that he did not become aware of his own Jewishness until after he went to Berlin in the spring of 1914. This is not as surprising as it sounds. The modern Zionist movement did not come into existence until 1897. The current for assimilation still continued to run swiftly through the Jewish community and Einstein himself noted in 1921 that "up till about a generation ago the Jews in Germany did not regard themselves as belonging to the Jewish people. They felt themselves only members of a religious community. . . ." Thus, despite the "nail from the Crucifix" brought into the Munich schoolroom, Einstein appears to have remembered no anti-Semitism from his student days, from his work in the Berne Patent Office, or from his years as a young professor in Zurich. "Different but equal" was the attitude of the liberal Swiss; so much so that the correspondence of Einstein's student days, of his early married life, and of his gradual integration into the scientific world contains barely a hint of his origin or of the religion into which he had been born.

In Prague, the Jewish community provided a power bloc in the struggle between the Czechs and the Germans into whose Austro-Hungarian Empire they had been brought. And here, for the first time it appears, Einstein became a member although certainly not a committed one, of a Jewish group. It met every Tuesday evening in the home of Bertha Fanta; but while almost every other member was an ardent Zionist, Einstein was completely uninterested.

The reason is not difficult to see once the viability of Zionism as a practical proposition in 1910 is soberly considered. Theodore Herzl had launched the movement little more than a decade previously, convening the first first to Cologne and then in 1911 to Berlin. The idea that Zionist Congress at Basel, where in 1897 it resolved "to secure for the Jewish people a home in Palestine guaranteed by public law." Led from Vienna until Herzl's death in 1904, the movement had been transferred to Germany, first to Cologne and then in 1911 to Berlin. The idea that the national home might be founded elsewhere than in Palestine, mooted more than once, was finally rejected in Basel at the Seventh Congress in 1905. Here the tentative offer made two years earlier by the British government, under which the Zionist organization was provisionally to be granted 6,000 square miles of East Africa, was firmly turned down. Zionists were concerned only with Palestine. But Palestine had for centuries been part of the Turkish Empire and when, even after the revolution of 1908, it became clear that the Turks had no intention of granting the Zionists a charter, "the movement, as Herzl had conceived it, came to a standstill."

To some Jews this was not altogether unwelcome. For while many saw their people as a potential nation, others saw them only as a group held together by theological beliefs and a personal code of behavior. "Thus," says Leonard Stein in his history of Zionism,

> while there was one school of thought which stoutly denied that the Jews were a nation at all, there was another which held that the Jews were a nation and nothing else—a nation precisely like any other, except that it happened to have been temporarily deprived of its national territory. Both sets of extremists oversimplified the Jewish problem, because both of them could only conceive of nationhood in terms of the nation-state. In calling upon the Jews to be fearlessly themselves, in reminding them that, for all their differences, they had precious possessions in common, in warning them that those possessions would be jeopardized if they failed to maintain and to enrich their corporate life, the nationalists performed a valuable and indeed an indispensable function. In suggesting, on the other hand, that the Jewish problem would be solved if the Jews would only imagine themselves to be something they were not, they were playing with fanciful analogies and using language which was sometimes least carefully thought out by those who used it most freely.

Einstein had no wish to be ground between these two millstones. In 1911 his common sense estimated Zionist prospects more as a chimera than a practical possibility. He was, moreover, already intellectually at odds with any movement which buttressed nationalism, however honorable its motives, and this intuitive feeling was to be strengthened by the experiences of the war years. Yet in 1920 Einstein emerges as the dedicated though sometimes qualified Zionist, adding the luster of his name to a cause still in need of luster despite its greatly improved prospects: speaking on platforms; warily putting a foot into the deep waters of Zionist politics; and making an exhausting tour of the United States for the cause. Something more than the magic of Weizmann's personality had been needed to bring this about.

One factor which influenced him was the transformation of Zionism from a pious hope to a practical possibility by the Balfour Declaration of 1917, the statement by the British Foreign Minister that "His Majesty's Government view with favor the establishment in Palestine of a national home for the Jewish people, and will use their best endeavors to facilitate the achievement of this object. . . ." It was true that the Declaration was issued at a fortunate moment and that, as H. A. L. Fisher has sagely noted, it "rallied to the Allied cause, at a time when money was urgently needed, the powerful and cosmopolitan community which, not from New York only, controls the loan market of the world." But it was also true that the ancient plain of Philistia, after almost 1,300 years of Persian and Turkish rule, was now being conquered by Allenby's armies. The hopes of the Jews looked high.

Moreover, as the significance of these hopes began to sink into the postwar German-Jewish consciousness, the attitude of Jewish intellectuals such as Einstein was inevitably affected by the influx of their fellow Jews from Eastern Europe, and by the reactions of many well-established German Jews who were happy to ignore their plight. With Einstein, the process had begun five years earlier, when he first moved to Berlin. In Switzerland, he wrote, there was "nothing that called forth any Jewish sentiments in me. When I moved to Berlin all that changed. There I realized the difficulties with which many young Jews were confronted. I saw how, amid anti-Semitic surroundings, systematic study, and with it the road to a safe existence, was made impossible for them." These difficulties were further intensified when the new Republican government contemplated expelling the new refugees from the east. "I stood up for them," Einstein later wrote, "and pointed out in the *Berliner Tageblatt* the inhumanity and folly of such a measure. Together with some colleagues, Jews and non-Jews, I started university courses for these eastern-born Jews, and I must add that in this matter we enjoyed official recognition and considerable assistance from the Ministry of Education." Here were some of the reasons for Einstein's enthusiasm for Zionism, quoted by him after conversion. They suggest that his interest was captured as much by the prospect of a Hebrew University, run by Jews, for Jews, as by the wider prospects of Zionism. They also make it easier to understand his reactions as the good cause hardened into the nationalism of which he was always suspicious rather than into the internationalism which he always supported.

Einstein's recruitment into the Zionist cause has been described by the man who carried it out, Kurt Blumenfeld. Two things are clear. First, that "until 1919 Einstein had no association with Zionism and Zionist ways of thought." Second, that the method of Einstein's recruitment was important not only in itself but by its example. "The method," says Blumenfeld, "found effective with him brought [other] friends and followers to Zionism: that is to say, the drawing out from a man of what is within him rather than the forcing from him of what is not truly within his nature."

Blumenfeld's account of his meetings with Einstein in February, 1919, is revealing both of Einstein and of the Zionist cause as it struggled into practical existence:

> Felix Rosenblueth [today Minister of Justice Pinhas Rosen] had prepared a list of Jewish scholars whom we wished to interest in Zionism. Einstein was among them. Scientists had known his importance for years but when we called upon him we did not know that his name would soon be resounding across the world. The abundance of interviews and photographs which later surrounded him had not yet started.
>
> I began to talk about the Jewish question. "What has that to do with Zionism?" Einstein asked. "The Zionism idea will give the Jew inner security. It will remove discord. Openness and inner freedom will be the result."
>
> These were the thoughts which interested Einstein. With extreme naïveté he asked questions, and his comments on the answers were simple and unconventional. "Is it a good idea to eliminate the Jews from the spiritual calling to which they were born? Is it not a retrograde step to put manual capabilities, and above all agriculture, at the center of everything Zionism does?"
>
> So far Einstein had avoided giving any specific opinions. Now opposition showed itself. "Are not the Jews, through a religious tradition which has evolved outside Palestine, too much estranged from the country and country life? Are not the talents which they have exploited with such scientific accomplishment perhaps the result of an innate spirituality; is it necessary to create a Jewish national movement which is circumscribed by the Jewish question?"

> We felt during our talk that we were dealing with a man of unusual gifts. There was nothing very surprising in his words, but I could see the thoughts of the man in the flash of his eyes and the look told me more than the words.

A few days later Einstein and Blumenfeld met again. "On this occasion," writes Blumenfeld, "he told me that Hermann Struck, the etcher, had tried to interest him in the Bible and the Jewish religion, but that he had refused to be drawn. 'I really don't know enough about my religious feelings,' he said. . . . 'I have always known exactly what I should do, and I feel satisfied with that.' "

Shortly afterwards, Blumenfeld noticed a change in Einstein's attitude. " 'I am against nationalism but in favor of Zionism,' he said. 'The reason has become clear to me today. When a man has both arms and he is always saying I have a right arm, then he is a chauvinist. However, when the right arm is missing, then he must do something to make up for the missing limb. Therefore I am, as a human being, an opponent of nationalism. But as a Jew I am from today a supporter of the Jewish Zionist efforts.' "

Einstein's support was to be complicated by the general situation in Germany. Support for assimilation was possibly even stronger among Jews there than it had previously been, partly as a result of the forces unleashed by the war, which tended to draw together all those living within the German Empire, partly as a reaction to what was considered the Jewish influence behind the Russian Revolution. Few wished to carry the policy as far as Einstein's colleague Haber, who had taken himself and his family into the Christian church. Yet there were many for whom the possibilities of Zionism had a double danger. It made more difficult their own attempts to become assimilated into the non-Jewish German community and it provided a weapon for those endemic anti-Semites whose attitude had helped to produce Zionism. Thus for every man who welcomed Einstein's espousal of the Zionist cause there was another among his friends who would warn that this was not really the way to further the cause of Jews in Germany; that pressure on them would be increased; and that if there were too much talk of a National Home outside Europe there would be increasing demands for Jews to be sent there.

The forces supporting assimilation were certainly strong, but so too were Einstein's feelings once he had become seized of the Zionist cause. Just how strong is shown by his letter of April 3, 1920, refusing to attend a meeting organized by the Central Association of German Citizens of Jewish Faith to help combat anti-Semitism in academic circles.

"I should gladly come if I believed it possible for such an undertaking to succeed," he wrote.

> First, however, the anti-Semitism and the servile disposition among us Jews in our own ranks would have to be combated by more knowledge. More dignity and more independence in our ranks! Not until we dare to regard ourselves as a nation, not until we respect ourselves, can we gain the esteem of others, or rather only then will it come of its own accord. There will be anti-Semitism in the sense of a psychological phenomenon as long as Jews come into contact with non-Jews—what does it matter? Perhaps we owe it to anti-Semitism that we can maintain ourselves as a race. I at least believe so.
>
> If I catch sight of an expression like "German citizens of Jewish faith" I cannot help smiling a little sadly. What is there to be found in this pretty label? What is Jewish faith? Does there exist a kind of unbelief by virtue of which one ceases being a Jew? There is not. But it suggests that the right people believe two things, i.e., (1) I don't wish to have anything to do with my poor (East European) Jewish brethren, and (2) I do not want to be taken for a child of my own people, but only as a member of a Jewish community.
>
> Is this sincere? Can the "Aryan" feel any respect for such underhand fellows? I am neither a German citizen, nor is there anything in me which can be designated as "Jewish faith." But I am a Jew and am glad to belong to the Jewish people, even if I do not consider them in any way God's elect. Let us calmly leave anti-Semitism to the non-Jew and retain our love for people of our kind.
>
> I hope that you will not frown on account of this confession. No harm or unkindness is meant.

Einstein was later to put his point of view even more pungently. "The German Jew who works for the Jewish people and for the Jewish home in Palestine no more ceases to be a German than the Jew who becomes baptized and changes his name ceased to be a Jew," he wrote in 1926. "The two attachments are grounded in realities of different kinds. The antithesis is not between Jew and German, but between honesty and lack of character. He who remains true to his origin, race, and tradition will also remain loyal to the state of which he is a subject. He who is faithless to the one will also be faithless to the other."

A further gloss on his position is given by a letter written on an unknown date in 1921 to the Prague pharmacologist Professor Starkenstein. Einstein stressed that denomination was itself unimportant, although for a Jew to embrace another faith was a symbolic action, indicating that he wished to cut himself off from his own people. Possibly he had Haber in mind. Freedom from any denomination at all was, however, a different matter. "I myself belong to no denomination and consider myself a faithful Jew," he went on. "In how far we Jews should consider ourselves as a race or a nation respectively, in how far we form a social community by tradition only, on this subject I have not arrived at a decisive judgment. It suffices that we form a social body of people which stands out more or less distinctly from the rest of humanity, and the reality of which is not doubted by anyone."

The lack of decision was shrewdly noted by Blumenfeld, whose frank account shows clearly the skill with which he brought Einstein into the Zionist camp. He realized that for Einstein, "Zionism and Palestine were only peripheral concerns," that these interests had not yet "become part of his specific pattern of life." Utilizing him for publicity purposes was thus a delicate matter and "was only successful if I was able to get under his skin in such a way that eventually he believed that words had not been put into his mouth but had come forth from him spontaneously."

If Einstein the Zionist thus found himself at odds with much of the Jewish community on matters of practical politics, he also had reservations about the character and methods of the key man in the Zionist movement. This was Chaim Weizmann, subsequently a good friend of Einstein but diametrically opposed to him in many ways. Weizmann was a Russian Jew who had emigrated to England before the war, became naturalized, and quickly achieved a position in the scientific world that owed nothing to his work as a propagandist for Zionism. In an ironic way Weizmann was the Allied counterpart of Fritz Haber. For while Haber found a method of supplying a blockaded Germany with unlimited explosives, Weizmann was a biochemist who discovered how one particular strain of bacterium could synthesize acetone, essential for the manufacture of the explosive cordite. On the outbreak of war he moved from Manchester University to government service. Subsequently he became director of Admiralty Laboratories under A. J. Balfour, First Lord of the Admiralty.

Thus Weizmann soon found himself well placed for staking the Zionist claim to Palestine. His connections with Whitehall increased still further as the naval war moved towards its crisis and as Balfour left the Admiralty for the Foreign Office in 1916. By September, 1917, his influence was such that the Prime Minister, "on Weizmann's representation of urgency, told Sutherland [one of Lloyd George's private secretaries] to put down 'Palestine' for the next War Cabinet." The Balfour Declaration followed on November 2. Thus it was in the accepted order of things that Weizmann represented the Zionist organization when this was given a hearing by the Council of Ten at the Peace Conference on February 27, 1919.

Positions of power are rarely gained or held by those who believe that all men are not only brothers but innocent ones. A good deal of ruthless wire pulling is required, a good deal of balancing and counter-balancing, and not occasionally the bland reassurance on facts which are not facts at all. All these, the common coin of getting things done, are required even of a statesman with the moral integrity of Weizmann. But to a man of Einstein's temperament this element of wheeling and dealing was repugnant. Thus, as Isaiah Berlin has noted,

> Weizmann's relationship with Einstein, despite their deep mutual admiration for each other, remained ambivalent; Weizmann was inclined to regard Einstein as an impractical idealist inclined to utopian attitudes in politics. Einstein, in his turn, looked on Weizmann as too much of a *Realpolitiker,* and was irritated by his failure to press for reforms in the [Hebrew] university away from what he

regarded as an undesirable American collegiate pattern. Nevertheless, they remained allies and friends to the end of their lives.

Along with these feelings which tended to qualify Einstein's enthusiasm for Zionism there was the essentially pacifist nature of his approach to the problems of the world. Even when it came to Zionism, a subject as emotionally close to his heart as anything ever was, he could never look on his opponents, in this case the Arabs, as the deep-dyed villains which the sentiments of the case demanded. He was all for the policy of live and let live. While many Zionists—possibly the majority of them—saw a Jewish National Home essentially as a political state created for political purposes, Einstein saw it rather as a cultural center. "For me," he wrote as late as 1938, "the value of the Zionist undertaking lies mainly in the educational and unifying effect on the Jews of different countries. I am not for the striving for a Jewish state, mainly because I am against the secularization (or becoming worldly) of Jewry." Many Zionists called for mass emigration to the Promised Land, but Einstein foresaw the way in which Arab opposition would be intensified. Thus the dichotomy which runs through so much of his life showed itself here also. To the demands of *Realpolitik* he would oppose the need for idealism; when force was demanded he would respond that pacifism was essential.

Despite these qualifications, however, he was drawn into the Zionist maelstrom by the climate of post-Armistice Germany, by the humiliations which the Jews from the east were suffering at the hands of Berliners, and by the impassioned advocacy of such German Zionists as Kurt Blumenfeld. His support had hardly been secured when a good chance of utilizing it arose.

Late in 1920 Weizmann decided to visit the United States to raise funds for the Keren Hayesod, to be formed in March, 1921, to take over from the Palestine Restoration Fund the main financial burden of constructive work. He quickly picked a strong party to accompany him. "I also approached Professor Albert Einstein, with special reference to the Hebrew University," he later wrote, "and to my great delight found him ready to help." It is clear from Blumenfeld's account and from Einstein's private correspondence that this was a description of his reaction more enthusiastic than accurate.

Blumenfeld had received a detailed telegraphed directive from Weizmann. "I was to stir up Einstein," he says,

> go with him to America, and there join in the propaganda for the Keren Hayesod. Einstein must be interested, above everything else, in the idea of the Hebrew University in Jerusalem.
>
> When I appeared before Einstein with this telegram he at first said No: "Do you think so much of the idea of a Hebrew University in Jerusalem?" It was unfortunate that I, for different reasons, was a bad advocate of the idea, and Einstein therefore said: "How is it that you are asking me to publicize an idea that you yourself do not wholeheartedly support? Besides, I consider that the role which is expected of me is an unworthy one. I am not an orator. I can contribute nothing convincing, and they only need my name which is now in the public eye."
>
> I did not reply, but read Weizmann's telegram aloud again. "It is irrelevant that we know what is necessary for Zionism today," I said. "We both know too little of all the factors involved. Wiezmann represents Zionism. He alone can make decisions. He is the president of our organization, and if you take your conversion to Zionism seriously, then I have the right to ask you, in Dr. Weizmann's name, to go with him to the United States and to do what he at the moment thinks is necessary."

Einstein had already begun to interest himself in politics and had joined the Republican League only a few days previously. But his concern with the peripheral left wing was parochial compared with the prospects that were now dangled before him. Did he really want to enter the dubious world of power politics which even he must have realized was the only world in which the great expectations of Zionism could be translated into reality? Surely his interrogation of the physical world would suffer? Surely it was all rather demeaning?

No doubt he pondered over these questions. If they had been asked two years previously he would almost certainly have given different answers. But he had emerged in the autumn of 1920 a different man from the almost lighthearted professor who only twenty-four months earlier had tried to talk the Berlin students into common sense while Born and Wertheimer had looked on. Now he was not only a scientist but one who might genuinely be able to influence world affairs. And by now he had watched the tide of anti-Semitism begin to rise again and had felt it lapping round his own feet in Berlin and Bad Nauheim. It seems more than likely that Lenard and the "Anti-relativity Company" were in his mind as he listened to Weizmann's telegram.

But there was also another factor. "I learned later," Weizmann has written, "that Haber had done all he could to prevent Einstein from joining me: he said, among other things, that Einstein would be doing untold harm to his career, and to the name of the institute of which he was a distinguished member, if he threw in his lot with the Zionists, and particularly with such a pronounced Zionist as myself." In Einstein's then state of mind, an appeal from a lapsed Jew who had helped the Germans so much in the war could have swung him in only one direction.

"To my boundless astonishment," Blumenfeld writes, "Einstein answered: 'What you say now is right and convincing. With argument and counterargument we get no further. To you Weizmann's telegram is a command. I realize that I myself am now part of the situation and that I must accept the invitation. Telegram Weizmann that I agree.'" Thus he prepared to take a major step towards the consolidation of his fame in America and of his notoriety in Germany as the focus of anti-Semitism.

Shortly after this meeting with Blumenfeld, Einstein wrote to Maurice Solovine, with whom he had kept up a desultory correspondence since the breakup of the Olympia Academy fifteen years earlier: "I am not going entirely willingly to America," he said, "but I am doing so only in the interests of the Zionists, who are obligated to ask for dollars for education in Jerusalem, and on this occasion I am to play the role of a little tin god and a decoy. If our places could be changed I would willingly let you go in my place." And to the same correspondent, shortly before he set off from Berlin, he wrote: "I, also, am not a patriot, and I firmly believe that the Jews, given the smallness and dependence of their colony in Palestine, will be immune from the folly of power."

As news of Einstein's acceptance leaked out, invitations from the United States began to arrive in Haberlandstrasse

—not only from Zionist organizations but from universities and other learned bodies eager to get the renowned Albert Einstein to explain his theories. By mid-March it must have been satisfactorily clear to Weizmann that whatever publicity would be coming to the Zionist cause would be doubled by the presence of Einstein.

However, all would not be plain sailing, and some of the problems are detailed in a letter which Blumenfeld wrote to Weizmann on March 15, 1921. This is extraordinarily revealing, showing as it does the way in which Einstein's enthusiasm for the Jewish cause was being manipulated, and highlighting his own ingenuous outlook, a characteristic which, it was clear, had to be put in the balance against the advantages of his name.

Einstein, Blumenfeld said, was no Zionist but he would always be willing to help at specific tasks so he should not be induced to join the organization. His interest arose from his aversion to assimilated Jewry. He had doubts about some of the Jewish leaders but there were none about the help which he would give to the efforts to be made in the United States. Already, at Elsa's request, 10,000 marks had been put at his disposal, and it was recommended that Weizmann should let him have further funds on the voyage. Einstein himself was worried about running up too many expenses, had seriously told his wife that he wanted to travel steerage, and had insisted that detailed accounts should be kept of all that was spent.

Then Blumenfeld gave a warning. Weizmann had been expecting Einstein to prepare speeches. But he was told to be particularly careful about this since Einstein was a bad speaker and often said things out of naïveté that caused trouble. In spite of this there was no doubt about his value, and Blumenfeld ended by saying how happy he was that he had aided the cause by winning over a man who would help to settle the American issue in their favor.

This issue was the difference in opinion between Weizmann and many leading Zionists as to how Zionist aims might best be pushed forward. On the question of tactics, many American Zionists, notably those led by Justice Brandeis, believed that the existing Zionist organization was adequate. Weizmann believed that in the long struggle ahead something more ambitious would be needed, and was already throwing his efforts into the creation of an enlarged Jewish Agency which would include not only Zionists but other Jews. Springing almost directly from this was the great contrast in the amount of cash which each group believed would be necessary. Brandeis and his supporters talked of raising $500,000 a year; Weizmann thought of $10,000,000. These divergent views might have been resolved more easily had it not been for the character of Weizmann, "overbearing and politically ruthless," according to one version of Brandeis' opinion. To many Americans he may well have looked like an embryonic dictator, carving out his own empire; to many European Jews who knew how close to the problems he had been, neither his ambition nor his ruthlessness seemed greater than was necessary.

The journey began on March 21, 1921, when the Einsteins left Berlin for Holland, where they were to embark on the *Rotterdam*. They were joined on board by the Weizmanns. "Einstein was young, gay, and flirtatious," says Mrs. Weizmann. "His wife, I recall, told me that she did not mind her husband's flirting with me as 'intellectual women' did not attract him; out of pity he was attracted to women who did physical work"—a remark substantiated by more than one of his intimate friends. During the voyage across the Atlantic, says Weizmann, Einstein "explained his theory to me every day and on my arrival I was fully convinced that he understood it." Weizmann utilized the journey to plan the tactics of his campaign.

From the comparative security of his home in Berlin, Einstein had already been burned by the hot wind of publicity, but only on arrival in New York did he meet its full blast. The effect was to last a lifetime and to give him a distrust of most newspapers, even though he showed an unexpected and masterly ease at handling a press conference when he took the trouble. First, he had to face the cameramen who came aboard with reporters as the ship docked, all of them anxious to forestall the official reception committee, which included New York's Mayor Hylan; Alfred E. Smith, soon to be elected Governor of New York State; and Fiorello La Guardia, president of the City Council. "I feel like a prima donna," said Einstein as he at last turned to the reporters and prepared for the worst.

One of the first questions had been a constant companion since November, 1919: "Can you explain relativity in a few sentences?" Ever anxious not to disappoint, and in this case doubly so out of loyalty to Weizmann, Einstein had an answer that became a classic. "If you will not take the answer too seriously, and consider it only as a kind of joke, then I can explain it as follows," he said. "It was formerly believed that if all material things disappeared out of the universe, time and space would be left. According to the relativity theory, however, time and space disappear together with the things."

From then on he had their confidence, a smiling, tousle-haired figure in his high wing collar and knitted tie, anxious to assure them that his theory would not change the ideas of the man in the street, claiming that every physicist who studied relativity could easily understand it, and as confounded as were his interrogators by the extraordinary interest which his work had aroused. "Well, gentlemen," he concluded, "I hope I have passed my examination."

There was the inevitable demand to know whether Mrs. Einstein understood the theory. "Oh, no," was the philosophical reply, "although he has explained it to me so many times—but it is not necessary to my happiness." She wished to protect him from the adulatory mob. "He does not like to be what you call a showcase," she explained. "He would rather work and play his violin and walk in the woods." And when he was deep into a problem, she added, "there is no day and no night."

The ordeal over, they went ashore. Awaiting them was more than the official reception committee. The Jewish areas of New York were gaily decorated, while Jewish Legionnaires who had fought with the British to liberate Palestine from the Turks were present in strength. Some of the crowds wore buttons with Zionist slogans, others waved the Jewish flag, then merely white and blue, without the star of David that it bears today.

What the crowds saw at the top of the gangway was Weizmann, smiling but stiff, almost a model for Lenin in physical features as in singlemindedness, and beside him the shorter figure of Einstein. He wore a faded gray overcoat, by no means new, and a black hat. In one hand he carried a briar pipe and in the other his violin. "He looked like an artist, a musician," wrote one reporter. "He is of medium height with strongly built shoulders, but an air of fragility and self-effacement." Under a broad, high forehead were the large and luminous eyes, almost child-like in their simplicity and unworldliness. "Great men, a very small family on earth, can unfortunately find nobody but themselves to imitate," Chateaubriand commented in his *Memoirs*. "At once a model and a copy, a real person and an actor playing that person, Napoleon was his own mime." In much the same way Einstein, the public figure now emerged from the chrysalis of the professor, unconsciously dropped into the role of Einstein playing Einstein.

The two men and their wives were driven between a police escort to the City Hall whose plaza was filled with more than 5,000 Zionists. Here they were formally received by New York, where there lived a third of all the Jews in the United States. And here, it had been tacitly arranged, Weizmann and Einstein would be given the freedom of the city.

At this point an unexpected hitch occurred. When the aldermen retired to vote the freedom of the city to their visitors, an Alderman Bruce Falconer objected. A dozen years previously, he pointed out, New York had granted its freedom to Dr. Cook, a gentleman whose claim to have reached the North Pole was as fraudulent as his earlier claim to have made the first ascent of Mount McKinley. How did they know that Einstein had really discovered relativity? Furthermore, while Weizmann was a British subject, Einstein was a German, a former enemy alien. Falconer successfully obstructed various attempts to push through the measure but his move was counterproductive. The following day the New York Senate in Albany gave Weizmann and Einstein the freedom of the state, without opposition. New York City eventually followed suit, while the Owasco Club, the democratic party organization of the Seventeenth Assembly District, passed a resolution noting that "the conduct of Alderman Falconer manifests a spirit of bigotry, narrowmindedness, and intolerance, and displays him as a champion of anti-Semitism, which is only a stepchild of anti-Americanism." Yet it is interesting to note that the resolution which gave Einstein the freedom of the state began—". . . Albert Einstein of Switzerland," a statement that conveniently ignored both his German birth and the fact that though he was a naturalized Swiss he was now also a German again.

As far as Einstein was concerned, there were three aspects to the tour that now followed. There was his involvement, inevitable although as slight as he could make it, in fund-raising and inter-Zionist argument. There was his own series of appeals for the Hebrew University, obviously closely linked with Weizmann's but launched at a slightly different level to a slightly different public. Thirdy there were his lectures on relativity, and the impression that they made on the American academic world.

From the first, it was clear that Weizmann's decision to invite Einstein had been more than justified. His appeals to the Jews of America struck deep down—even though many of them had radically different ideas on the financing of the Jewish Home. For he added more than the box-office draw of an international name and a mysterious theory. There was something romantic not only about his air of innocence but about the journey which had brought him from his study halfway round the world to what less than three years previously had been an enemy capital.

"To every person in America," says Frank, "it recalled the Holy Land and the legend of the Wandering Jew, thus striking a strongly responsive chord and evoking profound sympathies in many Christians." It needed no great stretch of the imagination to see in Einstein, trotting down the gangway with a pipe in one hand and a violin case in the other, the apotheosis of all that Jewry stood for. To the Americans, a nation of refugees, the figure had a double attraction.

As a member of the Weizmann party, Einstein could not stand aside entirely from the arguments about Jewish development in Palestine. But Weizmann had not ignored Blumenfeld's warning about Einstein's propensity for saying "things out of naïveté which cause us trouble." He had given his colleague broad hints about when to stay quiet. Einstein, for his part, kept himself well in hand. The classic example came on the evening of April 12, after Weizmann had spoken to 8,000 Jews at the 69th Regiment Armory. Einstein then rose. "Your leader, Dr. Weizmann, has spoken, and he has spoken very well for us all," he said. "Follow him and you will do well. That is all I have to say."

From the controversies that followed Weizmann's first

public appeal for funds on April 17 Einstein remained as aloof as possible. An open breach with the Brandeis party followed the next day. This was to be healed only after considerable wrangling, and it is difficult to estimate its effect on Weizmann's appeal. At a single meeting on April 20, $26,000 were donated and a total of $100,000 pledged. Next day a Keren Hayesod Bureau opened in Union Square and was visited by a constant stream of Jews giving cash—one man unrolling a thousand dollars worth of small notes and handing them over with the comment that he had saved them for his old age. However, it was not until years later that the larger contributions which were hoped for were extracted from American pockets, and it is clear both from the Einstein-Weizmann correspondence and from the recollections of Zionist historians that the results of the visit, though necessarily presented as successful, fell considerably short of what had been expected.

Meanwhile Einstein was addressing Jewish audiences on the needs of the Hebrew University, "the greatest thing in Palestine since the destruction of the Temple of Jerusalem," as he called it. The man who in Berlin had experienced the plight of Jews "knocking vainly at the doors of the universities of Eastern and Central Europe" was an ideal spokesman. "Others who have gained access to the areas of free research only did so by undergoing a painful, and even dishonoring process of assimilation which robbed them again and again of their cultural leaders," he said with feeling. "The time has now come for our spiritual life to find a home of its own." Here, speaking on his own ground, he could do no harm and much good, and after his first appeal Stephen Wise, rabbi of the Free Synagogue in New York who was later to become a close friend, pledged $10,000 for the university.

Einstein's lectures on relativity, which were to broaden the knowledge of his work in the United States, began on April 15 at Columbia University, which had awarded him the Barnard Medal the previous year. It was the first time he had spoken on relativity—or on anything else, it appears—to an English-speaking audience. He showed the same assured naturalness he used with allies and enemies, Presidents and street cleaners, Kings, Queens, and charwomen. "He several times brought chuckles and laughs from his audience by his references to the 'idiot' behavior of certain bodies in accelerated systems," the *New York Times* noted. "Also he caused much amusement when he wished to erase some diagrams he had drawn on the blackboard and made futile motions in the air with his hand until Professor Pupin came to his rescue."

At the City College of New York, where he lectured the following week, the lectures were translated. "I happened to be the most readily available person who understood both his language and his mathematics," writes Morris Raphael Cohen, "and so I was asked to translate his lectures. This gave rise to the altogether undeserved popular legend that I was one of the unbelievably few people in the world who understood the Einstein theory."

In Washington, where Einstein and Weizmann arrived soon afterwards, an unsuccessful attempt was made to read "a popular presentation of the relativity theory" into the *Congressional Record*. Here also they visited President Harding with a group from the National Academy of Sciences, at whose annual dinner Einstein spoke. The formal speeches went on and on, and as one scientist after another accepted the Academy's annual awards Einstein turned to his neighbor, the secretary of the Netherlands embassy who was representing the physicist Pieter Zeeman: "I have just got a new theory of eternity," he confided.

Another visit was to Princeton, where on Monday, May 9, an honorary degree was conferred and where he gave a lecture a day for the rest of the week. It was after one of these, during an evening discussion, that he heard of D. C. Miller's first announcement which appeared to refute the Michelson-Morley experiment. And here, believing that the truth did not lie in the convolutions demanded by Miller's results, he observed: "God is subtle but he is not malicious" ("Raffiniert ist der Herrgott, aber boshaft ist er nicht"). In Chicago, the next port of call, he made one contact which was greatly to affect his future. This was with Robert Millikan, who a few years previously had provided experimental evidence for Einstein's photoelectric equation. While Elsa was driven around the sights of Chicago with Mrs. Millikan, Einstein discussed the future of science with her husband.

Then, a few days before he was due to sail for Europe, leaving Weizmann to continue his Zionist work alone, the two men visited Cleveland. Most of the Jewish shops were closed for the occasion and the party was met at the Union Station by a 200-car parade headed by the band of the Third Regiment of the National Guard. "Only the strenuous efforts of a squad of Jewish war veterans, who fought off the people in their mad attempts to see them," the *New York Times* reported, "saved them from possible injury."

The near hysteria which had marked more than one phase of the visit was not entirely the result of the new-felt longing to be free which surged through the Jewish world with the hopes of a National Home raised by the Balfour Declaration, or of the intellectual cataclysm made by relativity. Both played their part. But both were reinforced by the extraordinary impact made by Einstein himself during what was for most practical purposes his first journey outside the academic world into the realm of the uninitiated. The curtains had parted and behind them there was seen not the austere and aloof leader of science, but an untidy figure carrying his violin, the epitome of the world's little man immortalized in different ways by Chaplin, Hans Fallada, and H. G. Wells' *Kipps*. Astonishment increased as it became clear that however steely keen Einstein's relentless dedication to science might be—and within the inner circle there was no doubt of that—here was the real article, genuinely humble, honestly surprised that so much fuss should be made of him. In Boston, where he was asked as part of a current "quiz" to give the speed of sound, he admitted he was sorry but he didn't know—and why should he, since it was a simple fact that could be looked up in a reference book? Speaking to the National Academy of Sciences, he said that "when a man after long years of searching chances upon a thought which discloses something of the beauty of this mysterious universe he should not therefore be personally celebrated. He is already sufficiently paid by his experience of seeking and finding."

For the Zionists the transparent sincerity of such remarks had turned out to be an invaluable asset, and as the Einsteins returned to Germany, breaking their journey in England, Weizmann had good reason to be satisfied. For Einstein, and his reputation, the results were more qualified. "Thank heaven, Yale did not give Einstein a degree," went a letter to Rutherford from Bertram Boltwood, then at the peak of his reputation. "We escaped that by a narrow margin. If he had been over here as a scientist and not as a Zionist it would have been entirely appropriate, but under the circumstances I think it would have been a mistake."

Back in Berlin, Einstein reflected on his experiences. There is no doubt that the Jews of America had given him a concept of Jewry quite different from the one he had grown up with in Europe. "It was in America," he wrote, "that I first discovered the Jewish people. I have seen any number of Jews, but the Jewish people I have never met either in Berlin or elsewhere in Germany. This Jewish people which I found in America came from Russia, Poland, and Eastern Europe generally. These men and women still retain a healthy national feeling; it has not yet been destroyed by the process of atomization and dispersion. I found these people extraordinarily ready for self-sacrifice and practically creative."

Einstein's optimism was further expressed when he spoke in Berlin's Bluthner Hall on work in Palestine a few days after his return, and in a letter to Ehrenfest on June 18 he noted that "our activities on behalf of the Hebrew University were very successful. . . . The university seems financially assured to the extent that the building of the particularly important medical facilities can soon be started. The middle classes, rather than the rich Jews, have made this possible and, in particular, the 6,000 Jewish doctors in America." This mood soon passed and the Zionist leader Selim Brodetsky, reporting on his visit to Einstein in Berlin shortly afterwards, relates that he was told "of the failure of his mission to the United States." Three months later Weizmann was writing almost plaintively asking Einstein to sign a letter to the Boston New Century Club where they had drummed up considerable support—"the Club has made difficulties regarding the handing over of the money collected; of the $20,000 promised, we have actually so far collected $4,000," he noted. The different views are not contradictory. Like the mythical bottle of whisky, half-full or half-empty, Weizmann's tour could be considered either failure or success according to expectations. But as the enthusiasm engendered by the visit began to slip away, the facts began to look less rosy. It was some years before the Hebrew University pulled in the really large contributions hoped for in 1921.

Einstein's already slightly jaundiced view of the tour was increased when he realized the price to be paid for the support gained. Forever the idealist, he could not stomach the shifts, the horse trading, and the accommodations necessary in an imperfect world. Above all, he could never reconcile himself to the fact that whoever pays the piper calls the tune: that the American Jews who provided most of the finance for the Hebrew University would in practice have a hand in the way it was run almost as powerful as the Board of Governors.

In 1921 this was still a small cloud on the horizon. Einstein remained the great Zionist capture; it followed therefore that he should be asked to visit Palestine on his return from the Far East early in 1923 and to give the inaugural address at the university. For Einstein himself the visit was a deeply emotional experience, doubly important to a man who had excluded emotion from his life whenever possible.

The Palestine Mandate, under which the former Turkish territory was administered by the British with the ultimate aim of creating a Jewish National Home, had been approved by the Council of the League of Nations only six months previously, and was not to become operative until the end of September, 1923. But the British High Commissioner had already been appointed, and Jewish immigration and reconstruction were being pushed ahead. The High Commissioner, with whom the Einsteins were to stay, was Sir Herbert, later Lord Samuel. Like Lord Haldane, he was both philosopher and statesman, a man who had been deeply moved by the implications of relativity, and one of the few outside the field of science to become a comparatively close friend. Samuel was not only a first-class administrator, he was also a Jew; and while his appointment had been intended to show the British government's favorable attitude towards Jewish aspirations, there were repercussions which only the most Machiavellian foresight could have predicted. For Sir Herbert was also a British official whose neutrality must be above suspicion. It was therefore almost inevitable that in the Jewish-Arab disputes that spattered the unhappy history of the country during the years of his appointment the High Commissioner should stress his impartiality by giving utmost consideration to the Arabs. In this he was no more than just; but among Jews it was often felt that he was so busy returning good for evil that he had little time to return good for good. Therefore his long friendship with Einstein, begun in the first months of 1923, was to be marked more than once by differences as to what should be done for Palestine.

Einstein arrived with his wife at Tel Aviv on February 2, 1923, and was greeted by Colonel Frederick Kisch, who had retired from the British army with a fine war record to join the Zionist Executive. "Found him rather tired as he had sat up all night," Kisch recorded in his diary, "but I later learned that this was his own fault, as he had insisted on traveling second class in spite of every effort to persuade him to go into a *wagon-lit* which had been reserved for him." Three days later he was formally received by the Palestine Zionist Executive. "He made," Kisch recorded, "a little speech explaining the nature of his brain which he said was such that he was afraid it would be unproductive work for him to attempt to learn Hebrew."

But there was no doubt about Einstein's almost embarrassing enthusiasm for Palestine—or of Palestine for him. This was shown the following day. That the most famous scientist in the world—if the most controversial one—should give such unqualified support to their efforts genuinely roused the inhabitants and emboldened them to think that the reward would be equally unqualified. Einstein responded with an answering enthusiasm. The interaction was shown when on February 6 he drove through streets lined with crowds of waving schoolchildren to a reception at the Lemel School organized by the Palestine Zionist Executive and the Jewish National Council. After he entered, there was, the *Palestine Weekly* reported, "no holding back the crowd who had assembled outside. The outer gates were stormed, and the crowd burst into the courtyard, and tried to force the inner gates which were stoutly held by three or four stalwarts."

Inside, Einstein was baring his soul. "I consider this the greatest day of my life," he said. "Hitherto I have always found something to regret in the Jewish soul, and that is the forgetfulness of its own people—forgetfulness of its being almost. Today I have been made happy by the sight of the Jewish people learning to recognize themselves and to make themselves recognized as a force in the world. This is a great age, the age of the liberation of the Jewish soul; and it has been accomplished through the Zionist movement, so that no one in the world will be able to destroy it."

The following day he was to perform his main task in Palestine: delivery of the inaugural address at the Hebrew University, which had been founded five years earlier as the British and Turkish guns still faintly boomed away fifteen miles to the north. Before the ceremony he had a long talk with Kisch, which reveals the state of his mind.

"Interview with Deedes," Kisch recorded; "then a walk back from Mount Scopus to the city with Einstein to whom I explained the political situation and some of the intricacies of the Arab question. Einstein spoke of Ussishkin's* attempt to persuade him to settle in Jerusalem. He has no intention of doing so, not because he would sever himself from his work and friends, but because in Europe he is free and here he would always be a prisoner. He is not prepared to be merely an ornament in Jerusalem."

At 4:30 the same afternoon some hundreds of men and women, including members of the consular corps and the newly created Palestine government and their wives, packed into the temporary building of the Hebrew University on Mount Scopus. "Many . . . like myself . . . could have no claim to understand his theory," wrote Helen Bentwich, wife of Norman Bentwich, then attorney general to the government. "But we all wanted to hear and meet this great man, probably to be able to say in the years to come that not only had we heard Einstein lecture about his theory, but that we had attended the first lecture given at the Hebrew University of Jerusalem."

The hall was hung with Zionist flags and the insignia of the twelve tribes. Above the platform hung the Union Jack with a portrait of the High Commissioner and a

*Menachem Ussishkin was president of the Zionist Executive and had been a member of the party which visited America in 1921.

Zionist flag with a portrait of Dr. Herzl, while from the ceiling descended a banner bearing the words *"Orah ve Torah"* ("Light and Learning").

Ussishkin introduced Einstein with the announcement that 2,000 years ago Titus and his avenging armies had stood where they now stood. But today they were inaugurating a temple of science. "Mount the platform which has been waiting for you for 2,000 years," he concluded grandly.

Einstein did so, delighting those present by giving what Samuel called "an opening sentence pro forma in a Hebrew that was evidently unfamiliar." Then he continued in French; and, at the end of the comparatively short address, repeated it in German. Nevertheless the first official words spoken from the university had been in Hebrew.

During the next few days Einstein toured the country, planting a tree in the garden on Mount Carmel outside Haifa and visiting the city's high school and technical college. "Suitably impressed by the work so far done," he wrote to Weizmann on a leaf torn from his notebook. "It would be of great benefit if teaching could start at the Tech. Coll. as everything is ready and the need is great. Here the difficulties are great, but the mood is confident and the work to be marveled at." In Tel Aviv he was created a free citizen and at a banquet held in his honor he spoke with an honesty that tact might have blue-penciled: "I have already had the privilege of receiving the honorary citizenship of the City of New York, but I am tenfold happier to be a citizen of this beautiful Jewish town." At Rishon Le Zion, which he visited from Jaffa, he promised to "rouse the Jewish world and tell them of the strength that has been invested here," adding that until his last hour he would "work for our settlement and for our country."

His enthusiasm for the opportunities which Palestine would now be able to offer was stressed as he walked on the Mount of Olives with the attorney general. "The Jews had produced no genius of rank in the nineteenth century save a mathematician—Jacoby—and Heine," he said, according to Bentwich. "The National Home in Palestine could release and foster their genius. For 2,000 years their common bond had been the past, the carefully guarded tradition. Now they had a new bond, the active cooperation in building up a country. Then he went on to talk of other things. He delighted in the beauty of the Arab peasant dress and the Arab village growing out of the rock, and equally in the beauty of life in Japan and in their sense of corporate union. The Japanese dinner made you understand the meaning of eternity. . . . On the journey from Japan, he had been thinking out a new theory of the relation of light to gravity. The ship gave the best conditions for thought; a regular life and no disturbing influence." And then, a decade before the same thought was to be awakened by solitude in England, Einstein commented: "For similar reasons he found lighthouses attractive; a man could be alone there."

Palestine strengthened his Zionist sinews, and the memory of it helped him during the difficult decade that lay ahead. When he dined with the attorney general and his wife, borrowing a violin and making up a quartet with Bentwich and his two sisters, he not only played remarkably well, but "looked so happy while he was playing that I enjoyed watching as much as listening," Mrs. Bentwich remembered. "We talked of books, and of one he said, with a happy twinkle in his eye: 'It's not worth reading. The author writes just like a professor.' "

This was but one side of the coin. The other was represented by the formality of Government House, by the mounted troops that accompanied the High Commissioner as he traveled with his guests, and by the boom of the cannon which echoed every time he left the official residence. All this worried him. He had already perfected a technique of behaving as if formality did not exist—a technique which was perfectly sincere but which at times gave a misleading impression of playing to the gallery or of being eccentric for eccentricity's sake. Elsa was also uncomfortable, but for her own reason. "I am a simple German housewife," she told Philipp Frank. "I like things to be cozy and comfortable and I feel unhappy in such a formal atmosphere. For my husband it is a different matter; he is a famous man. When he commits a breach of etiquette, it is said that he does so because he is a man of genius. In my case, however, it is attributed to a lack of culture."

Despite the contrasts between Samuel, the shrewd able statesman, and the less worldly Einstein, the two men were attracted to one another, and talking in the grounds of Government House their conversation ranged across the future not only of Israel but of relativity. Here Samuel quoted T. H. Huxley's famous remark: "Herbert Spencer's idea of a tragedy is a deduction killed by a fact." Einstein's reply was recorded by Samuel: "Every theory is killed sooner or later in that way. But if the theory has good in it, that good is embodied and continued in the next theory."

Einstein and his wife left Palestine for Europe in mid-February. His final impression, as he put it to Solovine in a letter that Easter, was that it would "become a spiritual center but will not be able to receive a big proportion of the Jewish people. I am, nevertheless, convinced that the colonization will succeed." His advice was severely practical. Kisch records that as he said good-bye to his visitor in Jerusalem, he asked Einstein "to let us know if during his tour he had observed that we were doing anything which in his opinion we should not do, or if we were leaving undone things which should be done. He answered: 'Ramassez plus d'argent' " ("Collect more money").

The journey to Palestine consolidated Einstein's feelings for Zionism and these remained strong—despite its nationalism, which he mistrusted as he mistrusted all nationalisms, despite its foundation stone of a religion which he could take no more seriously than he could take any other revealed religion. But there was a definite limit to the aid that he was prepared to give, and this was illustrated following his return to Europe. Later in the year Weizmann tried to coax him to London for a major Zionist meeting but was met with the plea that attendance at the League's committee meetings in Geneva would rule this out. In replying, on July 19, 1923, Einstein omitted to mention that he had by this time resigned from the committee for a second time and would not be going to Geneva at all that year.

Three months later, he felt it necessary to put down in black and white what he would do and what he would not. "I will do all that is asked of me, as long as I am not expected to travel around or to visit congresses," he wrote to Weizmann from Berlin on October 27. "I will gladly give my name and write letters, and talk to people *here*, but as for the rest, in order to preserve my rights as a thinker I have to stay quiet in order to work. (P.S. With this in mind I am prepared to join the J.A.) Therefore I cannot even now come to Holland for a meeting." But he showed sympathy. "I know the difficulties that are put in the way of your doing an already difficult job," he added. "It cannot be easy to be the Chosen of the chosen people."

Early the following year, he reinforced his attitude by refusing to make a second journey to the United States. "I have been there once and learned that the business was costly to me," he wrote on February 29. "In any case, I really cannot do any more. When one has dedicated one's life to thought, and is capable only of that, one should stick to it and should leave the 'worldlier' things to those who are better equipped to understand them." Instinctively, he wanted to stick to his physics. Emotionally, he was being tempted outside.

There were two other things which tended to make him qualify his support of Zionism. One was his belief that a first priority should be agreement with the Arabs. He was not alone in this opinion. "A few Jewish leaders, particularly Magnes, Hugo Bergmann, Ruppin, and Calvaresci, were convinced that the first political aim should be, not maximum immigration, but understanding with the Arabs," Norman Bentwich has written. "That conviction was expressed emphatically by Albert Einstein when I visited him in his cottage during my stay in Berlin in 1930. He would not remain associated, he said, with the Zionist movement unless it tried to make peace with the Arabs in deed as well as in word. The Jews should form committees with the Arab peasants and workers, and not try to negotiate only with the leaders." Earlier, in the *Jüdische Rundschau,* Einstein spelled out the lesson, saying that Jews were almost always forming a national group of certain characteristics. "This seems regrettable to Jews such as I, who consider membership of the human species as an ideal possible to attain even though difficult." As Arab feelings hardened, as Mandate policy appeared to be increasingly swayed by pro-Arab sentiment, and as practical Zionist aims were narrowed to nation-state or nothing, such internationalist and pacifist learnings began to make Einstein's position within the Zionist movement frequently difficult and sometimes anomalous.

There was also his guerrilla battle with the management of the Hebrew University, which continued from the university's formal opening in 1925 until the summer of 1934, a battle fought largely against the influence of Judah Magnes, the virtual ruler of the university who exercised his power in line with the U. S. interests which had so largely financed it.

Some months after Einstein gave his inaugural address early in 1923, the Institute of Chemistry was set up. The Institute for Microbiology followed in 1924. Early in April, 1925, the university was formally inaugurated by Lord Balfour and its property, until then vested in the Zionist organization, was subsequently transferred to a nine-man Board of Governors which met in Tel Aviv.

Einstein was elected one of the governors and the board met under his chairmanship in Munich in September, 1925. Here it was enlarged. An Academic Council was set up, and a "Palestine Executive" was created so that in future the university could almost be said to have two masters, one in London under the stern eye of Weizmann who was to be chairman of the board for the rest of his life, the second in Jerusalem under the chancellor who, as the man on the spot, alwavs had the option of acting first and asking afterwards. The chancellor was Judah Magnes.

Magnes exercised considerable influence in the Jewish community in New York, where he had been a rabbi before the First World War. He had been an uncompromising pacifist, critical both of Weizmann's work for the British Admiralty and of his willingness to base Zionist hopes on the promises of an imperial power. Thus it would not have been surprising if he and Einstein had been drawn together, two birds of the same feather. Yet during the decade between 1925 and 1935 the cards fell otherwise. Weizmann supported the choice of Magnes as chancellor; Einstein opposed it.

The battle was fought on gentlemanly lines, but with a good deal of hard hitting, and has the fascination of all battles which are struggles not of right against wrong but of right against right. The issue, which Weizmann was to admit to Einstein with astonishing frankness, was a simple one. For all practical purposes it was the Americans who had financed the Hebrew University. Magnes was their "nominee," and it was useless to complain about his performance in office. Einstein did complain—in general about Magnes' lack of academic experience and in particular about the way in which, from 1925 onwards, he ran the university.

The trouble started at the Munich meeting. Magnes later claimed that "when Einstein entered . . . he said: 'I find myself here among many financiers from America.' They were in fact myself, Judge Mack, and Dr. Schloessinger. It was on this occasion that difficulties were created with me at the beginning."

There were many difficulties, not the least delicate of which concerned the minutes of the Munich meeting. The situation is made clear by a letter which Einstein wrote to Magnes on December 29, 1925. "I possess the minutes of the meeting in Munich of the Board of Governors, which you have circulated, and feel obliged as the president of that meeting to protest strongly against the sending of these second minutes," he complained. "It goes against all business practice that after the acting secretary has circulated the minutes a member should take it upon himself to circulate to other members a different set of minutes differing on essential points, with the claim that these be the official minutes of the meeting." He went on to use the word "intolerable" and ended by demanding that the Magnes minutes be withdrawn.

Magnes declined. He was left in possession of the field, and Einstein wrote to him somewhat despairingly. "You declined—though politely—to withdraw the invalid minutes which you have no right to circulate. The contents belie the actual resolutions passed. In the circumstances I feel that it is useless to deal further with you."

However, he still continued to work for the good of the university, visiting Paris in January, 1926, to lecture on it before the Franco-Palestine Society and sparing for Zionist activities whatever time he could squeeze from his work. But a man in Einstein's position, brought onto committees and governing boards for the prestige of his name rather than for what he was expected to do, could always threaten to play the strong card of resignation. This he now did, in the first of a series of actions that strangely mirrors his indecisive turnabouts with the League committee.

Early in the summer of 1926 Weizmann visited Berlin

to discuss the unhappy university situation. Any ambiguity in Einstein's attitude was removed by a letter he wrote to Weizmann on July 6. "You will understand," Weizmann replied immediately,

> that my colleagues and I who discussed the situation with you in Berlin were most upset about its contents. Only a few days ago we discussed within the circle of the Zionist Executive that whatever it may cost we must, above all, avoid your resignation. A few days ago I wrote to Dr. Magnes and made it clear that under no circumstances will the Board of Governors allow you to resign because of him. I pointed out to him—without going into the details of your circulated address at the Munich Conference—that he cannot continue to act in this high-handed fashion with his continuous harking on the American moneybags, and that he would be more useful to the university were he not continuously dependent on the moods and threats of the donors. I think he will understand my hints, and I feel it is quite possible that when he receives your letter as well as mine he will feel it necessary to resign. I am quite determined, as I mentioned to you in Berlin, to stand behind you in this, even though your reasons—mentioned verbally in Berlin—may be somewhat inconvenient to me. But I am prepared to do this as I am fully convinced that your diagnosis of the situation is correct and that sooner or later Dr. M. will have to be got rid of.

Weizmann concluded by reiterating his appeal that Einstein should not resign, an act which would only leave Magnes in undisputed control. Einstein acquiesced, at least for the time being. But eighteen months later, on January 8, 1928, he felt it necessary to complain in stronger terms, noting to Weizmann that "in order to preserve the apparent authority of the Board of Governors, we have had constantly to accept and pass *faits accomplis*. . . ." Furthermore, there was a new proposal that Magnes should not only be head of administration but also the acadamic chief of the university.

As chairman of the board, Weizmann had mixed feelings. "Our income," he later stressed to Einstein, "is entirely from voluntary subscribers, and we had to depend on Magnes—as you yourself have admitted—because Magnes could secure at any rate a considerable proportion of the budget. The same argument covered even the choice of professors by the Board of Governors, who had to adopt the suggestions of those who controlled the purse of the university." To Weizmann, half a university was better than none. Einstein disagreed, and in his letter of January threatened to resign from the board unless action was taken within a year. Should this not happen, he went on, "I shall feel it my duty to sever all connections with the university and to say so publicly. It would be much better if we waited a generation before founding a Hebrew University, rather than, under the pressure which is apparent, build a botched-up one today."

These were tough words. They were implemented a few months later, although Einstein's concern for the university forced him to conceal this from the world at large. Weizmann wrote in midsummer, proposing what Einstein subsequently described as compromises. He did not agree with them. And on June 14, 1928, he wrote that in the circumstances he thought it best to retire completely from the university's affairs. "I will refrain from an official resignation from the Board of Governors and the Academic Council despite my earlier intentions because I do not wish to add to the possible failure of the university's development."

Six days later he decided to go. "Since you have kept me so fully informed on the development of university matters I most certainly feel it unnecessary for you and Mr. Brodetsky to visit me here," he wrote from Berlin. "As things stand I feel it impossible to be responsible any longer for matters concerning the university. Thus I ask you to strike me from the Board of Governors and the Academic Council and to inform the members of both accordingly. The public will certainly not be informed of this step by me." To Brodetsky, vice-chairman of the board, he wrote in explanatory terms. "Among my talkative Jewish brothers I appear like a wild man who can make himself understood only by means of gestures," he said.

> You must interpret my resignation in the same way, and not to a lack of mutual understanding. Even if I never see the day when I can revoke this act, I shall never cease to consider the welfare of the Jerusalem university as being

> close to my heart. I believe I was right to follow my instinct, without thinking too much—it has been the best way till now. I agree that you and Weizmann's conciliatory attitude may have been justified by your political needs. The main thing is that we all have the same aim: service to the university. I hope that my method will lead to the same fine end.

Einstein's genuine concern for the university was a measure of his own, individualistic Zionism. However much he might disagree on tactics, he kept in mind "the same fine end."

Thus Einstein was among those invited to attend, and to speak at, the crucial Sixteenth Zionist Congress held in Zurich in August, 1929. In the words of Weizmann's invitation, the congress would "be of an unusually momentous character in view of the fact that it will be called upon to ratify the measures taken by the Zionist Executive for the enlargement of the Jewish Agency, so that it may be possible for the first meeting of the Council of the Agency to be held immediately after the congress."

Einstein was, as always, only too happy to visit Zurich. He took the opportunity of visiting Mileva and his children, telling Eduard, who asked why he had come, that he was attending a Jewish conference and adding: "I am the Jewish Saint." Although he appears to have put up at the Grand Dolder Hotel on the Zurichberg, he was glad to shock Sir John and Lady Simon by telling them: "I am staying with my first wife." He visited the shop where he had bought "penny cigars" as a student. And he took the trolley car to visit his old landlady, Frau Markwalder, insisting that she should not be told of his coming since he "did not want to play the great man."

He had been invited to the congress because, as Weizmann assured him, he would "greatly enhance the importance of the proceedings and afford considerable gratification to all supporters." This was so, although he also gave great support to Weizmann whose name he quite justifiably linked with that of Herzl himself and whose past work, he said, gave him a moral right to influence their future. There had been bitter talk of "abdication" to the Jewish Agency, and it was claimed that the influential half of the new organization was concerned only with a much watered-down version of real Zionism. Little of this argument came through at the congress, although it is significant that in his speech Einstein, after speaking of "the brave and dedicated minority who call themselves Zionists," went on to say "we others. . . ."

The actual signing of the concordat with the enlarged Jewish Agency on August 12 was a moving moment. As it was completed Einstein took a sheet of Dolder Hotel notepaper from his pocket and wrote on it. "An diesem Tage ist die Saat Herzls und Weizmanns in wunderbarer Weise gereuft. Keiner von den Anwesenden blieb unbewegt." ("On this day the seed of Herzl and Weizmann has borne wonderful fruit. No one present was unmoved.") He pushed the note across the table to Weizmann, who added: "Mille amitiés. Je t'embrasse."

The Zurich meeting marked a climax in Zionist endeavor and, for overlapping reasons, the end of one phase of Einstein's support. The enlarged Jewish Agency with Weizmann at its head had barely come into existence when serious anti-Jewish riots broke out in Palestine. On September 11, Louis Marshall, who had been a mainstay of the non-Zionist section of the agency, died after an operation. The following month the Wall Street crash cut the hopes of major U. S. support and at the same time, by triggering off the great depression in Europe, provided the cue for the nationalist and largely anti-Semitic forces waiting in the wings of the Weimar Republic.

None of these developments directly affected Einstein, although they increasingly put him at odds with many orthodox Zionists. The complexities of the position were emphasized by Brodetsky, who spoke in Berlin in 1929. "Einstein was present," he said, "but I am afraid that what I said was not well received. I told them in the best German I could manage what we demanded of the Mandatory government, and I said that Arabs who had murdered Jews must be dealt with according to the law. The audience was shocked. Einstein complained to me afterwards that I had spoken like Mussolini. I had shown no spirit of conciliation; I had demanded that Arab murders should be punished. Most German Zionists agreed with Einstein."

Einstein's own reaction was given in a letter to Weizmann on November 25, 1929. He noted that "our leaders give me cause for concern," and then went on to criticize Brodetsky's Berlin speech. "The economic and psychological problems of the Judeo-Arabic symbiosis were completely bypassed, but handled as an episode of conflict," he said.

> This was even more damaging, as the more level-headed listeners would be totally convinced of incorrect facts. . . . Should we be unable to find a way to honest cooperation and honest pacts with the Arabs, then we have learned absolutely nothing during our 2,000 years of suffering, and deserve all that will come to us. Above all, in my opinion, we must avoid leaning too much on the English. If we fail to reach real cooperation with the leading Arabs, we will be dropped by the English, not perhaps formally but *de facto*. And they will, with their traditional "religious eye-opening," claim themselves innocent of our *débâcle,* and not raise a finger.

From Weizmann there came a pained reply. It brought a response from Einstein in which he stuck to his guns but did his best to be conciliatory. "I really believe that many opportunities have been missed here," he ended, "but we should consider them and not fight among ourselves. After all, even if we were not as good as defenseless it would be unworthy of us to maintain a nationalism *à la Prussienne.* Don't answer me now; you need your strength too much. I will keep quiet as much as I can and not meddle in anything."

The extent to which Einstein was not only willing but apparently eager to conciliate the Arabs, whatever provocation they might offer, was based not only on the expediency of working with the British but on a belief that turning the other cheek was morally right and practically workable. This tended to alienate him from at least a section of the Zionist movement. Yet in other ways events pushed him more firmly into the movement. From 1930 onwards, as he saw the growth of anti-Semitism in Europe and as his hopes of European peace began to fade, a sharper edge was given to the Zionist question by his own personal experiences. He now began to take a new pride in his background and on the evening of January 29, 1930, actually appeared in a Berlin synagogue, playing his violin in black skullcap with the augmented choir of the new building, to raise contributions for a Jewish community welfare center. He had once looked on assimilation as a mistake; now he began to think of it as an impossibility.

CHAPTER 15

PREPARING FOR THE STORM

By the early months of 1929, Einstein was recovering from his collapse of the previous spring. He had, says his stepson-in-law, Rudolf Kayser, "been very patient in his suffering. He never complained about the tediousness of his rest cure. Sometimes, indeed, he seemed to enjoy the atmosphere of the sick room, since it permitted him to work undisturbed." Of his long convalescence Einstein himself said in March, 1929: "Illness has its advantage; one learns to think. I have only just begun to think." He was still weak, his face drained of color so that he looked very different from the normally almost boisterous Einstein. Nevertheless it was clear that he was recovering. The man responsible was Janos Plesch, whose quick diagnosis and simple remedy had done the trick.

Plesch, who was to dedicate his *Physiology and Pathology of the Heart and Blood Vessels* to Einstein, was volatile and high-spirited, ambitious and successful. In some ways he was the complete contrast to Einstein who, in a letter commenting on a draft of his old friend's autobiography, wrote on February 3, 1944: "Finally my judgment about your work and yourself: talented to the fingertips, acutely sensitive and receptive, fine of feeling but disorderly and lacking a sense of duty. A genuine angel who was born fallen from heavenly grace through disorderliness and vanity." Yet for more than a quarter of a century the two men remained firm and mutually critical friends, a contrast in opposites in some way reminiscent of the friendship between Churchill and Lindemann.

When Einstein began to grow strong once more, he was past the age at which a scientist might be expected to produce original work; it was almost time to think of the administrative "plums" that academic life offered. After all, he was a European before he was a German, a man whose friendships, private and professional, linked him with the neighboring countries of Holland, Switzerland, and France; if he feared that the breeze of anti-Semitism blowing across Germany might soon rise to gale force, he could take any of the appointments in Leiden, Zurich, or Paris that would be offered at the drop of a hint. He did nothing of the sort. He not only continued the good fight against indeterminacy in physics where Born and Heisenberg could already claim substantial victories, but pressed vigorously on with what had for almost a decade been his main preoccupation, the construction of a field theory uniting the forces of electromagnetism and gravity.

And while he kept his European friendships in good repair he stretched out to make fresh and important contacts in both Britain and the United States. He wanted to get on with his work. He wanted to help push Europe away from the precipice of war. But as his fiftieth birthday came and went he seems to have felt the future, to have sensed that the Wehrmacht would one day reach the Channel and Atlantic coasts, and that in Europe the best he could hope for would be a place behind the wire. His work continued in Berlin; but from 1929 onwards there were increasing glances over the shoulder to countries not only beyond the Reich but beyond the continent itself.

The most important item in this work was his search for a unified field theory. He had studied the forces of electromagnetism and produced the Special Theory, a new and more accurate yardstick for measuring the characteristics of the physical world. He had studied the force of gravity, found it to be not quite what men had believed it to be, and had produced the General Theory. But, as he wrote in *Nature*, "the conceptual foundations of the [General] Theory have no relations with the electromagnetic field. These facts suggest the following question. Is it not possible to generalize the mathematical foundations of the theory in such a way that we can derive from them not only the properties of the gravitational field, but also those of the electromagnetic field?"

Some men answered this question with an unqualified "No." Wolfgang Pauli, who believed that such a marriage of the laws of electromagnetism and of gravitation was impossible, summed it up: "What God hath put asunder no man shall ever join." Others were more optimistic, notably Hermann Weyl and Eddington, both of whom produced plausible but by no means satisfactory theories which attempted to unify the two fields. One thing appeared certain: the scale of the task being attempted. "If the unification of physical theories was finally possible," said André Mercier years later, when such a prospect still looked remote, "its possession would put the human spirit in possession of an ideal instrument for making it master of the intellectual world. The scholar would find himself both powerful and bored, like an absolute monarch whose ideas could not be undone by human stupidity."

Einstein set out on the formidable venture soon after he had completed the General Theory and his correspondence of the immediate postwar years is spattered with references to it. In 1923 he published a preliminary paper on the subject based on an idea already put forward by Eddington; then, settling down after the return from his travels, gave the problem increasing attention. By 1925 he was able to confide to Millikan in Pasadena: "I am working with every effort on the wider shaping of the theory connecting gravitation and electricity. This theory is mathematically very evident; but I do not know if one can have confidence in it from a physical standpoint." His efforts were soon given a further spur by the birth of quantum mechanics; for it was part of his lifelong but unfilled hope that a unified field theory would help to remove the new, and for him uncongenial, statistical element which formed part of the new physics.

In some ways he was embarking on a search for the physicists' Hesperides, a scientific suicide mission on which even an Einstein might fail. This is perhaps more certainly the view today, when it is generally felt that the structure of the universe cannot be described by using a single set of equations. Yet even in the 1920s the prospects looked poor. Einstein himself knew this and the explanation he gave late in life for devotion to this particular task was as relevant in 1929 as in 1949. "He agreed that the chance of success was very small," as he told a colleague, Professor Taub of Berkeley, "but that the attempt must be made. He himself had established his name; his position was assured, and so he could afford to take the risk of failure. A young man with his way to make in the world could not afford to take a risk by which he might lose a great career, and so Einstein felt that in this matter he had a duty."

One paper giving the outline of a unified field was published in the *Proceedings* of the Prussian Academy of Sciences in 1928—probably the paper which caused Elsa to write of her husband to a friend: "He has solved the problem whose solution was the dream of his life." Then, on January 10, 1929, the Academy announced that Einstein had submitted a new paper on a unified field theory which was being examined. This immediately aroused the interest of the world, and not only because the Academy appeared to be suggesting that something important was coming. Einstein was by this time approaching his fiftieth birthday and the world was tickled by the fact that towards the end of his fiftieth year the man who had "caught light bending" might have perfected a set of equations which would, in the popular phrase, "solve the riddle of the universe."

It was announced that the paper would be published at the end of the month and extensive, ingenious, but unsuccessful efforts were made by the world's newspapers to secure an advance copy. In an age when liaison between newspapers and leading scientists was less happy than today, distortions and absurdities were more apt to creep in, and these were particularly irksome to Einstein, who knew that a real understanding of his work was beyond most laymen and many scientists. It was left to the chief Berlin correspondent of the *New York Times*, for which Einstein had developed a particular fondness, to explain that the spate of telephone calls and requests were solely the result of the theory whose publication was to be completed within a few days. Einstein could only murmur: "My God."

He was, however, persuaded to give an interview to the *Daily Chronicle*. The result was a nonmathematical explanation of what the theory was trying to do and a striking example of Einstein's ability to give explanations "so simple that a child could understand them." "For years," he said,

> it has been my greatest ambition to resolve the duality of natural laws into unity. This duality lies in the fact that physicists have hitherto been compelled to postulate two sets of laws—those which control gravitation and those which control the phenomena of electricity and of magnetism. . . . Many physicists have suspected that two sets of laws must be based upon one general law, but neither experiment nor theory has, until now, succeeded in formulating this law. I believe now that I have found a proper form. I have thought out a special construction which is differentiated from that of my relativity theory, and from other theories of four-dimensional space, through certain conditions. These conditions bring under the same mathematical equations the laws which govern the electromagnetic field and those which govern the field of gravitation. The relativity theory reduced to one formula all laws which govern space, time and gravitation, and thus it corresponded to the demand for simplification of our physical concepts. The purpose of my work is to further this simplification, and particularly to reduce to one formula the explanation of the field of gravity and of the field of electromagnetism. For this reason I call it a contribution to "a unified field theory." . . . Now, but only now, we know that the force which moves electrons in their ellipses about the nuclei of atoms is the same force which moves our earth in its annual course about the sun, and is the same force which brings to us the rays of light and heat which make life possible upon this planet.

The *Daily Chronicle* interview appeared on January 26. The unified field paper was to be published four days later and it now dawned on some newspapermen that its transmission by telephone or cable to staff who were as innocent of science as many scientists were innocent of newspapers would present abnormal difficulties. It had dawned slightly earlier to John Elliott, head of the *New York Herald Tribune*'s Berlin office. On his advice, a number of physicists from Columbia University were brought into the New York office for the occasion. Meanwhile, Elliott in Berlin sent a code to New York, which allowed the mathematical and scientific symbols to be cabled without fear of error. All went as planned on the thirtieth. When the Einstein paper arrived Elliott himself began the cabling, with the Columbia men in the New York office carrying out decipherment as the cable copy arrived.

The paper for which the press had been waiting consisted of six pages covered by fairly large print and including thirty-three equations. "To the layman," commented *The Times'* Berlin correspondent, "the paper conveys next to nothing." This was not surprising since, as Eddington noted, "for the present, at any rate, a nonmathematical explanation is out of the question, and in any case would miss the main purpose of the theory, which is to weld a number of laws into a mathematical expression of formal simplicity." Einstein himself did the next best thing. He wrote a 3,000-word two-part article, which was published in both the *New York* and the London *Times*, and which outlined "the chain of discovery." The most important feature of the new theory was its hypothesis that the structure of four-dimensional space could be described in terms of a synthesis of Riemannian and Euclidean geometry. On this rested the erection of unitary field laws for gravitation and electromagnetism. It was new, it was interesting, but during the next few years informed opinion tended to support the view of Eddington. "For my part," he wrote,

> I cannot readily give up the affine picture, where gravitational and electrical quantities supplement one another as belonging respectively to the symmetrical and antisymmetrical features of world measurement; it is difficult to imagine a neater dovetailing. Perhaps one who believes that Weyl's theory and its affine generalization afford considerable enlightenment may be excused for doubting whether the new theory offers sufficient inducement to make an exchange.

Einstein himself was soon dissatisfied and within a year was working on a fresh theory with a new assistant, Dr. Walther Mayer, an Austrian brought to see him in Berlin after publication of a book which Einstein greatly admired—*Lehrbuch der Differentialgeometrie*. There was at first some difficulty in getting support for Mayer—possibly an indication of the Kaiser Wilhelm's long memory of Einstein's attitude during the war—but eventually money for him was found by the Josiah Macy Jr. Foundation of New York. He then moved from Vienna to Berlin for what was to be more than three years of collaboration, and in October, 1931, the Macy Foundation issued details of a new unified field theory from Einstein and Mayer.

This too was eventually abandoned, as were the other attempts which Einstein continued to make for the rest of his life—most of them produced, as he wrote to an old friend, "in an agony of mathematical torment from which I am unable to escape."

The 1929 theory was published only a few weeks before his fiftieth birthday. This was to see the publication—although not in Germany—of what can almost be described as an authorized biography. The circumstances of publication were unusual. One of Einstein's two stepsons-in-law, Rudolf Kayser, was author as well as journalist and had a deep interest in philosophy. He got on well with his stepfather-in-law and as the fiftieth birthday approached Kayser asked if he could write Einstein's life. Einstein consented. But it was clearly a reluctant consent which he gave. For his wish to help his stepson-in-law had to struggle with his strong distaste for personal publicity. The result was a compromise that misled the reader. For the biography's author was disguised under the pseudonym of "Anton Reiser," and only the slightest hint of his identity was given in Einstein's foreword. "The author of this book," it said,

> is one who knows me rather intimately in my endeavor, thoughts, beliefs—in bedroom slippers. I have read it to satisfy, in the main, my own curiosity. What interested me was not a desire to know what I am or look like, but rather another's avowal of what I am.
>
> I found the facts of the book duly accurate, and its characterization, throughout, as good as might be expected of one who is perforce himself and who can no more be another than I can.
>
> What has perhaps been overlooked is the irrational, the inconsistent, the droll, even the insane, which nature, inexhaustively operative, implants in an individual, seemingly for her own amusement. But these things are singled out only in the crucible of one's own mind.
>
> This is as it should be. For, otherwise, how could the isolation of distance be approximated.

As far as it went this was fair enough, but it gave no indication that, as Reiser subsequently said, its factual contents rested entirely on personal information from Einstein.

Einstein's reaction to such biographies was apparent when, two years after the publication of Kayser's book, he wrote to David Reichinstein, a scientist whom he had known before the war in Zurich. Reichinstein had prepared a hotchpotch of a biography in which factual details of Einstein's life were interlarded with his own views on Zionism and the Jews, and with an attempt to give "A Piture of His Life and His Conception of the World." "Generally," Einstein wrote to him,

> I feel that it is in bad taste if biographical or autobiographical material is published while the person concerned is still living. The only exceptions concern the presentation of events or situations which the person concerned has allowed to be pushed into the background. I have also forbidden the publication of the Reiser book in the German language, and on the other hand have given you permission to publish your book in foreign languages. The latter I also consider, in fact, to be in bad taste. In both cases, however, it serves as an excuse that the authors really want to get the money and cannot wait until I am dead.

He then put forward a point that hinges directly on his relations with the Germans. "Apart from the aversion concerned solely with taste," he continued, "I cannot reconcile myself to publication in the German language, since this would alienate people from my personal background." His efforts were frustrated, and Reichinstein's book appeared in German as well as in Czech and English. But Kayser's life was different; and the book that rested "entirely on personal information from A. E." was not published in Germany.

Einstein's ambivalence to the Germans was equaled by their ambivalence to him, illustrated by the experience of his fiftieth birthday. On the one hand there was such international fame that he was driven to the refuge of Janos Plesch's house at Gatow by journalists who wanted a birthday interview. The German Chancellor described him as "Germany's great savant." The University of Paris conferred an honorary degree which he received later in the year, staying in the German embassy and meeting Briand with whom he discussed the need for Franco-German friendship. The Zionists announced that they were to plant an "Einstein wood" near Jerusalem. To the apartment in Haberlandstrasse there came presents from great men and small men alike—the first which Einstein acknowledged being an ounce of tobacco, sent by a German laborer with the apology that it was "a relatively small amount but gathered in a good field." To many friends he sent a mimeographed copy of his own doggerel verse, slipping it in the post without a covering letter:

> Everyone shows their best face today,
> And from near and far have sweetly written,
> Showering me with all things one could wish for
> That still matter to an old man.
> Everyone approaches with nice voices
> In order to make a better day of it,
> And even the innumerable spongers have paid their tribute.
> And so I feel lifted up like a noble eagle.
> Now the day nears its close and I send you my compliments.
> Everything that you did was good, and the sun smiles.

It was signed, as usual, "Peccavit," followed by signature and date.

Yet these birthday celebrations took place beneath the shadow of a significant tragicomedy. Some of those who played important roles in it are unindentified although the events in which they took part were a warning of things to come not lost on Einstein.

Early in 1929 Dr. Plesch approached the Berlin authorities, whom he describes as being typical middle and lower middle class. "I had to explain to Boess, the Mayor of Berlin, who and what Einstein was before I could convince him that his city numbered a really great man amongst its inhabitants and that it was his Council's obvious duty to show some recognition of the fact," he has written. "I am sure the worthy Boess was not entirely satisfied with what I told him, and pursued his inquiries further as to who this Einstein was. Apparently the result was satisfactory, for he finally agreed with me that it would be a good idea to acknowledge Einstein's birthday by presenting him with a house and garden as a mark of the deep esteem in which he was held by the Berlin municipality." This appears to be pitching the intellectual level of Berlin disparagingly low, but the outcome suggests that the judgment was justified.

Einstein's love of small boats had remained from the days when he had sailed the Zurichsee, tacking back and forth with the splendid panorama of the Alps before him. What better, the Berlin Municipal Council therefore decided, than to choose for him a country villa on one of the Berlin lakes? He was known to enjoy the Havel River and it was announced that as a birthday gift he would be presented with a fine house on its banks, a little way upstream from its junction with the Wannsee. Illustrated Berlin magazines quickly printed photographs of the "Einstein House" set among pines. Only when Elsa visited the site to make domestic inquiries did she learn that the house was already occupied. The innhabitants furthermore had no intention of leaving, even for a successor as illustrious as Einstein.

The Berlin Council certainly owned the property they had presented; but they had already let it on an inalienable lease. Realizing this, they changed their plans and hastily announced that a nearby plot would be presented to Einstein. Significantly, the gift was now to consist only of the land; Einstein would have to build his own house at his own expense. To this he readily agreed—only to be faced with another difficulty. For when other property on the estate had been leased, it had been agreed by the Council that no further building would be allowed to disturb the amenities or the view. Einstein might get his land; he would not be allowed to build on it.

At this point, doubts as to Berlin efficiency became mixed with darker suspicions. These were increased when the Council selected yet a third plot, only to discover after the bequest was announced that the property was not theirs to present. German humor is not always of its legendary stodginess and the Council was quickly made a laughing stock. To resolve the problem, Einstein was asked to select his own site; the Council would pay for it. Elsa was not long in choosing a site in the village of Caputh, a few miles from Potsdam. The Council agreed to the choice and a motion for the purchase of the land was moved at the next session. At last all seemed to be settled.

But now a member of a leading nationalist party came into the open. Did Einstein deserve this municipal gift, he demanded? The Council, forced to the vote, did not know. The subject was moved forward for further discussion at the next meeting.

It is difficult to disentangle the varying parts played in the sorry business by muddle, red tape, and the internal politics of the Berlin authorities. "The decisive power," says Frank, "lay in the hands of persons who sabotaged the work of the apparent rulers. The officials of the city of Berlin carried out the orders of the Municipal Council in such a way as to result in failure and to make the republican administration look ridiculous." This may well have been so. But there was also the ever-present groundswell of anti-Semitism, which like any other radical prejudice is likely to win support in a society where ballots govern by quantity rather than quality.

Einstein now acted with desperation but dignity, writing to the Mayor, thanking him for the Council's friendly intentions, noting that his birthday was now past. He declined the gift. By this time, however, he and Elsa had become fond of the plot they had chosen. So they bought it, and built their own house on it. "In this way, without wanting it, we have acquired a beautiful home of our own situated in the woods near the water," Elsa told Professor Frank. "But we have spent most of our savings. Now we have no money, but we have our land and property. This gives one a much greater sense of security." Einstein, unworldlywise in so many things, knew better. He had once warned Frank that no more than ten years might be left to him in Germany. Eight had already passed.

The new home had all the qualities of genuinely rural surroundings even though it lay only a few miles from the center of Berlin. Beyond Potsdam, on the road that led to Werder-on-the-Havel, Caputh was at that time little more than one straggling street, and was rarely visited by the weekend crowds from the capital. North of it stretched the sandy heaths and pine forests, interspersed by lakes and streams, which continue for mile after mile to the Baltic. Just outside the village the ground rises to the edge of the trees and here, only a few minutes from the Havelsee, on which white sails could usually be seen, the

Einsteins built what was to be for a few years a good deal more than a weekend cottage.

The young architect ingeniously combined sophistication with a simple style that fitted the surroundings, and the half-timbered construction concealed a comfortable roominess increased by smooth brown paneling and large windows giving on to the distant prospect of red Caputh roofs, the Havelsee, and the enclosing forest. This was also the view from the long upstairs room which Einstein used as combined study and bedroom. Books lined the walls, the bed filled a recess, while in front of the tall French windows which opened onto a balcony there stood the large paper-cluttered desk at which he worked. And on the Havelsee there was berthed the *Tummler*, the small boat given him as a fiftieth birthday present by friends. It was a fine scene. Had he known his Bishop Heber, he might have considered it as another Ceylon, where "every prospect pleases and only man is vile."

While the argument over his birthday present had been going on, the theory of relativity had been used to pull him into a religious controversy from which there emerged one of his much-quoted statements of faith. It began when Cardinal O'Connell of Boston, who had attacked Einstein's General Theory on previous occasions, told a group of Catholics that it "cloaked the ghastly apparition of atheism" and "befogged speculation, producing universal doubt about God and His Creation." Einstein, who had often reiterated his remark of 1921 to Archibshop Davidson—"It makes no difference. It is purely abstract science"—was at first uninterested. Then, on April 24, Rabbi Herbert Goldstein of the Institutional Synagogue, New York, faced Einstein with the simple five-word cablegram: "Do you believe in God?"

"I believe in Spinoza's God who reveals himself in the orderly harmony of what exists," he replied, "not in a God who concerns himself with fates and actions of human beings."

Years later he expanded this in a letter to Solovine, the survivor of the Olympia Academy. "I can understand your aversion to the use of the term 'religion' to describe an emotional and psychological attitude which shows itself most clearly in Spinoza," he wrote. "[But] I have not found a better expression than 'religious' for the trust in the rational nature of reality that is, at least to a certain extent, accessible to human reason."

In 1929 his statement was enough for Goldstein, who pointed out that "Spinoza, who is called the God-intoxicated man, and who saw God manifest in all nature, certainly could not be called an atheist. Furthermore," he went on, "Einstein points to a unity. Einstein's theory if carried out to its logical conclusion would bring to mankind a scientific formula for monotheism. He does away with all thought of dualism or pluralism. There can be no room for any aspect of polytheism. This latter thought may have caused the Cardinal to speak out. Let us call a spade a spade."

On this occasion Einstein was merely hinting tentatively at the belief which he held in common with many scientists who distrusted revealed religions and did not see that a future life was an essential for ethical behavior in this one: the belief that much if not all of both science and religion concerned complementary but separate aspects of human affairs. Like T. H. Huxley, he was aware that great though science was, it "could never lay its hands, could never touch, even with the tip of its finger, that dream with which our little life is rounded."

At Caputh, where he settled in during 1929, Einstein tried to isolate himself from unwanted visitors, newspaper correspondents, and the uncategorizable cranks who sought a few words with him. As there was no telephone, visitors took the train to Potsdam, the local bus to Caputh, then continued on foot, often arriving unannounced. Here came the group of Americans who wanted Einstein's advice on the organization of a Kellogg League that would appeal to all people opposed to war. Here came Otto Hahn from the Kaiser Wilhelm Institute to discuss the work which a few years later unlocked the door to nuclear fission. And here, in the summer of 1930, came Rabindranath Tagore, the Indian philosopher and mystic.

Einstein and Tagore talked for the afternoon in the grounds, and what was described as the "authorized version" of their conversation subsequently appeared in the *American Hebrew*. In view of Einstein's statement that the report "should, of course, never have been published," too much faith should not be put in the account, which was headed "The Nature of Reality." Nevertheless, it rings true, and there are exchanges which have the authentic Einstein touch as when, after Tagore had denied that truth or beauty was independent of man, his companion asked: "If there would be no human beings any more, the Apollo of Belvedere would no longer be beautiful?" To Tagore's "No," Einstein noted that he agreed "with regard to this conception of beauty, but not with regard to truth," adding: "I cannot prove that my conception is right, but that is my religion." The conversation, which ended with Einstein's exclamatory "Then I am more religious than you are!", contained two statements of dogmatic, if intuitive faith. "I cannot prove that scientific truth must be conceived as a truth that is valid independent of reality," he said, "but I believe it firmly. I believe, for instance, that the Pythagorean theorem in geometry states something that is approximately true, independent of the existence of man. Anyway, if there is a *reality* independent of man, there is also a truth relative to this reality; and in the same way the negation of the first engenders a negation of the existence of the latter." And later he continued: "Our natural point of view in regard to the existence of truth apart from humanity cannot be explained or proved. But it is a belief which nobody can lack—not primitive beings even. We attribute to truth a superhuman objectivity, it is indispensable for us, this reality which is independent of our existence and our experience and our mind—though we cannot say what it means."

Contemplation of first principles progressively occupied Einstein's attention. One visitor, Dr. Chaim Tschernowitz, has given a vivid account of a summer trip with him on the Havelsee during which their discussions were often metaphysical. "The conversation drifted back and forth from profundities about the nature of God, the universe, and man to questions of a lighter and more vivacious nature. . . . ," he has written. "Suddenly [Einstein] lifted his head, looked upward at the clear skies, and said: 'We know nothing about it all. All our knowledge is but the knowledge of schoolchildren.' 'Do you think,' I asked, 'that we shall ever probe the secret?' 'Possibly,' he said with a movement of his shoulders, 'we shall know a little more than we do now. But the real nature of things, that we shall never know, never.'" As Born said of Einstein after his death, "He knew, as did Socrates, that we know nothing."

Meanwhile he worked on, at the unified field theory, at the problems posed by quantum mechanics, intrigued by the prospects being opened up in cosmology by the new telescopes of California, and in nuclear physics by the accumulating knowledge of the atom. In his own specialty he was lucky; in the days before computers he demanded no equipment, and as for helpers, Dr. Mayer sufficed. "The kind of work I do can be done anywhere," he said when his friend Philipp Frank apologized that he might be late for a rendezvous near the Astrophysical Observatory. "Why should I be less capable of reflecting about my problems on the Potsdam bridge than at home?"

When the demon was with him nothing else mattered. Joffé, the Russian physicist, recalls how while staying in Berlin he visited Einstein to describe his recent work on the mechanical and electrical properties of crystals. "He asked me to explain in detail," Joffé has written.

> I remember that I arrived at his house about three o'clock and began the account of my work. After about an hour his wife came in and asked Einstein to see, about five o'clock, someone who had come fom Hamburg to make the acquaintance of the great man. Einstein hated this sort of thing, but he obviously got little support from his family. He therefore led me into a nearby park where we were able to continue the conversation undisturbed. As soon as the danger of a meeting had passed we returned to his study. In two hours I had explained all the essentials to him; and now Einstein began the process of turning the information to his own use. One can describe this process as the organic absorption of new information into an already existing uniform picture of nature.

"It was eight when we had our evening meal," Joffé goes on. "But even during this the discussion and mental probing of the subject did not cease. The intake of intellectual nourishment went on while the intake of material nourishment was left to instructions from his wife: what he should put on his fork and when he should put it into his mouth. For Einstein's attention was far from the macaroni we were eating."

After the meal, the discussion continued. Midnight

came and went—and so did the last train for Werder where Joffé was living. He tentatively remarked that the talk could be carried on at some other time, but the idea made no impression on Einstein. "Finally, at two in the morning," says Joffé, "the discussion ended; everything was settled, all doubts had been cleared up. Once again, a piece had been fitted into the contradictory jigsaw which was Einstein's picture of the world. Neither I nor many other scholars would have been capable of so long and so systematic an intellectual exercise. But for Einstein it was obviously commonplace."

It was natural that Joffé should go out of his way to consult the scientist who had by this time become, despite the reputation of Planck, Born, and von Laue, and the potential fame of Heisenberg, the man physicists most wished to see when they visited Berlin. And it was natural that after mathematicians and scientists throughout the world had contributed to a special award that was to bear Max Planck's name, Einstein should be the first to receive it.

The presentation was to take place at five in the afternoon and after a morning's work Einstein visited Plesch for a lunch over which they discussed the crisis in the theory of causality. Then Einstein lay down on a couch and went to sleep. He woke at four, said: "They'll expect me to say something or the other," sat down at the doctor's writing desk, took a bootmaker's bill which was the nearest piece of paper to hand, and scribbled away for twenty minutes. Half an hour later, in the packed hall of tlhe Institute of Physics, Planck took the platform and after a conventional speech handed over the medal.

"Then Einstein spoke," writes Plesch. " 'I knew that an honor of this sort would move me deeply,' he began, 'and therefore I have put down on paper what I would like to say to you as thanks. I will read it.' And out of his waistcoat pocket came my bootmaker's bill with the scribble on the back, and he read out what he had written about the principle of causality. And because, as he said, no reasoning being could get on at all without causality he established the principle of supercausality. The atmosphere was tense and most moving." Afterwards Plesch claimed his bootmaker's bill. Einstein also handed him the medal, of solid gold and with a bust relief of Planck. "It was still in the case," Plesch noted. "He never took it out or looked at it again."

This award, and the stream of comparable honors and invitations from abroad—a sign that Einstein's reputation was still uneroded despite his growing isolation in the crisis over indeterminacy—were fair enough indications of the position he still held in the German scientific community. Outside it, the situation was very different. In 1920 when he had been a convenient focus of attack for the nationalists and the anti-Semites, the battle had been fought on the extremist fringe, in an atmosphere exacerbated both by the humiliations of the German defeat and the aggravations aroused by Einstein's own war-time record and his left-wing pacifist beliefs. A decade later it was not merely the extremists who were involved. Now it was necessary to attract a larger audience and it was here that Einstein was such a useful weapon in the hands of those already optimistic of ending the Republic. For to the less discriminating and more credulous it was comparatively easy to portray the complexities of relativity as the culminating confidence trick of a Jewish conspiracy. Not everyone would believe this, of course. But Einstein as a symbol was far more vulnerable to attack than a hero of the medical sciences, a popular Jewish author, or a leader in any of the professions whose achievements were easy to understand and difficult to deride.

The dangers of the situation were increased by Einstein's own naïveté. This has been emphasized by Lancelot Law Whyte, a young British physicist studying in Berlin at the time. Whyte had met Einstein, greatly admired him, and had so gained the master's confidence as to become translator of the 3,000-word article on the unified field which Einstein wrote for *The Times* early in 1929. Whyte has put down what many were no doubt thinking. "Late in 1928," he says, "it seemed to me that, by giving favors to Jews and foreign visitors which he was not giving to German colleagues and students, Einstein was in a sense helping to produce anti-Semitism. I was disturbed by this; it did not correspond with my image of him as a noble and wise person, and it made me uncomfortable that he had been so kind to me."

Shortly afterwards Whyte consulted "a senior figure." "You do not understand," said this colleague.

> There is already so much anti-Semitism and jealousy of Einstein on the part of duller German scholars, and such a gulf between the German and modern sides of the university that it is impossible for Einstein to be above the battle, the same to all men. He is a Jew, he inevitably dislikes much that is going on, and he is already for many a hated symbol. A German teacher or student from some other German university could not approach him as you have done. The universities reflect a chasm in Germany; on the one side intellect and internationalism, and on the other the re-creation of something peculiarly German after the disaster of 1918.

From this situation it was possible to draw only one conclusion. "After this talk in 1929," Whyte says, "I had an uncomfortable feeling that since Einstein could not escape his outstanding responsibility as a symbol, he should not remain for longer than he could help in a university where he could not treat all alike. The fact was that his presence in Germany was acting as a focus and stimulant of anti-Semitism. He was the hero compelled by fate to become an instrument of evil, as again later in relation to nuclear energy."

Shortly afterwards Norman Bentwich, who as attorney general in Palestine had walked on Mount Scopus with Einstein seven years earlier, visited Berlin with his wife. "I was disturbed by grim signs of the rising anti-Semitic flood and the growing strength of the Nazi political party," he has written. "When we had spent a week there the previous year, on our tour through Europe, all seemed serene and hopeful. Now many Jewish shops had been sacked, and the Jews, who in 1929 were almost derisive about Hitler, were seriously alarmed. I visited Einstein in his sailing retreat on one of the lakes; and for all his serenity he was anxious." Soon he was more so, and a few months later was seriously advising a young correspondent not to become a mathematics master "because of the extraordinarily bad prospects . . . and the additional difficulty which is bound up with the 'jüdischen Nationalität' "—a difficult piece of advice since with him, "work with science means everything."

Good enough reason for his worry arrived soon afterwards, with the publication in Leipzig of an ill-tempered little book called *100 Authors Against Einstein* (*Hundert*

Autoren Gegen Einstein). With the exception of Lenard and Stark, few scientists of even middling reputation could be induced to condemn relativity, a fact which clearly made the Leipzig publication part of a careful propaganda drive. Some of the contents could be plausibly claimed as respectable, but the promoters had to scrape the bottom of the scientific barrel to find their quota of contributors. Professor Mellin of Helsingfors wrote on "The Untenability of the Relativity Theory" ("Die Unhaltbarkeit der Relativitätstheorie"); Professor Dr. Hans Driesch of Leipzig on "My Chief Objections to Relativity Theory" ("Meine Haupteinwände Gegen der Relativitätstheorie"); and Professor Dr. le Roux of Rennes on "The Bankruptcy of the Relativity Theory." "Der Bankrott der Relativitätstheorie"). Dr. Arvid Reuterdahl of Minnesota contributed a long disquisition on "Einsteinism: His Deceitful Conclusions and Frauds," in which he not only attacked the alleged priority of Einstein's theory but claimed that the bombastic style of his story had turned him into the Barnum of science.

Einstein was well aware that this was merely the tip of the anti-Semitic iceberg. More than once he spoke to his wife of taking a post abroad, of renouncing German nationality for the second time, and of holding up for public examination the attitude of Germany towards the Jews. Perhaps it would have been better for the Jews had he done so. But he hesitated; the magnet provided by the society of the Berlin physicists proved too powerful. Science über alles.

On July 17, 1931, he went so far as to draft a letter to Max Planck. "I feel impelled to call your attention to a matter which is closely related to the conditions of my employment," this went.

> You will surely recall that after the war I declared my willingness to accept German citizenship, in addition to my Swiss citizenship. The events of recent days suggest that it is not advisable to maintain this situation. Therefore, I should be grateful if you saw to it that my German citizenship were revoked, and to advise me whether such a change will permit me to maintain my position in the Academy of Sciences (which I sincerely hope).
>
> Concern for the many people who are financially

> dependent on me, as well as a certain need for personal independence, compels me to take this step. I very much hope that you will understand and that you will not interpret this request as an act of ingratitude towards a country and an institution which have granted me enviable living and working conditions during the best years of my life. So far, I have always rejected offers from abroad, however tempting, which would have forced me to leave the scene of my work. I hope I shall be able to maintain this attitude also in the future.

The letter was never posted and was still in its original envelope when in 1933, after Einstein's refusal to return to Germany following the rise of Hitler, his papers were retrieved from Germany by diplomatic bag through the French embassy. It is easy to infer what happened. With his built-in wish to cause the minimum trouble to everyone, Einstein would decide to have a private word with Planck before anything was put on record. And Planck, that figure of quintessential German loyalty, would have little difficulty in persuading his colleague, once again, where duty lay. He did not have to parade his national loyalty, nor his inner conviction that civil servants did not desert their posts in the hour of need. He had merely, from the scientific pedestal on which Einstein rightly placed him, to note that if a man genuinely wished to probe the secrets of nature there was no place better fitted for the work than Berlin.

Einstein genuinely agreed. Moreover he hoped that he would "be able to maintain this attitude." Since 1923 he had, it is true, been a visiting lecturer at Leiden. He had gladly given his services in Switzerland when required. But in spite of his feelings about Germans and Germany, he had remained faithful to the Kaiser Wilhelm Institute.

Yet now, as the 1930s started their disastrous course downhill, Einstein's faith in the future of Europe in general and of Germany in particular began to wane. This was revealed not only by his increasingly pessimistic utterances, publicly on platforms and privately to friends, in magazine and newspaper articles, but also in the new pattern of life soon produced by acceptance of two different sets of engagements. One was with the California Institute of Technology which he agreed to visit for a few weeks early in 1931 on what was mutually if loosely expected to be the start of a long-term regular engagement. The other was at Christ Church, Oxford, where he accepted a research fellowship which allowed him to spend one term a year in the university. His work in Berlin would of course continue as before; but it would dovetail conveniently into an annual program which would involve departure from Germany for the United States in December, return during the late winter or early spring, then summer in Oxford before a return to Berlin in the early autumn. This plan had the advantage of retaining his links with Planck, von Laue, and his other colleagues while providing two alternative refuges against the rise of anti-Semitism or the outbreak of war. Meanwhile, adding to the luster of German science, he continued to feed the hand that bit him.

Before the start of these series of visits to California and to Oxford, which developed under the increasingly sinister pressure of events in Germany, Einstein made three other significant journeys abroad, one to Holland and Belgium, two to Britain. The first was the most important. It led to one meeting which helped to topple him from his pacifist stance in the summer of 1933, but it was also a journey important to the world in general and to Japan in particular. In Belgium, Einstein forged a link which ran directly from the Belgian royal family to a study in Princeton, to the fear that Belgian uranium might come under German control, and thence to a letter alerting President Roosevelt to the possibilities of nuclear weapons.

In 1929 he made one of his regular trips to Leiden. He called as usual on his uncle Cäsar in Antwerp, just across the frontier. And here he received an invitation to visit the Queen of the Belgians at Laeken on Monday, May 20. King Albert, epitome of the liberal-minded constitutional monarch, still a symbolic figure from the First World War, a trench-coated King defying the German invaders in Flanders fields, had a genuine interest in science and was absent only because of an appointment in Switzerland. Queen Elizabeth, formerly Princess Elizabeth of Bavaria, was unconventional and artistic, and on May 20 Einstein and his violin spent the first of many musical afternoons at the Palace, Her Majesty "playing second fiddle." There followed, according to the Queen's own notes in her agenda book, tea under the chestnuts and a walk in the grounds, followed by dinner at 7:30. A few days later she sent him prints of the photographs she had taken, hoping he would come again soon, passing on the King's regrets that he had been away, and adding, according to her draft reply: "It was unforgettable for me when you came down from your peak of knowledge and gave me a tiny glimpse into your ingenious theory."

The meeting marked the start of an unusual friendship. During the next four years—as long as Einstein remained in Europe—he would rarely visit Belgium without being invited to the palace at Laeken. He was the usual Einstein, being missed at the railway station by the royal chauffeur who failed to recognize the drably dressed figure with violin case; alarming a small café by requesting the use of a telephone and then asking direct for the Queen; and generally behaving in the simple, unpremeditated way of a man with his mind on other things.

A full description of every visit went back to Elsa. In recounting one meeting he recorded that Her Majesty, an English guest, a lady-in-waiting, and he had played trios and quartets for several hours. "Then they all went away," he continued, "and I stayed behind alone for dinner with the King, vegetarian style, no servants. Spinach with hard-boiled eggs and potatoes, period." This casualness has been described by Antonina Vallentin, who records how one day at Caputh Einstein was searching for a piece of paper. "With impatient gestures he was emptying the contents of [his] pockets on the table," she writes.

> They were the pockets of a schoolboy; penknife, pieces of string, bits of biscuits, chits, bus tickets, change, tobacco dropped out of his pipe. At last, with a rustle of parchment, a large sheet of paper fell out. It was a poem that the Queen of the Belgians had dedicated to him. At the bottom of the large ivory-colored pages there were a few words and a few figures in Einstein's small, regular handwriting. I bent over the table. Immortal calculations side by side with the royal signature that cut across the page, I read: "Autobus 50 pfennig, newspaper, stationery, etc." Daily expenses, noted with care, entangled side by side with the loop of the regal 'E.'

King Albert died in a climbing accident in 1934. Queen Elizabeth lived on, and the quarter-century that followed her first meeting with Einstein was marked by a long series of letters. Einstein's were extremely outspoken—as though Her Majesty lived at such a far-removed level that he could write with a familiarity unusual in correspondence between royalty and commoner. Perhaps their mutual links with southern Germany—or the similarity of their experiences, Einstein rejecting the Fatherland and Her Majesty having her adopted country invaded by it—aroused a common sympathy. Whatever the particular fuel which kept the friendship alight, there were to be repercussions, unsuspected in 1929, of that first invitation and the walk under the chestnut trees.

The following year Einstein made two visits to England. Before he left Berlin for the first, he received a request from Professor Veblen whom he had met in Princeton nine years previously. A new faculty lounge was being built in the university for the mathematics and physics department. Could they have permission to use on it his phrase which had lodged in Veblen's memory—"God is subtle but he is not malicious"? Einstein consented, adding that what he had meant was that "Nature conceals her mystery by means of her essential grandeur, not by her cunning" ("Die Natur verbirgt ihr Geheimnis durch die Erhabenheit ihres Wesens, aber nich durch List"), and the original phrase was carved on the room's marble fireplace.

Shortly afterwards he left for England, going first to Nottingham where he gave to the university a general survey of relativity and the unified field theory. Then he traveled on to Cambridge to accept an honorary degree, a happy occasion since it enabled him to meet Eddington, whose knighthood was announced in the King's Birthday Honors during the visit. Einstein had been invited to stay at the Cambridge Observatory with Eddington and his sister in 1920, 1925, and 1926, but had been unable to accept due to pressure of work and official engagements. "I would like to come to England," he had written in 1926, "if for no other reason than the pleasure of talking with you. . . . I would so much like to talk with you that for this alone it would be profitable for me to learn the English language." Now the opportunity had arrived and the two men spent a week together.

In the autumn he came to London for a special dinner of the ORT—an organization for helping Jews in Eastern Europe—staying with Lord Samuel in Porchester Terrace where, as he later described it, he played a "star-guest role." In this way, he said, in accepting Samuel's invitation, "the business of a Jewish Holy One not only becomes easy for me but is even reduced to a pleasure." But he skillfully evaded a further invitation "to meet . . . many prominent men," pleading that he had a prior appointment in Switzerland where he was anxious to discuss the health of his younger son.

Samuel's notes of Einstein's visit, written a few hours after his guest's departure, cast some interesting sidelights on Einstein at the age of fifty. At luncheon one day the two men were joined by Edmond Kapp, who a decade previously had sketched Einstein lecturing in Vienna. By now a well-known portraitist, Kapp made roughs of Einstein's head, later marrying them with his action sketches of Vienna to produce one of his best studies. By this time Einstein was a habitual "subject." When Samuel remarked that he must be constantly troubled by painters or sculptors Einstein agreed; during his journey to England, he told them, he had got into conversation with a man who asked him his occupation. "Je suis modèle," he replied. During the meal he mentioned that he was still frequently being attacked in Germany—"parce que je suis Rouge et Juif." Samuel, knowing that Einstein's politics were pink rather than red, commented: "Mais pas très Rouge." "Et pas très Juif," added Einstein.

After the ORT banquet—where in his speech he paid tribute to his fellow guests, Bernard Shaw and H. G. Wells, "for whose conceptions of life I have a special sympathy" —he remarked on the difference in the way in which people had shaken hands with him. Some were nervous, some curious, some proud. The men were proud on account of their positions, the women on account of their beauty. "He said to me on the way to the station," Samuel continues, "that never in his early years had he imagined for a moment that he would take part in affairs of a public character such as this, which had brought him on this journey, or which arose from his interest in Palestine. He had expected that he should spend all his life in more solitary pursuits. He added that he did not really feel himself fitted for these tasks. 'Je suis pas "praktisch."'" The following day he "dropped in" on the Weizmanns. "He was much amused at the ORT dinner, where, he says, people made the impression of a monkeys' assembly," says Mrs. Weizmann. "They were mostly concerned over whom to shake hands with first—Lord Rothschild or Einstein himself."

Soon after he arrived back in Berlin he was visited by Arthur Fleming, chairman of the Board of Trustees of the California Institute of Technology. The visit appears to have been made on the suggestion of Richard Chase Tolman, the institute's professor of physical chemistry and mathematical physics for reasons which were soon self-evident. "The result was better than Tolman expected," Fleming wrote to a colleague, "so that when I first met Einstein at his home in the country, and invited him to come to us with the money provided by Mr. Thomas Cochran, his first question was, 'You have a man named Tolman at your institution?' I said we had, and he then asked if Tolman were a visitor or one of our men. I informed him that he was one of ours."

Tolman was handling much of the theoretical work at Mount Wilson Observatory concerning the nature and size of the universe. Einstein was eager to discuss this first-hand with the men concerned, and he quickly agreed to visit the institute as a research associate early in 1931.

When the news was announced he was soon brought up once more against the interest of the United States in all he said and did. By this time he was well aware of the power of his name; but nearly a decade had passed since his first visit to America and his recollection of the unrelenting eagerness with which the inhabitants seized their enthusiasms had faded. Before the end of the week, fifty cables a day were arriving from across the Atlantic. U. S. mail began to outnumber German letters. Elsa, who was left to handle the welter of invitations, stated firmly that the professor would be traveling purely on holiday; that he wished to be left alone; and, finally, that she would not allow him to land in New York, but would insist that he remained on board while their Belgian ship continued its journey south, through the Panama Canal, and up to California.

Despite these efforts at nonengagement, Einstein agreed

to one proposal which contributed an hors d'oeuvre of controversy before the start of his visit. This was a request to write for the *New York Times* an article on religion and science, a perennial subject on which the views of a nonpracticing Jew who had given a fresh description of the universe were particularly pertinent. Ever since he had been thrust into the limelight his views on religion had been sought not only by the press but by friends, colleagues, and acquaintances. Ernest Strauss, who worked with him in Princeton, quoted him in the Encyclopedia Americana as describing religious thought as "an attempt to find an out where there is no door." His friend Max Born observed that "he had no belief in the Church, but did not think that religious faith was a sign of stupidity, nor unbelief a sign of intelligence." There was a whiff of wishful thinking in some of the views credited to him. Thus Ben-Gurion, asked if he believed in God, replied: "I once talked to Einstein. Even he, with his great formula about energy and mass, agreed that there must be something behind the energy." And Prince Hubertus of Lowenstein reports him as saying, in the United States, before the Second World War: "In view of such harmony in the cosmos which I, with my limited human mind, am able to recognize, there are yet people who say there is no God. But what really makes me angry is that they quote me for support of such views."

Maybe. To some extent the differences between Einstein and more conventional believers were semantic, a point brought out in his "Religion and Science" which, on Sunday, November 9, occupied the entire first page of the *New York Times Magazine*. "Everything that men do or think," it began, "concerns the satisfaction of the needs they feel or the escape from pain." Einstein then went on to outline three states of religious development, starting with the religion of fear that moved primitive peoples, and which in due course became the moral religion whose driving force was social feelings. This in turn could become the "cosmic religious sense ... which recognizes neither dogmas nor God made in man's image." And he then put the key to his ideas in two sentences. "I assert that the cosmic religious experience is the strongest and noblest driving force behind scientific research." And, as a corollary, "the only deeply religious people of our largely materialistic age are the earnest men of research."

A leading article in the *New York Times* the following day was mildly noncommittal, a reasonable enough attitude in view of the obvious fact that the word "religion" had a different meaning for Einstein than for most people. By contrast, at opposite ends of the range, were Dr. Nathan Krass and Dr. Fulton Sheen. Dr. Krass, rabbi of the Temple Emanuel of 64th Street and Fifth Avenue, took it favorably: "The religion of Albert Einstein will not be approved by certain sectarians but it must and will be approved by the Jews." Dr. Sheen, on the other hand, told 1,200 members of the Catholic Teachers Association that the *Times* had "degraded itself" by publishing Einstein's article, which he described as "the sheerest kind of stupidity and nonsense." He asked whether anyone would be willing to lay down his life for the Milky Way, and concluded: "There is only one fault with his cosmical religion: he put an extra letter in the word—the letter 's.' "

Einstein's use of the usual word "religion" to cover his own unusual ethical attitudes was only one example of the way in which his outlook was contrary to that of the country he was now to visit for the second time; "An impersonal God, a deterministic universe, a churchless religion, disregard of money and material gains, world government, pacifism, and socialism—all of these are pretty generally thought to be un-American and more or less subversive." Einstein believed in the lot. In addition, he despised publicity, as he made clear to the American journalist he agreed to see on November 22, shortly before leaving for the United States. To him he deplored the letters which had been arriving at the Haberlandstrasse house from manufacturers of disinfectants, toilet waters, musical instruments, and clothes—dangling thousands of dollars for permission to say that Einstein had found their goods satisfactory. "Is it not a sad commentary on the commercialism and, I must add, the corruption of our time that business firms make these offers with no thought of wanting to insult me," he asked. "It evidently means that this form of corruption—for corruption it is—is widespread." He was still unable to realize that the enthusiasm for his presence, which was so frequently exploited to aid the causes of Zionism or of peace, could not be switched on or off at will. Much as he wished to utilize mass psychology in the battle for good causes, he yet deplored it. "My own case is, alas, an illustration," he said. "Why popular fancy should seize me, a scientist dealing in abstract things and happy if left alone, is one of those manifestations of mass psychology that are beyond me. I think it is terrible that this should be so and I suffer more than anybody can imagine." This was true. It was also ingenuous.

At Antwerp, where he and Elsa embarked on the *Belgenland* on December 2, 1930, he repeated that this was merely a holiday trip, although agreeing that he would be visiting the El Paso Observatory and would discuss with his American friends questions in which they were mutually interested. "If you really want to send a message to the press," he told reporters, "let it be that I want to be left alone. Personally I consider it indecent to delve into people's private affairs, and the world would certainly fare better if newspapers cared more for things that really matter instead of dealing with trifles." And to the news that he would be able to speak to his friends by radiotelephone he replied: "I hope these journalists are not going to call me up in the middle of the ocean and ask me how I slept the night before."

At Southampton, which according to a diary entry impressed him with England's might, the press appears to have been less importunate, and he noted that in England "even the reporters practice reserve. Honor to whom honor is due. A single 'no' is enough. The world can learn much from them—but not I who still dress carelessly, even for the holy sacrament of dinner. . . ."

As the liner pulled out into the Atlantic, Einstein was left comparatively at peace in the three flower-filled staterooms which had been allotted him and which went with "the excessive and pretentious attention [which] makes me uncomfortable." Here he was to work throughout much of the voyage with Dr. Mayer, permanently guarded from intrusion by a member of the crew stationed outside the door to his usite.

But the radiotelephone continued to bring news: of the *Völkischer Beobachter*, which was violently attacking him for traveling on a Belgian ship instead of the German

Europa, due to arrive in New York the same day (but not sailing on to the West Coast); and of the National German Jewish Union, taking up the old stick that Einstein was using his scientific fame to propagate Zionism, a charge which it would have been difficult to deny. Before the end of the voyage there came a further report from Berlin, quoting a Dr. Boris Brutzkus who recounted how Einstein had told him that he would settle in a quiet resort in the south of France if Hitler ever came to power.

On this final point, Einstein felt forced to comment. "One should not speak publicly about conditions which one hopes will not come to pass," he said. "Still less should one under such circumstances make any decision in advance or even make public such decisions." He refused to be drawn. But it seemed clear to others, if not to him, that he must be summing up the prospects in America should he be forced from Germany. There, after all, he could hope to continue his work in peace.

During the voyage, a working one for Einstein and Dr. Mayer, Elsa was persuaded that it would, after all, be better for them to go ashore in New York. Einstein himself agreed that it would be simpler for him to meet the press when the ship came into harbor. As the *New York Times* had already noted, "It is probably accurate for the Berlin paper to advise him that he cannot hope to keep his features out of the New York press unless he locks himself in the purser's safe. And even then there will be pictures taken of the safe."

The occasion, when it came, had an air of comedy. Fifty reporters and fifty photographers swooped on their victim. Einstein, good natured but bewildered, was called upon "within the brief quarter of an hour to define the fourth dimension in one word, state his theory of relativity in one sentence, give his views on prohibition, comment on politics and religion, and discuss the virtues of his violin." The German consul, Paul Schwarz, helped interpret; Elsa did her best to stage-manage the occasion, mothering her husband away from the trick questions, explaining, protecting, and sympathizing with those who wanted the theory of relativity described in a few one-syllable words.

"The reporters asked particularly inane questions to which I replied with cheap jokes that were received with enthusiasm," was Einstein's own diary account of the occasion. He proved remarkably adroit at handling his questioners, answering the scientific conundrums so that the replies were comprehensible, sidestepping the more irrelevant demands, and interspersing his remarks with the occasional debating point or colorful phrase. Asked whether there was any relation between science and metaphysics, he declared that science itself was metaphysics. And asked what he thought of Hitler, he replied: "I do not enjoy Mr. Hitler's acquaintance. Hitler is living on the empty stomach of Germany. As soon as economic conditions in Germany improve he will cease to be important."

He also broadcast from the ship, not once but twice, thus satisfying two companies and earning $1,000 for his welfare fund for the Berlin poor. The central message of his statement was, in effect, a challenge to America. This is how he put it:

> It is in your country, my friends, that those latent forces which eventually will kill any serious monster of professional militarism will be able to make themselves felt more clearly and definitely. Your political and economic condition today is such that if you ever set your hand to this job in all seriousness you will be able entirely to destroy the dreadful tradition of military violence under which the sad memories of the past and—to a certain extent—of the world continue to suffer even after the terrific warning of the Great War. It is along these lines of endeavor that your mission lies at the present moment, and should you be able and willing to accept this high duty I know that you will build for yourselves an enduring monument.

After the broadcasts Einstein went ashore, for five crowded days of speechmaking and sight-seeing, returning every night to the *Belgenland* where he could be protected from the hundreds of visitors who wished to invoke his personal aid. He received the keys of New York at a ceremony attended by Mayor Walker and President Butler of Columbia University. He saw his statue adorning Riverside Church overlooking the Hudson River—the only statue of a living man among the thinkers who had changed the world from the days of Socrates and Plato. He celebrated the Jewish festival of Hanukkah at a crowded meeting in Madison Square Garden, and on the fourteenth he gave his famous "two percent" pacifist speech to the New History Society at the Ritz-Carlton Hotel.* He visited the *New York Times* and he visited the Metropolitan Opera, where he was spontaneously cheered when the audience noticed him sitting quietly in a box. Here he was handed a slip of paper on which the Metropolitan's publicity director had written: "Relativity: There is no hitching post in the universe—so far as we know." Einstein studied it carefully, added: "Read, and found correct," and then signed it. And here, spying the press photographers who were awaiting him, he nimbly about-faced and escaped from them—a Marx brothers incident in which the publicity director was seen running after the world's most famous scientist plaintively calling: "Mr. Einstein, Mr. Einstein."

The dislike of publicity was genuine enough, even if at times it gave the impression of a Lawrence of Arabia backing into the limelight. But once the cordon had been broken through Einstein could be amiable enough. Thus a young Berliner, refused permission to sketch him when he returned on board, merely sat in the *Bergenland's* restaurant and sketched while Einstein ate. The great man was amused, signed the sketch, and added: "Dieses fette satte Schwien/Soll Professor Einstein sein" ("This fat, well-sated pig you see/ Professor Einstein purports to be"). He continued to evade the trail of autograph hunters, although those who wrote to him got strictly business treatment. "If the autograph is wanted very badly, if the letter brings, say, three dollars for the Berlin poor," Elsa said, "the doctor will be happy. And with pictures for autograph with, say, five dollars, the doctor will be happy." The little account book which she showed, containing the details of what Einstein sent to the Berlin poor, was, she claimed, his favorite reading.

The Einsteins sailed from New York on December 16, touched at Havana three days later—"luxurious clubs side by side with naked poverty, mainly affecting the colored people," he noted in his diary—then passed through the Panama Canal before turning northwards up the coast of

*See page 448.

California. As they neared their destination the other passengers made the most of the last opportunities of being photographed with Einstein. So much so that resignation at last gave place to annoyance. But there was of course one consolation. "The autograph business for the benefit of charity is flourishing," Einstein noted in his diary. He was reported to be charging a dollar a time.

At the end of the month, the *Belgenland* reached San Diego. Einstein gave a New Year's broadcast over the local radio, attended local festivities including one public reception at which local Jews presented him with an inscribed gold "*mezuzah*" containing a Hebrew prayer, and another at which he was given a floral float. "However crazy such things may look from the outside," Hedwig Born wrote to him, after watching the scene on a newsreel, "I always have the feeling that the Good Lord knows very well what he is up to. In the same way that Gretchen senses the Devil in Faust, so he makes people sense in you—well, just Einstein."

From San Diego the Einsteins were driven to Pasadena. Here they soon chose a small bungalow, the "shingled gingerbread house," as Einstein called it, where they were to live for their two-month stay at the institute. As a celebrity Einstein was much sought after even in a land of celebrities. Upton Sinclair, who took him to see Eisenstein's famous film about life in Mexico, later claimed a local millionairess had contributed $10,000 to Caltech on the promise of meeting him. He and Elsa dined with Charlie Chaplin "as a result of expressions of mutual desire on the part of himself and the professor to meet each other." And during a visit to Hollywood he was given a special showing of Remarque's *All Quiet on the Western Front*, already banned in Germany. "I thank you for all the things you have said of me," he said at the special dinner which followed. "If I believed them I would not be sane, and since I know I am sane, I do not believe them." Adulation was not unqualified, and Sinclair recalls a brief exchange when the Einsteins visited Professor Graham Laing and his wife. Mrs. Laing had queried Einstein's views on God, which had brought Elsa out of her corner with the declaration: "My husband has the greatest mind in the world." "Yes," came the reply, "but he doesn't know everything"—a statement with which Einstein himself would heartily have agreed.

All this, however, was the froth on an important working tour. The purpose of Einstein's visit, he announced on arriving, "would be to fit into the life of the California Institute of Technology and discuss problems with noted scientists more intimately than is possible by correspondence." The day after his arrival he gave a further clue to the reason for his visit. "New observations by Hubble and Humason"—both workers at the Mount Wilson Observatory above Pasadena—"concerning the red shift of light in distant nebulas make it appear likely that the general structure of the universe is not static," he said. "Theoretical investigations made by Lemaître and Tolman fit well into the General Theory of Relativity." Einstein had in fact traveled halfway round the world to see whether it was really necessary to revise the picture of the universe with which he had virtually founded modern cosmology in 1917; and, if so, in what way.

Only thirteen years separated his "Cosmological Implications" from 1930, but within that period a revolution had taken place in cosmology quite as shattering as the revolution in physics which separated the work of Lorentz and J. J. Thomson in the last years of the nineteenth century from that of Planck and Einstein in the first years of the twentieth. In 1917 the mathematical projections of the universe provided by Einstein and de Sitter were given due consideration, even though astronomers had not entirely abandoned a belief that the Milky Way, the galaxy which contains the sun and its solar system among millions of other stars, formed the entire universe. However, it was not denied that some of the faint mysterious patches of light scattered across the night sky might be other galaxies lying unimagined distances away. V. M. Slipher at the Lowell Observatory certainly thought so and suggested that at least some of them were receding from the Milky Way.

After the end of the war, evidence began to accumulate. Like evidence for the subnuclear world of the atom it came with the advance of technology, in this case with the use of ever more powerful telescopes, notably the 100-inch instrument on Mount Wilson above Pasadena. Here Edwin Hubble had from 1920 been probing into

Jean's "mysterious universe." It seemed clear to him that some of the light patches in the sky were merely clouds of gas illuminated from stars that lay within the galaxy of the Milky Way. But about others there was doubt that slowly began to be removed. In 1924 he was able to observe individual stars within the Andromeda M 31 nebula. Shortly afterwards it became evident that such stars were some 800,000 light-years away—eight times the distance of the farthest star in the Milky Way. Thus the galaxy of which the solar system formed part was but a portion of the universe: how small a portion became more and more obvious within the next few years as improvements in techniques and equipment revealed the existence of other galaxies millions and even billions of light-years away.

These discoveries were dramatically supported within two years, by both theoretical cosmology and observational astronomy. The story is chronologically tangled and has some similarity with the simultaneous but independent work on evolution by Darwin and Wallace and the near simultaneous but independent development of radar in Britain, the United States, and Germany.

Listening to Hubble's account of his Andromeda discoveries at a meeting of the National Academy of Sciences in Washington had been a young Belgian priest who, after studying astrophysics in Cambridge, had moved to the Massachusetts Institute of Technology. He was Abbé Lemaître, "the mathematician for whom symmetry was nearly as important as truth." Shortly afterwards, Lemaître returned to Belgium, and in a paper published in 1927 showed not only that the "Einstein world" would have to be unstable, but that it would in fact expand along the lines of de Sitter's world. A unique and startling feature of Lemaître's cosmology was that his presupposed world had started as a "primeval atom" or "cosmic egg," which had initially contained all the matter in the universe and whose disintegration had marked the beginning of time and space. Thus the contemporary universe was merely one phase in an evolving universe. This could have started as a greatly modified "Einstein world" before turning into a continuously expanding de Sitter world in which the galaxies were moving ever farther away from one another and in which the density of matter was becoming less while its amount remained static. Lemaître's paper passed virtually unnoticed at the time. But two years later Hubble at Mount Wilson made the sensational announcement that the galaxies were receding at a speed proportional to their distance—receding not only from the Milky Way but also from each other. All intergalactic distances were in fact increasing simultaneously, and the entire universe was expanding at a rate which doubled its dimensions roughly every 1,300 million years.

Spurred on by these revelations, Eddington began an inquiry with one of his research students into whether or not the "Einstein world" was stable. They soon received a copy of Lemaître's paper. This helped to convince them that the answer was "No." Thus by the middle of 1930 Hubble the astronomer, Lemaître the unknown theoretician, and Eddington the astrophysicist agreed that Einstein's formula for a stable universe could not be valid.

But there was an ironic corollary to this. The "Einstein world" had been produced with the aid of the cosmological constant and this had been necessary, in Einstein's own words, "only for the purpose of making possible a quasi-static distribution of matter, as required by the fact of the small velocities of the stars." But now Hubble's discoveries were revealing that some at least of the galaxies, and of course the stars within them, were moving at speeds which were sizable proportions of the speed of light. Thus there had been no need for the cosmological constant in the first place.

One other point was that Lemaître had included in his paper an equation which gave a term for the rate of recession of the galaxies. Hubble had put a figure to this term and with its aid the Lemaître equation could be used to provide a radius for the initial "Einstein world." This given, Einstein's original work could still give a figure for the total mass of the universe. What it could no longer do was give a picture of what was happening to that mass, for this depended on the character of the cosmological constant. If this were zero it was possible to postulate a universe which had begun some 10,000 million years ago with a "big bang" and which had been expanding uniformly ever since. If it were positive, as Lemaître had envisaged, then his primeval atom had begun to disintegrate some 60,000 million years ago and the result had begun to stabilize itself after some 50,000 million—the contemporary expansion being caused by an upsetting of that stabilization and not by the initial "big bang." While both these theories envisage the evolution of the universe as arising from a unique situation, use of a negative value for the cosmic constant provides a third blueprint: that of the alternately expanding and contracting universe. These possibilities—to which that of a universe constantly expanding, but kept in a steady state by the continuous creation of fresh matter, had not yet been added—formed the highlights of a development which had been going on since 1920. They were still under constant and sometimes acrimonious discussion in the scientific world when Einstein arrived in Pasadena.

He remained based there throughout January and February, meeting the aged Michelson of the Michelson-Morley experiment at a dinner given in honor of them both.* He was taken for short "rest" visits to a number of Californian ranches—sending back from one of them a delighted card to Queen Elizabeth of the Belgians, who had visited the ranch during a state visit to America in 1919—and he cruised off Long Beach with Millikan.

Real work started when he met Tolman and Dr. Paul Epstein, the professor of theoretical physics. Following this, he was driven up the long circuitous road which winds out above Pasadena and then back to the top of the Sierra Madre, from one of whose summits the Mount Wilson Observatory looks down upon the town. Here Elsa, when told that the giant telescope was required for establishing the structure of the universe, is claimed to have made a reply that may be apocryphal but is in true Elsa style: "Well, well, my husband does that on the back of an old envelope." Here Einstein conferred with Hubble.

*It was for long accepted that at this dinner Einstein directly attributed relativity to the work of Michelson, since a widespread version of his speech has him saying: "You uncovered an insidious defect in the ether theory of light, as it then existed, and stimulated the ideas of H. A. Lorentz and Fitzgerald, out of which the Special Theory of Relativity developed. Without your work this theory would today be scarcely more than an interesting speculation. . . ." Gerald Holton has by careful detective work (see *Iris,* Vol. 60, Pt. 2, No. 202, Summer, 1969) discovered that Einstein in fact put a third sentence between these two—"These in turn led the way to the General Theory of Relativity and to the theory of gravitation"—thus putting a slightly different gloss on the occasion.

And here, early in February, he officially announced that he had abandoned the idea of a closed spherical universe. Later he was to agree with the more complex theory of an alternately expanding and contracting universe, a decision which comforted Dean Inge, who noted that this was a "revolutionary change, for it means a return to the old theory of cosmic cycles" which had always attracted him. "Jeans and Eddington say that it is utterly impossible," he went on, "but if I may take refuge behind Einstein I am content." Early in 1930 Einstein did no more than agree that his initial idea had to be given up, and it is typical that he did so only after he had personally met Hubble and peered with him through the magnifiers at the revealing pictures of galaxies from what was then the largest telescope in the world.

In mid-February, a fortnight before he was to leave Pasadena, Einstein addressed several hundred students. His speech must have been startling to many members of the faculty, particularly to Millikan, whose natural inclination was to believe that all was for the best in the best of all possible worlds. For instead of singing the praises of scientific progress, Einstein asked why it had brought such little happiness. In war it had enabled men to mutilate one another more efficiently and in peace it had enslaved man to the machine. "You feel that this old chap in front of you is singing an ugly tune," he said.

> I do it, however, for the purpose of making some suggestions to you. If you want your life's work to be useful to mankind, it is not enough that you understand applied science as such. Concern for man himself must always constitute the chief objective of all technological effort, concern for the big, unsolved problems of how to organize human work and the distribution of commodities in such a manner as to assure that the results of our scientific thinking may be a blessing to mankind, and not a curse.

Millikan, who was to receive angry protests about the "two percent" speech which Einstein had made in New York on his way to Pasadena, was worried about what would happen during his guests' overland return to the East Coast. But nothing sensational did. On March 3 Einstein broke his journey in Chicago, where he was welcomed by a peace group and spoke from the rear platform of his train. In New York he found a waiting delegation from the War Resisters League, but the chance of an explosive afterdinner speech whose sentiments might brush off onto Caltech and discourage its wealthy supporters—and which would in any case have offended Millikan's conservative soul—was fortuitously removed by Weizmann.

The Jewish leader had cabled an urgent appeal for help which Einstein received before he left Pasadena. "Financial position movement and work Palestine extremely difficult in danger of immediate collapse especially harmful now that political situation much improved through satisfactory conclusion negotiations government," he had read.

> We are making all efforts here but as you know resources Europe limited. I am urged come America help drive. Serious work here and necessity going Palestine for negotiations with Arab friends prevents my undertaking trip now must be postponed till April. You are the only man to render real assistance this critical moment by responding invitation our American friends and attending very few banquets in States. I know this imposes heavy burden but having done so much for Palestine I hope you won't refuse come to its assistance at this anxious time.

Einstein did not refuse. He rarely did. And the whole of his evening in New York was spent in preparation for, and at, a fund-raising dinner organized by the American Palestine Campaign at the Hotel Astor.

When he returned to the docks he found banner-bearing pacifist groups awaiting him and he subsequently cabled the leaders a message of goodwill: "Only resistance to military service can bring success to the pacifist movement." Two years later he was urging that only resistance to the pacifist movement would bring success against Hitler.

In mid-March he arrived back in Berlin. Less than two months later he left Germany again, this time for Oxford to receive an honorary degree and give the Rhodes Lectures.

The Rhodes Trust had been set up only in 1926, and in 1927 Einstein had been asked to become the second lecturer. This was a singular honor and his efforts to dodge its acceptance have an almost contrived air. The first approach was made my Lindemann, on the urging of H. A. L. Fisher, Warden of New College and a Rhodes Trustee. In his letter to Berlin, Lindemann noted that acceptance would be "of great political significance" and "a conciliatory international gesture." If Einstein wished to "try the cloistered life," he could have rooms and service in college; if he wished to bring his wife, then a hotel would be found. The point that "even London and Cambridge" were within reach was added as a final inducement. Sir Otto Beit, one of the Rhodes Trustees, was conscripted to invoke the help of Lord Haldane, who supported the invitation, while the German ambassador in London, Count Bernstorff, wrote to "the competent authorities in Berlin and [had] asked them to urge Professor Einstein to accept the invitation."

However, this was rejected, partly because it had been proposed that the visit should be for a complete term of eight weeks. "Firstly, my current activities and obligations here do not permit me to absent myself for a long time as my work is too much interlaced with that of other people," Einstein replied from Berlin to Lord Haldane on July 8. "Secondly, my general health would scarcely permit of a transfer abroad for so long, a transfer which by want of verbal knowledge of the English language would put an exceptional strain upon me. Finally, I really do not have sufficient matter of real importance to submit, so that I cannot rid myself of the thought that my visit would be a case of carrying coals to Newcastle (Eulen nach Athen tragen)." He therefore asked to be excused, stressing that this was not due to any lack of sympathy for Britain, and ended with the expression: "If I could feel that I could come up to expectations I would accept the invitation."

To Lindemann Einstein replied in similar terms. But he did not want to disappoint him. "Perhaps," he therefore went on, "I can make amends and do what you ask at the same time. If you cannot find anyone else at Oxford and if a stay of four weeks in Oxford would be sufficient, I should be willing to come during next summer term. It is very important to me that I do not give an impression of ingratitude to England, where my work has received the greatest recognition."

By this time, however, other arrangements had been put in hand and the Trustees were, as Fisher wrote to Einstein, "put in the difficult position, which they understand has already been explained to you through Professor Lindemann, of having to wait till their offer elsewhere was refused or accepted, before they could write definitely to you."

However, although this first approach came to nothing, the Trust had the tenacious quality of its founder, and in 1930 its secretary, Philip Kerr, asked Lindemann whether he could induce Einstein to come in 1931, giving a single lecture if he felt unable to do more. At first Einstein accepted. Then, after arriving back in Berlin from Cambridge, he had second thoughts. "I unfortunately felt so unwell," he wrote to Lindemann on June 12, "that I find myself forced to withdraw my undertaking to Oxford. Also my doctor has advised me very strongly against it, and so I must, with heavy heart, give it up and at least I am glad to be able to write this to you now so that I shall not cause any fruitless preparations to be made."

However, Lindemann was not the man to give up easily. In October, 1930, he was in Berlin. He saw Einstein; almost as important, he saw Mrs. Einstein; and from the Adlon he wrote to Kerr—by now Lord Lothian. "I am glad to say that his health seems quite restored, and that he is in very good form," he said. ". . . He told me that he could understand English quite well now and although he does not speak it he had found no difficulty in discussions in America as he speaks very slowly and almost everybody knows either French or German. . . ." (And he added later that he would like to arrange for Einstein to have rooms in Christ Church, "which he told me he would like and which I think would be eminently conducive to obtain the object you have in view."

It seems clear that the visit was not yet finally settled, but that Lindemann had turned upon Elsa the considerable charm he could exercise when he wished. Drawing Einstein to Oxford was worth an effort, and in February, 1931, he learned that he had done the trick. On the twenty-fourth he wrote to Elsa saying how delighted he was that Einstein had finally agreed to come. "I will take every care that he has all he wants and will use my best endeavors to prevent his being bothered and troubled in any way," he went on. "He can of course have as many meals as he likes alone in his rooms and I will endeavor to preserve him as much as possible from importunate invitations.

"I am taking steps to see that he can get some sailing, so that I hope he will not feel that he is wasting his time here altogether."

There was little danger of that. But even before his departure from Berlin Einstein was trying to refuse engagements. "Dear colleague," he wrote to Lindemann,

> the Oxford Luncheon Club has written to me and, so to speak, twisted my arm to persuade me not only to fill my stomach in Oxford but also to make a speech. Unfortunately, the people there are so well educated that they not only know everything which in my ignorance I could not tell them but, what is more important, a great deal that I have never learned. In these circumstances I must ask you, nervously: must this be, or can it be avoided without offending tact or tradition: Write to me, please, quickly so that I need not cause them inconvenience by delay.

Lindemann intervened and there was no Luncheon Club address.

On arrival in Oxford Einstein was taken under Lindemann's wing and given the services of the latter's indefatigable servant and general factotum, James Harvey. In addition, Lindemann acted as his mentor and guide, showing him the sights, and introducing him to his various friends and acquaintances. Among these were John Scott Haldane the physiologist, and his wife Kathleen, parents of J. B. S. Haldane, *enfant terrible* among the geneticists. "We were such good friends that my husband took a great deal of trouble to ensure that the professor should have an appreciative audience . . . ," Mrs. Haldane has said. Efforts were necessary, since although the Milner Hall of the new Rhodes House was full at the inaugural lecture, many of the audience slipped away while it was still on. "I don't blame them," J. S. Haldane commented. "If their maths are good enough to follow him their German certainly is not." By the end, only a small audience was left and Einstein promised that the next time "the discourse should be in English delivered." Haldane was heard to murmur "Gott bewahre!"

The first lecture was on relativity, the second on cosmological theory, and the third on the unified field theory. While the first and last were largely syntheses of views which Einstein had already expounded at length, the second dealt with his recent abandoning of the cosmological constant. He admitted that this presented two problems. It would be difficult to know from what the expansion of the universe had started; and while its age worked out at about 10^{10} years, there was already considerable evidence that the earth itself was older than this. Another point was that his theory now limited the radius of the universe to 10^8 light-years, a distance to which the Mount Wilson telescope had already almost penetrated. As he said, if they went further, this would "put the varnish on" his theory.

Even in Oxford, where eccentrics are the rule rather than the exception, Einstein made his mark. The undergraduates loved him and Mrs. Haldane has recalled how a group of them helped him down from the pony trap into which he had been hurried when the Haldanes feared he would miss an important appointment. As he descended from the trap at Tom Gate a big button from his Ulster was torn off in the basketwork of the vehicle. The young girl driving him disentangled it and ran after him. "I wouldn't worry, Miss," said the college porter. "The gentleman will never miss it. He has one odd button on his coat already."

It was in Tom Quad that Einstein was discovered one day by Gilbert Murray with, as Arnold Toynbee describes it, a faraway look on his face. "The faraway thought behind that faraway look was evidently a happy one for, at that moment, the exile's countenance was serene and smiling," Toynbee has written. " 'Dr. Einstein, do tell me what you are thinking,' Murray asked. 'I am thinking,' Einstein answered, 'that, after all, this is a very small star.' All the universe's eggs were not in this basket that was now infested by the Nazis; and for a cosmogoner, this thought was convincingly consoling."

Some indication of Einstein's life during his first stay in Oxford is given in the letter which Lindemann received from Elsa after her husband had been at Christ Church a week. "He writes me enthusiastic letters," she said.

> Oxford, the calm cloisters of the college, and the noble suroundings combine to produce a refreshing and calming effect upon him. I am grateful to you for all the care and attention which you are so kindly showing him. I have, however, one request to make. My husband has no secretary or assistant. And a crowd of questions and letters of every kind come to him, although I keep back here everything I can, and send him virtually nothing. It is, therefore, unavoidably necessary for him to get some help. Don't ask him, please, because he will refuse out of his endless modesty. You would, however, be doing him a great kindness if you could simply arrange that every other day a secretary should appear and write his letters. We covet here things in his own handwriting but we get very little of it because he has so much else to write.

The "great kindness" was performed for the rest of his stay.

In Oxford he saw an England very different from the formality of Lord Haldane's London residence, an England where his Jewishness, his German ancestry, and his stature as a scientist all tended to be taken for granted and then passed over so that he could be weighed and considered as a human being. He liked the experience; he enjoyed Lindemann's friends, he soaked up the atmosphere of an Oxford that has largely disappeared in the last forty years; and whenever he wished he broke through the screens raised to ensure him privacy.

One typical picture has been drawn by Margaret Deneke, a leading figure at Oxford whose house was a mecca for music lovers. "We knew of his great interest in music," she says of Einstein.

> and we had great artists playing quartets and enjoying music in our house. They were people whose names were known to him and he was delighted to be invited to join. So he came to us. Afterwards we discovered that outsiders were not supposed to invite him, but he had found his way here and he chose to go on coming. We used to borrow instruments for him. He did not bring his violin. He played trios and quartets. He did not lead, and he

always preferred to be the second violin. Now and again he would lose his place or they had to repeat something so that he came in at the right moment.

On May 23 he received an honorary doctorate of science. He spent a few days making final courtesy calls. Then he left for home, arriving in Berlin during the first days of June. "The situation here is horrible," he wrote to Lindemann, after thanking him for all his help. "All money values have disappeared, and the people are disturbed and embittered against the government. The future that lies ahead is threatening and dark."

These words, written casually in a thank-you letter, may well have had their impact on Lindemann who during the next few years was to be the savior of so many German Jews. Touring Germany in his chauffeur-driven Mercedes, one of the few physicists whom the headwaiters of Europe's grand hotels would automatically bow to the best table, Lindemann did a great deal to extricate the cream of the country's scientists from the Reich as Hitler rose to power. Some at least of this was foreshadowed as he wrote to Lord Lothian in June, commenting on the success of Einstein in Oxford. "He threw himself into all the activities of Oxford science, attended the Colloquiums and meetings for discussion and proved so stimulating and thought-provoking that I am sure his visit will leave a permanent mark on the progress of our subject," he noted. ". . . I have hopes that this period as Rhodes Lecturer may initiate more permanent connections with this university which can only prove fertile and advantageous in every respect."

The first move came quickly. It was proposed that Einstein should be made a "Research Student," the most honorific post to which the college could elect him. This was a personal triumph for Einstein on more than one count. Inside Christ Church a considerable internal fight was being carried on about endowing research at all: on one side was the party mobilized by Lindemann and the Senior Censor, Roy (now Sir Roy) Harrod, the economist; against them was ranged a body of opinion which insisted that research men were unclubbable and would completely upset Common Room life. The latter party was supported by one college official, who stated strongly that the college endowments had not been given to subsidize "some German Jew."

Then, without obvious reason, it became clear that Einstein's candidacy was being favored. The reason for the change of balance is interesting. Einstein had in Christ Church used the rooms of R. H. Dundas, who was traveling. On his return Dundas opened his Visitor's Book to find the following written in German by Einstein:

Dundas lets his rooms decay
While he lingers far away,
Drinking wisdom at the source
Where the sun begins its course.

That his walls may not grow cold
He's installed a hermit old,
One that undeterredly preaches
What the Art of Numbers teaches

Shelves of towering folios
Meditate in solemn rows;
Find it strange that one can dwell
Here without their aid so well

Grumble: Why's this creature staying
With his pipe and piano-playing?
Why should this barbarian roam?
Could he not have stopped at home?

Often, though, his thoughts will stray
To the owner far away,
Hoping one day face to face
To behold him in this place

With hearty thanks and greetings

Dundas was charmed with the verses. So much so that he became a keen supporter of Einstein's research fellowship. All at once everyone remembered how they had taken to Einstein, what good company he had been. Einstein's doggerel ensured that the Dean was able formally to make the proposal with no chance of its being rejected. In fact there was only one protester—a former student who wrote to say that such appointments endangered his pension rights. The letter was ill-received.

News of the offer came on June 29 through Lindemann, who pointed out that Einstein would be able to stay in Oxford for one term a year without giving up his Berlin appointments. The appointment as a senior member of Christ Church—"called 'Fellows' (Socii) in most Colleges, 'Students' at Christ Church (not in the sense of Studiosum)" as Lindemann explained—would be for five years at a stipend of £400 per year with the use of a set of rooms in college and dinner allowance when he dined in Hall: and it was hoped that he "would be able to visit Oxford for something like a month during term time in the course of the year at such periods as may be convenient."

Einstein accepted quickly, "very pleased," as he wrote to Lindemann, "to be able to keep in contact with Oxford and with you personally so regularly." But already, in the summer of 1931, there was more to it than mere love of Oxford. "Extraordinary things are happening here," he continued in his letter from Berlin. "Parliament has to a certain extent renounced its authority and inevitably a kind of dictatorship has been set up. Let us hope that this will not lead to intolerable internal stresses." As events turned out, he was to appear as a Student at Christ Church during only two years of his appointment. To what must have been the chagrin of some men in Oxford, the outstanding £1,200 of his stipend went to help other German Jews.

The Christ Church offer had formally come as Einstein was completing arrangements for a second visit to the California Institute of Technology. Earlier in the year Fleming had proposed that he should come to Pasadena on a regular basis and Einstein had tentatively accepted. Fleming appears to have acted largely on his own initiative, a circumstance common to his later years and one which added an air of chaos to some of the institute's proceedings, and details of the offer are not clear. However, he gave his own version at a meeting called to consider the proposed appointment in the early autumn of 1931, and this was described in a long letter to Hale from A. A. Noyes, director of chemical research at Caltech. "Fleming," this said,

> read *not* his own letters to Einstein, but two replies he had received from Einstein, the second one written in July stating that he (Einstein) had definitely accepted the permanent appointment, with $5,000 annually plus $15,000 in any year when he comes for ten weeks to the institute plus a $3,000 annuity to his widow. Einstein himself proposed reducing the annual payment from the $25,000 proposed by Fleming to $20,000, and the proposed annuity from some larger sum to $3,000. Fleming said that Einstein cabled him in August asking to know whether the arrangement was definite, as his plans for the present year must be consummated, but we have never been able to get out of Fleming just what reply he made to that last cablegram of Einstein, though I made two attempts. It seems *probable,* however, that Fleming told Einstein that the arrangement was definite for this year, but that the permanent plan must await action by the trustees.

This was in fact what happened. Millikan, who would shortly be in Europe, was given the job of ensuring that the institute netted Einstein for the coming season but that any offer of a permanent post was evaded for the time being. In addition, he was given an even more delicate task. "Board is of opinion commitment of $20,000 all inclusive has been made for coming year," he was informed soon after reaching Europe by E. C. Barrett, the institute secretary. "If Einstein thinks so, board will carry out this commitment. If Einstein does not feel we have made such commitment board voted that you offer $15,000 or thereabouts all inclusive."

However, Millikan the faithful servant of the institute took a worldly view of Einstein's vagueness about money. "Now the $7,000 figure which we talked about for a ten or twelve weeks' annual stay in Pasadena," he wrote on October 11,

> was one which I had already suggested to some of my financial friends as a dignified and suitable one for such a service as Professor Einstein would there render, and I hope soon to be in a position to suggest such an arrangement as a continuing one—and that too without putting a strain upon the finances of the institute. . . . For the present year, in view of some previous correspondence which I believe has already been had, I am sure the trustees expect us to decide upon a considerably larger

figure and they are prepared to meet it whatever it is that we have determined upon. In other words, they want you, and we all want you very much to come.

Despite Einstein's apparent otherworldliness, despite the fact that he once used a check as a bookmarker instead of paying it into the bank, his character yet contained a strong streak of peasant awareness that quickly noted any attempt at financial sleight of hand.

His reply to Millikan, written from Caputh on October 19, 1931, was not, therefore, as surprising as it probably appeared to Millikan. "Thank you very much for your friendly and full letter," he wrote. "But I have now decided to remain here for this winter and have informed Herr Fleming and confirmed it in the following letter.

Dear Herr Fleming,

Herr Professor Millikan has laid your new proposals before me. On the strength of that, we have made up our minds to remain in Europe this winter. We have decided this chiefly because it is repugnant to me, in the present difficult situation, to accept this invitation. Besides, I must confess to you frankly that the ways and means with which the negotiations have been conducted with me, are, to say the least of it, somewhat peculiar. After your first written offer, you received from me a detailed counterproposal. To this I received no answer at all. After five weeks I finally sent you a telegram in which I asked you to inform me of your decision concerning the establishment of our winter program. Your telegraphed reply promised the forwarding of a contract at the latest on September 3. But nothing came of this.

Now recently Professor Millikan came with entirely new proposals which entirely ignore our previous negotiations. So it is not to be wondered at if I have decided to recover from the harassing negotiations during the winter in the south European sun, and to gather new strength for the future.

With most sincere greetings, Yours, A. Einstein

"I am very pleased about your and [your wife's] friendly visit," he continued to Professor Millikan. "It was very good of you to let me know some days in advance so that I was certain to be free."

So far so good. But this was not the end of the encounter. What happened next is not entirely clear. But the outcome was revealed when Elsa wrote to Millikan almost a month later, on November 14, sending the contract, signed by Einstein. She added details about the secretarial help that would be required after they arrived in Pasadena at the end of December, and referred to the domestic arrangements which involved the renting of the same private house in Pasadena that they had occupied the previous year.

The sudden change on Einstein's part may well have been due to a further appeal on the part of Fleming. It is certainly true that when the Einsteins arrived in Pasadena at the end of 1931 they were accommodated not in private quarters but in the splendid premises of the Athenaeum, the faculty club where Fleming had given up his own apartment for the occasion.

Einstein's second journey to Pasadena was thus made in the same one-visit circumstances as the first. But the question of a journey each year had now been raised. He had been led by Millikan to assume that this was still a distinct possibility if not a likelihood, and this was no doubt in his mind when in December he made a significant entry in his diary; "I decided today," it went, "that I shall essentially give up my Berlin position and shall be a bird of passage for the rest of my life." It was in this frame of mind that he arrived in Pasadena for the second time, a significant condition in view of a meeting which was shortly to come.

This was with Abraham Flexner, the American educationalist then preparing to set up a new kind of educational institute, made possible when Mr. Louis Bamberger and Mrs. Felix Fulds had two years previously provided $5 million for what Flexner called a "haven where scholars and scientists may regard the world and its phenomena as their laboratory without being carried off in the maelstrom of the immediate." Its small number of selected staff would have no duties in the usual sense of the word and the Institute for Advanced Study, as it was to become, thus offered something comparable to the conditions which had drawn Einstein to Berlin two decades previously: no routine and a lot of time to think.

It had been agreed that the institute, whose location had not yet been decided, would first concentrate on mathematical studies, and early in 1932 Flexner visited

Pasadena to get the advice of Millikan. There was one obvious suggestion—why not have a word with Einstein? "I drove over to the Athenaeum where he and Mrs. Einstein were staying and met him for the first time," Flexner has written. "I was fascinated by his noble bearing, his simple charming manner, and his genuine humility. We walked up and down the corridors of the Athenaeum for upwards of an hour, I explaining, he questioning. Shortly after twelve, Mrs. Einstein appeared to remind him that he had a luncheon engagement. 'Very well,' he said in his kindly way, 'we have time for that. Let us talk a little while longer.'"

Before they parted, Flexner said that he would be in Europe later in the year. Einstein would be spending the spring term at Oxford with Lindemann and it was agreed that they would meet again. "I had no idea," Flexner later recorded, "that he would be interested in being concerned with the institute, but he gave me the best of reasons for thinking that an informal organization such as I had in mind would be much more important at this stage of our development and at the stage of the world's development than another organized university." This then was Flexner's story: that at this point he entertained no idea of attracting Einstein from Caltech to his new institute. Nevertheless, he left Pasadena having carefully made his arrangements for a further meeting.

During this visit to Pasadena Einstein lectured on space curvature and in a joint statement issued with de Sitter, also visiting the institute, said that recent studies further strengthened the idea of an expanding universe. Hand in hand with his scientific work went a long series of pacifist statements which gravely worried Millikan and which were to have their effect on Einstein's visit the following year. To a mass disarmament meeting in the high school at Whittier he spoke of the grave danger of militarism, and pinned his hopes on the Disarmament Conference, due to start soon in Geneva. At a meeting on world affairs sponsored by the Los Angeles University of International Relations held in Pasadena, in February, he claimed that "disarmament cannot take place by easy stages but must come in one swoop *or not at all.*" The following day he told a mass meeting in Santa Barbara that renunciation of at least some political sovereignty was essential to peace, while at the end of the month he recommended to listeners in the Pasadena Civic Auditorium that the decisions of an international court should "be enforced by all the nations acting in common." Here, although his pacifist friends may not have noticed it, were indications that Einstein's renunciation of force had a qualification: that it should be outlawed for national but not necessarily international ends.

He returned to Berlin in the spring, and early in May set out for England once again, first to deliver the Rouse Ball Lecture on Mathematics in Cambridge and then to make his first visit to Oxford as a Research Student. He was given rooms in Christ Church and dined at High Table most evenings. "He was a charming person," says Sir Roy Harrod,

> and we entered into relations of easy intimacy with him. He divided his time between his mathematics and playing the violin; as one crossed the quad, one was privileged to hear the strains coming from his rooms. In our Governing Body I sat next to him; we had a green baize tablecloth; under cover of this he held a wad of paper on his knee, and I observed that all through our meetings his pencil was in incessant progress, covering sheet after sheet with equations. His general conversation was not stimulating, like that of the Prof. I am afraid I did not have the sense that, so far as human affairs were concerned, I was in the presence of a wise man or a deep thinker. Rather I had the idea that he was a very good man, a simple soul, and rather naive about worldly matters. He had his little fund of amusing stories on an unsophisticated level.

On one occasion Lindemann was able to shine before his guest. "Einstein happened to mention at High Table some mathematical proposition which he took to be well established but for which he had never been able to furnish himself with the proof," says Harrod. "The Prof returned the next day, claiming to have thought of the proof in his bath; Einstein was satisfied with it." What is more, Einstein remained satisfied. Twelve years later, writing to Lindemann, by this time Lord Cherwell and Churchill's personal scientific adviser, he added as a P. S.

to his letter: "Do you remember the beautiful proof about prime factors you found while sitting in your bathtub?"

It appears to have been on this visit that Einstein was finally conscripted by Lindemann into the forces fighting for the site of the new Radcliffe Observatory, which it was claimed should be situated in Oxford rather than in South Africa. This bitter contest of university politics was being fought on grounds which were more parochial than scientific, and it is difficult not to believe that Einstein's involvement was a tribute to his innocence rather than to deep convictions. As Lindemann's biographer says, "The Prof must have felt a glow of triumph when he induced the great Einstein to testify emphatically upon the university side." Einstein's testimony was certainly unqualified.

"I have examined the affidavits of Professors Lindemann, Milne, and Plaskett, and am in complete agreement with the arguments and views expressed therein," it ran.

However, not even this was enough. When Lindemann and others took the issue to court, they lost their case. The telescope was built near Pretoria.

Before Einstein left Oxford, Flexner arrived. They met in Christ Church and on a fine morning began pacing the lawn of the quadrangle, coming closer and closer to grips with the problem of the new institute. "As it dawned on me during our conversation," Flexner has written, "that perhaps he might be interested in attaching himself to an institute of the proposed kind, before we parted I said to him: 'Professor Einstein, I would not presume to offer you a post in this new institute, but if on reflection you decide that it would afford you the opprtunities which you value, you would be welcome on your own terms.'" Einstein was apparently noncommittal: but he agreed that as Flexner was visiting Berlin later in the year they could well meet again.

He returned from England at the end of May, 1932. Berlin was already ominously different from the city of even a few months previously. In April there had taken place what was, on the face of it, an encouraging presidential election. For the octogenarian Field Marshal Hindenburg, representing the Democrats and Socialists, had been reelected, defeating the leader of the National Socialist party, Adolf Hitler. However, the President soon showed where his sympathies lay. In May he forced

Brüning, the Reich Chancellor, on whose support he had largely won the election, to give way to von Papen, a man determined to end the Weimar Republic. Von Papen's ostensibly non-party, but in fact ultra-right wing, cabinet was formed a few days later. It quickly expelled the Socialist-Center Prussian cabinet under a form of martial law and dissolved the Reichstag. Rule by bayonet had arrived.

What this landslide to the right meant to Jews in general and Einstein in particular was indicated when on June 2 Deputy Kube announced to the Prussian Diet that "when we clean house the exodus of the Children of Israel will be a child's game in comparison." To leave do doubt of his meaning, he added that "a people that possesses a Kant will not permit an Einstein to be tacked onto it." Human wisdom, noted Edgar Mowrer, "whispered that a people that refused an Einstein would be unworthy of a Kant."

Many in Germany still hoped that a quasi-military government with strong monarchist leanings would keep the Nazi party in its place. Einstein had no such illusions. Frank records that when a professor expressed the hope one evening at Caputh during this summer of 1932, Einstein replied: "I am convinced that a military regime will not prevent the imminent National Socialist revolution. The military dictatorship will suppress the popular will and the people will seek protection against the rule of the Junkers and the officers in a right-radical revolution."

It was against this background that Abraham Flexner made his promised visit to Berlin. "It was a cold day," he has written.

> I was stll wearing my winter clothes and heavy overcoat. Arriving at Einstein's country home, beautiful and commodious, I found him seated on the veranda wearing summer flannels. He asked me to sit down. I asked whether I might wear my overcoat. "Oh, yes," he replied. "Aren't you chilly?" I asked, surveying his costume. "No," he replied, "my dress is according to this season, not according to the weather; it is summer."
>
> We sat then on the veranda and talked until evening, when Einstein invited me to stay to supper. After supper we talked until almost eleven. By that time it was perfectly clear that Einstein and his wife were prepared to come to America. I told him to name his own terms and he promised me to write within a few days.

Einstein accompanied his guest back to the bus for Berlin, walking through the rain hatless and in an old sweater. "I am full of enthusiasm (Ich bin Feuer und Flamme dafür)," he said as they parted.

The following Monday Flexner prepared a memorandum covering the details of what was to become Einstein's official appointment for virtually the rest of his life. These included, in Flexner's words, location of the new institute "contiguous to Princeton University, residence from autumn until about the middle of April, salary, pension, etc., and an independent appointment for Professor Mayer."

When the question of salary had first been raised Einstein said that he wanted $3,000 a year. "Could I live on less?" he asked, according to Flexner's later recollections. "You couldn't live on that," he had replied. "Let Mrs. Einstein and me arrange it." The result was a salary of $16,000 a year, to be continued after retirement.

Einstein had been careful to explain two things: that he would once again be spending the winter months in Pasadena, and that he still had his obligations both to the Prussian Academy of Sciences and to Christ Church, Oxford. Judging by the memories of Hermann Weyl, who was to join him in the institute, there were other reservations. Recalling a meeting between Einstein and himself, Flexner, and Dr. Frank Aydelotte, a trustee of the new institute and later successor to Flexner, Weyl declared that whatever doubts and thoughts they had about turning their backs on Germany to join Flexner's new institute were soon dispelled by Hitler's rise to power.

On June 22, Elsa explained the situation in a letter to California. "My dear Professor Millikan," she wrote,

> you are aware how much my husband wishes to obtain an appointment for Dr. Mayer, and therefore, almost as a matter of course, my husband has accepted the post which offers this to Dr. Mayer. In addition my husband values his work very much. So the die is cast; my husband has accepted Flexner's offer. I know what a wonderful time we had in Pasadena. We shall never forget it. But Albert has felt the burden of not being able to take care of Mayer. And he was so relieved when this was done. Will you, under the circumstances, still want my husband in Pasadena next winter? I doubt it.

It is clear from this, even it not from Einstein's own careful letter, that acceptance of Flexner's offer was a significant change of emphasis from West Coast to East, from the old Caltech to the new institute. That Millikan himself saw it in this light is obvious from the disgruntled letter which he wrote to Flexner. With an air of surprise—that ignored his introduction of Flexner to Einstein the previous year—he noted that he had "just had a letter from Dr. Einstein saying that you are establishing in Princeton a theoretical research institute and that he has accepted some sort of a permanent part-time annual commitment to participate in the work of this institute beginning in the fall of 1933, and that this is likely to make his continued association with the corresponding institute which has been laborously [*sic*] built up during the past ten years impossible."

Millikan was not, he implied, thinking of his own institute, but of more important things. "Whether the progress of science in the United States would be advanced by such a move, or whether Professor Einstein's productivity will be increased by such a transfer, is at least debatable," he went on. "The work in which his interest and his activity lies is certainly much more strongly developed here than it is at Princeton, and I am inclined to think that with the astrophysical advances that are in prospect here this will continue to be the case." He concluded with the hope that Flexner might still collaborate with his own institute in some joint venture and that, even if this were not possible, Einstein might be able to "spend half the time which he would normally be in this country in Princeton and half the time here. . . ."

Flexner, with the Einstein contract safely in his pocket, could afford the lofty reply. After noting that "altogether by accident" he had been in Oxford at the same time as Einstein—a remark ingeniously dissimilar from the account which he was to write when Millikan was dead—he defended himself in slightly injured terms. "I cannot believe that annual residence for brief periods at several places is sound or wholesome. Looking at the entire matter from Professor Einstein's point of view, I believe that you and all his friends will rejoice that it has been possible to create for him a permanent post of the character above indicated."

The question of the coming autumn visit was soon resolved: Millikan would be as glad as ever to see Einstein—not least, one must feel, because this would strengthen his hand against whatever blandishments Flexner was offering. What was to happen after Einstein had begun to visit Princeton—"maybe a solution will be found so that he can from time to time come to Pasadena," Elsa wrote to Millikan on August 13—was left in the air. But Einstein never visited Pasadena after the winter of 1932–33.

Some comment must be made on this battle for Einstein's last years. The first is that vacillation over Fleming's initial offer, and then its supersession by Millikan's, left a nasty taste in the mouth for Einstein. Had he known the truth about Flexner's cutting-out operation against Caltech, he might have had much the same feeling about the offer from Princeton. In any case, he was shrewd enough to see how the land lay and will have had no qualms against playing off such opponents against each other. With Einstein, getting the best conditions for his work justified anything. He was certainly anxious to take Mayer with him wherever he went, and this was a useful point for Elsa to make. Just how she made it was immaterial, for once he had come to a decision, Einstein left the details to her, not worrying overmuch how his decision was implemented.

The appointment was, moreover, still only a part-time winter affair. This feature of the contract was made clear in a statement from Berlin. "I have received leave of absence from the Prussian Academy for five months of the year for five years," this explained. "Those five months I expect to spend at Princeton. I am not abandoning Germany. My permanent home will still be in Berlin."

And now, prepared for the worst as he continued to hope for the best, he began to get ready for his third trip to Pasadena.

Before his departure he again visited Belgium, calling on the King and Queen at Laeken. In a letter of thanks to Her Majesty dated September 19 he wrote that "it was a great happiness for me to explain to you something of the mysteries in front of which physicists stand silent."

Then, unexpectedly, he received news from Weizemann about the Hebrew University. There had been a meeting between Magnes and Weizmann. The details were not passed on but the upshot was that an impartial Structure Committee was to investigate the whole situation. From this fact, Weizmann went confidently on. "Now I come to a request for you to rejoin the Board of Governors," he wrote.

> a request which I know would be backed by everyone who really has the university at heart. I remind you of a promise you gave me, that you would do so under my leadership. All those who have fought for reforms, which now look like being successfully carried through, would see a great moral boost in your return, quite apart from the other good it would do. We cannot lose you, although we cannot offer you a "scientific home" as Princeton can. But who knows! Now that I shall be spending a longer time in Jerusalem I have every intention of improving the physics and chemistry, and perhaps you will then visit us.

Einstein replied that he was delighted to hear the news. He poured out advice about the department of physics almost as though he was already back on the Board of Governors. But this was merely physics taking control. He added that he would be glad to rejoin the board if there were university reforms; but he made it clear that he did not take Weizmann's assurances entirely at their face value, and implied that the new committee would first have to produce results. As for visiting Palestine, this was studiously ignored. Weizmann, as well as Flexner and Millikan and Lindemann, was shopping for Einstein as events in Germany made it less and less likely that he would be able to remain in the country much longer. Einstein measured all the offers and hints by the usual yardstick: the extent to which they would enable him to get on with his work.

Now, in the late autumn, he prepared for Pasadena again. For a short while it looked as though there might not be any need. For while anti-Semitic opposition to Einstein was increasing in Germany, a ground swell of protest was building up in the United States. The board of the National Patriotic Council issued a statement describing him as a German Bolshevist and adding that his theory "was of no scientific value or purpose, not understandable because there is nothing to understand," an assessment that brought an immediate response from Einstein: "Wouldn't it be funny if they didn't let me in? Why, the whole world would laugh at America." The possibility was less ludicrous than it sounded, for the American Women's League now issued a formal statement demanding that the U. S. State Department should not grant an entry visa to a man such as Einstein, a member of the War Resisters International whom they described as a Communist.

Common sense suggested that the protest should be ignored, but Einstein's delight at making the opposition look foolish came to the top. "Never before have I experienced from the fair sex such energetic rejection of all advances; or if I have, never from so many at once," he said in a public statement.

> But are they not quite right, these watchful citizenesses? Why should one open one's doors to a person who devours hard-boiled capitalists with as much appreciation and gusto as the Cretan Minotaur in days gone by devoured luscious Greek maidens, and on top of that is low down enough to reject every sort of war, except the unavoidable war with one's own wife? Therefore give heed to your clever and patriotic womenfolk and remember that the Capitol of mighty Rome was once saved by the cackling of its faithful geese.

As far as pacifism was concerned the protests from America were sound enough. But they were wildly out regarding Einstein's attitude to communism and to Soviet Russia. Only a few months previously he had refused to sign an appeal from Henri Barbusse, a man with whose pacifist views he greatly sympathized, solely on account of its "glorification of Soviet Russia." He had, he told Barbusse, reached some somber conclusions about the country. "At the top there appears to be a personal struggle in which the foulest means are used by power-hungry individuals acting from purely selfish motives. At the bottom there seems to be complete suppression of the individual and of freedom of speech. One wonders what life is worth under such conditions." But these views were unknown. What was known was Einstein's view that the Russia of the interwar years had no aggressive intentions. More than once he said that he believed Lenin was a great man; and a decade earlier he had tried to intercede in the cause of Zionism with the Russians in Berlin. But he would have been as ready to intercede with the devil had he thought that good would come of it. His view of the Revolution was a complex if balanced one in which he weighed the bad against the good with considerable judgment; but the balance was concealed by his own default and if he was wrongly accused he had no one to blame but himself.

The visa was finally granted, and early in December he and Elsa completed their preparations. Despite the earlier statement that he intended to keep a permanent home in Berlin, despite his unwavering hope and brave front, he was under no illusions as he spent the final days of November in the house at Caputh that he had come to love. As he left it for Berlin and the train to Antwerp where he and his wife were to board ship for the States he turned to her with the warning: "Before you leave our villa this time, take a good look at it." When she asked why, he replied: "You will never see it again." Elsa, says Philipp Frank, thought he was being rather foolish.

CHAPTER 16

GOOD-BYE TO BERLIN

Einstein and Elsa arrived in California early in January, 1933, the third visit in three years. It now looked as though this might be a regular thing, even though the summer months were securely earmarked for Princeton and commitments in Berlin would further limit his free time. Millikan certainly hoped so, and had gone to great lengths to land his catch for this visit when it seemed that the institute might not find the necessary money.

Salvation eventually came from the Oberlaender Trust of Philadelphia, set up "to enable American men and women without regard to race, creed, or color, who are actively engaged in work that affects the public welfare, to become better acquainted with similar activities in German-speaking countries." In 1931 Millikan had been given an Oberlaender grant "to contact German scholars, lecturers, and universities." The following year, after further contacts with Millikan, the Trust voted "to appropriate the sum of $7,000 to cover the expenses of Professor Einstein in America some time during the academic year 1932–33. The money to be forwarded through Professor Millikan as a grant to Professor Einstein, exclusively for scientific work." However, there was a rider to the exclusivity. For while Millikan was completing arrangements with Einstein, he wrote to the Trust agreeing that his guest should make "one broadcast which will be helpful to German-American relations." This was the fee which was to be paid by Einstein for the support which made possible his third visit to Pasadena. Whether he fully appreciated this before setting out is not recorded. But Millikan's wish to keep faith with the Trust certainly increased anxiety that Einstein might queer the pitch for what was to be in many ways a propaganda broadcast.

Dourly conservative, faintly militarist, and with more than a touch of right-wing enthusiasm, Millikan had cause for worry. Einstein's persistence in advocating his pacifist ideal during earlier visits had done much to foster the undercurrent of objection which flowed through the American scene and which not even the general adulation could entirely conceal. And it had already caused more than one of his scientific colleagues to perform verbal gymnastics in his defense. Thus Millikan himself, a man who lacked pacifist learnings as much as Einstein lacked the aggressive instinct, had been forced to reply to an impassioned appeal from Major General Amos A. Fried, who wrote to him to "protest against Americans who, in the name of science, are aiding and abetting the teaching of treason to the youth of this country by being hosts to Dr. Albert Einstein." Fried went on to say that when he had last talked with Millikan, $100,000 worth of radium was being presented to Madame Curie who was, he ended, in his opinion worth a million Albert Einsteins.

The answer to General Fried throws interesting light on Einstein and also helps to explain Millikan's somewhat panic-stricken efforts to prevent him from speaking on nonscientific matters. "It is quite true," he replied on March 8

> that Einstein has been exploited by all sorts of agencies that had their special axes to grind. Part of these have been of the Charlie Chaplin type and part of the Upton Sinclair type. The latter in particular have misquoted him to such an extent that I am not very much suprised that a man like yourself should have been misinformed by the flood of literature of this type.
>
> I am not saying that Einstein has not made blunders of his own, for he has. He is an exceedingly straightforward, honest, and childlike sort, and has only recently, through rather bitter experience, been learning the lesson of the danger of trusting everybody who pretends to be actuated by high motives. Even more than that, he has not always been wise in his utterances, and in one or two instances has made very bad slips which I think he now realizes himself, and I think in practically all the speeches and interviews which he has made out here he has been often times extraordinarily profound, pene-

> trating, and wise. But when he went east last year he is reported by the papers to have said a number of things which I would condemn as unsound as hard as you do—for example, the two percent comment, if he ever made it, is one which no experienced man could possibly have made. It takes all of us some time to learn wisdom.
>
> Of course I am only writing to you now to let you know that I think you have fallen into the same error that Einstein has fallen into, and have trusted to reports of designing people who are not trustworthy, and because of that trust have made a fundamental error in your estimate of the man. I should not have confidence in my own judgment alone, but it is that he is a man of the finest qualities and character, who has made errors, indeed, but not so many as most of us have.

Millikan did what he could. He stood up in honorable fashion to defend what he had no particular wish to defend. But underneath his confident exterior he was seriously worried that his guest might make another "two percent" speech that would invalidate the coming broadcast or affect the flow of money into the institute from rich patrons. This much is clear from his private comments to the Trust after Einstein had met reporters on arrival in Pasadena. He "handled himself," wrote Millikan "with a skill which, I am sure if your trustees had seen, would help to relieve their minds as to any possible adverse influence which he might exert in the way of furnishing additional ammunition to those who have been spreading these grotesquely foolish reports about his connection with influences aimed at the undermining of American institutions and ideals. . . ."

The broadcast to "help German-American relations" was to be made on January 23 and until then Millikan's security measures worked, although only at the cost of revealing to Einstein how limited his freedom of action really was. He had agreed to make no public appearances except those personally arranged by Millikan "under dignified auspices." "But even after this conversation," Millikan informed the Trust.

> I suddenly found that some wholly nonrepresentative group of so-called "War Resisters" at the University of California at Los Angeles had come over to see him, representing that it was just a private gathering of no

> public significance, and he had been unwise enough to believe them and agree to say something. I then found that this group had issued handbills which they had spread all over the institutions of southern California that he was to appear last Sunday and speak. I saw at once that this situation was full of dynamite, and went straight to him and told him that he would have to cancel the engagement, and he then saw the necessity and authorized me to cancel it for him. I accordingly telephoned UCLA and got the whole thing eliminated, with the Los Angeles press explaining the cancellation in a way which was really helpful, I think. The form in which it went in was, as a matter of fact, prepared in our office. . . .

Einstein appears to have acquiesced without protest at this adroit piece of manipulation. Millikan, had he remembered his guest's reaction to the institute's sleight of financial hand the previous year, might have felt some qualms about the future. However, the present had been saved and Einstein's broadcast "On German-American Agreement" was the one-shot success which everyone had hoped it would be.

The broadcast was preceded by a full-dress dinner at the Athenaeum and here Einstein first met Leon Watters, a wealthy Jewish biochemist who was to become an intimate friend for the last two decades of his life. Watters, a New Yorker, had the previous month begun to finance work at the institute and as a result found himself and his wife placed by Millikan at the top table, separated from Einstein only by a woman of considerable wealth who was also supporting the institute financially. "I soon noted," Watters later wrote,

> that, while the lady was doing considerable talking, Einstein was only nodding. He seemed somewhat ill at ease. I leaned over and offered him a cigarette from my case. He hesitated, then smiled, took one, lighted it, and consumed it in three strong puffs. While the coffee was being served I took a cigar from my pocket and wrote the following verse on a card which I attached to the cigar and proffered it to him. He shook his head and said: "No thanks: I prefer my pipe." But he noticed the card, read it, and burst out laughing. On the card I had written a verse from a poem by Bert Leston Taylor, reading: "When men are calling one another names and making faces/

> And all the world's a jangle and a jar/ I mediate [sic] on interstellar space/ And smoke a mild segar."
>
> That seemed to loosen his tongue. He asked me to spell out my name for him and I showed him my place card. He asked me if I were teaching at California Institute of Technology and I explained that I was not and that I was only a visitor. Was I alone?

In some ways Watters, with his chauffeur-driven car and his apartment on Fifth Avenue, with his dilettante approach to science, was the antithesis of all that Einstein believed in. Yet an interior practical kindness was enough to bind him both to Einstein and to Elsa as the long and deeply personal correspondence between them was later to show. The foundations for it were laid that evening as Watters and the rest of the carefully picked guests followed Einstein to the Pasadena Civic Auditorium. Here the program, entitled "Symposium on America and the World," sponsored by the Southern California College Student Body Presidents' Association, was to be broadcast by the National Broadcasting Company.

Einstein began by speaking of two obstacles. "The first of these," he said, "is the obstacle of the black dress suit. When men come together on ceremonial occasions attired in their dress clothes, they create about themselves as a matter of routine an atmosphere from which the realities of life with their severity are excluded. There is an atmosphere of well-sounding oratory that likes to attach itself to dress clothes. Away with it." After this typical Einsteinian opening he discussed the emotion-laden content of some words—"heretic" in relation to the Inquisition, "Communist" in the United States, "Jew" among the reactionary group in Germany, and "bourgeois" in Russia. "I should like to call it the obstacle of the taboo," he said of this feature of human relationships. He then went on, in mild and rational words, to speak of the prospects for American-German relations, and of the economic situation. "It was," the *New York Times* noted in an editorial, "exactly the same kind of thing that we had got hundreds of times from other people. The spirit of the Einstein address was fine, even lofty; but it cast not a single fresh ray of light upon a dark situation." Meanwhile, in Germany, Hitler was preparing to accept the call of the Germans.

Einstein remained in Pasadena for another seven weeks, obeying Millikan's injunction to hold his tongue and paying occasional rest visits to places such as the Rayben Farm Hope Ranch, from which he sent this brief poem on a card to the Queen of the Belgians: "A tree stands in the cloister garden/ Which was planted by your hand./ It sends a little twig as greeting/ Because there it must forever stand./ It sends a friendly greeting with Yours, A. Einstein."

However humiliating his enforced silence may have been, he could be grateful to Millikan for extricating him from one embarrassing situation. For it was on his host's instructions that he finally declined to be guest of honor at a banquet of the Arts, Literature, and Science National Convention. Earl C. Bloss, the convention's first vice-president, had written to Millikan explaining that many of the invited guests were withholding acceptance and adding that it had recently been "unanimously decided that the success of our banquet would be unquestioned if we were to replace Professor Einstein's presence with some other outstanding gentleman." A suitably high-ranking naval officer was finally obtained. Millikan was duly informed that the convention more than appreciated "what you have done by withholding the presence of Professor Einstein."

Such exhibitions of the anger and distrust which Einstein's pacifist and left-wing statements aroused in Americans did much to explain Millikan's apprehension as the time for his visitor's departure approached. Earlier he had written to the Oberlaender Trust saying that he feared "the possible efforts of all kinds of radical groups to exploit him when he gets away from Pasadena, especially if he goes east—as I think perhaps he plans to do—by train instead of by boat." Early in February his worst fears were realized. Einstein was to return east by train. Moreover, he was to make one address in Chicago and another in New York. In view "of the near slips which we have been fortunate enough to avoid making," Millikan wondered what the Trust in Philadelphia could do.

The answer was that it could do very little. The secretary, Mr. Thomas, wrote from the Trust to Einstein, noting that he had had no reply to earlier letters, stating that he had heard of plans to make addresses, and saying rather plaintively that he would like to know about them as soon as possible. The scanty evidence suggests that if Einstein gave Mr. Thomas' letters any attention at all he stuffed them into his pocket determined that on leaving Pasadena he would make up for the silence so far forced upon him. As it turned out, other events were to dominate his thoughts. Looking back, the reasons are self-evident. For while Einstein was again discussing the riddle of the universe with Hubble and Tolman at Mount Wilson, lecturing to students, and generally acting as a scientific liaison officer between Caltech and the Berlin of the Kaiser Wilhelm Institute, events in Germany had rolled forward with ominous inevitability. During the last month of 1932 Kurt von Schleicher had become Chancellor; for some weeks he had desperately tried to form a stable government. He failed, the third man to do so in as many years. On January 30, President Hindenburg turned to the one leader he felt might at least square the circle—Adolf Hitler.

The effect on Einstein was immediate and unqualified, perhaps surprisingly so for a man so mild mannered, so uninterested in the balances and counterbalances of politics, so eternally hopeful that with goodwill the worst might be avoided. But now he knew that his "Never see it again" prophecy on leaving Caputh was more likely to be borne out than the return to Germany foreshadowed in his October statement. His first action was to cancel the lecture due to be given at the Prussian Academy on his return to Berlin. By February 27 he was writing to a friend, Mrs. Margarete Lebach, that he "dare not enter Germany because of Hitler." A few hours later the Reichstag was in flames, set alight by the subnormal Dutchman van der Lubbe. Within a few days the incident had been exploited by the new Nazi government to rush through emergency decrees which gave them totalitarian powers. And on March 2 any remaining doubts that Einstein's unique position might guard him from the government's growing anti-Jewish wrath were dispelled by a leading article in the *Völkischer Beobachter* on "cultural internationalism," "international treason," and "pacifist excesses." In it, Einstein was singled out for attack, together with Heinrich and Thomas Mann, Arnold Zweig, and a short list of Germany's leading intellectuals, academics, and artists.

On March 10, Einstein made his decision public. In a long interview with Evelyn Seeley of the *New York World Telegram* on the eve of his departure from Pasadena he said: "As long as I have any choice in the matter, I shall live only in a country where civil liberty, tolerance, and equality of all citizens before the law prevail. Civil liberty implies freedom to express one's political convictions, in speech and in writing; tolerance implies respect for the convictions of others whatever they may be. These conditions do not exist in Germany at the present time."

Concluding the interview, Einstein said that he would probably settle in Switzerland. He then rose to attend a final seminar at the institute. As he left the room, Los Angeles, a score of miles away, was shaken by the worst earthquake in its history. Symbolically, the reporter was able to note that "as he left for the seminar, walking across the campus, Dr. Einstein felt the ground shaking under his feet."

Thus in mid-March, 1933, Einstein arrived at the position he had correctly forecast to Infeld little more than a decade previously. He was no longer able to live in what was both the country of his birth and, since 1919, the country of his voluntary adoption. As in 1920, there were no doubt elements in Germany which were national, civilized, and libertarian; as in 1920, they formed a minority, helpless and silent. Einstein's disillusion was thus compounded. For the rest of his life he felt a double grudge against Germany: first that he had been born there and, worse still, that he had been misguided enough to take German nationality again when he might easily have remained simply a Swiss.

Even so, it is clear that he had not even begun to comprehend the nature of the revolution that was sweeping Germany. Had he done so he would not have written to Planck as he wrote on March 9—not only suggesting that specialists might leave Germany to work on an international scientific committee, but asking whether Planck would put up the idea to the Academy.

"I was recently with Professor Hale of the Mount Wilson Observatory, who is the current president of the Research Council," he wrote.

He said that he wants to make an attempt to cut out politics entirely from the work of international scientific cooperation. This is what he wants to do:

First he wishes to set up a working committee of specialists from all countries, with the aim of transferring scientific methods from one discipline to another (for example, the transfer of physical methods into the biological sciences). He naturally wants to give a share of this work to German research workers. But he does not want it to seem as if such invitations bypass, as it were, the German scientific institutions. He wishes to attract from every country only those genuinely interested specialists who have no political axes to grind. He hopes that all really well-disposed scientists will help him and also that the institutions of individual countries will approve of it, if one takes care to remove all political influences from the scientific work, and so to bring about again the state of affairs which was once taken as a matter of course.

Herr Hale wants to know your view about this. He wants to know whether you would be prepared to submit the idea to the Academy in a friendly way. He thinks that I should write to you first since you, writing to me, can truly express your opinion. I will use your answer only in so far as you wish, and as it is needed to express your point of view.

Then, if you and the Academy are well disposed to this, we will consider the people who might be able to carry out useful work on the problems to be handled by the commission. Any suggestions as to names would be valuable to the commission or to Herr Hale; this, then, would be the second exercise.

I myself would be very happy if Herr Hale, with all his efforts for science, were successful. There cannot be the slightest doubt about the genuineness of his wish; his ideals, governed by devotion to research, are more than a guarantee of this.

Please send your answer c/o Herr Ehrenfest, Leiden, Holland, as I am not yet sure where I shall pitch my tent.

The answer, in the negative, arrived towards the end of April and Einstein sent it off without delay to Hale from the Belgian resort where he had temporarily made his home.

He and Elsa had left Pasadena on March 11, traveling overland to New York by way of Chicago, as expected. The repercussions were less than Millikan had feared, partly because he had agreed to attend a birthday luncheon arranged by a local committee in aid of the Hebrew University, and his time for other matters was therefore limited. But he did what he could, and finally agreed to attend a pacifist meeting on the morning of the fourteenth. "After he came and found us interested in serious discussions he would not leave us even when eleven o'clock came, the hour for the luncheon to claim him," according to a report by Mrs. Lloyd, one of the organizers. "At eleven fifteen Mrs. Einstein rose and reminded him of the committee. He asked her to sit down and said he wanted another quarter of an hour with us. So we enjoyed a full hour of his valuable discussion on international, political, and psychological subjects."

Thus far there appears to have been no crack in his pacifist armor. "His firm faith in the decent impulses of the human heart is evident and inspiring," wrote Mrs. Lloyd. "The peace campaign must go on. Let the Youth Peace Council whose representatives sit with us note his plain teaching. Let all pacifists take courage and be as extreme as they like. Einstein will never abandon the peace movement because it is too bold." Only thirteen weeks later the plain teaching was to be different. Were he a Belgian, Einstein then declared, he would give military service "cheerfully, in the belief that I would thereby be helping to save European civilization."

From the pacifist meeting he went on to the luncheon, attended by, among others, Arthur Compton of the University of Chicago, and the governor of Illinois. He spoke of the problem of "finding a method of distribution which would work as well as that of production" and he spoke of organizing international affairs so that war could be abolished. But this was subdued stuff, very different from the "two percent" speech of 1931. It was, already, almost as if Einstein were beginning to doubt his own pacifism.

The following day he traveled on to New York where he arrived shortly after Weizmann had left for Palestine—one of those missed meetings which might have altered history. In New York he spoke at a function held for the joint good of the Jewish Telegraph Agency and the Hebrew University. Dr. Rosenbach, the noted American bibliophile, was in charge and had organized a dinner for more than 600 at the Commodore Hotel.

"He wrote to Dr. Karl Compton of the Massachusetts Institute of Technology and Dr. Harlow Shapley of Harvard asking them to speak on the program," says Rosenbach's biographer.

> They sent out invitations, and in his name a barrage of promotional publicity went out to the press. Both the eminent American scientists accepted the invitation, but Shapley was concerned about the position of the microphone (he could not have picked a worse person to whom to mention details of that kind), was worried lest "the publicity submerge the spirit," was upset by rumors that Einstein's genial gullibility had been taken advantage of by high-pressure fund raisers; in fact, he wanted detailed assurance that the whole program would be on a dignified level. Dr. Rosenbach gave him that assurance.

It was on a dignified level; Einstein's Zionism was quickly submerged in physics and Rosenbach's lost in the world of books. Congressman Sol Bloom had given up his seat beside Einstein to Harlow Shapley, and the two scientists were soon absorbed in the universe, Einstein using his body to illustrate a point, the ribs being the heavens and his backbone the Milky Way. Soon afterwards he made a sketch for his dinner companion on the back of a place card—only to find it snatched away as a souvenir by an onlooker. Rosenbach was not long in reaching his true love and, after mentioning the two good causes for which the dinner was being held, presented Einstein with a first edition of Napier's *Rabdologiae.*

The following day Einstein squeezed in a visit to Princeton, conferred there with Oswald Veblen, and went on a preliminary round of house hunting in preparation for his return in the autumn. Back in New York he was driven with his wife to a synagogue where the eight-day-old son of the Jewish Telegraphic Agency's managing director became their godchild, and where Einstein wrote on the back of a photograph of himself a poem "To little Albert Landau on the occasion of his entering the world."

> If others often plague thee
> And do or say evil of thee,
> Think also they came here
> Without having asked for it.

Think, though you may not like it,
You, too, plagued others often.
As this cannot be altered,
Think gently of everyone.

That duty performed, Einstein had but a few more hours in New York. So far, his only public reaction to the news from Germany had been his measured statement that he would not be returning. This was reasonable enough; and it gave no weapons to his enemies. Now, with only a few hours to go before sailing for Europe, he attended a reception at the Waldorf-Astoria to launch *The Fight Against War,* an anthology of his pacifist writings to be published later in the year. So far, he had spoken openly only of his own personal position in relation to the new German government; he had given the world no other reaction of the world's most famous Jew to the rise of the world's most famous Jew-baiter. That was the way he wanted it.

Now, at the Waldorf-Astoria, he stepped into the ring, attacking the German Academy of Arts, pointing out that in Germany pacifists were considered enemies of the state, and saying that the world should be made more aware of the dangers of Hitlerism. All this made it easier for the German authorities to attack him. They would of course have done so anyway. But his honesty in speaking out, without reserve and while on a "mission of molding public opinion to better German-American relations," as Millikan had put it in one letter to the Oberlaender Trust—made their task that much simpler. He issued no plea for U. S. intervention, and he was not atrocity-mongering; but by the time reports reached Germany via the New York correspondents it could easily enough be represented as such, and it was fuel for the virulent anti-Einstein campaign exemplified by the *Berliner Lokal-Anzeiger*. "Good news from Einstein—he's not coming back," this said. ". . . Relativity is in little demand by us now. On the contrary. The ideals of national honor and love of country which Herr Einstein wanted to abolish have become absolute values to us. So the outlook for Einstein here is very bad."

It was in this atmosphere that he and his wife left for Europe. It appears that they had been given a final warning by the German consul in New York, Dr. Paul

Schwarz, whom Einstein had known in Berlin. Details of the meeting are vague, and the secondhand accounts contradictory. But the truth seems to be that Schwarz formally told Einstein that it would be safe for him to return to Germany but informally warned him against it. His warning may not have been as blunt as one reported version: "If you go to Germany, Albert, they'll drag you through the streets by the hair," but it was strong enough to convince him that his decision had been not only ethical but wise.

As the *Belgenland* crossed the Atlantic, Einstein playing the violin at benefit concerts for refugee musicians, there came more news from Germany. Bruno Walter, the Jewish conductor, had fled to Austria. The offices of the Zionist Federation of Germany had been searched. In Ulm, the state commissioner for the city's administration had ordered that Einsteinstrasse, named eleven years previously should in future be known as Fichtestrasse, after the German nationalist philosopher. Preparations were being made for the purge of the Civil Service which was soon to remove everyone of even partial Jewish descent, and for control of the universities by Bernard Rust, Minister for Education, who was to oust more than 1,600 Jewish lecturers and professors from their jobs. The time was coming when all books by Jews would have to be marked "Translated from the Hebrew"—and when only a daring professor would declare: "It is a mistake to believe that Einstein's original papers were translated from the Hebrew."

In mid-ocean, news came that the Einstein's home in Caputh had been searched, the pretext being that an arms cache might be found there. "The raid . . . by an armed crowd is but one example of the arbitrary acts of violence now taking place throughout Germany," said Einstein in a statement issued on the ship. "These acts are the result of the government's overnight transfer of police powers to a raw and rabid mob of the Nazi militia. My summer home has often in the past been honored by the presence of guests. They were always welcome. No one had any reason to break in."

The *Belgenland* docked on March 28 at Antwerp, where the Einsteins were welcomed by the mayor, Camille Huysmans, and a group of professors from Ghent University. The latter was headed by Professor A. de Groodt, and Einstein and his wife gratefully accepted the offer of a temporary refuge at "Cantecroy," a historic manor house outside Antwerp which was the de Groodt's family home.* Their next move had now to be decided.

*Frans G. L. A. de Groodt, Professor de Groodt's eldest son, says that his parents, in consultation with a number of friends, had telegraphed to Einstein on the *Belgenland*, begging him not to sail on to Hamburg but to come ashore in Antwerp. "I remember that it needed some insistence to persuade Einstein not to return to his country," he says. This is curious, but may well indicate the turmoil of Einstein's mind during these critical days.

CHAPTER 17

SHOPPING FOR EINSTEIN

Between the spring and the autumn of 1933 Einstein was driven to action in three different fields. Virtually barred from Germany, he had to decide where to settle. Faced with a Third Reich under Hitler, he had to reconsider his pacifist beliefs. And as the future of the Jewish scholars driven from Germany grew into a major issue, he felt forced to bring into the open his long-standing argument with the Hebrew University. These climaxes in his life, all the direct result of Hitler's rise to the chancellorship, developed simultaneously as he continued with his work, amiably agreed to lecture to all and sundry, and was reluctantly transformed into a symbol of the anti-Nazi forces which began to form throughout the continent. They give to his life a muddled and incoherent pattern paralleled by Europe as it reacted in its own way to the rise of the National Socialist party.

One of Einstein's first actions after reaching Antwerp revealed how the events of the previous few weeks had hardened his opinions. In Pasadena, talking to Miss Seeley of the *New York World-Telegram*, he had remarked that his citizenship (of Germany) was "a strange affair" but had gone on to say that "for an internationally minded man, citizenship of a specific country is not important. Humanity is more important than national citizenship."

Now he was convinced that the Nazi actions satisfied some urge in the Prussian character. He remembered his youth in Munich and he remembered what he had done then. How right he had been thirty-seven years ago! How wrong he had been to believe that Weimar had changed everything! Once again, he decided to renounce his German citizenship.

He was driven to Brussels and here in the German embassy he formally surrendered the rights of full German citizenship he had taken with such determination after the war. He retained his Swiss nationality so he could hand in his German passport. Descending the steps of the German embassy, Albert Einstein, the Swabian from Ulm, left German territory for the last time.

At the same time he unknowingly set a riddle for the German authorities. For without their consent a German continued to remain a German whatever he said or did; and within a few months, as Einstein's formal withdrawal from Prussian nationality was being considered, the authorities began to ask whether it might not be better for them to refuse his renunciation, and then themselves take away his nationality. Two points of view emerged at a meeting held at the Ministry of the Interior in Berlin on the morning of August 16, when officials met to discuss the first list of men whose citizenship, it was proposed, should be taken away under new regulations passed the previous month. There were seven of them: George Bernhardt, Rudolf Breitscheid, Albert Einstein, Lion Feuchtwanger, Heinrich Mann, the Communist leader Munzenberg, and Philipp Scheidemann. Of Einstein it was proposed, in the words of the minutes, that "in view of the world position which he holds, the withdrawal of his citizenship rights should not be announced, at least not immediately, even though he could be accused of the same crimes as the others; instead, his application for the ending of his Prussian citizenship should be accepted. Reasons for this are: the prejudicial reaction of other countries towards Germany, particularly England, which has made provision for giving him English nationality should he be expelled." The Gestapo representative was among those who objected, especially as Einstein's possessions had already been confiscated. "As Einstein allows his world-famous name to be used as the cover for lying propaganda, his omission from the first list would not be understood and would be sharply criticized in Germany," ran this argument. One compromise suggested by the Foreign Office was that he should be deprived of his citizenship but that his scientific equipment should be freed. Finally the meeting ended without a decision being taken, the Gestapo representative repeating his concern that "the postponement should not take too long, in case Einstein's actions made it impossible to put him in the first list that was to be issued."

Einstein was of course to know nothing of this, now or in the future. His immediate problem was to decide where to go. A return to Switzerland seemed likely. His personal feeling for the country and its people remained strong, and Zurich would have welcomed him back. Yet he had firm links with Holland, where Lorentz had died only five years previously, and the ties with Switzerland were tangled by the fact that Mileva was still living in Zurich. For the moment therefore he remained in Belgium.

Here, in the last days of March, he received a letter which was to have considerable repercussions later in the year. It came from one of the more colorful, if more enigmatic, characters who was to cross Einstein's path. This was Commander Locker-Lampson. English barrister and journalist, Member of Parliament for the Handsworth Division of Birmingham, he was the younger son of Frederick Locker, the Victorian poet, and in the First World War had pursued an adventurous career, first in the Royal Naval Air Service and then in armoured cars, which he commanded in Belgium, Lapland, Prussia, Austrian Galacia, and Russia. It was in character that Locker-Lampson should have served under the Grand Duke Nicholas and later been invited to murder Rasputin by one of the men who eventually carried out the assassination.

On the face of it, the mutual attraction of Einstein, the natural-born pacifist, and Locker-Lampson, the natural-born fighter who had "Combative" as the first word of his telegraphic address, seems almost absurd. On the face of it, their only similarity was that both were "outsiders" in the same way that Churchill and Lloyd George—both of whom were introduced to Einstein by the politician—were "outsiders" who hunted without the pack. The simplest explanation of their friendship is probably the most accurate: mutual support for the underdog which had produced in Locker-Lampson a hatred of the Nazi government equaled only by his hatred of the Communists. In addition, the commander must fully have appreciated that association with Einstein would bring his name into the news, where he was not averse to seeing it. This fact, though too plain in the record to be smudged, should not hide the genuine feeling with which he acted.

Locker-Lampson, writing from the House of Commons, began by recalling a chance meeting with Einstein at Oxford a few years previously. "This letter," he continued,

> is first of all to assure you, my dear professor, of how sincerely a great number of my people sympathize with you and your German fellow believers in your sufferings. That even Einstein should be without a home has moved me deeply and perhaps this justifies me, a modest M.P., in approaching you, the greatest scientist of our age. I hope, my dear professor, that you will therefore see nothing more in my humble offer than a simple tribute of my boundless respect and the wish to be allowed to serve you in my way. And so, my dear professor, would you do me the great happiness—I venture to ask simply this—of you, and your wife, taking over my small house in London, such as it is, for about a year, whenever it is convenient to you? It consists of a hall, a dining room, a sitting room and drawing room, two or three bedrooms, three staff bedrooms, as well as well-appointed kitchens. It goes without saying that you would live in the house as my guest, that is, there would be no cost and the service would be at my expense. My house would naturally not be as comfortable as your own, but who knows whether England's own "ether" with its atmosphere of Fair Play might not help you to explore still more deeply the mysteries of Relativity. With sincere regards, Your truly, Oliver Locker-Lampson.

Einstein politely declined the offer and moved with his wife to Le Coq-sur-Mer, a small resort near Ostend built, like the other beads on the long chain of Belgian coast villages, between the sand dunes and the network of streams and irrigation channels that stretches north-eastwards towards the Leopold Canal and the Dutch frontier. Here he made a base for his last six months in Europe. And from here he severed his link with the Prussian Academy, the magnet whose distinguished company had first drawn him to Berlin almost exactly two decades earlier.

For although German nationality had been discarded, membership of the Prussian Academy of Sciences—that "greatest benefit . . . which you can confer on me," as he described it when first addressing his fellow members—still remained. He might indeed be expelled in due course. But it was not only to avoid this that he now, on March 28, wrote to Berlin formally announcing his resignation on the grounds that he was no longer able to serve the Prussian state. A more important reason was the embarrassing position into which he feared that his old friends Nernst and Planck would be thrust. If he were expelled they would find it dangerous to protest yet disloyal not to.

Not all of Einstein's faith was justified. Nernst, it is true, declared that the Academy was proud of such non-German members as Voltaire, d'Alembert, and Maupertuis, and need not, under all circumstances, demand service to the Prussian state. Yet Planck's reply, which reached Einstein early in April, was of a rather different character. He felt that Einstein's resignation was the only way of resolving the situation "honorably," and that this "spared Einstein's friends immeasurable grief," a clear enough indication that not all these friends were willing to stand up and be counted.

This was only the first disillusionment. Early in April Einstein learned how the Academy was dealing with the situation. On the first of the month one of its permanent secretaries, Dr. Ernst Neymann, issued the following statement:

> The Prussian Academy of Sciences heard with indignation from the newspapers of Albert Einstein's participation in atrocity-mongering in France and America. It immediately demanded an explanation. In the meantime Einstein has announced his withdrawal from the Academy, giving as his reason that he cannot continue to serve the Prussian state under its present government. Being a Swiss citizen, he also, it seems, intends to resign the Prussian nationality which he acquired in 1913 simply by becoming a full member of the Academy.
>
> The Prussian Academy of Sciences is particularly distressed by Einstein's activities as an agitator in foreign countries, as it and its members have always felt themselves bound by the closest ties to the Prussian state and, while abstaining strictly from all political partisanship have always stressed and remained faithful to the national idea. It has, therefore, no reason to regret Einstein's withdrawal.

Anyone who doubted what the coming of the Nazis meant might have been warned by this miserable fudge of the facts, perpetrated by what had once been a proud institution. Einstein was the last man to shrink from trying to put the record straight, and he now wrote to the Academy the first of a series of crossing letters which passed between Le Coq and Berlin. He denied atrocity-mongering, while admitting to what, in the newly created hysteria of the German times, would be considered little else. He had, he admitted, "described the present state of affairs in Germany as a state of psychic distemper in the masses," and also made some remarks about its causes. He had also, in a document which he had allowed the International League for Combating Anti-Semitism to use, "called upon all sensible people, who are still faithful to the ideals of a civilization in peril, to do their utmost to prevent this mass psychosis, which is exhibiting itself in such terrible symptoms in Germany today, from spreading further."

He ended with a protest and an appeal.

> It would have been an easy matter for the Academy to get hold of a correct version of my words before issuing the sort of statement about me that it has. The German press has reproduced a deliberately distorted version of my words, as indeed was only to be expected with the press muzzled as it is today. I am ready to stand by every word I have published. In return, I expect the Academy to communicate this statement of mine to its members and also to the German public before which I have been slandered, especially as it has itself had a hand in slandering me before that public.

But before the Academy could deal with this letter, H. von Ficker, its senior permanent secretary, had already replied officially to Einstein's resignation, which had been accepted on March 30. His letter deplored Einstein's action in "disseminating erroneous views and unfounded rumors. We had confidently expected that one who had belonged to our Academy for so long would have ranged himself, irrespective of his own political sympathies, on the side of the defenders of our nation against the flood of lies which has been let loose upon it," it concluded. "In these days of mudslinging, some of it vile, some of it ridiculous, a good word for the German people from you in particular might have produced a great effect, especially abroad. Instead of which your testimony has served as a handle to the enemies not merely of the present government but of the German people. This has come as a bitter and grievous disappointment to us, which would no doubt have led inevitably to a parting of the ways even if we had not received your resignation."

In his reply, Einstein protested against the idea of speaking up on behalf of the German people. "By giving such testimony in the present circumstances," he concluded, "I should have been contributing, even if only indirectly, to the barbarization of manners and the destruction of all existing cultural values. It is for this reason that I felt compelled to resign from the Academy, and your letter only shows me how right I was to do so."

This exchange—closely followed by his expulsion from the Bavarian Academy of Sciences—drew a sharp line across his life. While the Berlin of 1933 could hardly have been foreseen from the Berlin of 1913, the rallying of the Academy behind the new German government reinforced the question mark which had hung over the offer from Nernst and Planck two decades previously. It suggested, by implication, that his acceptance had been wrong, and that his original suspicions of the Prussian spirit had been right. Moreover it sharpened and deepened his feelings about the German people as a whole, so that from now onwards he would find it less easy to look on them as did the easygoing British or the even more easygoing Americans. From now onwards the words "German menace" had for Einstein a significance more readily understood by the French and by the Russians. From now onwards, moreover, there could be no doubt about his public position as a martyr. As his old friend Rabbi Wise wrote from the United States on May 9, "We are all very proud of the part you have played and, above all, the distinction which has been yours in being expelled from the [Nazified] Prussian Academy."

Yet even Einstein, percipient though he was about the future, can have had little idea of the wrath to come. Hitler's purge of the civil service—whose laws automatically applied to the universities—began on April 1 with the removal from office of those of Jewish descent. Bernard

Rust, the Minister of Education in Prussia who was soon to be given control by Hitler over all education in Germany, had no remorse about the scores of professors and lecturers who were summarily sacked. "It is less important that a professor make discoveries," he noted, "than that he train assistants and students in the proper views of the world."

These measures went virtually unopposed. Thirteen years earlier, the anti-Jewish movement of which Einstein became the focal point had brought nodding acquiescence, if not downright approval, from a sizable percentage of the German people. They had not changed. And on May 10 in Berlin—even Berlin, where cosmopolitanism and culture had always been a little higher up the scale than elsewhere in Germany—here in Berlin 40,000 inhabitants watched and cheered what William Shirer has called "a scene which had not been witnessed in the Western world since the late Middle Ages": the sight of 5,000 swastika-bearing students burning in a massive pile before the Opera House 2,000 volumes that included the works of Einstein and Freud, Thomas Mann, Remarque and Stefan Zweig, and of Americans such as Helen Keller and Upton Sinclair. After the flames had leaped upwards, wrote one observer later, there was a sudden silence. Perhaps it was not only conscience. Perhaps some among the crowd caught a psychic glimpse of the flames that exactly a decade later would be sweeping through far larger parts of Berlin.

However, it was not only the mob that acquiesced. Thirteen days later, on May 23, Professor Ernst Krieck asserted during his investiture as the new rector of the University of Frankfurt that the German universities could never have struggled from their paralysis without a folk renascence. "The chief characteristic of this renascence is the replacement of the humanistic ideal by the national and political," he said. "Nowadays the task of the universities is not to cultivate objective science but soldierlike militant science, and their foremost task is to form the will and character of their students."

Nor was Krieck alone among the academics in such sentiments. On the day that he spoke in Frankfurt, the twenty-second annual meeting of the Kaiser Wilhelm Society was held in Berlin. Planck presided. No one in Germany could be permitted to stand aside, "rifle at rest," he said. There should be only one ideal—"the consolidation of all available forces for the reconstruction of the Fatherland." And he then read the following message sent by the society to Chancellor Hitler: "The Kaiser Wilhelm Society for the Advancement of the Sciences begs leave to tender reverential greetings to the Chancellor, and its solemn pledge that German science is also ready to cooperate joyously in the reconstruction of the new national state."

Although a shock to Einstein, it was perhaps hardly surprising that Planck should have stood firm for his country and seen Einstein's resignation from the Academy as the only honorable solution to a problem which Einstein had apparently created for himself. Even Max von Laue had written to him stating that the scientist should keep silent on political matters. "In general," Einstein wrote to Ehrenfest, "the lack of courage on the part of the educated class in Germany has been catastrophic."

It was in this climate that between April 4 and May 15 no less than 164 German professors resigned or were dismissed—25 from Berlin; 23 from Frankfurt; 6, including Max Born and James Franck, from Göttingen; 7 from Hamburg; and others from Heidelberg, Bonn, Jena, Leipzig, and Kiel. And it was in this climate that the Nazi attack on Einstein gathered weight.

On April 2 his Berlin bank account was taken over by the authorities and cash and securities totaling 30,000 marks confiscated on the grounds that they would otherwise be used for treasonable purposes. His Haberlandstrasse apartment was formally closed and a lock put on the door. Shortly afterwards his summer house at Caputh was seized. On April 12 his two stepdaughters left Germany for France and on the same day Dr. Walther Mayer arrived at Le Coq. Dr. Plesch, the man who had discovered the real cause of Einstein's heart trouble a few years earlier, also left. And in Le Coq there arrived a special album published in Germany and containing photographs of leading opponents of the Nazi government. On the first page was a portrait of Einstein. Underneath it were the words: "Discovered a much-contested theory of relativity. Was greatly honored by the Jewish press and the unsuspecting German people. Showed his gratitude by lying atrocity propaganda against Adolf Hitler abroad." And then, in parentheses, there were the words "Noch ungehangt"—"Not yet hanged."

As with the more general attack on science, so with the specific attack on Einstein: a German Nobel Prize winner supported the case. "The most important example of the dangerous influence of Jewish circles on the study of nature has been provided by Herr Einstein with his mathematically botched-up theories consisting of some ancient knowledge and a few arbitrary additions," Lenard asserted in the *Völkischer Beobachter*. "This theory now gradually falls to pieces, as is the fate of all ideas that are estranged from nature. Even scientists who have otherwise done solid work cannot escape the reproach that they have allowed the theory of relativity to get a foothold in Germany because they did not see, or did not want to see, how wrong it is, quite apart from the field of science itself, to regard this Jew as a good German."

Throughout all this, and the worse that was to come, despite his strong feelings and his personal involvement, Einstein continued to keep part of himself outside the battle, interestedly looking on. He was still, in some ways, the man of 1920 in the Berlin opera box, loudly applauding the anti-Einstein tirades on the stage. The external, impersonal attitude remained. There still exists one of the hideously anti-Semitic cartoons then published in Germany which shows Einstein as a Jewish vulture; across the bottom of it is Einstein's autograph, superimposed possibly for a friend, possibly for a collector, a signature without comment, inscription, or emotion. He felt deeply about the irrationality of anti-Semitism, he deplored its cruelties and its humiliations long before the extermination programs of the Final Solution got under way. But his reaction was disdainful. As with so many other human problems, he was the outsider looking in. He could afford to be dispassionate; so long, that is, as he was able to get on with his work.

As he sat on the Belgian dunes with Dr. Mayer in the spring of 1933, doggedly searching for an answer to the riddle of a unified field theory, the question of where he was to work in future was still the one that mattered most. There were many ways of answering it, since the news that Einstein would not be returning to

Germany had been quickly followed by a flood of academic offers. Some of them were, as he wrote to Paul Langevin, "political demonstrations which I considered important and did not want to spoil." The result was that he accepted them indiscriminately, without much thought, and to the eventual embarrassment both of himself and of those who made the offers.

He agreed to lecture to the Foundation Universitaire in Brussels; a week later accepted the offer of a chair at the University of Madrid and agreed to move to Spain in April, 1934—an acceptance from which he withdrew following an attack by the Spanish Catholic press. Meanwhile his friends in France had been active, and on April 14, the government started to rush through a special bill to create a new chair of mathematical physics for him at the Collège de France. In its preamble, the bill noted that in 1840 the chair of Slavonic literature had been founded for Adam Mieckiewicz, and it was recommended that the Third Republic should not be less liberal than the July Monarchy. However, early in May the dates of the lectures in Brussels were fixed. "Since I cannot do any of these things during the summer vacation, it is not clear to me when and for how long I could come to Paris," Einstein wrote rather plaintively to Langevin on May 5.

Both his perplexity with the present and his plans for the future were expressed in a letter to his old friend Solovine: "I have not got round to replying to your letter, so great has been the flood of letters and of men," he said. "I am afraid that this epidemic of hatred and violence is spreading everywhere. It comes like a tidal wave from below, so that the upper layers are isolated, anguished, demoralized, and swelled up by the flood. I now have more professorial chairs than reasonable ideas in my head. The devil makes a fool of himself with their size!

"But enough of nonsense. We hope to see you again one day when everything around me is calm once more." And then, as a P.S.: "If you meet any academic refugee Jews from Germany, tell them to get in touch with me. I want, with some friends, to try to start a liberal university abroad (in England?) for Jewish *dozents* and professors, so that we can at least do something for the most urgent needs, and create a kind of intellectual refuge."

Two days later, Einstein put down his ideas for this

"intellectual refuge" in a letter to Leo Szilard, his former student-colleague from Berlin, who was himself organizing help from England for the wave of Jewish intellectuals moving from Germany. Szilard was a man of almost infinite imagination and *panache*, packed with ideas for the salvation of the world and equally at home in science, technology, or international morality. A few years earlier he had tried to launch a scheme for "Twelve Just Men" who by the wisdom of their arguments would bring peace to a world reluctant to have it. Szilard put up the scheme to H. N. Brailsford, the British Socialist leader with whom Einstein had been in contact in 1919, and Brailsford in turn asked Einstein's opinion. He gave cautious approval but noted that Szilard might "exaggerate the significance of reason in human affairs."

Now Szilard, who was to play an important, although largely unsung, part in creating the Academic Assistance Council, entered Einstein's life once again. Typically, he had an ambitious plan for helping refugee Jewish professors. "Your plan doesn't really set me on fire," Einstein wrote to him from Belgium on April 26. "I have the strong feeling that in this way the only men who will be placed are already known, and that one will not be able to take care by this method of the university teachers who are still unknown, or of the students. I believe, rather, that one ought to try to form a kind of refugee Jewish University which would be best placed in England. A visit to me now would not be useful, as I am tremendously overworked."

Szilard was not a man easy to discourage, and the following month he crossed the Channel to Belgium where he saw Einstein on May 14. "Though he is still at some sympathy for his original plan," he wrote on the same day to an unidentified correspondent, "he is perfectly willing to cooperate in view of the fact that our plan is further advanced than the other one. I shall stay in touch with him and will ask for his help in such a way as I think fit." He did stay in touch, even though Einstein's own interest in founding a "Jewish Refugee University" in England soon evaporated. There were many reasons for this, including pressure of other work and, probably more influential, the fact that in both England and the United States academic aid organizations sprang up and showed every sign of being able to handle the worst of the problem.

Perhaps the winds which shifted Einstein out of this particular field as quickly as they had blown him in were really favorable, for he was singularly ill equipped to handle the complicated task involved in the resettlement of refugee academics. He himself quickly appreciated this, for by mid-July he was stating the position accurately enough to his friend Dr. Gustav Bucky, a Leipzig radiologist whom he had known in Berlin, and who had already moved to New York. "Your belief that I stand at the center of organized relief is not correct," he wrote. "I am here in an out-of-the-way place and I have neither the talent for organization which is required nor close contact with the necessary people. I can intervene only occasionally, and in very special cases, by means of the trust which people put in me." As his friend Philipp Frank has said: "Einstein might have done more for the refugees if he had undertaken to study the situation at various universities and to take advantage of the personal, economic, and political factors involved, but such action was not possible for him. The people who are the most outstanding intellectually and also the kindest are not always very practical."

He might also have done more had his guerrilla war with the administration of the Hebrew University not suddenly erupted into a major engagement. For now, as the situation in Germany made it essential for the Jews to form a united front, he brought his breach with the university into the open with an unthinking timing that had the quality of Greek drama.

In August, 1932, the Board of Governors, meeting in London, had elected the committee for the purpose, in Weizmann's words, "of drawing up a constitution for the university, and of introducing into that constitution as many practical reforms as possible, with a view to making the young and struggling university into an institution rather more worthy of the name." Sir Herbert Samuel, Professor Norman Bentwich—who a decade earlier had seen much of Einstein during his visit to Palestine—Sir Philip Hartog, and Weizmann himself were members. Despite the cautious description by Weizmann, the committee represented a first step towards dealing with Einstein's criticisms of the way Magnes was running the university; and when Weizmann met Einstein in Berlin in the autumn of 1932, shortly before he was to leave for the United States, Einstein tentatively agreed that on certain conditions he might rejoin the Board of Governors. But these had not yet been brought about.

This was the situation when, soon after his arrival in Belgium in the spring of 1933, Einstein received a cable from Weizmann in Jerusalem which invited him to join the university. Weizmann had received no reply when he left Palestine on April 19. "But on my arrival in Cairo the following day," he wrote to Einstein on reaching London, "I was met by a statement in the press to the effect that you had considered this invitation and had refused it because you were dissatisfied with the management of the university." Only half-believing, Weizmann telephoned Magnes in Jerusalem. "He read out to me, over the telephone," Weizmann continued, "the letter just received from you in which you state that you are refusing our invitation because you have been informed from four different and independent sources that the position of the university is so deplorable that it is undesirable for you to allow your name to be associated with it."

Weizmann's shock would have been all the greater had he known that Einstein had already unburdened himself to Samuel, who had recently invited him to a banquet to be held in London in support of the university. In his refusal Einstein made the same points he was to make to Weizmann.

"I think Dr. Magnes is most responsible for the enormous damage and disadvantages which have been brought to the university by his leadership, an opinion which I have already openly expressed several times. Whatever might be said in his favor, that which must be said in his disfavor predominates," he wrote.

"If ever people want my collaboration his immediate resignation is my condition *sine qua non*. Only after that could I consider the conditions which might lead to successful work. The need of Jewish knowledge is immense; I receive letters, inquiries, and proposals every day proving to me that swift assistance is necessary.

"Changes should be made," he repeated, before concluding: "If this is not possible, I think it best to leave the university to its fate. In this case I shall try to help in other ways in the present emergency."

This private attack was supported in public by interviews which were a good deal more damaging than the statements Weizmann had heard in Cairo. Einstein had told the Jewish Telegraph Agency that he had turned down the Jerusalem offer in view of his "long-standing differences with the university management," and had then added: "I declined in strong terms to accept this invitation because I feel that the conditions prevailing at the university are such as to make fruitful work impossible until some radical improvement in the management is introduced."

To the representative of the *Jewish Chronicle* he had been even more outspoken, declaring that "it was deplorable that this university, on which such great hopes had been based, was not in a position to play the role and to cater for spiritual needs in the way that might have been expected of it at this critical time." He spoke of deficiences of the administrative and directing boards. "It really depends on those professors who have been driven out of Germany, whether they would care to associate themselves with the Hebrew University," he concluded. As far as he was concerned, he had resigned five years ago and he did not wish to be "responsible" for it any longer.

Such statements, awaiting Weizmann in London, were almost certainly justified by conditions in Jerusalem. But they were doubly damning at a time when the Jews in general and the Jerusalem authorities in particular were being overwhelmed by the refugee tide from Germany. But for Einstein's indisputably open character, it would be easy to assume that he had merely got his blow in first, that his denunciations were a clever move by a master of tactics. This was not so. He had acted with innocent intent, repeating the unthinking carelessness of his resignation from the League's commission when news of his about-face had come secondhand to those most concerned. As then, his attitude arose merely from the combination of thoughtlessness and innocence that so often satisfied Einstein even though it spread dismay among his friends.

Weizmann's immediate response to the news that he had made his criticisms so public was a bitter four and a half page letter in which he recapitulated the details of what Einstein had said and done. "In commenting on them," he continued.

> I feel that I must begin by saying quite frankly that the action you have thus taken seems to me to be so surprising, and so unjust even, in substance and in manner, alike towards the university and towards me personally, that the only thing I can do is to ask you to explain it, and, if you are satisfied (as I hope you will be) that it is unjust, to withdraw it. You are the bearer of a great name, and so the injustice cuts more deeply, especially as I am so entirely at a loss to account for it.

Years earlier, Max Brod had in his novel made Tycho Brahe confront Kepler/Einstein: "You are no serpent, you never lie or constrain yourself," he says. "Thus you really serve, not truth, but only yourself; that is to say, your own purity and inviolateness. But I see not only myself, I see also my relations with those among whom I must live in the determination to serve truth with the aid of adroitness and every shrewd device." One can almost hear Weizmann speaking.

Einstein did not withdraw. Neither did he back up his charges in detail; the only informant he named was Professor Yahuda, the scholar who had brought the Spanish offer from Madrid, who had been refused a chair at the Hebrew University by Magnes, and who can hardly be considered an impartial witness. Furthermore, in his reply to Weizmann on May 7, he reaffirmed his action. For good measure he suggested that Weizmann had committed a breach of faith by not resigning from the university board when he himself had done so.

The cat had now been firmly put among the pigeons. Samuel and Hartog, who had planned a dinner to raise funds for German Jewish refugees already at the university, had to call it off. From Jerusalem, Magnes wrote to Weizmann and to Einstein saying to both that an inquiry should be set up and that he was willing to withdraw from the univeristy if any charges against him were proved.

Throughout this imbroglio, which was to continue unabated in one form or another until he finally left Europe for the United States in the autumn, Einstein moved as though not fully aware of the turmoil he had created. He had simply done and said what he thought was right. That completed, he got on with the things that mattered to him; detached and, if not exactly serene, at least a good deal less worried than most of those around him. "In spite of all the agitations and distractions," he wrote to Solovine in mid-May, "I have carried out with my scientific colleagues here a beautiful piece of work which makes me most happy."

As Weizmann grappled with realities, as the Jewish exodus continued to France and the temporary security of Austria and Czechoslovakia, and as Hitler prepared the Third Reich for its thousand years of power, Einstein, his future still undecided, began to get ready for his visit as a Research Student to Christ Church.

"Could I come to Oxford this year in June?" he wrote to Lindemann. "Do you think that Christ Church could find a small room for me? It need not be so grand as in the two previous years." It was a simple letter, innocent in the typical Einstein way of the fact that the Oxford term ended in mid-June, and adding that he had "worked out with Professor Mayer a couple of wonderful new results of a mathematical-physical kind." But there was one sentence which came oddly and humanly from Einstein, the self-styled Swiss and the man who did not put down roots anywhere. He thought Lindemann had probably heard of his "little duel with the Prussian Academy"; and he added: "I shall never see the land of my birth again."

Lindemann replied by return, hoping that Einstein would be able to come at the beginning of June. "I was in Berlin for four or five weeks at Easter," he went on,

> and saw a great many of your colleagues. The general feeling was much against the action taken by the Academy, which was the responsibility of one of the secretaries without consultation with the members. I can tell you more about it when you come. Everybody sent you their kind regards, more especially Schrödinger, but it was felt that it would be damaging to all concerned to write to you, especially as the letter would almost certainly not be forwarded. Conditions there were extremely curious. It seems, however, that the Nazis have got their hands on the machine and they will probably be there for a long time.

Lindemann concluded with an outline of what was to become a scheme greatly affecting not only Oxford but Britain's scientific effort in the Second World War. "It appears to me," he wrote,

> that the present circumstances in Germany might provide us with an opportunity to get one or two good theoretical physicists to Oxford, at any rate for two or three years. Professor Sommerfeld told me that many of the *privatdozenten* of Jewish origin would be deprived of their positions and in the circumstances would be ready to come here at a very small salary. I need scarcely say that very little money is available and that it would cause a lot of feeling, even if it were possible to place them in positions normally occupied by Englishmen. The only chance is to get extra supernumary jobs. These may be feasible and it occurred to me that if the unmarried were given rooms and food in college, only a very small amount of actual cash would be required for them to be reasonably comfortable for the time being. Sommerfeld suggested Bethe and London as possible men. I wonder whether you think well of them and whether you would be prepared to support their candidature. If so, a line from you would be invaluable in persuading colleges to make the offer.

The offer was a generous one, genuinely made. But the unnamed Berlin scientist quoted by Frank was also right. "What we are now doing in Germany is organizing a bargain sale of good merchandise at reduced prices," he had said of the Nazis' summer purges. "Shrewd persons will certainly seize this opportunity to buy something from us."

Einstein replied noncommitally, agreed to come to England as soon as his three lectures were given in Brussels, and added despondently: "I think the Nazis have got the whip hand in Berlin. I am reliably informed that they are collecting war material and in particular airplanes in a great hurry. If they are given another year or two the world will have another fine experience at the hands of the Germans."

A fortnight later he left Le Coq and its sand dunes for Brussels, speaking on three separate evenings to invited audiences at the Fondation Universitaire. After the first packed lecture, he was asked whether he thought he had been understood by everyone: "By Professor D., perhaps," he replied, "certainly by Le Chanoine Lemaître, but as for the rest I—don't think so." He was right. The second lecture was given in a half-empty room, the third to a mere handful of listeners.

He had planned to travel direct from Brussels to Oxford but a few days before leaving Le Coq learned that his younger son Eduard was ill in Zurich. "I could not wait six weeks before going to see him," he wrote to Lindemann. "I should never have had a quiet moment in England. You are not a father yourself, but I know you will understand."

On June 1 he arrived in Oxford. Despite the disagreement which had prefaced his election to the Research Fellowship he was extremely popular and an ambitious program had been prepared for him. The first day after his arrival he attended the Boyle Memorial Lecture, given to the Junior Scientific Society in the University Museum by Rutherford, and proposed the vote of thanks. It was an impressive occasion, Rutherford the big booming extrovert who had searched the interior of the atom contrasting once again with the smaller figure of Einstein whose mind had grappled with the immensities of space.

"I can almost see Einstein now," writes one of the undergraduates who attended the meeting.

> a poor forlorn little figure, obviously disappointed at the way in which he had just been expelled from Germany by the Nazis. As he delivered his speech, it seemed to me that he was more than a little doubtful about the way in which he would be received in a British university. However, the moment he sat down he was greeted by a thunderous outburst of applause from us all. Never in all my life shall I forget the wonderful change which took place in Einstein's face at that moment. The light came back into his eyes, and his whole face seemed transfigured with joy and delight when it came home to him in this way that, no matter how badly he had been treated by the Nazis, both he himself and his undoubted genius were at any rate greatly appreciated at Oxford.

Three days later he received a letter from Weizmann, about to leave Britain for an important visit to the United States but suggesting that Einstein and he should meet.

Einstein, preparing the Herbert Spencer Lecture, the Deneke Lecture which was to follow, and the first George Gibson Lecture which he was to give in Glasgow on the twentieth, replied that he could not spare the time. He did not wish to be wooed away from his better judgment by oratory and personal pleas.

Weizmann replied with a three-page letter that is a minor masterpiece. He repeated his amazement at the stories of maladministration at the Hebrew University, while admitting that many things there were "far from satisfactory." He admitted that the university was dependent on Magnes since he alone could secure the hard cash necessary to keep it afloat. "The same argument covered even the choice of professors by the Board of Governors, who had to adopt the suggestions of those who controlled the purse of the university," he went on. Having thus presumably drawn Einstein into his line of argument, he came out with two propositions. The first was simple. "Would you," he asked, "support a proposal to dismiss some of the Jerusalem people whom we have now an opportunity of substituting by much more distinguished people?"

The second proposal was more subtle. Weizmann himself was "trying to create a completely independent institute in Rehovot, which will be able to make a fresh start, and will not be involved in the past of the Jerusalem University." Then he dangled what he hoped was the bait. "What I hope and believe is this," he went on

> that this institute will definitely replace, and within a relatively short period of time, the chemistry department of the university in Jerusalem. If you undertake to do something on the same lines for physics and mathematics . . . what could we not do for the university? And physics would, in a way, be easier because physics does not yet exist in Jerusalem. Two great faculties would do much to raise the status of the university.

He concluded by rounding up the arguments, pleading forgiveness for inflicting such a long letter on his friend, and finally made a moving appeal for Einstein's cooperation.

The letter exhibits all the skill of the master political advocate. If anything could have drawn Einstein to Palestine it was probably this. Yet its failure was inevitable. The Hebrew University was important; but to Einstein it was less important than physics. And as far as physics was concerned, his present arrangements with Flexner had two great advantages over anything dangled by Weizmann. Einstein was not a political animal, and he had no wish to become entangled in the skein of diplomatic maneuvers which would inevitably hamper the scientific work of a man building a new department in such conditions. Secondly, he was not by nature the team worker, the man who excelled in directing the energies of younger men. He did not want to direct; he wanted to get on with his thinks.

"Dear Mr. Weizmann," he replied by return,

> The people who (unconnected with each other) have informed me have my fullest confidence and I know them to be upstanding and to have insight in regard to the situation at the university. I am therefore convinced that only a decisive change of personnel would alter things. If this is not done, then one cheats the people who have donated the money. The creation of an independent institute of chemistry is probably the best thing for you, in order to make it work. But to create it with the existing one still intact is a wasteful thing that I cannot condone. I also feel that the splitting up of the different departments, especially geographically, is most unwelcome. In these circumstances I feel it to be a waste to meet to talk, even at a larger committee. I am not able to negotiate or to influence; I only see the facts regarding the men and their objective and their moral insufficiency. My point of view in these circumstances can only be that I take no responsibility whatsoever. There is no ill feeling on my part; I just can't see a way in which I can be of any use. Friendly greetings, yours, A. E.

The letter was as decisive as Einstein could make it. Weizmann realized it was so. He also realized that the outspoken refusal gave him an opportunity that could be exploited by a series of Byzantine maneuvers.

Shortly afterwards he left for the United States. One of his first engagements was at a dinner of the American Jewish Physicians Committee founded by Einstein and himself in 1921. He addressed its 500 members on June 29 and for the first time he brought the argument fully into the open in the United States.

One of the speakers proposed—as one of them was almost certain to propose—that Einstein should join the Hebrew University. This was just the opportunity for which Weizmann was waiting. Einstein, he said, had refused. "Without wishing to enter on a controversy," he went on, "I must say that, unfortunately, Professor Einstein has severely criticized the university recently. The criticism was provoked by the invitation of Chancellor Judah Leon Magnes and myself, sent to him from Jerusalem. He had been offered a chair in Madrid (which he has since accepted), a chair in the Collège de France, a chair in Leiden, a chair in Oxford; and we did not want to compete with those four distinguished universities; yet we thought Jerusalem, although it cannot offer him the same facilities, has certainly a claim on him—particularly since he does not need any special equipment but only a pencil and a piece of paper—and that we could afford him in Jerusalem." He concluded with the hope that they would still be able to draw him to Jerusalem—and with the brusque comment that Einstein's idea of founding a refugee university was "a fantastic project . . . [that] would mean the creation of a Jewish intellectual concentration camp."

Einstein responded immediately through the Jewish Telegraphic Agency and in what he no doubt thought were uncompromising terms. "Dr. Weizmann knows very well that, by his declaration, he has misled public opinion," he replied from Belgium. "He knows only too well the reasons for my refusal, and he has repeatedly recognized them to be justified in our private conversations. He knows, too, under what circumstances I would be prepared to undertake work for the Hebrew University."

Weizmann's ingenuity in interpreting this statement was shown three days later when, at the annual convention of the Zionist Organization of America, he blandly announced that Einstein had "made peace with the Hebrew University in Jerusalem and agreed to accept a chair at the institution." This was stretching interpretation a little far. His only justification for the statement appears to have been a further promise of investigation into the university which Weizmann now made, and his extrapolated assumption that this would satisfy Einstein.

But the upshot was as anticipated. With Einstein's attitude openly criticized by Weizmann, an investigation would now be favored. Later in the month Sir Philip Hartog wrote that he was willing to chair a committee or commission which would specifically inquire into conditions in the university. Weizmann agreed, and the Survey Committee was finally set up in the autumn. Its members visited Jerusalem at the end of 1933 to investigate "with a view as to such reform as may be found desirable, and to the framing of plans for the development of the university." In the words of Magnes' biographer, Norman Bentwich, the committee "proposed radical changes in the administration and in his position. Action was shelved for a year; but things could never be the same to him thereafter, and he accepted a change in his functions."

On September 23, 1935, Rabbi Stephen Wise, returning from Palestine, reported to Einstein the outcome of the crucial meeting of the university's Board of Governors. "It retired Magnes from the academic direction of things and made him the president, which means that he becomes a more or less decorative figure," he said. In his place there was appointed as Rector Professor Hugo Bergmann, whom Einstein had, quite coincidentally, known in Prague two decades earlier. Writing in *New Palestine,* Einstein trusted that the university would "now exert that power of attraction on our young scholars which it has failed to do in the past because of previous circumstances." Doing a vice-chancellor's job, Magnes had been known as chancellor; now, ostensibly upgraded to a presidency, he was to have powers comparable to a chancellor at a British university. These powers were in some ways considerable, and he remained a trusted link with the British administration; yet effectually the move gave game, set, and match to Einstein, who had proposed almost this very thing a decade previously.

From the evidence that remains—the extensive Weizmann correspondence, the Report of the Survey Committee with Magnes' replies to its conclusions, and the reminiscences of those who still survive—it is clear that throughout the whole episode, spread across the decade from 1925 to 1935, Einstein made the worst of a good case. His motives were impeccable. But vacillating over his membership of the Board of Governors and then detonating his own charges in the spring of 1933, he substantiated Magnes' claim that the Survey Committee was appointed almost solely because of Einstein's complaints. "Even the events in Germany, which required united Jewish action to make the university worthy of its mission as a sanctuary for Jewish scholars, scientists, and students from Germany, did not cause Professor Einstein to abate his public and private attacks," Magnes noted. "On the contrary he was persuaded to make them even more bitter." The result was that Weizmann, coping with the day-by-day practical problems of leading the Zionist cause, was able to bring in the reforms he wanted only after a good deal of unnecessary negotiating, subterfuge, and delay. Throughout it all, Einstein's integrity could not be faulted, but it was not enough. ["His] faith has the stirring and driving quality of all truly spiritual leaders who are in the world but not of it," his old friend Morris Raphael Cohen concluded in reviewing *The World As I See It*. "It needs to be supplemented by a more realistic vision of the brute actualities of our existence." Einstein's outspoken honesty could be a formidable weapon; but it was double-edged and during the argument with Magnes it was sometimes wielded to the danger of friend and foe alike.

CHAPTER 18

OF NO ADDRESS

The end of the long disagreement about the Hebrew University still lay two years ahead as Einstein dissuaded Weizmann from visiting him at Oxford and prepared to put the finishing touches to his Herbert Spencer Lecture.

He spoke in Rhodes House, "On the Method of Theoretical Physics," from an English translation, and he surprised many of the audience with his opening sentence. "If you want to find out anything from the theoretical physicists about the methods they use, I advise you to stick closely to one principle," he said. "Don't listen to their words, fix your attention on their deeds. To the discoverer in this field the products of his imagination appear so necessary and natural that he regards them, and would have them regarded by others, not as creations of thought but as given realities." The emphasis on imagination was maintained as he went on. "I am convinced," he said in one much-quoted passage,

> that we can discover by means of purely mathematical constructions the concepts and the laws connecting them with each other, which furnish the key to the understanding of natural phenomena. Experience may suggest the appropriate mathematical concepts, but they certainly cannot be deduced from it. Experience remains, of course, the sole criterion of the physical utility of a mathematical construction. But the creative principle resides in mathematics. In a certain sense, therefore, I hold it true that pure thought can grasp reality, as the ancients dreamed.

Two days later, to a packed audience in Lady Margaret Hall he gave the Deneke Lecture, dealing with the inner meaning of physics and apparently concluding with the comment: "The deeper we search, the more we find there is to know, and as long as human life exists I believe it will always be so." The "apparently" is necessary. On this occasion Einstein spoke only from notes, and no script of the lecture survives despite the efforts made at the time to coax some form of written version from him.

From Oxford he traveled north to Glasgow to give the first George Gibson Lecture. He arrived in the city unexpectedly and found himself, totally unrecognized, in the center of a huge crowd which had gathered to welcome the film star Thelma Todd. Luckily, he was soon seen by a local reporter who telephoned the university. A rescue operation soon brought Einstein safely home to port. Miss Todd, speaking of the incident later, was contrite: "I wish I had known," she said. "I'd have lent Einstein some of my crowd."

That afternoon he spoke for twenty minutes in the university's Bute Hall, addressing the attentive audience in English on "The Origins of the General Theory of Relativity." He began by saying that he was glad to talk about the history of his own scientific work. "Not that I have an unduly high opinion of the importance of my own endeavors," he went on.

> But to write the history of the work of another requires an understanding of his mental processes which can be better achieved by professional historians; while to explain one's own former way of thinking is very much easier. In this respect one is in an incomparably more favorable position than anyone else, and it would be a mistake from a sense of false modesty to pass by an opportunity to put the story on record.

His exposition was one of the clearest ever given of the process which led from the Special to the General Theory and which, after numerous errors, led Einstein "penitently to the Riemann curvature, which enabled [him] to find the relation to the empirical facts of astronomy." He himself was impressed with the seeming simplicity of the work he had described. For he ended his lecture with words which stuck in many memories.

> Once the validity of this mode of thought has been recognized, the final results appear almost simple; any intelligent undergraduate can understand them without much trouble. But the years of searching in the dark for a truth that one feels, but cannot express; the intense desire and the alternations of confidence and misgiving, until one breaks through to clarity and understanding, are only known to him who has himself experienced them.

A few days later, after receiving the by now customary honorary degree, he returned to Belgium, turning down the offer of a stay in Canterbury which had come from Hewlett Johnson, the "Red Dean," who recalled that twelve years earlier he had listened to Einstein's lecture in Manchester. "This is a large, quiet, and very beautiful deanery," Johnson wrote, "and nothing would please me more than that you should come here for a month or more and work in undisturbed surroundings. You could have your own rooms and see me, or anybody else, just as often or as seldom as you liked."

Einstein's refusal is significant. In his invitation, Johnson stressed Einstein's "Labors for peace," a hint of his own long-term efforts for the Communist version of pacifism. But at this particular moment in his life, Einstein was anxious to dissociate himself from the smear of communism as well as worried about his own pacifism.

Both points were crystallized soon after his return to Le Coq. In Britain and the United States it was frequently claimed that he was a member of the Communist International, and how he himself tended thoughtlessly to give support to the charge is described by Dr. Max Gottschalk, a Belgian Jewish scholar who recalls that Einstein now decided to give his patronage to the peace congress in Amsterdam. "When we pointed out that it was really a Communist congress," he says, "Einstein replied: 'I saw that it was a peace congress and I didn't concern myself with the organizer.' He also signed during these same months a protest organized by Flemish youth. We told him about the subversive character of the group. He said that he had only seen in the protest a claim for equality before the law and in the light of the facts as he understood them [that] was justified."

But now the weapon that he so generously presented to his enemies was being wielded against him. He had to do something about it. On July 7 he therefore wrote to *The Times* and to the *New York Times.* "I have received a copy of a circular issued by the Better America Federation, containing photographs of me purporting to show that I am connected with the Third [Communist] Internaional," he said. "I have never had anything to do with the Third International, and have never been in Russia. Furthermore, it is manifest that the pictures purporting to be my photographs do not resemble me. The pictures are probably an attempted forgery inspired by political motives."

While he thus became the center of one storm, he was busy creating a second, struggling with his own conscience and finally confirming one of the most agonizing decisions of his life. For now, to the alarm of his friends and the dismay of his supporters, he crossed the great divide between pacifism and nonpacifism, renouncing his earlier conviction that the use of force was never justified; implying, in the words of his former colleagues, that he lined himself up with those who would "save European civilization by means of fire bombs, poison gas, and bacteria"; announcing without a flicker, like the cool customer he was, that the change was not in himself but in the European situation, and that nonviolence was no longer enough.

Einstein's rejection of the pacifist cause did not come suddenly. The blunt statement which he issued in the late summer of 1933 may give this impression, but the truth is more complex. The first hint of a change in his all-out pacifist beliefs came in November, 1932, when, shortly before leaving Berlin for the United States, he issued a statement on certain disarmament proposals put forward by Edouard Herriot, the French Premier. Included in these was one for an international police force, and Einstein agreed that this should be armed with—and would presumably be allowed to use—truly effective weapons. The idea appears to have become even less objectionable during the next few months, and while in America he even raised it with the War Resisters International.

Th genuine pacifist reaction was summed up by Lord Ponsonby in a letter to the secretary of the International. "I am quite sure we should avoid advocating anything like new forms of military organization," he said. "Professor Einstein's mention of the fusing of small professional armies and the eventual establishment of an international police force reminds me of the French proposals and is a policy advocated here by Lord Davies and others. I personally have always strongly opposed it for two main reasons." It would be an admission that force could help solve international disputes; and it would not work. A copy of Ponsonby's letter had little effect on Einstein, whose doubts about the current practicality of pacifism were further increased during his visit to Britain in June. For in Glasgow he met Lord Davies, head of the New Commonwealth Society, whose books on an international force he later described as "the best and most effective publications in their field. I could not have expressed my own position as well or as completely as you have."

Thus Einstein was already moving away from his unqualified pacifism when he returned to Le Coq from Britain late in June. This is apparent in a letter he wrote on July 1 to the Rev. J. B. Th. Hugenholtz, who had visited him the previous summer at Caputh, and who now revived his idea of an International Peace House in The Hague. It was a long shadow of attitudes to come.

"I must confess freely that the time seems inauspicious for further advocacy of certain propositions of the radical pacifist movement," Einstein wrote. "For example, is one justified in advising a Frenchman or a Belgian to refuse military service in the face of German rearmament? Ought one to campaign for such a policy? Frankly, I do not believe so. It seems to me that in the present situation we must support a *supranational* organization of force rather than advocate the abolition of all forces. Recent events have taught me a lesson in this respect." Support for this "*supranational* organization," a body that would give existing military alliances a new uniform, was indeed spitting in the temple.

Einstein sent a statement to the *Biosophical Review* of New York which reiterated the position outlined to Hugenholtz, but this was not published until the autumn. Outwardly, therefore, the attitude of Albert Einstein, the most famous of those who had expelled themselves from Germany on the rise of Hitler, was still that of the confirmed pacifist. The revelation came before the end of the month.

While he had been lecturing in Oxford, two Belgians

had been arrested for refusing to undertake military service. Their case had been taken up by Alfred Nahon, a young French pacifist living in Belgium who now appealed to Einstein to appear for the defense.

Before Einstein had time to reply, intervention came from an unexpected quarter. "The husband of the second fiddler," said a letter delivered to Einstein at Le Coq, "would like to see you on an urgent matter." The second fiddler was Queen Elizabeth, with whom Einstein had been playing quartets on at least three occasions during May; her husband had faced a German invasion twenty years previously and had every reason to fear the power of a Germany led by the National Socialist party.

Einstein traveled to Brussels and met King Albert in the palace at Laeken. The audience was handled circumspectly, and for good reason. For in some quarters Einstein's continued presence in Belgium was regarded as a distinctly mixed blessing. It would be unfair to suggest that the country harbored any sizable pro-German party; yet there existed—as indeed there existed in England—an overall wish to mollify rather than to criticize dictators. Nowhere in Belgium was much more than three hours' drive from the German frontier, and if threats that Einstein might be kidnapped or assassinated were exaggerated, this was not certain at the time. International incidents should be avoided, and it is significant that no offers of a permanent appointment appear to have been made to Einstein from any Belgian university.

In this climate, intervention by a constitutional monarch in a matter involving military service had to be handled with care, and the King appears to have kept no record of the views which he put to Einstein, or of Einstein's reaction. These are, however, clearly implied in the exchange of letters that followed the audience. The comment of the editors of *Einstein on Peace* that "the discussion with the King apparently helped Einstein to come to a decision on the crucial matter of war resistance" seems justified. If so, the Queen's invitation that Einstein should bring his violin to Laeken four years earlier had produced its first ripple on public affairs.

"Your Majesty," Einstein wrote on July 14,

The matter of the conscientious objectors is constantly on

my mind. It is a grave question, far transcending the special case before me.

I have already indicated why, despite my close association with the War Resisters' movement, I shall not intervene:

1. In the present threatening situation, created by the events in Germany, Belgium's armed forces can only be regarded as a means of defense, not an instrument of aggression. And now, of all times, such defense forces are urgently needed.

2. If anyone is to intervene in the case, it should not be one who enjoys your country's hospitality.

I should like to venture some additional remarks, however. Men who, by their religious and moral convictions, are constrained to refuse military service should not be treated as criminals. Nor should anyone be permitted to sit in judgment on the question of whether such a refusal is rooted in deep conviction or in less worthy motives.

In my view there exists a more dignified and more effective way of testing and utilizing such men. They should be offered the alternative of accepting more onerous and hazardous work than military service. If their conviction is deep enough, they will choose this course; and there will probably never be many of such people. As substitute work I have in mind certain types of mine labor, stoking furnaces aboard ships, hospital service in infectious-disease wards or in certain sections of mental institutions, and possibly other services of a similar nature.

Anyone who voluntarily accepts such service without pay is possessed of remarkable qualities and really deserves even more than merely being accepted as a conscientious objector. Certainly, he should not be treated as a criminal. Were Belgium to enact such a law or merely establish such a custom, it would constitute noteworthy progress toward true humanity.

This was a letter typical of Einstein; humane and courteous, thoughtful of the wider services which men might render to one another. Yet it was still a letter written on the brink of decision; it burked the entire issue of whether "mine labor, stoking furnaces aboard ships," and such services might not be quite as essential to a country's war effort as service in the armed forces.

The King's reply, dated from Ostend on the twenty-fourth, was friendly but noncommittal and to avoid the accusation of being unconstitutional he was careful to speak of anonymous "Belgian governments" rather than the specific current administration. "My dear professor, I have received with great pleasure the letter you have so kindly written me, and I send you my warmest thanks," His Majesty began.

> I am most responsive to what you say about Belgium and the sincerity of its foreign policy.
>
> Belgian governments intend to stay out of the conflicts that are taking place in or among its neighbor countries; under no circumstances will they consent to discriminatory practices which the great majority of Belgians consider unacceptable. As you have said it so well, our army is defensive in character. To serve in it means to serve the will of a free people intent on maintaining the place which is legitimately theirs in the society of nations.
>
> We are delighted that you have set foot on our soil. There are men who by their work and intellectual stature belong to mankind rather than to any one country, yet the country they choose as their asylum takes keen pride in that fact.
>
> The Queen joins me in sending you best wishes for a pleasant stay in Belgium. Please accept my expression of high esteem. Albert.

There is an air of fencing about the exchange and it seems likely that the King was still not certain of what Einstein would do next. Judging by past record, he had every reason to keep his fingers crossed.

However, Einstein's mind had already been made up. On July 20 he wrote to Nahon. He asked that the contents of his letter should be publicized—a letter in which Albert Einstein, who had once declared that he "would rather be hacked in pieces than take part in such an abominable business" as war, had changed his tune.

"What I shall tell you will greatly surprise you," he said.

> Until quite recently we in Europe could assume that personal war resistance constituted an effective attack on militarism. Today we face an altogether different situation. In the heart of Europe lies a power, Germany, that is obviously pushing toward war with all available means. This has created such a serious danger to the Latin countries, especially Belgium and France, that they have

come to depend completely on their armed forces. As for Belgium, surely so small a country cannot possibly misuse its armed forces; rather, it needs them desperately to protect its very existence. Imagine Belgium occupied by present-day Germany! Things would be far worse than in 1914, and they were bad enough even then. Hence I must tell you candidly: were I a Belgian, I should not, in the present circumstances, refuse military service; rather, I should enter such service cheerfully in the belief that I would thereby be helping to save European civilization.

This does not mean that I am surrendering the principle for which I have stood heretofore. I have no greater hope than that the time may not be far off when refusal of military service will once again be an effective method of serving the cause of human progress.

Please bring this letter to the attention of your friends, especially the two who are now in prison.

"The friends" were not the only ones whose attention was now drawn to his changed attitude. At first the news was passed round only in pacifist circulars, but on August 18 Einstein's letter was published in *La Patrie Humaine*. Protests were pained and vociferous. Three days later, Lord Ponsonby wrote expressing his "deep disappointment." H. Runham Brown, secretary of the War Resisters International, declared Einstein's letter to be "a great blow to our cause," while the Press Service of the International Antimilitaristic Commission claimed that "The apostasy of Einstein is a great victory for German National Socialism," a statement whose line of reasoning is perverse rather than obscure. Romain Rolland bitterly remarked in his diary that Einstein was now failing the very objectors whom he had encouraged only two years previously. The International League of Fighters for Peace, the Belgian War Resisters Committee, and many other organizations felt that Einstein's disavowal of all they stood for had the sniff of treason. To all, he replied in much the same terms: Germany was now a threat to the peace of Europe and could only be resisted by force. Circumstances altered cases.

As the protests continued to arrive, Einstein felt forced to issue a general statement. "My ideal remains the settlement of all international disputes by arbitration," he proclaimed. "Until a year and a half ago, I considered refusal to do military service one of the most effective steps to the achievement of that goal. At that time, throughout the civilized world there was not a single nation which actually intended to overwhelm any other nation by force. I remain wholeheartedly devoted to the idea that belligerent actions must be avoided and improved relations among nations must be accomplished. For that very reason I believe nothing should be done that is likely to weaken the organized power of those European countries which today represent the best hope of realizing that idea."

Fourteen years later he admitted that "England, France, and the United States had to pay dearly for remaining more or less unarmed from 1925 to 1935; this fact merely served to encourage the arrogance of the Germans." For long he also had encouraged them. Now he decided, as H. G. Wells had decided in the First World War, that "Every sword that is drawn against Germany is now a sword of peace."

The justification that Einstein gives for his *bouleversement* is valid as far as it goes. The European situation of the 1920s was indeed very different from the situation a decade later, when for the first time since 1919 a European country was deliberately turning to the threat of war to achieve its aims. Decent men did reluctantly admit that pacifism had to be abandoned. Circumstances did alter cases. But there is an important rider to the situation, and it lies in the contradiction between Einstein's admission that comparative disarmament had encouraged the Germans—a polite euphemism for muddled good intentions helping to bring about the very situation it was hoped to avoid—and his hope that "refusal of military service" would "once again be effective." For the essence of his argument was that after pacifism had been tucked away for a while in order to deal with an aggressive Germany, it could be pulled from the drawer and worn once again, a garment for fine days when all was set fair.

There are two other significant points that should not be smudged. Despite his readiness to abandon pacifism at the very point when it was put to the test, and despite his support for an international force, Einstein continued to regard himself as a pacifist, an attitude to which many of his former friends not unnaturally took exception. In addition it is notable that he concentrated his new-found belief in military defense against Germany in particular rather than against dictators in general. Certainly it was Germany which in 1933 represented the major threat to the peace of the world. Yet even in later years his admission that tyranny must be met by force only rarely flowed over to deal with the cases of Italy or Japan, let alone Russia. His vigor was concentrated to the exclusion of almost all else against the Germany whose evils he saw as a natural extension of his experiences at the Luitpold Gymnasium. His honesty, his international standing, his Jewishness, all helped to reinforce the anti-Nazi figurehead into which this vigor had turned him. As such he had his uses. But after 1933 not only Zionists and members of the League but also pacifists could plainly see his limitations as well. And after 1933 Wilfred Trotter's warning became even more self-evident "It is necessary," he once said, "to guard ourselves from thinking that the practice of the scientific method enlarges the powers of the human mind. Nothing is more flatly contradicted by experience than the belief that a man, distinguished in one or even more departments of science, is more likely to think sensibly about ordinary affairs than anyone else."

Einstein's position as a symbol of the anti-German forces now beginning to coalesce was emphasized while the affair of the two Belgian conscripts was still under way. For during the second half of July he became the centerpiece of what was essentially a political operation. The prime instigator is not known, but on July 20 the indefatigable Locker-Lampson wrote to Lindemann, whom he had first met during his time as private secretary to Winston Churchill. "My dear Prof," he said, "someone has seen Einstein and is bringing him to England and has asked me to put him up at my cottage this weekend. I have therefore arranged to do this and am taking him to Winston's on Saturday. I do hope you are likely to be there."

Einstein arrived a few days later and was taken first to Locker-Lampson's home at Esher, Surrey, a few miles from London. From here he was escorted not to one interview but to a trio. First he met Churchill, with whom he was photographed in the gardens of Chartwell. "He is an eminently wise man," he wrote to his wife the same day; "it became very clear to me that these people have made their plans well ahead and are determined to act soon." Next he had lunch with Sir Austen Chamberlain, whom Locker-Lampson had accompanied to the Peace Conference in Paris fourteen years earlier. Finally he was taken to Lloyd George's country home at Churt, and it was here that Einstein, signing the visitor's book in the rambling Surrey house before meeting the former Prime Minister, paused for a moment when he came to the column "Address." Then he wrote "Ohne"—"Without any."

The following day Locker-Lampson made the most of the incident when he spoke in the House of Commons, seeking leave to introduce a bill "to promote and extend opportunities of citizenship for Jews resident outside the British Empire." Einstein, grave and silent in white linen suit, looked on from the Distinguished Visitors' gallery. It was a moving incident, taking place at a time when Europe had reached a watershed of history, and oddly reflecting both the best and the worst in contemporary England—the eccentric outsider taking up arms for the downtrodden, and the House which agreed in principle, but quickly moved on to other things.

"I do not happen to possess a drop, as far as I know, of Jewish blood in my veins," Locker-Lampson began. He had, he pointed out, spoken up for the Germans after the war but he thanked God that they had not won—"they might have treated England as they have treated the Jews today." Then he came to Einstein, "the man without a home." "The Huns have stolen his savings. The roadhog and the racketeer of Europe have plundered his place. They have even taken away his violin." It was not very eloquent. But what it lacked in finesse it made up for in sincerity—which no doubt encouraged the *Völkischer Beobachter* to describe the incident a few days later as an "Einsteinian Jew Show in the House of Commons."

Locker-Lampson's private bill was the victim partly of apathy, partly of the British parliamentary system, since there was no chance of a second reading before the session ended on November 17. This, in turn, meant the automatic lapsing of the bill. There is no doubt of Locker-Lampson's sympathy for Einstein. Yet it would be ingenuous to believe that the invitation to Britain and the attempted introduction of the citizenship bill was the result only of disinterested goodwill. In the Britain of July, 1933, a few keen-sighted men, anti-Fascists before their time, sensed the dangers to come; among them were Churchill, Lindemann, and Locker-Lampson. To them Einstein was not only a man deserving of honest support but, as so often, a pawn in the great game.

Now he returned to Belgium, apparently accepting an open invitation from Locker-Lampson to visit him again before leaving Europe for his winter visit to Princeton. He had only a short time to wait before being thrust into a more glaring limelight.

On August 31, *The Brown Book of the Hitler Terror* was published by the World Committee for the Victims of German Fascism—by coincidence on the same day that Professor Theodor Lessing, a German who had fled to Czechoslovakia, was tracked down by Nazi thugs and murdered in Marienbad. The central core of the book was the allegation that the Nazis had themselves instigated the burning of the Reichstag, a claim which looked plausible enough in 1933 whatever doubts can be thrown on it today. Einstein had given his name as head of the committee in his usual generous way. Now he found himself saddled with part authorship and was forced to issue a retraction. "My name appeared in the French and English editions as if I had written it," he said.

> That is not true. I did not write a word of it. The fact that I did not write it does not matter, and [*sic*] the truth has a certain importance. I was on the committee which authorized the book, but I certainly did not write any of it, although I agree with the spirit of it. The cause of all this is that the regime in Germany is one of revenge; and I happen to be chosen as one of the victimized.

Naturally enough, this disclaimer had little effect on those who were baying for blood. "Einstein's Newest Infamy," a German newspaper banner underlined in red, was typical, and early in September it was reported that "Fehme," the extreme German nationalist organization, had earmarked $5,000 for the man who would kill Einstein. The news that this sum had been "put on his head" caused him to touch his white hair and remark smilingly: "I did not know it was worth so much."

Ellen Wilkinson, the British Labour M.P. who was a member of the committee which had published the book, traveled to Le Coq where she met Einstein on September

2. "I implored him to resign, to let us take his name off our notepaper," she said. " 'No,' he said quietly. 'They shall not force me to do that. The work your committee has done is good.' "

All this provided a dramatic context for the events of the next few weeks. For Einstein was now to return to England, and to remain there as Locker-Lampson's guest until, a month later, he spoke at a packed meeting in the Royal Albert Hall before leaving Britain and Europe for the last time. Sensational overtones were given to the story. Thus it was subsequently claimed that Einstein had fled from the continent on hearing of the assassination of Lessing; that he had been brought to England secretly in Locker-Lampson's yacht; that an armed guard had constantly kept watch over him in England; and, inevitably, that special police protection was given in England after warnings of assassination attempts. The truth is that when he left England for Belgium in July Einstein had said that he expected to be returning in September; that Locker-Lampson never had a yacht; that the "armed guards" consisted of Locker-Lampson's two girl secretaries and a farm hand who were given sporting rifles partly as a joke, partly as local color for photographers; and that neither Scotland Yard nor the Special Branch were warned of any murder threats. The assassination story was, in fact, made up by Locker-Lampson and "leaked" to a London evening paper when the sale of tickets for the "Einstein meeting" at the Royal Albert Hall was flagging.

Bearing all this in mind, the seriousness of any personal threat to Einstein in the late summer of 1933 appears questionable. With the Final Solution so well documented, there is no need to believe that this particular assassination would have been beyond the infamy of the Nazis, and their record suggests that it would not have been beyond their stupidity. But Einstein himself had the most common-sense comment. "When a bandit is going to commit a crime he keeps it a secret," he remarked on first hearing of the threats. The Belgian police had much the same attitude and their chief, quoted by the Jewish Telegraphic Agency, gives an impression of what is usually regarded as British phlegm: "The professor is taking everything quietly. When he was told that there was reputed to be a price upon his head he was only mildly surprised. He knows he is being guarded by police, but he gives me to understand that he does not wish to discuss the measures that are being taken. He told me that he is not afraid. I went this morning to ask him if he thought any further measures were required for his protection. He replied they were not needed."

This lofty disregard for his own safety was in the marrow of the man. All that worried him was the interference with his work that police surveillance often caused. Elsa was another matter and it was Elsa who on Friday, September 8, asked a visiting reporter from England—Patrick Murphy of the *Sunday Express*—to telephone Locker-Lampson and ask whether Einstein could come back as a guest without delay. Locker-Lampson swung into action, eager to be host once more, especially in such dramatic circumstances, and on Saturday Einstein was driven with Murphy to Ostend. In the cabin of the Channel boat he soon had out his notebook and was hard at work.

Arrived in London, he was taken for the night to a small boardinghouse in Earl's Court run by Locker-Lampson's former housekeeper, thankful that for once the hurried departure had enabled him to travel light. "If I traveled with two huge trunks my wife would still have a little paper parcel with excess luggage," he confided to Murphy.

The following morning, he was driven by the commander's two girl secretaries northeast from London, through Newmarket where the three lunched, Einstein making himself understood as well as he could with his slight conversational English, and then on to Cromer on the east coast. Here Locker-Lampson ran a holiday hotel in which a room had been reserved. But Einstein was taken instead to Roughton Heath, a sandy stretch of moorland three miles from the town where the commander owned a stretch of land. Here he was installed in one of the holiday chalets. His stay was surrounded by a grotesque mixture of pseudo-secrecy and publicity. "If any unauthorized person comes near they will get a charge of buckshot," threatened the commander. But the local Cromer photographer was allowed to take pictures of Einstein in his sweater and sandals, while the girl "guards," carrying sporting guns, posed for the agencies whose pictures went round the world.

Here Einstein stated significantly to a reporter:

> I shall become a naturalized Englishman as soon as it it possible for my papers to go through. Commander Locker-Lampson has already suggested to your Parliament that England should adopt me immediately instead of my having to wait the usual five years. Parliament will give us the answer when it reassembles. I cannot tell you yet whether I shall make England my home. I do not know where my future lies. I shall be here for a month, and then cross to America to fulfill engagements for a lecture tour.
>
> Professor Millikan, the great American research worker, has invited me to make Pasadena University [*sic*], in California, my home. They have there the finest observatory in the world. That is a temptation. But, although I try to be universal in thought, I am European by instinct and inclination. I shall want to return here.

Einstein spent about a month on Roughton Heath, living and eating in the small wooden building allocated to him, working with Dr. Mayer, who soon joined him from Belgium, and sometimes walking for an hour or more over the rough heathlands, "talking to the goats," as he told one of the commander's secretaries.

His presence outside Cromer had become an open secret and there were many visitors to the Locker-Lampson "encampment." One was Sir Samuel Hoare, the former British foreign minister. With Hoare Einstein discussed the European situation; and, invigorated by the comparative solitude of Roughton Heath, he brought up again the idea that he had made to Norman Bentwich in Jerusalem a decade ago—that lighthouses would be good places in which young scientists could carry out routine work because the loneliness encouraged them to think.

Another visitor was Einstein's stepson-in-law Dmitri Marianoff, commissioned by a French paper to produce a popular article on relativity and a little uncertain of what his stepfather-in-law's reaction would be to yet another request for potted science.

To Roughton Heath there also came Jacob Epstein, who was able to obtain three sittings for a bust. These were the only meetings of sculptor and scientist and recall one of the more famous pieces of doggerel which grew in such profusion round Einstein:

> Three wonderful people called Stein;
> There's Gert and there's Ep and there's Ein.
> Gert writes in blank verse
> Ep's sculptures are worse
> And nobody understands Ein.

"Ein" appeared in a pullover with his wild hair floating in the wind, Epstein remembered in his autobiography. "His glance contained a mixture of the humane, the humorous, and the profound. This was a combination which delighted me. He resembled," he added in a phrase which was later to be echoed elsewhere, "the aging Rembrandt."

The sittings took place in Einstein's small hut which already contained a piano and was hardly the best place for the job. "I asked the girl attendants, of which there were several, secretaries of Commander Lampson, to remove the door, which they did," writes Epstein. "But they facetiously asked whether I would like the roof off next. I thought I should have liked that too, but I did not demand it, as the attendant 'angels' seemed to resent a little my intrusion into the retreat of their professor. After the third day they thawed and I was offered beer at the end of the sitting."

Each session lasted two hours. At the first Einstein was so surrounded with smoke that work was almost impossible. "At the second I asked him to smoke in the interval," says Epstein. "His manner was full of charm and *bonhomie*. He enjoyed a joke and had many a jibe at the Nazi professors, one hundred of whom in a book had condemned his theory. 'Were I wrong,' he said, 'one professor would have been quite enough.' "

When the sittings were over he relaxed at a piano. On one occasion, he took out his violin and scraped away happily. "He looked altogether like a wandering gypsy, but the sea air was damp and the violin execrable and he gave up," Epstein wrote.

If these were the days of men who were anti-Nazi before their time, there were others who were still rabidly anti-Jewish. Briefly left unattended while on exhibition in

London a few weeks later, the bust of the world's greatest scientist by the world's greatest sculptor—both Jews—was discovered on the floor of the gallery. Fortunately, the damage was easily repaired.

The vandalism was explicable. For while Einstein was thus living in isolation, a transformation had been taking place comparable to that which fourteen years earlier had lifted him from the obscurity of academic science to the center of the world stage. For more than a decade he had symbolized the otherworldliness of the theoretical physicist, a figure whose sometimes comic appearance was redeemed and made real by the transparent honesty of his beliefs, the depth of his humanity, and the earthiness of his humor which touched a chord of sympathy in ordinary men. Now, as Hitler proclaimed that the Third Reich would last for a thousand years, and the lamps really began to go out in Europe, the image changed once again. Now, despite himself, he became the symbol of men who had at last, reluctantly, been forced to take up arms. But not all felt that it was right to fight against Hitler and the Nazi threat. Just as there were those in Britain, in France, and even in the Reich who felt that the time had arrived to make a stand against the growing rearmanent of Germany, so did others believe that the new German government must be built up as a bulwark against the Russian threat from the East. Thus in Europe, more poignantly than in the United States, Einstein became a symbol of that ideological schism that three years later, with the outbreak of the Spanish Civil War, was to split Britain down the mental middle.

The position was neatly summarized by the *New Statesman*, which stated in "Miscellany" that ". . . to our generation Einstein has been made to become a double symbol."

> . . . a symbol of the mind traveling in the cold regions of space, and a symbol of the brave and generous, outcast, pure in heart and cheerful in spirit. . . . See him as he squats on Cromer beach doing sums, Charlie Chaplin with the brow of Shakespeare, whilst yet another schoolboy, Locker-Lampson, mounts guard against the bullies. So it is not accident that the Nazi lads vent a particular fury against him. He does truly stand for what they most

dislike, the opposition of the blond beast—intellectualist, individualist, supernationalist, pacifist, inky, plump. It is unthinkable that the nasty lads should not kick Albert.

But it was not only the nasty lads. Some of the comparatively nice ones, the pacifists who considered themselves dishonorably betrayed, by this time regarded Einstein as "an evil renegade," as he described it the day after he arrived in England.

During the golden month of September, 1933, Einstein was thus a man beset from all sides: by the German establishment, by the "Hands Off Hitler" movement in Britain, and by his former pacifist friends with their accusations of betrayal. And now there came a more bitter personal blow; the news from Leiden that Paul Ehrenfest, perhaps after Lorentz the man for whom he felt the deepest affection and respect, had committed suicide. The circumstances were tragic. He had first shot his young son, whom he only blinded, and then himself. The immediate cause of the suicide, Einstein was later to suggest, lay deep in "a conflict of conscience that in some form or other is spared no university teacher who has passed, say, his fiftieth year."

The message from Holland snapped one of Einstein's links with the days before the First World War and with his crucial move to Berlin in the spring of 1914. Before he left Europe he received other news which in the most ironic of ways concerned another friend of the same period.

Earlier in the summer he had received a note from Haber, who had saved Germany on two counts during the First World War. In spite of being the blondest and least distinguishable of Jews; in spite of having himself and his entire family baptized into the Christian faith, he was not to be spared. On April 30 he was forced to resign from the Kaiser Wilhelm. One report—from the Jewish Telegraphic Agency—said that he appealed to the authorities to let him retire on pension in five months' time. If this was the case, the appeal failed. "For more than forty years," said his letter to the authorities, "I have selected my collaborators on the basis of their intelligence and their character and not on the basis of their grandmothers, and I am not willing to change, for the rest of my life, this method which I have found so good." In his farewell letter to the staff he stressed that for twenty-two years the institute had striven under his leadership to serve mankind in peace and the Fatherland in war. "So far as I can judge the result, it has been favorable and has brought things of value both to science and the defense of our land."

Now the man who had helped the Fatherland in its hour of need turned to his fellow member of the Kaiser Wilhelm who had wished only for the Fatherland's downfall. "He informs me of his intention to apply for a position at the Hebrew University in Jerusalem," Einstein told Philipp Frank. "There you have it, the whole world is topsy-turvy."

But Einstein, who had been warned by Haber against supporting the Zionists in 1921, now dissuaded Haber from going to Palestine. His reason was simple. While Weizmann was trying to induce well-known men such as Weyl, James Franck, and Einstein himself to the university, Einstein believed that the young and potentially brilliant among the flood of refugees had first call on any posts which the university had to offer. Older men, whose names were already made, should be farther down the queue.

Einstein's discouragement was effective and Haber came to England. But here his past caught up with him and, settling in Cambridge, he found that England liked him as little as he liked England. "Lord Rutherford," says Max Born, himself a refugee in Cambridge by this time, "declined an invitation to my house when Haber would also be there, because he did not want to shake hands with the inventor of chemical warfare." Haber moved to Switzerland and in the late summer he traveled up the Visp Valley to meet Weizmann in Zermatt. Here the Zionist leader persuaded him to take a post in the Seiff Institute in Palestine. "The climate will be good for you," he said. "You will find a modern laboratory, able assistants. You will work in peace and honor. It will be a return home for you—your journey's end." Now Weizmann passed the news to Einstein. "I am happy that despite my warnings, he has decided to go to Jerusalem," he replied. "It can only be a good thing in connection with the situation, as he can only be a good influence and would do nothing that would smack of foul compromise."

There was a postscript of which Einstein heard only in

the United States. Early in 1934 Haber set out on the first leg of his journey to the promised land. He reached Basel. And there he died, alone, and still incredulous that his services to the Fatherland did not give him a privileged shelter from the gale which was sweeping Europe.

Haber was still preparing for the move to Palestine when Einstein left Roughton Heath during the first days of October. He was bound for London, billed as star speaker at a mass meeting in the Royal Albert Hall, organized with typical thrust by Locker-Lampson. The initiative had come from the Academic Assistance Council, the prototype of so many rescue organizations which the Hitler purge brought into existence. As the *Belgenland* with Einstein on board was docking in Antwerp six months earlier, William (later Lord) Beveridge, director of the London School of Economics, had been sitting in a Vienna café reading the long list of German professors already being dismissed from their posts under the new Nazi statutes. He wished to help them and he was encouraged during a meeting with Leo Szilard, who had arrived in the city one step ahead of the German authorities. "It was agreed," Szilard has written.

> that Beveridge, when he got back to England, and when he got the most important things he had on the docket out of the way, would try to form a committee which would set itself the task of finding places for those who have to leave German universities. He suggested that I come to London and that I occasionally prod him on this, and that if I were to prod him long enough and frequently enough, he thought he would do it. Soon thereafter he left, and soon after he left, I left and went to London.

Arrived back in England, Beveridge formed the Academic Freedom Fund to which members of the L.S.E. could contribute. In May, staying with George Trevelyan, Master of Trinity, he had discovered that Rutherford was ready to head an organization to help refugees from German universities. When he first heard of Einstein's exchange with the Prussian Academy, Rutherford's reaction had perhaps lacked the indignation that might have been expected, and he had written to de Hevesy: "I see that Einstein has resigned his Berlin post but I presume he is financially well fixed in the U.S.A. due to the special endowment there." Now, however, he swung his energies unreservedly behind the Academic Assistance Council—the forerunner of similar organizations in France, Switzerland, and Holland, and of the Emergency Committee for Aid to Displaced German Scholars in the United States.

The council met in June, but the Albert Hall meeting of October 3 was its first major attempt to reveal to the nonacademic public the size and scope of the purge now thrusting from Germany so many of the men who might have saved her in the war that lay only six years away. A meeting of some sort had been the idea of the council's secretary, Walter Adams, then a lecturer in history at University College, London, and later director of the London School of Economics.

Adams drove out to Cromer a few days after Einstein had arrived. "First we were confronted by one beautiful girl with a gun," he says. "Then there was a second one, also with a gun. Finally we saw Einstein who was walking round inside what seemed to be a little hedged compound."

He quickly came to the point. Einstein as quickly agreed to speak on behalf of the council. But it appears that neither then, nor for some while, did he fully appreciate what was involved. As he understood it, there would be a smallish meeting at which a number of well-known people would be asked to speak and would appeal for funds. But, in Adams' words, "once he had agreed, Locker went away, picked up the telephone, and hired the Albert Hall." Organization was then prodded forward by the commander and carried out by the Refugee Assistance Fund, an amalgamation of the Academic Assistance Council, the International Students Service, the Refugee Professionals Committee, and the German Emergency Committee of the Society of Friends.

On the evening of October 3 Lord Rutherford was in the chair; others on the platform included not only Einstein but also Sir James Jeans, now at the height of his fame; Sir William Beveridge; and Sir Austen Chamberlain. The hall was packed; its 10,000 seats were all taken and the overflow of hundreds sat or stood in the gangways. It was not only the famous names that had brought them. Locker-Lampson's carefully leaked story that an attempt might be made on Einstein's life had drawn those in search of drama. For some there was the spicy attraction of a declaration on the back of each ticket, which had to be signed before its holder was allowed in: "I hereby undertake not to create any disturbance or in any way impede the progress and proper conduct of the meeting."

The danger of trouble, if only local trouble, was real enough, and large numbers of police were stationed outside the hall to deal with protests from the British Union of Fascists. More than 1,000 students, many from the University of London, acted as stewards—largely to handle the expected protests from Nazi sympathizers inside the hall. There were none.

Despite the big names on the platform, it was Einstein most of them wanted to hear. There is some disagreement about what he said and the published versions differ considerably. A truncated text appears in Einstein's own *Out of My Later Years*, and the version printed in *Einstein on Peace*, revised by the editors from the German manuscript in Einstein's papers, omits the famous "scientists and lighthouse keepers" statement which he interpolated apparently on the spur of the moment.

He spoke in English and all versions agree that he succeeded in outlining the German menace without mentioning Germany. This was largely at the instigation of the council itself, whose manifesto noted that "the issue raised at the moment is not a Jewish one alone; many who have suffered or are threatened have no Jewish connection. The issue, though raised acutely at the moment in Germany, is not confined to that country." Einstein thought it wrong, he later noted, specifically to condemn the country of which he had until recently been considered a national and he spoke, therefore, "as a man, as a good European, and as a Jew." He omitted a reference in his prepared notes to "the seizure of power, which results from preaching doctrines of hate and vengeance in a great country," and he also omitted a reference to "stories of clandestine German rearmament."

These reasons for describing the German purge without mentioning Germany were supported by those who did not wish to anger if it were still possible to appease, that is, to "pacify by satisfying demands." Thus Sir William

Bragg, by this time one of the key figures in the scientific establishment, noted to Rutherford on being asked to become treasurer of the Academic Assistance Council that "it is possible I suppose to do more harm than good by angering the people in power in Germany." Sir Austen Chamberlain felt even more strongly that while it might be right to protest it was wrong to protest too definitely. He was, Rutherford was informed, "particularly anxious that there should be no implication in the speeches of hostility to Germany and would prefer that the word 'Germany' should not occur."

Towards the end of his speech Einstein extemporized, remembering back to his recent days in Norfolk. "I lived in solitude in the country and noticed how the monotony of a quiet life stimulates the creative mind," he said.

> There are certain callings in our modern organization which entail such an isolated life without making a great claim on bodily and intellectual effort. I think of such occupations as the services in lighthouses and lightships. Would it not be possible to fill such places with young people who wish to think out scientific problems especially of a mathematical or philosophical nature? In this way, perhaps, a greater number of creative individuals could be given in opportunity for mental development than is possible at present. In these times of economic depression and political upheaval such considerations seem to be worth attention.

Einstein's performance was direct, simple, and moving. He radiated the personal magnetism that typified the born actor and the natural politician. Like them, he believed what he said at the moment he said it, and he gained by contrast with the platitudinous comments of the other speakers. Only Sir James Jeans pushed through to the uncomfortable truth: that men such as Einstein—comparable to those whom the council might help—"do not labor for private gain, neither for themselves, nor for their family, nor for their tribe, nor for their country." The meeting certainly consolidated the position of those seeking help for academic refugees, and it brought in not only hard cash but offers of aid from universities throughout the country. Yet Britain's sneaking feeling that a strong Germany would be a bulwark against Russia, and the strong business, political, and traditional links which since Victorian times had stretched into Germany, combined with an innocent trust in the English Channel to limit the impact of such appeals on the general public.

There were certainly those for whom Einstein was now, even more than before, a symbol of intellectual freedom. But there were certainly others in Britain who would have agreed with Einstein's old colleague Dufour-Feronce, former German secretary of the League to whom he had explained his resignation in 1932. "I am convinced that in time things will right themselves and meetings such as the Albert Hall meeting for Einstein will only tend to inflame the situation and not improve it...," he wrote to Lloyd George's secretary: "It is a pity that so great a scientist should lend his name for propaganda against the country of his birth. But although born in Bavaria, he was never really a German in sentiment."

The meeting over, Einstein completed his preparations for leaving Europe, apparently unaware that one of the figures from his Zurich days was in Britain—the Friedrich Adler whose flat had once been above his own, who had helped push him into the Zurich chair, and whose antiwar feelings had culminated in 1916 in his assassination of the Austrian Prime Minister. After being released from prison, Adler had quickly been elected to the Austrian National Assembly. And while Einstein had been preparing his Albert Hall speech, Adler had been addressing the British Socialist party conference at Hastings as secretary of the Labour and Socialist International, defending his assassination of Sturgkh on the grounds that it offered the best chance of ending the war. An exchange of views between the two former colleagues would have been interesting.

One of Einstein's last meetings in England was with Rabbi M. L. Perizweig, chairman of the World Union of Jewish Students of which Einstein was honorary president. After the meeting, Einstein issued a statement that had a slightly ominous ring. "The value of Judaism," this went,

> lies exclusively in its spiritual and ethical content, and in the way in which it has found expression in the lives of individual Jews. Study has therefore always rightly been regarded among us as a sacred activity. That, however, does not mean to say that we ought to strive to earn a

livelihood through the learned professions, as is now unfortunately too often the case. In these difficult times we must explore every possibility of adjusting ourselves to practical needs, without thereby surrendering our love for the things of the spirit or the right to pursue our studies.

To make not too fine a point, he was indicating that not all refugees from Germany would be able to follow the academic lives they planned.

Before Einstein sailed from England another meeting failed to materialize. It is tantalizing to speculate on what might have happened had it done so. On October 4 Lindemann drove to London from Oxford, telephoned Locker-Lampson, and made it clear that he hoped to meet Einstein the following day. With his firm intention of building up Oxford science in general and the Clarendon in particular with the help of refugee scientists, it is inconceivable that he was not now hopeful of strengthening the existing links with Einstein.

What happened next is not clear. But on the fifth Einstein wrote to Lindemann saying he had learned of the attempt to speak to him on the telephone, "but as I heard nothing more I take it that you have returned to Oxford." He ended, "in the hope of our next happy meeting," and it is evident that he expected to return to Oxford, as scheduled, in the summer of 1934.

On the seventh he emphasized to reporters that he was only going to the United States for six months although he did not know what he would do when he returned. Only a couple of months earlier he had prefaced his Herbert Spencer Lecture with the assurance that the links between himself and Oxford University were "becoming progressively stronger," and many at Oxford expected that he would soon be added to the select band already settling there under Lindemann's auspices. Lindemann himself, according to Christ Church legend, claimed for years afterwards that "Locker-Lampson frightened Einstein from Europe."

Einstein left Southampton for New York on the evening of the seventh, joining the *Westernland* on which Elsa had already embarked at Antwerp. As the liner made its way down Southampton Water, past the clustered lights of the Isle of Wight, he apparently still believed that in due course he might be offered British nationality.

The voyage was uneventful. During its later stages plans were completed for disembarkation. In the months that had elapsed since the *Belgenland* sailed from New York Einstein had learned a lot about avoiding publicity—both the personal kind, which genuinely irked him, and the even less pleasant publicity of the pro-Nazi and anti-Nazi groups. There would be no repetition of the earlier occasions on which he had been cornered; this time he was determined to avoid those interviews which had, as *The Times* said, "in 1930 made relativity seem even less comprehensible than it is."

As the *Westernland* sailed up the approaches to New York Harbor Einstein and his wife, Dr. Mayer and Miss Dukas, completed their preparations. At the Battery a tugboat came aside. In it were two trustees of the Institute for Advanced Study, who now helped their visitors aboard. The *Westernland* continued on its way and long before it docked Einstein and his party had been transferred to a car and were, unknown to those awaiting him at the 23rd Street Pier in Manhattan, being driven to Princeton.

He was taken to the temporary home rented for him. He changed into casual clothes and walked out alone to explore his new environment.

On Nassau Street, which runs the length of the town, there stood the Baltimore, at which was sold "The Balt," a special ice-cream cone which was a favorite among students. "Einstein's boat was not yet at the pier in New York," says the Rev. John Lampe, then a divinity student at Princeton Seminary, who had just entered the Balt.

> Yet Einstein walked through the doorway just as the waitress behind the counter handed me my special ice-cream cone! The great man looked at the cone, smiled at me, turned to the girl, and pointed his thumb first at the cone and then at himself.
>
> I wish I could say that I had the generosity of presence of mind to pay for Einstein's first typically American treat. But that would not be the truth. When the waitress handed his cone over the counter, Einstein gave her a coin and she made change, muttering something like "This one goes in my memory book."
>
> Einstein and I stood there together, then, nibbling our ice-cream cones and looking out the window into Nassau

Street. Neither of us said anything. We finished the cones about the same instant and I think I held the door for him as he stepped out.

Einstein had arrived in the United States for good.

PART FIVE

THE ILLUSTRIOUS IMMIGRANT

CHAPTER 19

LIVING WITH THE LEGEND

When Einstein came to Princeton he was still a Research Student of Christ Church, due to visit Oxford for some weeks during 1934, 1935, and 1936. A Private Member's Bill still lay on the table of the House of Commons which could make it possible for him to be granted British nationality. The attractions of Europe were still great and nothing could quite replace the intellectual climate of the Berlin he had known, the closeness to Bohr in Copenhagen, the ease with which he could visit Leiden, Zurich, or Oxford. Years previously, Rutherford had told a friend that leaving England for Canada, after three years with J. J. Thomson at the Cavendish, had been leaving "the Physical World," meaning the world of physics. And when Einstein had first confided to Janos Plesch his plans to go to Princeton, the latter had asked: "Do you want to commit suicide?" Einstein always remembered the remark. Thus his advent in the town was simply the arrival of the "bird of passage" he had described in his diary two years before.

At first the settling in was not necessarily permanent. The "bird of passage" would have a six-months' perch with the institute every year. Not much more was absolutely certain during the autumn of 1933. He might still return to the continent for visits, long or short, even if he did not live there regularly for a part of the year. Gradually this prospect faded, eventually merging into an unspoken acceptance that he would never again see Europe.

That he should finally have decided to settle permanently in New Jersey says much for the treatment he was accorded in Princeton, and for the quality of life there in the 1930s. Set conveniently midway between New York and Philadelphia, the town meanders along its one main street much as it did when Washington dated his farewell address to the army from the town. White-painted wooden-frame houses stretch into undulating country that is not unduly North American. The nostalgic pseudo-English buildings of the university, in one respect a monument to architectural poverty, provide some solace to those who have crossed the Atlantic from necessity rather than choice. Einstein, never particularly partial to human beings, had some feeling for places, preferring the quieter demonstrations of nature, the hills rather than the heights, the areas where the formal transition from winter through spring to summer, and from the blaze of the dying fall to winter came regularly and without commotion. Princeton satisfied these comparatively simple yearnings, and he settled down to the winter months as content as any refugee could expect to be.

He was helped by one other accident of circumstance. Princeton was then, even more than today, surrounded by a "green belt" of estates owned by former university alumni. These in turn created the atmosphere which permeated the town, one of rich, conservative-Republican businessmen, some faintly anti-Semitic. As a group they were rather displeased with the sudden descent on their town of distinguished refugees whose intellectual eminence tended to overshadow their own social position. With a few notable exceptions they made no attempt to establish contact with the newcomers. That suited Einstein.

The upheaval from Europe was not as great as it would have been for most people. "I have never known a place that to me was a homeland," he regretted a few years later to his friend Leon Watters. "No country, no city has such a hold on me." Even Zurich, even Berlin, did not have quite that. Later, when he had lived in Princeton for two decades, as long as he had lived anywhere, he found that its tree-lined streets and quiet houses, each a comfortable island in its own garden, had almost begun to have the quality of home.

In addition, the atmosphere of the institute itself had its attractions. There were no undergraduates, no fraternities, no football teams, no grants, no degrees. Instead there was an intellectual monasticism which allowed him and other scholars—who already included among refugees from Germany Erwin Panofsky, Ernst Herzfeld, and Dr. Otto Nathan, who became Einstein's friend and literary executor—to get on with their thoughts without interruption. There was another side to the coin, however. In Berlin Einstein had enjoyed the best of both worlds with his freedom from responsibilities and his equal freedom to hold seminars when he wished and to put the impress of his ideas wherever he thought the results might justify the trouble. In Princeton, where the only "students" were men who had already acquired their doctorates, he tended to regret the lack of contact with younger minds which batted about ideas with the uninhibited pleasure of inexperience. He thus had some mixed feelings, quite in accord, as his friend Frank put it, "with his divided attitude towards contact with his fellow men in general."

In the winter of 1933 the institute was the work place for eighteen academics whose only obligation was the nominal one of being in residence from October until the end of April. The elegant building which eventually housed the institute on the outskirts of the town was not started until 1938, and the new organization was divided between the big frame house on Alexander Street, near the center of the town, and the university buildings where Einstein was given quarters.

He and Elsa were soon established nearby, in No. 2, Library Place, a small rented house only a few hundred yards from the university campus. Around it, and around the tousled head of Einstein, which was already haloed by the saintly white aureole that was to become his hallmark, there began to evolve a new set of legends. Within a few months he had been given a special place in American mythology, a place occupied not by the master of incomprehensible relativity but by the valiant David shaking his fist at Goliath-Hitler. When the young political scientist David Mitrany arrived in the United States to join the institute the questioning of the customs officer ended as he explained his destination. "Oh, you mean the *Einstein* Institute," said the officer, and, pointing to his package of books: "That's all right, brother, take them away."

As Einstein became a part of the Princeton scene, he became also the great man to whom the small girl down the street was claimed to bring her "sums" regularly, the man to whom the local bus driver said in desperation as the stranger fumbled with his new money: "Bad at arithmetic." With his reputation for having changed man's ideas of the universe, his pervasive humility, and his built-in ability to let the world make a fool of itself, he was tailor-made for apocrypha, and from the winter of 1933 onwards this grew round him just as it had grown in Berlin in the 1920s. The stories are illuminating, not for their truth but for what Einstein was expected to be and to do. His kindliness was as well established as his physical presence and if the small girl with her sums had not existed she would have been invented. He was a genuinely humble man, and it was natural that the earlier "Can't you count" story, almost certainly starting as a chance aside before being embroidered into a score of variations which traveled wherever he played his violin, should be transferred across the Atlantic.

Sometimes nature apes art, sometimes the real man is more than any legend would dare claim. Churchill Einsenhart, son of the former dean of Princeton University's Graduate School, tells how a telephone call was taken in the dean's office shortly after Einstein's arrival. "May I speak with Dean Eisenhart, please?" the speaker asked. On being told that the dean was out, the caller said: "Perhaps *you* can tell me where Dr. Einstein lives." But it had been agreed that everything should be done to protect him from inquisitive callers, so the request was politely refused. "The voice on the telephone dropped to a near whisper," writes Eisenhart, "and continued: 'Please do not tell anybody, but I *am* Dr. Einstein. I am on my way home and have forgotten where my house is.' " So, too, there were occasions on which he could not remember his unlisted phone number.

The absentmindedness was no more assumed than the untidiness. It did not have to be. What looked like caricature was the man himself, merely amused as the Princeton University students, puzzled as well as honored by the settler in their midst, chanted: "The bright boys, they all study maths/And Albie Einstein points the paths./Although he seldom takes the air/We wish to God he'd cut his hair." For Einstein was the practical Bohemian, the man who genuinely acted the way he did because his mind and his time were devoted to essentials. "We are slaves of bathrooms, Frigidaires, cars, radios, and millions of other things," said Infeld, who joined Einstein in Princeton in 1936 and soon became an intimate. Einstein tried to reduce them to the absolute minimum. Long hair minimizes the need for the barber. Socks can be done without. One leather jacket solves the coat problem for many years. Suspenders are superfluous, as are nightshirts and pajamas. It is a minimum problem which Einstein has solved, and shoes, trousers, shirt, jacket are the very necessary things; it would be difficult to reduce them further."

This was the Einstein, sockless and suspenderless, who soon settled in, protected by the agreement that he should be left in peace to acclimatize. Both he and Elsa gradually became accepted, not least because he was always good company while Elsa, despite her obvious enjoyment of Princeton's "high society," had a naturalness that soon won confidence. Thus Einstein, asked at a dinner given by Dean Eisenhart which historical person he would most like to meet, was expected to choose Newton or Archimedes. But his choice was Moses—"I would like to ask him if he ever thought that his people would obey his law so long." And Elsa, invited to tea by the wife of the president of the university, took a long time to speak on finding that she was the guest of honor. At last she was coaxed into a conversation with a group of faculty wives who were liberally quoting their husbands: "Well," she said, "*My* husband always says . . . he's a physicist . . . and he always says. . . ."

A hint of this new status that they were being given in the United States came at the beginning of November when Roosevelt invited Einstein to dine at the White House. The way this was handled by the institute was a warning of things to come, and of the battle with Abraham Flexner that was only to end when the director was replaced by Dr. Frank Aydelotte.

Early in November, Colonel MacIntyre, President Roosevelt's secretary, telephoned the institute, where Einstein's secretary accepted the President's invitation on his behalf. Shortly afterwards, MacIntyre was surprised to receive a telephone call from Flexner. In the words of a memorandum from the White House Social Bureau, he "stated very strongly that appointments could not be made for Professor Einstein except through him." Lest there should be any doubt about the implication, Flexner followed up the call with a letter to the President. "With genuine and profound reluctance I felt myself compelled this afternoon to explain to your secretary, Mr. [*sic*] MacIntyre, that Professor Einstein had come to Princeton for the purpose of carrying on his scientific work in seclusion and that it was absolutely impossible to make any exception which would inevitably bring him into public notice," he wrote.

> You are aware of the fact that there exists in New York an irresponsible group of Nazis. In addition, if the newspapers had access to him or if he accepted a single engagement or invitation that could possibly become public, it would be practically impossible for him to remain in the post which he has accepted in this institute or in America at all. With his consent and at his desire I have declined on his behalf invitations from high officials and from scientific societies in whose work he is really interested.

This was not good enough. Far from failing to accept "a single engagement," Einstein made his American debut as a violinist at a public concert, attended as guest of honor a dinner given by Governor Lehmann, was officially welcomed as a resident of New Jersey, and attended public celebrations to set the first type for an enlarged edition of the *Jewish Daily Bulletin*, all within a few months of his arrival. But it gives some idea of Flexner's proprietorial attitude towards the scholars and scientists he had brought up and it suggests that the "irresponsible group of Nazis" was an excuse for keeping Einstein from a President who might expect him to spread his energies across the United States—possibly even to the California Institute of Technology. Certainly the implication of Flexner's letter was that Einstein had personally agreed to refuse the President's invitation.

Roosevelt himself might have continued to think this had not Henry Morgenthau, then Undersecretary of the Treasury, written casually to Einstein mentioning the invitation that had been refused. "You can hardly imagine," Einstein wrote to Mrs. Roosevelt on learning the news, "of what great interest it would have been for me to meet the man who is tackling with gigantic energy the greatest and most difficult problem of our time. However, as a matter of fact, no invitation whatever has reached me. I only learned that such an invitation was intended but believed that the plan had been dropped." He ended by saying that he was writing "because it means a great deal to me to avoid the ugly impression that I had been negligent or discourteous in this matter." The incident foreshadowed what he later described to a colleague as his "little war in the beerglass" with Flexner. And it helps to explain his later comment to his friend Leon Watters: "When I first came to Princeton I thought I understood Flexner; since then I find him an enigma. I feel that I am not kept advised as to what is going on. There is anti-Semitism at Princeton."

A second invitation to the White House quickly followed Einstein's letter, and he and Elsa arrived in Washington on January 24. They dined with the President and Mrs. Roosevelt and stayed the night, their long afterdinner conversations being in German which, Einstein later recalled, the President spoke very well. There is no direct record of what they talked about. But there is indirect evidence in eight lines of doggerel which Einstein wrote before leaving, a copy of which is preserved in the White House archives.

The German runs as follows:

In der Hauptstadt stolzer Pracht
Wo das Schicksal wird gewacht
Kämpfet froh ein stolzer Mann
Der die Lösung schaffen kann
Beim Gerpräche gestern Nacht
Herzlich Ihrer wird gedacht
Was berichtet werden muss
Darum sende ich diesen Gruss.

The translation by the White House Bureau runs:

In the Capital's proud magnificence
Where destiny is made
Cheerfully fights a proud man
Who can provide the solution.
In our conversation of last night
There were cordial thoughts of you
Which must be spoken
So I send this greeting.

But the copy in the White House archives is written by Elsa; it gives, moreover, no clue to the "you" of whom Einstein and Roosevelt had cordial thoughts. But this is clear from the original verses, written in Einstein's hand on a small postcard. The card, now in the Royal Archives, Brussels, was addressed to Queen Elizabeth of the Belgians.

The situation in Europe—and presumably Belgium's position next to a swiftly rearming Germany—is unlikely to have been the only subject discussed that evening and the question of U. S. nationality appears to have been raised. This may have been so. A few weeks earlier Roosevelt had received a letter from Representative F. H. Shoemaker suggesting that he should "by Executive Order extend to Professor Einstein citizenship in the United States, thus making it possible for Professor Einstein to continue his scientific work and research, thus extending the helping hand, instead of perhaps the reproachful word." Roosevelt's secretary replied that Congress had never provided for U. S. citizenship to be given by Executive Order, but that no doubt the Secretary of Labor would write to Einstein telling him how to take out naturalization papers if he wished to do so. However, Einstein was at this date quite satisfied to hold only Swiss nationality—and until the summer of 1936 continued to live in the United States only on a temporary visitor's visa.

The question of nationality was publicly raised two months later. On Wednesday, March 28, Congressman Kenney of New Jersey proposed a Joint Resolution in the House of Representatives to admit Einstein to U. S. citizenship. It went as follows:

> Whereas Professor Einstein has been accepted by the scientific world as a savant and a genius; and
> Whereas his activities as a humanitariun have placed him high in the regard of countless of his fellowmen; and
> Whereas he has publicly declared on many occasions to be a lover of the United States and an admirer of its Constitution; and
> Whereas the United States is known in the world as a haven of liberty and true civilization: Therefore be it
> 1. Resolved by the Senate and House of Representatives

> of the United States of America in Congress assembled, That Albert Einstein is hereby unconditionally admitted to the character and privileges of a citizen of the United States.

The following day, presumably by coincidence, it was officially announced in Berlin that Einstein had been formally deprived of German citizenship by an order promulgated by Wilhelm Frick, Minister of the Interior. By this time the list of the previous summer had lengthened. When Einstein's name had been put on the first list of men who might be deprived of their nationality, there had been only six more. Now his name appeared with thirty-six others.

Einstein made no public comment although years later he drew a grisly parallel to the German action. "The Hitler regime pompously threw me out after I had already renounced my nationality," he wrote. "To me it is analogous to the case of Mussolini who was hung up even when it was known he was dead." As far as the congressman's action was concerned, Einstein's feeling was made plain to his friends: he was quite satisfied with his Swiss citizenship—a point which he made to Kenney on April 11 in a letter asking him to drop the motion.

This move came as Einstein's plans for the immediate future were, according to his own evidence written at the time, still in the balance. On Friday, March 30, he and Elsa went to New York and met a number of Elsa's relatives arriving from Europe on the S. S. *Albert Ballin*. On the Sunday he attended a Carnegie Hall concert at which he was presented with a scroll of honor before going on to a dinner of the National Labor Committee for the Jewish Worker in Palestine. Both were announced as farewell occasions, and Einstein was reported to be sailing for Antwerp on Tuesday, April 3. But on Monday the second the Jewish Telegraphic Agency—always among the best-informed sources on Einstein's activities—announced that he had changed his plans and would be staying indefinitely in the United States. The New York papers announced that he had been about to leave for a visit to France and Belgium, and the Agency quoted a statement from his secretary saying: "Many different circumstances had entered into his decision."

In fact Einstein had been hovering for some months. Plans for his visit to Oxford, due in the spring or summer of 1934, had been discussed with Lindemann from November, 1933, onwards. But he was increasingly anxious to cancel it and on December 17 wrote saying that conditions in the United States were so favorable that he was able to forego the £400 from Christ Church. Could it not be used elsewhere, he asked; a suggestion that was finally to harden into the proposal that it should support Jewish refugees from Germany. However, Lindemann was a determined fighter and early in 1934 Einstein received an invitation from Locker-Lampson almost certainly written at Lindemann's instigation, urging him to come to England.

He was still reluctant to leave America. But he had written to Mrs. Roosevelt earlier on inferring that he would be in Princeton only "until the end of March, 1934"; as late as March 22 he told Max Born that "if at all possible [he was] going to fritter away the summer somewhere in America. Why should an old fellow like me not enjoy relative peace and quiet for once?" It is clear, therefore, that his final decision was not made until the end of March. Judging by a letter to Lindemann written by Erwin Shrödinger, it was made on the twenty-eighth.

Schrödinger had by this time been awarded a Fellowship at Magdalen. But he was visiting America and had called on Einstein partly out of friendship, partly as an emissary from Lindemann. Now, on March 29, he reported back:

> Dear Lindemann, I suppose you are waiting for news from me concerning our friend A. E. and his coming to Oxford. I did not want to write to you before I had the feeling that his answer was really definitive—and of course I did not wish to urge him, because I feared that might still reduce the likeliness of a positive answer. But now I asked him once more, adding that it would of course be wishable for you to know as soon as possible. Well, I am sorry to say, that he asked me to write to you a definite *no.* I really wanted to cable but unfortunately I said so and he had objections to it. The reason for his decision is really

> that he is frightened of all the ado and the fuss and the consequent duties that would be laid upon him, if he came to Europe at all. He considers the only way of escaping is to stay in America this summer—I also told him that his idea of so to speak transferring the grant, that was at his disposition for this purpose, on another or some other refugees, who need it, was not feasible. He understands this of course, though he regrets it.

Einstein not only regretted it. He refused to take No for an answer. He himself now wrote to Christ Church, stating that he did not propose to visit Oxford that year. He did not therefore consider himself entitled to the £400 that went with his Studentship, but hoped that the governing body would apply all or part of this to help scientific refugees. The request was repeated for two more years. "I fear," he wrote to Lindemann at the beginning of 1935, when asked whether he would be visiting Oxford, "that I shall not be able to come to Europe again so soon because if I come to Oxford I must also go to Paris and Madrid and I lack the courage to undertake all this. And so I am going to remain here. . . . You can use the money which was granted to me, therefore, in the same way as last year."

Had Einstein returned to Europe in the spring of 1934, he would have been involved at two levels. As a public symbol of opposition to Hitler he would have had to speak, to lobby, to steep himself in the political ferment, an occupation for which he had no liking, even when deeply committed to a cause. Further, there were personal involvements which would inevitably take up his time and his energies. His first wife and his two sons were safe in Switzerland; his eldest stepdaughter, Ilse, had gone to Amsterdam with her husband while Margot had remained in Belgium. There were other relatives, his and Elsa's, scattered across Europe. If he crossed the Atlantic he would inevitably be drawn more directly into discussion about their future.

Now, with the decision, in Schrödinger's words, "to stay in America this summer," there came the search for a cottage away from Princeton, preferably where he could sail. Elsa handled the search, turning for help to Leon Watters, whom they had first met at Pasadena in January, 1933. Like Dr. Bucky, the radiologist from Leipzig with whom the Einsteins renewed their friendship during their first months in the United States, Watters left a large collection of letters and reminiscences which throw valuable light on the last two decades of Einstein's life. Early in 1933 plans were being made to celebrate the fiftieth anniversary of the Hebrew Technical Institute for Boys which Watters ran in New York, and he hoped that Einstein might be induced to attend. "In considering how I might approach him," Watters later wrote,

> I recalled that in the course of my conversation with him at Pasadena I had mentioned a somewhat rare book which I had acquired. Its title was *Memorabilia Mathematica* and it contained interesting anecdotes concerning famous mathematicians and physicists. Einstein had expressed a desire to see it and I thought that presenting it to him might afford an excuse for calling on him.
>
> Arriving [at Einstein's house in Princeton] I asked my chauffeur, Martin Flattery, to go to the door, ring the bell, and ask if I might see the professor. He came back to the car promptly and reported that a lady had told him that the Einsteins were not at home. I wrote a short note and asked the chauffeur to leave it at the house with the book I had brought. While thus engaged, I thought I discerned someone looking through the curtained window of the house and motioning to Martin. He went to the door again and came running back with a broad grin on his face, saying I was to come in. As I crossed the threshold Mrs. Einstein grasped my hand warmly and was most abject in apologizing for having sent out word that they were not at home. She said that she had not recognized the name and explained that she had to resort to subterfuge to shield themselves from incessant annoyance by visitors. I apologized on my part for coming unannounced. After a short chat she called out "Albert!" and in a moment Einstein came down the stairs. He had on a worn gray sweater, a pair of baggy trousers, and slippers, holding a pipe in his hand, and greeted me warmly. I continued to stand till he invited me to sit down, he taking a chair opposite me while fondling the book I had brought him.

Einstein was by now being deluged by demands to speak for charity, to attend dinners for charity, to give his name to a multitude of good causes. He usually declined;

the exceptions were to help either the growing stream of Jewish refugees from Europe or the Jews in Palestine. "For a cause like yours I will gladly come," he told Watters.

The meeting sealed a friendship which quickly developed. Within three weeks the Einsteins had visited Watters' institute, spent some time with him at his New York home, and accepted his offer of help in their search for a country cottage. "Both of us feel," Elsa wrote to him on April 5, "that we have found a friend in you. If our life were not so hectic and busy we would very much like to have your company more. We will meet again as soon as it is possible."

They did meet again, and often, and in April, 1934, there began a long and revealing correspondence between Elsa—always eager to push her husband into what she thought of as "society"—and the rich biochemist. Einstein wrote too, but it is his wife's letters which paint the homely picture of the great man, anxious to avoid public appearances, intent on getting on with work, being coaxed into a synagogue for "the first time in his adult life," and relaxing only in the small boat which he would sail with a ferocious intensity that drew admiration from the experts and fear from his friends.

Watters himself is for a few years a minor Boswell in his recording of the extrovert Einstein. This is the Einstein arriving with his friend at what turned out to be a New York charity party and remarking of his host's floral exhibition: "One flower is beautiful, a surfeit of flowers is vulgar." It is the Einstein stopping Watters' chauffeur-driven car, jumping out to post his own letters, and replying to the obvious question with the answer that he "didn't wish to incommode us." It is also the Einstein who cannot or will not see that his own idea of equality can be embarrassing. "Just as we were all seated at the table," writes Watters in describing how they arrived back at the Einstein home after one Sunday drive, "Einstein rose from his chair, went outside, came back with my chauffeur, and seated him at the table next to himself. Flattery, a decidedly modest person, felt ill at ease, and just as soon as the meal was finished, he made the excuse that he had to do some work on the car and thus escaped. This was the second time that he had been an unwilling guest at their table."

Watters also records an incident which casts light on the aloofness which permeated so many of Einstein's personal relationships. One evening he said, with a sense of regret and longing, that he had never put down roots. "As a youth," Watters says, "he had never enjoyed the companionship of other youths, as a student he had never become intimate with his fellow students and took no part in their activities; as a noted scientist people did him homage; he never met them on a scale of equality that leads to lasting friendship. From all this I realized his craving for someone in whom he could confide." The statement does little justice to Einstein's close personal friendship with Ehrenfest which continued for more than twenty years or that with Besso which went on for more than twice as long. It reflects the lonely exile in his fifties rather than the younger man at the center of things, dashing off his friendly postcards to all and sundry. Yet it also indicated that Einstein knew what he had lost through a combination of temperament and determination to plow his own furrow.

But such confidences came only some years after their meeting in 1934. During the first months of their acquaintanceship, Elsa conscripted Watters' help in the choice of the summer sailing retreat. Before the matter could be finally decided there came news from Europe that her daughter Ilse was seriously ill in Paris. Elsa announced that she must go to her at once.

What would happen to Einstein? For seventeen years, broken only by short unaccompanied journeys abroad, he had been guided and cosseted by Elsa through the minefields of everyday life. Now he was to be left, if not on his own—for there was always the incomparable Miss Dukas—at least without Elsa, in a country where he was still something of a stranger. He had no wish to stay in Princeton, and it was finally arranged that he should go after his wife's departure to "The Studio" at Watch Hill, Rhode Island, standing on the Sound just where it meets the sea. Here he would share their rented cottage for the early summer with Dr. and Mrs. Bucky, their two sons, and Miss Dukas, who would keep house and deal with correspondence that would not wait.

At noon on May 19 Elsa sailed from New York on the

French liner *Paris*. Her husband, having seen her off, was taken by Watters to his apartment and instructed to lie down before lunch. "I am not tired but I will not be insubordinate," he said, relaxing while Liszt's "Lorelei" was played on the Ampico. "Was it restful?" Watters asked as they went into lunch. "The sofa yes, the music not much—too sugary." Einstein replied. He was driven to a brief interview with his old friend Dr. Schwarz, the former German consul who had by this time been dismissed; then back to Princeton to prepare for his move to Watch Hill with the Buckys.

While Einstein's friendship with Watters reflects his unwavering interest in Jewish causes, and the determined fight that American Zionists carried on for the use of his name, that with Bucky shows something different. The doctor was not only a radiologist and physician but also an inventor, and the correspondence shows that Einstein's intuition for seeing the strengths and weaknesses of a good idea, developed in the Patent Office thirty years earlier, had not left him. The two men patented a camera, discussed means of using gravitation to measure altitudes, and also of "obtaining a proportional description of sound waves by magnetic means."

Some of the father's ingenuity seems to have been shown by the Bucky boys. At "The Studio" they had, says Watters,

> set up an excellent short-wave radio set with a directional antenna. On the porch was a signboard showing at what time each country would broadcast: England, France, Holland, Germany, etc. This was during the period when Hitler was occupying the center of the world stage. When we heard his turgid, shrieking voice come over the air, we all agreed that his antics, had they not had tragic consequences, could have been rightly designated as comic.

Watters visited the Rhode Island ménage early in July. He learned much about Einstein's habits. When no visitors were present, he was served first and alone. The Buckys dined by themselves later. Miss Dukas did most of the cooking which consisted usually of macaroni, noodles, other soft foods, and little meat.

At Watch Hill, Einstein spent most of his available time in the 17-foot boat which he kept at a small quay within walking distance of the cottage. His boat on the Havelsee outside Berlin had been, wrote Plesch, "perhaps the one thing that it hurt him to have to leave behind when the time came to shake the dust of Germany from his feet"; and until old age joined forces with ill-health he continued to sail, not only on Princeton's Carnegie Lake but throughout the summer vacation. His choice would be sometimes a hamlet on the eastern coast, sometimes a spot on one of the seaboard's inland lakes. Once he was persuaded by his friend to go to Florida instead. They had a hard time. Florida, as far as Einstein was concerned, was "too snobbish."

Sailing, like music, was with Einstein not so much a hobby as an extension of himself in which the essentials of his character and temperament were revealed. Thus it was inevitable that he should politely return an outboard motor which had been presented to him. He never drove a car—"the Herr Professor does not drive. It is too complicated," Elsa explained to one visitor—was over fifty when he handled a camera for the first time and barely learned to use a typewriter. A motor of any sort was a mechanical barrier. "The natural counterplay of wind and water delighted him most," says Bucky, who often sailed with him. "Speed, records, and above all competition were against his nature. He had a childlike delight when there was a calm and the boat came to a standstill, or when the boat ran aground."

He carried his passion for bare essentials to the point of refusing to have life jackets or belts on board—even though he never learned to swim. He would have liked gliding, he would have loved skiing, and it was possibly only a lack of facilities which kept him from the first and a built-in physical laziness—"I like sailing," he said, "because it is the sport which demands the least energy" —which kept him from the second. He never studied navigation and never looked at a compass when in a boat, making up for this with a good sense of direction —which he rarely showed on land—and what Watters called "the ability to forecast a storm with uncanny accuracy." Wind and weather had an obvious link with stress and strain, action and reaction, and the basis of physics, and his long theoretical experience clearly gave him an intuitive knowledge of how to handle a boat. This was appreciated by the designer, W. Sterling Burgess, who some years later, when Einstein was on holiday at Newport, came to confer with him. "Burgess had made a number of drawings from which to determine the best configuration of the hull of the new American yacht, and he had several pages of computations and equations," says Watters. "Einstein patiently listened while Burgess read his notes; then he sat for a few minutes in thought and, taking pencil and paper, gave Burgess his answer."

Two other traits were revealed to friends who sailed with him. One was his indifference to danger or death, reflected in such fearlessness of rough weather that more than once he had to be towed in after his mast had been blown down. Another was his perverse delight in doing the unexpected. "Once when out sailing with him," writes Watters, "and while we were engaged in an interesting conversation, I suddenly cried out 'Achtung' for we were almost upon another boat. He veered away with excellent control and when I remarked what a close call we had had, he started to laugh and sailed directly toward one boat after another, much to my horror; but he always veered off in time, and then laughed like a naughty boy." On another occasion Watters pointed out that they had sailed too close to a group of projecting rocks; Einstein replied by skimming the boat across a barely submerged shelf. In his boat, as in physics, he sailed close to the wind.

Einstein enjoyed his first summer in America, even though the news, both from his wife in France and from friends who had succeeded in leaving Germany, grew steadily worse. Elsa arrived in Paris to find her younger daughter, Margot, caring for a sister who was dying. Within a few weeks she was returning across the Atlantic with her elder daughter's ashes, kept in a casket in the Einstein home until it disappeared after her own death two years later.

Ilse's husband was Rudolf Kayser, who after the Nazis' rise to power had emigrated to Holland, where he edited his stepfather-in-law's writings published as *Mein Weltbild*. Kayser now crossed the Atlantic and in due course joined the Einsteins in Princeton. Margot also came, with her husband, from whom she subsequently obtained a divorce. Eventually they were joined by Hans Albert, Einstein's elder son, who left Mileva in Zurich to care for his younger brother, already diagnosed as a schizophrenic for whom there was in those days little hope of cure. Two years later, only a few months before the outbreak of the Second World War, Einstein was reunited with his sister Maja, who arrived in America from Italy. Of the relatives who remained in Europe the closest were Uncle Cäsar and his two children, with whom Einstein kept up a lively correspondence that continued into the first years of the war.

The emigrants typified the growing stream of Jews from Germany—and later from Austria and Czechoslovakia—who crossed the Atlantic during the second half of the 1930s. Einstein could not isolate himself from their fortunes—the personal fortunes of his own family or the fate of the refugee Jewry in general—however much the voice of physics encouraged him to do so.

From his arrival in the United States until that country's entry into the war with Germany in 1941 his research in Princeton was therefore carried on against a background of extracurricular work. This ranged from fund raising to giving confidential advice on posts into which particular men might be fitted. He wrote letters, pulled strings, and unashamedly used all the considerable force of the small tidy "A. Einstein" at the foot of the page. He was as lavish with money as with time. "I am in a somewhat difficult situation because I am supposed to help in bringing the fiancé of a relative of mine over here, and I have already given too many affidavits for my financial status," he wrote to Watters on one occasion. "I would be forced to put $2,000 for months into a foreign account." There is no record of the response. It would be surprising if Watters had not come to the rescue.

Einstein disliked all that this work involved, and for several reasons. "My husband is, as you will understand, surfeited with publicity," Elsa wrote on his behalf in reply to one request to speak in New York for a $2,000 charity fee. "Public appearance is, for him, impossible for the moment. I hope he will make some again next season. But now every public activity and appearance is repugnant to him. He has had so much of it." He disliked soft-soaping people, a dislike epitomized when he pleaded with a friend to speak in his place: "You know I can't make speeches. I can't lie." But this did not mean that his colleague could do so. "Oh, no. You know how to be gracious."

He disliked wasting his time, writing to Weizmann on one occasion that "it really is a scandal that people who could occupy their time far better, have to attend at such a money-raising circus." His health limited what he could do, so that in 1937 he had to reject an invitation to visit London—"My physical condition . . . is so bad that I am treated like an egg without a shell and can under no circumstances entertain traveling either to England or to Palestine." He was now satisfied with the post-Magnes Hebrew University—"it tickles my vanity to know that through my stubbornness I contributed a little towards this improvement"—but there were still occasions when his views failed to chime with official Zionist policy. Thus in 1938 some of his comments about "narrow nationalism" in Palestine brought forth a letter from Weizmann. He politely assumed that Einstein's "thoughts were being misrepresented"; but used nearly 2,000 words in an attempt to put the matter straight. Nevertheless, Einstein did what he could, and from 1934 his speeches, appeals, and letter-signings multiply. During the first half of the 1930s he had pleaded that England and France should remain unarmed. Now he helped cope with the results.

"Politically," he wrote to Lindemann on December 17,

> I have voiced my opinion much less than it may seem, since the press makes a great deal of fuss over me without my intending it or wishing it. All the same I am of the opinion that a conscientious person who has a certain amount of influence cannot in times like the present keep completely silent, since such silence can lead to wrong interpretation which is undesirable in the present circumstances.

The circumstances were not only the increasing persecution of the Jews but also a process which Einstein knew would move Lindemann as much as it moved him: the division of physics into Aryan right and Jewish wrong.

The first attempts at this, made in the backwash of the 1918 defeat, had been deepened by political propaganda during the decade that followed. But the straight condemnation of relativity as a Jewish theory seemed almost sane compared with the huge edifice of mumbo jumbo being created as Einstein settled into Princeton. At one end of the German academic spectrum stood Professor Mueller of the Technical College of Aachen, seeing Einstein and his work as part of a Jewish plot to pollute science. "The [relativity] theory was," he stated in *Jewry and Science*,

> directed from beginning to end towards the goal of transforming the living—that is, the non-Jewish—world of living essence, born from a mother earth and bound up with blood, and bewitching it into spectral abstraction in which all idividual differences of people and nations, and all inner limits of the races, are lost in unreality, and in which only an unsubstantial diversity of geometric dimensions survives which produces all events out of the compulsion of its godless subjection to laws.

At much the same level was Professor Tomaschek, director of the Institute of Physics at Dresden. "Modern physics," he claimed, "is an instrument of [world] Jewry for the destruction of Nordic science. True physics is the creation of the German spirit.... In fact, all European science is the fruit of Aryan, or, better, German thought." Presumably this sounded like common sense to a writer who could claim that "statistical laws in physics must be racially understood."

At a higher level were the men whose reputation automatically gave them a hearing. Not all had the comparative harmlessness of Professor Stark, who had been forced to retire from his chair in the University of Wurzburg in 1922 because of his polemics against Einstein, but who now bounced back with the claim that "the founders of research in physics, and the great discoverers from Galileo to Newton to the physical pioneers of our time, were almost exclusively of Aryan, predominantly of the Nordic, race." There was also the irrepressible Lenard, who had ordered that the word "ampere," commemorating the French physicist in the unit of electrical current, should be replaced by the German "weber" after Wilhelm Weber on the instruments in his Heidelberg laboratory. His four-volume *Deutsche Physik*, printed in Gothic type to epitomize "the German spirit," illustrated his paranoia. "Jewish science soon found many industrious interpreters of non-Jewish or practically non-Jewish blood," he said. "One may summarise them all by calling to mind the probably pure-minded Jew, Albert Einstein. His 'theories of relativity' seek to revolutionize and dominate the whole of physics. In fact these theories are now down and out [*ausgespielt*]. They were never even intended to be true."

This line of attack was epitomized by the opening words of Lenard's fourth volume. "German physics? one asks. I might rather have said Aryan Physics or the Physics of the Nordic Species of Man. The Physics of those who have fathomed the depths of Reality, seekers after Truth, the Physics of the very founders of Science. But, I shall be answered, 'Science is and remains international.' It is false. Science, like every other human product, is racial and conditioned by blood." Bruno Thurring, lecturing to the Heidelberg Association of Students of Science on September 4, 1936, pointed up the same argument. Einstein, he claimed, was not the pupil of Copernicus, Galileo, Kepler, and Newton, but their determined opponent. "His theory is not the keystone of a development, but a declaration of total war," he went on, "waged with the purpose of destroying what lies at the basis of this development, namely, the world view of German man."

If this negation of scientific inquiry had been confined to the lunatic fringe of the universities fewer men would have decided to pull up their emotional roots and leave quietly in the night for an unknown future wherever fortune provided it. But its implications stretched out wider, corrupting all they touched. Some did decide to fight on within Germany itself. Von Laue, visiting Einstein in Princeton shortly before the outbreak of war, explained why he had to return: "I hate them so much I must be close to them. I have to go back." Others concluded that it was their duty to acquiesce, others remained enigmatic, while yet others decided it was their duty to pack their bags and go.

Among those who had been Einstein's colleagues, the most notable to leave Germany with honest speed was Max Born, as unyielding in his opposition to Hitler as he later was to nuclear weapons, coming first to Cambridge and then to Edinburgh. In Hamburg, Einstein's old colleague Otto Stern declared on Hitler's accession to power that he would resign from his chair. He was dissuaded by his staff, but reiterated that he would leave at the first hint of interference with his department. It came in June.

Stern walked from his laboratory, never to return. Shortly afterwards he left Germany for the United States where, at the Carnegie Institute of Technology, he was awarded the Nobel Prize, acted as adviser to the Manhattan Project, which built the first nuclear weapons—and later helped awaken Einstein to the problems they posed for the postwar world. Erwin Freundlich left the Einstein Tower at Potsdam—going first to Istanbul, where a brave but unsuccessful effort was made to create a new center of Western learning; then to Prague: and, after the *débâcle* of the Munich Agreement, to St. Andrews, Scotland, where he was offered a post on the initiative of Eddington and spent the rest of his working life. Schrödinger went to Oxford and, subsequently, to Belgium and Dublin. Leo Szilard, one of the first Hungarians to see the implications of Hitler's conquest of the chancellory, came to England via Austria and subsequently, for lack of support in Britain, crossed the Atlantic.

Szilard highlights the most momentous result of the year which brought Hitler to power, Einstein to Princeton, and drove no less than six Nobel Prize winners from Germany; a result which can be seen in any story of the world's first nuclear weapons. Einstein, Szilard, Teller, Wigner, Peierls and Frisch, Otto Stern, Hans Bethe, and Victor Weisskopf—these are only a few of the men who left Europe under attack, or threat of attack, from the Nazi government; who played their part in the work which led to Hiroshima and Nagasaki; and who might, but for the policy of the National Socialist party, have written a very different opening chapter to the story of the nuclear age.

The grotesque Nazi interpretation of the new physical theories produced during the first third of the century, the expulsion of the Jews and the effect of this on the situation in Palestine, together with what seemed to be the inevitable approach of world war, formed the background against which Einstein settled into his work at the Institute for Advanced Study. He was much sought after. The prospect of a musical evening or of some new development in science were the bait most commonly used to draw him from the relative seclusion of Princeton. But he was not in demand solely because he was the most famous scientist in the world. He was in his mid-fifties, unsociable rather than the reverse, a dropper of bricks as much by intent as by accident. Yet in the true dictionary definition of "a favor specially vouchsafed by God," a charisma did not only set him apart but made almost any meeting with him a memorable occasion. There would invariably be some attitude, some phrase, that would be remembered long afterwards and which could be attached to him alone.

When Harvard wanted to confer an honorary degree on him, he was coaxed to the occasion by Harlow Shapley, who at Mount Wilson had laid the foundations for galactic astronomy, offering a private evening of chamber music at his house. Elsa, unable to come, gave her usual list of instructions. "He is a sensitive plant," she wrote. "He should smoke no cigar. He can have coffee for breakfast, but in the evening he must have Sanka; otherwise he will not sleep well." Einstein followed his instructions, says Shapley. "When we rose from the dinner table and the men went into the library, he said "no" to the proffered cigar. Sadly he got out his pipe. Later I tempted him again. This time he took a cigar, saying softly, 'Ach, mein Weib.' "

At the end of the evening the guests began to go, but not rapidly. "Who would want to go away hastily from an Einstein evening?" says Shapley.

> He might say something—and indeed he did. He whispered it to me as I was sending the fiddlers along. "They remind me of time," he said.
>
> "But it is only eleven o'clock. The time is not late: they will be gone in a few minutes."
>
> "But they remind me of time," he persisted.
>
> "How so?"
>
> "Always going—but never gone."

Once he was induced to visit Rockefeller Medical Center in New York, then run by Abraham Flexner's brother. Here Dr. Alexis Carrel, whose extracurricular interests were spiritualism and extrasensory perception, was working with Lindbergh on an apparatus for the perfusion of human organs, a device which helped open the way to the modern heart transplant. Carrel had invited Einstein to inspect the apparatus with its pulsating exhibits. Thirty years later Lindbergh still remembers Einstein coming into the room with Carrel. The latter, expounding his spiritualism, was saying: "But doctor, what would you say if you observed this phenomenon yourself?"

"I still would not believe it," Einstein replied.

By the start of 1935 he had become reconciled to the fact that Europe would never again be his home; even a sentimental visit would present problems—"so many obligations would await me there that I seem unable to find the courage for such a project," he wrote to the Belgian Queen-Mother in February. Three months later he arrived in Hamilton, Bermuda, with his family and Miss Dukas. He played the usual hide-and-seek with reporters, stayed long enough to make formal visa applications to the U. S. consul necessary under U. S. law since they still held only visitors' permits, and returned to Princeton at the end of a week. Now they were able to take out the papers which eventually meant naturalization. Long before this Einstein had put down his first real roots in the United States. In August, 1935, he bought 112 Mercer Street, the comfortable two-story house in its own piece of ground that was to become in time one of the most famous houses in the world—the "very old and beautiful house with a long garden," as Elsa described it in a letter to Uncle Cäsar in Belgium. Mercer Street is a rib which runs from the university site on Princeton's main backbone, a broad tree-lined avenue making for open parklike country in which the Institute for Advanced Study was built. No. 112, 120 years old, quiet and comfortable behind its veranda and green shutters, had little to distinguish it from many similar white-painted houses. Tidy hedge, neat lawn, five-stepped approach to the porch, broad interior stairs leading up to the bedrooms—all these were the hallmarks of anonymity as were the trees back and front which enclosed the house in its own personal countryside.

The first change in the house came with the creation of Einstein's study, an upper room overlooking the back garden. Half the wall was replaced with a huge window, which seemed to bring the trees into the room, so that Einstein could say it was hardly like being indoors. Two of the remaining walls were transformed into floor-to-ceiling bookshelves. The center of the room was almost filled with a large low table, usually covered with a debris of pencils, pads, and pipes. In front of the window stood his desk. For ornaments there were portraits of Faraday, Maxwell and, soon afterwards, of Gandhi, "the only statesman," in Einstein's opinion, "who represented that higher conception of human relations in the political sphere to which we must aspire with all our powers." On the walls hung a simple diploma: that of his honorary membership of the Berner Naturforschende Gesellschaft. In the rooms below, contrasting grotesquely with the colonial-style surroundings, was the bulky and outmoded furniture from 5, Haberlandstrasse, surprisingly released by the Nazis and finally brought to the United States on Elsa's instructions.* It seems that Einstein hated it.

With this home as headquarters, he became a feature of the Princeton scene. First reactions had been qualified. "Princeton is a wonderful little spot," he wrote to Queen Elizabeth of Belgium soon after his arrival, "a quaint and ceremonious village of puny demigods on stilts. Yet, by ignoring certain special conventions, I have been able to create for myself an atmosphere conducive to study and free from distraction. Here, the people who compose what is called 'society' enjoy even less freedom than their counterparts in Europe. Yet they seem unaware of this restriction since their way of life tends to inhibit personality development from childhood." And, more than a year later, he could write, to the same correspondent: ". . . as an elderly man, I have remained estranged from the society here. . . ." As always, he would have been unhappy as the odd man in.

This early frigidity between Einstein and the inhabitants of the small New Jersey township was easy to understand. Never the most gregarious of men, he felt a shy European reserve among this nation of extroverts; on their side, even the most friendly were slightly put off by an isolating whiff of genius as they considered this quiet eccentric-looking fellow who had in some mysterious fashion convinced the experts that neither space nor time was what they thought it was.

*Einstein's scientific papers were taken from the Haberlandstrasse apartment to Rudolf Kayser's flat, and from there to the French Embassy. They then left Germany in the diplomatic bag. Treatment of refugees was still haphazard, and one Jewish Physicist who left Germany in 1933—and who was to play a key role in the Allies' nuclear war effort—was followed by his scientific equipment some months afterwards.

The phase passed. Long before the outbreak of war, Einstein had been accorded his own niche inside the Princeton community. They still felt that he was uncomfortably unique. A good many held reservations about his uncompromising views on politics and his unconventional views on religion. But it was tacitly agreed that these matters could be ignored, that Einstein could be accepted in spite of them. His greatness would be overlooked as a pardonable eccentricity. They would pass the time of day with him, allow their children to make friends, and would generally agree that however outrageous his views, however shy and retiring he might be, he was yet a decent neighbor. As opinion softened, they began to regard their genius as after all a man of flesh and blood, tortured by the usual human anxieties and fears. They were almost right.

The tragedy which began as he and Elsa were settling into the new home was a human enough link with other men's lives. Only a few months after they had moved in, Elsa was affected by a swelling of the eye. Specialists confirmed that this, as she had feared, was a symptom of heart and kidney troubles. Hospital treatment in New York was proposed. But she soon came back to Mercer Street, to a drastic cure which involved complete immobilization. "I was very, very ill," she wrote in December to Watters, "and I do not believe that I will ever again be completely well. It has fagged me too completely. But it goes a little better now and with that I must be satisfied. I have lain almost two months now and naturally I cannot stand up, let alone walk. That I must learn all over again." Einstein, she added, "sticks frightfully to his problems. I have never before seen him so engrossed in his work. Even at night he is without rest and his problems plague him."

Einstein's devotion to physics throughout these trying months was not a sign of callousness. With such dedicated men—whether their interests be politics or science or art—the normal emotions take their turn. Compared with the problems of the universe, family duties were small beer, a priority that was reinforced as he grew older. Talking late one evening with Watters, he looked intently at a picture of Watters' recently dead wife. "The individual," he reflected, "counts for little; man's individual troubles are insignificant; we place too much importance on the trivialities of living." Yet despite this there was still a subtle difference between the first wife with whom he lived for a decade and the second with whom he lived for two. Elsa herself sensed it, observing after Einstein had boasted to Watters that he wore the same clothes all the year round: "For his first wife he dressed up: for me, he will not." Beneath this she enjoyed his genius despite the hardships that went with it. "You cannot analyze him, otherwise you will misjudge him," she wrote in one percipient letter to a friend. "Such a genius should be irreproachable in every respect. But no, nature doesn't behave like this. Where she gives extravagantly, she takes away extravagantly. You have to see him all of one piece. You cannot put him under one heading or another heading. Otherwise you have unpleasantness. God has given him so much nobility, and I find him wonderful, although life with him is exhausting and complicated, and not only in one way but in others."*

At the start of their twenty years together, they had achieved a working arrangement. While he devoted himself to discovering how God made the world, she reduced to an absolute minimum the mundane problems of life. To an extent which offended the matriarchal society of the United States, he thought while she toiled, a division illustrated by a homely incident when they dined outdoors with two friends one summer night. As the air freshened, the hostess asked her husband to fetch her coat. Elsa was horrified: "I would never ask the Professor to do that."

For his part, "the Professor" supported the family and irradiated genius from his own private world. "Your wife," Mrs. Eisenhart, wife of the dean of Princeton University Graduate School, said to him soon after his arrival, "seems to do absolutely everything for you. Just

*"Man darf ihn nicht zergliedern, sonst kommt man auf 'Ausfallserscheinungen.' Solch ein Genie hat solche, oder glaubt man, er sei untadelig nach jeder Hinsicht mit nichten, so verfährt die Natur nicht. Wo sie so uferlos verschwendet, da nimmt sie in anderer Beziehung auch fort, und das kommt dann zu Ausfallserscheinungen! Man muss ihn als 'Ganzes' betrachten, darf ihn nicht einreihen in diese oder jene Rubrik! Sonst erlebt man Unerquickliches. Aber der Herrgott hat schon viel Schönes in ihn hineingelegt, und ich find ihn wundervoll, trotzdem das Leben an seiner Seite aufreibend u. komplicirt ist, nicht nur in dieser, in jeder Hinsicht. . . ."

exactly what do *you* do for her?" Einstein replied: "I give her my understanding."

The understanding was tested in 1936. At first Elsa seemed to recover and when the summer came they both traveled to Saranac Lake, 300 miles north of New York and high in the Adirondacks. But here, as she wrote to Leon Watters, she passed a very sad summer. To Watters, Elsa confided a great deal. "Einstein," he later wrote, "absorbed in his intellectual pursuits, found little time to fulfill the duties expected of a husband." It was true, he went on, that Elsa "enjoyed the sharing of the many honors which were bestowed on him and the many travels with him, but she missed the sympathy and tenderness which she craved, and found herself much alone in these respects." This sounds harsh—particularly as Elsa's friend Antonina Vallentin quotes her as writing of her husband during the illness, "He had been so upset by my illness. He wanders about like a lost soul. I never thought he loved me so much." The impression given in her letters to Watters is rather different. And now, in September, writing to him from Saranac Lake after hearing that Watters is to remarry following the death of his first wife, she says how sure she is that Mrs. Watters will accustom herself to New York; and, in any case, Watters was a most considerate and loving husband. She would, she makes clear, have been happy to send Einstein to Watters for lessons; but, dear God, it was too late for that to be of use. The two versions of Einstein the loving husband and the Albert who had to be taught are not mutually exclusive. Elsa had to pay her price, although she paid it willingly.

Back in Princeton her condition continued to deteriorate. The ground floor of the Mercer Street home began to resemble a hospital ward. Einstein, forsaking the institute, worked on in his first-floor study. No more could be done and Elsa died on December 21, still grieving for the daughter she had lost in Paris two years previously, still proud of what Albert was accomplishing. "He is in very good form. He has accomplished a lot lately," she had said during her illness. "He himself believes his latest work to be the best he has ever done."

After her death he got down to it with even more self-centered concentration. "I have settled down splendidly here," he wrote to Born. "I hibernate like a bear in its cave, and really feel more at home than ever before in all my varied existence. This bearishness has been accentuated further by the death of my mate, who was more attached to human beings than I."* From the beginning of 1937 he once more, and without distraction, devoted himself to the institute. His absorption had been intense since his first days at Princeton. Asked by the Buckys to pass a long weekend with them, he had replied that he could not, for the time being, think of such an undertaking because he did not want to interrupt the work at the institute for so long a period of time. Offered a brief break by Leon Watters, he rejected it on the grounds that "in the near future my theoretical experiments will take up so much of my time that an interruption of such length would constitute a real damage. It is a sad fact that Man does not live for pleasure alone." And even in the summer of 1935 when he was working hard during the August holidays at Old Lyme, Connecticut, he refused a similar invitation, saying: "I cannot leave my work and my sailing boat so long. . . . When a man is as well off as I am he should be grateful and not ask for more."

He had plunged into pacifist waters and plunged out when he found they were taking him the wrong way. He was still a Zionist at heart and as far as the Hebrew University was concerned he was about to win a considerable victory at considerable cost. He still hoped to do good, although by slightly more judicious means. But now, thank God, he could for most practical purposes concentrate on his cobbler's last, a physicist devoting himself to physics in a new world which might in due course, with only passing help from him, help to redress the balance of the old. "One must be happy," he had written to his Uncle Cäsar in Belgium in 1935, "if one has one's peaceful little room in which one can forget the bustle of life."

Thus he was always anxious to get back—even from his beloved sailboat—to the intellectual workshop of Princeton. He could of course work anywhere—"as well on a Potsdam bridge as at my home." Nevertheless his room in

*After noting that "the incidental way in which Einstein announces his wife's death . . . seems rather strange," Born comments: "For all his kindness, sociability, and love of humanity, he was nevertheless totally detached from his environment and the human beings included in it."

the institute or his study in Mercer Street was his natural habitat. It was here that he could best carry on his main work and continue his stubborn rearguard battle against the new movements in physics which he had started nearly a third of a century before.

Einstein's attitude to quantum mechanics drew him further and further from the mainstream of theoretical physics. He himself was well aware of this. To Solovine, the member of the Olympia Academy with whom he kept up a sporadic correspondence, he wrote of being "highly appreciated as a genuine old museum piece and a curiosity." He told his old friend Infeld, who arrived in the United States in 1935, that "in Princeton they regard me as an old fool." Infeld, at first incredulous, later agreed. "Einstein, during my stay in Princeton, was regarded by most of the professors here more like a historic relic than as an active scientist," he wrote. The Princeton professors were not alone, and Max Born, noting that Einstein was unable to get him an invitation to the institute, saw one obvious explanation: "Probably I was regarded there as a fossil, as he was himself, and two such relics from times past were too much for the modern masters of Princeton."

This view was widespread throughout physics and was summed up after Einstein's death by Robert Oppenheimer, who became director of the institute in 1947. His judgment is that during that last twenty-five years of Einstein's life his tradition in a certain sense failed him. "They were the years he spent at Princeton and this, though a source of sorrow, should not be concealed," he said.

> He had a right to that failure. . . . He spent those years first in trying to prove that the quantum theory had inconsistencies in it. No one could have been more ingenious in thinking up unexpected and clever examples, but it turned out that the inconsistencies were not there: and often their resolution could be found in earlier work of Einstein himself. When that did not work, after repeated efforts, Einstein had simply to say that he did not like the theory. He did not like the elements of indeterminacy. He did not like the abandonment of continuity or of causality. These were things that he had grown up with, saved by him, and enormously enlarged;

> and to see them lost, even though he had put the dagger in the hand of their assassin by his own work, was very hard on him. He fought with Bohr in a noble and furious way, and he fought with the theory which he had fathered but which he hated. It was not the first time that this has happened in science.

Thus Einstein's scientific position in Princeton, the aura of greatness which he radiated, and the extraordinary influence of his personality on the minds of his assistants and collaborators continued in spite of his contemporary standing in theoretical physics rather than because of it. A decade and a half earlier, when he was at the height of his powers in Berlin, his idea of how scientific problems should be tackled, his facility for "making physics melt in his mouth," had created an overwhelming impression on his listeners. Now, even though many of his firmly held beliefs were fighting for their lives, the magic still remained.

"As I look back to our work," says Professor Nathan Rosen, who succeeded Mayer as Einstein's assistant,

> I think that the things which impressed me most were the simplicity of his thinking and his faith in the ability of the human mind to understand the workings of nature. Throughout his life, Einstein believed that human reason was capable of leading to theories that would provide correct descriptions of physical phenomena. In building a theory, his approach had something in common with that of an artist; he would aim for simplicity and beauty (and beauty for him was, after all, essentially simplicity). The crucial question that he would ask, when weighing an element of a theory, was: "Is it reasonable?" No matter how successful a theory appeared to be, if it seemed to him not to be reasonable (the German word that he used was *"vernunftig"*), he was convinced that the theory could not provide a really fundamental understanding of nature.

A strikingly similar picture of Einstein during the later 1930s, as one part of him remained above the contemporary scientific battle, is given by another assistant, Banesh Hoffmann, who stressed that Einstein's method, though based on a profound knowledge of physics, "was essentially aesthetic and intuitive. Watching him, and talking with him," he says, "I came to understand the nature of science in a way that I could not possibly have understood it merely from reading his writings or the writings of other great physicists or of philosophers and historians of science. Except for the fact that he was the greatest physicist since Newton, one might almost say that he was not so much a scientist as an artist of science."

When Elsa died, Einstein was only a few months from his fifty-eighth birthday. By all the rules of the game his creative life was finished. He had what lesser men could have regarded as a well-paid sinecure, beyond students, beyond competition, beyond the need to struggle upward. Yet the extraordinary thing was that now, at a time when most scientists were ready to drop into administration, and those with a dislike for it were happy enough to potter on, Einstein stuck to his last with the fierce determination of a master craftsman determined not to waste a minute of the waking day.

At the institute until his retirement in 1945 and at Mercer Street until his death a decade later, he worked with a succession of colleagues and assistants on three different but closely interlocked areas of research. First, and certainly the most important in his own view, was his persistent search for a unified field theory. He never found it. He worked on a variety of solutions; each seemed to offer hope; each had eventually to be discarded. As he himself has said, only a man with his name already made could afford to do the job. Only a man with Einstein's deep vision would have found satisfaction in it.

His attitude to what even the comprehending scientist tended to see as a thankless task is highlighted by two stories. One day his accountant and friend, Leo Mattersdorf, asked whether he felt he was nearing his goal. "He replied 'No,'" says Mattersdorf, "and he added: 'God never tells us in advance whether the course we are to follow is the correct one.' He had tried at least 99 solutions and none worked but he had learned a lot. 'At least,' he said, 'I know 99 ways that won't work.'"

There was also his statement to David Mitrany, one of the few people in Princeton who became a genuine confidant. The friendship had started after Mitrany, walking to the institute one morning, gave a friendly wave to Einstein on the other side of the street. The same thing happened the following morning, and the next. "After that," says Mitrany, "we decided to walk together." To this figure from the older happier Europe—who as a young journalist had in 1921 reported Einstein's first speech in England for the *Manchester Guardian*—Einstein confided a great deal. He even talked about his work, which he did not usually discuss with men outside the subject. One day he thought he was at last on the track of a satisfactory unified field theory. Six months later he mentioned, almost casually, that the path led into a dead end; but he would, he threw off, be publishing it soon. Mitrany asked why. "To save another fool from wasting six months on the same idea."

Second only to the problems of a unified field was development of the General Theory of Relativity, particularly so that it could accommodate the new discoveries and speculations of cosmology. Here Einstein was moving from the fringes of his own field into an area already being transformed by technological advance. Here, with his conception of the universe as he had first described it in 1917 and as he had later amended it, Einstein had much to offer. But he was now one man among many.

The third subject was the quantum theory as it had been developed a decade earlier, a theory which now seemed to satisfy the apparent duality of nature, but which in the process allowed indeterminacy to lord it over the universe. Here Einstein obstinately stuck. He refused to accept the possibility that the new order was satisfactory, and over the years made successive efforts to demolish it.

One of the most important of these efforts came when, together with two colleagues, B. Podolsky and Nathan Rosen, he at first appeared to have struck a mortal blow at Heisenberg's uncertainty principle, the idea that had become if not the backbone at least an important item in the body of quantum mechanics. The paper which Einstein produced with his two fellow workers asked: "Can Quantum-Mechanical Description of Physical Reality Be Considered Complete?" When the article is stripped of its essential mathematics, it is easy to see how its simple statements constituted a major attack on the new ideas which had almost displaced those of Einstein's youth.

Heisenberg had claimed that in the study of very small

objects, such as subatomic particles, their systems were inevitably disturbed in such a way that it was impossible to measure at the same time with equal accuracy two associated quantities. As measurement of position increased in accuracy, measurement of momentum became more uncertain; increasing certainty about the time of a subatomic event would inevitably be matched by increasing uncertainty about the energy involved.

Einstein and his colleagues began by pointing out that in judging the merits of any theory one had to consider both its agreement with human experience and the completeness which the description gave of the physical world. After this preliminary statement they went on to what was the nub of their ingenious exposition. They took a situation which could arise in quantum mechanics of two interacting systems, called for convenience system *A* and system *B*. After a while the interaction was allowed to stop. But by taking a measurement of one quantity in system *A*, it was still possible to get its value in system *B*; and by measuring an associated quantity in system *A* it was possible to get its value in system *B*. But according to Heisenberg's uncertainty principle this was not possible; therefore, it was concluded, the description provided by quantum mechanics was incomplete.

The new physics had an answer to this. "I have used this opportunity to take up my old discussions with Einstein in the hope that we once may reach to an understanding regarding the actual position in atomic theory, which to my mind he does not quite realize," Bohr wrote to Rutherford. This attempt appeared in the next issue of the *Physical Review*, Bohr asking the same question as Einstein and providing the answer "Yes." Einstein refused to be convinced, clinging to the attitude which he maintained to the end of his life: that the description of nature provided by quantum mechanics was not incorrect but incomplete, a temporary makeshift which would eventually be superseded.

The problems took up most of Einstein's working days at the institute. But he was as much on the lookout for fresh ideas and bright young people as he had been in Berlin. The institute was until 1940 virtually a part of the university, and Einstein would often sit in on student seminars. Sometimes he learned with surprise how his own theoretical work of the prewar years had been absorbed into common practice. This was the case even with his famous $E=mc^2$. In his original paper he had noted that it was "not impossible that with bodies whose energy content is variable to a high degree (e.g., with radium salts) the theory may be successfully put to the test." He had sown the seed and left it at that. And he was hardly aware that by the 1930s many physicists were making such tests. "One of my most vivid memories," writes Professor A. E. Condon,

> is of a seminar at Princeton (1934) when a graduate student was reporting on researches of this kind and Einstein was in the audience. Einstein had been so preoccupied with other studies that he had not realized that such confirmation of his early theories had become an everyday affair in the physical laboratory. He grinned like a small boy and kept saying over and over, "Ist das wirklich so?" (Is it really true) as more and more specific evidence of his $E = mc^2$ relation was being presented.

In addition to listening, he sometimes lectured, and he still displayed his mastery of the subject. One instance is recalled by Churchill Eisenhart. "When he had finished," he says,

> one of the other mathematicians present proceeded to deduce Professor Einstein's principal result in short order from certain results of other authors in the then available scientific literature. The audience waited breathlessly for Professor Einstein's response. He rose, thanked his colleague for this very concise and elegant derivation of his own principal result, reminded all present that the assumptions underlying the results upon which the discussant's short proof had been based were somewhat different from those which he himself had started, and concluded by thanking his colleague for thus revealing that his result had a somewhat broader base of validity than he himself had appreciated. The approving buzz of the audience testified to the fact that Albert Einstein had clearly not lost but gained from the intended criticism.

His ability as a lecturer, together with his reputation as the most famous scientist of the century, made him a natural choice as guest speaker when the American Association for the Advancement of Science held its annual meeting at Pittsburgh, even though he was still dubious about addressing large public audiences in English. Leon Watters stage-managed the occasion, organizing Einstein's stay with mutual friends in the city, taking him there by train and later recording how Einstein, sitting in one train and watching another on a neighboring track, said that he had never before had the chance of watching how connecting rods worked.

The meeting was remembered for Einstein's Willard Gibbs Lecture on "Elementary Derivation of the Equivalence of Mass and Energy," given in English after a great deal of persuasion had been brought to bear. Legend claims that on the morning of the great day a notice appeared in the personal columns of the local paper, inserted by a well-wisher and reading: "Don't be afraid, Albert, I am sure you can do it." Einstein did do it, speaking before two long blackboards which filled most of the stage. Watters and a colleague sat in the front row, ready to prompt if he stumbled over his English. It was not necessary. The only hitch came when he remarked that his line of reasoning was simple. He was greeted by shouts of "No."

Before the lecture there was the press conference. Between 30 and 40 correspondents were invited and it was agreed that none of them should try to get an exclusive statement. One girl reporter, ignoring this, succeeded in getting Einstein alone and asked whether he ever conversed about subjects other than physics. He gave her a quick comprehending look and replied: "Yes, but not with you."

The conference, with reporters providing the usual barrage of questions, was to produce one historic reply, repeated with various renderings over the years, and much quoted a decade later. "Do you think that it will be possible to release the enormous amount of energy shown by your equation, by bombardment of the atom?" he was asked. "I feel that it will not be possible for practical purposes," he replied. "Splitting the atom by bombardment is like shooting at birds in the dark in a region where there are few birds."

Most physicists agreed, although one of the few who did not was Leo Szilard, Einstein's former collaborator in

Berlin, who had already lodged his secret patent with the British Admiralty. But most still held the view of Lord Rutherford, given at the Leicester meeting of the British Association for the Advancement of Science in 1933, where he issued a word of warning ". . . to those who look for sources of power in atomic transmutations—such expectations are the merest moonshine."*

Einstein's ability to think simply about physics and describe its essentials in terms that ordinary men and women could understand was further deployed in *The Evolution of Physics*, which he wrote in 1937 with Leopold Infeld. During 1935, towards the end of the one-year appointment of his assistant Nathan Rosen, he received a letter from Infeld, by this time a lecturer in the Polish university of Lvov. Poland's recent nonaggression pact with Germany augured ill for men of left-wing opinions and Infeld feared that he might soon be forced to leave. On Einstein's instigation he was given a small grant which enabled him to work at Princeton, where he arrived early in 1936.

It was sixteen years since the two men had met. "Quietly he took a piece of chalk, went to the blackboard and started to deliver a perfect lecture," Infeld later wrote.

> The calmness with which Einstein spoke was striking. There was nothing of the restlessness of a scientist who, explaining the problems with which he has lived for years, assumed that they are equally familiar to the listener and proceeds quickly with his exposition. Before going into details Einstein sketched the philosophical background for the problems on which he was working. Walking slowly and with dignity round the room, going to the blackboard from time to time to write down mathematical equations, keeping a dead pipe in his mouth, he formed his sentences perfectly. Everything he said could have been printed as he said it and every sentence would make perfect sense. The exposition was simple, profound, and clear.

Infeld's grant at the institute was for one year: it was not renewed, even though Einstein intervened on his friend's behalf. Having burned his bridges in Europe, Infeld was thus in danger of being left financially high and

*But see page 662.

dry. He realized that there was one way out of his problem. He had been working for a year with Einstein. Why should they not collaborate in writing a popular book on science? There would obviously be no difficulty in finding a publisher, half of the advance might cover another year's stay in the United States, and who knew what might not turn up during that time? With a great deal of hesitation he put forward the idea, adding that it might possibly be a stupid proposition. Einstein knew that his colleague was desperate. "This is not at all a stupid idea. Not stupid at all," he replied. Then he got up, stretched out his hand to Infeld, and said: "We shall do it."

Between them, the two men produced what they modestly called "a simple chat between you and me." Yet the book, describing the rise and fall of the mechanical view of the natural world, the concept of field, the idea of relativity, and the development of the quantum theory, is far more than a survey of physics as the subject was understood in the 1930s. Just as Einstein discerned a link between the values of science and the values of art, just as he thought a simple theory was better than a complicated one, and just as he would have appreciated the later use of the word "elegant" to describe an experiment, so did he and Infeld describe the "connection between the world of ideas and the world of phenomena." They had, they wrote, "tried to show the active forces which compel science to invent ideas corresponding to the reality of our world . . . to give some idea of the eternal struggle of the inventive human mind for a fuller understanding of the laws governing physical phenomena."

The success of *The Evolution of Physics* in 1938 was a bright spot in a grim period. Einstein still had his science, and the consolation which it brought can be judged from a letter he wrote to the Belgian Queen-Mother early in 1939. "The work has proved fruitful this past year," he said.

> I have hit upon a hopeful trail, which I follow painfully but steadfastly in company with a few youthful fellow workers. Whether it will lead to truth or fallacy—this I may be unable to establish with any certainty in the brief time left to me. But I am grateful to destiny for having made my life into an exciting experience so that life has appeared meaningful . . .

But even Einstein could not isolate himself entirely from the march of events in the outside world. In March, 1938, Austria found herself nipped between Nazi Germany on the north and Fascist Italy on the south, and the German army was ordered in—to the cheers of what was probably a majority of the population, ignorant of what was being prepared for them. In October, Czechoslovakia was offered up to the same occupiers, a democratic passenger thrown to the pursuing wolves in an effort to gain time for the building of fighter forces and the erection of the vital radar chain.

For Einstein, ignorant of the arguments which might justify appeasement—but, arguably, did not—this mounting record of capitulation, followed in March, 1939, by the abandonment of Prague itself, was particularly painful. He, after all, had learned his lesson even if he had learned it late. "A strange breed of pacifist, you will probably say to me!" he had written when asked to address a world peace congress. "But I cannot shut my eyes to realities. It is no exaggeration to say that the British and, to some extent, French pacifists are largely responsible for the desperate situation today because they prevented energetic measures from being taken at a time when it would have been relatively easy to adopt them." But while he had learned that pacifism was no answer to the dictators, Britain and France still appeared to be beating the retreat as unashamedly as ever.

In April, 1938, unsuccessfully trying to launch a new scheme to save the Jews after the German invasion of Austria, he regretted the breakdown of the system of collective security and "that this deplorable retrogression in the life of nations can be reversed only by paying a heavy price in human life." Less than a year later, writing to the Queen-Mother in the letter already quoted, he noted that he had been too troubled to write in good cheer. "The moral decline we are compelled to witness, and the suffering it engenders, are so oppressive that one cannot ignore them even for a moment. No matter how deeply one immerses oneself in work, a haunting feeling of inescapable tragedy persists."

To the sense of coming doom there was added, as his sixtieth birthday came and went, a feeling of personal limitation. This he confided to Watters, as he confided much else. After an introspective evening, his host jotted down what he remembered of their conversation. "I find my physical powers decreasing as I grow older," he remembers Einstein saying.

> I find that I require more sleep now. I doubt if my mental capacity has diminished. I grasp things as quickly as I did when I was younger. My power, my particular ability, lies in visualizing the effects, consequences, and possibilities, and the bearings on present thought of the discoveries of others. I gasp things in a broad way easily. I cannot do mathematical calculations easily. I do them not willingly and not readily. Others perform these details better. . . .

He would go on with his work, of course. He would continue to help all and sundry: unknown Jewish refugees, disestablished professors whom he could guide into temporary positions, relatives such as his sister Maja who arrived in the United States from Florence, fearing the future too much to continue living under Mussolini. There seemed to be prospects of little else as the summer of 1939 approached.

CHAPTER 20

EINSTEIN, THE BOMB, AND THE BOARD OF ORDNANCE

By the start of 1939 Einstein had spent more than five years in the United States. He had settled in satisfactorily, a self-styled bird of passage which had at last come to rest. He was a part of the Princeton scene, a landmark figure whose worldwide fame was ignored by the local inhabitants partly for decency's sake, partly because of the genuine affection in which many of them had come to hold him. At times the man who was essentially European missed the familiar sights and sounds of Leiden, the Kaiser Wilhelm Institute, and the gray buildings of the ETH in Zurich where so many corners reminded him of his earlier days. Nevertheless, Einstein liked America. He liked the openness and the natural generosity of the people. He liked their willingness to be lavish about research. At times he almost felt comfortable, less a refugee from Europe.

His work still concentrated on the search for a unified field theory, a point which he drove home on his sixtieth birthday in March, 1939. Answering a questionnaire from the National Association of Science Writers, he said he had been engaged on the work for more than twenty years but that the mathematical constructions so far devised had not stood the test of experiment. "A year ago I discovered a new solution and I am now engaged with two collaborators in developing the results to a point where they could be checked with experimental facts," he went on. "From this statement the layman can at least recognize one thing; namely, that the pursuit of such a goal requires almost unlimited patience, particularly in view of the fact that there is nothing to give assurance of the attainment of this goal." The lack of assurance did not worry him. He was content enough and he frequently noted that "every man may draw comfort from Lessing's fine saying that the search for truth is more precious than its possession."

But as the Germans prepared to follow up the Munich victory, things went from worse to worst. One consequence was that Einstein now found himself permanently joined in America by his old friend and colleague from Prague, Philipp Frank. Late in 1938 Frank had been invited to Harvard as visiting professor, and had begun a series of lectures on the quantum theory and the philosophical foundations of modern physics when the Germans marched into what was left of Czechoslovakia. He was to remain in the United States for the rest of his life.

Meanwhile, the Wehrmacht prepared for the late summer's campaign across the plains of Poland. And meanwhile scientists throughout the world debated the implications of an event which had taken place in the Kaiser Wilhelm during the last weeks of 1938. For here Einstein's old friend Otto Hahn had split in two the nucleus of the uranium atom. The event not only ushered in the nuclear age and ended the age of innocence in physics; it also drew Einstein into the mainstream of world events—and in circumstances still shrouded by a good deal of mythology, ignorance, and special pleading.

The importance of Hahn's discovery of nuclear fission in the long trail of events which led to atomic weapons is well known. So is Einstein's later involvement in that trail, even though its significance is often misunderstood. Less appreciated is the ironic way in which theoretical research produced the prospect of an ultimate weapon just as the world was preparing for war. No dramatist would have dared to arrange such fortuitous events in such apparently contrived order.

If one is to appreciate where Einstein stands, and to assess what he did during the crucial periods of 1939–41 and 1944–45 as well as what he did not do, it is necessary to recapitulate these events and to explain their significance. The interpretation of Hahn's experiments early in 1939 by Lise Meitner and her nephew Otto Frisch led on to applications far more important than any others which sprang from that generation of investigators that included the Curies and J. J. Thomson, Planck, Rutherford, Bohr, and Einstein. It is true that their work had already changed the world in many ways which it would have been difficult to forecast at the start of the century. The electron of Lorentz and Thomson was already becoming the basis of great industries. The electromagnetic waves forecast by Maxwell and discovered by Hertz had already made near instantaneous communication practicable across the globe. The X rays discovered by Röntgen were giving advance warning of disease where none would have before been possible. The effect of the radium so laboriously purified and investigated by the Curies was giving the hope of life to patients who before had no hope. Einstein's explanation of the photoelectric effect had already helped to prod forward television from experiment to reality. The revolutionaries who had gathered in Brussels for the First Solvay Congress less than three decades earlier already had ample practical results to show for what had seemed, so recently, to be largely theoretical discussions.

Yet it was only now that physics began to touch with the tips of its fingers that most stupendous of possibilities: the use of the energy locked within the nucleus of the atom. It was not that this awesome prospect had lain beyond the imagination. As early as 1903 Rutherford had made what a correspondent, Sir William Dampier-Whetham, called his "playful suggestion that, could a proper detonator be found, it was just conceivable that a wave of atomic disintegration might be started through matter, which would indeed make this old world vanish in smoke." Planck, mulling over Einstein's $E = mc^2$, declared in 1908 of the atom's "latent energy" that "though the actual production of such a 'radical' process might have appeared extremely small only a decade ago, it is now in the range of the possible. . . ." They thought about the possibility often enough. Yet throughout the first part of the century, ignorance of the subnuclear world was a barrier stout enough to keep such projects within the realm of science fiction, or of those apparently impractical optimists who declared that a lump of fuel no bigger than a man's hand might one day drive a liner across the Atlantic.

The problem was transformed as knowledge increased. From being a theoretical conundrum it became a problem of practical technology. How would it be possible to penetrate the heart of the atomic nucleus with a bullet which would split the nucleus apart and release the energy which bound it together as one piece? How, moreover, could this be done not once or twice but on a vast multiplicity of occasions so that the immense number of atoms comprising the material under attack would release their energy in the minimum of time? The great steps forward in experimental physics made by Rutherford at Manchester in 1919 and by Cockcroft and Walton in 1932 had little direct effect on this central and tantalizing problem. Rutherford bombarded nitrogen with the particles which were constantly being naturally ejected by radium. About one in every million of the ejected particles penetrated a nitrogen nucleus and transmuted it into the nucleus of an oxygen atom. But although the energy released by this transformation was greater than that of the bullet particle, most particles missed the target and passed between the clouds of electrons encircling the nucleus. Much the same happened in Cambridge when Cockcroft and Walton used streams of hydrogen protons, artificially speeded up by the use of high voltages, to bombard targets of lithium. The "bullets" were not natural but artificially produced, and the "hits" were far more numerous than those which Rutherford had obtained; but the result still remained a net loss of energy. It was still true that more had to be put into the nuclear stockpot than could be obtained from it. Einstein's comment on the problem still held—"like shooting at birds in the dark in a region where there are few birds."

In public, Rutherford held much the same view, dismissing the use of nuclear energy as "moonshine" almost until his death in 1937. In private, he had doubts, warning Lord Hankey, then secretary of Britain's Committee of Imperial Defence, that the work of the Cavendish on nuclear transformations might one day have an important impact on defense and that someone should "keep an eye on the matter."* Rutherford's scepticism had something in

*It is generally believed that Rutherford publicly maintained his "moonshine" attitude to the use of atomic energy to the end of his life. This is not entirely true. Giving the Watt Anniversary Lecture in Greenock in January, 1936, he noted that "the recent discovery of the neutron, the proof of its extraordinary effectiveness in producing transformations at very low velocities, opens up new possibilities if only a method could be found of producing slow

common with Einstein's views on indeterminacy, and his reluctance to admit that God might "play dice with the world." Both men, investigating nature as they found it, had pushed science along particular paths; with the years, both became increasingly reluctant to follow that path to the end.

Yet by the later 1930s, events were slowly moving towards the situation in which men like Einstein were to be faced with an agonizing choice. Only a few days before Cockcroft and Walton's experiments in Cambridge, the first performances of *Wings Over Europe* had taken place in London. Writing of the play—which asks but does not answer the questions posed by nuclear weapons—Desmond McCarthy set the scene for the main involvement of Einstein's later years. "The destiny of man," he said, "has slipped (we are all aware of it) from the hands of politicians into the hands of scientists, who know not what they do, but pass responsibility for results on to those whose sense of proportion and knowledge are inadequate to the situations created by science."

Not yet, maybe. But the following year of 1933, which was to mark a crisis in human affairs with the coming of Hitler, and in Einstein's with his final departure from Europe, was also to see a new turn given to physics by Leo Szilard. In England he noted a newspaper account of Rutherford's "moonshine" description of the prospects of liberating atomic energy. A few days later, he says, "It suddenly occurred to me that if we could find an element which is split by neutrons and which would emit *two* neutrons when it absorbed *one* neutron, such an element, if assembled in sufficiently large mass, could sustain a nuclear chain reaction."

Szilard's flash of inspiration was to have its consequences. One was the filing in the spring of 1934 of a patent which described the laws governing such a chain reaction. "I assigned this patent to the British Admiralty because in England a patent could at that time be kept secret only if it was assigned to the government," he has said. "The reason for secrecy was my conviction that if a

---

neutrons in quantity with little expenditure of energy." He went on to point out that "at the moment" natural radioactive bodies were the only known sources of getting useful energy from atoms and that this was too small a scale to be of more than scientific interest. But he was obviously already thinking about the "new possibilities."

nuclear reaction can be made to work it can be used to set up violent explosions." With this in mind he had previously approached the British War Office. But the War Office was not interested. Neither, for that matter, was the Admiralty. More important than the patent itself was the conviction behind it, a conviction which was to produce its own chain reaction six years later.

As important as Szilard among the figures now gathering in the wings was Enrico Fermi, a refugee from Fascist Italy. While Szilard had postulated the splitting of the nucleus but had failed to find experimental facilities in Britain for seeing if this could be done, Fermi had gone through a similar experience. In Italy he had used the chargeless neutrons discovered by Chadwick to bombard the heaviest known element, the metal uranium. The result had been a transformation of the uranium; but it was a transformation which took place in only a minute percentage of the atoms involved, and its true nature was missed by Fermi. What had happened, he believed, was the creation of a few atoms not found naturally on earth, the first of what came to be known as the transuranic elements.

Among those physicists not so sure about this was Lise Meitner, the young Austrian who had listened in rapt attention to Einstein in Salzburg almost three decades earlier, and Otto Hahn and Fritz Strassman, the two German chemists with whom she worked in the Kaiser Wilhelm Institute. All three began to repeat the Fermi experiments, which had also been carried out by Irene and Frédéric Joliot-Curie in Paris with what appeared to be comparable results. Grotesquely, the operation was disturbed by the German invasion of Austria; for the Anschluss automatically brought Fräulein Meitner German citizenship. Since she was a Jewess it also brought the threat of the concentration camp. She moved on, first to Holland and then to Sweden.

Meanwhile the work continued in Berlin under Hahn and Strassman. It finished a few days before Christmas, 1938, and Hahn immediately sent to Lise Meitner a copy of his paper describing the findings. By the first of a long series of coincidences which mark the release of nuclear energy, Lise Meitner's nephew, Otto Frisch, a worker in

Niels Bohr's Copenhagen Institute, was spending the Christmas with her in Sweden.

Aunt and nephew discussed Hahn's paper during a long walk in the snow-covered woods outside Stockholm, a walk that was to help shape the future of the human race. For Lise Meitner and her nephew discerned what Hahn had done: split the nucleus of the uranium atom into two roughly equal parts, and released a staggering amount of energy. "The picture," Frisch says, "was that of two fairly large nuclei flying apart with an energy of nearly two hundred million electron volts, more than ten times the energy involved in any other nuclear reaction." Bohr, about to leave Europe for the Fifth Washington Conference on Theoretical Physics, was immediately telephoned the news, which he took across the Atlantic. Within a few hours of his statement at the Conference, the Berlin experiments were being repeated, notably by Szilard and by Fermi who had both arrived in the United States by this time.

But an important uncertainty remained. The fission of a uranium nucleus in a microscopic specimen certainly released an immense amount of energy. But for the process to be developed into a weapon such fissions would have to be repeated through a block of the metal. Fissions had been produced at the Kaiser Wilhelm Institute by neutrons, and the crucial question was whether the process released other neutrons which would, in their turn, produce further fissions. Would the flicker of nuclear fire act as a detonator or would it merely peter harmlessly out?

Only a few weeks after Bohr had spoken to the packed and excited meeting in Washington this question was answered in Paris by a Collège de France team led by Joliot-Curie. For in Paris it was confirmed that the fission of the uranium nucleus with the resulting immense release of energy did unloose neutrons hitherto locked inside the nucleus. The number was not yet certain; but it appeared obvious that in the right conditions it would be sufficient to cause yet further fissions. These, in turn, would create still more, feeding the nuclear fire until in a minute fraction of a second the release of energy would be indescribably more damaging than that of a chemical explosion.

Thus it seemed, in the early spring of 1939, as though the world might at last be at the start of a nuclear arms race. In the United States George B. Pegram, dean of graduate faculties at Columbia University, urged on by Szilard and Fermi, wrote to Admiral Hooper of the U. S. Navy, warning him of "the possibility that uranium might be used as an explosive that would liberate a million times as much energy per pound as any known explosive." In France, the members of the Collège de France team filed five patents covering the use of nuclear energy, number three being for the construction of a uranium bomb. In Holland, the physicist Uhlenbeck informed his government of the situation and the Minister of Finance ordered 50 tons of uranium ore from Belgium's Union Minière, remarking: "Clever, these physicists." And in Britain, where in April research into the possibility of a nuclear weapon was officially brought under the charge of Sir Henry Tizard, both the Treasury and the Foreign Office were approached by the Committee of Imperial Defence with one object in mind: to secure the necessary uranium for research and to ensure that, as far as was possible, stocks were kept from the Germans. In 1939 the greatest known supply lay in the Belgian Congo, where it was mined as ore by the Union Minière, and on May 10, 1939, Tizard met the company's president, M. Edgar Sengier, from whom he obtained certain assurances.

In Germany Dr. Siegfried Flugge, one of Hahn's colleagues, produced a paper for *Naturwissenschaften* in which the building of a "uranium device" was considered. "Available quantitative calculations have too great a margin of error to allow us to raise this possibility into a certainty," he concluded. "Be this as it may, it is nevertheless a remarkable advance that such possibilities can be considered at all, an advance sufficient to justify thorough discussion in this paper, even if our hopes should not be fulfilled." And on April 24 Paul Harteck in Hamburg wrote with his colleague W. Groth to the German War Office, proposing that nuclear explosives should be investigated. Shortly afterwards, two separate groups, neither of whom acknowledged the existence of the other, began work in Germany on "the uranium problem." One was headed by Professor Erich Schumann, director of the research section of the German army's ordnance department, the other by Professor Abraham Esau, the official in charge of physics in the German Ministry of Education.

All this—the French patents, British earmarking of uranium stocks, and German preparations—took place months before Einstein signed the famous letter to Roosevelt. Vannevar Bush, director of the U. S. Office of Scientific Research and Development, and later the key man in America's wartime defense science, has summed up the situation neatly: "The show was going before that letter was even written." Nevertheless, Einstein's intervention was to be significant for reasons that have nothing to do with the chauvinism of national priorities.

The role which Einstein was to play was singularly dramatic. For fate now compounded the joke it had perpetrated in 1919. Then the introverted scientist, only too anxious to keep to his study, had been propelled into the center of public affairs. Now Einstein, until recently the dedicated pacifist and still a man who detested the use of force, was to help launch the weapons which killed more than 130,000 men, women, and children in a few seconds. However, this is only part of the story. The truth, more complicated and more ironic, has been obscured for a quarter of a century by romantic misconceptions, failure to examine the documents, and a good deal of special pleading and dodgery.

New material, including the extensive Szilard Archives in San Diego, and fresh papers unearthed in Washington and elsewhere, shows that Einstein's initial letter to Roosevelt was written when he believed the prospect of nuclear weapons to be slight—but when the first moves towards them had already been taken elsewhere. It shows that Charles Lindbergh was the first choice of intermediary with the President. It shows that Einstein signed not one letter but three, of which the third, which helped to spark off the creation of the Manhattan Project, was arguably the most important. It shows that he produced a theoretical study for gaseous diffusion, later an important process in the Manhattan Project—although it is not certain that he fully realized what the study was for—and that he would have been more deeply involved had Washington suspicions of his history not made this "utterly impossible." Moreover, it shows that by December, 1944, he was almost certainly aware in general terms of the progress that had been made in the Manhattan Project and that he was stopped only by Niels Bohr from what might have been a disastrous political step. As final irony, a second memorandum which he tried to bring to Roosevelt's notice in March, 1945, included not only the suggestion that a bomb should not be dropped on Japan, but also the idea that the United States might build up an "overwhelming superiority" vis-à-vis the Russians. All these were milestones on a road opened in July, 1939, by Leo Szilard, who comprehensively stage-managed Einstein not only in 1939 but in 1945.

Following Bohr's initial description of fission in January, Szilard had been almost continuously at work in Columbia and had become even more convinced that a nuclear chain reaction was possible. Like Tizard in Britain, he appreciated the danger of Germany's acquiring stocks of uranium, and like Tizard he knew that the Union Minière controlled virtually the world stocks of uranium ore. At this point he discussed the situation with Eugene Wigner of Princeton University, also a physicist of note, also a refugee from Hungary. "Both Wigner and I began to worry about what would happen if the Germans got hold of some of the vast quantities of the uranium which the Belgians had in the Congo," Szilard has written.

> So we began to think, through what channels we could approach the Belgian government and warn them against selling any uranium to Germany.
>
> It occurred to me that Einstein knew the Queen of the Belgians [by now the Queen-Mother], and I suggested to Wigner that we visit Einstein, tell him about the situation, and ask him whether he might not write to the Queen. We knew that Einstein was somewhere on Long Island but we didn't know precisely where, so I phoned his Princeton office and I was told he was staying at Dr. Moore's cabin at Peconic, Long Island. Wigner had a car and we drove out of Peconic and tried to find Dr. Moore's cabin. We drove around for about half an hour. We asked a number of people, but no one knew where Dr. Moore's cabin was. We were on the point of giving up and about to return to New York when I saw a boy of about seven or eight years of age standing at the curb. I leaned out of the window and I asked, "Say, do you by any chance know where Professor Einstein lives?" The boy knew and he offered to take us there, though he had never heard of Dr. Moore's cabin.

It is typical that Szilard, the skilled operator-by-unconventional-means, should feel that a quiet private note from Einstein to Queen Elizabeth might help prevent Germany from acquiring raw materials for the most violent explosive in the world.

Once in Dr. Moore's house, the two visitors explained their fears and their hopes, and Szilard described what Einstein later called "a specific system he [had] devised and which he thought would make it possible to set up a chain reaction." According to a letter written by Szilard to Carl Seelig in 1952, Einstein said that he "had not been aware of the possibility of a chain reaction in uranium." A few years later Einstein's statement was given by Szilard as, "that never occurred to me (Daran habe ich gar nicht gedacht)."

Eugene Wigner, the only member of the trio still alive, does not in fact recollect Einstein's remark, although he does have a feeling that he had discussed chain reactions with Einstein some weeks earlier. These had been a major subject of debate among physicists since Bohr's dramatic announcement at the end of January. Bohr himself had spoken with Einstein in Princeton and it might seem unlikely that chain reactions were not talked about. In addition, many articles, comments, and papers on the subject had by July, 1939, appeared in scientific journals, more than twenty in *Nature* alone. Furthermore, Einstein's old friend Rudolf Ladenburg, who had invited him to the Salzburg meeting just thirty years previously, was himself carrying out work on fission problems in Princeton University's Palmer Laboratory only a few hundred yards from Einstein's home.

Bearing all this in mind, Einstein's remark seems at first glance to have been an extraordinary one. Is it really possible that in the summer of 1939 he should never have considered the possibility of a chain reaction, even though the subject had been the nub of controversy in the physicists' world? The answer is that it is not only possible but likely. To think otherwise is to misjudge the extent to which Einstein had by this time isolated himself from the mainstream of physics. The weekly copies of *Nature* and of *Science* arrived regularly at 112 Mercer Street but they were usually filed away without being looked at unless they contained some paper Einstein had been specially recommended to read. He no longer joined in the seminars and discussions that his colleagues held. In some ways he was comparable to the Berne Patent Office clerk of 1905 whose strength lay partly in his isolation from the detail of current developments. His continuing preoccupation with the unified field theory made him once again the man whose life demanded, above all, "time for quiet thought and reflection." Professor Aage Bohr, Niels Bohr's son and today head of his father's institute in Copenhagen, says that Einstein "was deeply involved in his own work and I hardly think that he was following the current developments in nuclear physics." Furthermore, Professor Rosenfeld, working with Bohr in Princeton in the Spring of 1939, believes that "during that visit Bohr and Einstein hardly discussed the matter of possible military implications of the nuclear developments."

Even had they done so, Einstein might still have been extremely sceptical about the practicability of nuclear weapons. For as early as February 15, Bohr had put forward in the *Physical Review* the sobering proposal that only the U-235 nuclei could easily be split; and that the nuclei of the U-238—which comprised the overwhelming bulk of the element—would usually absorb any of the neutrons which hit them. Experimental proof of this theory was not to be given for another year. It was, Frisch has said, "a surprising conclusion based on rather subtle arguments." Not all scientists agreed with it, and even those who did so included many who still believed that it would be possible to make a nuclear explosion by using a block of the element which contained the different isotopes in their naturally occurring proportions. But if Bohr were right it would be necessary to separate a substantial quantity of U-235 before a "nuclear fire" could be produced. This problem of isotope separation—comparable to sorting a vast number of particular sand grains from their chemically identical companions on the seashore—looked totally insoluble in 1939. Indeed, it looked totally insoluble four years later, even to Bohr. When, in spring, 1943, he was invited to England from German-occupied Denmark by James Chadwick, Bohr sent back a secret message through intelligence channels: "I have, to the best of my judgment, convinced myself that in spite of all future prospects any immediate use of the latest marvelous discoveries of atomic physics is impracticable." He thought at the time, says his son, "that isotope separation on the needed scale was beyond industrial potentialities and it was a surprise for him on his arrival in England in October, 1943, to learn how far the project had advanced."

The exact depth of Einstein's scepticism as he sat in the Long Island cottage with Szilard and Wigner on that summer afternoon is unknown. Yet he himself has gone on the record with one revealing statement about nuclear energy: "I did not, in fact, foresee that it would be released in my time. I only believed that it was theoretically possible." Scientific scepticism, however great or little it was, may well have been increased by wishful thinking. Einstein's old friend Lindemann was so repelled by the idea of such destructive power being available to human hands that "he could scarcely believe that the universe was constructed in this way." Sir Henry Tizard, who had launched precautionary measures in England, had raised the question to a colleague in surprisingly similar terms: "Do you really think that the universe was made in this way?"

There is no evidence to suggest that Einstein was any less sceptical about the chance of nuclear weapons in the summer of 1939 than Bohr was to be four years later; but if he could not genuinely share his visitors' scientific views, he could share their fears. There was always the one-in-a-million chance that a bomb would prove feasible. Since nuclear fission had been discovered in the Kaiser Wilhelm Institute, it was wise to take precautions. If there were even a bare chance that nuclear weapons could be made, then the Americans should not lag behind the Germans.

Here Einstein parted company with his old friend Max Born, who worked in Edinburgh throughout the war and took no part in the Allied nuclear effort since, as he has said, "my colleagues knew that I was opposed to taking part in war work of this character which seemed so horrible." Had his attitude convinced his colleagues, post-war history might have been different. For one day a young German working in his laboratory was asked to join the British nuclear team. "He was inclined to accept," Born has said. "I told him of my attitude to such kind of work, and tried to warn him not to involve himself in these things. But he was filled with tremendous hatred of the Nazis, and accepted." Thus Klaus Fuchs, who was to provide Russia—and possibly Britain—with vital details of the H-bomb, left Edinburgh for Birmingham and Los Alamos.

In retrospect, too late, Einstein agreed with Born. "I made one great mistake in my life—when I signed the letter to President Roosevelt recommending that atom bombs be made," he said in old age to Linus Pauling, "but there was some justification—the danger that the Germans would make them." The mistake was in fact a double one. The danger from the Germans never materialized; but in America an almost superhuman technological effort gave the lie to Bohr's "impracticable."

At this first meeting with Szilard and Wigner in July, 1939, Einstein agreed that Belgian stocks of uranium should not be allowed to fall into German hands. But the situation was delicate, even for native-born Americans, let alone for two Hungarians and a German-born Swiss who had relinquished his first nationality but had not yet become American. Szilard therefore proposed a transitional step. "Before contacting the Belgian government," he says, "it seemed desirable to advise the State Department of the step we proposed to take. Wigner suggested that we draft a letter to the Belgian government, send a copy to the State Department, and give the State Department two weeks in which to object if they are opposed to Professor Einstein's sending such a letter." Thus, as a first step, the Queen-Mother was bypassed. Instead, Einstein dictated a letter to a Belgian cabinet minister, mentioning "the danger to the Belgian state" that seemed to be apparent, and it was agreed that a copy should be sent to the Belgian ambassador in Washington.

On his return to Columbia University, Szilard typed out a draft and put it in the post to Einstein, together with the letter which he felt should be sent to the State Department.

Here the process might have stuck. But now history nudged the project back on course; ironically using for its *deus ex machina* Dr. Gustav Stolper, not only a German refugee but a former member of the Reichstag.

"Somehow," says Szilard, referring to what had been arranged before he left Einstein's house,

> this procedure seemed to be an awkward one and so I decided to consult friends with more experience in things practical than we were. I went to see in New York Dr. Gustav Stolper and told him of our need to establish contact in this manner with the U. S. government. He recommended that I talk with Dr. Alexander Sachs. Dr. Sachs seemed very much interested and said that he would be willing to take a letter in person to President Roosevelt if Professor Einstein were willing to write such a letter.

It is probable that Alexander Sachs, a well-known economist and an intimate of the President, did not at the time know much of Einstein's earlier history, since he has gone on record as saying that he has "always been of the view that the real warmongering, combined with defeatism, is done by the pacifists." However, Sachs was helpful. Szilard recognized a useful contact and on July 19 wrote again to Einstein, saying that Sachs had recommended a direct approach to Roosevelt and that he himself would be willing to help. Enclosed, Szilard added, was a draft of the letter he felt should be sent to the White House. Would Einstein make any proposed corrections over the telephone or did he think that a second meeting was necessary?

Einstein favored a meeting, and a few days later Szilard was at Peconic once again. This time, Wigner having left for the West Coast, his companion was Edward Teller of George Washington University, another of the brilliant Hungarians who had found refuge in the United States, and one later to become famous, or notorious, as "the father of the H-bomb."

There is, understandably enough, some difference in recollection about the details of this second meeting. According to Teller, "at the time [of the visit] Szilard had a final formulation of the letter with him. We had tea with Einstein. Einstein read the letter, made very little comment, and signed it." Later Szilard wrote: "As I remember, Einstein dictated a letter in German which Teller took down and I used this German text as a guide in preparing two drafts of a letter to the President, a shorter one and a longer one, and left it up to Einstein to choose which he liked best. I wondered how many words we could expect the President to read. How many words does the fission of uranium rate?"

As far as they go, Szilard's recollections appear accurate on this point. But his papers reveal more. For when he sent the short and the long versions to Einstein on August 2—the date he put on both—he accompanied them with a note saying that Sachs now thought Bernard Baruch or Karl Compton might be the best man to get the letter to Roosevelt, but that he personally favored Colonel Lindbergh.

The last suggestion was unexpected, since it was felt in some quarters that Lindbergh was not particularly allergic to the Nazis. However, Einstein dutifully complied. He returned to Szilard not his own choice of letters, but both of them, both signed. Szilard could make up his own mind which one to send, but Einstein's accompanying note urged him to curb his inner resistance and not to "be too clever"—another inclination that Einstein's views about the practicability of a bomb were different from Szilard's. At the same time he wrote, as requested, a note to Lindbergh, whom he had last met at the Rockefeller Center.

"Dear Herr Lindbergh," says the copy which Szilard made of this letter before sending it on.

> I would like to ask you to do me the favor of receiving my friend Dr. Szilard and think very carefully about what he will tell you. To one who is outside of science, the matter he will bring up may seem fantastic. However, you will certainly become convinced that a possibility is presented here which has to be very carefully watched in the public interest, even though the results so far are not immediately impressive. With all respects and friendly wishes, A. E.

Szilard acknowledged Einstein's letters on August 9 and said he would note the "admonition" about being too clever. Five days later he wrote to Lindbergh, enclosing Einstein's letter of introduction and suggesting that Lindbergh might approach Roosevelt. At the same time he sent to Sachs the longer of the two letters which Einstein had signed.

This letter, by now famous, ran as follows:

Sir: Some recent work by E. Fermi and L. Szilard, which has been communicated to me in manuscript, leads me to expect that the element uranium may be turned into a new and important source of energy in the immediate future. Certain aspects of the situation seem to call for watchfulness and, if necessary, quick action on the part of the administration. I believe, therefore, that it is my duty to bring to your attention the following facts and recommendations.

In the course of the last four months it has been made probable—through the work of Joliot in France as well as Fermi and Szilard in America—that it may become possible to set up nuclear chain reactions in a large mass of uranium, by which vast amounts of power and large quantities of new radium-like elements would be generated. Now it appears almost certain that this could be achieved in the immediate future.

This new phenomenon would also lead to the construction of bombs, and it is conceivable—though much less certain—that extremely powerful bombs of a new type may thus be constructed. A single bomb of this type, carried by boat or exploded in a port, might very well destroy the whole port together with some of the surrounding territory. However, such bombs might very well prove to be too heavy for transportation by air.

The United States has only very poor ores of uranium in moderate quantities. There is some good ore in Canada and the former Czechoslovakia, while the most important source of uranium is the Belgian Congo.

In view of this situation you may think it desirable to have some permanent contact maintained between the administration and the group of physicists working on chain reaction in America. One possible way of achieving this might be for you to entrust with this task a person who has your confidence and who could perhaps serve in an unofficial capacity. His task might comprise the following:

(a) To approach government departments, keep them informed of further developments, and put forward recommendations for government action, giving particular attention to the problem of securing a supply of uranium ore for the United States.

(b) To speed up the experimental work which is at present being carried on within the limits of the budgets of the university laboratories, by providing funds, if such funds be required, through his contacts with private persons who are willing to make contributions for this

cause, and perhaps also by obtaining the cooperation of industrial laboratories which have the necessary equipment.

I understand that Germany has actually stopped the sale of uranium from the Czechoslovakian mines which she has taken over. That she should have taken such early action might perhaps be understood on the ground that the son of the German Undersecretary of State, von Weizsäcker, is attached to the Kaiser Wilhelm Institute of Berlin, where some of the American work on uranium is now being repeated.

Yours very truly,
A. Einstein.

Whatever the details of how it was written, it is clear that this letter, with its "possible" and "almost certain," was the work of Szilard. And it is interesting that despite all his intuition he was still thinking of fission in terms of creating mere "bombs," while "extremely powerful bombs of a new type" were apparently in a different category and were still "much less certain." As far as Einstein was concerned, this was an understatement. But, making "the greatest mistake" of his life, he signed on the dotted line.

Szilard now had two irons in the fire—the potential introduction to Lindbergh and the letter which reposed in Sachs' office. Neither appeared to be getting hot. Lindbergh does not today recall the letter from Einstein. "If such a note was written and forwarded it may have been lost in the heavy mail that came in that year," he says. The same presumably happened to the reminder which Szilard sent him on September 13. No record remains of what happened next, but on September 27 Szilard wrote to Einstein saying: "Lindbergh is not our man." By this time the Germans had not only invaded Poland but had effectively conquered most of it, and he gloomily added that as Belgium would eventually be overrun the Americans should try to buy 50 tons of uranium as soon as possible.

Six days later he wrote with equal gloom that "Sachs confessed that he is still sitting on the letter," and that it was "possible that Sachs was useless."

However, this was far from so. Sachs knew the way official machinery works and was merely biding his time. "Our system is such that national public figures . . . are, so to speak, punch-drunk with printer's ink," he has said. "So

I thought there was no point in transmitting material which would be passed on to someone lower down." The outbreak of war, with Roosevelt's resulting involvement in the neutrality laws, caused initial delay and it was not until October 11 that Sachs saw Roosevelt and handed over the Einstein letter with a memorandum prepared by Szilard. This memorandum, rather oddly in view of all that had prefaced it, mentioned first the possibility that nuclear fission might be used to provide power; went on to suggest potential uses in medicine; and only then stated that it might be utilized in a weapon. It mentioned also that in the previous March an unsuccessful attempt had been made to hold up publication of information on fission—an attempt frustrated by the French—and that a further attempt might now be made.

At the meeting with Roosevelt, Sachs, according to the official American history of events, "read aloud his covering letter, which emphasized the same ideas as the Einstein communication but was more pointed on the need for funds. As the interview drew to a close, Roosevelt remarked, 'Alex, what you are after is to see that the Nazis don't blow us up.' Then he called in 'Pa Watson' "—General Edwin M. Watson, the President's secretary—"and announced. 'This requires action.' " Sachs left the room with Watson and by evening the Briggs committee had been set up, a small group of men presided over by Dr. Lyman J. Briggs, director of the U.S. Bureau of Standards, charged with investigating the potentialities of nuclear fission.

The first meeting of the committee was held ten days later and was attended by Szilard, Teller, and Wigner. A conspicuous absentee was Einstein. The official history of the U. S. bomb project implies that he had been invited but had declined to come; but it seems clear from Szilard's papers that no invitation had been issued. At the meeting it was decided to set up an expanded group to coordinate the research being carried out in American universities. Einstein was formally invited to become a member of this group. He just as formally declined.

However, any assumption that Einstein, having started the official machinery, was willing to let it move at its own leisurely pace is contradicted by the events of the next few months. For Einstein, far from writing only the first letter to Roosevelt and then letting affairs take their course, did very much more.

In the new year there was, as Sachs stated in his postwar evidence to the Senate, "pressure—by Einstein and the speaker—for a new framework and an accelerated tempo for the project. . . . Dr. Einstein and myself were dissatisfied with the scope and the pace of the work and its progress." The pressure began after Sachs visited Einstein at Princeton in February. Here they discussed, among other things, the report in a current issue of *Science* of the latest work by Joliot-Curie's team at the Collège de France in Paris. "While we felt that it was very important that . . . this exchange of ideas among free scientists should be carried on because they served as links and as stimuli to future work," says Sachs, "their accessibility through publications to Germany constituted an important problem."

However, the most important outcome of this meeting was the further nudge which it gave to the U. S. work. "Dr. Einstein said that he thought the work at Columbia was the more important," says Sachs. "He further said that conditions should be created for its extension and acceleration." There were further meetings between the two men within the next few weeks and Einstein then agreed to write another letter outlining the current situation. "I had felt," says Sachs, "that Dr. Einstein's authority was such that, combined with his insight and concern, it would affect the tempo of the work."

The letter, written to Sachs for transmission to Roosevelt, was dated March 7, 1940.

"In view of our common concern in the bearings of certain experimental work on problems connected with the national defense," it said,

> I wish to draw your attention to the development which has taken place since the conference that was arranged through your good offices in October last year between scientists engaged in this work and governmental representatives.
>
> Last year, when I realized that results of national importance might arise out of the research on uranium, I thought it my duty to inform the administration of this possibility. You will perhaps remember that in the letter which I addressed to the President I also mentioned the

fact that C. F. von Weizsäcker, son of the German Undersecretary of State, was collaborating with a group of chemists working upon uranium at one of the Kaiser Wilhelm Institutes—namely, the Institute of Chemistry.

Since the outbreak of the war, interest in uranium has intensified in Germany. I have now learned that research there is carried out in great secrecy and that it has been extended to another of the Kaiser Wilhelm Institutes, the Institute of Physics. The latter has been taken over by the government and a group of physicists, under the leadership of C. F. von Weizsäcker, who is now working there on uranium in collaboration with the Institute of Chemistry. The former director was sent away on a leave of absence, apparently for the duration of the war.

Should you think it advisable to relay this information to the President, please consider yourself free to do so. Will you be kind enough to let me know if you are taking action in this direction?

Dr. Szilard has shown me the manuscript which he is sending to the *Physics Review* in which he describes in detail a method of setting up a chain reaction in uranium. The papers will appear in print unless they are held up, and the question arises whether something ought to be done to withhold publication.

I have discused with Professor Wigner of Princeton University the situation in the light of the information available. Dr. Szilard will let you have a memorandum informing you of the progress made since October last year so that you will be able to take such action as you think in the circumstances advisable. You will see that the line he has pursued is different and apparently more promising than the line pursued by M. Joliot in France, about whose work you may have seen reports in the papers.

This letter is of interest for two reasons. It emphasizes, once again, how fear of a German atomic bomb was the main spur to the early nuclear work, American as well as British. And it also—no doubt at Szilard's instigation—recommends by implication the censorship of scientific discovery in the nuclear field, a proposal which had been put by Szilard to the French team in the Collège de France almost exactly a year earlier and had been curtly turned down. In fact, as Sachs later said, "Dr. Szilard, Dr. Wigner, and Dr. Einstein were all of the same view, that there had to be secrecy against leaks to the enemy."

From the Szilard papers one gets the impression that Sachs' comment was a polite gloss on the situation. What Szilard and Einstein were saying was obvious: either "the uranium question" was of importance, in which case the government should take it more seriously; alternatively, it was of little importance, in which case Szilard would publish information that could be of considerable consequence to the future. It is inconceivable that Szilard, who knew what he was doing, would implement such a threat; nevertheless, arm-twisting sometimes works. It worked in this case.

Even so, the first reaction to the Einstein letter of March 7 was tepid. The Briggs committee recommended that until a report of the work going on at Columbia University had been received, "the matter should rest in abeyance." Sachs disagreed, and finally persuaded Roosevelt to call another meeting between Briggs and army and navy representatives at which the question of enlarging the project should be thrashed out. Roosevelt, writing to Sachs on April 5 and noting that Watson would fix "a time convenient to you and Dr. Einstein," took it for granted that Einstein was part of the organization. Watson himself, who noted that "perhaps Dr. Einstein would have some suggestions to offer as to the attendance of the other professors," apparently thought so as well.

Sachs again visited Einstein at Princeton. "It became clear," he subsequently told the Senate, "that indisposition on account of a cold, and the great shyness and humility of that really saintly scientist, would make Dr. Einstein recoil from participating in large groups and would prevent his attendance. So he delegated me to report for him, too."

Precisely. As usual, Szilard had the situation well in hand. "In case you wish to decline," he had written to Einstein on April 19, "we shall prepare a polite letter of regret in English which you can use if you think it advisable." Here, as at more than one other point during the prologue to the Manhattan Project, Szilard emerges as a combination of stage manager and producer, organizing into their correct places not only Sachs, Briggs, and Watson, but also Albert Einstein.

In his letter, Einstein regretted his absence and referred

to the work of Wigner and Szilard. "I am convinced," he went on,

> as to the wisdom and the urgency of creating the conditions under which that and related work can be carried out with greater speed and on a larger scale than hitherto. I was interested in a suggestion made by Dr. Sachs that the Special Advisory Committee supply names of persons to serve as a board of trustees for a nonprofit organization which, with the approval of the government committee, could secure from governmental or private sources or both, the necessary funds for carrying out the work. Given such a framework and the necessary funds, it (the large-scale experiments and exploration of practical applications) could be carried out much faster than through a loose cooperation of university laboratories and government departments.

This letter was implemented less than two months later. For then the drastically reorganized Briggs committee was brought under the wing of the National Defense Research Committee (NRDC) which Roosevelt created, and a special committee of the National Academy of Sciences set up to inform the government of any developments in nuclear fission that might affect defense.

Two points should be made. The first is that Einstein's demand for "large-scale experiments and exploration of practical applications" does not mean that he necessarily thought the bomb was now a likely proposition. What he was after was the facts. If a self-sustaining chain reaction proved impossible then, as he had said when publishing his own negative results on the unified field theory, "at least it will prevent other people from making the same mistakes."

The second point is that this letter, foreshadowing the setting up of the Manhattan Project in 1942—the "nonprofit organization which . . . could secure . . . the necessary funds for carrying out the work"—was perhaps even more important than the initial letter to Roosevelt. And like the rest of the pressure that Einstein had exercised since the summer of 1939 it contrasts strongly with his later claim: "My participation in the production of the atomic bomb consists of one single act: I signed a letter to President Roosevelt."

The initial approach to Roosevelt produced the Briggs committee, which in turn produced the new organization under the National Defense Research Committee; this led to the Manhattan Project and the bombs on Japan. With this in mind, what is the meaning of the statement by Oppenheimer, scientific head of the project, that Einstein's letter "had very little effect"; of the evaluation of Arthur Compton, a key worker in the field, that the result of the Government Committee set up following Einstein's letter "was to retard rather than to advance the development of American uranium research"?

The explanation lies partly in the momentum which research into nuclear fission had already gained throughout the world, partly in the results of research carried out in Britain by workers who convincingly showed that a nuclear weapon was possible even if their own country was unable to make it. By the summer of 1940, when the Briggs committee was transformed, Hans Halban and Lew Kowarski, two important members of the French team which a year previously had shown a chain reaction to be possible, had reached England and were contemplating going to America. In the United States itself Szilard and Fermi were only two of the workers at the head of research teams which owed comparatively little to official help. In Germany research was known to be going ahead. In Britain, where Frisch and Rudolf Peierls had made the discovery that the amount of separated uranium required for a bomb weighed pounds rather than tons, numbers of physicists were at work on detailed studies of the time, money, labor, and raw materials required to make a specific nuclear weapon. All this would have carried the world into the nuclear age whether or not Einstein had signed a letter to Roosevelt.

There was also the specific impact of the Maud Report, the account of Britain's plans for building a bomb, which was completed in the summer of 1941. On October 3, copies were handed to Dr. Vannevar Bush. On the ninth, according to James Baxter, official historian of the Office of Scientific Research and Development, Bush "had a long conversation with the President and the Vice-President in which he reported the British view that a bomb could be constructed from U-235 produced by a diffusion plant." And two days later Roosevelt wrote to Churchill proposing that the British and the U. S. should work together. It would appear chauvinistic for a British writer to assess the significance of these dates. But two Americans may be allowed to speak: "Though the Americans were aware of this weapon as a possibility," Arthur Compton has written, "it was more than a year later that it became for us the focus of attention. In 1940 it was still difficult for us in America to concentrate our thoughts on war, while for the British it was their prime concern." And the official historians of the American effort, writing in *The New World*, have this to say of the Maud Report: "[It] gave Bush and [Dr. James] Conant what they had been looking for: a promise that there was a reasonable chance for something militarily useful during the war in progress. The British did more than promise; they outlined a concrete program. None of the recommendations Briggs had made and neither of the two National Academy reports had done as much."

All this fills out Bush's bare statement that "the show had been going long before Einstein's letter." But it does not relegate the letter to a place of no importance. Donald Fleming, writing in *An American Primer* of the British scientists who sat on the Maud Committee, and of the visit to England of Pegram and Urey in the autumn of 1941, puts the situation in perspective. "Their optimistic report of July, 1941, and the detailed case they made to American scientists who visited England in the fall, played a major, perhaps critical, part in the American decision to make a big push on the eve of Pearl Harbor rather than later. It does not follow that Einstein's letter of August, 1939, served no purpose. The decision of December 6, 1941, would have been comparatively empty if the Americans had no base to build upon." In other words, America would have built the bomb without Einstein. But they might not have had it ready for the war against Japan. Instead, the bomb would have been ready for Korea; by which time, without much doubt, the Russians would have had one too.

Einstein's letter of April, 1940, setting the U. S. administration along the road towards what was to become the Manhattan Project, ended the first phase of his wartime involvement with nuclear weapons. The second, which came a year and a half later, is one of extraordinary irony. For it shows Einstein eager to help the war effort —but kept from it by men unaware that Einstein himself had set the whole U.S. machine moving two years earlier.

On December 6, 1941, a few hours before the Japanese attack on Pearl Harbor, the Office of Scientific Research and Development began a greatly expanded program of research into nuclear weapons. A key technological problem for it was the separation of U-235 from its chemically identical isotopes. One likely method was gaseous diffusion, in which uranium in gaseous form is passed through an immense number of barriers pierced with extremely small holes. The U-235, with three fewer neutrons than the almost ubiquitous U-238, is able to pass through more quickly, and the lighter isotope can eventually be concentrated. Many purely theoretical problems are associated with the barriers. They had to be solved without delay and early in December Bush turned to Einstein for help.

The request was made through Dr. Frank Aydelotte, by this time in Dr. Flexner's shoes as Director of the Institute for Advanced Study. Einstein worked at the problem which Bush gave him and on December 19, 1941, Aydelotte sent the handwritten solution to Bush at the Office of Scientific Research and Development in Washington. "As I told you over the telephone," he said in his covering letter,

> Einstein was very much interested in your problem, has worked at it for a couple of days and produced the solution, which I enclose herewith. Einstein asks me to say that if there are other angles of the problem that you want him to develop or if you wish any parts of this amplified, you need only let him know and he will be glad to do anything in his power. I very much hope that you will make use of him in any way that occurs to you, because I know how deep is his satisfaction at doing anything which might be useful in the national effort.
>
> I hope you can read his handwriting. Neither he nor I felt free, in view of the necessary secrecy, to give the manuscript to anyone to copy. In this, as in all other respects, we shall be glad to do anything that will facilitate your work.

Bush passed on Einstein's calculations to Dr. Harold Urey, head of the American gaseous-diffusion project, and

Urey in due course discussed them with Bush. One thing quickly became clear: if Einstein's work was to be really useful, the problem would have to be presented to him in much more detail. But this was impossible. And it was impossible for reasons which Bush gave Aydelotte in a letter on December 30. "I am not going to tell him any more than I have told him, for a number of reasons," he wrote.

> If my statement of the problem is not sufficient to make it clear, I will of course be very glad to make the statement as precise as possible, but I really believe that my statement placed the problem in its exact form. The reason that I am not going farther is that I am not at all sure that if I place Einstein in entire contact with his subject he would not discuss it in a way that it should not be discussed, and with this doubt in my mind I do not feel that I ought to take him into confidence on the subject to the extent of showing just where this thing fits into the defense picture, and what the military aspects of the matter might be. If I were to explain more than I already have, I feel sure that the rest of the story would immediately follow. I wish very much that I could place the whole thing before him and take him fully into confidence, but this is utterly impossible in view of the attitude of people here in Washington who have studied into his whole history.

So Einstein, who had put his name to a letter warning that a single nuclear weapon might destroy a whole port, was to be kept from knowing "where this thing fits into the defense picture"! The extraordinary contradiction is in fact simply explained. For as Bush has written of Einstein's letter, "in my many discussions with President Roosevelt on the subject he did not mention it."

Trying to get an answer from Einstein without telling him too much, unaware of his earlier involvement, Bush asked for help on a subject that was academic—even though it was clearly so secret that Einstein thought it unwise to have the answer copied. Thus it is not absolutely certain that when he produced the solution, and showed his "deep . . . satisfaction at doing anything which might be useful in the national effort," Einstein knew that he was working towards a nuclear weapon. But it is a strong assumption. He would, after all, have been "glad to do anything in his power" now that the United States was at last at war with Germany.

The exclusion of Einstein from the inner counsels of the scientists who drove the Manhattan Project to its conclusion was to have one important result in 1945. For it effectively prevented him from using his enormous prestige when the future of the bomb was being discussed. By that time he was the outsider, unable even to declare openly that he knew of the bomb's existence without betraying what his friends and acquaintances had let him know, consciously or unconsciously. Thus the prophet of $E = mc^2$ did not, in theory, know of the bomb's existence until it was dropped in anger. Sometimes this has been too much for history to bear. One account mentions "Dr. Einstein" at Los Alamos—which Einstein never visited—without spoiling the story by adding that the name was a local soubriquet for someone else. And one biography not only has a drawn frontispiece showing Einstein "at the first test of the atomic bomb" but soberly has him speaking a farrago of nonsense there. In fact, Einstein remained officially—although not unofficially—unaware of America's nuclear effort until, on August 6, 1945, he heard at Saranac Lake the radio announcement of the Hiroshima bombing.

This, the most publicized period of Einstein's connection with nuclear weapons, runs from July, 1939, until, very approximately, the American entry into the war in December, 1941. Before the end of it he had taken U. S. citizenship, together with his stepdaughter Margot and Helen Dukas. Not every American was pleased. A letter in *The Tablet* complained of "Einstein the refugee Jewish Communist taking an oath of allegiance to the U. S. government," while a long article in a book entitled *The Fifth Column in Our Schools* attacked Einstein's right to become a U. S. citizen at all. "If Albert Einstein is right and there is no personal God, then America is founded on fable and falsehood," this went.

> If there is no God then the citizen has no God-given rights. Then all the rights set forth in the Constitution are sham and delusion. If man has no Creator, then our fathers fought for a lie; then the rights of citizenship are based on a lie. Then Professor Einstein has subscribed to

> a lie, in the very act of pledging allegiance to a form of government which—according to his philosophy—is founded on a lie.

The reasoning was tortuous; it was not uncommon, and fuel was added to the criticism with Einstein's support for Bertrand Russell, who was first appointed to, and then sacked from, a professorship at the City College of New York. Russell's *Marriage and Morals* was used as the cudgel to belabor him in a savage attack which described the distinguished philosopher as "lecherous, libidinous, lustful, venerous, erotomaniac, aphrodisiac, irreverent, narrow-minded, untruthful, and bereft of moral fiber." Einstein was no longer surprised by this attitude of the Christian mob. "It keeps repeating itself," he wrote in a doggerel verse to Russell. "In this world so fine and honest;/the parson alarms the populace/; The genius is executed. (Es wiederholt sich immer wieder/ In dieser Welt so fein und bieder/ Der Pfaff den Poebel alarmiert/ Der Genius wird executiert.)"

The institute buildings were finally completed in 1940 and before the end of the year Einstein moved from his rooms in the university to the new and rather splendid quarters in their parklike setting on the outskirts of the town. Here he was allocated an imposing room with leaded windows, long curtains, and even an Oriental rug on the floor.

In Princeton, where familiarity had bred acceptance, his presence was taken for granted. Everywhere else in the United States Einstein was still a name which made news, and in 1944 there was a flurry of excitement when there appeared a biography by his former stepson-in-law, Dmitri Marianoff, with the aid of another professional writer. Marianoff had separated from Margot in the summer of 1934, soon after arriving in America. Now he was cashing in on the Berlin days. "He is said to have lived with the Einstein family for eight years," Einstein said in a public denunciation of the book. "He never lived at my house for even a year, only for a few months at a time." The book was popularly written and harmless enough. But it was, Einstein stated, "generally unreliable," and the bits which he had read were "not true at all."

He was naturally enough sensitive about his name. After all, it was often his name which did the trick; as, for instance, in prizing a message from Roosevelt for the American Fund for Palestinian Institutions when it held a dinner in his honor at the Waldrof-Astoria in the summer of 1944. Roosevelt declined a first request to send a message "stressing the important work of the beneficiary institutions in contemporary life and in the war effort of Palestine." But a second appeal produced a Roosevelt message extending "hearty greetings to all who gather at the dinner in honor of Professor Albert Einstein." This, in the words of a memorandum from the White House, was "a compromise—a little compliment to Professor Einstein—silence about the fund raising."

He was, inevitably, the much sought-after distinguished guest for all manner of scientific gatherings, and he was drawn from the oasis of Princeton to attend the Carnegie Hall meeting celebrating the 400th anniversary of Copernicus' death. Since Copernicus was a revolutionary, a number of modern revolutionaries were invited. They included Einstein, T. H. Morgan the geneticist, Igor Sikorsky the helicopter designer, and Henry Ford. Einstein was one of the two who made brief speeches.

"It was in broken English, and Einstein's English had been pretty badly broken," says Harlow Shapley, who helped to organize the occasion.

> He pointed out that it was not inappropriate for him to appear "because Copernicus was the great leader of scientists and he was our teacher"—or some such connection. It was a modest talk in pidgin English and the audience just roared. Carnegie Hall rattled with applause. In the front row were some of my friends from the Century Club. I had sent them tickets so they could come, and they did and applauded wildly. They are of course good Republicans and careful clubmen; that they would applaud this relativity man and his doings was a little surprising. That night I asked some of them about it and was told: "Well, I think the reason we applauded was that we'd always insisted that we couldn't understand one damn word of this relativity nonsense. And here we hear Relativity himself talking about it and still we couldn't understand it."

The members of the Century Club may have shown little logic. They accurately reflected lay opinion in midwar—Einstein was still "Relativity himself." He was also the most famous living Jew, and it is a revelation of his attitude to nonscientific affairs that during the early years of the war his letters to relatives in German-occupied Belgium exposed them to considerable risk. They exist today, full of local gossip and still in the envelopes that had been twice slit open for the contents to be approved first by the American and then by the German censors. To conceal who they came from, the sender was given as Marianoff, Margot's married name; but the address was "112 Mercer Street, Princeton," a straight pointer to the Koch family's kinship with Hitler's *bête juive*.

During these wartime years, Einstein was to many scientists the ultimate court of appeal and this fact drew him, the most amiable of men, into some cantankerous disputes. One was with the supporters of Felix Ehrenhaft, who had been turned out of Vienna after the Nazis came to power and forced to abandon the great electromagnet whose construction had been the light of his life. The experience may have pushed him beyond reason. Certainly his power of rational argument decreased and his insistence that the electronic charge was not constant was maintained against all comers. A capable experimenter who had "gradually developed into a kind of swindler" was one description by Einstein; a later one was "a strongly paranoiac creature." Einstein thought that some of Ehrenhaft's claims were nonsense, and openly said so. This brought down on his head requests to "repair the great injustice done to Felix Ehrenhaft by your attitude towards him and through the unfounded and defaming reports about his discoveries which you spread not only among his colleagues but also in financial circles, among bankers who wanted to help him carry on with his research." Einstein had little time for such complaints. As far as he could, he ignored them.

He also tried to ignore his involvement with Wilhelm Reich. This eccentric distraught figure seems already to have slipped down the slope towards charlatanry or madness by the time he asked Einstein to investigate his discovery of "a specific biologically effective energy which behaves in many respects differently to all that is known about electromagnetic energy." Reich first wrote to Einstein on December 30, 1940, informing him that he had been Freud's assistant at the Polyclinic in Vienna from 1922 until 1930, and was now teaching "experimental and clinical biopsychology" in New York. Anyone other than Einstein would have been warned by the letter, which continued with the admission that he had not reported his discovery to the Academy of Physics because of "extremely bad experience." But Reich added that it might possibly "be used in the fight against the Fascist pestilence." Einstein, who had encouraged the country forward in what still seemed to be the one-in-a-million chance of using nuclear fission for this very purpose, was the last man to resist such a bait.

Reich called on Einstein in his Mercer Street home on January 13, 1941. "He told me," his wife wrote later, "that the conversation with Einstein had been extremely friendly and cordial, that Einstein was easy to talk to, that their conversation had lasted almost five hours. Einstein was willing to investigate the phenomena that Reich had described to him, and a special little accumulator would have to be built and taken to him." Certainly there was a further visit, and certainly Einstein tested the apparatus. But his query "What else do you do?" when told by Reich that he was not a physicist but a psychiatrist, probably contained an unnoticed hint of scepticism.

Einstein found a commonplace explanation of the phenomena which Reich had noted, and said so in polite terms. The postscript—contained in *The Einstein Affair*, a privately printed booklet from Reich's own press—was spread across the following three years of their correspondence. Reich disputed Einstein's findings and Einstein was dismayed that his name might be wrongly used to support Reich's theory. Briefly, the theory "has not my confidence," as he put it. Reich took the easy way out, and blamed the Communists.

It was not only in the United States that Einstein's name meant a lot, and the British Association requested a message from him for their 1942 meeting. The text was prepared in German, but was broadcast by Einstein in English, from the United States; reception in England was poor and the published text was a compromise of printed German and spoken English. One result was a long-lasting rumor that Einstein had traveled to Britain in wartime to deliver an address.

At the time, what he said sounded conventional enough. But an inner significance comes from the fact that it was given by the man who had written the letter to Roosevelt. "What hopes and fears does the scientific method imply for mankind?" Einstein asked towards the end of it.

> I do not think that is the right way to put the question. Whatever this tool may produce in the hands of men depends entirely upon the nature of the aims alive in mankind. Once these aims exist, the scientific method furnishes means to realize them. But it cannot furnish these aims itself. The scientific method itself would not have led to anything, it would not even have been born at all, without a passionate striving for clear understanding. Perfection of means and confusion of aims seem, in my opinion to characterize our age. If we desire passionately the safety, the welfare, and the free development of all men, we should not lack the means to approach such a state. Even if only a small part of mankind strives for such an aim, their superiority will prove itself in the long run.

Anything that would aid the "fight against the Fascist pestilence" drew Einstein's immediate support. In 1943 he was asked by the Book and Author Committee of the Fourth War Loan drive to donate his original paper of 1905 for sale. Like many others, it had been destroyed when he received printed copies. However, he agreed to write it out once more in longhand, adding above it: "The following pages are a copy of my first paper concerning the theory of relativity. I made this copy in November 1943. The original manuscript not [*sic*] longer exists having been discarded by me after its publication. The publication bears the title 'Elektrodynamik bewegter Körper' (*Annalen der Physik;* vierte Folge, Vol. 17, 1905). A. Einstein 21. X1. 1943." Miss Dukas dictated it to him from his published paper. "I could have said this more simply," he said more than once.

He also handed over an unpublished manuscript on "The Bivector Field," and the two manuscripts were auctioned in Kansas City on February 4, 1944, the Kansas City Insurance Company investing $6.5 million in war bonds for the relativity paper—and subsequently presenting it to the Library of Congress—while W. T. Kemper,

Jr., a custodian of insurance funds, invested $5 million of impounded funds to obtain the second paper.

By this time Einstein had again become directly involved in defense work. On August 13, 1943, he had written to his friend Gustav Bucky that he now had "closer relations with the navy and Office of Scientific Research and Development in Washington." And Vannevar Bush, the organization's director, writes: "Some friends of Einstein visited me and told me that he was disturbed because he was not active in the war effort. I accordingly appointed him a member of a committee where it seemed to me his particular skills would be most likely to be of service." What the committee was has never been discovered, but from internal evidence it is unlikely to have been concerned with nuclear research.

No such question mark hangs over Einstein's engagement with the U. S. Navy's Bureau of Ordnance. An announcement from Washington on June 24, 1943, stated that "his naval assignment will be on a part-time contractual basis and he will continue his association with the Institute for Advanced Study, Princeton, N. J., where most of his studies on behalf of the Bureau of Ordnance will be undertaken." Records of the General Services Administration, St. Louis, Missouri, show that Einstein "was intermittently employed in Special Service Contract of the Department of the Navy, Washington, D. C., as a Scientist from May 31, 1943, to June 30, 1944. As a Technicist from July 1, 1944, to June 30, 1945, and also as a Consultant for Research on Explosives from July 1, 1945, to June 30, 1946." *Star Shell,* the Bureau of Ordnance publication, later stated that his work concerned "the theory of explosion, seeking to determine what laws govern the more obscure waves of detonation, why certain explosives have marked directional effect and other highly technical theories," while the St. Louis records further add that Einstein's service "was performed in the development of bombs and underwater weapons."

His duties were on a personal services basis which, according to Admiral Furer's official history, "allowed the Bureau to secure the services of persons which it would not otherwise have attracted." Among the eminent scientists thus employed were Dr. von Neumann, who furnished the theoretical foundation for the air-burst principle used in the atomic bomb attack on Hiroshima; Dr. John Kirkwood, who developed theoretical methods for determining the relative effectiveness of explosives; and Dr. George Gamow, who worked on the theory of initiation and detonation of explosives.

Einstein said, on accepting the consultantship, that he would be unable to travel to Washington regularly and that someone from the Division of High Explosives for which he would be working must come to him at Princeton. "Since I happened to have known Einstein earlier, on nonmilitary grounds, I was selected to carry out this job," writes George Gamow.

> Thus on every other Friday I took a morning train to Princeton, carrying a briefcase tightly packed with confidential and secret Navy projects. There was a great variety of proposals, such as exploding a series of underwater mines placed along a parabolic path that would lead to the entrance of a Japanese naval base, with "follow-up" aerial bombs to be dropped on the flight decks of Japanese aircraft carriers. Einstein would meet me in his study at home, wearing one of his famous soft sweaters, and we would go through all the proposals, one by one. He approved practically all of them, saying, "Oh yes, very interesting, very, very, ingenious," and the next day the admiral in charge of the bureau was very happy when I reported to him Einstein's comments.

One other idea was that of producing a certain effect by using a convergent detonation wave formed by combining two explosives with different propagation velocities. After Einstein had approved it, plans were made for a model test at Indian Head, the navy proving grounds on the Potomac River. But then, recalls Gamow, the high-explosives factory in Pittsburgh which was to make the device shied away from it. "On the next day my project was moved from the top of the priority list to the bottom," he says, "and I suddenly realized what was being worked on at a mysterious place in New Mexico with the address: P. O. Box 1663, Santa Fé. Years later, when I was fully cleared for work on the A-bomb and went to Los Alamos, I learned that my guess had been correct." Gamow gives no indication of whether he mentioned the incident, or passed on his guess, to Einstein. It seems likely.

Einstein's attitude to this work was by no means half-hearted. He wrote to Bucky in July, 1943 saying he would be staying in Princeton for the summer and commenting: "So long as the war lasts and I work for the navy I do not wish to begin anything else." The following year he was reported to have spent his sixty-fifth birthday hard at work, and his colleagues, according to the *New York Times*, said "he preferred it that way in view of the amount of work to be done."

Only part of his time was devoted to the navy but there is no indication that he shirked it or shrank from that part. Indeed, there was no reason why he should. Events had taught him, in the words of his friend Max Born, "that the ultimate ethical values, on which all human existence is based, must, as a last resort, be defended even by force and with the sacrifice of human lives." This reluctant admission had first been made in the summer of 1933. Now "his satisfaction at doing anything which might be useful in the national effort" pressed his actions yet further against the grain of his normal inclinations. Circumstances altered cases; even in pacifism there were no absolutes. The war had to be won. All this was commonplace enough. Many decent men did what they did in wartime only with reluctance, admitting ruefully that at times life offers only a choice between evils.

Yet the real tragedy of Einstein's situation can be judged not by the record of the war years, when his work for the Services was openly acknowledged, but by the postwar period when he banished to the back of his mind what he had done as though it were a nightmare rather than the reality. Writing in 1950 to A. J. Muste, a leading American pacifist who was opposing production of the hydrogen bomb, he stated that his only contribution to the atomic bomb had been "a letter to Roosevelt." Furthermore, he went on, it would "be quite ridiculous if I were to issue a statement declaring my refusal to participate in armament work. Since the military authorities are well aware of my position, it would never occur to them to invite me to participate in such work." It can be claimed, perhaps only with special pleading, that Einstein had by this time overlooked his two significant letters to

Dr. Briggs; that he was unaware of what lay behind the manuscript, too secret to be copied, which he prepared for Bush in December, 1941; and that his pacifism vis-à-vis armament work referred to peacetime rather than wartime. Yet in 1952, replying to a correspondent who raised the question of the atomic bomb, he went further. "You are mistaken in regarding me as a kind of chieftain of those scientists who abuse science for military purposes," he replied. "I have never worked in the field of applied science, let alone for the military. I condemn the military mentality of our time just as you do. Indeed, I have been a pacifist all my life and regard Gandhi as the only truly great political figure of our age."

Were Einstein different from the man who emerges so clearly both from the archives and from reminiscence, the discrepancy between what he did and what he later said would be simple to explain. But his weakness in a predatory world was that of the man who speaks the truth by an inner compulsion; thus his ability to disregard his wartime activity suggests a psychological failing rather than dishonesty.

His reluctance to think back to the war must also be seen in association with two other things. One was his natural, and later almost paranoiac, distrust of the Germans, a distrust which he finally appreciated had paved the road to Hiroshima and which, when he considered the Japanese holocaust, must have filled him with mixed emotions. The other was his decision in December, 1944, when he had learned of the peril of nuclear weapons, to "abstain from any action" which might "complicate the delicate task of the statesmen."

For as the war rose to its climax with the Allied invasion of Europe and the prospect of the Wehrmacht being driven back to Germany in defeat, the consequences of his action in July, 1939, became even more difficult to ignore.

It is generally believed that Einstein was totally ignorant of the progress made by the Manhattan Project until the announcement that the first bomb had been dropped on Hiroshima. He himself never pushed such a claim—a fact adequately explained by the evidence now available. He cannot have failed to note the permanent disappearance from the academic scene of such men as Szilard, Fermi, Compton, Teller, Wigner, and a host of others who had been involved in uranium research during 1939 and 1940. He could not fail to have noted the sudden dropping from academic discussion of all news about nuclear fission. And if he took more than a cursory interest in the subject of uranium itself—the very nub of his initial worry—he may even have noted the reference on page 825 of the *U. S. Minerals Yearbook* of 1943 which said: "The uranium industry in 1943 was greatly stimulated by a government program having materials priority over all other mineral procurement, but most of the facts were buried in War Department secrecy."

In addition, there was the case of his own Danish *alter ego.* In October, 1943, Niels Bohr had made one of the most spectacular escapes of the war, sailing with his son across the Kattegat to Sweden in a small boat and being taken first to England in a high-flying Mosquito and then to the United States. Bohr spent most of the summer of 1944 at Los Alamos, where he "instigated some of the most important experiments on the velocity selector ... enlivened discussions on bomb assembly, and ... participated very actively in the design of the initiator."

Bohr also visited Einstein in Princeton. He arrived while other friends were there, and only as these friends were leaving did Einstein hurry downstairs and warn them that on no account must they mention that Bohr was in the United States. His presence in America was officially secret since he was traveling in the name of John Baker, and had even been given a British passport for the purpose—reportedly the only foreigner ever to have been granted one.

Bohr was a man of honor. He kept confidences. He no doubt denied himself the pleasure of describing to Einstein the technological successes with which he had been brought face to face at Los Alamos. But he now knew that two years previously Fermi had succeeded in producing the first self-sustaining chain reaction in the famous squash court in Chicago. He knew that the forecast he had made in his secret message to Chadwick a year earlier was incorrect. And it is clear from subsequent events that he was one of the first scientists to become genuinely concerned with postwar control of whatever new weapons the war produced.

It is unlikely that Einstein knew much of the technological details involved in the Manhattan Project. For one thing, General Groves' policy of compartmentalization made it difficult for any one man to know more than the necessary minimum—or to impart it, even if he wished to do so. More important, Einstein would not have been interested in purely technological detail. However, by the winter of 1944 he had talked on many occasions with an adviser to the Manhattan Project, had discussed with him the need to prevent a postwar arms race for weapons that would cause "destruction even more evil than that of today," and had desperately written to Bohr invoking his aid. The evidence is not that Einstein knew how, or even if, the new weapons were to be used to finish the war; but it implies beyond all reasonable doubt that by the end of 1944 he knew that they were nearing completion.

The adviser was Otto Stern, Einstein's old colleague from the Prague days, who had crossed the Atlantic in 1934. Soon after America entered the war, Stern had served as consultant to one of the early radar schemes. Then, following the start of the Manhattan Project, he had become a consultant assigned to the Metallurgical Laboratory at the University of Chicago, where the first nuclear pile went into operation in 1942. He continued to live in Pittsburgh, working as adviser to the other Manhattan Project consultants at the Carnegie Institute of Technology. Perhaps more important, he traveled to Chicago for the information meetings held there about every six weeks. Exactly how much he knew about the detailed progress of the bomb is not certain; there is every indication that it was considerable.

Stern paid a number of visits to Einstein, who after one of them said how terribly worried he was about the development of new weapons after the end of the war. No record of their discussions is likely to have been made, but their nature can be inferred from the climax which they produced.

This came in mid-December, 1944. Stern visited Einstein on Monday, December 11. Once again they discussed weapons. This time Einstein appears to have become gravely alarmed. The following day he sat down and wrote to Bohr. He wrote to him at the Danish Legation in Washington, and he appears to have dropped the "John Baker" pseudonym and addressed him plainly as Professor Niels Bohr.

Writing of the news which so greatly disturbed him, he said that his reaction had been that

> when the war is over, then there will be in all countries a pursuit of secret war preparations with technological means which will lead inevitably to preventive wars and to destruction even more terrible than the present destruction of life. The politicians do not appreciate the possibilities and consequently do not know the extent of the menace. Every effort must be made to avert such a development. I share your view of the situation but I see no way of doing anything promising.

He then referred to the visit from Stern of the previous day. "It seemed to us," he continued,

> that there is one possibility, however slight it may be. There are in the principal countries scientists who are really influential and who know how to get a hearing with political leaders. There is you yourself with your international connections, Compton here in the U.S.A., Lindemann in England, Kapitza and Joffe in Russia, etc. The idea is that these men should bring combined pressure on the political leaders in their countries in order to bring about an internationalization of military power—a method that has been rejected for too long as being too adventurous. But this radical step with all its far-reaching political assumptions regarding extranational government seems the only alternative to a secret technical arms race.
>
> We agreed that I should lay this before you. Don't say, at first sight, "Impossible" but wait a day or two until you have got used to the idea. [He concluded by saying that if there was even a chance in a thousand of something being done, there should be further discussion.]

This letter could hardly have been more fortuitously ill timed; the names it mentioned could hardly have been more fortuitously ill chosen. In April, Bohr had received in London a letter from Kapitza which had invited him and his family to settle in Russia. He had shown it to the British intelligence authorities, who had vetted his warm but innocuous reply. In May he had secured a meeting with Churchill in London, largely through Lindemann's intervention, and had tried to impress on the British Prime Minister the need for bringing the Russians into a scheme for postwar control of nuclear energy. The interview was a tragic failure; Bohr was unable to explain and Churchill was unwilling to listen. In August Bohr was better received by Roosevelt, who listened sympathetically for an hour, agreed that an approach should be made to Russia, and promised to raise the matter direct with Churchill whom he was due to meet at Hyde Park the following month. But in September Roosevelt and Churchill did more than rule out any idea of an approach to the Russians. They also initialed an *aide-mémoire* the last clause of which said: "Enquiries should be made regarding the activities of Professor Bohr and steps taken to ensure that he is responsible for no leakage of information particularly to the Russians." Bohr's friends loyally rallied to his support but he was "distressed that the whole business had now become enmeshed in the interstices of American politics. . . ." He had moved, both in Britain and the United States, among the men who pulled the levers of power and he had put to them proposals that were well thought out and practical where Einstein's were by comparison unreal. Nevertheless, he had been brusquely brushed off.

Bohr was in an awkward situation. He knew his Einstein. He knew that to a man of such trusting idealism the niceties of diplomatic protocol meant little. Whether he feared that Einstein might himself try to write to Kapitza or Joffé is not certain, but if he did the fear—with all his knowledge of how "the secret" of the bomb was being kept from the Russians—must have haunted him. What is beyond doubt is that when Bohr received Einstein's letter from the embassy he hastened to Princeton; that in a long interview he persuaded Einstein to keep quiet; and that in an official capacity he reported on the incident to Washington in a private note that must have done much to vindicate the attitude of the "people . . . in Washington" who three years earlier decided to restrict Einstein's knowledge of the Manhattan Project.

He arrived at Mercer Street on Friday, December 22, and his report of what happened, dated merely "December, 1944," was typed on quarto paper, apparently by

Bohr himself and certainly in his own brand of English, with himself referred to as "B" and Einstein referred to as "X." It began by stating that he had visited Einstein, to whom he had explained that it "would be quite illegitimate [*sic*] and might have the most deplorable consequences if anyone who was brought into confidence about the matter concerned, on his own hands should take steps of the kind suggested."

The note then continued as follows;

> Confidentially B could, however, inform X that the responsible statesmen in America and England were fully aware of the scope of the technical development, and that their attention had been called to the dangers to world security as well as to the unique opportunity for furthering a harmonious relationship between nations, which the great scientific advance involves. In response X assured B that he quite realized the situation and would not only abstain from any action himself, but would also—without any reference to his confidential conversation with B—impress on the friends with whom he had talked about the matter, the undesirability of all discussions which might complicate the delicate task of the statesmen.

There is no reason to doubt the accuracy of Bohr's note. There is no reason to doubt that Einstein was here, as elsewhere, a man of his word. And the inevitable conclusion is that from December, 1944, until the dropping of the bombs on Japan eight months later Einstein not only knew far more of the developing nuclear situation than any of his scientist friends realized but used his confidential and undisclosable information from Bohr to impress on them "the undesirability of all discussions which might complicate the delicate task of the statesmen."

First he had to deal with Otto Stern. He waited until the Christmas celebrations were half over. Then, on December 26, he sat down to write what must have been, even for Einstein, an extraordinarily difficult letter—one that would prevent Stern from making any ill-advised move yet would not reveal the visit from Bohr; a letter, moreover, that would be innocuous if it fell into the wrong hands.

"Dear Stern," it went,

> A cloud of deep secrecy has settled on me following my letter to B. so that I can report no more on the matter than that we are not the first who have faced similar things. I have the impression that one must strive seriously to be responsible, that one does best not to speak about the matter for the time being, and that it would in no way help, at the present moment, to bring it to public notice.
>
> It is difficult for me to speak in such a nebulous way, but for the moment I cannot do anything else.
>
> With the best of wishes,

Here, as on previous occasions, Einstein had stepped into a dark arena and been tripped by his own ignorance of what was going on. Furthermore his freedom of action, already limited by lack of official knowledge about the Manhattan Project, was now further hampered by what he had been told only in confidence. This was to be important in more ways than one. These arguments, and the earlier exchanges between Otto Stern and Einstein, were concerned with what was to happen after the war. Yet for practical purposes they also made it more difficult for Einstein to make his voice heard in any discussion which might be raised about use of the bomb in the Pacific or even in Europe, where a week before Bohr's visit the Germans had launched the Ardennes offensive, a salutary reminder that they were not yet beaten.

First questions about the actual use of the bomb were raised in March, 1945, by Leo Szilard, who since February, 1942, had been chief physicist at the Metallurgical Laboratory in Chicago. Germany was now seen to be within a few weeks of defeat, while it was already known to a few men, almost certainly including Szilard, that the Third Reich was nowhere near producing a nuclear weapon.

The story there had been strange. In the United States Einstein had been kept virtually outside the nuclear effort once he had started it; in Germany there had been, by contrast, a movement which tended to rehabilitate the much-condemned "Jewish physics" which he represented. Certainly a number of German physicists, fearful that the current denigration of theoretical physics would seriously hamper their country, held a meeting in Munich in November, 1940, and officially agreed that:

> 1. Theoretical physics is an indispensable part of all physics. 2. The Special Theory of Relativity belongs to the experimentally verified facts of physics. Its application to cosmic problems, however, it still uncertain. 3. The theory of relativity has nothing to do with a general relativistic philosophy. No new concepts of time and space have been introduced. And 4. Modern quantum theory is the only method known to describe quantitatively the properties of the atom. As yet, no one has been able to go beyond this mathematical formalism to obtain a deeper understanding of the atomic structure.

Two years later another meeting was held, this time in Seefeld, in the Austrian Tyrol. Here a somewhat similar compromise was achieved, softening the decision that relativity had to be accepted with the consolation that "before Einstein, Aryan scientists like Lorentz, Hasenohrl, Poincaré, etc., had created the foundations of the theory of relativity and Einstein merely followed up the already existing ideas consistently and added the cornerstone."

Not all Germans were happy that such intellectual convolutions should remain unnoticed outside the Third Reich, and at least one effort was made to inform Einstein of what was going on. It consisted of a single typed sheet posted from Hamburg in 1942. It found its way onto the desk in the Foreign Office of Einstein's old friend, David Mitrany, who on the outbreak of war had come back across the Atlantic to work for the British. The note asked that the following message should be passed on to Einstein:

> In his article W. Lenz (Hamburg), puts forward the thesis that you were not the only one responsible for the Relativity Theory, but rather that Henri Poincaré was a fellow culprit. He does this with the explicit purpose of clearing it of the reproach that it sprang solely from a Jewish mind, and thereby, so to speak, of making it "hoffähig" [presentable] in the Third Reich. For if it was established also by Poincaré, then it is proved that physicists were bound to come upon it, and to it is really Aryan after all.
>
> There is no way of preventing the publication of the article. It will appear in the *Naturwissenschaften*. Possibly they will add as a postscript and commentary certain quotations from Poincaré's lecture called "La

> Mécanique Nouvelle 1909—10" which in my opinion proves absolutely that the author had indeed known the mathematical aspect of the theory, but that he did not take the steps which were really decisive in the establishment of the theory. But it is not certain whether this postscript will appear together with the article.

The need to cloak relativity in particular and "Jewish physics" in general with a respectability enabling them to be used without reproach by German physicists was part and parcel of the nuclear research which in Germany paralleled the work being carried out in the United States and Britain. In all three countries the crucial decision whether to follow up laboratory work with industrial exploitation had to be taken in 1942. In Britain it was decided that industrial resources were inadequate, and the British effort was moved across the Atlantic. In the United States, America embarked on the multimillion-dollar Manhattan Project. In Germany, where the theoretical results were discussed at a high-level Berlin conference on June 4, 1942, the decision was the reverse. For a variety of reasons, Heisenberg and his colleagues had not been as successful in their theoretical work as the Allies. But they had achieved quite a lot: they had demonstrated the theoretical possibility of a weapon. Yet no serious attempt to move on to the higher ground of industrial production was now made. This was sensible enough. During the first two years of the war the Germans had been so militarily successful that no need for nuclear weapons was foreseen. But now the balance had swung too much the other way. "At the time," says Heisenberg of the 1942 meeting,

> the war situation was already too tense for long-term technical projects. An order is supposed to have been issued prohibiting technical developments which would require more than half a year for completion. This situation spared the German physicists the decision whether to plead for an attempt to produce atom bombs; they knew, on the basis of their technical experience, that such an attempt could not lead to success in less than three or four years. An attempt of this sort would have undoubtedly hastened German defeat, because the extensive manpower and materials necessary for it would have to be borrowed from other sources, thereby lessening the production of tanks and aeroplanes.

In addition there were two other reasons: Hitler could not be interested in nuclear fission; and the anti-Jewish purges of the previous decade had skimmed off from Germany too much of the country's scientific cream.

Heisenberg and his colleagues carried on. During the last months of the war he and the Kaiser Wilhelm Institute for Physics of which he had been made director in 1941 were evacuated to Hechingen, bringing the end of Germany's wartime nuclear fission story back to the little village where Elsa Einstein had been born. But they were still only at the stage of academic research—a fact which had become plain to an American mission in December, 1944. Code-named "Alsos"—a curious choice since "groves," its translation from the Greek, was a lead to General Groves of the Manhattan Project—it had followed up the Allied advance across Europe. With the capture of von Weizsäcker's papers in Strasbourg, it discovered that the Allies need fear no nuclear weapons from Germany. As Heisenberg himself said later, "Whatever one may think about the motives, it remains a fact that a serious attempt to produce atom bombs in Germany was not undertaken, although in principle—but perhaps not in practice—the path to it had been open since 1942."

It seems that this was the case. But clinching evidence, fortuitously provided, has been as fortuitously withheld. After the collapse of Germany in May, 1945, the leading German physicists who had been involved on nuclear research—Heisenberg, Hahn, and about a dozen others—were taken to France, and then unexpectedly brought to a house on the outskirts of Cambridge by Professor R. V. Jones, then director of scientific intelligence in the British Air Ministry. "I had them brought to Farm Hall," he has written, "to save them from a threat they never knew—for I had been told that an American general proposed to solve the problem of nuclear energy in postwar Germany by having them shot while they were still in 'Dustbin,' the special transit camp in France." In England their rooms were fitted with secret microphones. Their conversations were recorded and their reactions to the news of Hiroshima, provided by the radio, were taken down in detail. Small sections of the transcripts have been printed in English in General Groves' reminiscences; but the Germans have maintained that these are mistranslations. The original texts have not been made available—due largely, it appears, to British reluctance to admit that the incident ever took place.

During the closing months of 1944 information on the position of German nuclear research was made available in Washington to a few members of the Manhattan Project. It is most unlikely, says Goudsmidt, the Alsos leader, that Einstein was aware of it until well after the war. But Szilard was no doubt informed. And in the spring of 1945, Szilard began to ask himself, he records: "What is the purpose of continuing the development of the bomb, and how would the bomb be used if the war with Japan has not ended by the time we have the first bomb?" As in 1939, he wished to bring the matter to the notice of the President. As in 1939, he approached Einstein, visiting him in Princeton—and presumably being trailed by the Manhattan Project's intelligence agents, who followed him as they followed other leading members of the Project.

In Princeton Einstein gladly wrote another letter of introduction to the President. "Unusual circumstances which I shall describe further below induce me to take this action in spite of the fact that I do not know the substance of the considerations and recommendations which Dr. Szilard proposes to submit to you," he said. After recalling the circumstances of his approach in 1939, he continued.

> The terms of secrecy under which Dr. Szilard is working at present do not permit him to give me information about his work; however, I understand that he now is greatly concerned about the lack of adequate contact between scientists who are doing this work and those members of your cabinet who are responsible for formulating policy. In the circumstances I consider it my duty to give Dr. Szilard this introduction, and I wish to express the hope that you will be able to give his presentation of the case your personal attention.

Just how much additional information Einstein had by this time gained either from Stern or from others is not clear. But there is a significant statement given in the June, 1945, edition of the *Contemporary Jewish Record*. This contains an interview with Einstein which took place "shortly before" he retired from the institute in April,

1945, four months before the bombs on Japan. The interviewer asked "whether the disintegration of atoms would not soon be able to release the tremendous atomic energies for warfare." "Unhappily," Einstein replied, "such a possibility is not entirely in the utopian domain. When military art is able to utilize nuclear atomic energies it will not be houses or blocks of houses that will destroyed [*sic*] in a few seconds—it will be entire cities." Taken with the correspondence of the previous December, this suggests that Einstein's assumed ignorance of what Szilard's memorandum concerned was no more than a euphemism to protect the author from the allegation of having talked too much.

However, this does not mean that Einstein knew the details of Szilard's proposals. It is unlikely that he did. And this was probably just as well. For while the memorandum did question the use of the bomb in the war against Japan, it did so for reasons with which Einstein would not necessarily have sympathized. The consequence of its use, Szilard warned, might be that in the ensuing arms race the United States would lose its initial advantage. And he asked whether the chances of eventual international control of nuclear weapons might not be obtained "by developing in the next two years modern methods of production which would give us an overwhelming superiority in this field at the time when Russia might be approached."

Four months later Szilard was to be one of those who went clearly and unmistakably on record in opposition on moral grounds to the use of these bombs "in the present phase of the war." But the memorandum that Einstein supported was something different. "Scrambling his technology to cloak his reference to the hydrogen bomb," say the official U. S. historians, "Szilard divided atomic development into two stages.* The first was reaching fruition. If the United States were well along on the second when it approached Russia, the better the chances of success. If international control proved a vain hope, the worst possible course would be to delay developing the second stage." This, one feels, was not exactly what Ein-

*Dr. Gertrud Weiss Szilard, Leo Szilard's widow, questions the view that he was in fact referring to the hydrogen bomb.

stein had in mind as Szilard left Mercer Street in March with his letter to the President.

However, the effort was to be abortive as far as Roosevelt was concerned. Einstein's letter was dated March 25. "I decided to transmit the memorandum and the letter to the President through Mrs. Roosevelt, who once before had channeled communications from the Project to the President," Szilard has written. "I have forgotten now precisely what I wrote to Mrs. Roosevelt. I suppose that I sent her a copy of Einstein's letter—but not the memorandum. This I could not do. The memorandum I couldn't send her, because the memorandum would have been considered secret."

Mrs. Roosevelt gave Szilard an appointment for May 8. Shortly afterwards Szilard showed his memorandum to A. H. Compton, director of the Metallurgical Laboratory. "I hope that you will get the President to read this," he said. "Elated by finding no resistance where I expected resistance, I went back to my office," says Szilard. "I hadn't been in my office for five minutes when there was a knock on the door and Compton's assistant came in, telling me that he had just heard over the radio that President Roosevelt had died."

Some weeks later, Szilard took his memorandum to President Truman. Einstein's letter went too, but there is no evidence that it had any influence on Truman, who read Szilard's document and said: "I see now this is a serious matter." He then referred it to Byrnes, the new Secretary of State. "President Truman asked me to see Szilard, who came down to Spartanburg [South Carolina, Byrnes' home], bringing with him Dr. H. C. Urey and another scientist," Byrnes had written.

> As the Einstein letter had indicated he would, Szilard complained that he and some of his associates did not know enough about the policy of the government with regard to the use of the bomb. He felt that scientists, including himself, should discuss the matter with the cabinet, which I did not feel desirable. His general demeanor and his desire to participate in policy-making made an unfavorable impression on me, but his associates were neither as aggressive nor apparently as dissatisfied.

Szilard, like many other scientists who attempted to influence U. S. policy during the next few months, failed in his purpose. In the words of the Frank memorandum, signed by many of the Manhattan Project scientists, and as summarized in the official U. S. history, "statesmen who did not realize that the atom had changed the world were laying futile plans for peace while scientists who knew the facts stood helplessly by." And after July 16, when the nuclear weapon was successfully tested in the New Mexico desert, the statesmen went ahead with plans for its use over Japan.

Einstein left Princeton for his usual summer holiday. At Saranac on August 6 he heard on the radio the news that his earlier views had, indeed, been a mistake: a chain reaction had given a proof of his $E = mc^2$ far more spectacular than any given in the laboratory. To a *New York Times* reporter who visited Einstein's house to tell him the news, he said, "The world is not yet ready for it." It is also claimed by the editors of *Einstein on Peace* that he exclaimed: "Oh, weh!" At first he refused to make any public comment. Instead, Miss Dukas made a statement on his behalf. "Although it can be said that the professor thoroughly understands the fundamental science of the atomic bomb," this went, "military expediency demands that he remain uncommunicative on the subject until the authorities release details."

On August 11, he made his first public comment on the bomb, during a half-hour interview with Richard Lewis, an *Albany Times-Union* staff writer. He began by trying to damp down the hysteria which had swept the world. "In developing atomic or nuclear energy, science did not draw upon supernatural strength, but merely imitated the actions of the sun's rays," he said. "Atomic power is no more unnatural than when I sail a boat on Saranac Lake." He was asked about reports of secondary radiation which might cause sterilization or leukemia and answered: "I will not discuss that." He continued: "I have done no work on the subject, no work at all. I am interested in the bomb the same as any other person; perhaps a little more interested. However, I do not feel justified to say anything about it." He added that he thought it would be many years before atomic energy could be used for commercial purposes, but that substances other than uranium-235 might be found "and probably would be found" to accelerate its commercial use, an indication that he knew of the great U. S. achievement in manufacturing, on a commercial scale, the plutonium which had been used in the test bomb and in the second of those dropped on Japan. "You will do everyone a favor by not writing any story. I don't believe anyone will be interested," he concluded.

With this exhortation and belief he faced the future, unaware that within a few days the Smyth Report, issued in Washington, would describe the genesis of the American nuclear effort and reveal to the world at least some of the part he had played in it.

Einstein's wartime attitude towards the bomb has sometimes been described as muddled and ambivalent. It was, on the contrary, quite logical; once he had reluctantly agreed that force could only be met by force, as he had agreed in 1933, all the rest followed. When there seemed a chance that the Germans might be able to utilize a new weapon of frightening proportions it followed that he should encourage the United States to counter it—even though he personally rated the danger very slight. When, in the summer of 1940, the nuclear project seemed likely to be stillborn, it was natural that he should further urge the authorities into the action that produced the Manhattan Project. When he learned in the winter of 1944 that the new weapon was in fact a practical proposition, this must have seemed to justify his earlier action: what was possible in the United States might well be possible in the Third Reich. But when the war had been won, postwar control would be essential.

Later, as the background to the bombing of Hiroshima and Nagasaki began to be known, Einstein supported those scientists who claimed that the bombs should not have been used. This also followed. He agreed that force had to be met by force, and he supported the Allied bombing of German civilians as morally justified, yet he believed that justification could be stretched only to cover the minimum force necessary to achieve desired moral ends. On the facts available this did not include the Japanese bombings.

However, Einstein was the last man to wriggle. During the war he wrote to a conscientious objector saying that he had given up pacifism since he could maintain it only at the risk of allowing the whole world to fall into the hands of the most terrible enemies of mankind. "Organized power can be opposed only by organized power," he went on. "Much as I regret this, there is no other way." And twelve years later, replying to the Japanese journal *Kaizo* which had reproached him for involvement with nuclear weapons, he wrote: "While I am a convinced pacifist there are circumstances in which I believe the use of force is appropriate—namely, in the face of an enemy unconditionally bent on destroying me and my people."

It is not absolutely certain that he would have agreed, even reluctantly, with the use of nuclear weapons against Germany if only this could have prevented her conquest of the world; but it is a very strong assumption.

CHAPTER 21

THE CONSCIENCE OF THE WORLD

When the war with Japan ended in August, 1945, with the destruction of Hiroshima and Nagasaki by atomic bombs—and the threat of more to come although no more were yet ready—Einstein was sixty-six. He had officially retired from the Institute for Advanced Study in April, but the change in status was more formal than real. He still retained his study there. He still worked on, as he had for more than twenty years, at his search for the elusive field theory, always a step ahead of him like a scientific will-o'-the-wisp. In some ways he appeared to have shrunk back into the Einstein of pre-1914 days, an almost quaint survival of the day before yesterday, smiling to the Princeton children from his own private world, occupied only with his science and the ways in which the laws of nature were ordered.

He was still the symbol of relativity, but that was an old song, as distant from the world of the United Nations and postwar problems as Queen Victoria or the Louisiana Purchase. In 1933 he had been a symbol of the world's distaste for what was happening in Germany; a rallying point for Jewish efforts to deal with the practical problems of the refugees. But all that, too, was now part of the past. The world had eventually taken up arms, fought the good fight, and was now faced with the problem of clearing up the mess. A defeated Germany and a defeated Japan had to be dealt with, an Italy whose status was what you liked to make it had to be encouraged to work her passage back into the council of nations. In Palestine it was becoming more and more clear that the British would be unable to hold Arabs and Jews apart much longer, and a question mark hung over what was to follow the Mandate. Dominating all, there loomed the riddle of Russia's intentions and the grim thought that the worst of American and British suspicions might be justified. None of this seemed to belong to the world of Albert Einstein, a combination of the century's greatest brain and dear old gentleman.

The situation was transformed by the publication on August 11 of the Smyth Report—*Atomic Energy for Military Purposes*. The quiet recluse of Mercer Street suddenly became the man who had revolutionized modern warfare and upset both the applecart of military power and the accepted morality of war. What is more, the $E = mc^2$ of 1905 and the 1939 letter to President Roosevelt came from the man whose reputation in science had once been equaled by his position as a vociferous pacifist. This was some consolation to scientists who did not really like responsibility for the death of 120,000 civilians, even in the best of causes, and to the nonscientific population, most of whom were glad that the decision to drop the bombs was no business of theirs. The outcome was inevitable. Almost overnight Einstein became the conscience of the world.

As such he wrote, spoke, and broadcast throughout the ten years that remained to him. His attitude to all that had gone before August 6, 1945, was virtually limited to two points: the claim that his only action had been to sign a single letter to Roosevelt, and his statement that had he known about the Frank memorandum, pleading that the bomb should not be used on Japan without warning, then he would have supported it. Instead of holding an inquest on the past he looked to the future.

Towards the end of August, 1945, he had written a laudatory letter to Raymond Gram Swing of the American Broadcasting Company. This brought about a meeting between the two men. The result was Einstein's first major public statement on nuclear affairs, "Atomic War or Peace, by Albert Einstein as told to Raymond Swing." Although the "as told to" formula is often open to suspicion, there is no reason to doubt the accuracy of this example; Einstein's views as outlined to Swing were those which he held for the rest of his life. They are extremely revealing, not least in the parallel they show between his atttiude to the United Nations and to the League of Nations twenty years earlier.

Everything was in clear black and white. "I do not believe that the secret of the bomb should be given to the Soviet Union. . . . The secret of the bomb should be committed to a world government, and the United States should immediately announce its readiness to do so. Such a world government should be established by the United States, the Soviet Union, and Great Britain, the only three powers which possess great military strength." All the rest sprang from this: the invitation to the Russians to present the first draft of a world government, "since the United States and Great Britain have the secret of the atomic bomb and the Soviet Union does not"; and the power of the world government "to interfere in countries where a minority is oppressing the majority and, therefore, is creating the kind of instability that leads to war."

Einstein himself admitted in the same article that the current advantage of the United States and Britain was a wasting asset since "we shall not have the secret of the bomb for very long." And he admitted that conditions in Spain and the Argentine "should be dealt with since the abandonment of nonintervention in certain circumstances is part of keeping the peace." Each of these two qualifications drove a coach and horses through his main argument. If Russia would soon have "the secret," there would be no incentive for her to surrender her hard-earned sovereignty to a world government whose two other members she had every reason to distrust. And "dealing with" Spain—or with the Argentine—would mean an aggressive war which would have been given little support by any world government.

Here, as on other occasions, Einstein handed a weapon to his enemies. Shortly before publication of the *Atlantic Monthly* article, Representative John Rankin, a Mississippi politician of ultraconservative views, strongly attacked Einstein in the House of Representatives for allegedly supporting an anti-Franco organization. "This foreign-born agitator would have us plunge into another European war in order to further the spread of communism throughout the world," he claimed. ". . . . It is about time the American people got wise to Einstein." The slightly hysterical attack was off target since Einstein had made every effort to prevent the organization concerned from using his name. A few weeks later Rankin could more reasonably have asked how Spain could be "dealt with" without war.

However, this was a minor point when compared with Einstein's assumption that Russia would be willing to cooperate in the creation of a world government. In the prewar years, he had certainly condemned a Russia which denied the freedoms taken for granted in a democracy. But now the story was changed; now the heroic actions of the Red army, without which even the power of America might have been overstretched in the struggle against the Axis nations, blinded him to the facts of political life. Russia had been "the most loyal supporter of the League of Nations." He complained that the United States, on the question of supranational control of atomic energy, "made only a conditional proposition, and this on terms which the Soviet Union is determined not to accept." And when the defection of Igor Gouzenko laid bare the scope of Russian espionage in North America he complained, almost with an air of surprise, that this seemed to have adversely affected U. S.—Russian relations. He still criticized the Soviet Union; he still deplored her denial of academic and scientific freedom. But in his reactions to the grave nuclear problems of the immediate postwar years, he was unwilling to face the unpleasant truth: that Russia, far from being amenable to joining any supranational organization that genuinely wielded nuclear power, was determined to go it alone and get the bomb as well.

Not all physicists were so remote from real lfie. Szilard had revealed in his March, 1945, letter to Roosevelt that he had a keen awareness of practicalities; even Bohr, in many ways the epitome of the idealist with his head in the clouds, had been brushed by circumstances into hard contact with the reality of what could, and could not, be accomplished in the immediate postwar world. And Einstein's friend Bertrand Russell also shared the vision he lacked. "I have no hope of reasonableness in the Soviet government," Russell wrote to him on November 19, 1947, after Einstein had suggested alterations in a statement on nuclear weapons that Russell was preparing.

I think the only hope of peace (and that a slender one) lies in frightening Russia. I favored appeasement before

1939, wrongly, as I now think; I do not want to repeat the same mistake. . . . Generally, I think it useless to make any attempt whatever to conciliate Russia. The hope of achieving anything by this method seems to me "wishful thinking." I came to my present view of Soviet government when I went to Russia in 1920; all that has happened since has made me feel more certain that I was right.

Einstein's attitude was very different. Just how different was revealed by an interview which he gave in the summer of 1946 to Norman Thomas, the veteran socialist leader. Einstein personally approved a record of the interview which shows that in discussion of an international security force he "suggested that it might be well to have Russians in the service of the world organization stationed in America, and Americans stationed in Russia." An analogy was given of "the way in which the old Austro-Hungarian empire allocated the troops of the different nationalities comprising it." It is difficult to know whether public raising of the idea would have done world government more harm in the United States or in the Soviet Union.

Einstein's implied confidence that the Russians would cooperate is doubly surprising since he had only recently been given a good illustration of the reverse. He had agreed, together with a number of other scientists and intellectuals, to contribute to *One World or None*, a book designed to inform the American public of the new situation created by the bomb, and a message asking Russian scientists to do so was sent over his name to the president of the Academy of Sciences in Moscow. After considerable delay, and apparently much lobbying, the request was refused. President Vavilov, replying for those who had been asked, noted that "because of technical difficulties they are deprived of the possibility to express their concrete opinion with respect to the facts proposed for publication."

Any doubts about the Russian attitude were dispelled in November, 1947, after Einstein had written an "Open Letter to the General Assembly of the United Nations" for *United Nations World*. This called for a strengthening of the United Nations, criticized the veto with which the

Russians were hamstringing operations, and made a further plea for world government. Russian reaction came the following month in an Open Letter on "Dr. Einstein's Mistaken Notions. . . ," signed by four leading Russian scientists, including Vavilov and A. F. Joffé, Einstein's old friend of Berlin days. There was fulsome praise for Einstein, followed by a recapitulation of Russia's struggle against Allied intervention after the First World War, and of her fight against Germany in the Second. "And now," the letter continued, "the proponents of a 'world superstate' are asking us voluntarily to surrender this independence for the sake of a 'world government' which is nothing but a flamboyant signboard for the world supremacy of the capitalist monopolies."

The reply—regarded even by Einstein as a "semiofficial statement"—would have been enough to knock most men from the argument. Einstein hung on. But it is significant that when in April, 1948, the Emergency Committee of Atomic Scientists endorsed the idea of world government in a major policy statement, it noted that "this cannot be achieved overnight." Einstein had argued that something almost as instant was essential.

The Emergency Committee, the most prestigious of the early postwar bodies which attempted to guide the public into the nuclear age, was one over whose activities Einstein at first appears to have exercised considerable influence. He had been an early member of the National Committee on Atomic Information, formed to represent more than fifty educational, religious, and civic organizations. In 1946 this took on the job of satisfying the ever-growing demand for information about the real implications of the bomb. It was soon clear that this was a professional task demanding a new organization headed by an impressive name to give it moral and scientific standing. Harold Oram, a New York fund raiser, believed that $20,000 a month might be raised, and was soon in Princeton visiting Einstein. "What happened next is not entirely clear," says Alice Kimball Smith in her detailed analysis of the scientists' movement in America, *A Peril and a Hope.* "Perhaps Oram and Einstein together proposed an 'emergency committee,' though one observer suspects that the vagueness of the original proposals left Einstein somewhat out on a limb from which Szilard, Urey, and others united to rescue him." Whatever the details, the outcome was the Emergency Committee of Atomic Scientists, with Einstein as president and chairman of trustees. Harold Urey as vice-president and vice-chairman, and Szilard, Weisskopf, Linus Pauling, and Hans Bethe among the other trustees.

With headquarters in Princeton and offices in Chicago and Madison Avenue—the latter soon graced by the Epstein bust of Einstein—the committee went into action. On May 23, 1946, an appeal went out over Einstein's signature for $200,000 to be spent on "a nationwide campaign to inform the American people that a new type of thinking is essential if mankind is to survive and move toward higher levels," and less than a fortnight later he recorded a similar appeal for the newsreels. Later, in June, his views were given in a long interview with Michael Amrine published in the *New York Times*. It stressed the need for "a great chain reaction of awareness and communication," and made the point that to "maintain the threat of military power" was to "cling to old methods in a world which is changed forever." Soon afterwards came formal incorporation in the state of New Jersey of the Emergency Committee, followed by a conference in Princeton in November; and, early in 1947, another appeal over Einstein's name, this time for $1 million to enable the trustees "to carry to our fellow citizens an understanding of the simple facts of atomic energy and its implications for society." But the appeal also noted that "this basic power of the universe cannot be fitted into the outmoded concept of narrow nationalisms." Whether true or not, this immediately added political overtones to what was basically an appeal for educational funds, and produced a critical reaction from those who did not believe that peace would be made more secure by appeals to world government. Not all protests came from the backwoodsmen. Thus Dr. Charles G. Abbot of the Smithsonian Institution wrote to Einstein saying:

> A long life has satisfied me that the pledged word of treaties, public opinion, and confederations are all powerless to prevent unscrupulous leaders from aggressive measures. As for world government, I regard the very idea as chimerical for centuries to come. Also one country, now

> and for many years, has been at war with us by spying methods.
>
> Recognizing fully the truth of your two propositions *(a)* no secret *(b)* no defense (that is materially), I feel that our only chance lies in T. Roosevelt's famous saying "Walk softly but carry a big stick." That has a psychological power. . . .
>
> With these convictions, I think the Emergency Committee will be doing a disservice to this nation. For they will tend to cause people to rely on agreements, which will be broken reeds,—no better.

Another correspondent, arguing that the Russians would "continue to bicker and refuse to submit to any kind of disarmament and [would] insist on impossible demands from the Western world only to gain time to perfect their own weapons," claimed that the time to press demands for a genuinely free world had been when the Russians were hard put to it at Stalingrad.

Despite criticisms which made the most of the Emergency Committee's tendency, difficult to avoid, of mixing straight nuclear education with political implications, the work went on successfully until the immediate postwar need for it ended. The committee gave widespread support to educational work and kept the incomparable *Bulletin of the Atomic Scientists* afloat through a stormy financial period. As its chairman, Einstein in November, 1947, received the annual award of the Foreign Press Association "in recognition of his valiant efforts to make the world's nations understand the need of outlawing atomic energy as a means of war, and of developing it as an instrument of peace." He wrote, spoke, gave interviews, and drew on his often scanty reserves of health and energy to an extent which went beyond the call of duty. His output, always well intentioned and sometimes extremely percipient, if inevitably repetitious and usually unavailing, is well chronicled in *Einstein on Peace.*

Yet it is clear from the papers of the committee, as from the detailed analysis of the scientists' movement in America given by Alice Kimball Smith, that the effect of what Einstein said and did during this period was extremely limited. After the great wash of words subsided the breakwaters still remained. Weisskopf, a member of the committee, puts it this way: "I do not remember that

Einstein ever had any influence on our discussions. He very rarely took part in them. His only help was the influence of his name. He was not much informed about the details of the problems and tried to stay away from any decision-making discussions."

As far as the U. S. manufacture of the hydrogen bomb was concerned, Einstein's honesty combined with his common sense to limit his effectiveness. He was of course against it. But when asked to use his influence to delay the decision he replied that such an idea "seems to me quite impracticable. As long as competitive armament prevails, it will not be possible to halt the process in one country." As with immediate postwar control of atomic bombs, he saw the issue in all-or-nothing terms; and it was even more difficult to dissuade the authorities now than it had been to encourage them to carry out work "with greater speed and on a larger scale" in the spring of 1940.

Apart from his obsession for getting back to the scientific work forever playing round in his brain—as dominant now as it had been when in a letter to Weizmann he had qualified the hlep he could give Zionism*—Einstein's personal role was circumscribed by two other factors. One was his ignorance of the scientific-military machinery that had been built as the Manhattan Project grew from 1942 onwards. Szilard and Weisskopf and Bethe, as well as Compton and many others, knew how the machine worked. Einstein hardly knew what its parts were. This ignorance was compounded by his instinctive dislike of mixing with the men in command. As J. Robert Oppenheimer once put it, "he did not have that convenient and natural converse with statesmen and men of power that was quite appropriate to Rutherford and Bohr, perhaps the two physicists of this century who most nearly rivaled him in eminence."

Einstein's strength lay less in diplomatic haggling and compromise than in the bold imaginative gesture outside the normal round. Thus it is doubly galling that he should have missed by a hair's-breadth one great chance of making a decisive impact on the postwar nuclear debate. The chance was all but presented by Weizmann, who in December, 1945, conceived an ambitious idea for bringing

*See page 481.

Einstein to what was still Palestine. He planned to utilize Alexander Sachs, who had been brought in by Szilard six years previously, and if it was probably bad tactics to remind Einstein of the part he had played in prodding forward nuclear weapons, this is the only flaw in the scheme outlined in Weizmann's "Suggested Draft Letter to Professor Einstein." "Reflecting upon the impetus that you gave in 1939 to an enterprise that telescoped in a few years what otherwise might have taken a generation to accomplish," this said, "I have been moved to ask our good friend Alex to play once more an intermediary role and to submit to you some thoughts of mine regarding a unique service that I fervently hope you will find yourself in a position to render to the *Yishur* [general settlement] in Palestine and to the furtherance of science." The service was a visit to the country in the spring of 1946, and Weizmann quickly tried to deal with the obvious objections.

> Such a visit can be arranged to conform to the very requirements of your personal physician by assuring that the travel is direct from here to Haifa, that is, without any change, under the most comfortable accommodation available for yourself together with medical and other aides, not only for the journey but also in Palestine. For this we would consult with and be guided by what your physician recommends. Indeed, a stay of a month to six weeks in Palestine—say from the middle of April to the end of May—could be made to be beneficial for your health, as it would certainly tone up the body and the spirit of Jewry.

However, this was not all. The cornerstone of a new Institute of Science was to be laid that spring. "In connection with the inauguration of this institute," Weizmann went on,

> it has occurred to me that a select number of those who had contributed importantly to the telescoped fruition of atomic research and its application could be invited for the occasion, jointly by the Hebrew University and the Institute, and to contribute to a symposium on the import of that research for human progress and peace. Such a group to be selected, with your aid, as representative of the œcumenical order of science instead of only the nations

involved in the atomic bomb production, might thus issue from Palestine not only a synthesis of the current scientific view but a message "for the healing of the nations and humanity."

This was the grand scheme which Weizmann conceived. He finally wrote on December 28, and shortly afterwards the letter was in Sachs' hands. Sachs drove to Princeton, handed it over, and then took a short stroll with Einstein. During the walk they discussed the proposal, and on their return to Mercer Street Einstein said he would consider making the journey if Sachs would come too. "But then," says Sachs, "some twinge experienced by him and reflected in his face led him to say: 'But my poor health doesn't permit.' The letter was handed back to me. . . ."

But the rejected invitation contained only the first half of Weizmann's initial idea, the visit to Palestine. There was no mention of atomic research, of a symposium on the importance of nuclear research for human progress and peace, or of a message "for the healing of the nations and humanity." What Einstein rejected was the idea of a simple visit—thinking, no doubt, of "the ado and the fuss and the consequent duties" which he had spoken of to Schrödinger in 1934. Whether he would have rejected the more significant appeal is another matter.

Einstein's influence on the development of postwar nuclear attitudes was thus at first glance a good deal less than mythology suggests. His ideas for world government, in which he wrapped up so tightly the solution of the nuclear dilemma, were considered wildly impractical by those with experience of day-to-day international relations, while those who favored them rarely appreciated that they rested on force as surely as the policies of the Pentagon or the Kremlin. The hamstringing of the May-Johnson Bill, which would have put nuclear energy in the hands of the military and which Einstein disliked, was largely the work of men from the Manhattan Project, spurred on by Szilard. And it is difficult to point to any one act of government, any decisive swing of public opinion, and unhesitatingly declare: "Without Einstein, things would have been different."

Yet Einstein was, to most, the one figure inextricably linked with the bomb, the man who sincerely regretted the way in which it had been used. His name still caught the eye. Even without the resplendent halo of hair which made him a photographer's delight, he retained more than a touch of the guru. Ordinary people listened to him. So, to varying extents, did the men who were in the front line of the postwar battle to control nuclear energy. It was not a popular battle to fight and it was one in which their opponents could summon up—with different degrees of justification—patriotism, common sense, and the will of the people. It was fortifying, therefore, that they could count on the moral support of a man like Einstein; however wooly his proposals for action might be, he was a man whom most people felt, and usually with good reason, sensed right from wrong with almost uncanny intuition. Therefore it would not be right to underrate the unrecorded influence that Einstein may well have had on others: although he can be credited with no great victory, his mere presence added to the moral muscle of those who claimed that the great issues of nuclear weapons should be argued out with reason rather than emotion. Thus there are two perfectly defendable views of Einstein's influence on nuclear thinking during the postwar decade. He did more than his adversaries claimed even if he did less than his well-wishers sometimes imagine.

Einstein's concern with the nuclear debate logically drew him out into two other discussions which spread across America as scientists discovered themselves unexpectedly in the corridors of power and as the nation began to argue about the new situation which had been created. One dealt with the social responsibilities of science and scientists; the other with civil liberties and academic freedom, a subject which grew in importance as the rights and wrongs of nuclear rearmament became inextricably entangled with both national and international politics.

As far as science was concerned, the nature of Einstein's work had from the early days tended to shield him from the ways in which science could be exploited for good or evil. For him science was an investigation of the laws of nature. Certainly his old friend Haber exploited these laws in the cause of gas warfare, but that was surely only a temporary aberration? Surely the "small group of scholars and intellectuals" whom he had described to Ehrenfest in 1915 as forming "the only 'fatherland' which is worthy of serious concern to people like ourselves," was a group which must be above the battle?

This attitude had begun to change in the years that immediately followed the First World War. The movement was speeded up by the coming of the Nazis, and when even his good friend von Laue told him in 1933 "that the scientist should observe silence in political matters, i.e., human affairs in the broader sense," he had been forced to reply that he did not share the view. The evolution continued. From regarding scientists as a group almost aloof from the rest of the world, he began to consider them first as having responsibilities and rights on a level with the rest of men, and finally as a group whose exceptional position demanded the exercise of exceptional responsibilities. "By painful experience," he wrote in a message to the World Congress of Intellectuals held in Wroclaw (Breslau) in 1948,

> we have learned that rational thinking does not suffice to solve the problems of our social life. . . . We scientists, whose tragic destiny it has been to help make the methods of annihilation ever more gruesome and more effective, must consider it our solemn and transcendent duty to do all in our power in preventing these weapons from being used for the brutal purpose for which they were invented. What task could possibly be more important to us? What social aim could be closer to our hearts?*

"The bomb" lay at the heart of the problem. But Einstein well knew that the position of the scientist in society had been radically altered by other developments and that in many fields other than nuclear physics new guidelines had to be drawn. Here his views were realistic rather than starry-eyed. Just as he saw science and religion as complementary, one searching for the "whats" while the other sought the "whys," so did he look upon an understanding of science as necessary to good govern-

*Einstein's friend, Otto Nathan, took the message to the Congress. The tone of the meeting was anti-American and Nathan was asked to delete a number of passages from Einstein's message, notably those dealing with the need for a supranational organization. He refused. The organizers thereupon read as "Einstein's message" a totally different letter which he had previously written to the Franco-Polish Organizing Committee.

ment. But he was willing to render unto Caesar only those things which were Caesar's; and he would have experienced little of the fashionable shock at the view that scientists should be "on tap but not on top." Einstein's own position was put squarely in his address at the Nobel anniversary dinner in New York in December, 1945. "We physicists are not politicians, nor has it ever been our wish to meddle in political affairs," he said. "However, we happen to know a few things that the politicians do not know, and we feel it our duty to speak up and remind those in responsible positions that there can be no easy escape into indifference; that there is no time left for petty bargaining and procrastination." Yet Einstein himself provides no guide to the place that scientists should or should not occupy outside their own fields. Einstein was, even more obviously than most human beings, a one-off model. His genius was linked with attributes not only of the saint but also of the rogue elephant, and scientists in government, at whatever level they operate or advise, must be counter-balanced by the more humdrum qualities. As Rutherford showed, they need not lack the sparks of the great imaginative mind; as Szilard showed, they can retain a quirkiness fringing on eccentricity. But if they are to serve without disaster they must have something less than Einstein's white-hot fanaticism and must devote more time than he did to ordinary men and women.

On academic freedom, on the right of minorities to disagree, and on what he considered the almost sacred duty of dissent, emotion tied in with intellect, for his life had been marked by a long series of rear-guard actions in support of temporarily retreating causes. In Germany, between the wars, his attitude was epitomized by the Gumbel case in which he publicly supported the pacifist professor of Heidelberg University's department of philosophy, almost harried from his post by nationalist attacks. In the United States, after 1945, he threw his support wholeheartedly behind those who defied the draft law on grounds of conscience and, later, those who refused to incriminate themselves before the House Un-American Activities Committee. But the editors of *Einstein on Peace* have stressed that "Einstein, who passionately defended the intellectual and moral freedom of the individual, frequently emphasized with equal conviction the obligations which a truly free individual must assume toward the community of which he is an integral part." Thus the long list of cases and letters which they quote exhibits a splendid reserve. Einstein is as careful to be fair, to hold the balance between individual and public interest, as he had been almost forty years earlier when helping to draw up the "Manifesto to Europeans."

Not until 1953 did he at last boil over. The case was that of William Frauenglass, a Brooklyn teacher called to give evidence before one of the congressional committees investigating political beliefs and associations. Frauenglass approached Einstein and Einstein replied with a letter which he said "need not be considered 'confidential.' " It was published in the *New York Times* on June 12 and its point was made in three central paragraphs. "The problem with which the intellectuals of this country are confronted is very serious," he began.

> Reactionary politicians have managed to instill suspicions of all intellectual efforts into the public by dangling before their eyes a danger from without. Having succeeded so far, they are now proceeding to suppress the freedom of teaching and to deprive of their positions all those who do not prove submissive, i.e., to starve them out.
>
> What ought the minority of intellectuals to do against this evil? Frankly, I can only see the revolutionary way of noncooperation in the sense of Gandhi's. Every intellectual who is called before one of the committees ought to refuse to testify, i.e., he must be prepared for jail and economic ruin, in short, for the sacrifice of his personal welfare in the interests of the cultural welfare of his country.
>
> However, this refusal to testify must not be based on the well-known subterfuge of invoking the Fifth Amendment against possible self-incrimination, but on the assertion that it is shameful for a blameless citizen to submit to such an inquisition and that this kind of inquisition violates the spirit of the Constitution.

The claim that it is wrong to obey the law when it is a really bad one brought down on Einstein's head the anticipated bucketload of hot coals. The *New York Times* said in an editorial that "to employ the unnatural and illegal forces of civil disobedience, as Professor Einstein advises, is in this case to attack one evil with another." A majority of papers followed suit, while in academic circles support was less than Einstein might have expected. "If enough people are ready to take this grave step," he had concluded after advocating a refusal to testify, "they will be successful. If not then the intellectuals of this country deserve nothing better than the slavery which is intended for them."

He continued to be unhappy and in November, 1954, commenting on *The Reporter's* articles on the situation of scientists in America, made one of his most quoted statements: "If I would be a young man again and had to decide how to make my living, I would not try to become a scientist or scholar or teacher. I would rather choose to be a plumber or a peddler in the hope to find that modest degree of independence still available under present circumstances." This brought down a rebuke for being so willing to abandon the scientific ship. He replied in a letter published only after his death. "I want to suggest," he said,

> that the practices of those ignoramuses who use their public positions of power to tyrannize over profesional intellectuals must not be accepted by intellectuals without a struggle. Spinoza followed this rule when he turned down a professorship at Heidelberg and (unlike Hegel) decided to earn his living in a way that would not force him to mortgage his freedom. The only defense a minority has is passive resistance.

Just where some of the intellectuals stood was not quite clear and earlier in the year there had been an incident whose significance was not appreciated at the time. On March 13, 1954, some 200 educators, clergymen, and authors met in Princeton for a conference on "The Meaning of Academic Freedom," held by the Emergency Civil Liberties Committee in observance of Einstein's seventy-fifth birthday the following day. He answered, in writing, a number of questions which had been put to him. But he did not attend the conference, held in the Nassau Inn only a few hundred yards from Mercer Street. Norman Thomas, the veteran socialist leader, has given a clue to the reason. Thomas had intervened in the celebrations, he has written, at the request both of the American Committee for Cultural Freedom and the American Jewish Committee, and with the approval of J. Robert Oppenheimer, the Director of the Institute for Advanced Study. At that juncture in American affairs, he has said, there was worry that Dr. Einstein's name would be exploited, not for the defense of civil liberties but for the aggrandizement of a committee, some of whose members and spokesmen were stated to have been at last pretty indiscriminate apologists for communism. Almost to the end Einstein remained the object of manipulation and countermanipulation.

Thus on the central problem of the bomb, which had transformed the world even though the world was reluctant to admit it, on the responsibilities of science and the academic freedom to discuss what should be done about them, his attitude was forecastable and clearcut. As the conscience of the world he might be naïve but he was morally impregnable. But Einstein was also the German who had turned from his country twice, the German Jew who was appalled at the way the Germans had treated the Jews. Here, if anywhere, was the touchstone of how he really felt about the human race. And here, as he had written to Ehrenfest in another context thirty years previously, "impulse was stronger than judgment." Here Einstein, as though reflecting the dichotomy that so often marks his life, succeeded in matching white with black. His first impulse, conditioned by the Luitpold Gymnasium if not entirely governed by it, and certainly remembered with disadvantages through the years, had been to detest the Prussians and the Prussian spirit, an attitude which during the First World War had substituted "German" for "Prussian." A transformation had been worked by Weimar and reinforced by the events of the immediate postwar year, so that by September, 1919, he was writing that it was "*a priori* incredible that the inhabitants of a whole great country should be branded as morally inferior." Soon he was subordinating early impulse to fresh judgment, stressing how wrong it was to categorize men by the places in which they had been born. And throughout the 1920s, shunning Solvay because Germans were excluded as Germans, happy to be fêted in Berlin as the republic's unofficial ambassador returned from America and Britain, innocently thinking that bygones were bygones, Einstein became a symbol of the international man for whom condemnation of a nation as a nation was a mistake as much as a crime.

The coming of Hitler brought impulse to the fore again. With the fervor of all lapsed converts, Einstein once more began to see the problem in terms of unshaded black and white. "The Germans," he told one visitor seeking his views in 1935, "are cruel. No people in the world take such delight in cruelty as they do. I thought I knew Germans, but during the past two years I have learned to know better the cruelty of which they are capable." After Hitler had reoccupied the Rhineland, he wrote that "Germans believe in an unwritten tradition that good faith and compliance with agreements should be practiced only among themselves, but are not extended to foreigners and foreign countries." And, forgetting his own reactions to Weimar, he noted of Germany that "The nation has been on the decline mentally and morally since 1870." The outbreak of war reinforced his feeling. "Behind the Nazi party," he said, "stands the German people, who elected Hitler after he had in his book and in his speeches made his shameful intentions clear beyond the possibility of misunderstanding." And asked what educational measures should be taken in Germany after the war, he had a simple reply: "The Germans can be killed or constrained, but they cannot be re-educated to a democratic way of thinking and acting within a foreseeable period of time."

All this was understandable, even if it was not rational. In wartime it had a stern plausibility, and the horrors of the concentration camps revealed by the defeat of Germany did not make it less so. Yet if the catalogue of war and recrimination was not to continue forever, generation by generation, someone had to stretch a hand across the gap that appeared to separate two different kinds of human and discover what was reality and what mirage. Two decades back Einstein had not looked on "reconciliation" as a dirty word.

Yet now, with the peace, his black detestation of all things German reasserted itself. It was not only the rearming of Germany as a providentially supplied weapon against Russia that he detested. That was enough to stick in the gullets of many decent men. Einstein's detestation went deeper, was more irrational, ignored the forgiveness of both Jews and Germans who had suffered far more than he. At heart, perhaps he could never forgive the fact that he himself had been born a German. The result looks today like a deep chink in his humanity.

He thought it was essential to prevent Germans from obtaining great political power and noted that "this cannot be accomplished if the Germans are once more allowed to own and exploit their raw materials resources without outside control." And the Einstein who had resigned from the League committee when the French marched into the Ruhr now wrote: "If the Ruhr is left to the Germans the terrible sacrifices of the English-speaking world will have been in vain." Einstein, with Morgenthau, would have been happy to see the Reich transformed from an industrial nation into an agricultural country, and his old friend James Franck, appealing for a relaxation of postwar restraints in Germany, received a dusty answer: "I am firmly convinced that it is absolutely indispensable to prevent the restoration of German industrial power for many years," he was told. ". . . I firmly object to any attempt from Jewish quarters to reawaken the kind of soft sentimental feelings which permitted Germany to prepare a war of aggression without any interference on the part of the rest of the world—and this long before the Nazis came to power. . . . Should your appeal be circulated, I shall not fail to do whatever I can to oppose it." And the merest hint that Churchill, not notably soft on the Germans, might let them work their passage back to respectability brought a brusque comment in a letter to Janos Plesch. "Cannot you see to it that your Churchill is put into cold storage until the next national calamity," he wrote. "Otherwise his activity will cause one unnecessarily."

His attitude towards Germany at the personal level was even more revealing than his views on the position that the country should occupy in the postwar world. Its tone was set in his uncompromising reply to Arnold Sommerfeld, who in October, 1946, invited him to rejoin the Bavarian Academy. "It was a real joy for me to receive your letter after all these dark years," Einstein replied. "None of us would have dreamed of all the horror we have been through." He went on, "The Germans slaughtered my Jewish brethren; I will have nothing further to do with them, not even with a relatively harmless academy. I feel differently about the few people who, insofar as it was possible, remained steadfast against Nazism. I am happy to learn that you were among them." Others were presumably von Laue and Planck, as well as Hahn and Heisenberg, by now president and director respectively of the Max Planck Institute with which the Allied occupation authorities had replaced the Kaiser Wilhelm Institute.

Otto Hahn himself asked whether Einstein would become a foreign member of the new organization. He was met with a firm "No." Although Hahn was "one of the few men who remained decent," Einstein said, "the conduct of the German intellectuals—seen as a group—was no better than that of the mob." He refused to become an honorary member of a society much after his own heart, the German Association of World Government. He refused to become an honorary citizen of Ulm, or of West Berlin. His resolution was shown in a letter written by his secretary about a German Foreign Office official. "As he did not resign from his office when Hitler came to power," she said, "Professor Einstein has no interest in him whatsoever—despite his Jewish wife." And when President Heuss told him of plans to reform the Peace Section of the former Prussian order "Pour le Mérite," he was told by Einstein: "Because of the mass murder which the Germans inflicted upon the Jewish people, it is evident that a self-respecting Jew could not possibly wish to be associated in any way with any official German institution. The renewal of my membership in the Pour le Mérite order is therefore out of the question."

The same unforgiving spirit was shown in a letter to his old friend Born in September, 1950. "I have not changed my attitude to the Germans which, by the way, dates not just from the Nazi period," this went. "All human beings are more or less the same from birth. The Germans, however, have a far more dangerous tradition than any of the other so-called civilized nations. The present behavior of these other nations towards the Germans merely proves to me how little human beings learn from their most painful experiences." And two years later, when Born retired from his post at Edinburgh and moved to Bad Pyrmont in northern Germany, he was taken to task for "migrating back to the land of the mass murderers of our kinsmen." Born, noting that the German Quakers had their headquarters in Bad Pyrmont, replied in a letter that contained two points. "They are no mass murderers," he said, and "many of our friends there suffered far worse thing under the Nazis than you or I." And then, no doubt remembering his own refusal to work on nuclear weapons and Einstein's letter to Roosevelt, he went on: "The Americans have demonstrated in Dresden, Hiroshima, and Nagasaki that in sheer speed of extermination they surpass even the Nazis."

This was perhaps a failure to compare like with like; and Einstein's feelings, like Born's, were those of the now-distant 1950s. Memories of the gas chambers, of Dresden and Hiroshima, were then stronger. Some of Einstein's friends, putting in a plea of mitigation for his attitude, believe that maybe a few more years would have made a difference. Later events might, just possibly, have discouraged what was dangerously near an inverted *Herrenvolk* doctrine that appealed to race as much as to the history of that last 100 years. In particular, Einstein might have been swayed—irrationally, but swayed nevertheless—by the eventual accession to power of the Social Democrats. He had been swung round full circle in 1919 and although he later wrote that "the postwar democratic constitution of the Weimar Republic fitted the German people about as well as the giant's clothes fitted Tom Thumb," he might well have admitted that Brandt's Germany could turn over a new leaf, a concession he would never give to Adenauer's or to Ulbricht's.

This is possible; but it looks unlikely. By the end of the Second World War Einstein was refusing to see Hitler as the scapegoat of the popular papers; what was wrong was not a madman but that such a figure could express the will of the thousands burning deep. What he had experienced at the Luitpold Gymnasium was not the exception but the norm. If he thought back seriously to the halcyon days of Weimar, when for a few years it seemed that a new Germany was rising from the old, he thought also of the old saying, "Once bitten, twice shy." Even had he experienced a twinge of doubt, even had he started to be influenced by Born's arguments, by the dictates of common sense or by the growing evidence of a postwar German spirit very different from the old, he might have thought it wrong to change his stance. By now he was too much a symbol of all that Jewry had suffered at Germany's hands; by now, for Einstein, reason would have been treason.

It was in this frame of mind that in the autumn of 1947 he heard of the death of Max Planck, that servant of the state whose first son had been killed at Verdun and whose second had been executed by his own countrymen after the attempt to kill Hitler in 1944. Einstein's attitude was curiously in contrast to that of Born. The physicist who had returned to live in "the land of mass murderers" wrote somewhat critically of Planck as the man in whom "the Prussian tradition of service to the state and allegiance to the government was deeply rooted . . . I think he trusted that violence and oppression would subside in time and everything return to normal. He did not see that an irreversible process was going on." Einstein remembered another side to Planck. He had, significantly enough, not written to him since the end of the war. Now the man who hated the Prussian spirit wrote to the widow of the man who typified at least some elements of that spirit.

"Your husband has come to the end of his days after doing great things and suffering bitterly," he wrote.

> It was a beautiful and fruitful period that I was allowed to live through with him. His gaze was directed on eternal truths, yet he played an active part in all that concerned humanity and the world around him. How different, and how much better it would be for mankind, if there were more like him. But this cannot be; it seems that fine characters in every age and continent must remain apart from the world, unable to influence events.
>
> The hours which I was allowed to spend in your house, and the many close conversations which I had with your dear husband, will remain among my happiest memories for the rest of my life. Nothing can alter the fact that a tragic event has affected us both. May you draw comfort in your days of loneliness from the thought that you brought happiness and contentment into the life of your respected husband. From this distant place I share your grief and greet you with all the former affection.

When it came to Planck, and to the scientific spirit that he stood for, it was as if the years between 1913 and 1947 had not existed. Even so, it was a generous letter.

Yet Einstein, who ruled out any reconciliation between

Germany and the rest of the world in general, let alone between Germany and the Jews, still hoped for something comparable between Jews and Arabs. For this reason he had campaigned against the creation of yet another nation-state, putting his views clearly in one typical statement to the National Labor Committee for Palestine. "My awareness of the essential nature of Judaism resists the idea of a Jewish state with borders, an army, and a measure of temporal power, no matter how modest," he said. "I am afraid of the inner damage Judaism will sustain—especially from the development of a narrow nationalism within our own ranks, against which we have already had to fight strongly, even without a Jewish state." But in the postwar world other ethnic and religious groups were trying to give themselves the covering of political independence. Now it was certain that a Jewish state would arise from the ruins of the Mandate.

Nor was this all. With the British desperately trying to restrict immigration during the last months of their control, extremists increasingly took the law into their own hands. It was not only the rise of Hitler that justified the use of force; in Palestine the situation quickly degenerated into guerrilla warfare. And now Einstein decided to swallow his pacifism once again.

In the spring of 1948 Lina Kocherthaler, Einstein's cousin in Montevideo, was approached by those wishing to raise funds for the Haganah, the Jewish resistance movement in Palestine. Would Einstein send them a letter which could be sold by auction? Einstein not only replied by return mail, on May 4, 1948, ten days before the end of the Palestine Mandate, but enclosed a declaration headed: "To my Jewish brothers in Montevideo" which revealingly outlines his position.

> If we wait until the Great Powers and the United Nations fulfill their commitments to us then our Palestinian brothers will be under the ground before this is accomplished. These people have done the only thing possible in the present deplorable conditions of the world. They have taken their destiny in their own hands and fought for their rights. This they may be able to do successfully in the long run, if the rest of the world's Jews help them. Our Palestinians show themselves in this just as capable and resolute as in the economic field.

> On the destiny of our Palestinians will depend, in the long run, the destiny of the remaining Jews in the world. For no one respects or bothers about those who do not fight for their rights. We may regret that we have to use methods which are repulsive and stupid to us, methods of which the human race has not yet been able to free itself. But to help bring about better conditions in the international sphere, we must first of all maintain our existence by all means at our disposal.

On the arrival of this letter it was decided to form in Montevideo a committee of Jewish academics, and to hold a banquet at which the letter could be auctioned. The banquet was on July 17; and most of the money—roughly $5,000—came from the buyer of the Einstein letter.

Thus the instinctive pacifist was once more driven into admitting that force was necessary. Further, the arms which he detested were now to create a nation-state which he believed to be contrary to genuine Jewish needs. "In this last priod of the fulfillment of our dreams there was but one thing that weighed heavily upon me," he said in a statement to the Hebrew University in 1949; "the fact that we were compelled by the adversities of our situation to assert our rights through force of arms; it was the only way to avert complete annihilation." This regret, mixed with perplexity at the juxtaposition of good ends and evil means, remained with him for the rest of his life. With his failure to move opinion an inch along the road to nuclear control through world government, and his refusal to budge from an almost draconian approach to Germany, it completes a trilogy. Only science mitigated these tragedies, a field in which he was both humble enough to see his life as a link in a long chain, and confident enough to know that he had been essential.

CHAPTER 22

TWO STARS AT THE END OF THE ROCKET

Einstein's nonscientific interests after the Second World War were parallel to those which followed the war of 1914–18. Then he had wanted to abolish all weapons, to bring Germany back into the comity of Europe and help create a Jewish homeland that would not be a nation-state; now his aims were control of nuclear weapons, a Germany safe within an economic straitjacket, and the survival of Israel. There were other comparisons which suggest that outside science as well as inside it, Einstein would always be cast as the lonely and tragic figure. Not least was the feeling that America of the later 1940s was tying him with the bonds he had first felt in the Germany of the 1920s. The country of his adoption seemed to be going the same way as the country of his birth.

Pessimism about America, an intuitive fear for its future, developed in Einstein long before it was felt by most of his American colleagues. There was reason enough for this. He worked on at the institute as he had worked on at the Kaiser Wilhelm. He listened to the distortions of his own stand on nuclear weapons much as he had listened to descriptions of the General Theory as part of an international Jewish conspiracy. And as Senator Joseph McCarthy swam into power, kept afloat on a sea of ignorance, he no doubt remembered that "the great masses of the people . . . will more easily fall victims to a great lie than to a small one." The whole scene began to look uncomfortably familiar.

"America," he wrote to Janos Plesch in the autumn of 1947, "has changed pretty much since 1928. It has become pretty military and aggressive. The fear of Russia is the means of making it digestible to the plebs. As one of the younger Don Quixotes I preach against it even here, but without any prospect of success." Not only was there no prospect of success, but his reaction to the pressures which built up as the cold war grew in intensity made him again the target for attack. In Germany he had thought of emigration many times before he had been forced to go. Now, according to his relatives in South America, to whom he confided his feelings and fears in a long series of intimate letters, he "considered leaving the United States and finding another home in which scholarship and the things of the spirit were guaranteed more freedom."

He decided to stay. One cannot be sure how serious was his thought of emigrating once again. But however deep his misgivings about America, however strongly he at times felt that the lunatic fringe was in control, he retained some faith that the country would eventually solve its dilemmas without the episodes of self-destruction which seemed such a recurrent feature of German history. He hoped on, so that five years after his Don Quixote letter to Plesch, he could write to him more equably. I still lose my temper dutifully about politics," he said, "but I no longer flap my wings—I only ruffle my feathers. The majority of fools remain invincible." He had got over the hump. He was determined to stick it out in Princeton, and a note of resignation was beginning to creep into his letters. "It is a curious drama in which we all appear," he wrote to his cousin Lina in South America, a relative on the Koch side of the family; "good, when one does not take it too seriously. The play has neither beginning nor end and only the players change." And to Fräulein Markwalder, the daughter of his old landlady in Zurich, with whom he had sailed on the Zurichsee half a century before: "I have been in America now for seventeen years without having adopted anything of this country's mentality. One has to guard against becoming superficial in thought and feeling; it lies in the air here. You have never changed your human surroundings and you can hardly realize what it is to be an old gypsy. It is not so bad."

Attempts were made to coax him to Israel. "He said he was too old," reports Brodetsky, who visited him in 1948. "I told him that according to Jewish tradition, as he was only sixty-nine, he had another fifty-one years to live to reach the age of Moses. He repeated that he was too old.

But I could see that he had many other claims at Princeton."

Quite apart from claims—notably those of people with whom he still worked at the institute—there were ties, the most important being his own poor health. Since the breakdown of 1928, when he was approaching his fiftieth birthday, he had been forced to take life more easily. His smoking which had always been strictly rationed by Elsa, was now more drastically cut. He compromised by keeping a tiny pipe and tobacco hidden in his desk, and would occasionally be tempted to half-fill it. Then he would go outside and borrow a match—not a box, for that would be too tempting and sinful, but a single match with which he might or might not get the pipe going. He had also been put on first a fat-free and later a salt-free diet by Dr. Ehrmann, his regular Berlin doctor who had emigrated to New York before the war. Einstein hated it all, but he was never one to kick against the pricks, and his good-humored resignation comes out in two incidents.

When a box of candy was being passed round after dinner at Mercer Street one night he took merely a deep sniff. "You see, that's all my doctor allows me to do," he said. "The devil has put a penalty on all things we enjoy in life. Either we suffer in our health, or we suffer in our soul, or we get fat." A friend asked him why it was the devil and not God who had imposed the penalty. "What's the difference?" he answered. "One has a plus in front, the other a minus." On another occasion his doctor came to Mercer Street with medicine in the form of both pills and drops, not knowing which his patient would prefer. He chose the drops. "I still remember him standing there, counting the drops into a water glass and handing it over to Einstein," says a colleague. "He swallowed the whole thing down, then turned a little green in the face, and started to throw up. After that he turned to his doctor and asked him: 'Do you feel better now?' "

Until 1945 his poor health was inconvenient rather than crippling. But ever since his illness in 1917 he had suffered periodically from stomach cramp, nausea, and vomiting, and in 1945 it was decided that an operation was necessary. He recovered normally but was much weakened and even by the end of the following year still found it necessary to take a rest after lunch. In 1948 a second operation in the Brooklyn Jewish Hospital revealed an aneurysm in the main artery and two years later an examination showed that the condition had worsened. From 1950 Einstein knew that time was running out.

The threat made little difference. He was as careless of himself now as he had been as a youth or in the hungry days of the First World War. As long as he could get on with his work nothing else mattered. He got on with it relentlessly and with an inner determination which contrasted strongly with the outer picture of a frail old man. Those who saw him in his working habitat were impressed. "One unforgettable memory," says a visitor during these last years,

> is of Einstein slightly ill and forced to keep to his bed. It occupied almost the entire room. The blinds were drawn. The light attached to the head of the bed lit up the back of his head and the board on which were the sheets of paper which he covered with lines of regular writing. He was covered with an eiderdown from which his naked body emerged at one end and his feet at the other. The picture was that of an impressive Rembrandt.

The slow but steady deterioration in his condition would alone have tied him to Princeton. But there was also his work. Here his principal worry was still the removal of indeterminacy from physics, which had been the main epistemological result of quantum mechanics, a result which to the end of his life he continued to regard as merely transitory. He suffered from no illusions. He knew that he was fighting a rearguard action against his colleagues, and he had no doubts about how they regarded him. To Conrad Habicht, a survivor of the Olympia Academy, he wrote in 1948: "I still work indefatigably at science but I have become an evil renegade who does not wish physics to be based on probabilities."

And with Max Born he continued to discuss, in the greatest detail, and with an almost pathetic attempt to reconcile the irreconcilable, the chasm which had opened up between him and so many of his contemporaries. The two men had been intimates since 1916. They had agreed to differ in the twenties; unknown to both, their paths had diverged when Einstein had helped launch the U. S. nuclear weapons project and Born had refused to join the British enterprise. They differed over the Germans. Yet they remained mutual fathers-confessor for their hopes and fears in physics, and it was to Born that Einstein gave the fullest explanation of how he saw the situation during the last decade of his life. "I cannot make a case for my attitude in physics which you would consider at all reasonable," he wrote.

> I admit, of course, that there is a considerable amount of validity in the statistical approach which you were the first to recognize clearly as necessary, given the framework of the existing formalism. I cannot seriously believe in it because the theory cannot be reconciled with the idea that physics should represent a reality in time and space, free from ghostly actions at a distance. I am, however, not yet firmly convinced that it can really be achieved with a continuous field theory, although I have discovered a possible way of doing this which so far seems quite reasonable. The difficulties of calculation are so great that I will be biting the dust long before I myself can be fully convinced of it. But I am quite convinced that someone will eventually come up with a theory, whose objects, connected by laws, are not probabilities but considered facts, as was until recently taken for granted. I cannot, however, base this conviction on logical reasons, but can only produce my little finger as witness, that is I offer no authority which would be able to command any kind of respect outside of my own hand.

This stubborn belief continued to keep him the outsider, the old man mirroring the young rebel who had dared claim that light could be both wave and corpuscle and that time and space were not what they seemed to be. There were occasions when he was humorously sceptical of what was going on in science. Thus at his seventieth birthday celebrations he sat all day in the lecture hall of the institute listening to a series of invited papers, and at the end was asked if he had found them tiring. "They would have been tiring if I had understood them," he replied.

Yet it was accepted that few men knew as much as Einstein about the nature of the physical world. Few were to have one of the new artificially created elements named after them, the einsteinium which as the ninety-ninth was added to lawrencium, mendelevium, fermium, and curium—and was later joined by rutherfordium and hahnium. Even fewer knew as much about the spurs to creative scientific activity, and it followed as a matter of course that when Aydelotte retired from the directorship of the institute in 1947, Lewis Strauss, one of the trustees, should seek his advice on a successor. Einstein would neither comment on the names put forward nor himself suggest any candidates. "I besought him to tell me, at the very least, what ideal qualities the trustees should seek in a director of the institute," Strauss has written." 'Ah, that I can do easily,' he replied with a smile. 'You should look for a very quiet man who will not disturb people who are trying to think.' "

He might succeed in recommending a quiet man—it turned out to be J. Robert Oppenheimer—but his powers failed when it came to persuading the institute to invite Max Born to Princeton. And Born, however hard he tried, could never coax Einstein back across the Atlantic. Thus their basic disagreements had to be shuttled back and forth through the post. It was different with Einstein and Bohr, since Bohr, a nonresident member of the institute, could visit Princeton whenever he wished. He came once in 1946, for the bicentennial celebrations of Princeton University, and again in 1948 for the spring semester at the institute. On both occasions he had long exchanges with Einstein, carrying on the argument which had started at the Solvay Congresses two decades previously. They were not particularly happy exchanges and Abraham Pais, then a temporary member of the institute, has described how one day Bohr came into his room "in a state of angry despair," saying "I am sick of myself." Pais asked what was wrong. "He told me," he has written, "he had just been downstairs to see Einstein. As always, they had got into an argument about the meaning of quantum mechanics. And, as remained true to the end, Bohr had been unable to convince Einstein of his views. There can be no doubt that Einstein's lack of assent was a very deep frustration to Bohr."

Those lucky enough to be present at the meetings watched an interplay between master and master that had an heroic quality quite distinct from its relevance to physics. Both the 1946 and the 1948 visits also produced those dramatic highlights which seemed inseparable from contact between the two men, as though their mere presence in a room together was enough to strike flint against iron and make the sparks fly.

One such engagement occurred when Einstein attended a major address by Bohr in the institute's main mathematics building. He was collected from Mercer Street by Dr. Mitrany who, accustomed to his friend's sweatered informality, was surprised to see him in dark suit, collar, and tie. They took their places in the lecture hall amongst an august company. Everyone settled down for a highly technical two-hour lecture which only Einstein and a handful of others could follow with more than polite interest. Bohr progressed towards the heart of the epistemological and scientific argument. Einstein listened, attentive from the start, then more than attentive, then with obviously mounting impatience. Finally the strain was too much. He rose from his seat, and walked to the platform in front of the long roller blackboard that covered the entire wall. Then, chalk in hand, he interrupted the lecturer. What had been a monologue became a dialogue. Bohr understood. He, like Einstein, knew this was not arrogance but submission to fate. Only Einstein could adequately contradict what he believed was wrong even if he could not prove it was wrong. Not to do so would be dereliction of duty.

During the 1946 visit Bohr had been asked to contribute to *Albert Einstein—Philosopher-Scientist*, a volume being prepared in honor of Einstein's seventieth birthday three years later. He agreed to write a history of their epistemological arguments and completed it during his stay at the institute in 1949. While at work on the article he invited Pais to his office. "We went there," says Pais.

> ... After we had entered, Bohr asked me to sit down ("I always need an origin for the coordinate system") and soon started to pace furiously around the oblong table in the center of the room. He then asked me if I could put down a few sentences as they would emerge during his pacing. It should be explained that, at such sessions, Bohr never had a full sentence ready. He would often dwell on one word, coax it, implore it, to find the continuation. This could go on for many minutes. At that moment the word was "Einstein." There Bohr was, almost running

around the table and repeating: "Einstein . . . Einstein . . ." It would have been a curious sight for someone not familiar with Bohr. After a little while he walked to the window, gazed out, repeating every now and then: "Einstein . . . Einstein. . . ."

At that moment the door opened very softly and Einstein tiptoed in.

He beckoned to me with a finger on his lips to be very quiet, his urchin smile on his face. He was to explain a few minutes later the reason for his behavior. Einstein was not allowed by his doctor to buy tobacco. However, the doctor had not forbidden him to steal tobacco, and this was precisely what he set out to do now. Always on tiptoe he made a beeline for Bohr's tobacco pot which stood on the table at which I was sitting. Meanwhile Bohr, unaware, was standing at the window, muttering "Einstein . . . Einstein. . . ." I was at a loss what to do, especially because I had at that moment not the faintest idea what Einstein was up to.

Then Bohr, with a firm "Einstein," turned around. There they were, face to face, as if Bohr had summoned him forth. It is an understatement to say that for a moment Bohr was speechless. I myself, who had seen it coming, had distinctly felt uncanny for a moment, so I could well understand Bohr's own reaction. A moment later the spell was broken when Einstein explained his mission and soon we were all bursting with laughter.

Bohr and Einstein continued their argument. They agreed to go on differing, Bohr confident that he had reached bedrock, Einstein as confident that they were still dealing with the lower subsoil of physics. Below, he continued to believe, lay the ideas which would bring back the world he had known half a century ago. If it were based on anything more than elderly optimism, the hope of restoring the images he had helped destroy during an iconoclastic youth was based on that old panacea for a fragmented physics, a satisfactory unified field theory. He still intuitively believed that this would allow the laws of quantum mechanics to be derived from nonstatistical laws governing not probabilities but facts and he had pressed on relentlessly during his early years at the institute, throughout the war and into the peace, still in hot pursuit of the set of equations which would show that God did not really play dice with the world.

In 1942 he had written to an old Jewish friend, Hans Muhsam: "I am an old man mainly known as a crank who doesn't wear socks. But I am working at a more fantastic rate than ever, and I still hope to solve my pet problem of the unified physical field. I feel as if I were flying in an airplane high in the skies without quite knowing how I will ever reach the ground." Two years later he told Muhsam that he might still live to see whether he was a hope, as every variant entails tremendous mathematical justified in believing in his equations: "It is no more than a hope, as every variant entails tremendous mathematical difficulties. I did not write to you for so long because, despite my conscience pricking and a sincere desire to write, I am in an agony of mathematical torment from which I am unable to escape." The comparison with the early months of the First World War, when he had struggled with the complexities of the General Theory, is striking.

That there was so little to show for the work had been explained in a letter to Solovine years earlier. "For me, interest in science is restricted to the study of principles, and this offers the best explanation of my work. That I have published so few papers derives from the same circumstance: in consequence of my ardent desire to understand the principles is that much of my time has been spent on fruitless efforts." He still had doubts, which were not concealed from his old friends. Thus to Solovine he also wrote: "You seem to think that I look back upon my life's work with serene satisfaction. Viewed more closely, however, things are not so bright. There is not an idea of which I can be certain. I am not even sure that I am on the right road." To Hermann Weyl he conceded that, after all, "who knows, perhaps He is a little malicious."

Yet he never completely despaired. He worked on, past his seventieth birthday, and at last began to see what he thought was light at the end of the tunnel. By the autumn he was ready with "A Generalized Theory of Gravitation." A typewritten copy of the manuscript was exhibited at the Christmas meeting of the American Association for the Advancement of Science and the theory, with its twenty-eight mathematical formulas, was published two months later as a fourteen-page appendix to the fourth edition of *The Meaning of Relativity*.

A new theory from Einstein, offering at the age of seventy a key to the riddle of the universe to replace the one he had provided at the age of fifty, caused a major stir in the scientific world and its ground-swell reached out to the man in the street. Low drew a cartoon which quickly became famous showing Einstein bringing a giant key on New Year's Day to a Father Time who was exclaiming: "About time, too!" There were numerous headlines; phrases such as "master theory" were freely bandied about. Some of the more weighty journals began to outline what Einstein's thirty years of thought had yielded, a new and more convenient tool with which it was hoped that the laws of nature could be described.

What no one attempted to explain was how the tool could be used. The reason was simple. Infeld considered that he would need a year to understand it and added: "Like Chinese, you have to study it first."

However, it was not only the remoteness of the theory from even most scientific minds that was a stumbling block to acceptance. Unlike the General Theory of 1915, it could not apparently be tested. Thus in the new edition of *The Meaning of Relativity* Einstein was forced to preface his fresh set of equations with the statement: "In the following I shall present an attempt at the solution of this problem which appears to me highly convincing although, due to mathematical difficulties, I have not yet found a practicable way to confront the results of the theory with experimental evidence."* He knew the limitations of what had been half a lifetime's work; typically, he made light of them, replying to an inquiry about the chances of experimental evidence: "Come back in twenty years' time."

His real feelings were expressed in a letter to Carl Seelig. "The mathematical conclusiveness of the theory cannot be opposed," he wrote.

*Only a few months before his death, in December, 1954, Einstein signed a note for the sixth edition of the book, which was to be published in 1956. "For the present edition," he said, I have completely revised the 'Generalization of Gravitation Theory' under the title 'Relativistic Theory of the Nonsymmetric Field.' For I have succeeded—in part in collaboration with an assistant B. Kaufman—in simplifying derivations as well as the form of the field equations. The whole theory becomes thereby more transparent, without changing its content."

> The question of its physical validity, however is still completely undecided. The reason for this is that comparison of calculated solutions with experiment entails field equations that cannot be formulated. This position can last for a very long time. From this you can see clearly in what direction my efforts lie. There is little prospect that I shall see any success in the short time that remains to me.

Almost two decades later, Einstein's theory of a unified field remains unsubstantiated and current thought veers away from the idea of the universe being built in this way. Tough realist that he was, Einstein would be only moderately put out by the view. He knew that at the least he was clearing a good deal of scientific scrub. He might be regarded as a scientific curiosity; nevertheless, he was spending his last years doing a job which could be attempted by only a handful of men in the world. Therefore Einstein, a familiar figure on the treelined streets of Princeton in his shabby coat, old muffler, and black knitted cap, was still fired by an inner certitude no less invincible than in the days in Berne and Zurich. Then he had been the silent dark horse, content to work on alone, confident of Albert Einstein. The older version of the man was quite as sure of the work needing to be done, happy to ignore how the rest of the world regarded him. For half a century he had stuck to his last, a Mr. Standfast of physics. He had no cause to regret the decision now.

His routine was simple. He would breakfast between nine and ten, at the same time taking his "adrenalin cure"—reading the current political situation in the daily papers. In the winter he would be picked up from Mercer Street at about 10:30 by the green station wagon from the institute. He would usually walk home. In the summer he would go on foot and ride back in the early afternoon heat. On the way to the institute, says Ernst Strauss, his assistant from 1944 until 1947, who accompanied him on occasions, a stranger would sometimes waylay him, and say how much he had wanted to meet him. "Einstein would pose with the waylayer's wife, children, or grandchildren as desired and exchange a few good-humored words. Then he would go on, shaking his head, saying:

'Well, the old elephant has gone through his tricks again.' "

At the institute, he would work until one o'clock, sometimes alone, sometimes with his assistant, soaring up into the mathematical stratosphere where the battle had to be fought, always with his forces well disposed, always optimistic of eventual success, even optimistic about failures which he would face with: "Well, we've learned something." Soon after one o'clock he would put his notes into a thin worn briefcase and make for Mercer Street, sometimes stopping to chat with the two Oppenheimer children; occasionally he was accompanied by one of the younger faculty members or by one of the visiting professors. More frequently he walked alone. He did not like keeping good men from their duty and Helen Dukas, asking him on one occasion whether she should bring home a brilliant young mathematician just appointed to the institute, was told: "No: let him get on with his work."

At 1:30 he would eat, then rest until the late afternoon when after a cup of tea he would work, see visitors, or more frequently deal with the correspondence which had been sorted by Helen Dukas earlier in the day. Supper came soon after 6:30 and then there would be another bout of work or more letters. Sometimes he would listen to the radio, and occasionally there were private visitors. He had by this time given up his violin, saying that he was not good enough, but continued to play Bach or Mozart each day on his Bechstein grand. Nor was this all. "It is true that I have improvised much on the piano with delight," he wrote early in 1954 to the coordinator of a group of amateur musicians at Harvard Observatory, "but I discovered without much astonishment that it was not worth the paper and ink to be written down." On Sundays, friends would collect him for a drive into the country or to the coast which was only an hour away. He still hated to be seen in public, and he often repeated his old claim that like Midas he changed everything he touched—but in his case it turned not into gold but into a circus.

Such was the life that went on behind the barrier raised against inquisitive callers, visitors who wanted only a glimpse of the great man or of the place where he worked and lived, and correspondents who produced an echo of the crankeries with which he had had to deal during his first days of fame in Berlin. "Thank God," Miss Dukas once wrote of his morning post, "most of it can go straight into the wastepaper basket."

But there were sometimes unexpected repercussions. Thus when the IBM Corporation invited him to the unveiling of a new computer they failed to receive an answer. Dean Eisenhart of the Graduate School, Princeton University, was asked to investigate when a follow-up invitation, immaculately typed like the first one on an IBM executive machine, also failed to produce a reply. "He explained," says his son, Churchill Eisenhart,

> that something must be amiss, because Dr. Einstein was scrupulous about replying to all such invitations. He walked over to Dr. Einstein's house and explained the situation. Dr. Einstein dumped the contents of a very large wastebasket on the floor and examined an item here and there. Finally his face lighted up. He handed one of the invitational letters to my father, saying: "It looks as if it were printed. I never read printed circulars."

Life at Mercer Street was quiet and unpretentious, homely and unaffected, not blatantly the life of a genius—in fact a life in surroundings which were sometimes unexpected. "My eye," said one visitor, "was immediately caught by two inlaid cabinets containing various objects of religious art. On a canopied central shelf of one was a rather beautiful Madonna and Child; on a side table was a statuette of a Chinese philosopher beggar man; on the wall hung a picture of the period of early Italian Christian painting."

In this house, more home of artist or polymath than theoretical physicist, Einstein was the centerpiece of a trio of women. Dominating it was Helen Dukas, since Elsa's death the person on whom the main burden of the household had fallen—the housekeeper and shopper, the cook and secretary, the organizer of peace and quiet, the filer of correspondence who for lack of space was forced to store boxes of letters in the cellar and who often wished that Gutenberg had never lived. Only after Einstein's death was the priceless collection taken to the institute to be housed in the room safe, guarded with entry door and combination lock, that had once held the miscellaneous nuclear secrets of the former director, J. Robert Oppenheimer.

Also at Mercer Street there was Margot, the stepdaughter who had grown so like Einstein in attitude and outlook that it was difficult to think of them as linked only by collateral lines on the family tree. Thirdly there was Maja, two years younger than her brother, for whom Einstein possibly felt more affection than for anyone. "Her manner of speaking and the sound of her voice, as well as the childlike and yet sceptical formulation of every statement, are unusually similar to her brother's mode of expression," Frank noted; "it is amazing to listen to her; it arouses a sense of uneasiness to find a replica of even the minor traits of a genius."

Brother and sister read much together in what Einstein called "our enviable peaceful den." From 1946, when she began to be crippled by arteriosclerosis, he would read to her every evening and he continued to do so as, from the end of 1950, her condition became more critical. Margot nursed her. But, with intelligence scarcely impaired by advancing illness. Maja died in December, 1951. "Now I miss her more than I can easily explain," wrote Einstein to his cousin in South America.

Since the start of the century, his life had presented a series of unexpected contradictions. The Patent Office official had been hoisted into academic life. The hater of all things German had been tempted to Berlin. The man who wanted only a quiet life had in 1919 had become the most famous scientist in the world. The pacifist had been forced to support armed resistance, and the man who regarded all war as murder had helped push the buttons that killed 120,000. Now there was to come a final twist. In 1952 the image of the old eccentric, pottering along in his seventies, was to be brusquely shattered. Albert Einstein, the man who had always decried force, was invited to become President of Israel, that realization of Zionist hopes, the state which had successfully staked out its frontiers by force of arms and was defending them against all comers.

The proposal, practical, outrageous, or pathetic according to viewpoint, splendid in its audacity if grotesque in its implications, followed the death of Chaim

Weizmann, who had become first President soon after declaration of the state of Israel in May, 1948. Weizmann died on Sunday, November 9, 1952, and a few days later Einstein was mooted as successor in the Tel Aviv newspaper *Maariv*. It seems likely that this was a trial balloon to discover public reaction. If so, it was flown by the Prime Minister, David Ben-Gurion. "The presidency in Israel is a symbol," he said later.

> It carries with it no power. I thought to myself: if we are looking for a symbol, why not have the most illustrious Jew in the world, and possibly the greatest man alive—Einstein? That's all there was to it. Had he accepted, I would have submitted his name to the Knesset—in Israel the Knesset elects the President—and I am quite sure that the motion for his election would have been carried by acclamation.

Einstein, like most of his friends, refused to take the idea seriously and when the *New York Times* asked for his reaction on the evening of Sunday the sixteenth, he refused to comment. Shortly afterwards, the telephone in Mercer Street rang again and the operator said that Washington was on the line. "Herr Gott," exclaimed Helen Dukas, who had answered: "Washington! What is wrong now?" This time it was Abba Eban, the Israeli ambassador to the United States, who was making an informal inquiry. Would Einstein accept the presidency if it were offered by a vote of the Knesset?

His reply was in keeping with his reputation. "His main and urgent thought," says Professor Mitrany, who was with him when the call came through "was how to spare the ambassador the embarrassment of his inevitable refusal."

To Eban the situation was equally clear: "Einstein was visibly moved by the splendor and audacity of the thought," he has said, "but his rejection was firm and vehement: 'I know a little about nature,' he said, 'and hardly anything about men.' He implored me to accept his negative decision as final and do everything possible to divert and banish the press whose representatives were laying siege to his house in Mercer Street."

But Eban's instructions had come direct from the Prime Minister. He finally convinced Einstein that it would be improper for him to reject the proposal on the telephone, and the following day made a formal telegraphed request that he should receive his deputy to seek his "reaction on a matter of the utmost urgency and importance."

Einstein telephoned Eban, again declining the invitation. However, on Tuesday the eighteenth a formal letter was brought to Princeton by the Israeli Minister, David Goiten. "Acceptance would entail moving to Israel and taking its citizenship," said the letter. "The Prime Minister assures me that in such circumstances complete facility and freedom to pursue your great scientific work would be afforded by the government and people who are fully conscious of the supreme significance of your labors."

It was a persuasive appeal to a man for whom the creation of Israel was a political act of an essentially moral quality. Its refusal illuminates a good deal of Einstein's life in three starkly honest paragraphs. "I am deeply moved by the offer from our state of Israel, and at once saddened and ashamed that I cannot accept it," this said.

> All my life I have dealt with objective matters, hence I lack both the natural aptitude and the experience to deal properly with people and to exercise official functions. For these reasons alone I should be unsuited to fulfill the duties of that high office, even if advancing age was not making increasing inroads on my strength.
>
> I am the more distressed over these circumstances because my relationship to the Jewish people has become my strongest human bond, ever since I became fully aware of our precarious situation among the nations of the world.
>
> Now that we have lost the man who for so many years, against such great and tragic odds, bore the heavy burden of leading us towards political independence, I hope with all my heart that a successor may be found whose experience and personality will enable him to accept the formidable and responsible task.

Thus the matter ended—after the editor-in-chief of *Maariv* had made an impassioned entreaty for reconsideration of the idea, and after Einstein had pointed out that however formal his functions, as President he would be responsible for the country's actions and these might conflict with his conscience.

Einstein as President was a prospect which aroused diverse emotions among those who knew him best. Weizmann had been a biochemist by profession. Therefore it might be claimed that the idea of a theoretical physicist holding such a post was nothing to startle the world. Yet their links with learning and their support for Zionism were the only things which the two men had in common; in many ways their qualities were diametrically contrasted. Certainly the very characteristics of steely determination and ruthlessness which had enabled Weizmann to bring Zionism safely home to port were, except when applied to science, not in Einstein's makeup. It is possible to claim that such a world figure, transparently remote from the petty squabbles of nationalism, would never be suspected of ulterior motives, that he would be listened to where other men would be ignored. It is more likely that his innocence of public affairs would have made him easy meat for the predators of the international scene, however symbolic his appointment. The proposal was, in any case, stillborn. "In order to preserve my rights as a thinker, I have to stay quiet in order to work," Einstein had written to Weizmann in circumscribing his Zionist activities nearly thirty years previously. That still held. He still put science first, second, and third.

As his seventy-fifth birthday approached there were still many ways in which it seemed that while age had matured him it had hardly changed him basically. It was more than sixty years since he had decided to devote his life to a single quest, to order his days to an almost inhuman sense of priorities; nearly forty since he had reluctantly been drawn out into contact with the world of politics and power by the demands of Zionism and European peace. Yet what Einstein now stood for echoed his earlier beliefs in remarkable fashion, so that the *obiter dicta* of his last years ring like crystallized and polished examples of the casual ideas he had tossed off to fellow students at the ETH or to colleagues who broke in on his thoughts while he was remaking man's picture of the universe. He had tossed Mach overboard after long and careful thought, but most of the rest remained.

Luckily, he was almost as unstinting in his writing to a few close friends as of the time he devoted to work; thus it is possible to glean from his letters as adequate picture of how he regarded the world towards the end of his life. About the great central issue, he was in no doubt. "I have read with great interest your timely remarks about the fact that science in itself is by no means a moral leader and that something is needed that you call religion," he wrote to Leon Watters. "I must confess, however, that in my opinion the main problem begins here. Without a remarkable change in the traditions concerning moral values, nothing can be achieved. The old religions are, in my opinion, no longer influential and there is no general formula which can bring about moral revival."

About the problem of force, the dichotomy of ends and means, he appears to have returned to his instinctive pacifism, looking on the need to oppose Hitler and to sustain Israel by arms as exceptions which proved the rule. But they were, of course, the only two cases with which he had personally to deal. "I miss no occasion," he wrote to a friend in Paris, "to try to make the people aware of the great possibilities offered by Gandhi's method, which gives strength to the minority of morally and intellectually independent people."

As far as his own life was concerned, one thing seemed quite clear. "I made one great mistake in my life," he said to Linus Pauling, who spent an hour with him on the morning of November 11, 1954, ". . . when I signed the letter to President Roosevelt recommending that atom bombs be made; but there was some justification—the danger that the Germans would make them." In a message to the American Friends of the Hebrew University, he stressed the Jewish ideal of the person who enriched the spiritual life of his people and added: "This implies a definite repudiation of what is commonly called materialism." It was a temptation to which he had never succumbed; enjoyment of "the pleasures that nature provides" was the nearest he came to it. So too with the more insidious temptations of great success. "The only way to escape the personal corruption of praise is to go on working," he said. "One is tempted to stop and listen to it. The only thing is to turn away and go on working. Work. There is nothing else."

Some of his last scientific judgments have been put on record by the Canadian astronomer, Dr. A. Vibert Douglas, Eddington's biographer, who traveled to Princeton in January, 1954. Einstein began by paying a striking tribute to Eddington, whose *The Mathematical Theory of Relativity* he considered the finest presentation of the subject in any language. "He spoke," says Dr. Douglas,

> of the literary value, the beauty, and brilliance of Eddington's writing in those books aimed at giving to the intelligent lay reader at least some understanding, some insight into the significance of the new scientific ideas—but with a smile he added that a scientist is mistaken if he thinks he is making the layman understand: a scientist should not attempt to popularize his theories, if he does "he is a fakir—it is the duty of a scientist to remain obscure."

This point, which Einstein also made in other places during his later years, was in strong contrast to his earlier attempts to explain relativity in simple language. It is difficult not to see here a reflection of the disillusion with the masses which surfaced during the latter part of his life.

"In regard to the developments in the early years made by Weyl and Eddington, the later theories of the expanding universe of Friedmann, Lemaître, and Eddington, the still later kinematic relativity of E. A. Milne, and the yet more recent theories of continuous creation of matter of Jordan, Bondi, and Hoyle, the comments of Dr. Einstein were brief and critical," says Dr. Douglas. "He definitely disliked the hypothesis of continuous creation, he felt the necessity for a 'beginning'; he regarded Milne's brilliant mathematical mind as lacking in critical judgment; he was not attracted by the idea of Lemaître's primeval atom; and he concluded by saying of his own and all the others: 'Every man has his own cosmology and who can say that his own theory is right.' " Thus, after two decades, what Thomson had said as a joke* was repeated by Einstein in earnest.

Dr. Douglas knew that in Einstein's Berlin study there had once hung portraits of Newton and of Maxwell. Now all she saw was a portrait of Gandhi and another of a German musician. "The greatest man of our age," was how Einstein now described Gandhi; and, of Dr. Schweitz-

*See page 301.

er, whose name was mentioned: "Yes, he too is a very great man."

"There remained one special thing I wanted to ask him—Who were the greatest men, the most powerful thinkers whom he had known?" writes Dr. Douglas. "The answer came without hesitation, 'Lorentz.'" None of the other theoretical physicists and cosmologists named were on the same level. "No, this one was too uncritical, that one was uneven, another was of a lesser stature . . . but, he added, 'I never met Willard Gibbs; perhaps, had I done so, I might have placed him beside Lorentz.'" There was one other name in Dr. Douglas' thoughts: Minkowski, whose work almost half a century earlier had lifted the Special Theory of Relativity from a physical to a mathematical concept. Where would Einstein place him? "He was my very great teacher in Zurich," he said, "but I am not a good enough mathematician to know where to place him."

His near idolatry for Lorentz had lasted all his life, and a few weeks before his death he described what the magnetism was. "Everything that emanated from his supremely great mind was as clear and beautiful as a good work of art," he wrote in a contribution to a memorial volume published in Holland. There was his humor, his smile, his mastery of physics and mathematics. Nevertheless, Einstein went on, he "was perfectly aware that the human intellect cannot penetrate very deeply into the essential core of things. It was not until my later years that I was able fully to appreciate this half-sceptical, half-humble disposition."

Just as he dotted the *i*'s and crossed the *t*'s of his scientific beliefs during the last year or so of his life, so did he recapitulate his religious convictions. To Dr. Douglas he stated: "If I were not a Jew I would be a Quaker." And in an interview with Professor William Hermanns, he said: "I cannot accept any concept of God based on the fear of life or the fear of death or blind faith. I cannot prove to you that there is no personal God, but if I were to speak of Him I would be a liar."

As to what one could believe in, the answer was simple enough. "I believe in the brotherhood of man and the uniqueness of the individual. But if you ask me to prove what I believe, I can't. You know them to be true but you could spend a whole lifetime without being able to prove them. The mind can proceed only so far upon what it knows and can prove. There comes a point where the mind takes a higher plane of knowledge, but can never prove how it got there. All great discoveries have involved such a leap." Thus, fifty years on from the papers of 1905, there came the unequivocal renunciation of Mach and his concept of divination through sensation alone.

As to the spur which pricked all men onwards, that too was simple enough to explain. "The important thing is not to stop questioning," he said. "Curiosity has its own reason for existence. One cannot help but be in awe when [one] contemplates the mysteries of eternity, of life, of the marvelous structure of reality. It is enough if one tries merely to comprehend a little of this mystery each day. Never lose a holy curiosity."

Einstein had tried to comprehend. Looking back from the vantage point of 1954 he could rightly claim to have played a major part in two achievements as great as man had ever accomplished. He had helped show that time and space were not the inelastic things which they were thought to be, but were relative to the sum total of circumstances in which they were considered. Thus he had changed the meaning attached to the word "reality." He had also encouraged physicists into accepting the dual nature of matter, that matter which had, as Sir Lawrence Bragg so percipiently stated, the perverse characteristic of being "coagulated from waves into particles by the advancing sieve of time."

These were important achievements at an intellectual level where few dared tread. Einstein had reached that level carrying little of the emotional baggage that lumbers most men. In some ways, of course, it made his task easier. He travels fastest who travels not only alone, but light; yet even in science this had brought items on the debit side. His inability to feel the human tragedy emotionally as well as intellectually had helped to disrupt his first marriage, a troublesome vexatious mistake which seems at times to have driven him to the point of desperation just when he wished to concentrate on the job in hand. These personal troubles had been overcome with his marriage to Elsa, who from 1919 helped to clear the path of greatness without complaint. To this extent the disabilities produced by his emotional isolation—by being, as he had described it to Besso as a young man, "rather cool and a bit of a hard nut"—had been overcome. He could get on with his work without worrying too much about anyone else. Outside that work, however, the aloofness which he did little to discourage brought its own reward: a man genuinely eager to do good, he found the best of his intentions frustrated with maddening regularity.

Early in 1955 he was invited to conferences in Berne and Berlin to celebrate the fiftieth anniversary of his most famous paper. He declined. His excuses were in character. "Old age and poor health make such a trip impossible," he replied to von Laue in Berlin,

> and I must say that I am not sorry, for anything resembling a personality cult has always been distasteful to me. In the present case, moreover, many people have contributed to the advance of this theory, and it is far from completed. . . . If many years of search have taught me anything, it is that we are much farther from an understanding of elementary particles than most men realize (yourself excluded), and a festive pageant would hardly benefit the present state of affairs.

To Pauli, who invited him to the Swiss conference, he replied: "It would seem that the expectations attached to the General Theory of Relativity are extraordinarily diverse. This is good, for with us scientists the philosophical expression 'War is the father of all things' has not the fatal flavor that is usually attached to it."

He would have enjoyed the Berne meeting, even though its appraisal of the General Theory lacked the initial scientific rapture of 1919. For the unqualified acceptance and the experimental verification that had long ago put the Special Theory beyond all dispute were still lacking here. While there was no doubt that gravity did affect light, the extent of its effect had become increasingly questioned as experimental methods improved. "A lot of work will have to be done before the astronomers really can say what is the value of the observed light deflection and whether the red shift is in existence at all," noted Freundlich at the conference. Some of this work now has been done. But Born, to whom the General Theory continued to remain "the greatest feat of human thinking about nature," voiced qualifications which still hold.

Einstein would have accepted the point. More than thirty years before, walking in the grounds of the Governor's House in Jerusalem, he had remarked of Herbert Spencer's idea of tragedy—"a deduction killed by a fact"—"Every theory is killed sooner or later in that way. But if the theory has good in it, that good is embodied and continued in the next theory."

The jubilee meetings could carry on well enough without him. Others could glitter in the scientific limelight while he, the man who had started it all, wound quietly towards the end of his life without fuss, an onlooker more than ever removed from the affairs of the world. At least, that was the way it looked. Yet now, at almost the last minute of the last hour, Einstein was again to be drawn into the whirlpool of public affairs, willingly and almost excitedly, as though determined to refute the idea that his life would end not with a bang but a whimper. The offer of the Presidency of Israel had come unexpectedly, a star blazing out through the twilight at the end of a long life. Now another arrived, and one which lit up a possible road to peace in a way that even now is not fully appreciated.

In mid-February he received a letter from Bertrand Russell. Both men had, in Russell's words "opposed the First World War but considered the Second unavoidable." Both distrusted orthodoxy and both had been appalled by the destructive possibilities of the hydrogen bomb. Yet if both had in general sought the same objectives their methods had been as diametrically opposed as their characters. While Einstein had been content to continue with his work under the aegis of the Kaiser Wilhelm, Russell had gone to prison. While Einstein had aloofly despaired of the intelligence of mankind, Russell had reacted by sitting as a protest in public squares. Einstein, for all his genuine feeings, had rarely stepped from behind the protection of his own interior world; Russell had insisted that he too should be heard, tormented, anguished, and combative.

But now Russell turned to Einstein for help. He was, he wrote on February 11, profoundly disquieted by the nuclear arms race. "I think that eminent men of science ought to do something dramatic to bring home to the public and governments the disasters that may occur. Do you think it would be possible to get, say, six men of the very highest scientific repute, headed by yourself, to make a very solemn statement about the imperative necessity of avoiding war?" The statement would best be signed by men of opposing political creeds, and should deal not merely with the dangers of the hydrogen bomb but with those of bacteriological warfare, thus emphasizing "the general proposition that war and science can no longer coexist." The letter added that the statement might appeal to neutral countries to set up commissions of their own nationals to investigate the effect, on them, of a third world war.

Einstein replied on February 16, 1955, with a letter which took Russell's proposal one step further. What he suggested was "a public declaration, signed by a small number of people—say, twelve persons, whose scientific achievements (scientific in the widest sense) have gained them international stature and whose declarations will not lose any effectiveness on account of their political affiliations." Such men might even include Joliot-Curie, a leading Communist, "provided they were counterbalanced by men from the other camp." Bohr was an obvious candidate from the uncommitted countries which Einstein hoped would supply half the signatures.

There followed another letter from Russell and a further reply from Einstein who had by this time written to Bohr. Thus Russell's initial idea was considerably influenced by Einstein and the outcome was quite rightly known as the Russell-Einstein Declaration. This was sent to Einstein by Russell on April 5; it recapitulated the dangers of contemporary war, with special emphasis on hydrogen bombs. And it ended with the following resolution, to be put to a world convention of scientists:

> In view of the fact that in any future world war nuclear weapons will certainly be employed, and that such weapons threaten the continued existence of mankind, we urge the governments of the world to realize, and to acknowledge publicly, that their purposes cannot be furthered by a world war, and we urge them, consequently, to find peaceful means for the settlement of all matters of dispute between them.

While Russell's declaration was still in the post with its accompanying letter, Einstein struck out on his own, writing to Nehru and in effect asking for his intervention in the area where an East-West war seemed most likely. This was in China, where the Nationalist government's toehold on the offshore islands of Quemoy and Matsu threatened to lead the United States into an Asiatic quagmire. He enclosed with his letters a plan, prepared by Szilard, for the evacuation of the two islands for a definite period. Superficially this appeared the most obvious of nonstarters but Einstein presumably felt that nothing but good would come of Nehru's intervention, whatever form it might take.

Three officers of the Society for Social Responsibilities in Science now fortuitously called on him with a proposal for an open letter which they hoped he might sign. He explained that something similar was already afoot, that Russell was behind the move, and that he had written to Russell saying: "You understand such things. You are the general. I am just a foot soldier; give the command and I will follow." But he seems to have known that he had little time left. "He was on the porch of his house as he spoke," writes one of his visitors. "Though it was not cold he was wrapped in a blanket. And somehow the air of parting was around." The intuition was justified.

Russell's letter had stirred Einstein in a way which few things had stirred him during recent years, and he now decided that the time had come to make a major statement on the position of Israel, whose Independence Day in May was to be held in circumstances even more ominous than usual. The threats from her ring of Arab neighbors were growing while the announcement that Czechoslovakia and Russia were both to supply Egypt with arms added a new and more dangerous menace. Countermeasures were in fact already under way and Mr. Dulles had agreed to release to the Israelis a dozen Mystére fighters from the U. S. contingent to NATO as well as twenty-four Sabrejets from another source. But these measures were still unknown to the general public. This included Einstein—who only a few weeks earlier had claimed that the current Eisenhower adminstration was seeking "to win the sympathy of the Arab nations by sacrificing Israel."

He was therefore particularly receptive when, early in April, the Israeli authorities in Washington asked if he would make an Independence Day statement dealing with the country's scientific and cultural activities and stressing the peaceful uses of atomic energy. "I should very much like to assist the cause of Israel in the difficult and dangerous conditions prevailing today," he replied on April 4. But, in the present circumstances, cultural and scientific developments were hardly relevant. What Einstein thought might be most effective was "a somewhat critical analysis of the policies of the Western nations with regard to Israel and the Arab states." He went on to say that if such a statement was to be meaningful it would have to be prepared in cooperation with responsible Israeli officials.

Here was a unique opportunity. The Israeli ambassador, Abba Eban, seized it with both hands and on April 11 arrived at Mercer Street with the Israeli consul, Reuven Dafni. "Professor Einstein told me," he later wrote,

> that he saw the rebirth of Israel as one of the few political acts in his lifetime which had an essential moral quality. He believed that the conscience of the world should, therefore, be involved in Israel's preservation. He had always refused the requests of television and radio networks to project his views to public opinion. This issue, however, seemed to him to be of such importance that he was actually taking the initiative, through me, of seeking the opportunity to address the American people and the world. He showed me the draft which he had begun to prepare. He had reached the end of a long preamble on the cold war and wished to hear my views at greater length before discussing the political aspects of the Middle Eastern situation.

Eban and his colleague talked with Einstein for some while, and it was agreed that Dafni should return in a few days when Einstein had put the draft of his proposed address into more finished form.

On the same day, the eleventh, he received the expected statement from Russell, and an accompanying list of scientists who would be asked to sign it. "I am gladly willing to sign your excellent statement," he replied without delay. "I also agree with your choice of the prospective signers." Thus in one sentence he helped launch the manifesto calling for a conference to appraise the perils of war and leading directly to the long series of influential Pugwash conferences attended by prominent scientists from the United States, Britain, and Russia, among more than a dozen countries.*

The following day Einstein was in pain. But he refused to allow the doctor to be called and it was without his knowledge that Helen Dukas telephoned Margot, then ill in the local hospital, and said that Einstein's personal doctor should be told.

Despite the pain, Einstein worked on his Independence Day broadcast, to be further discussed with the Israeli consul the next day. The five paragraphs which survive presented the conflict between Israel and Egypt as interdependent with larger problems. "And the big problem in our time," he went on in characteristic style, "is the division of mankind into two hostile camps: the Communist World and the so-called Free World. Since the significance of the terms 'Free' and 'Communist' is in this context hardly clear to me, I prefer to speak of a power conflict between East and West, although, the world being round, it is not even clear what precisely is meant by the terms 'East' and 'West.' "

On the thirteenth, he was still in pain. But in the morning he received both the Israeli consul and Janos Plesch, who had come from New York. He went over his draft with Dafni. He also made additional notes. Some mystery surrounds their fate. The editors of *Einstein on Peace*, one of whom was Einstein's literary executor, describe them as "not available"; but they could find nothing to support a later rumor that the notes had been stolen from the Princeton hospital. And they criticize a "reconstruction" of Einstein's planned address, based on information provided by Dafni, subsequently published in the *New York Times*. The most likely conclusion is that the notes, whatever happened to them, were too critical of "East," of "West," or of both sides in the power game, to be openly admitted as coming from Einstein.

*Full details of the course and influence of the Pugwash conferences are given in *Pugwash: A History of the Conferences on Science and World Affairs*, by J. Rotblat (Prague: Czechoslovak Academy of Sciences, 1967).

Dafni left Mercer Street by midday. Soon afterwards, Einstein complained of extreme tiredness and lack of appetite. After a light meal he lay down to rest; in midafternoon he collapsed. Helen Dukas, managing the situation singlehanded, called the doctor who soon arrived with two colleagues, helped as an electrocardiogram was taken, fixed up a bed in the study, and prepared for a long vigil. The patient, given morphia injections, passed a quiet night.

Dr. Dean, who found Einstein "very stoical" and "his usual kind shy self," had diagnosed a small leakage of blood from a hardened aorta, and on the morning of Thursday the fourteenth Dr. Frank Glenn, the cardiac and aortic surgeon, arrived from New York. So did Dr. Ehrmann and Dr. Bucky. One question had to be settled quickly: whether or not to operate. By 1955 this was possible although the chances of survival during such an operation were still low. Some experts put it at fifty percent; but without it they were minimal.

Years earlier, when Einstein had first learned of his condition and been told that his aorta might burst unless he took care, he had brusquely replied: "Let it burst." Now he was similarly uncompromising. He asked how long death would take and was told that it might come in a moment, might take hours, or might take days. He was, his doctor said, "violently opposed" to surgery. To Helen Dukas, the later protested: "The end comes some time: does it matter when?" Just as in physics he had developed into the conservative revolutionary, so in medicine he tended to distrust what he thought of as radical innovations; it had once been impossible to operate on a man in his condition, and he would have none of it now.

Friday night passed quietly and on Saturday morning he seemed to be better. Then, once again, there was intense pain and he was unable to move. On the arrival of the doctor, hastily called by Helen Dukas, he at first refused to budge. Most patients would have been quickly overruled, but even now it was not easy to overrule Einstein. Finally, he was persuaded that hospital was best; characteristically, the argument which counted was that the nursing was too much for Miss Dukas.

On the way to the hospital he talked animatedly to one of the volunteer ambulance men. After arrival he began to feel better and he soon telephoned Mercer Street. First he wanted his spectacles; then he wanted writing material. If there was still time left it should not be wasted.

On Sunday, Margot was wheeled in to see him. "I did not recognize him at first, so changed was he by the pain and the lack of blood in his face," she wrote to Hedwig Born. "But his manner was the same. He was glad that I was looking a little better, joked with me, and faced his own state with complete superiority; he talked with perfect calm, even with slight humor about the doctors, and was waiting for his end as if for an expected 'natural phenomenon.' "

He would go in his own time, and insisted on one thing: "Do not let the house become a museum." He had already asked that his office at the institute should not be preserved as he had used it, but passed on for the use of others. He did not want Mercer Street turned into a place of pilgrimage and he would have had little sympathy for those who in later years called at No. 112 asking to see his study; for those who were to write to the institute for mementos; or for the correspondents who from as far away as India wrote to his son Hans Albert pleading for a piece of anything that Albert Einstein had touched. He would have been surprised that an opera based on his life should be written for presentation in East Berlin, and been astonished at the million words that were cabled out of Princeton as the press moved in after his death. He would have exploded in one of his hearty gusts of laughter at the value of his signature and the hundreds of dollars which were soon to be the market price of his letters. He had wanted all this to die with him.

He had insisted that his brain should be used for research and that he be cremated; but his ashes were to be scattered at an undisclosed place. Again, no point of pilgrimage. He would have agreed with his literary executor, Otto Nathan, who was to write that the less published about Einstein's illness and the developments that led to his death, the better; Nathan did not see why the public should have an interest in the details, or why he and others should satisfy it if they had.

Hans Albert and Nathan arrived in Princeton on Sunday. With the first, Einstein discussed science; with the latter, politics and the danger of German rearmament. He was equable now, and late in the afternoon Dr. Dean even felt that the aneurysm might be repairing itself. With a recurrence of pain in the evening Einstein was given another injection; but he was sleeping peacefully when Dean took a final look at him at 11 P.M.

In the small hours, soon after midnight, nurse Alberta Roszel noticed a difference in his breathing. Becoming alarmed, she called for assistance, and with the aid of another nurse cranked up the head of the bed.

He was muttering in German, the language of his despised compatriots, still the only tongue with which he felt comfortable. It was with Germans that he had first won his spurs and in Berlin that he had first become world famous. It was only in German that he could contemplate the course of his life: his dedication to science and subjugation of everything else; the self-imposed emotional asceticism; his belief that the human race was naturally aggressive and Germans more aggressive than the rest. It was in German that the last thoughts of one of the greatest brains since Newton's came to the surface through the unconscious mind.

Perhaps he should not have been so bearish about people? Perhaps he should never have gone to Berlin, made the way that much easier for the aggressors with his pacifism, or hated the Germans so much that he encouraged Roosevelt into the nuclear age? Perhaps he should not always have put science first? But on this there was of course no room for doubt, no cause for regret. As he took two deep breaths and died, it is unlikely that Einstein regretted very much, if he regretted anything at all. But Mrs. Roszel did not understand his German. And anyway, as Elsa had felt nearly twenty years before, dear God it was too late now.

SOURCES AND BIBLIOGRAPHY

The original material for a life of Albert Einstein is scattered throughout the libraries and archives of Europe, the United States, and the Middle East. The largest single collections are the Einstein Archives in Princeton, currently housed at the Institute for Advanced Study, and the Einstein-Sammlung der ETH Bibliothek in Zurich. The Princeton collection is particularly rich in records of Einstein's later years, but as his executor, Dr. Otto Nathan, has written: "Einstein himself was not greatly concerned with a systematic collection of his papers and correspondence; only in the last few decades of his life was sufficient attention paid to the preservation of the many important documents and letters that crossed his desk." The collection in the Eidgenossische Technische Hochschule, Zurich (ETH), where Einstein both studied and taught, is naturally strong in the records of his years in Switzerland. These however are only two of the sources of original material. Much of Einstein's long correspondence with Lorentz is divided between the Algemeen Riiksarchiv in The Hague and the Rijksmuseum voor de Geschiedenis der Natuurwetenschappen in Leiden. His meeting and early relationship with Erwin Freundlich is dealt with in the correspondence held until recently by Frau Freundlich. His friendship with Professor Lindemann—later Lord Cherwell—which began at the Solvay Congress in 1911 and continued to within a few years of Einstein's death, is covered by the Cherwell Papers in Nuffield College, Oxford. Light is thrown on his connections with the Solvay Institute by the papers at present being used by Professor Jagdish Mehra for a history of the congress, and on his move to Prague by the Adler Archives in Vienna. The

Hale Papers and the Millikan Papers are among important material in the California Institute of Technology dealing with Einstein's early visits to the United States.

The archives of the League of Nations Library in Geneva contain much new information on Einstein's membership of the International Committee on Intellectual Cooperation, "while the Royal Library in Brussels contains his correspondence with H.M. Queen Elizabeth of the Belgians and details of his early visits to the Royal Palace at Laeken." The 190 pages of correspondence in the Weizmann Archives, Rehovot, and the Samuel Papers in the House of Lords Record Office, London, deal with Einstein's connections with Zionism from 1918 until the year of his death. And the Stadtarchiv, Ulm; the Israelitische Kultusvereinigung, Württembergund Hohenzollern; the Geheimes Staatsarchiv, Berlin; and many other German sources provide the documentary evidence for his birth, background, and citizenship.

The Rutherford Papers in the University of Cambridge; the Haldane Papers in the National Library of Scotland; the Bibliothèque Nationale, Paris; the Curie Laboratory Archives, Paris; the Russell Archives, McMaster University, Hamilton, Ontario; the Roosevelt Library, Hyde Park, N.Y.; and the archives of the University of Utrecht all provide material dealing with his life and work. Two important unpublished manuscripts are Ehrenhaft's "My Experiences with Einstein" held by the Burndy Library, Norwalk, Connecticut; and "Comments on the Letters of Professor and Mrs. Albert Einstein to Dr. Leon L. Watters," copies of which are held by the American Jewish Archives and by the California Institute of Technology. Useful collections of private letters include the correspondence of Professor and Mrs. Einstein with Leon L. Watters, held by the American Jewish Archives; the Bucky letters, held by the University of Texas; the Koch letters, written by Einstein to his relatives in the Koch—Ferrard family in Belgium; the Kocherthaler letters, written to relatives in South America, in private hands in Montevideo; the correspondence with Dr. Janos Plesch, held by the Plesch family; and, in some ways the most important of all, the long correspondence with Michelangelo Besso, continuing for almost half a century, copies of which are held by Dr. Jagdish Mehra of the University of Texas at Austin.

The Szilard Archives in San Diego contain much valuable background to the famous letter to Roosevelt, while the U. S. Atomic Energy Commission, the Office of the Chief of Naval Operations, and the National Archives and Records Service are among the official sources which hold material dealing with Einstein's work during the Second World War.

All these sources have been drawn upon, as well as the following:

Allgemeines Staatsarchiv, Munich; American Institute of Physics, New York; Auswärtiges Amt, Bonn; Bureau Fédéral de la Propriété Intellectuelle, Berne; University of Chicago, Chicago; Christ Church Library, Oxford; Library of Congress, Washington, D.C.; "Deutsche Staatsbibliothek, Berlin;" Deutsches Zentralarchiv, Potsdam; Perkins Library, Perkins Duke University, Durham, North Carolina; University of Edinburgh, Edinburgh; Geheimes Staatsarchiv, Berlin; University of Göttingen, Göttingen; Landesarchiv, Berlin; MacArthur Memorial Archives, Norfolk, Virginia; University of Manchester, Manchester; Max-Planck-Gesellschaft, Berlin and Munich; John Murray Archives, London; National Personnel Records Center, St. Louis, Missouri; "Rhodes Trust, Oxford;" Royal Netherlands Academy of Sciences and Letters, Amsterdam; Schweizer Schuler, Milan; Senatsverwaltung der Stadt, Berlin; University of Sheffield, Sheffield; Staatsbibliothek der Stiftung Preussischer Kulturbesitz, Berlin; Stanford University, Palo Alto, Calif.; Records of Swiss Federal Council, Berne; Swiss National Library, Berne; University of Syracuse; UNESCO Archives, Paris.

PRINTED MATERIAL

The bulk of Einstein's scientific work is contained in the papers listed in *Albert Einstein: A Bibliography of His Scientific Papers. 1901–1930* by E. Weil (London, 1937). Later bibliographies include that given in *Albert Einstein: Philosopher-Scientist,* edited by Paul A. Schilpp (Evanston, Ill., 1949), and *A Bibliographical Checklist and Index to the Collected Writings of Albert Einstein*, Readex Microprint edition compiled by Nell Boni, Monique Russ, and Dan H. Laurence (New York, 1960); both include Einstein's nonscientific writings and bibliographical details of many interviews.

Einstein's key papers on relativity are printed, together with other relevant papers by H. A. Lorentz, H. Minkowski, and H. Weyl, in *The Principle of Relativity* (London, 1923 and New York, 1952) while his own *Relativity: The Special and the General Theory* is available in a succession of editions and translations from 1920 onwards. His major papers on Brownian motion are contained in *Investigations on the Theory of the Brownian Movement,* edited by R. Furth (London, 1926). Important material dealing with the birth of quantum mechanics is contained in *Letters on Wave Mechanics—Schrödinger, Planck, Einstein, and Lorentz* edited by K. Przibram (New York, 1967), while Einstein letters dealing with science in general and with nonscientific subjects are contained in *Briefwechsel—Albert Einstein/Arnold Sommerfeld,* edited and with commentary by Armin Hermann (Basel and Stuttgart, 1968), and in *Briefwechsel 1916–1955—Albert Einstein/Max Born* (Munich, 1969; *Born—Einstein Letters,* London, 1971).

Books explaining relativity and putting Einstein's work in the larger context of science are as numerous as their quality is varied. Among the best are *Relativity Theory: Its Origins and Impact on Modern Thought,* edited by L. Pearce Williams (New York, 1968); Max Born's *Einstein's Theory of Relativity* (London, 1924); Pai's *Theory of Relativity* (New York 1958); Clement V. Duell's *Readable Relativity* (London 1966); Lincoln Barnett's *Universe and Dr. Einstein* (London 1949); Freundlich's *The Foundations of Einstein's Theory of Gravitation* (Cambridge 1924); Russell's *The ABC of Relativity* (London 1925); Bob's *Relativity and Commonsense* (London 1964); Charles Nordmann's *Einstein and the Universe* (London 1922); and Cornelius Lanczos' *Albert Einstein and the Cosmic World Order* (London, 1965).

A number of Einstein's miscellaneous writings are contained in *The World As I See It* (London, 1935) and *Out of My Later Years* (London, 1950), and a selection of speeches and letters in *About Zionism* (London, 1930). Many of his early pacifist writings are included in *The*

Fight Against War, edited by Alfred Lief (New York, 1933), and the bulk of them in *Einstein on Peace*, edited by Otto Nathan and Heinz Norden (London, 1963).

Einstein's autobiographical writings are limited to the—exclusively scientific—account of his development in Schilpp's *Albert Einstein: Philosopher-Scientist* (Evanston, Ill., 1949), and the brief notes in *Helle Zeit; Dunkel Zeit* (Zurich, 1956), a volume of reminiscences edited by Carl Seelig. The first attempt to give him a biographical background was made by Alexander Moszkowski in *Einstein the Searcher: His Work Explained from Dialogues with Einstein* (Berlin, 1921), a book which Einstein's friends ineffectively urged him to suppress. It was the first of many. The husband of one stepdaughter produced a psudonymous biography—*Albert Einstein*, by Anton Reiser (London, 1931)—to which Einstein gave his cachet; the husband of the other produced, together with a journalist colleague, a book— *Einstein* (New York, 1944)—which he repudiated. His doctor friend, John Plesch, devoted two chapters of his autobiographical *Janos* (London, 1947) to Albert Einstein; a writer friend of his second wife, Antonina Vallentin, wrote a personal account of his life; while a Berlin acquaintance, David Reichinstein, wrote an *Albert Einstein* which its subject unsuccessfully tried to suppress. Three lives written with varying degrees of blessing from their subject are: Philipp Frank's *Einstein: His Life and Times* (London, 1948), Carl Seelig's *Albert Einstein* (London, 1956), and Leopold Infeld's *Albert Einstein* (New York and London, 1950). In certain of the above volumes, as well as in various journal articles, some of Einstein's letters appear in stylistically different translations.

The files of *Annalen der Physik, Nature, Science, The Times* (London), and the *New York Times* have been used extensively, as have many other journals, magazines, and papers to which individual reference is made in the "Notes," which begin on page 785. The following is a select bibliography of the books and journal articles which have been found useful or to which specific reference is made below. For convenience, the bibliographical details of Einstein's main papers are given here; but the full list of his scientific publications runs to nearly forty pages and should be consulted, if required, in one of the bibliographies referred to above.

ADAMS, Walter S. "George Ellery Hale," *Astrophysical Journal*, Vol. 87, 1938.

BADASH, L. (ed.). *Rutherford and Boltwood: Letters on Radioactivity*, New Haven, 1969.

BARKER, Sir Ernest. *Age and Youth*, Oxford, 1953.

BARNETT, Lincoln. *The Universe and Dr. Einstein*, London, 1949.

BAXTER, James Phinney. *Scientists Against Time*, Boston, 1946.

BELL, E. T. *Men of Mathematics*, London, 1965.

BELL, G. K. A. *Randall Davidson, Archbishop of Canterbury;* London, 1935.

BEN-GURION, David. *Ben-Gurion Looks Back in Talks with Moshe Pearlman*, London, 1965.

BENTWICH, Norman. *The Hebrew University of Jerusalem 1918–60*, London, 1961.

BENTWICH, Norman. *Judah L. Magnes*, Philadelphia, 1954.

BENTWICH, Norman. *My Seventy-Seven Years: An Account of My Life and Times 1881–1960*, London, 1962.

BENTWICH, Norman. *The Rescue and Achievement of Refugee Scholars*, The Hague, 1953.

BENTWICH, Norman. *Wanderer Between Two Worlds*, London, 1941.

BENTWICH, Norman and Helen. *Mandate Memories 1918–1948*, London, 1965.

BIRKENHEAD, The Earl of. *The Prof in Two Worlds*, London, 1961.

BLUMENFELD, Kurt. *Erlebte Judenfrage*, Stuttgart, 1962.

BOHR, Niels. *Essays 1958–1962 on Atomic Physics and Human Knowledge*, New York, 1963.

BONDI, Hermann. *Assumption and Myth in Physical Theory*, Cambridge, 1965.

BONDI, Hermann. *Relativity and Commonsense*, London, 1964.

BOORSTIN, Daniel (ed.). *An American Primer*, Chicago, 1966.

BORK, Alfred H. "The Fitzgerald Contraction," *Isis*, Vol. 57 (1966), pp. 199-207.

BORN, Max. *Einstein's Theory of Relativity*, New York, 1962.

BORN, Max. *Natural Philosophy of Cause and Chance* (The Waynflete Lectures, 1948), Oxford, 1949.

BORN, Max. *Physics in My Generation*, London, 1956, and New York, 1969.

BRAUNTHAL, Julius. *In Search of the Millennium*, London, 1945.

BRODETSKY, Selig. *Memoirs: From Ghetto to Israel*, London, 1960.

BUBER, Martin. *The Knowledge of Man*, London, 1965.

BYRNES, James F. *All in One Lifetime*, New York, 1958.

CAMPBELL, Lewis, and W. Garnet. *James Clerk Maxwell*, London, 1884.

CLARK, Ronald W. *The Birth of the Bomb*, London, 1961.

CLARK, Ronald W. *Tizard*, London, 1965.

CLINE, Barbara Lovett. *The Questioners: Physicists and the Quantum Theory*, New York, 1965.

COHEN, Harry A. "An Afternoon with Einstein," *Jewish Spectator*, January, 1969, p. 13.

COHEN, I. Bernard. "An Interview with Einstein," *Scientific American*, Vol. 193 (1955), p. 69.

COHEN, Morris Raphael. *A Dreamer's Journey*, Boston, 1949.

COHEN, Morris Raphael. "Einstein and His World," *The Menorah Journal*, Vol. 24 (Spring, 1936), p. 107.

COHEN, Morris Raphael. *The Faith of a Liberal*, New York, 1946.

COMPTON, Arthur H. "The Scattering of X-Rays," *Journal of the Franklin Institute*, Vol. 198, 1924.

DAMPIER, Sir William. *A Shorter History of Science*, London, 1945.

DE BROGLIE, Louis. *New Perspectives in Physics*, Edinburgh, 1962.

DE BROGLIE, Louis. *The Revolution in Physics: A Non-Mathematical Survey of Quanta*, London, 1954.

DE SITTER, W. "Einstein's Theory of Gravitation,"

Monthly Notices of the Royal Astronomical Society, Vol. LXXVI.

DE SITTER, W. *Kosmos: A Course of Six Lectures on the Development of Our Insight into the Structure of the Universe,* Cambridge, 1932.

DEUEL, Wallace. *People Under Hitler,* London, 1942.

DOUGLAS, A. Vibert. "Forty Minutes with Einstein," *Journal of the Royal Astronomical Society of Canada,* Vol. 50, No. 3, p. 99.

DOUGLAS, A. Vibert. *The Life of Arthur Stanley Eddington,* London, 1956.

DURRELL, Clement V. *Readable Relativity,* London, 1966.

EDDINGTON, Arthur. *Relativity* (Eighth Annual Haldane Lecture, May 26, 1937), London, 1937.

EDDINGTON, Arthur. *Report on the Relativity Theory of Gravitation,* London, 1918.

EDDINGTON, Arthur. *Space, Time and Gravitation,* London, 1920.

EDDINGTON, Arthur. *The Theory of Relativity and Its Influence on Scientific Thought* (Romanes Lecture, May 24, 1922), Oxford, 1922.

EHRENHAFT, Felix. "My Experiences with Einstein" (unpublished).

EINSTEIN, Albert. *About Zionism: Speeches and Letters by Professor Albert Einstein* (edited and translated by Leon Simon) London, 1930.

EINSTEIN, Albert. *The Fight Against War,* Alfred Lief, ed., New York, 1933.

EINSTEIN, Albert. *Ideas and Opinions,* London, 1964.

EINSTEIN, Albert. *Investigations on the Theory of the Brownian Movement,* London, 1926.

EINSTEIN, Albert. *Letters à Maurice Solvine,* Paris, 1956.

EINSTEIN, Albert. *Out of My Later Years,* London, 1950.

EINSTEIN, Albert. *The Theory of Relativity,* London, 1924.

EINSTEIN, Albert. *Why War?,* London, 1934.

EINSTEIN, Albert. *The World As I See It,* London, 1935.

EINSTEIN, Albert, and Max Born. *Briefwechsel 1916–*

1955, Munich, 1969 (*Born-Einstein Letters*, London, 1971).

EINSTEIN, Albert, and Leopold Infeld. *The Evolution of Physics*, Cambridge, 1938.

EINSTEIN, Albert, Erwin Schrödinger, Max Planck, and H. A. Lorentz. *Letters on Wave Mechanics*, K. Przibram, ed., New York, 1967.

EINSTEIN, Albert, and Arnold Sommerfeld. *Briefwechsel*, Basel and Stuttgart, 1968.

The following are among Einstein's more famous scientific papers and lectures:

1905: "Über einen die Erzeugung und Verwandlung des Lichtes betreffenden heuristischen Gesichtspunkt," *Annalen der Physik*, Ser. 4, Vol. 17, 1905, pp. 132–148.

1905: "Über die von der molekularkinetischen Theorie der Wärme geforderte Bewegung von in ruhenden Flüssigkeiten suspendierten Teilchen," *Annalen der Physik*, Ser. 4, Vol. 17, pp. 549–560.

1905: "Zur Elektrodynamik bewegter Körper," *Annalen der Physik*, Ser. 4, Vol. 17, 1905, pp. 891–921.

1905: "Ist die Trägheit eines Körpers von seinem Energieinhalt abhängig?" *Annalen der Physik*, Ser. 4, Vol. 18, 1905, pp. 639–641.

1907: "Die Planck'sche Theorie der Strahlung und die Theorie der spezifischen Wärme," *Annalen der Physik*, Ser. 4, Vol. 22, 1907, pp. 180–190 and p. 800 (Berichtigung).

1907: "Über das Relativitätsprinzip und die aus demselben gezogenen Folgerungen," *Jahrbuch der Radioaktivität und Elektronik*, Vol. 4, 1907, pp. 411–462, and Vol. 5, 1908, pp. 98–99 (Berichtigungen).

1909: "Über die Entwicklung unserer Anschauungen über das Wesen und die Konstitution der Strahlung," *Physikalische Zeitschrift*, Vol. 10, 1909, pp. 817–825.

1911: "Über den Einfluss der Schwerkraft auf die Ausbreitung des Lichtes," *Annalen der Physik*, Ser. 4, Vol. 35, 1911, pp. 898–908.

1913: "Entwurf einer verallgemeinerten Relativitätstheorie

und eine Theorie der Gravitation," I. Physikalischer Teil von A. Einstein. II. Mathematischer Teil von M. Grossmann. Sonderdruck aus *Zeitschrift für Mathematik und Physik*, Vol. 62, 1913, pp. 225–261 (Physikalischer Teil, pp. 225–244).

1915: "Erklärung der Perihelbewegung des Merkur aus der allgemeinen Relativitätstheorie," *Preussische Akademie der Wissenschaften, Sitzungsberichte,* 1915, Pt. 2, pp. 831–839.

1916: "Die Grundlage der allgemeinen Relativitätstheorie," *Annalen der Physik*, Ser. 4, Vol. 49, 1916, pp. 769–822.

1917: "Zur Quantentheorie der Strahlung," *Physikalische Zeitschrift,* Vol. 18, 1917, pp. 121–128.

1917: "Kosmologische Betrachtungen zur allgemeinen Relativitätstheorie," *Preussische Akademie der Wissenschaften, Sitzungsberichte,* 1917, Pt. 1, pp. 142–152.

1924: "Quantentheorie des einatomigen idealen Gases," *Preussische Akademie der Wissenschaften, Phys.-math. Klasse, Sitzungsberichte*, 1924, pp. 261–267.

and

1925: "Quantentheorie des einatomigen idealen Gases. 2. Abhandlung," *Preussische Akademie der Wissenschaften, Phys.-math. Klasse, Sitzungsberichte,* 1925, pp. 3–14.

1928: "Fundamental Concepts of Physics and Their Most Recent Changes," *St. Louis Post-Dispatch,* December 29, 1928. (*A translation of the Davos Hochschule Lecture, not printed elsewhere.*)

1929: "Zur Einheitlichen Feldtheorie," *Preussische Akademie der Wissenschaften, Phys.-math. Klasse, Sitzungsberichte*, 1929, pp. 2–7.

1933: *On the Method of Theoretical Physics*. The Herbert Spencer Lecture delivered at Oxford, June 10, 1933. Oxford, 1933.

1933: *Origins of the General Theory of Relativity*. Lecture of the George A. Gibson Foundation in the University of Glasgow, June 20, 1933. Glasgow (Glasgow University Publications, No. 30), 1933.

1935: "Can Quantum-Mechanical Description of Physical Reality Be Considered Complete?", with B. Podolsky and N. Rosen. *Physical Review*, Ser. 2, Vol. 47, 1935, pp. 777–780.

EISENHART, Churchill. "Albert Einstein, As I Remember Him," *Journal of the Washington Academy of Sciences*, Vol. 54 (1964), pp. 325–328.

EPSTEIN, Jacob. *Let There Be Sculpture*, London, 1940.

EVE, A. S. *Rutherford*, Cambridge, 1939.

FERMI, Laura. *Illustrious Immigrants: The Intellectual Migration from Europe 1930–1941*, Chicago, 1968.

FIERZ, M., and V. F. Weisskopf. *Theoretical Physics in the Twentieth Century: A Memorial Volume to Wolfgang Pauli*, New York and London, 1960.

FISHER, H. A. L. *The History of Europe*, London, 1936.

FITZROY, Sir Almeric. *Memoirs, Vol. II*, London, n.d.

FLAMMARION, Camille. *Lumen*, Paris, 1873.

FLEXNER, Abraham. *I Remember*, New York, 1940.

FLUCKIGER, Max. *A. E. in Bern*, Berne.

FRANK, Philipp. *Einstein: His Life and Times*, London, 1948.

FRANK, Philipp. *Interpretations and Misinterpretations of Modern Physics*, Paris, 1938.

FRANK, Philipp. *Modern Science and Its Philosophy*, Cambridge, Mass., 1949.

FRANK, Philipp. *Relativity—A Richer Truth*, London, 1951.

FREUD, Sigmund. *Letters of Sigmund Freud, 1873–1939*, London, 1961.

FREUNDLICH, Erwin. *The Foundations of Einstein's Theory of Gravitation*, Cambridge, 1920.

FURER, Admiral. *Administration of the Navy Department in World War Two*, Washington, D.C., 1959.

GAMOW. George. *My World Line*, New York, 1970.

GEORGE, Hereford. *The Oberland and Its Glaciers, Explored and Illustrated with Ice-Axe and Camera*, London, 1866.

GILPIN, Robert. *American Scientists and Nuclear Weapons Policy*, Princeton, N.J., 1962.

GOLDMAN, Nahum. *Memories*, London, 1970.

GORAN, Morris. *The Story of Fritz Haber*, Norman, Okla., 1967.

GOUDSMIT, Samuel A. *Alsos*, New York, 1947.

GOWING, Margaret. *Britain and Atomic Energy 1939–1945*, London, 1964.

GROSSMANN, Kurt R. "Peace Movements in Germany," *South Atlantic Quarterly* (July, 1950), Durham, N.C.

HAAS-LORENTZ, G. J. de(ed.). *H. A. Lorentz: Impressions of His Life and Work*, Amsterdam, 1957.

HADAMARD, Jacques. *An Essay on the Psychology of Invention in the Mathematical Field*, Princeton, N.J., 1945.

HAHN, Otto. *My Life*, London, 1970.

HALDANE, R. B. *The Reign of Relativity*, London, 1921.

HANNAK, Dr. J. *Emanuel Lasker: The Life of a Chess Master*, London, 1959.

HARROD, R. F. *The Prof*, London, 1959.

HARTSHORNE, Edward Yarnall, Jr. *The German Universities and National Socialism*, London, 1937.

HEISENBERG, Werner. *Physics and Philosophy: The Revolution in Modern Science*, New York, 1962.

Helvetica Physica Acta, Supplementum IV, Basel, 1956.

HERNECK, Friedrich, "Über die deutsche Reichsangehörigkeit Albert Einstein," *Die Naturwissenschaften*, Heft 2, S 33, 1961.

HEWLETT, G., and E. D. Anderson, Jr. *The New World, 1939–1946*, University Park, Penn., 1962.

HOFFMAN, Banesh. *The Strange Story of the Quantum*, New York, 1959.

HOLTON, Gerald. "Einstein, Michelson and the Crucial Experiment," *Isis*, Vol. 60, Pt. 2, No. 202, 1969.

HOLTON, Gerald. "Influences on Einstein's Early Work in Relativity Theory," *American Scholar*, Vol. 37, No. 1, Winter 1967–68.

HOLTON, Gerald. "Mach, Einstein, and the Search for Reality," *Daedalus* (Spring, 1968), Cambridge, Mass.

HOLTON, Gerald. "On the Origin of the Special Theory of Relativity," *American Journal of Physics*, Vol. 28, 1960.

HUBBLE, Edwin. *The Observational Approach to Cosmology* (The Rhodes Memorial Lectures, 1936), Oxford, 1937.

INFELD, Leopold. *Albert Einstein: His Work and Its Influence on Our World*, New York and London, 1950.

INFELD, Leopold. "As I See It," *Bulletin of the Atomic Scientists*, February, 1965.

INFELD, Leopold. *Quest: The Evolution of a Scientist*, New York, 1941.

INGE, The Very Rev. W. R. *Diary of a Dean: St. Pauls 1911–1934*, London, 1949.

INGE, William Ralph. *God and the Astronomers*, London, 1933.

JAFFE, Bernard. *Michelson and the Speed of Light*, London, 1961.

JEANS, Sir James. *The New Background of Science*, Ann Arbor, Mich., 1959.

JEANS, Sir James. *The Universe Around Us*, Cambridge, 1930.

JONES, R. V. "Thicker than Heavy Water," *Chemistry and Industry*, August 26, 1967.

KARMAN, Theodore von. *The Wind and Beyond*, Toronto, 1967.

KISCH, F. H. *Palestine Diary*, London, 1938.

KLEIN, Martin J. "Einstein's First Paper on Quanta," *The Natural Philosopher*, Vol. 2, New York, 1963.

KLEIN, Martin J. "Einstein and the Wave-Particle Duality," *The Natural Philosopher*, Vol. 3, New York, 1964.

KLEIN, Martin J. *Paul Ehrenfest*. Vol. 1. *The Making of a Theoretical Physicist*, Amsterdam, 1970.

KUZNETSOV, B. *Einstein*, Moscow, 1965.

LEMAÎTRE, Georges. "The Beginning of the World from the Point of View of the Quantum Theory," *Nature*, Vol. 127 (1931), p. 706.

LEMAÎTRE, Georges. *The Primeval Atom: An Essay on Cosmogony*, New York, 1950.

LIEF, Alfred (ed.), *The Fight Against War*, New York, 1933.

LINDEMANN, F. A. "Einstein's Theory: A Revolution in Thought," *Times Educational Supplement*, January 29, 1920.

LINDEMANN, A. F. and F. A. "Daylight Photography

of Stars As a Means of Testing Equivalence Postulate in the Theory of Relativity," *Monthlv Notices* of the Royal Astronomical Society, Vol. LXXVII, December 2, 1916.

LODGE, Sir Oliver. "Einstein's Real Achievement," *Fortnightly Review,* DCLVII, new series, September, 1921.

LORENTZ, H. A. *H. A. Lorentz: Impressions of His Life and Work* (ed. G. J. de Haas-Lorentz), Amsterdam, 1957.

LORENTZ, H. A., Albert Einstein, H. Weyl, and A. Minkowski. *The Principle of Relativity, A Collection of Original Memoirs on the Special and General Theory of Relativity,* New York, 1952.

LOVELL, Sir Bernard. *Our Present Knowledge of the Universe*, Manchester, 1967.

LOWENSTEIN, Prince Hubertus of. *Towards the Farther Shore,* London, 1968.

MACH, Ernst. *The Science of Mechanics,* Chicago and London, 1907.

MARIANOFF, Dimitri, and Palm Wayne. *Einstein: An Intimate Study of a Great Man*, New York, 1944.

MARTIN, Kingsley. *Editor; a Second Volume of Autobiography, 1931–1945*, London, 1968.

MEITNER, Lise. "As I Remember," *Bulletin of the Atomic Scientists,* November, 1964.

MICHELMORE, Peter. *Einstein: Profile of the Man,* London, 1963.

MILLIKAN, Robert A. *The Autobiography of Robert A. Millikan*, London, 1951.

MILLIKAN, Robert A. *The Electron*, Chicago, 1917.

MILLIKAN, Robert A. *Time, Matter and Values*, Chapel Hill, N.C., 1932.

MILNE, E. A. *The Aims of Mathematical Physics*, Oxford 1930.

MILNE, E. A. *Modern Cosmology and the Christian Idea of God*, Oxford, 1952.

MILNE, E. A. *Sir James Jeans: A Biography*, Cambridge, 1952.

MOORE, Ruth. *Niels Bohr: The Man and the Scientist,* London, 1967.

MOSSE, George L. *Nazi Culture: Intellectual, Cultural and Social Life in the Third Reich*, London, 1966.

MOSZKOWSKI, Alexander. *Einstein the Searcher: His Work Explained from Dialogues with Einstein*, Berlin, 1921.
MOWRER, Edgar Ansel. *Germany Puts the Clock Back*, London, 1933.

NATHAN, Otto, and Heinz Norden (eds.). *Einstein on Peace*, London, 1963.
NEWTON, Sir Isaac. *Mathematical Principles of Natural Philosophy*, Berkeley, 1960.
NEWTON, Sir Isaac. *Opticks*, New York, 1952 (based on the Fourth Edition, London, 1730).
NOBEL FOUNDATION (ed.). *Nobel: The Man and His Prizes*, Stockholm, 1950.
NORDMANN, Charles. "Einstein in Paris," *Revue des Deux Mondes*, Vol. 8, 7th series, Paris, 1922.
NORDMANN, Charles. "Einstein à Paris," *L'Illustration*, April 15, 1922.
NORDMANN, Charles. *The Tyranny of Time: Einstein or Bergson*, London, 1925.
NORTH, J. D. *The Measure of the Universe*, Oxford, 1965.

OPPENHEIMER, J. Robert. "On Albert Einstein" (Lecture delivered at UNESCO House, December 13, 1965), reprinted in *The New York Review*, March 17, 1966.
OPPENHEIMER, J. Robert. *The Flying Trapeze: Three Crises for Physicists* (The Whidden Lectures for 1962), Oxford, 1964.

PAULI, W. *The Theory of Relativity*, New York, 1958.
PLANCK, Max. *The Origin and Development of the Quantum Theory*, (Nobel Prize Address, June 2, 1920), Oxford, 1922.
PLANCK, Max. *Scientific Biography and Other Papers*, London, 1950.
PLANCK, Max. *Where Is Science Going?*, London, 1933.
PLESCH, John. *Janos: The Story of a Doctor*, London, 1947.
POLANYI, Michael. *The Logic of Liberty: Reflections and Rejoiners*, London, 1951.
POLANYI, Michael. *Personal Knowledge*, London, 1958.
PRZIBRAM, K. (ed.). *Letters on Wave Mechanics:*

Schrödinger, Planck, Einstein, Lorentz, translated and with an introduction by Martin J. Klein, New York, 1967.

RAYLEIGH, Lord. *The Life of Sir J. J. Thomson, O.M.*, Cambridge, 1942.

REICH, Ilse Ollendorff. *Wilhelm Reich*, London, 1969.

REICH, Wilhelm. *Biographical Material: History of the Discovery of Life Energy—the Einstein Affair*, Orgonon, Rangeley Maine, 1953.

REICHINSTEIN, David. *Albert Einstein: A Picture of His Life and His Conception of the World*, Prague, 1934.

REISER, Anton. *Albert Einstein: A Biographical Portrait*, London, 1931.

RINGER, Fritz K. *The Decline of the German Mandarins*, Cambridge, Mass., 1969.

ROBB, Alfred A. *The Absolute Relations of Time and Space*, Cambridge, 1921.

ROBB, Alfred A. *A Theory of Time and Space*, Cambridge, 1914.

ROLLAND, Romain. *Le Bund Neues Vaterland (1914–1916)*, Lyon and Paris, 1952.

ROLLAND, Romain. *Journal des Années de Guerre 1914–1919*, Paris, 1953.

ROSENFELD, L. *Niels Bohr: An Essay*, Amsterdam, 1961.

ROSENFELD, Leonora Cohen. *Portrait of a Philosopher: Morris R. Cohen in Life and Letters*, New York, 1948.

ROTBLAT, J. *Pugwash*, Prague, 1967.

ROZENTAL, S. (ed.). *Niels Bohr*, Amsterdam, 1967.

RUSSELL, Bertrand. *The ABC of Relativity*, London, 1925.

RUTHERFORD OF NELSON, Lord. "The Transformation of Energy." (Watt Anniversary Lecture for 1936 delivered before the Greenock Philosophical Society, January 1, 1936.)

SACHS, Alexander. *Background and Early History, Atomic Bomb Project in Relation to President Roosevelt*, Washington, D.C., 1945.

SAMUEL, Viscount. *Belief and Action: An Everyday Philosophy*, London, 1937.

SAMUEL, Viscount. *Essay in Physics*, Oxford, 1951.

SAMUEL, Viscount. *Memoirs*, London, 1945.

SAMUEL, Viscount, and Herbert Dingle. "*A Threefold Cord: Philosophy, Science, and Religion.*" *A Discussion Between Viscount Samuel and Professor Herbert Dingle*, London, 1961.

SCHILPP, Paul Arthur (ed.). *Albert Einstein: Philosopher-Scientist*, Evanston, Ill., 1949.

SCHONLAND. Sir Basil. *The Atomists*, Oxford, 1968.

SCHRÖDINGER, Erwin. *Mind and Matter* (The Tarner Lectures, 1956), Cambridge, 1958.

SCOTT, C. P. *The Political Diaries of C. P. Scott, 1911–1928*, London, 1970.

SEELIG, Carl. *Albert Einstein: A Documentary Biography*, London, 1956.

SEELIG, Carl (ed.). *Helle Zeit; Dunkel Zeit*, Zurich, 1956.

SHANKLAND, R. S. "Conversations with Albert Einstein," *American Journal of Physics*, Vol. 31 (1963), pp. 47–57.

SHAPLEY, A. *Through Rugged Ways to the Stars*, New York, 1969.

SHIRER, William. *The Rise and Fall of the Third Reich*, New York, 1960.

SMITH, Alice Kimball. *A Peril and a Hope: the Scientists' Movement in America, 1945–47* Chicago, 1965.

SMITH, Jean, and Arthur Toynbee, (ed.). *Gilbert Murray: An Unfinished Autobiography*, London, 1960.

SMYTH, H. D. *Atomic Energy for Military Power*, Washington, D.C., 1945.

SOMMER, Dudley. *Haldane of Cloan: His Life and Times 1856–1928*, London, 1960.

SPEIGHT-HUMBERTSON, Clara E. *Spiritism: The Hidden Secret in Einstein's Theory of Relativity*, Kitchener, Ontario, n.d.

STEIN, Leonard. *Zionism*, London, 1925.

STERN, Alfred. "An Interview with Einstein," *Contemporary Jewish Record*, VIII (June, 1945), pp. 245-49.

STRAUSS, Lewis. *Men and Decisions*, London, 1963.

STUART, James. *Within the Fringe*, London, 1967.

SZILARD, Leo. *Perspectives in American History*, Vol. II, Cambridge, 1968.

TALMEY, Max. *The Relativity Theory Simplified and the Formative Period of Its Inventor*, New York, 1932.

TEMPLEWOOD, Viscount. *Nine Troubled Years*, London, 1954.

THIRRING, J. H. *The Ideas of Einstein's Theory*, London, 1921.

THOMSON, Sir J. J. *Recollections and Reflections*, London, 1936.

TOYNBEE, Arnold J. *Acquaintances*, Oxford, 1967.

TSCHERNOWITZ, Chaim. "A Day with Albert Einstein," *Jewish Sentinel*, Vol. I (September, 1931).

ULITZUR, A. *Two Decades of Keren Hayesod*, Jerusalem, 1940.

VALLENTIN, Antonina. *Einstein: A Biography*, London, 1954.

VOSS, Carl Hermann (ed.). *Servant of the People* (the letters of Stephen Wise), Philadelphia, 1969.

WATTERS, Leon L. "Comments on the Letters of Professor and Mrs. Albert Einstein to Dr. Leon L. Watters" (unpublished).

WEIL, E. *Albert Einstein: A Bibliography of His Scientific Papers, 1901–1930*, London, 1937.

WEISGAL, Meyer W., and Joel Carmichael (eds). *Chaim Weizman: A Biography by Several Hands*, New York, 1963.

WEIZMANN, Chaim. *Trial and Error*, London, 1950.

WEIZMANN, Vera. *The Impossible Takes Longer*, London, 1967.

WEYL, Hermann. *The Open World* (Three Lectures on the Metaphysical Implications of Science), New Haven, Conn., 1932.

WHITEHEAD, A. N: *Science and the Modern World*, London, 1926.

WHITROW, G. J. (ed.). *Einstein: The Man and His Achievement*, London, 1967.

WHITTAKER, Sir Edmund. *Albert Einstein, Biographical Memoirs of Fellows of the Royal Society*, Vol. 1, 1955.

WHITTAKER, Sir Edmund. *From Euclid to Eddington*, New York, 1958.

WHITTAKER, Sir Edmund. *History of the Theories of the Aether and Electricity*, 2 vols., London, 1951 and 1953.

WHYTE, L. L. *Focus and Diversions*, London, 1963.

WILSON, Margaret. *Ninth Astronomer Royal: The Life of Frank Watson Dyson*, Cambridge, 1951.

WOLF, Edwin, II (with John F. Fleming). *Rosenbach: A Biography*, London, 1960.

NOTES

PAGE

19 "one of the follies of my life": Einstein–Plesch, February 3, 1944, material in hands of the Plesch family (afterward referred to as "Plesch correspondence").

20 "pas très Juif": private note by Lord Samuel of conversation, October 31, 1930, Samuel Papers, House of Lords Records Office (afterward referred to as "Samuel Papers").

21 Genealogical details: "Der Stammbaum Prof. Albert Einsteins" by Rabbiner Dr. A. Tanzer, *Jüdische Familien-Forschung*, Jahrgang VII, December 1931, and Israelitische Kultusvereinigung Württemberg und Hohenzollern. Genealogical trees of both the Einstein and the Koch families also exist in the Einstein Archives in Princeton (afterward referred to as "Princeton").

21 "my husband mystical": G. K. A. Bell, *Randall Davidson*, p. 1052.

22 "His mode of life": Philipp Frank, *Einstein: His Life and Times* (afterward referred to as "Frank"), p. 15.

22 "exceedingly friendly": Einstein–Bela Kornitzer, *Gazette & Daily*, York, Pa., September 20, 1948 (afterward referred to as "Kornitzer").

22 "no particular talent": Carl Seelig, *Albert Einstein* (afterward referred to as "Seelig"), p. 11.

23 Ulm birthplace details: Stadtarchiv, Ulm.

24 "excellent, reliable, incorruptible": Max Born, obituary notices, *Fellows of the Royal Society*, Vol. 6, No. 17, November 1948, p. 161.

26 "every reminiscence": autobiographical notes in *Albert Einstein: Philosopher-Scientist*, Paul A. Schilpp, ed. (afterward referred to as "Schilpp"), p. 3.

26 "marvelous memory": John Plesch, *Janos* (afterward referred to as "Plesch"), p. 200.

27 "something for psychoanalysts": Einstein–Plesch, February 3, 1944, Plesch correspondence.

27 "Leonardo da Vinci . . . Einstein, and Niels Bohr": *News Letter No. 1* of The North Surrey Dyslexic (Word Blind) Society, September 1968, p. 3. Letter from Mrs. V. W. Fisher to author, November 9, 1968.

27 "I sometimes ask myself": Einstein–James Franck, quoted Seelig, p. 71.

28 "A true story": Kornitzer.

29 "man has little insight": questionnaire on seventy-fourth birthday, Seelig, p. 211.

29 "algebra is a merry science": Frank, p. 24.

30 "my best-loved uncle": Einstein–Cäsar Koch, March 28, 1924. Documents in possession of the Suzanne Gottschalk–Jean Ferrard family, Brussels. Translation by Dr. Jagdish Mehra.

31 "teachers . . . like sergeants": quoted in B. Kuznetsov, *Einstein*, p. 22.

31 "keep your manuscript": Einstein, *The World As I See It*, p. 21.

32 "could not . . . say that he hated it": Antonina Vallentin, *Einstein* (afterward referred to as "Vallentin"), p. 8.

32 "Respect for Planck": Kornitzer.

33 "the happy, comfortable . . . Einstein home": Max Talmey, *The Relativity Theory Simplified and the Formative Period of Its Inventor* (afterward referred to as "Talmey"), p. 161.

33 "a pretty, dark-haired boy": Talmey, p. 161.

34 "worked through the whole book of Spieker": Talmey, p. 164.

34 "living matter and clarity": Einstein–Hedwig Born, January 15, 1927, *Born–Einstein Letters*, London, 1971 (afterward referred to as "Born Letters"), p. 95.

34 "biological procedures": Carl Seelig, ed., *Helle Zeit; Dunkel Zeit* (afterward referred to as "*Helle Zeit*"), p. 64.

34-35 "how primitive physics still is": Einstein–Szilard, July 12, 1947, Szilard Papers, San Diego (afterward referred to as "Szilard Papers").

35 "they follow beams": "Comments on the Letters of Professor and Mrs. Albert Einstein to Dr. Leon L. Watters," unpublished MS, American Jewish Archives (afterward referred to as "Watters"), p. 4.

35 "reasonable view": Einstein–Samuel, undated, believed October 1937, Samuel Papers.

36 "Fanatic [orgy of] freethinking": Schilpp, p. 3.

36 "the Hebrew mind has been obsessed": Abba Eban, *The Jewish Chronicle*, October 2, 1959, p. 33.

37 "a great eternal riddle": Schilpp, p. 5.

37 "the *arcana* of nature": Hereford George, *The Oberland and Its Glaciers, Explored and Illustrated with Ice-Axe and Camera*, London, 1866.

37 "to draw His lines after Him": Martin Buber, *The Knowledge of Man*, p. 156.

37 "how God created the world": Esther Salaman, "A Talk with Einstein," *The Listener*, September 8, 1955 (afterward referred to as "Salaman").

38 "God is subtle but he is not malicious": for origin of phrase, see p. 390.

38 "God does not play dice": for origin of phrase, see p. 340.

38 "Spinoza's God": *New York Times*, April 25, 1929.

38 "something behind the energy": David Ben-Gurion, *Ben-Gurion Looks Back*, p. 217.

39 "your presence . . . disruptive": Frank, p. 27.

40 "the ordinary Italian": Harry A. Cohen, "An Afternoon with Einstein," *Jewish Spectator*, January 1969, p. 16.

41 " 'sensible trade' of electrical engineering": Hans Einstein, quoted in Kornitzer, *Ladies Home Journal*, April 1951, p. 136.

41 "My dear Uncle" and (p. 23) "Concerning the Investigation of the State of Aether in Magnetic Fields": undated letter and MS, Einstein–Cäsar Koch, authenticated c. 1950 by Einstein. Documents in possession of the Suzanne Gottschalk–Jean Ferrard family, Brussels. Translation by Dr. Jagdish Mehra. Pre-print no. of "Albert Einstein's 'First' Paper" by Jagdish Mehra, CPT-82: AEC-31, January 8, 1971.

42 "spatially oscillatory electromagnetic field at rest": Schilpp, p. 53.

44 "his influence to let Albert jump a class": Plesch, p. 219.

44 "entirely his own fault": Plesch, p. 219.

45 "supposed to choose a practical profession": Kornitzer.

45 "the most pleasing example": Einstein, *Aargauer Tageblatt*, February 19, 1952.

46 "pretty much the same to me": Seelig, p. 19.

46 "Sure of himself, his gray felt hat": Seelig, p. 14.

47 "I should certainly not have understood": Dr. Hans Mühsam in *Helle Zeit*, p. 57.

48 "he was by nationality a German": André Mercier, quoted G. J. Whitrow, ed., *Einstein: The Man and His Achievement*, BBC Third Programme Talks (afterward referred to as "Whitrow"), p. 17.

48 "give up his passport": Walter Jens, "Albert Einstein," *Universitas*, Vol. 11, No. 3, 1969, p. 243.

48 "formally ended Einstein's German nationality": Stadtarchiv, Ulm.

48 "Between the ages of fifteen and twenty-one": Einstein–Plesch, February 3, 1944, Plesch correspondence.

50 "When I was a very young man": Watters, p. 26.

50 "he did not care for large, impressive mountains": Hans Einstein, quoted Whitrow, p. 21.

50 Fräulein Markwalder, quoted Seelig, p. 36.

51 "It's in my blood": Seelig, p. 15.

52 "masculine good looks": Vallentin, p. 3.

52 "he was attracted to women who did physical work": Vera Weizmann, *The Impossible Takes Longer*, pp. 102–03.

53 "Personal matters": *The Observer*, London, April 24, 1955.

53 "the experience of the exterior world": "Jubilee of Relativity Theory," *Helvetica Physica Acta*, Supplementum iv, Basel, 1956 (afterward referred to as "*Physica Acta*"), p. 19.

53 "not been embarrassed by much learning": Morris R. Cohen, "Einstein and His World." *The Menorah Journal*, Vol. 24, Spring 1936 (afterward referred to as "*Menorah*"), p. 107.

54 "saw that mathematics was split up": Schilpp, p. 15.

54 "approach to a more profound knowledge": Schilpp, p. 17.

54 "fascinated by the direct contact with experience": Schilpp, p. 15.

55 "to construct an apparatus": Anton Reiser, *Albert Einstein* (afterward referred to as "Reiser"), p. 53.

55 "excellent teachers": Schilpp, p. 15.

55 "His lectures were outstanding": Die Einstein-Sammlung der ETH Bibliothek, Zurich (afterward referred to as "ETH"), and Seelig, p. 29.

55 Maxwell's work was not touched upon: Gerald Holton, "Influences on Einstein's Early Work in Relativity Theory," *American Scholar*, Vol. 37, No. 1, Winter 1967–68 (afterward referred to as "Holton"), p. 63.

55 "the most fascinating subject": Schilpp, p. 33.

56 "explanations of new discoveries fitted together": Sir William Dampier, *A Shorter History of Science*, p. 92.

58 "Maxwell's theory . . . not a part": Max Born, "Physics in the Last 50 Years," *Nature*, Vol. 168, 1951, p. 625.

58 "In the beginning": Schilpp, p. 19.

59 "to study at home": Schilpp, p. 15.

59 "the last man": E. T. Bell, *Men of Mathematics*, Vol. 2, p. 581.

60 "These are the only realities": quoted Holton, "Mach, Einstein, and the Search for Reality," *Daedalus*, Spring 1968, p. 659.

60 "not speculative in origin": typically, lecture, King's College, London, 1921, quoted *The Nation*, London, June 18, 1921.

60 "great influence on my development": Einstein–Herr Dr. Ing. Armin Weiner, September 18, 1930, Burndy Library.

60 "a long philosophical pilgrimage": see Holton, *Daedalus*, p. 636.

60 "exercised a profound influence": Schilpp, p. 21.

61 "to warn you in your own interest": quoted "Erinnerungen an Einstein" by Margarete Niewenhuis von Uexküll, *Frankfurter Allgemeine Zeitung*, March 10, 1956; also "Albert Einstein nach meiner Erinnerung" by Uexküll, ETH.

61 "had not published anything": Einstein–Plesch, February 2, 1944, Plesch correspondence.

62 "The coercion had such a deterring effect": Schilpp, p. 17.

62 "I, a pariah": Einstein–Frau Grossmann, Seelig, p. 207.

63 "I was unable to attend": Einstein–Hurvitz, September 26, 1900, Seelig, p. 49. (Since numerous early Einstein letters appear in Seelig, page references to English edition are given. Some letters appear elsewhere with stylistic differences and Seelig translation is not always used.)

63 "not have taken the liberty": Einstein–Hurvitz, September 23, 1900, Seelig, p. 48.

63 "happy in Switzerland": Infeld, *Albert Einstein*, p. 119.

63 "I commend my application": Stadtarchiv, Zurich.

64 "perfectly in agreement": Stadtarchiv, Zurich.

64 "The Zurich city fathers": Reiser, p. 65.

65 "I love the Swiss": Einstein–Wisseler, August 24, 1948, Swiss National Library, Berne.

65 "opponents of military imperialism": *Menorah*, p. 53.

66 "I hear through a student friend": Einstein–Kamerlingh Onnes, April 12, 1901. Rijksmuseum voor de Geschiedenis der Natuurwetenschappen, Leiden (afterward referred to as "Leiden").

67 "offered a position . . . at Winterthur": Einstein–Professor Alfred Stern, May 3, 1901, ETH.

68 "I, the undersigned": Bureau Fédéral de la Propriété Intellectuelle, Berne (afterward referred to as "Bureau Fédéral").

69 "deeply moved by your devotion": Einstein–Grossmann, April 14, 1901, Seelig, p. 52.

70 "Albert was examined": Reiser, p. 65.

70 "Thorough academic education": Bureau Fédéral.

73 "proved himself very useful": quotation from Haller and details of salary and gradings, Bureau Fédéral.

73 "as the principal achievement of Einstein's" and "crudeness in style": reports, ETH.

74 "good deal of poverty": Talmey, p. 167.

75 "More severe than my father": "Erinnerungen an Albert Einstein, 1902–1909," Bureau Fédéral.

75 "besides eight hours of work . . .": Einstein–Habicht, apparently dated summer 1905, Seelig, p. 75.

75 "the opportunity to think about physics": Einstein, *Helle Zeit*, p. 12.

76 "My major aim . . .": Schilpp, p. 47.

76 "more as a visualizing symbol": Schilpp, p. 19.

77 "first two papers": "Folgerungen aus den Kapillaritätserscheinungen," *Annalen der Physik*, Vol. 4, Series 4, pp. 513–23, and "Thermodynamische Theorie der Potentialdifferenz zwischen Metallen und vollständig dissoziierten Loesungen ihrer Salze, und eine elektrische Methode zur Erforschung der Molekularkraefte," *Annalen der Physik*, Vol. 8, Series 4, pp. 798–814.

77 "my two worthless beginner's works": Einstein–Stark, December 7, 1907, quoted A. Hermann, *Albert Einstein und Johannes Stark: Briefwechsel und Verhältnis der beiden Nobel-Preisträge*, Suddhoffs Archiv, Bd 50, 1966.

77 "I have got a few wonderful ideas": Seelig, p. 53.

78 "three more papers": "Kinetische Theorie des Wärmegleichgewichtes und des zweiten Hauptsatzes der Thermodynamik," *Annalen der Physik*, Vol. 9, Series 4, pp. 417–33, "Theorie der Grundlagen der Thermodynamik," *Annalen der Physik*, Vol. 14, Series 4, pp. 170–87, and "Allgemeine Molekulare Theorie der Wärme," *Annalen der Physik*, Vol. 14, Series 4, pp. 354–62.

78 "Walking in the streets of Berne one day": Einstein, *Lettres à Maurice Solovine*, (afterward referred to as "Solovine"), p. vi.

79 "Very often I met Einstein": Solovine–Seelig, April 14, 1952, ETH.

80 "Einstein is 1.76 meters tall": Seelig, p. 40.

80 "It's all the same to me": Solovine, p. x.

81 "a man's private life": Princeton.

82 "a modest unassuming creature": Seelig, p. 38.

83 "her dreamy, ponderous nature": Seelig, p. 46.

83 "she has such a lovely voice": Seelig, p. 38.

83 "How it came about": Watters, p. 14.

84 "He was sitting in his study in front of a heap of papers": Dr. Hans Tanner–Seelig, Seelig, p. 104.

85 "one hand rocking the bassinet": Reichinstein, *Albert Einstein: A Picture of His Life and His Conception of the World*, p. 25.

86 "blazing rockets": Louis de Broglie, in Schilpp, p. 110.

87 "promise you in return four works": Einstein–Habicht, early 1905, Seelig, p. 74.

88 "a movement of suspended microscopic particles open to observations": Schilpp, p. 47.

88 "These motions were such as to satisfy me": *Philosophical Magazine*, Pt. 4, 1828.

88 "M. Gouy": *Journal de Physics* (2), 7.561, 1888.

88 "Franz Exner": *Annalen der Physik*, 2.843, 1900.

88 "an impressive sight . . . contradictory to all previous experience": Einstein and Infeld, *The Evolution of Physics* (afterward referred to as "Einstein and Infeld"), p. 64.

89 "On the Motion of Small Particles": "Über die von der molekularkinetischen Theorie der Wärme geförderte Bewegung von in ruhenden Flüssigkeiten suspendierten Teilchen," *Annalen der Physik*, Vol. 17, Series 4, pp. 549–60.

89 "To appreciate the importance of this step": Max Born, *Natural Philosophy of Cause and Chance* (afterward referred to as "Born, *Cause and Chance*"), p. 63.

89 "the old fighter against atomistics": Sommerfeld, in Schilpp, p. 105.

89 "The accuracy of measurement": Born, *Cause and Chance*, p. 63.

90 "The antipathy of these scholars": Schilpp, p. 49.

90 "like a bolt from the blue": de Broglie, *New Perspectives in Physics*, p. 134.

90-91 "end his scientific life in sad isolation": de Broglie, *New Perspectives in Physics*, p. x.

91 "On a Heuristic Viewpoint": "Über einen die Erzeugung und Verwandlung des Lichtes betreffenden heuristischen Gesichtspunkt," *Annalen der Physik*, Vol. 18, Series 4, pp. 132–48.

94 "something fundamental . . . missed by both": Schonland, *The Atomists*, p. 70.

94 "clearness began to dawn upon me": Max Planck, *The Origin and Development of the Quantum Theory*, Nobel Prize Address, p. 3.

94 "my nature is peace-loving": Planck–R. W. Wood, July 10, 1931, American Institute of Physics.

95 "a discovery as important as that of Newton": Max Born, obituary notices, *Fellows of the Royal Society*, Vol. 6, No. 17, November 1948, p. 161.

97 "killing of two birds by one stone": quoted E. A. Milne, *Sir James Jeans*, p. 54.

97 "a novel kind of complementary relationship": Niels Bohr, "The Solvay Meetings and the Development of Quantum Physics," in *Essays 1958–1962 on Atomic Physics and Human Knowledge*, p. 80.

98 "practically no convinced adherents": R. A. Millikan, *Autobiography*, p. 83.

101 "On the Electrodynamics of Moving Bodies": "Electrodynamik bewegter Körper," *Annalen der Physik*, Vol. 17, Series 4, pp. 891–921.

103 "a magnificently precise and beautiful science": J. R. Oppenheimer, *The Flying Trapeze: Three Crises for Physicists* (afterward referred to as "Oppenheimer, *Flying Trapeze*"), p. 10.

103 "absolute, true, and mathematical time": Sir Isaac Newton, *Mathematical Principles of Natural Philosophy*, p. 6.

103 "Absolute motion is the translation from one relative place into another": Newton, p. 7.

105 "expressed intention only to investigate *actual facts*": Ernst Mach, *The Science of Mechanics*, tr. Thomas J. McCormack, p. 229.

107 "If Michelson-Morley is wrong": Viscount Samuel and Herbert Dingle, *A Threefold Cord*, pp. 52–53.

107 "Trouton and Nobel had tried": *Philosophical Transactions*, A, Vol. 202, 1903, p. 165.

107 "Lord Rayleigh and Brace had looked": *Philosophical Maga-*

zine, December 1902, p. 678, and *Philosophical Magazine*, April 1904, p. 317.

109 "happy in the knowledge of a good instrument maker": quoted L. Campbell and W. Garnet, *James Clerk Maxwell.*

109 "the enormous stream of discoveries": Hermann Bondi, *Assumption and Myth in Physical Theory*, p. 5.

110 "for me personally . . .": Einstein in Haas-Lorentz, *H. A. Lorentz*, p. 8.

111 "a logical consequence of several simultaneous hypotheses": Philipp Frank, *Interpretations and Misinterpretations of Modern Physics*, p. 39.

114 "a spatially oscillatory electromagnetic field at rest": Schilpp, p. 53.

114 "all sorts of nervous conflicts": Alexander Moszkowski, *Einstein the Searcher*, p. 4.

115 "time was suspect": Shankland, "Conversations with Albert Einstein," *American Journal of Physics*, Vol. 31, January 1963 (afterward referred to as "Shankland"), pp. 47–57.

115 "there elapsed five or six weeks": Einstein–Seelig, March 11, 1952, ETH.

115 "I pestered him for a whole month": Sauter–Seelig, Seelig, p. 73.

115 "You are the second": "Erinnerungen," Bureau Fédéral.

115 "a better sounding board": Einstein, quoted Seelig, p. 71.

115 "Einstein the eagle": Besso, quoted Seelig, p. 71.

116 "as impersonalized a piece of writing": Bondi, *Assumption and Myth*, p. iv.

116 "but nobody had taken offense": Born, *Physica Acta*, p. 251.

117-18 "If you are on an escalator": Russell, *The ABC of Relativity*, p. 28.

118 "eternal struggle of the inventive human mind": Einstein and Infeld, p. vi.

118 "fey": Schonland, p. 56.

118 "gift of fantasy": Plesch, p. 207.

119 "we cannot attach any *absolute* signification": "Elektrodynamik bewegter Körper, *Annalen der Physik.*

120 "the notorious controversy": Born, *Einstein's Theory of Relativity*, p. 254.

120 "the bearing of the Lorentz transformation": Einstein, *Technische Rundschau*, No. 20, 47, Jahrgang, Berne, May 6, 1955.

120 "It is as real as anything we can observe": H. A. Lorentz at Mount Wilson Observatory, quoted *Contributions from the Mount Wilson Observatory*, Vol. XVII, Carnegie Institute of Washington, April 1928–November 1929, p. 27.

120 "length is not a property of the rod": Eddington, quoted by H. L. Brose, in *The Foundations of Einstein's Theory of Gravitation* by Erwin Freundlich, p. viii.

121 Voigt: *Über das Dopplersche Prinzip*, Nachr. Ges. Wiss., Göttingen (1887), p. 41.

124 "because the old conceptions are so nearly right": Lindemann, "Einstein's Theory: A Revolution in Thought," *Times Educational Supplement*, January 29, 1920.

124 "Nature, always economical": Russell, *The Observer*, April 24, 1955.

124 "gross change, a rather sharp change": Oppenheimer, *Flying Trapeze*, p. 22.

125 "the most fundamental terms in physics": Eddington, Romanes Lecture, 1922.

127 "a further consequential development": Einstein, "Fundamental Concepts of Physics and Their Most Recent Changes," lecture given Davos Hochschule, printed *St. Louis Post-Dispatch*, December 29, 1928.

127 "the harmony of the universe": Reichenbach, quoted Vallentin, p. 106.

127 "the work of the individual": Speaking to National Academy of Sciences, Washington, D.C., April 26, 1921, quoted *New York Times*, April 27, 1921.

128 "the desire to make physical theory fit observed fact": typically, lecture King's College, London, quoted *The Nation*, London, June 18, 1921.

128 "pretty much convinced of the validity of the principle": Einstein–Jaffe, March 17, 1942; Jaffe–author, January 10, 1970.

128 "*only after 1905*": Shankland.

129 "The Michelson-Morley experiment had no role": Polanyi, *The Art of Knowing*, p. 11.

129 "the experimental works of those preceding me": *Jewish Observer*, February 22, 1955.

129 "ripe for discovery": Einstein–Seelig, *Technische Rundshau*, No. 20, 47, Jahrgang, Berne, May 6, 1955.

130 "adopted Poincaré's Principle of Relativity": Whittaker, *Biographical Memoirs of Fellows of the Royal Society*, Vol. 1, 1955, p. 42.

130 "Everybody does what he considers right": Einstein–Born, October 12, 1953, Born Letters, p. 199.

131 "a particularly welcome task": H. A. Lorentz, *Physikalische Zeitschrift*, Vol. 11, 1910, p. 1234, quoted Born, *Physica Acta*, p. 225.

131 "The genius of Einstein": *The Times* (London), editorial, May 25, 1931.

132 "a result of the electrodynamic work": Einstein–Habicht, Summer 1905, Seelig, p. 76. Neither original nor copy of this letter appears to exist in either the Princeton or the ETH archives.

132 "The results of the previous investigation": "Ist die Trägheit

eines Körpers von seinem Energieinhalt abhängig?" *Annalen der Physik*, Vol. 18, Series 4, pp. 639–41.

133 "gross Bodies and Light convertible": Newton, *Opticks*, p. 374.

134 "the dormant energy of a single brick": Thirring, *The Ideas of Einstein's Theory*, p. 92.

135 "Its foolishness is evident": Frank, p. 211.

135 "in almost every branch of nuclear physics": Oppenheimer, *Flying Trapeze*, p. 20.

136 "the introduction of a richer language": Frank, *Relativity—A Richer Truth*, pp. 29–30.

136 "Physical science does not . . . suggest": Sir James Jeans, *The New Background of Science*, p. 98.

137 "the viewpoint of a man, not from that of an angel": *The Tablet*, London, April 23, 1955.

139 "They've turned Catholic": Seelig, p. 113.

140 "obsessional concentration . . . one of the keys to his [Churchill's] character": James Stuart, *Within the Fringe*, p. 96.

141 "refuge in music": Whitrow, p. 21.

141 A copy of the *Annalen* in his hand: Laub–Seelig, September 11, 1959, ETH.

142 "the first lecture . . . was one by Planck on Einstein's work": Von Laue–Seelig, March 13, 1952, ETH.

142 "A new Copernicus": Infeld, *Albert Einstein*, p. 44.

142 "neither Born nor anyone else there had heard about Einstein": Infeld, *Albert Einstein*, p. 44.

142 "Einstein's reasoning was a revelation": Born, *Physica Acta*, p. 247.

143 "*the results are not compatible with the Lorentz–Einsteinian fundamental assumptions*": Kaufmann, *Annalen der Physik*, Vol. 19, 1906, p. 495.

143 "both . . . have a rather small probability": Einstein, "Relativitätsprinzip und die aus demselben gezogenen Folgerungen," *Jahrbuch der Radioaktivität und Elektronik*, Vol. 4, 1907, pp. 411–62, and Vol. 5, 1908, pp. 98–99 (Berichtigungen).

143 "is the more impressive the greater the simplicity of its premises": Schilpp, p. 33.

144 "The young man . . . made such an unexpected impression": Von Laue–Seelig, March 13, 1952, ETH.

145 "Einstein kneeling in front of the oven": Seelig, p. 72.

145 "ceaselessly occupied with the question of the constitution of radiation": Einstein–Laub, dated "Monday," 1908 added by hand, ETH.

146 "greatest hopes of solving the radiation problem": Einstein–Laub, November 4, 1910, and "the Devil played a wicked trick": Seelig, p. 116.

146 "opportunity of working with Lenard": Einstein–Laub, dated "Monday," 1908 added by hand, ETH.

146–47 "explaining the deviations of the specific heat of solids from the classical law": Einstein, "Planck'sche Theorie der Strahlung und die Theorie der spezifischen Wärme," *Annalen der Physik*, Vol. 22, Series 4, pp. 180–90, 800.

148 The law of causality: Frank, "Kausalgesetz und Erfahrung" (Causal Law and Experience), published in Ostwald's *Annalen der Naturphilosophie*, Leipzig, 1907, Vol. 6, p. 443.

148 "He approved the logic of my argument": Frank, *Modern Science and Its Philosophy*, p. 10.

149 "Since I am keen that the time I spend on teaching": Einstein–Gruner, February 11, 1908, Seelig, p. 88.

150 "an amusing example of academic red tape" and "decision was revised shortly afterwards": Einstein–Plesch, February 3, 1944, Plesch correspondence.

151 "we feel compelled at the present juncture to grant a kind of absolute physical reality to nonuniform motion": Einstein, *Theory of Relativity*, p. 62.

151-52 "displeasing to Einstein": Dr. Sciama in Whitrow, p. 34.

152 "I was, of course, familiar with Mach's idea": Einstein, *Origins of the General Theory of Relativity*, George A. Gibson Lecture, delivered Glasgow, June 20, 1933 (afterward referred to as "Gibson"), p. 6.

152 "when I endeavored to include the law of gravity in the framework of the Special Theory of Relativity": Gibson, p. 6.

155 "airplane pilot in a cloud": Lindemann, *Times Educational Supplement*, January 29, 1920, p. 59.

156 "reasonable theory of . . . relativity": Gibson, p. 8.

157 "great and brilliant period": Weyl, "David Hilbert" obituary notices, *Fellows of the Royal Society*, Vol. 4, No. 18, November 1944, p. 547.

158 "whether he would ever have done it without . . . Minkowski": E. Cunningham, *Nature*, February 17, 1921.

158 "the natural laws . . . assume mathematical forms": Einstein, *Theory of Relativity*, p. 57.

159 "a mysterious shuddering": Einstein, *Theory of Relativity*, p. 55.

159 "a 'happening' in three-dimensional space": Einstein, *Theory of Relativity*, p. 122.

159 "from the engineer-scientist to the mathematician": Sir James Jeans, quoted Leon Watters, Vol. 4, p. 30, *The Universal Jewish Encyclopedia*, New York, 1941.

159 "The people in Göttingen": Frank, p. 249.

160 "so busy discussing relativity": Theodore von Karman, *The Wind and Beyond*, p. 51.

161 "every moment . . . servant of society": statement for Curie Memorial Celebration, Roerich Museum, New York, November 23, 1935, reprinted Einstein, *Ideas and Opinions*, p. 76.

162 "never met a real physicist": Infeld, *Albert Einstein*, p. 119.

162 "a splendid chap": Einstein–Laub, December 31, 1909, ETH.

162 "Axalp . . . and he and Einstein . . . to have met": Princeton.

162 "presumptuous on his part": Planck, *Where Is Science Going?*, p. 16.

163 "Special Relativity . . . left to minor prophets": Born, *Physics in My Generation*, p. 197.

163 "one of the landmarks": Pauli in Schilpp, p. 154.

163 "an extensive group of data concerning radiation": Einstein, "Entwicklung unserer Anschauungen über das Wesen und die Konstitution der Strahlung," *Physikalische Zeitschrift*, Vol. 10, 1909, pp. 817–25.

164 "two facts . . . so overwhelmingly new and surprising": Meitner, "As I Remember," *Bulletin of the Atomic Scientists*, November 1964, p. 4.

165 "enough schoolmasters without me": Einstein–Laub, July 30, 1908, ETH.

165 "absurd to appoint me": Frank, p. 95.

165 "I hope to have achieved this": Fritz Adler–Viktor Adler, November 28, 1908, Adler Archives, Verein für Geschichte der Arbeiterbewegung, Vienna.

166 "Teaching is always satisfying": Einstein–Fräulein Melanie Serbu, April 21, 1948, Leiden.

161 "my prospects . . . look very rosy": Einstein–Ehrats, February 15, 1909, Seelig, p. 91.

161 "Einstein was not mentioned": Fritz Adler–Viktor Adler, April 16, 1909, Adler Archives.

161 "The departure means a loss": Haller–Federal Council, July 12, 1909, Bureau Fédéral.

167 "I send you my *Dienstbüchlein*": Einstein–Chavan, October 19, 1909, Max Fluckiger, *A.E. in Bern*, p. 27.

168 "In my relativity theory": Frank, p. 96.

168 "spend all his time in more solitary pursuits": note by Lord Samuel, October 31, 1930, Samuel Papers.

169 "not recovered the balance of mind": Einstein–Besso, November 19, 1909, Besso correspondence.

169 "future was being brewed": Einstein–Plesch, February 3, 1944, Plesch correspondence.

170 "The more I speak with Einstein": Fritz Adler–Viktor Adler, October 28, 1910, Adler Archives.

170 "He repeatedly asked the class": Dr. A. Fisch–Seelig, February 28, 1952, ETH; Seelig, p. 100.

171 "people must go and listen to Einstein": Fritz Adler–Viktor Adler, October 5, 1909, Adler Archives.

171 "Teaching also gives me great pleasure": Seelig, p. 117.

171 "Einstein only got stuck once": Dr. Hans Tanner–Seelig, ETH; Seelig, p. 101.

172-76 The details of Einstein's move to Prague are provided mainly by the Adler letters and are supplemented by Frank, pp. 98–101, who as Einstein's successor gives the most reliable general account of the move. Einstein's letter to Ehrenfest on p. 136 was written on April 25, 1912, and is quoted by Klein, *Paul Ehrenfest*, p. 180.

176 "I am having a good time here": Einstein–Chavan, July 5, 1911, Seelig, p. 129.

177 Einstein–Pick correspondence: Princeton.

178 "the relation of the Jews to the other Germans": Frank, p. 106.

179 "philosophical and Zionist enthusiasts": Einstein–Born, September 8, 1916, Born Letters, p. 4.

179 "The problems of nationality": Frank, p. 107.

180 "Once in his strolls": Marianoff and Wayne, *Einstein: An Intimate Study of a Great Man*, p. 49.

181 "another paper for the *Annalen der Physik*: "Über den Einfluss der Schwerkraft auf die Ausbreitung des Lichtes" (On the Influence of Gravitation on the Propagation of Light), *Annalen der Physik*, Vol. 35, Series 4, 1911, p. 898–908.

181 "bodies act upon light": Newton, *Opticks*, p. 339.

181 Soldner: *Astronomisches Jahrbuch*, Berlin, 1804, p. 161.

184 "The whole undertaking pleases me": Einstein–Nernst, June 20, 1911, Solvay Institute.

185 "Einstein all calculation": Chaim Weizmann, *Trial and Error*, p. 153.

185 "They have too much sense": A. S. Eve, *Rutherford*, p. 193.

185 "concentrated on speculative theories": Einstein–Seelig, n.d., Seelig, p. 188.

185 "I well remember my co-secretary": original draft of obituary published *Daily Telegraph*, April 22, 1955, Cherwell Archives, Nuffield College, Oxford (afterward referred to as "Cherwell Archives").

185 "I got on very well with Einstein": Birkenhead, *The Prof in Two Worlds*, p. 52.

186 Lindemann formed an opinion of Einstein's character: Birkenhead, p. 37.

186 Einstein contributed a paper: "On the Current Situation Regarding the Problems of Specific Heat," *Deutsche Bunsengesellschaft*, Abhandlungen nr. 7, 1913, pp. 330–64.

186 "the clearness of his mind": Curie–ETH, November 17, 1911, ETH.

186 The wish of his first wife: Frank–Seelig, May 13, 1952, ETH.

187 "to lecture on experimental physics": Hans Einstein statement to author.

187 Correspondence between Einstein and Utrecht, University of Utrecht, collection Julius papers, correspondence Julius, University Museum, Utrecht, vacature Windt, 1911.

187 "artistically fine-spirited man": *Astrophysical Journal*, Vol. 63, 1926, pp. 196–98.

190 "The prospect of returning to Zurich": Einstein–Grossmann, November 18, 1911, Seelig, p. 132.

190 "despite my long silence": Lorentz–Einstein, December 6, 1911, Leiden.

191 A further misunderstanding: Klein, *Paul Ehrenfest*, pp. 183–84.

191 "I much admire the work": Curie–Professor Weiss, November 17, 1911, ETH.

191 "The role of mathematical physics": Poincaré–ETH, undated, ETH.

192 "your coming would be welcomed": Pegram–Einstein, January 9, 1912, and "loaded with . . . work": Einstein–Pegram, January 29, 1912, Columbia University.

192 "Two days ago (Hallelujah!)": Einstein–Stern, February 2, 1912, ETH.

193 "he infected his students with his own enthusiasm": *Nature*, Vol. 132, October 26, 1933, p. 667.

193 "Whatever I can do for you": Einstein–Ehrenfest, February 12, 1912, Klein, *Paul Ehrenfest*, p. 176.

194 "Two days of continual scientific dispute": Klein, *Paul Ehrenfest*, pp. 176–77.

194 "Nature created us for each other": Einstein, "Nachruf Paul Ehrenfest" in *Almanak van het Leidsche Studentencorps*, Leiden, 1934.

195 When he saw Einstein: Von Laue–Seelig, March 13, 1952, ETH.

195 "the small journey into the mountains": Einstein–Curie, April 3, 1913, ETH.

196 "That is absolute nonsense": Levy, in Whitrow, p. 43.

197 "opposed to all metaphysical undertakings": Full text of manifesto quoted *The Journal of Philosophy, Psychology and Scientific Methods*, Vol. ix, No. 16, August 1, 1912, p. 419.

198 "actually superhuman exertions": Einstein–Ehrenfest, May 28, 1913, Klein, *Paul Ehrenfest*, p. 293.

198 Einstein and Grossmann published jointly a paper: *Zeitschrift für Mathematik und Physik*, Vol. 62, 1931, pp. 225–61.

198 "were not compatible with experience": Gibson, p. 11.

199 "as matter-of-factly as others speak of sandwiches": N. Goldman, *Memories*, p. x.

199 "German-speaking men of science": *Nature*, Vol. 175, May 28, 1955, pp. 926–27.

200 "The blackboard moves": Felix Ehrenhaft, "My Experiences

with Einstein," unpublished MS (afterward referred to as "Ehrenhaft").

201 "leaning directly on Einstein's treatment": Bohr, p. 84.

202 "he had once similar ideas": Hevesy–Rutherford, October 14, 1913, Rutherford Papers, University of Cambridge.

202 "it means the end of physics": Bohr, in *Nauka i Zhzn (Science and Life)*, No. 8, 1961, p. 77, Kuznetsov, p. 271.

202 "appeared to me like a miracle": Schilpp, p. 47.

202 "a stream of knowledge": Planck Nobel Prize Address, p. 16.

203 "A half-good-natured, half-cunning expression": Frank, p. 131.

204 "Einstein asked Mach": I. Bernard Cohen, "An Interview with Einstein," *Scientific American*, Vol. 193, 1955, p. 73.

204 "Mach recognized clearly": *Physikalische Zeit*, XVII, 1961, p. 107.

205 Reversed his views: Mach, *The Principles of Physical Optics*, London, 1908, p. vii.

205 "un bon mécanicien": *Bulletin de la Société Française de Philosophie*, Vol. 22, 1922, p. 111.

205 "a result of his advanced years": Einstein–Herr Dr. Ing. Armin Weiner, September 18, 1930, Burndy Library.

205 "At the solar eclipse next year": *Forschungen und Fortschritte*, Vol. 37, 1963, quoted in Gerald Holton's "Mach, Einstein, and the Search for Reality," *Daedalus*, Spring 1968, p. 645.

206 Details of Einstein's early friendship with Freundlich are contained in a long series of letters between the two, including the following, until recently held by Frau Freundlich:

"It would give me great pleasure": Einstein–Freundlich, September 1, 1911.

"If the speed of light is . . . affected": Einstein–Freundlich, August 1913.

"a nice letter from Einstein": Freundlich–Frau Freundlich, August 26, 1913.

208 "no possibility of detecting the effect": Hale–Einstein, November 8, 1913, Hale Papers, California Institute of Technology.

208 "I immediately wrote to Planck": Einstein–Freundlich, December 7, 1913.

211 "at a profound disadvantage with the Germans": R. B. Haldane, *An Autobiography*, London, 1929, p. 232.

211 "the weakness of human beings for decorations and titles": Plesch, p. 129.

212 "going to Berlin": Einstein–Besso, March 26 (no year, but apparently 1911), Princeton.

212 "his childlike vanity and self-complacency": Einstein, "The Work and Personality of Walther Nernst," *Scientific Monthly*, LIV, 1942, p. 196.

214 "This new interpretation of the time concept": statement dated Berlin, June 12, 1913, ETH.

216 "Einstein will move to Berlin": Nernst–Lindemann, August 18, 1913, Cherwell Archives.

216 "each working day": Einstein–Prussian Academy, December 7, 1913, ETH.

217 "this peculiar sinecure": Einstein–Ehrenfest, undated Winter 1913–14, Klein, *Paul Ehrenfest*, p. 296.

217 "personal factors": Frank, p. 136.

218 "when a great idea is at stake": Reichinstein, p. 28.

218 "the true artist will let his wife starve": George Bernard Shaw, *Major Barbara.*

218 "Prussian nationality . . . acquired in 1913": Dr. Ernst Heymann, April 1, 1933, quoted Einstein, *The World As I See It*, p. 86.

218 "no change in my nationality": Einstein–Prussian Academy, March 23, 1923 (18 Akad. Arch. II: IIIa, Bd. 23, B197), quoted Herneck, *Naturwissenschaften.*

219 "errors of thinking": Gibson, p. 11.

220 A farewell supper for him in the Kronenhalle: Kollros, *Physica Acta*, p. 280.

220 "Kieks": Rudolf H. Hertz–author, April 12, 1969.

220 "By electing me to your Academy": *Sitzungsberichte der Koeniglich, Preussischen Akademie der Wissenschaften*, XXVIII, 1914, pp. 739–42.

221 "I remained unburdened": Einstein–Plesch, February 3, 1944, Plesch correspondence.

221 "Life is better here": Einstein–Hurwitz, May 4, 1914, Seelig, p. 150.

221 "honored to receive him in their homes": Frank, p. 153.

222 "kneel down on the floor": Samuel, *Memoirs*, p. 254.

222 "I no longer doubt": Einstein–Besso, March 1914, Besso correspondence.

223 "My dear astronomer Freundlich": Einstein–Ehrenfest, August 19, 1914, Princeton.

224 Out of sight and out of mind: Einstein–Besso, July 14, 1916, Besso correspondence.

225 "problem from the Ordnance Department": Morris Goran, *The Story of Fritz Haber*, p. 66.

225 "lack of a higher military title": Goran, p. 75.

225 "I am a sergeant": Goran, pp. 75–76.

226 "they stunk first": Sommerfeld, quoted Schilpp, p. 103.

226 "a few educated Germans": Fritz K. Ringer, *The Decline of the German Mandarins: The German Academic Community 1890–1933*, p. 180.

227 "given the money for my salary": Einstein–Freundlich, December 7, 1913, Freundlich correspondence.

227 "my academic remuneration": Einstein–Hedwig Born, September 1, 1919, Born Letters, p. 12.

228 "Manifesto": quoted Nathan and Norden, *Einstein on Peace*, p. 4–6.

228 "without your participation": George Nicolai–Einstein, May 18, 1918, quoted Nathan and Norden, p. 7.

231 "Einstein . . . very active": Kurt R. Grossmann, "Peace Movements in Germany," *South Atlantic Quarterly*, July 1950, p. 294.

231 "equivalent to treason": Grossmann, p. 294.

232 "started something unbelievable": Einstein–Ehrenfest, August 19, 1914, Princeton.

232 "this 'great epoch' ": Einstein–Ehrenfest, December 1914, Princeton.

232 "men always need some idiotic fiction": Einstein–Lorentz, August 2, 1915, Allgemeine Rijksarchief, The Hague (afterward referred to as "Hague").

232 "Impulse was stronger": Einstein–Ehrenfest, August 23, 1915, Princeton.

233 "the fateful misunderstandings": Einstein–Rolland, March 22, 1915, Romain Rolland, *Journal des Années de Guerre 1914–1919*, p. 289.

233 "brilliant physicist and mathematician": Rolland, pp. 510–15.

236 "The Kaiser meant well": *Saturday Evening Post*, October 26, 1929.

237 "the worst side of his own nation": Rolland, p. 514.

237 "The psychological root of war": *Das Land Goethes 1914–1916*, Berliner Goethebund, 1916, Dokumentsammlung der Preuss, Staatsbibliothek, Berlin-Dahlem.

239 "irrevocable" decision: Einstein–Besso, July 14, 1916, Besso correspondence.

239 They went up to Lorentz' study: undated draft by Ehrenfest, Klein, *Paul Ehrenfest*, p. 303.

240 Adler–Einstein correspondence: Princeton.

240 "Adler was mentally deranged": Frank, p. 212.

242 "follows no set rules": Plesch, p. 206.

242 "His utter independence": Hedwig Born, *Helle Zeit*, p. 36.

242 "You are complaining": Einstein–Ehrenfest, June 3, 1917, Klein, *Paul Ehrenfest*, p. 305.

243 "thankful every hour of my life": Bucky, *Helle Zeit*, p. 65.

244 "My first wife did": Salaman.

244 "women . . . attached to their furniture": Frank, p. 156.

245 "I am touched by the warm interest": Einstein–Rolland, August 22, 1917, Rolland, *Journal des Années de Guerre*, p. 1205 (given as Wednesday 21st, but Wednesday was the 22nd).

246 "the extreme injustice": Rolland, p. 1303.

246 Financial details: Einstein–Besso, May 15, 1917, Besso correspondence.

247 The move to Haberlandstrasse: Einstein–Besso, September 3, 1917, Besso correspondence.

247 "look after his outside affairs": *The Manchester Guardian*, June 14, 1921.

247 "he has a good wife": Chaim Tschernowitz, "A Day with Albert Einstein," *Jewish Sentinal*, September 1931.

248 Divorce papers and evidence before tribunal: Einstein–Besso, December 12, 1919, Besso correspondence.

249 "The great event has happened": Nathan and Norden, p. 24.

249 Einstein and the Berlin student council: Born Letters, p. 150.

252 "the most exacting period of my life": Einstein–Sommerfeld, November 28, 1915, quoted *Briefwechsel–Albert Einstein/Arnold Sommerfeld* (afterward referred to as "Sommerfeld"), p. 32.

252 "the greatest feat of human thinking about nature": Born, *Physica Acta*, p. 253.

252 "not merely a background for events": Wolfgang Yourgrau, "On Invariance Principles," in *Entstehung, Entwicklung und Perspektiven der Einsteinschen Gravitationstheorie*, Berlin, 1966 (report of Einstein Symposium, November 2–5, 1965).

252 "I want to reflect": *Aufsätze und Vorträge über Physik und Erkenntnis-theorie*, Braunschweig, 1961, p. 88.

254 "When the blind beetle": Seelig, p. 80.

255 "last nail in the coffin of absolute space": E. T. Bell, p. 561.

256 "responsible for a great deal of popular misconception": Sir Edmund Whittaker, *From Euclid to Eddington*, p. 39.

256 "the expression 'Taum-Krummung,' space-curvature": Talmey, "Einstein's Theory and Rational Language," *Scientific Monthly*, Vol. XXXV, 1932, p. 254.

257 "old theory from the higher level of the new one": Einstein and Infeld, pp. 251–52.

258 Found by Flinders Petrie: O. G. S. Crawford, *Archaeology in the Field*, London, 1953, p. 269.

258 "the assumption of hypotheses": Einstein, *Theory of Relativity*, p. 103.

259 "I hope to account . . . secular changes": Einstein–Habicht, December 24, 1907, Seelig, p. 76.

259 "full agreement between theory and experience": Einstein–Mrs. Whitney, July 15, 1926, Stanford University.

259 "speechless for several days": Einstein–Ehrenfest, January 1916, Seelig, p. 156.

259 "I did not . . . doubt": Moszkowski, p. 5.

259 Schwarzschild published a description: Berlin, Sitzungsberichte (1916), p. 189.

260 L. F. Jewell: *Journal of Physics*, vi (1897), p. 84.

261 "a recent experiment conducted at Harvard": Oppenheimer, *Flying Trapeze*, p. 27.

262 "to use tensors as a tool": A. Vibert Douglas, *The Life of Arthur Stanley Eddington* (afterward referred to as "Douglas"), p. 39.

262 "an enormous progress": Wilhelm de Sitter, "Einstein's Theory of Relativity," *Monthly Notices* of the Royal Astronomical Society, Vol. LXXVII, December 2, 1916.

263 "a view to testing Einstein's theory": F. A. Lindemann and A. F. Lindemann, "Daylight Photography of Stars As a Means of Testing the Equivalence Postulate in the Theory of Relativity," *Monthly Notices* of the Royal Astronomical Society, Vol. LXXVII, December 2, 1916.

263 "wait some thousands of years": Eddington, *Space, Time and Gravitation*," p. 113.

264 "an unusual number of bright stars": *Monthly Notices* of the Royal Astronomical Society, Vol. LXXVII, March 2, 1917.

264 Two important papers: "Quantentheorie der Strahlung," *Physikalische Zeitschrift*, Vol. 18, pp. 121–28, and "Kosmologische Betrachtungen zur allgemeinen Relativitätstheorie," *Preussische Akademie der Wissenschaften, Sitzungsberichte*, 1917, Pt. 1, pp. 142–52.

265 "an electron . . . *of its own free will*": Einstein–Born, April 24, 1924, Born Letters, p. 82.

265 "I have once more broken a little ground": Seelig, p. 157.

266 "a superstructure including other principles": E. Hubble, *The Observational Approach to Cosmology*, The Rhodes Memorial Lectures, 1936 (afterward referred to as "Hubble"), p. 53.

268 ". . . all must see the universe alike": Hubble, p. 53.

268 "The whole universe": Moszkowski, p. 127.

270 "Friedmann noticed": G. Gamow, *My World Line*, pp. 149–50.

271 "It solved the mysterious fact": Born, *Physica Acta*, p. 254.

273 "I have become deeply disillusioned": Einstein–Ehrenfest, March 22, 1919, Nathan and Norden, p. 29.

273 "men's moral qualities": Einstein–Lorentz, August 1, 1919, The Hague.

273 "borne the collapse with calm and dignity": Einstein–Ehrenfest, December 6, 1918, American Philosophical Society.

273 "branded as morally inferior": Einstein–Lorentz, September 21, 1939, The Hague.

274 "to plead with the Allies": Einstein–Ehrenfest, December 6, 1918, American Philosophical Society.

275 He had turned down the offer: Einstein–Besso, August 20, 1918, Besso correspondence.

275 An incident recalled by Hermann Weyl: Weyl–Seelig, May 19, 1952, ETH.

276 "It is not for me to lecture": Einstein–unknown correspondent,

quoted catalogue, autograph auction, February 18 and 19, 1969, J. A. Stargardt, Marburg.

276 If he ever wished to leave his second wife: Einstein–Besso, July 29, 1918, Besso correspondence.

277 "crimes . . . committed by the German High Command": Einstein–unnamed correspondent, August 17, 1919, Nathan and Norden, p. 31.

277 "Germany's conduct in the war": Einstein–Lorentz, April 26, 1919, The Hague.

278 "Einstein . . . in no way 'German' ": Lorentz–Solvay, January 10, 1919, Solvay Archives, quoted unpublished MS "Historique des Instituts Internationaux de Physique et de Chimie Solvay depuis leur fondation jusqu'à la 2e guerre mondiale" by Jean Pelseneer (afterward referred to as "Pelseneer"), p. 37.

278 "You must not deceive yourself": Lorentz–Einstein, May 4, 1919, The Hague.

278 "Germans will not be invited": Lorentz–Einstein, July 26, 1919, Leiden.

279 "Einstein who . . . spent the whole war in Berlin": Brillouin–Tassin, June 1, 1919, Solvay Institute documents.

279 "an exception . . . made for Einstein": Tassel–M. Huisman, March 23, 1921, Solvay Institute documents.

279 "The only German invited is Einstein": Rutherford–Boltwood, February 28, 1921, quoted Badash, p. 342.

279 "Einstein 'accepted with great pleasure' ": Einstein–Lorentz, June 15, 1920, The Hague.

279 Lorentz informed Rutherford: Lorentz–Rutherford, December 16, 1920, Rutherford Papers.

279 "the rich American Jews": Einstein–Lorentz, February 22, 1921, The Hague.

280 "it is not right for me to take part": Einstein–Lorentz, August 16, 1920, The Hague.

280 "unworthy of cultured men": Einstein–Curie, December 25, 1923, Bibliothèque Nationale, Paris.

280 "I am able to write to Einstein": Lorentz note on telegram, quoted in Pelseneer, p. 41.

281 "feelings . . . should be gradually damped down": report, Lorentz–Solvay, Pelseneer, p. 41.

281 Einstein "quite startled": Einstein–Lorentz, September 21, 1919, The Hague.

282 "spend as much time as you want in Switzerland": Ehrenfest–Einstein, September 2, 1919, Klein, *Paul Ehrenfest*, p. 310.

282 "Your offer is so fabulous": Einstein–Ehrenfest, September 12, 1919, Klein, *Paul Ehrenfest*, p. 311; also partially quoted, Nathan and Norden, p. 36.

283 Trying to induce Einstein to remain in Switzerland: Planck–Einstein, July 20, 1919, Princeton.

284 "Eddington found star displacement": Lorentz–Einstein, September 22, 1919, Leiden.

284 "experimental confirmation has been ample": *Monthly Notices* of the Royal Astronomical Society, Vol. LXXVII, February 1917, p. 377.

284 "an end . . . of boycotting German science": A. S. Eddington, quoted in obituary notices, *Fellows of the Royal Society*, Vol. 3, No. 8, January 1940, p. 167.

285 "Eddington will go mad": Douglas, p. 40.

285 "programme of photographs on faith": Douglas, p. 40.

285 "We developed the photographs": Douglas, p. 40.

286 "This . . . Eddington never forgot": Douglas, p. 40.

286 "The Clock no question makes": Douglas, p. 43.

287 "definitely confirming . . . value of the deflection": Wilson, *Ninth Astronomer Royal*, p. 193.

287 "so far nothing precise": Einstein–Hartmann, September 2, 1919, Leiden.

287 "good news from H. A. Lorentz": Einstein–Pauline Einstein, September 27, 1919, Nathan and Norden, p. 27.

287 "this will . . . interest you": Holton, *Daedalus*, p. 653.

288 "I have heard of Eddington's results": Lorentz–Einstein, October 7, 1919, The Hague.

289 "Hertzsprung showed me": Einstein–Planck, October 23, 1919, Seelig, p. 160.

290 "that of the Greek drama": A. N. Whitehead, *Science and the Modern World*, p. 13.

290 "a whole continent": quoted in *The Times* (London), November 8, 1919.

290 "not need to observe an eclipse": Eddington, *Relativity*, Eighth Annual Haldane Lecture, May 26, 1937.

295 "so bad that I can hardly breathe": Einstein–Born, December 9, 1919, Max Born, *Physics in My Generation*, p. 158.

296 "These . . . are sold for the benefit": *Daily Chronicle*, January 15, 1920.

296 "talk . . . of almost nothing but Einstein": Lawson–Berliner, November 1919, Nathan and Norden, p. 27.

297 "It cannot do any harm": *Nature*, Vol. 175, May 28, 1955, p. 927.

298 "After the lamentable breach": *The Times* (London), November 28, 1919.

299 "I should like to congratulate you": Einstein–Eddington, December 15, 1919, Douglas, p. 41.

299 "I was myself a sceptic": Dyson–Hale, December 29, 1919, Hale Papers.

299 "too much for my comprehension": Hale–Dyson, February 9, 1920, Hale Papers.

300 It might tend to draw scientific men away: Rutherford–Hale, January 13, 1920, Hale Papers.

300 "a typical case of mathematical . . . development": Rutherford, Presidential Address, British Association, 1923, Eve, p. 296.

300 "a magnificent work of art": Rutherford, Royal Society of Arts, 1932, Eve, p. 353.

300 "he never seemed particularly enthusiastic on the subject": Rayleigh, *The Life of Sir J. J. Thomson*, p. 202.

301 "an individualist . . . can have a universe of his own": Thomson, *Recollections and Reflections*, p. 431.

301 Like the Mad Hatter, experience time standing still: Douglas, p. 117.

302 "the really essential physical consideration": Robb, *A Theory of Time and Space*, p. 1.

302 "Hymn to Einstein": Robb, Rutherford Papers.

304 "all England has been talking": Eddington–Einstein, December 1, 1919, Princeton.

305 "I am going to England": Einstein–Born, January 27, 1920, Born Letters, p. 22.

305 "a rebuff from reaction": Eddington–Einstein, January 9, 1920, Princeton.

305 "Saying 'no' ": Einstein–Hopf, February 2, 1920, Seelig, p. 162.

306 "universal theme which had taken possession of humanity": Moszkowski, pp. 13–14.

306 "To those who have the vision": *Nature*, Vol. 106, November 11, 1920, p. 337.

307 "crowd . . . queued up on a cold . . . night": Infeld, "Einstein," *American Scholar*, Vol. 16, 1946–47.

309 "People were weary of hatred": Infeld, *Quest*, p. 264.

309-10 "the dethronement of time as a rigid tyrant": E. Schrödinger, *Mind and Matter*, p. 82.

311 Correspondence on proposed freedom of Ulm: Stadtarchiv, Ulm.

312 "a proof of your affection": Einstein–Lorentz, November 15, 1919, The Hague.

313 "just as keen on him as you are": Einstein–Ehrenfest, Seelig, p. 185.

313 "my admiration for Einstein": Bohr, in Schilpp, p. 206.

313 "the first . . . opportunity of meeting Planck and Einstein": Bohr–Rutherford, July 27, 1920, Rutherford Papers.

314 "the man who introduced the idea": *Nauka i Zhzh (Science in Life)*, No. 8, 1961, p. 73, quoted Kuznetzov, pp. 279–80.

314 "certain difference in attitude and outlook": Schilpp, p. 206.

314 "Given me such happiness": Einstein–Bohr, May 2, 1920, Princeton.

314 "one of the great experiences of life": Bohr–Einstein, June 29, 1920, American Institute of Physics.

315 Swearing into Weimar and Prussian constitution: dates given by Herneck.

315 "one of the follies of my life": Einstein–Plesch, February 3, 1944, Plesch correspondence.

316 "anti-Semitism is strong here": Einstein–Ehrenfest, December 4, 1919, Nathan and Norden, p. 37.

316 The press and other rabble: Einstein–Born, December 9, 1919, Born Letters, p. 18.

317 "secret groups round Krupp": Grossmann, p. 292 et seq.

317 A high opinion of Einstein's photoelectric paper: Laub–Seelig, September 19, 1959, ETH.

318 "a university lecturer": Infeld, *Die Wahrheit*, March 15–16, 1969.

319 "My Answer to the Antirelativity Theory Company Ltd.": *Berliner Tageblatt*, August 25, 1920.

320 "rather unfortunate reply": Hedwig Born–Einstein, September 8, 1920, Born Letters, p. 34.

320 "My wife and I . . . cannot believe": Ehrenfest–Einstein, September 2, 1920, Klein, *Paul Ehrenfest*, p. 321.

320 "I had to do it": Einstein–Ehrenfest, September 10, 1920, Klein, *Paul Ehrenfest*, p. 323.

321 "men such as Lenard and Wolf of Heidelberg": Von Laue–Sommerfeld, August 25, 1920, Sommerfeld, p. 65.

321 "With real fury": Sommerfeld–Einstein, September 3, 1920, Sommerfeld, p. 65.

323 "referred to his lecturing at Oxford": Everett Skillings, "Some Recent Impressions in Germany," *The Oxford Magazine*, Vol. XXXVIII, No. 23, June 11, 1920.

323 "need of a first-class applied mathematician": Jeans–Rutherford, September 1, 1920, Rutherford Papers.

323 "too much importance to that attack": Einstein–Sommerfeld, September 6, 1920, Sommerfeld, p. 69.

324 "the man in the fairy tale": Einstein–Born, September 9, 1920, Born Letters, p. 35.

324 Einstein might lose patience: Planck–Einstein, September 5, 1920, Princeton.

325 "most respected professor": Haenisch–Einstein, quoted in *New York Times*, September 26, 1920.

326 Bad Nauheim meetings: As with the famous confrontation between T. H. Huxley and Bishop Wilberforce at the Oxford meeting of the British Association in 1860, no complete verbatim record of the Lenard–Einstein exchange appears to have

survived. Eye-witness accounts, recalled after half a century, are conflicting. The overall impression is that Planck just managed to keep the occasion in hand.

326 "guaranteed a very large sum": Ehrenhaft, p. 3.

326 Lenard, Einstein, and (p. 264) other speakers: *Physikalische Zeitschrift*, Vol. XXI, 1920, pp. 666–68.

326 "When Lenard began": Friedrich Dessauer–Seelig, September 9, 1953, ETH.

326 "the simple understanding of the scientist": Lenard, *Physikalische Zeitschrift.*

326 "provoked into making a caustic reply": Born Letters, p. 36.

326 "I . . . will not allow myself to get excited": Einstein–Born, undated, Born Letters, p. 41.

328 "the closest human and scientific ties": Frank, p. 206.

328 "presented him to the fifty or sixty thousand people": Grossmann.

328 Founder member of the Republican League: *New York Times*, January 9, 1921, 3:3.

329 "That power/Which erring men call Chance": John Milton, *Comus.*

331 "thorns in the side": Einstein–Plesch, February 3, 1944, Plesch correspondence.

332 "Calm yourself": Frank, p. 211.

332 "developed into a kind of phony": Einstein–Plesch, February 3, 1944, Plesch correspondence.

332 "Einstein stayed in my house": Ehrenhaft, p. 5.

333 "Every time . . . he travels": Elsa–unidentified correspondent, March 12, no year, Stargardt Catalogue, No. 384, Marburg.

333 "my English is practically nonexistent" and following Manchester correspondence: Manchester University Archives.

335 "the excellence of his diction": *The Manchester Guardian*, June 10, 1921.

335 "The man in the street": *The Manchester Guardian*, June 10, 1921.

336 "a more condensed distribution": Eddington–Lindemann, April 24, 1932, Cherwell Archives.

337 "admiration for the power of systematic reflection": Haldane, p. 283.

337 "Haldane is doing for Einstein": Sir Oliver Lodge, "Einstein's Real Achievement," *Fortnightly Review*, DCLVII, new series, September 1, 1921, p. 353.

337 "a poor compliment": Eddington, Eighth Annual Haldane Lecture, 1937.

337 "a cloud descended": Sommer, *Haldane of Cloan: His Life and Times 1856–1928*, p. 381.

337 "make a market for us": Haldane–John Murray, May 12, 1921, John Murray Archives.

337 "Will you do me the honor": Haldane–Einstein, Princeton.

338 Haldane's comments to his mother on the Einstein visit are taken from the Haldane correspondence in the National Library of Scotland. Sources for the dinner party on the 10th include G. K. A. Bell and Sommer. Randall Davidson appears to have made a detailed record of the meeting.

338 "neither head nor tail of Einstein": Sanderson–Thomson, April 7, 1921, quoted in Rayleigh, p. 203.

339 "typical scientific lion": Randall Davidson, quoted in G. K. A. Bell, p. 1052.

340 "It is purely abstract–science": G. K. A. Bell, p. 1052.

340 "relativity . . . widely misunderstood": *Saturday Evening Post*, October 26, 1929, p. 17 et seq.

340 "clergymen are interested": Philipp Frank, "Einstein's Philosophy of Science," *Reviews of Modern Physics*, Vol. 21, No. 3, July 1949, p. 349.

340 "My husband mystical!": G. K. A. Bell, p. 1052.

340 "Mysticism is in fact": Seelig, p. 79.

340 "the non sequitur is obvious": Eddington, Eighth Annual Haldane Lecture, 1937.

341 "events . . . of the Norman Conquest": Sir Almeric Fitzroy, *Memoirs, Vol. II*, p. 756.

341 "his palatial residence": Kuznetsov, p. 237.

342 "Feeling against Germany": Barker, *Age and Youth*, p. 136.

342 "no notes, no hesitations": *The Nation*, June 18, 1921.

343 "not speculative in origin": *The Nation*, June 18, 1921.

343 "the harmony of the universe": Reichenbach, quoted in Vallentin, p. 106.

343 "Each of these two nations": *The Nation*, June 18, 1921.

344 "One of the most memorable weeks": Einstein–Mrs. Haldane, June 15, 1921, Haldane Papers, 6082 (131–32), National Library of Scotland.

345 "the German ambassador was right": Haldane–Lindemann, June 15, 1921, Cherwell Archives.

345 "no room for question that Einstein 'explained' gravitation": Sampson–Lindemann, June 16, 1921, Cherwell Archives.

347 "No intelligent Englishman": Einstein–Sommerfeld, July 4, 1921, Sommerfeld, p. 81.

347 "a markedly unfriendly feeling": *New York Times*, July 2, 1921.

348 "no right to reproduce utterances": Einstein–Sommerfeld, January 28, 1922, Sommerfeld, p. 99.

352 "Rathenau has told me": Einstein–Langevin, Vallentin, p. 73.

352 "Langevin has got a roof": Einstein–Solovine, March 14, 1922, Solovine, p. 37.

352 The two fullest accounts of Einstein's Paris visit are given by Charles Nordmann in *Revue des Deux Mondes*, Vol. 8, 7th series, 1922, and *L'Illustration*, April 15, 1922.

352 "impression . . . of astonishing youth": Nordmann, *L'Illustration.*

355 "Mach was a good mechanic . . . a deplorable philosopher": *Bulletin de la Société Française de Philosophie*, Vol. 22, 1922, pp. 92–113.

355 "I see red": quoted Jaffe, *Michelson and the Speed of Light*, p. 101.

356 "Relativity is an interesting word": *The Times* (London), April 3, 1922.

357 "all the students of the world": Nordmann, *L'Illustration.*

358 "another movie on the same terms": Cohen, *A Dreamer's Journey*, p. 189.

358 "an old Zurich boy": Einstein–Weyl, June 6, 1922, quoted Weyl–Seelig, May 19, 1952, ETH.

359 "get in touch with one another across their frontiers": quoted Einstein, *The Fight Against War*, Alfred Lief, ed., p. 13.

360 "conduct in public . . . one of proud reserve": *Neue Rundschau*, Vol. 33, Pt. 2, pp. 815–16.

360 "no longer the right person for the job": Einstein–Curie, July 4, 1922, Bibliothèque Nationale, Paris.

361 Dangerous for him . . . to stay in Berlin: Nathan and Norden, p. 54.

361 Madame Curie wrote pleading: Curie–Einstein, July 7, 1922, Curie Laboratory Archives, Paris.

361 "I accept the full consequences": Einstein–Curie, July 11, 1922, Bibliothèque Nationale, Paris.

361 "one lives through exciting days": Einstein–Solovine, July 16, 1922, Solovine, p. 43.

362 "not so important where you live": Einstein–Born, March 3, 1920, Born Letters, p. 26.

364 Einstein's nationality: A major source is Herneck in *Die Naturwissenschaften*, which quotes extensively from government and Academy documents.

364 "The Swiss ambassador was surprised": Nadolny, quoted in Herneck.

365 Award was received by the German ambassador: Nobel Foundation.

365 Handed over at Einstein's request by the Swiss ambassador: Princeton.

365 Ministerial report January 13, 1923: quoted Herneck.

365 "my colleague Haber informed me": Einstein–Ministry, March 24, 1923, quoted Herneck.

365 "Einstein . . . always appears as German": report of German consul general, Barcelona, May 2, 1923, Deutsches Zentralarchiv, Potsdam.

365 Einstein statement, February 7, 1924: quoted Herneck.

367 "a material side to the Nobel Prize": Lorentz–Einstein, May 1, 1923, Leiden.

367 "a cunning publisher": Einstein–Plesch, February 3, 1944, Plesch correspondence.

367 "We rode in small one-man carriages": Einstein diary, October 28, 1922, quoted Nathan and Norden, p. 56.

369 "Japan is wonderful": Einstein–Solovine, Easter 1923, Solovine, p. 45.

372 "When I say it three times": Douglas, p. 44.

372 "reluctance of many leading men of science": Douglas, p. 44.

372 "still controversial": Born, *Physica Acta*, p. 225.

372 Alleged "trip to Russia": Frank, pp. 245–46.

373 Blumenfeld has . . . told the story: Blumenfeld has described his recruitment of Einstein into the Zionist ranks in his autobiography, *Erlebte Judenfrage*; in a lengthy article in the Belgian Zionist paper *La Tribune Sioniste*; and in various documents now in the ETH. They differ in wording, but not in significant detail.

373 Leaving the country . . . and canceling a dinner date with Planck: Princeton.

378 "I have to stay quiet": Einstein–Weizmann, October 27, 1923, Weizmann Archives.

380 "Poor old Joffe": Plesch, p. 235.

381 "never mind the dust and disorder": Plesch, p. 201.

381 The salaries of scholars and teachers: *New Leader*, October 6, 1922.

382 "grievous privations": *The Oxford Magazine*, Vol. XXXVIII, No. 23, June 11, 1920.

382 "no hope of working our way": *New Leader*, October 6, 1922.

382 "seven more books on relativity": *Nature*, Vol. 109, June 17, 1922, pp. 770–72.

383 "if misunderstandings are to be avoided": Einstein–Freundlich, undated, Stargardt Catalogue, No. 378, autograph auction, February 18 and 19, 1969.

383 "old ideas . . . in the melting pot": Douglas, p. 42.

385 "Poor people beg for money": Reiser, p. 202.

386 "the great Pyramid of Egypt": Speight-Humbertson, *Spiritism: The Hidden Secret in Einstein's Theory of Relativity*, p. 23.

386 "When you are twenty": Letter to author, October 22, 1968.

386 "dressed in a morning coat and striped trousers": Infeld, *American Scholar.*

387 "his great kindness": Infeld, *American Scholar.*

388 "already disclosed the secret": Ehrenhaft, p. 11.

388 "I retire to the back of my mind": Marianoff, p. 85.

388 "Why tails?": Vallentin, p. 15.

389 "I want nothing from anyone": George Sylvester Viereck, "What Life Means to Einstein," *Saturday Evening Post*, October 26, 1929, p. 17 et seq.

390 "Einstein could do so": Frau Freundlich statement to author.

390 "Anything is allowed to Einstein": Tatiana–Ehrenfest–Afanasyeiva–Seelig, June 4, 1952, ETH.

390 "start an argument": Infeld, *Bulletin of the Atomic Scientists.*

391 Einstein Tower: For details see Erwin Finlay–Freundlich, "How I came to Build the Einstein Tower." *Physikalische Blätter*, Vol. 12, 1969.

392 "Einstein looking at me": Salaman.

394 Crest of the wave: A. S. Eve and J. Chadwick, obituary notices, *Fellows of the Royal Society*, Vol. 2, No. 6, January 1958, p. 422.

395 "discussions were . . . unforgettable": Herzberger–author, January 22, 1970.

395 "Physics melted in his mouth": Gabor–author, November 15, 1969.

396 "it can be used to set up violent explosions": Szilard, *Reminiscences* (afterward referred to as "Szilard"), p. 102.

396 "who create intellectual and spiritual life": Einstein–Professor Donnan, August 16, 1933, Szilard Papers.

397 "He could sleep when he was tired": Uexküll. (Margarete Niewenhuis von Uexküll's "Reminiscences of Einstein" have been given the *Frankfurter Allgemeine Zeitung*, March 10, 1956, and in a memorandum dealing with the same events, although slightly different in detail, in the ETH.)

398 Life in Leiden: Uexküll.

399 "ten years of my life": *Review of Modern Physics*, Vol. 21, No. 3, July 1949, p. 344.

399 "X rays . . . consist of discrete units": A. H. Compton, *Journal of the Franklin Institute*, Vol. 198, 1924, p. 70.

400 "Otherwise the whole relativity theory collapses": Einstein–Millikan, July 13, 1925, Millikan Papers, California Institute of Technology.

400 "sent Miller home": Polanyi, *The Logic of Liberty*, p. 11.

401 No readings were possible: Born Letters, p. 74.

401 "The Einstein and The Eddington": Professor W. H. Williams' poem was discovered among Eddington's papers by Professor

A. Vibert Douglas when writing his life, and is published in her biography, p. 116.

403 "Strange people, these Germans": Einstein diary, Princeton.

403 "my nerves so bad": Einstein–Millikan, July 13, 1925, Millikan Papers.

404 "the future, that is only a gamble": Einstein–Millikan, September 18, 1925, Millikan Papers.

404 "my husband hesitated": Elsa–Millikan, September 18, 1925, Millikan Papers.

404 "I have become a vegetable": Einstein–Millikan, January 8, 1927, Millikan Papers.

405 "he gropes his way in loneliness": Born, in Schilpp, p. 163.

405 "a tantalizingly incomplete and confused tangle": See Klein, *Letters on Wave Mechanics*, K. Przibram, ed., p. x.

406 "The question of causality worries me . . . a lot": Einstein–Born, January 27, 1920, Born Letters.

407 "after a long absence": de Broglie, *New Perspectives in Physics*, p. 80.

408 "purely on grounds of intellectual beauty": Polanyi, *Personal Knowledge*, p. 148.

408 "In the months that followed": de Broglie, *New Perspectives in Physics*, p. 139.

409 Two papers for the Prussian Academy: "Quantentheorie des einatomigen idealen Gases," *Preussische Akademie der Wissenschaften, Phys.-math. Klasse, Sitzungsberichte*, 1924, pp. 261–67, and 1925, pp. 13–14.

409 "The scientific world of the time": de Broglie, *New Perspectives in Physics*, p. 140.

409 "to exterminate mankind": Schrödinger, "Our Image of Matter," *On Modern Physics*, London, 1961, p. 43.

409 "your second paper on gas degeneracy": Schrödinger–Einstein, April 23, 1926, Klein, *Letters on Wave Mechanics*, Przibram, ed., p. 26.

410 "the top of Fujiyama": Rosenfeld, *Niels Bohr: An Essay* (on Einstein's sixtieth birthday, October 7, 1945), p. 15.

413 "the monumental stability of an enormous life insurance company": Schonland, p. 188.

413 "is no objectively existing situation": Born, "Physics and Metaphysics," *The Scientific Monthly*, Vol. 82, No. 5, May 1956, p. 234.

413 "unhappy over what they have been forced to do": Oppenheimer, *Flying Trapeze*, pp. 5–6.

414 "A new fashion . . . in physics": Frank, p. 260.

414 "A good joke . . .": Frank, p. 261.

414 "I . . . am convinced that He does not throw dice": Einstein–

Born, December 12, 1926, Born Letters, p. 91, and *Physics in My Generation*, p. 204.

414 "laws which compel the Good Lord to throw the dice": Seelig, p. 209.

415 "never be possible to decide whether the world is causal or not": Einstein–Samuel, October 1937, Samuel Papers.

416 "came to the conference with great anticipations": Schilpp, p. 211.

416 "the impossibility of any sharp separation": Schilpp, p. 210.

418 "Einstein mockingly asked us": Schilpp, p. 218.

418 "his sweet disposition . . . his general kindness": de Broglie, *New Perspectives in Physics*, p. 182.

420 "Einstein, who had forgotten to apply his own General Theory of Relativity": Cline, p. 240.

420 "On Mondays, Wednesdays, and Fridays": Sir William Bragg, *Electrons and Ether Waves*, 23rd Robert Boyle Lecture, Oxford, 1921, p. 11.

420 "The advancing sieve of time": Lawrence Bragg–author, May 30, 1970.

420 "power to restore unison": *Nature*, Vol. 119, 1927, p. 467.

421 "You believe in the God who plays dice": Einstein–Born, September 7, 1944, Born Letters, p. 149.

421 "the right to go to the limit": Born, *Physica Acta*, p. 259.

422 "we all dance to a mysterious tune": *Saturday Evening Post*, October 26, 1929, p. 17 et seq.

423 "faith in unbroken causality is threatened": "Fundamental Concepts of Physics and Their Most Recent Changes," translation of the Davos Hochschule Lecture, published in the *St. Louis Post-Dispatch*, December 29, 1928. No other printed version believed to exist.

424 "Einstein never took any exercise": Plesch, p. 216.

424 "oar of a difficult sailing boat": Einstein–Plesch, February 3, 1944, Plesch correspondence.

425 "The professor lay reading in bed": Helen Dukas, *Bucherwagen*, Zurich, 1969.

427 "pacifism . . . an instinctive feeling": Paul Hutchinson, *Christian Century*, July/August 1929.

428 "unconditionally refuse to do war service": *Die Wahrheit*, 1929, quoted Lief, p. 26.

428 "pacifists are largely responsible": Einstein–Thirring, August 12, 1936, Nathan and Norden, p. 273.

429 "not as representatives": League Files, 13C/20823X/14297, Geneva.

430 "a conversation with leading members": Murray–Russell, May 4, 1955, Smith and Toynbee, *Gilbert Murray*, p. 200.

430 "the idea of building up international understanding": Einstein–Curie, May 30, 1922, Bibliothèque Nationale, Paris.

430 "the example of . . . Newton": *Menorah.*

431 "no desire to represent people": Einstein–Comert, July 4, 1922, League Archives.

431 "your letter, which has caused me a great disappointment": Curie–Einstein, July (date unclear), 1922, Institut de Physique Nucleaire, Paris.

432 "Einstein resigns": Nitobe–Murray, League Archives.

432 "resignation . . . cannot become definitive": Bergson–Nitobe, League Archives.

432 "your sudden and motiveless retreat": Comert–Einstein, April 10, 1923, League Archives.

433 "from French friends": Einstein–Haldane, August 30, 1922, Haldane Papers.

434 "As a convinced pacifist": Einstein–League, March 21, 1923, League Archives.

434 "a condemnation, without appeal": Comert–Einstein, April 10, 1923, League Archives.

435 "no action, no matter how brutal": *Die Friedenswarte*, June, 1923.

436 "I know that . . . I annoyed you": Einstein–Curie, December 25, 1923, Bibliothèque Nationale, Paris.

437 "If I should not be elected": Einstein–Murray, May 30, 1924, League Archives.

437 "singular broadmindedness and magnanimity": Einstein–Drummond, June 25, 1924, League Archives.

438 "guided by narrow nationalism": speech at inauguration of Institute of Intellectual Cooperation, June 26, 1926.

439 "We had no funds": Smith and Toynbee, p. 202.

440 "immense intellectual power, perfect goodwill": Smith and Toynbee, p. 200.

440 "very reluctant to believe evil": Murray–Bertrand Russell, May 4, 1955, quoted Smith and Toynbee, p. 200.

440 "fighting the chauvinistic influence": Einstein–Millikan, January 9, 1925, Millikan Papers.

441 "sole communication to the proceedings": Trowbridge–Millikan, January 14, 1926, Millikan Papers.

442 "a horror of platonic declarations": Steinig–Bonnet, October 29, 1931, League Archives.

443 "an expression of the same revolutionary phase": *Why War?.*

443 "hasten to answer your letter": *Letters of Sigmund Freud, 1873-1939*, Ernst L. Freud, ed., p. 267.

445 Long discursive answer: printed in *Why War?.*

446 "an utterly futile task": Einstein–Women's International League for Peace and Freedom, January 4, 1928, quoted Nathan and Norden, p. 90.

447 "the solemn and unconditional obligation": Einstein–British No More War movement, November 25, 1928, quoted Nathan and Norden, p. 91.

447 "Einstein considered . . . governments . . . justified": *War Resistance*, Vol. 2, No. 23, 4th Quarter, p. 11.

447 "to meet Einstein at his lakeside summer house": *War Resistance*, Vol. 2, No. 23, 4th Quarter, p. 11.

448 "Even if only two percent": speech, Ritz–Carlton Hotel, New York, December 14, 1930, quoted Lief, p. 35.

448 "there are two ways of resisting war": Hewlett and Anderson, *The New World*, July 1931 issue, quoted Nathan and Norden, p. 139.

449 "resolve to go no more to Geneva": Einstein–Dufour-Feronce, July 1930, League Archives.

449 "I was not suitable for doing useful work": Einstein–Montenach, April 20, 1932, League Archives.

450 "his colleagues . . . would greatly appreciate": Montenach–Dufour-Feronce, League Archives.

450 "This little corner of Balfourian jobs and gentility": quoted Kingsley Martin, *Editor*, p. 94.

451 "I believe [it] should take place": *Paix Mondiale*, November 17, 1931.

451 Henderson "engineered" Einstein's appearance: "The Comedy of Peace," *Pictorial Review*, February 1933.

452 "One does not make wars less likely": quoted Nathan and Norden, pp. 168–70.

453 "This is not a comedy": Einstein, quoted in Konrad Bercovici, *Pictorial Review*, February 1933.

455 A bad speaker: Blumenfeld–Weizmann, March 15, 1921, ETH.

456 "the Jews in Germany did not regard themselves": *Jewish Chronicle*, June 17, 1921.

457 "the movement . . . came to a standstill": Leonard Stein, *Zionism*, p. 98.

457 "denied that the Jews were a nation at all": Stein, p. 82.

458 "the . . . community, which . . . controls the loan market of the world": Fisher, p. 1147.

458 "nothing that called forth any Jewish sentiments": *About Zionism*, p. 27.

458 "I stood up for them": *About Zionism*, p. 28.

461 "the anti-Semitism . . . among us Jews": Reichinstein, p. 137.

461 "the Jew who . . . changes his name": *About Zionism*, p. 37.

462 "I myself belong to no denomination": Reichinstein, p. 137.

463 "put down 'Palestine' for the next War Cabinet": Scott, entry for September 28, 1917, p. 306.

463 "Weizmann's relationship with Einstein . . . remained ambivalent": Isaiah Berlin, in *Chaim Weizmann*, Weisgal and Carmichael, eds., p. 42.

464 "the value of the Zionist undertaking": Einstein–Andrew Young, October 12, 1938.

464 "I also approached . . . Einstein": Weizmann, p. 331.

465 "I was to stir up Einstein": Blumenfeld, see note to p. 303.

466 "Haber had done all he could": Weizmann, p. 435.

466 "Telegram Weizmann that I agree": Blumenfeld, see note to p. 303.

466 "I am to play the role of a little tin god": Einstein–Solovine, March 8, 1921, Solovine, p. 27.

467 A letter which Blumenfeld wrote to Weizmann: March 15, 1921, ETH.

468 "Overbearing and politically ruthless": Weisgal and Carmichael, p. 41.

468 "Einstein . . . gay and flirtatious": Vera Weismann, pp. 102–03.

468 "I was fully convinced he understood it": Weizmann–Ossip Dymow, quoted in Seelig, p. 81.

468 New York arrival: The main record of Einstein's day-to-day activities is taken from the *New York Times*.

471 "To every person in America": Frank, p. 219.

473 "I was asked to translate": Morris R. Cohen, *A Dreamer's Journey*, p. 187.

473 "a new theory of eternity": Shapley, p. 78.

473 "God is subtle": The famous remark, later to be carved into the mantelpiece of a Princeton University common room was, says Miss Dukas, overheard and remembered by Professor Veblen. See p. 422.

475 "We escaped . . . by a narrow margin": Boltwood–Rutherford, July 14, 1921, Badash, p. 342.

475 "I first discovered the Jewish people": *About Zionism*, p. 34.

475 "the university seems financially assured": Einstein–Ehrenfest, June 18, 1921, Seelig, p. 171.

475 "the Club has made difficulties": Weizmann–Einstein, June 30, 1922, Weizmann Archives.

477 "insisted on traveling second class": Kisch, p. 29.

477 "outer gates were stormed" and "made happy by the sight of the Jewish people": *Palestine Weekly*, February 9, 1923.

478 "Interview with Deedes": Kisch, p. 30.

478 "attended the first lecture": Bentwich, *Mandate Memories*, pp. 88–89.

479 "a Hebrew that was evidently unfamiliar": Samuel, *Memoirs*, p. 253.

479 "Suitably impressed": Einstein–Weizmann, February 11, 1923, Weizmann Archives.

479 "I am tenfold happier": *Palestine Weekly*, February 23, 1923.

479 "rouse the Jewish world": *Palestine Weekly*, February 23, 1923.

479 "no genius of rank . . . save a mathematician": Bentwich, *Wanderer Between Two Worlds*, p. 133.

480 "writes just like a professor": Bentwich, *Mandate Memories*, p. 88.

480 "a simple German housewife": Frank, p. 243.

481 "good . . . embodied and continued in the next theory": Einstein, quoted by Samuel, February 5, 1923, Samuel Papers.

481 "convinced that colonization will succeed": Einstein–Solovine, Easter 1923, Solovine, p. 45.

481 "Ramassez plus d'argent": Kisch, p. 30.

482 "learned that the business was costly": Einstein–Weizmann, February 29, 1924, Weizmann Archives.

482 "the first political aim": Bentwich, *My Seventy-Seven Years: An Account of My Life and Times*, p. 99.

482 "membership of the human species": *Jüdische Rundschau*, Vol. XXX, 1925, p. 129.

484 "many financiers from America": Hebrew University Report.

484 "I possess the minutes of the meeting": Einstein–Magnes, December 29, 1925, Weizmann Archives.

484 "you declined—though politely": Einstein–Magnes, March 6, 1926, Weizmann Archives.

485 "my colleagues and I . . . were most upset": Weizmann–Einstein, July 9, 1926, Weizmann Archives.

485 "to preserve the apparent authority of the Board of Governors": Einstein–Weizmann, January 8, 1928, Weizmann Archives.

485 "Our income . . . entirely from voluntary subscribers": Weizmann–Einstein, June 8, 1933, Weizmann Archives.

486 "sever all connections with the university": Einstein–Weizmann, January 8, 1928, Weizmann Archives.

486 "I will refrain from an official resignation": Einstein–Weizmann, June 14, 1928, Weizmann Archives.

486 "impossible to be responsible any longer": Einstein–Weizmann, June 20, 1928, Weizmann Archives.

486 "I appear like a wild man": quoted Brodetsky, *Memoirs* (afterward referred to as "Brodetsky"), p. 130.

487 "of an unusually momentous character": Weizmann–Einstein, May 29, 1929, Weizmann Archives.

487 "I am the Jewish Saint": statement to Simon: visit to Markwalder—personal information and Grand Dolder Hotel.

488 "the brave and dedicated minority": Einstein, quoted official report, 1. Council-Sitzung: Eroffnungsreden, p. 578.

488 A sheet of Dolder Hotel notepaper: August 11, 1929, Weizmann Archives.

488 "Arabs who had murdered Jews": Brodetsky, p. 137.

489 "handled as an episode of conflict": Einstein–Weizmann, November 25, 1929, Weizmann Archives.

489 "many opportunities have been missed": Einstein–Weizmann, December 1929, Weizmann Archives.

491 "very patient in his suffering": Reiser, p. 200.

491 "only just begun to think": *Nature*, Vol. 123, March 23, 1929, p. 464.

491 "talented to the fingertips": Einstein–Plesch, February 3, 1944, Plesch correspondence.

492 "the conceptual foundations of the [General] Theory": *Nature*, Vol. 112, September 22, 1923, p. 448.

493 "master of the intellectual world": Mercier, "Sur L'Identification des Theories Physiques," in *Entstehung, Entwicklung, und Perspektiven der Einsteinschen Gravitationstheorie*, Berlin, 1966 (report of Einstein Symposium, November 2–5, 1965).

493 A preliminary paper: "Zur affinen Feldtheorie," *Preussiche Akademie der Wissenschaften, Phys.-math. Klasse, Sitzungsberichte*, 1923, pp. 137–40.

493 "I am working with every effort": Einstein–Millikan, January 9, 1925, Millikan Papers.

493 "his position was assured": Taub, quoted Whitrow, p. xii.

494 The outline of a unified field: "Neue Möglichkeit für eine einheitliche Feldtheorie von Gravitation und Elektrizität," *Preussische Akademie der Wissenschaften, Phys.-math. Klasse, Sitzungsberichte*, 1928, pp. 224–27.

494 "the dream of his life": Elsa Einstein–Hermann Struck, December 27, 1928, quoted Stargardt Auction Catalogue, November 1969.

495 "it has been my greatest ambition": *Daily Chronicle*, January 26, 1929.

495 The unified field paper: "Einheitlichen Feldtheorie," *Preussische Akademie der Wissenschaften, Phys.-math. Klasse, Sitzungsberichte*, 1929, pp. 2–7.

496 "a nonmathematical explanation is out of the question": *Nature*, Vol. 123, February 23, 1929.

496 "I cannot readily give up the affine picture": *Nature*, Vol. 123, February 23, 1929, p. 281.

497 "an agony of mathematical torment": *Helle Zeit*, p. 51.

497 "The author of this book": Reiser, p. 11.

497 Factual contents . . . on personal information from Einstein: Kayser–Seelig, October 31, 1955, ETH.

498 "I have also forbidden the publication of the Reiser book in the German language": Reichinstein, p. 251.

499 "Everyone shows their best face today": Einstein's doggerel on his fiftieth birthday, mimeographed on a card to many of his friends.

499 "I had to explain to Boess": Plesch, p. 224.

501 "The decisive power": Frank, p. 270.

501 "we have spent most of our savings": Elsa Einstein–Frank, Frank, p. 270.

502 O'Connell, Goldstein, and "I believe in Spinoza's God": *New York Times*, April 25, 1929.

502 "your aversion to . . . the term 'religion' ": Einstein–Solovine, January 1, 1951, Solovine, p. 103.

503 "the 'authorized version' ": *American Hebrew*, September 11, 1931.

503 "should . . . never have been published": Einstein–Tagore, October 10, 1930, Nathan and Norden, p. 112.

504 "The conversation drifted back and forth": Tschernowitz.

505 "The kind of work I do": Frank, p. 147.

505 "I arrived at his house about three o'clock": *Die Wahrheit*, Berlin, March 15–16, 1969.

506 "Then Einstein spoke": Plesch, p. 210.

507 "by giving favors to Jews": Whyte, p. 99.

508 "grim signs of the rising anti-Semitic flood": Bentwich, *My Seventy-Seven Years*, p. 95.

508 "the additional difficulty . . . the jüdischen Nationalität": Rosentiel–author, December 2, 1968.

509 "a matter . . . closely related to the conditions of my employment": draft, Einstein–Planck, July 17, 1931, Princeton.

511 The Queen's own notes in her agenda book: Royal Archives, Brussels.

512 "dinner with the Kings": Einstein–Elsa, quoted Nathan and Norden, p. 662.

512 "the pockets of a schoolboy": Vallentin, p. 81.

513 "Nature conceals her mystery": Einstein–Veblen, April 1930, Princeton.

513 "the pleasure of talking with you": Einstein–Eddington, quoted Douglas, p. 102.

514 "the business of a Jewish Holy One": Einstein–Samuel, September 25, 1930, Samuel Papers.

514 "Je suis modèle" and "pas très Juif": note by Samuel, Samuel Papers.

515 "the impression of a monkeys' assembly": Vera Weizmann, p. 113.

515 "when I first met Einstein": Fleming–Allan Balch, December 5, 1934, Millikan Papers.

516 "religious thought 'an attempt to find an out' ": Ernst G. Strauss, *Encyclopedia Americana*, Vol. 10, New York, 1969, p. 42a.

516 "he had no belief in the Church": Born Letters, p. 203.

516 "something behind the energy": quoted in Ben-Gurion, p. 217.

516 "they quote me for support of such views": Lowenstein, *Towards the Farther Shore*, p. 156.

517 At opposite ends of the range: Sheen, Krass, *New York Times*, November 16, 1930.

517 "An impersonal God . . .": William Kent, "Einstein's Reflections on Life and Religion," *The Western Humanities Review*, Vol. IX, No. 3, Summer 1955, p. 189.

517 "a sad commentary on . . . commercialism . . . and corruption": *New York Times*, November 23, 1930.

518 "I want to be left alone": *New York Times*, December 3, 1930.

519 "One should not speak publicly": *New York Times*, December 17, 1930.

519 "to define the fourth dimension": *New York Times*, December 12, 1930.

519 "particularly inane questions": Einstein diary, December 11, 1930, quoted Nathan and Norden, p. 115.

520 "It is in your country": translation provided by Mrs. Einstein, quoted Lief, pp. 32–33.

520 "five crowded days": details, *New York Times*.

522 "The autograph business . . . flourishing": quoted Nathan and Norden, p. 119.

522 "the Good Lord knows very well": Hedwig Born–Einstein, February 22, 1931, *Briefwechsel 1916–1955*, Munich, 1969, p. 154.

522 "the greatest mind in the world": Upton Sinclair, "As I Remember Him," *Saturday Review*, April 14, 1956.

523 "New observations by Hubble and Humason": *New York Times*, January 3, 1931.

524 "symmetry . . . nearly as important as truth": North, p. 118.

526 "the back of an old envelope": As with many stories of the Einsteins in Pasadena, this is firmly believed even though evidence is lacking.

527 "if I may take refuge behind Einstein": Inge, *God and the Astronomers*, p. 50.

527 "singing an ugly tune": *New York Times*, February 17, 1931.

528 "Financial position . . . extremely difficult": cable, Weizmann–Einstein, February 4, 1931, Weizmann Archives.

528 "Only resistance": Nathan and Norden, p. 124.

528 The Rhodes Lectures: the Einstein Archives in Princeton, the

Cherwell Archives, and the present Warden of the Rhodes Trust are the main sources for details of Einstein's negotiations with the Trust.

529 "my current activities and obligations": Einstein–Haldane, June 8, 1927, Rhodes Trust.

529 "perhaps . . . I can make amends": Einstein–Lindemann, August 8, 1927, Cherwell Archives.

530 Trustees "put in the difficult position": Fisher–Einstein, October 14, 1927, Princeton.

530 "withdraw my undertaking to Oxford": Einstein–Lindemann, June 12, 1930, Cherwell Archives.

530 "his health seems quite restored": Lindemann–Lothian, October 4 and 13, 1930, Cherwell Archives.

530 "every care that he has all he wants": Lindemann–Mrs. Einstein, February 24, 1931, Cherwell Archives.

531 "the Oxford Luncheon Club has written to me": Einstein–Lindemann, March 23, 1931, Cherwell Archives.

531 "my husband took a good deal of trouble": Mrs. Haldane, *The Manchester Guardian*, April 28, 1955.

532 The first lecture: Einstein's Rhodes Lectures have never been printed. They are summarized in *Nature*, Vol. 127, pp. 765, 790, 826.

532 "The faraway thought behind that faraway look": Toynbee, *Acquaintances*, p. 268.

533 "the calm cloisters of the college": Mrs. Einstein–Lindemann, May 11, 1931, Cherwell Archives.

533 "his great interest in music": Whitrow, p. 58.

534 "The situation here is horrible": Einstein–Lindemann, June 9, 1931, Cherwell Archives.

534 "He . . . proved so stimulating": Lindemann–Lord Lothian, June 27, 1931, Cherwell Archives.

534 Proposed that Einstein should be made a "Research Student": details from Christ Church, Sir Roy Harrod, C. H. Collie, Cherwell Archives.

535 Einstein's thank-you: translated by J. B. Leishman, *The Times* (London), May 17, 1955.

536 "able to visit Oxford for something like a month": Lindemann–Einstein, June 29, 1931, Cherwell Archives.

536 "Extraordinary things are happening here": Einstein–Lindemann, July 15, 1931, Cherwell Archives.

537 "Fleming read *not* his own letters": Noyes–Hale, October 8, 1931, Hale Papers.

537 "commitment of $20,000 all inclusive": telegram, Barrett–Millikan, Millikan Papers.

537 "the $7,000 figure which we talked about": Millikan–Einstein, October 11, 1931, Millikan Papers.

538 "decided to remain here for this winter": Einstein–Millikan, October 19, 1931, Millikan Papers.

539 Sending the contract: Mrs. Einstein–Millikan, November 14, 1931, Millikan Papers.

539 "I shall essentially give up my Berlin position": Einstein diary, December 1931, Princeton.

540 "I drove over to the Athenaeum": Flexner, p. 381.

540 "I had no idea that he would be interested": Flexner, p. 382.

540 "in one swoop": Lief, p. 56.

541 "we entered into relations of easy intimacy with him": Harrod, p. 47.

541 "some mathematical proposition which he took to be well established": Harrod, p. 48.

542 "the beautiful proof about prime factors": Einstein–Lindemann, June 19, 1944, Cherwell Archives.

542 "a glow of triumph": Birkenhead, p. 140.

542 "I have examined the affidavits": Birkenhead, p. 140.

542 "I would not presume to offer you a post": Flexner, p. 383.

543 "a people that refused an Einstein": Mowrer, *Germany Puts the Clock Back*, p. 238.

543 "The military dictatorship will suppress the popular will": Frank, p. 273.

543 "I found him seated on the veranda": Flexner, p. 384.

544 "Let Mrs. Einstein and me arrange it": Flexner, quoted *New York Times*, April 19, 1955.

544 "Whatever doubts and thoughts they had": Weyl–Seelig, May 19, 1952, ETH.

544 "my husband has accepted Flexner's offer": Mrs. Einstein–Millikan, June 22, 1932, Millikan Papers.

545 "you are establishing in Princeton a theoretical research institute": Millikan–Flexner, July 25, 1932, Millikan Papers.

545 "annual residence for brief periods at several places": Flexner–Millikan, July 29, 1932, Millikan Papers.

546 "maybe a solution will be found": Mrs. Einstein–Millikan, August 13, 1932, Millikan Papers.

546 "leave of absence from the Prussian Academy": *New York Times*, October 16, 1932.

546 "something of the mysteries": Einstein–Queen Elizabeth of Belgium, September 19, 1932, Royal Archives, Brussels.

547 "to a request for you to rejoin the Board of Governors": Weizmann–Einstein, November 8, 1932, Weizmann Archives.

547 Einstein delighted to hear the news: Einstein–Weizmann, November 20, 1932, Weizmann Archives.

548 "funny if they didn't let me in": *New York Times*, December 4, 1932.

548 "these watchful citizenesses": statement to Associated Press, December 3, 1932.

548 "a personal struggle in which the foulest means are used": Einstein–Barbusse, June 1932, Nathan and Norden, p. 178.

549 "You will never see it again": Frank, p. 273.

550 "to cover the expenses of Professor Einstein in America": Wilber K. Thomas, Oberlaender Trust–Millikan, January 14, 1932, Millikan Papers.

551 "aiding and abetting the teaching of treason to the youth of this country": Fried–Millikan, March 4, 1932, Millikan Papers.

551 "Einstein has been exploited by all sorts of agencies": Millikan–Fried, March 8, 1932, Millikan Papers.

552 "a skill which . . . would help to relieve their minds": Millikan–Thomas, January 16, 1933, Millikan Papers.

552 "some wholly nonrepresentative groups of so-called 'War Resisters' ": Millikan–Thomas, January 24, 1933, Millikan Papers.

553 "Einstein was only nodding. He seemed somewhat ill at ease": Watters, p. 3.

554 "the obstacle of the black dress suit": *Bulletin* of the California Institute of Technology, Vol. XLII, No. 138, February 1933, pp. 4–12.

555 "a tree stands in the cloister garden": Einstein–Queen Elizabeth of Belgium, February 19, 1933, Royal Library, Brussels.

555 "the success of our banquet . . . if we were to replace Professor Einstein's presence": Earl C. Bloss–Millikan, February 18, 1933, Millikan Papers.

555 "efforts of all kinds of radical groups to exploit him": Millikan–Oberlaender Trust, January 16, 1933, Millikan Papers.

555 Wrote from the Trust: Thomas–Einstein, February 7, 1933, Millikan Papers.

556 "dare not enter Germany because of Hitler": Einstein–Mrs. Margarete Lebach, February 27, 1933, Nathan and Norden, p. 210.

557 "As long as I have any choice in the matter": interview, *New York World-Telegram*, Evelyn Seeley, March 10, 1933.

557 "I was recently with Professor Hale": Einstein–Planck, March 9, 1933, Leiden.

559 "would not leave us": Lola Maverick Lloyd, *Unity*, March 27, 1933, p. 59.

559 "helping to save European civilization": Einstein–Nahon, July 20, 1933, *La Patrie Humaine*, August 18, 1933.

560 "rumors that Einstein's genial gullibility had been taken advantage of": Edwin Wolf, II (with John F. Fleming), *Rosenbach*, p. 380.

560 A visit to Princeton: details from the *New York Times* and the Jewish Telegraphic Agency.

565 Details of Berlin meeting, August 16, 1933: German Foreign Office, Bonn.

567 "taking over my small house in London": Locker-Lampson–Einstein, March 25, 1933, Princeton.

568 Planck's letter: Planck–Einstein, March 1933, Princeton.

568 "The Prussian Academy of Sciences heard with indignation": The correspondence with the Academy has been published in various versions. That used here follows the text used in *The World As I See It*, pp 85–92.

570 "we are all very proud of the part you have played": Wise–Einstein, May 9, 1933, *Servant of the People* (the letters of Stephen Wise), Carl Hermann Voss, ed., p. 187.

571 "less important that a professor make discoveries": quoted Fermi, *Illustrious Immigrants: The Intellectual Migration from Europe 1930–1941*, p. 51.

571 "a scene . . . not . . . witnessed . . . since the late Middle Ages": William Shirer, *The Rise and Fall of the Third Reich*, p. 241.

571 "the task of the universities": Professor Ernst Krieck, quoted *Science*, May 23, 1933.

572 "reverential greetings to the Chancellor": *Science*, Vol 77, No. 2005, June 2, 1933, p. 529.

572 "the lack of courage . . . has been catastrophic": Einstein–Ehrenfest, April 14, 1933, Nathan and Norden, p. 219.

573 "not yet hanged": private information.

573 "the dangerous influence of Jewish circles on the study of nature": Lenard, *Völkischer Beobachter*.

573 "one of the hideously anti-Semitic cartoons": letters from owner to author.

574 "political demonstrations": Einstein–Langevin, May 5, 1933, Nathan and Norden, p. 221.

574 "it is not clear to me when . . . I could come to Paris": Einstein–Langevin, May 5, 1933, Nathan and Norden, p. 221.

574 "this epidemic of hatred and violence": Einstein–Solovine, April 23, 1933, Solovine, p. 67.

575 "Your plan doesn't really set me on fire": Einstein–Szilard, April 25, 1933, Szilard Papers.

575 "he is still at some sympathy for his original plan": Szilard–unknown correspondent, May 14, 1933, Szilard Papers.

576 "I am here in an out-of-the-way place": Einstein–Bucky, July 15, 1933, Bucky correspondence.

576 "the kindest are not always very practical": Frank, p. 333.

577 "on my arrival in Cairo the following day": Weizmann–Einstein, May 3, 1933, Weizmann Archives.

577 "I think Dr. Magnes is most responsible": Einstein–Samuel, April 4, 1933, Samuel Papers.

578 Einstein had told the Jewish Telegraphic Agency: Jewish Telegraphic Agency Bulletins.

578 "it was deplorable that this university": *Jewish Chronicle*, April 8, 1933.

579 "the action you have thus taken . . . so surprising, and so unjust even": Weizmann–Einstein, May 3, 1933, Weizmann Archives.

579 His reply to Weizmann of May 7—see Weizmann–Einstein, May 11, 1933.

580 "In spite of all the agitations and distractions": Einstein–Solovine, May 19, 1933, Solovine, p. 69.

580 "Could I come to Oxford this year in June": Einstein–Lindemann, May 1, 1933, Cherwell Archives.

580 "I was in Berlin for four or five weeks at Easter": Lindemann–Einstein, May 4, 1933, Cherwell Archives.

581 "Shrewd persons": Frank, p. 318.

581 "the whip hand in Berlin": Einstein–Lindemann, May 7, 1933, Cherwell Archives.

582 "certainly by Le Chanoine Lemaître": Dr. M. Gottschalk, *Bulletin de la Centrale d'Oeuvres Sociales Juives,* June 1955, p. 4.

582 "I could not wait six weeks": Einstein–Lindemann, May 9, 1933, Cherwell Archives.

582 "I can almost see Einstein now": C. H. Arnold–author, October 8, 1968.

582 Suggesting that Einstein and he should meet: Weizmann–Einstein, June 4, 1933, Weizmann Archives.

583 A three-page letter: Weizmann–Einstein, June 8, 1933, Weizmann Archives.

584 "only a decisive change of personnel": Einstein–Weizmann, June 9, 1933, Weizmann Archives.

585 "Einstein has severely criticized the university": *New York Times,* June 30, 1933.

585 "Dr. Weizmann . . . has misled public opinion": Einstein, July 3, 1933, Jewish Telegraphic Agency.

585 "made peace with the Hebrew University": Weizmann, *New York Times,* July 5, 1933.

586 "things could never be the same to him thereafter": Bentwich, *Judah L. Magnes*, p. 168.

586 "a more or less decorative figure": Voss, pp. 206–07.

586 "power of attraction on our young scholars": Einstein, *New Palestine*, XXV, No. 36, September 2, 1934.

587 "Even the events in Germany": Magnes, reply to the Report of the Hebrew University Survey Committee.

587 "[His] faith has the stirring and driving quality": *Menorah.*

590 "you should come here for a month or more": Hewlett Johnson–Einstein, June 3, 1933, Cherwell Archives.

590 "I saw that it was a peace congress": Gottschalk, *Bulletin de la Centrale d'Oeuvres Sociales Juives,* June 1955.

591 "the fusing of small professional armies": Lord Ponsonby–Runham Brown, February 6, 1933, quoted Nathan and Norden, p. 225.

592 "best and most effective publications": Nathan and Norden, p. 226.

592 "time seems inauspicious": Einstein–Hugenholtz, July 1, 1933, Nathan and Norden, p. 226.

593 "The husband of the second fiddler": quoted Nathan and Norden, p. 227.

593 "The matter of the conscientious objectors": Einstein–King Albert of Belgium, July 14, 1933, Royal Archives, Brussels.

595 "responsive to what you say about Belgium": King Albert–Einstein, July 24, 1933, Royal Archives, Brussels.

595 "would rather be hacked in pieces": Einstein, *Ideas and Opinions,* p. 10.

595 "What I tell you will greatly surprise you": Einstein–Nahon, July 20, 1933; *La Patrie Humaine,* August 18, 1933.

596 "The apostasy of Einstein": Press Service of the International Antimilitaristic Commission.

596 "Until a year and a half ago": Einstein public statement at Le Coq, Nathan and Norden, p. 234.

597 "encourage the arrogance of the Germans": Einstein–Arthur Squires and Cuthbert Daniel, December 15, 1947, quoted Nathan and Norden, p. 456.

597 "a sword of peace": quoted Kingsley Martin, p. 94.

598 "to guard ourselves from thinking": Wilfred Trotter, "Has the Intellect a Function?" *Lancet,* i, June 24, 1939, p. 1419.

598 "seen Einstein . . . bringing him to England": Locker-Lampson–Lindemann, July 20, 1933, Cherwell Archives.

598 "an eminently wise man": Einstein–Elsa, Nathan and Norden, p. 236.

599 "I do not . . . possess a drop . . . of Jewish blood": Locker-Lampson, House of Commons, July 26, 1933.

599 "Einsteinian Jew Show": *Völkischer Beobachter.*

600 "I did not write a word of it": quoted press reports, Britain and America.

601 "I implored him to resign": Ellen Wilkinson, quoted *Daily Express,* September 12, 1933.

601 "When a bandit is going to commit a crime": Jewish Telegraphic Agency.

601 "The professor is taking everything quietly": Jewish Telegraphic Agency, September 8, 1933.

602 A small boardinghouse: Information on Einstein's third, and final, journey to England in 1933 provided by Locker-Lampson's widow; Sir Walter Adams, former secretary of the Academic

Assistance Council; the Rutherford Papers; contemporary newspapers; and other sources cited.

603 "I shall become a naturalized Englishman": *Daily Express*, September 11, 1933.

604 "Three wonderful people called Stein": It has been impossible to trace the printed source of this. It may well be a folk creation, springing from "Precious Steins," 15 lines which appeared in *Punch*, September 11, 1929.

604 "a mixture of the humane, the humorous, and the profound": Epstein, pp. 77–78.

605 "made to become a double symbol": *New Statesman*, Vol. VI, October 21, 1933, p. 481.

606 "a conflict of conscience": Einstein, "Nachruf Paul Ehrenfest," *Almanak van het Leidsche Studentencorps*, Leiden, 1934.

606 "For more than forty years": Goran, p. 161.

607 "things of value": Haber–Kaiser Wilhelm, in Bentwich, *The Rescue and Achievement of Refugee Scholars*, p. 4.

607 "a position at the Hebrew University": Frank, p. 292.

607 "did not want to shake hands": Born, *Universitas*, Vol. 8, No. 2, 1966, p. 104.

607 "The climate will be good for you": Weizmann, p. 437.

607 "nothing that would smack of foul compromise": Einstein–Weizmann, undated (penciled "9.6.33"), Weizmann Archives.

608 "I see that Einstein has resigned": Rutherford–de Hevesy, April 3, 1933, Eve, p. 371.

609 Lord Rutherford was in the chair: details from official and press accounts of the meeting; also Walter Adams to author.

611 "it is possible . . . to do more harm than good": Bragg–Rutherford, May 4, 1933, Rutherford Papers.

611 "no implication . . . of hostility to Germany": Adams–Rutherford, Rutherford Papers.

612 "so great a scientist should lend his name": Dufour-Feronce–Sylvestor, September 27, 1933, Beaverbrook Library, London.

612 "The value of Judaism": *New York Times*, October 1933.

613 "I take it that you have returned to Oxford": Einstein–Lindemann, October 5, 1933, Cherwell Archives.

614 "Einstein's boat was not yet at the pier in New York": Rev. John Lampe, July 7, 1956.

619 Leaving "the Physical World": Cline, p. 15.

619 "Do you want to commit suicide?": Einstein–Plesch, September 22, 1947, Plesch correspondence.

620 "never known a place that to me was a homeland": Watters, p. 26.

621 "his divided attitude towards contact": Frank, p. 325.

622 "but I *am* Dr. Einstein": Eisenhart.

622 "We are slaves of bathrooms": Infeld, *Quest*, p. 293.

623 His choice was Moses; and "*My* husband always says" (page 513); private source.

623 Colonel MacIntyre telephoned the institute: report to White House Social Bureau, December 7, 1933, Roosevelt Library.

624 "With genuine and profound reluctance": Flexner–Roosevelt, November 3, 1933, Roosevelt Library.

624 "no invitation whatever has reached me": Einstein–Mrs. Roosevelt, November 21, 1933, Roosevelt Library.

625 "there is anti-Semitism at Princeton": Watters, p. 27.

625 In eight lines of doggerel: The copy in the Roosevelt Library in Elsa's handwriting was translated by the Department of State Translating Bureau which provided a close and a rhymed version and was "careful not to fold or otherwise tamper with the original sheets." The original card, written by Einstein and addressed to Queen Elizabeth, is in the Royal Library, Brussels.

626 A letter from Rep. F. H. Shoemaker: Shoemaker–Roosevelt, December 1, 1933, Roosevelt Library.

627 "analogous to the case of Mussolini": Einstein–Wisseler, August 24, 1948, Swiss National Library, Berne.

628 "Many different circumstances": Jewish Telegraphic Agency.

628 Discussed with Lindemann from November 1933 onwards: Princeton and Cherwell Archives.

628 Written to Mrs. Roosevelt: Einstein–Mrs. Roosevelt, December 21, 1933, Roosevelt Library.

628 "fritter away the summer": Einstein–Born, March 22, 1934, Born Letters, p. 122.

628 "news from me concerning our friend A. E.": Schrödinger–Lindemann, March 29, 1934, Cherwell Archives.

629 The governing body considered his letter: Christ Church Records.

629 "if I come to Oxford I must also go to Paris and Madrid": Einstein–Lindemann, January 22, 1935, Cherwell Archives.

630 "I recalled that . . . I had mentioned a somewhat rare book": Watters, p. 5.

631 "we have found a friend in you": Mrs. Einstein–Watters, April 5, 1934, American Jewish Archives.

631 "One flower is beautiful": Watters, p. 20.

631 "Einstein . . . came back with my chauffeur": Watters, p. 10.

632 "never enjoyed the companionship": Watters, p. 26.

633 "Liszt's 'Lorelei' . . . played on the Ampico": Watters, p. 20.

633 Bucky–Einstein correspondence: The collection of letters is owned by the University of Texas at Austin.

633 "a signboard showing at what time each country": Watters, p. 19.

634 "the one thing . . . it hurt him . . . to leave behind": Plesch, p. 224.

634 Was "too snobbish": Bucky, *Helle Zeit*, pp. 60–65.

634 "the Herr Professor does not drive": Harry A. Cohen, *Jewish Spectator*.

634 "a childlike delight": Bucky, *Helle Zeit*, pp. 60–65.

635 "Burgess had made a number of drawings": Watters, p. 21.

635 "suddenly cried out 'Achtung' ": Watters, p. 21.

636 "the fiancé of a relative of mine": Einstein–Watters, July 13, 1938, American Jewish Archives.

636 "Public appearance is . . . impossible": Mrs. Einstein–Watters, April 21, 1934, American Jewish Archives.

637 "You know how to be gracious": quoted *New York Times*, March 12, 1944, VI, p. 16.

637 "a scandal . . . to attend at such a money-raising circus" and "it tickles my vanity": Einstein–Weizmann, March 24, 1937, Weizmann Archives.

637 Einstein's "thoughts . . . being misrepresented": Weizmann–Einstein, April 28, 1938.

637 "a conscientious person . . . cannot . . . keep completely silent": Einstein–Lindemann, December 17, 1933, Cherwell Archives.

638 "born from a mother earth and bound up with blood": quoted Shirer, p. 250.

638 "True physics . . . the creation of the German spirit": quoted Shirer, p. 250.

638 "the founders of research in physics . . . were almost exclusively of Aryan": *Nature*, Vol. 141, April 1938, p. 772.

639 "the probably pure-minded Jew, Albert Einstein": Lenard, *Deutsche Physik*, Vol. 1, 1934.

639 "the world view of German man": Bruno Thurring, reprinted in *Deutsche Mathematik*, Theodor Vahlen, ed., Leipzig, 1936, pp. 706–11.

639 "I hate them so much. . . . I have to go back": personal information.

641 Private evening of chamber music at his house: Shapley, p. 111.

641 "Always going—but never gone": Shapley, p. 112.

642 "I still would not believe it": Lindbergh–author, December 12, 1969.

643 Gandhi . . . "the only statesman": public statement by Einstein, February 11, 1948, following Gandhi's assassination.

643 "a quaint and ceremonious village": Einstein–Queen Elizabeth of Belgium, November 20, 1933, Royal Archives, Brussels.

644 "I was very, very ill": Mrs. Einstein–Watters, December 10, 1935, American Jewish Archives.

645 "The individual counts for little": Watters, p. 27.

645 "God has given him so much nobility": Mrs. Einstein–Hermann Struck, 1929, quoted F. A. Stargardt Auction Catalogue, November 1969.

645 "never ask the Professor to do that": Mayer–author, December 4, 1968.

646 "I give her my understanding": Eisenhart.

646 Passed a very sad summer: Mrs. Einstein–Watters, September 10, 1936, American Jewish Archives.

646 "little time to fulfill the duties": Watters, p. 15.

646 "never thought he loved me so much": Vallentin, p. 175.

646 To send Einstein to Watters: Mrs. Einstein–Watters, September 10, 1926, American Jewish Archives.

646 "He is in very good form": Vallentin, p. 175.

647 "This bearishness . . . accentuated further by the death of my mate": Einstein–Born, undated, Born Letters, p. 128.

647 "the incidental way": Born, Born Letters, p. 128.

647 "Man does not live for pleasure alone": Einstein–Watters, February 2, 1935, American Jewish Archives.

647 "I cannot leave my work": Einstein–Watters, August 15, 1935, American Jewish Archives.

647 "One's peaceful little room": Einstein–Cäsar Koch, November 30, 1935, Koch–Ferrard correspondence.

648 "a guaranteed museum piece": Einstein–Solovine, April 10, 1938, Solovine, p. 70.

648 "more like a historic relic": Infeld, *Bulletin of the Atomic Scientists*, February 1965, p. 9.

648 "two such relics from times past": Born, *Physics in My Generation*, p. 164.

648 "He had a right to that failure": lecture to UNESCO, Paris, December 13, 1965, printed *New York Review*, March 17, 1966.

649 "beauty for him was, after all, essentially simplicity": Rosen–author, January 26, 1970.

650 "the nature of science": Hoffman–author, March 24, 1970.

650 "God never tells us in advance": Mattersdorf–author, May 7, 1969.

651 "To save another fool": Mitrany statement to author.

651 "Can Quantum-Mechanical Description of Physical Reality Be Considered Complete?": *Physical Review*, Vol. 47, Series 2, pp. 777–80.

652 "I have used this opportunity": Bohr–Rutherford, June 3, 1935, Rutherford Papers.

652 Bohr published a paper: "Can Quantum-Mechanical Description of Physical Reality Be Considered Complete?" *Physical Review*, Vol. 48, October 15, 1935, p. 696.

653 "He grinned like a small boy": A. E. Condon, quoted in Samuel Rapport and Helen Wright, *Mathematics*, New York, 1963, p. 90.

653 "his result had a somewhat broader base of validity": Eisenhart.

654 "Elementary Derivation of the Equivalence of Mass and Energy": American Mathematical Society, *Bulletin*, Vol. 41, pp. 223–30.

655 "he . . . went to the blackboard": Infeld, *Quest*, p. 255.

656 "We shall do it": Infeld, *Quest*, p. 311.

656 "I have hit upon a hopeful trail": Einstein–Queen Elizabeth of Belgium, January 9, 1939, Royal Library, Brussels.

657 "A strange breed of pacifist": Einstein–Hans Thirring, August 12, 1936, quoted Nathan and Norden, p. 273.

658 "my physical powers decreasing": Watters, p. 39.

659 "the layman can at least recognize one thing": questionnaire from National Association of Science Writers (on Einstein's sixtieth birthday).

661 "a wave of atomic disintegration": Sir William Dampier-Whetham–Rutherford, July 26, 1903, quoted Eve, p. 102.

661 " 'radical' process . . . now in the range of the possible": Planck quoted in Born's obituary, p. 5.

662 Rutherford's warning to Lord Hankey: Ronald W. Clark, *The Birth of the Bomb*, p. 153.

663 "The destiny of man has slipped": Desmond McCarthy, *New Statesman*, Vol. III, May 7, 1932, p. 585.

663 "an element which is split by neutrons": Szilard, p. 100.

663 "I assigned this patent to the British Admiralty": Szilard, p. 102.

664 The threat of the concentration camp: The story of Lise Meitner's escape from Germany is told in Otto Hahn's *My Life*.

665 "two fairly large nuclei flying apart": Clark, *The Birth of the Bomb*, p. 15.

666 "Clever, these physicists": Oppenheimer, *Flying Trapeze*, p. 52.

666 "Tizard met the company's president": Clark, *The Birth of the Bomb*, p. 23.

666 Building of a "uranium device": *Naturwissenschaften*, Nos. 23/24, June 9, 1933.

667 "the show was going on": Vannevar Bush, *Boston Globe*, December 2, 1962.

667 New material: Leo Szilard's archives are the most important single source of fresh information on the Roosevelt letter. Another is Alexander Sachs.

668 "Both Wigner and I began to worry": Szilard, pp. 111–12.

669 Einstein "had not been aware": Szilard–Seelig, August 19, 1955, ETH.

669 "that never occurred to me": Szilard–Nathan and Norden, quoted in *Einstein on Peace*, p. 291.

669 That he himself had discussed chain reactions: Wigner statement to author.

670 "deeply involved in his own work": Professor Aage Bohr–author, September 23, 1970.

670 "a surprising conclusion": Clark, *The Birth of the Bomb*, p. 39.

670 "any immediate use . . . is impracticable": message, Bohr–Chadwick, quoted Cockcroft, *Biographical Memoirs of Fellows of the Royal Society*, Vol. 9, p. 45.

671 "a surprise for him on his arrival in England": Professor Aage Bohr–author, September 23, 1970.

671 "I did not . . . foresee that it would be released": Einstein, "Atomic War or Peace," *Atlantic Monthly*, November 1945.

671 "scarcely believe that the universe was constructed in this way": quoted Clark, *Tizard*, p. 301.

671 "Do you really think that the universe was made in this way?": Clark, *Tizard*, p. 301.

671 "my colleagues knew that I was opposed": Born–author, 1960, quoted Clark, *The Birth of the Bomb*, p. 83.

672 Born and Klaus Fuchs: Clark, *The Birth of the Bomb*, p. 83.

672 "one great mistake of my life": Einstein–Pauling, recorded same day in Pauling's diary; Pauling–author, July 28, 1969.

672 "Before contacting the Belgian government": Szilard–Seelig, August 19, 1955, ETH.

672 "the danger to the Belgian state": Szilard Papers.

673 "I decided to consult friends": Szilard–Seelig, August 19, 1955, ETH.

673 "the real warmongering": Sachs before Special Committee on Atomic Energy, U. S. Senate, November 27, 1945; *Background to Early History, Atomic Bomb Project in Relation to President Roosevelt*, Washington, D. C., 1945, pp. 553–73 (afterward referred to as "Senate").

673 "Szilard had a final formulation": Teller–author, May 19, 1969.

674 Bernard Baruch or Karl Compton: Szilard–Einstein, August 2, 1939, Szilard Papers.

674 Not "be too clever": Einstein–Szilard, undated but apparently August 9, 1939, Szilard Papers.

674 "Dear Herr Lindbergh": Einstein–Lindbergh, copy made by Szilard, apparently August 16, 1939, Szilard Papers.

675 "Some recent work by E. Fermi and L. Szilard": Einstein–Roosevelt, August 2, 1939, Roosevelt Library.

676 "lost in the heavy mail": Lindbergh–author, December 12, 1969.

676 "Lindbergh is not our man": Szilard–Einstein, September 27, 1939, Szilard Papers.

676 "Sachs confessed": Szilard–Einstein, October 3, 1939, Szilard Papers.

676 "national public figures . . . punch-drunk": Senate.

677 Sachs "read . . . his covering letter": Hewlett and Anderson, *The New World*, p. 17.

678 "pressure–by Einstein and the speaker": Senate.

678 "their accessibility . . . to Germany constituted an important problem": Senate.

678 "our common concern in the bearings of certain experimental work": Einstein–Sachs, March 7, 1940, Senate.

679 "there had to be secrecy against leaks": Senate.

680 "the matter should rest in abeyance": Senate.

680 "a time convenient to you and Dr. Einstein": Roosevelt–Sachs, April 5, 1940, Senate.

680 "perhaps Dr. Einstein would have suggestions to offer": Senate.

680 "the great shyness and humility of that really saintly scientist": Senate.

680 "a polite letter of regret": Szilard–Einstein, April 19, 1940, Szilard Papers.

681 "the wisdom . . . of creating the conditions under which . . . work can be carried out": Einstein–Briggs, April 25, 1940, Senate.

681 "my participation . . . [only] one single act": Nathan and Norden, p. 584.

682 Government Committee . . . "was to retard rather than advance": Compton, p. 29.

682 Bush "had a long conversation with the President": Baxter, p. 427.

683 "In 1940 it was still difficult for us": Compton, p. 60.

683 "gave Bush and Conant what they had been looking for": Hewlett and Anderson, p. 43.

683 "detailed case they made to American scientists": Boorstin, p. 862.

684 Bush turned to Einstein for help: Aydelotte–Bush, December 19, 1941; Bush–Aydelotte, December 22, 1941; Bush–Urey, December 22, 1941; Urey–Bush, December 29, 1941; Bush–Aydelotte, December 30, 1941; U. S. Atomic Energy Commission, Documents No. 327–331.

685 "Roosevelt . . . did not mention it": Bush–author, December 27, 1968.

687 "It keeps repeating itself": undated verse, Russell Archives.

687 "He never lived at my house": *New York Times*, August 5, 1944.

688 "stressing the important work": Julius Loeb–Roosevelt, May 15, 1944, Roosevelt Library.

688 "silence about the fund raising": memo, W. D. H.–Judge Roseman, May 27, 1944, Roosevelt Library.

688 "Einstein's English had been pretty badly broken": Shapley, p. 132.

689 "gradually developed into a kind of swindler": Einstein–Plesch, February 3, 1944, Plesch correspondence.

689 "a strongly paranoiac creature": Einstein–Plesch, September 22, 1947, Plesch correspondence.

690 "fight against the Fascist pestilence": Reich–Einstein, December 30, 1940, Reich, *Wilhelm Reich* (before start of pagination).

690 "Einstein was easy to talk to": Reich, *Wilhelm Reich*, p. 58.

691 "What hopes and fears": *Advancement of Science*, Vol. 2, No. 5, 1942, p. 109.

692 "closer relations with the navy": Einstein–Bucky, August 13, 1943, Bucky correspondence.

692 "Einstein . . . disturbed because he was not active in the war effort": Bush–author, December 27, 1968.

692 Signed on as a scientist: dates and details from the National Personnel Records Center, General Services Administration.

692 "persons which it would not otherwise have attracted": Furer, p. 147.

693 "I took a morning train to Princeton": Gamow, p. 151.

693 "project was moved from the top of the priority list": Gamow, p. 151.

694 "the amount of work to be done": *New York Times*, March 15, 1944.

694 "defended . . . with the sacrifice of human lives": Born Letters, p. 147.

694 Only contribution to the atomic bomb: Einstein–A. J. Muste, January 23, 1950, quoted Nathan and Norden, p. 519.

695 "never worked in the field of applied science": Einstein–A. Steiner, October 1, 1952, quoted Nathan and Norden, p. 569.

696 "the uranium industry . . . was greatly stimulated": *U. S. Minerals Yearbook*, 1943, p. 825.

696 "enlivened discussions on bomb assembly": Gowing, p. 264.

698 "when the war is over": Einstein–Bohr, December 12, 1944, diplomatic source.

698 A letter from Kapitza: the fullest account of the Kapitza incident, the meetings with Churchill and Roosevelt, and the Hyde Park *aide-memoire* is given in Gowing, pp. 350–60.

700 Bohr memorandum, December 1944: diplomatic source.

701 "A cloud of deep secrecy": Einstein–Stern, December 1944, Princeton.

701 A meeting in Munich: details and quotations, Goudsmit, *Alsos*, p. 152.

702 "before Einstein": Goudsmit, p. 153.

703 "the war situation was already too tense": Heisenberg, "The Third Reich and the Atomic Bomb," *Frankfurter Allgemeine*

Zeitung, December 1967, reprinted *Bulletin of the Atomic Scientists*, June 1968.

703 "a serious attempt to produce atom bombs in Germany": Heisenberg, "The Third Reich and the Atomic Bomb."

704 "I had them brought to Farm Hall": R. V. Jones, "Thicker Than Heavy Water," *Chemistry and Industry*, August 26, 1967, p. 1419.

705 "how would the bomb be used": Szilard, p. 123.

705 Trailed by intelligence agents: Byrnes, p. 285.

705 "Unusual circumstances which I shall describe further": Einstein–Roosevelt, March 25, 1945, Senate.

706 "a possibility . . . not entirely in the utopian domain": *Contemporary Jewish Record*, VIII, June 1945.

706 "an overwhelming superiority in this field": Szilard memorandum, Szilard, p. 147.

706 "Scrambling his technology": Hewlett and Anderson, p. 342.

707 "I decided to transmit the memorandum": Szilard, p. 124.

707 "hope that you will get the President to read this": Szilard, p. 124.

707 "Truman asked me to see Szilard": Byrnes, p. 284.

708 "statesmen who did not realize": Hewlett and Anderson, p. 342.

708 "The world is not yet ready": *New York Times*, August 7, 1945.

708 "Oh weh": Nathan and Norden, p. 308.

708 "the professor thoroughly understands": Dukas, quoted in *New York Times*, August 8, 1945.

708 "science did not draw on supernatural strength": Einstein interviewed by Richard Lewis, *New York Times*, August 12, 1945.

709 Supported the Allied bombing of German civilians: *Atlantic Monthly*, November 1947.

710 "Organized power . . . organized power": Einstein–student at Missouri University, July 14, 1941, quoted Nathan and Norden, p. 319.

710 "the use of force is appropriate": Einstein–*Kaizo*, February 22, 1953, quoted Nathan and Norden, p. 585.

712 "Atomic War or Peace, by Albert Einstein as told to Raymond Swing": *Atlantic Monthly*, November 1945.

713 "This foreign-born agitator": Rep. John Rankin, October 5, 1945.

714 "the most loyal supporter of the League of Nations": Einstein's draft of message for National Congress of Scientists, quoted Nathan and Norden, p. 343.

714 "no hope of reasonableness in the Soviet government": Russell–Einstein, November 24, 1947, Russell Archives.

715 "Russians . . . stationed in America": interview, June 22, 1946; Thomas–Einstein, June 26, 1946, Einstein–Thomas, June 27, 1946; Perkins Library, Duke University.

715 "Open Letter to the General Assembly of the United Nations": Einstein, *United Nations World*, October 1947.

716 "Dr. Einstein's Mistaken Notions": *New Times*, November 26, 1947.

716 "What happened next": Alice Kimball Smith, p. 325.

717 "a nationwide campaign to inform the American people": This, and other appeal quotations, are taken from the Emergency Committee papers, University of Chicago.

717 "a great chain reaction of awareness": Michael Amrine, "The Real Problem Is in the Hearts of Men," *New York Times*, June 23, 1946.

717 "pledged word of treaties, public opinion": Abbot–Einstein, May 3, 1947, Emergency Committee.

718 "refuse to submit to any kind of disarmament": V. H. Van Maren–Emergency Committee, April 29, 1947, Emergency Committee.

718 "I do not remember that Einstein ever had any influence": Weisskopf–author, May 14, 1970.

719 "As long as competitive armament prevails": Einstein–Muste, January 30, 1950, Nathan and Norden, p. 520.

719 "that convenient and natural converse with statesmen": Oppenheimer, "On Albert Einstein."

720 "Suggested Draft Letter to Professor Einstein": undated (penciled "December 1945"), Weizmann Archives.

721 Finally wrote on December 28: Weizmann–Einstein, December 28, 1945; Alexander Sachs.

721 During the walk they discussed the proposal: Sachs–author, May 7, 1970.

723 "By painful experience": *Bulletin of the Atomic Scientists*, September 1948.

724 "on tap but not on top": The phrase is credited to the British junior minister who said: "We must keep the scientists on tap but never let them get on top"; Sir Thomas Merton, "Science and Invention," *The New Scientist*, Vol. 25, p. 377.

724 "Einstein . . . passionately defended the intellectual and moral freedom": Nathan and Norden, p. 541.

725 "The problem with which the intellectuals . . . confronted": *New York Times*, June 12, 1953.

725 "the unnatural and illegal forces of civil disobedience": *New York Times*, June 12, 1953.

726 "I would rather choose to be a plumber": *The Reporter*, November 18, 1954.

726 "those ignoramuses who use their public positions of power": *The Reporter*, May 5, 1955.

727 Worry that Dr. Einstein's name would be exploited: Thomas–Seelig, July 28, 1955, ETH.

728 "The Germans are cruel": Harry Cohen, "An Afternoon with Einstein," *Jewish Spectator*, p. 14.

728 "Germans believe in an unwritten tradition": Einstein–Leslie Buell, March 18, 1936, quoted Nathan and Norden, p. 269.

728 "nation . . . on the decline mentally and morally": *Survey Graphic*, August 1935.

728 "Behind the Nazi party": message "To the Heroes of the Battle of the Warsaw Ghetto," *Bulletin of the Society of Polish Jews*, 1944.

728 "The Germans can be killed or constrained": *Free World*, VIII, 1944, pp. 370–71.

729 "if the Germans are once more allowed": Einstein–Eleanor Roosevelt and Edgar Mowrer, January 9, 1947, as quoted in Nathan and Norden, p. 400.

729 "If the Ruhr is left to the Germans": Einstein–Council for German Democracy, October 1, 1945.

729 "prevent the restoration of German industrial power": Einstein–Franck, December 6, 1945, Nathan and Norden, p. 366.

729 "see . . . that your Churchill is put into cold storage": Einstein–Plesch, October 26, 1946, Plesch correspondence.

729 "the Germans slaughtered my Jewish brethren": Einstein–Sommerfeld, December 14, 1946, Sommerfeld, p. 121.

730 "the conduct of the German intellectuals": Einstein–Hahn, January 28, 1949, Nathan and Norden, p. 577.

730 "Professor Einstein has no interest in him whatsoever": Dukas–Harison Brown, October 28, 1949, Emergency Committee.

730 "the mass murder which the Germans inflicted": Einstein–Heuss, January 16, 1951, Nathan and Norden, p. 578.

730 "I have not changed my attitude to the Germans": Einstein–Born, September 15, 1950, Born Letters, p. 189.

730 "the land of the mass murderers": Einstein–Born, October 12, 1953, Born Letters, p. 199.

731 "they are no mass murderers": Born–Einstein, November 8, 1953, Born Letters, p. 204.

731 "fitted the German people . . . as the giant's clothes . . . Tom Thumb": unpublished MS, quoted Nathan and Norden, p. 263.

732 "Your husband . . . the end of his days": Einstein–Frau Planck, Princeton.

733 "If we wait . . . then our Palestinian brothers will be under the ground": Einstein–Kocherthaler, May 4, 1948, Kocherthaler correspondence.

734 "one thing that weighed heavily upon me": Einstein statement to Hebrew University, March 15, 1949.

735 "fall victims to a great lie": Adolf Hitler, *Mein Kampf*.

735 "America has changed pretty much": Einstein–Plesch, September 22, 1947, Plesch correspondence.

736 "considered leaving the United States": Kocherthaler broadcast, German language radio, 1968, Montevideo, Uruguay.

736 "lose my temper dutifully about politics": Einstein–Plesch, 1952.

736 "a curious drama in which we all appear": Einstein–Lina Kocherthaler, undated, Kocherthaler correspondence.

736 "One has to guard against becoming superficial": Einstein–Markwalder, December 23, 1950, Seelig, p. 39.

736 "He said he was too old": Brodetsky, p. 289.

737 "The devil has put a penalty on all things": personal information.

738 "an impressive Rembrandt": Max Gottschalk, *Bulletin de la Centrale d'Oeuvres Sociales Juives*, June 1955.

738 "I still work indefatigably at science": Einstein–Habicht, Summer 1948, Seelig, p. 209.

739 "case for my attitude in physics": Einstein–Born, March 3, 1947, Born Letters, p. 158.

739 "tiring if I had understood them": private information.

740 "what ideal qualities the trustees should seek": Strauss, p. 271.

740 "a state of angry despair": Abraham Pais, "Reminiscenses of the Post-War Years," in *Niels Bohr*, Rozental, ed., p. 224.

741 What had been a monologue became a dialogue: Dr. Mitrany, statement to author.

742 "Einstein . . . Einstein": Pais, in Rozental, p. 225.

743 "an old man mainly known as a crank": Muhsam, in *Helle Zeit*, p. 50.

743 "no more than a hope": Muhsam, in *Helle Zeit*, p. 51.

743 "interest is restricted to the study of principles": Einstein–Solovine, October 30, 1924, Solovine, p. 49.

743 "There is not an idea of which I can be certain": Einstein–Solovine, March 28, 1949, Solovine, p. 95.

743 "perhaps He is a little malicious": Einstein–Weyl, quoted Seelig, p. 183.

744 "Like Chinese, you have to study it": Infeld, quoted *New York Herald Tribune*, January 1, 1950.

744 "not yet found a practicable way to confront the results of the theory": Einstein, *The Meaning of Relativity*, 6th ed. rev., London, 1956, p. 128.

745 "its physical validity . . . still completely undecided": Einstein–Seelig, September 14, 1953, ETH.

745 "His routine was simple": Details of Einstein's postwar life are taken from conversations with Miss Helen Dukas, letters from Miss Dukas to Seelig (ETH), and the more reliable of the correspondents who visited him.

746 "improvised much on the piano": Einstein–Miss Frances W. Wright, January 12, 1954, quoted *Sky and Telescope*, June 1955.

747 "dumped the contents of a very large wastebasket": Eisenhart.

747 "various objects of religious art": Douglas, "Forty Minutes with Einstein."

748 "Her manner of speaking and the sound of her voice": Frank, p. 351.

748 "I miss her more": Einstein–Lina Kocherthaler, undated, Kocherthaler correspondence.

749 "The presidency in Israel is a symbol": Ben-Gurion, p. 203.

749 "Herr Gott. . . . What is wrong now": Mitrany statement.

749 There is some conflict of evidence about the details of how the offer of the presidency was made, as remembered by those directly concerned. The main facts are clear.

749 "Einstein was visibly moved by the splendor and audacity of the thought": Abba Eban, "Albert Einstein and Israel," *Jewish Chronicle*, October 2, 1959.

750 "Acceptance would entail moving to Israel": Eban–Einstein, November 17, 1952, Nathan and Norden, p. 571.

750 "I am deeply moved by the offer": Einstein–Eban, November 18, 1952, Nathan and Norden, p. 572.

752 "science in itself by no means a moral leader": Einstein–Watters, September 29, 1954, American Jewish Archives.

752 "the great possibilities offered by Gandhi's method": Einstein–Rosenthal, July 12, 1953, Rosenthal–author.

752 "I made one great mistake": Einstein–Pauling, quoted in Pauling's diary.

752 "repudiation of . . . materialism": message to American Friends of the Hebrew University, 1954, quoted Bentwich *Hebrew University*, p. 148.

752 "The only thing is to . . . go on working": Einstein–Hermanns, interview by William Miller, *Life*, May 2, 1955.

753 "the beauty and brilliance of Eddington's writing": Doublas, "Forty Minutes with Einstein."

754 "his supremely great mind": Einstein, in Haas-Lorentz, p. 8.

754 "I cannot prove . . . there is no personal God": "the brotherhood of man"; "never lose a holy curiosity": Einstein–Hermanns, interview by William Miller, *Life*, May 2, 1955.

756 "anything resembling a personality cult": Einstein–von Laue, February 1955, Kuznetsov, p. 305.

756 "the expectations attached to the General Theory": Einstein–Pauli, February 10, 1955, *Physica Acta*, p. 27.

756 "A lot of work will have to be done": Freundlich, *Physica Acta*, p. 112.

757 "Every theory is killed": Einstein, quoted note by Samuel, February 5, 1923, Samuel Papers.

757 "opposed the First World War": Russell, quoted Nathan and Norden, p. xv.

757 "eminent men of science ought to do something dramatic": Russell–Einstein, February 11, 1955, Russell Archives.

758 "A public declaration, signed by a small number of people": Einstein–Russell, February 16, 1955, Russell Archives.

758 "we urge the governments of the world to realize": Russell–Einstein, April 5, 1955, Russell Archives.

759 He had written to Russell; and "He was on the porch of his house": Paschkis–author, January 5, 1969.

760 "very much like to assist the cause of Israel": Einstein–Israeli Consul, April 4, 1955, Nathan and Norden, p. 639.

760 "Professor Einstein told me": Abba Eban, "Albert Einstein and Israel", *The Jewish Chronicle*, October 2, 1959.

760 "willing to sign your excellent statement": Einstein–Russell, April 11, 1955, Russell Archives.

761 "the big problem in our time": Einstein draft, Nathan and Norden, p. 640.

763 "I did not recognize him at first": Margot Einstein-Hedwig Born, Born Letters, p. 234.

INDEX

Aarau, Switzerland, 45, 47, 49–50
Abbott, Charles G., 717
ABC of Relativity, The (Russell), 384
Absolute Relations of Time and Space, The (Robb), 302
Academic Assistance Council, 575, 608–11
Academic Freedom Fund, 608
Académie des Sciences, 355, 408
Academy of Science (Sweden), 363–64
Academy of Sciences (Madrid), 370
Academy of Sciences (Moscow), 715
"Actual State of the Problems of Specific Heats, The" (Einstein), 186
Adams, Sir Walter S., 609
Adams, Walter S., 401
Adamson Lecture, 333
Adenauer, Konrad, 731
Adler, Annika, 170
Adler, Friedrich, 165–66, 170–75, 240–41, 612
Adler, Katya, 174–76
Adler, Viktor, 172–75, 241
Albert, King of the Belgians, 281, 511–13, 546, 593–95
Albert Einstein—Philosopher-Scientist (ed. Schilpp), 741
All Quiet on the Western Front (Remarque), 522
Alphonso XIII, King of Spain, 370
"Alsos," 704
Althoff, Friedrich, 211
American Association for the Advancement of Science, 653–54, 743
American Committee for Cultural Freedom, 727
American Friends of the Hebrew University, 752
American Fund for Palestinian Institutions, 688
American Hebrew, 503
American Jewish Committee, 727
American Jewish Physicians Committee, 584
American Palestine Campaign, 528
American Primer, An, 683
American Women's League, 548
Andrade, Edward Neville da Costa, 195
Andromeda nebulae, 524
Annalen der Physik, 66, 74, 86, 98, 101–2, 132, 141–42, 150, 181, 200, 252, 261, 691
Anti-Germanism, 20, 32, 47–49, 217, 234–36, 245–46, 273, 281, 302, 557, 570, 598, 695, 727–32
"Antirelativity Company," *see* "Study Group of German Natural Philosophers"
Anti-Semitism, 216, 315–29, 359–62, 373–74, 397, 431, 456, 458–62, 466, 470, 489, 501, 507–9, 547, 556, 561–62, 565, 570–73, 600, 604, 625
Antwerp, Belgium, 511, 563
Appleton, Sir Edward Victor, 108, 363, 378
Arago, Dominique, 107, 258
Art of Knowing, The (Polanyi), 129
Arts, Literature and Science National Convention, 555
Asquith, Herbert Henry, 1st Earl of Oxford and, 337
Astronomische Nachrichten, 207
Athenaeum, 347, 384
Athenaeum, Pasadena, 539, 553
Atlantic Monthly, 713
Atomic Energy for Military Purposes (Smythe Report), 712

"Atomic War or Peace, by Albert Einstein as told to Raymond Swing," 712
Atomists, The (Schonland), 412
Autobiography (Einstein), 35
Aydelotte, Frank, 544, 623, 684–85, 740

Bad Nauheim, Germany, 320, 325–27, 362, 466
Bad Pyrmont, Germany, 730
Balazs, N., 129
Balfour, A. J., 1st Earl of, 463, 483
Balfour Declaration, 455, 458, 463, 474
Barbusse, Henri, 548
Barker, Sir Ernest, 342–44
Barnard Medal, 472
Baruch, Bernard, 674
"Basic Equations for the Electromagnetic Phenomena in Moving Bodies" (Minkowski), 157
Bavarian Academy of Sciences, 570, 729
Baxter, James, 682
Becquerel, Antoine, H., 58
Beit, Sir Otto, 529
Belgenland (ship), 518–19, 562, 608
Belief and Action (Samuel), 415
Bell, E. T., 255
Ben-Gurion, David, 38, 129, 516, 749–50
Bentwich, Helen, 478, 480, 508
Bentwich, Norman, 478–80, 482, 508, 576, 586, 603
Bercovici, Konrad, 452–54
Bergmann, Hugo, 178, 482, 586
Bergson, Henri, 354, 429, 432, 437–38, 440
Berkeley, Bishop, 152, 266, 297
Berlin, Isaiah, 463
Berlin, University of, 37, 211, 214, 230, 236, 250, 261
Berlin Observatory, 206–7
Berlin Physical Society, 94–95, 264, 390
Berliner, Arnold, 296–97
Berliner Borsenzeitung, 372
Berliner Lokal-Anzeiger, 561
Berliner Tageblatt, 318, 321–23, 349, 372, 433, 458
Berne, Switzerland, 72–76, 85
Berne, University of, 149–50
Berner Naturforschende Gesellschaft, 643
Bernstein, Eduard, 235
Bernstorff, Count, 529
Besso, Michelangelo
  relationship with Einstein, 115, 632
  other references, 52, 60, 82, 101, 169, 219, 222, 245–48, 275, 756
Besso, Mrs. Michelangelo, 187
Bethe, Hans, 581, 640, 717, 719
Better America Federation, 591
Beveridge, William Henry, 1st Baron, 608–9
Bing, Harold, 447
Biology of War, The (Nicolai), 228
Biosophical Review, 592
"Bivector Field, The" (Einstein), 691
Blondin, Charles, 118
Bloss, Earl C., 555
Blumenfeld, Kurt, 373, 378, 459–60, 462, 464–67, 471
Bohr, Aage, 670–71, 696
Bohr, Niels
  attitude to nuclear weapons, 200, 670–71
  birth of quantum mechanics, 416–19
  brings news of nuclear fission to U.S., 665
  escape from Denmark, 696
  first meeting with Einstein, 312–14
  and Kapitza, 698
  and the nuclear atom, 200–3
  at Solvay Congress, 416–18
  visits to Princeton, 696, 699, 740–42
  other references, 96–97, 266, 314–15, 384, 396, 406–7, 410–13, 416, 619, 649, 652, 660, 667–70, 698, 714, 719, 758
Bolton, Lyndon, 307
Boltwood, Bertram Borden, 475
Bondi, Hermann, 109, 116, 753
Bonnet, Henri, 442–43
Book and Author Committee of the Fourth War Loan Drive, 691
Born, Hedwig, 320, 522, 763
Born, Max
  attitude to nuclear weapons, 671–72
  correspondence with Einstein, 738–40

early life of, 225
and Einstein's anti-Germanism, 730–32
first meeting with Einstein, 162
leaves Germany, 639
other references, 58, 89, 116, 120, 142, 147, 157, 226, 238, 250, 252, 265, 270–71, 281, 295, 305–6, 316, 319, 324, 362, 383, 401, 405–6, 411–14, 416, 419–21, 446, 492, 503–6, 516, 572, 607, 628, 646–48, 694, 756
Born, Mrs. Max, 242
Bosch, Dr., 391
Bose, S. N., 408–9
"Bose-Einstein statistics," 409
Boston New Century Club, 475, 688
Boyle Memorial Lecture (Oxford), 582
Brace, De Witt Bristol, 107
Bradley, James, 110
Bragg, Sir William Henry, 416, 420, 610–11
Bragg, Sir William Lawrence, 416, 420, 755
Brahe, Tycho, 173, 180
Brailsford, H. N., 575
Brandeis, Louis Dembitz, 467–68
Brandt, Willy, 731
Briand, Aristide, 498
Briggs, Lyman J., 677, 680, 683, 695
Briggs committee, 680–82
Brillouin, Léon, 279, 304
British Association for the Advancement of Science, 288, 325, 655, 690
Brockway, Archibald Fenner, Baron, 448
Brod, Max, 178, 579
Brodetsky, Selig, 475, 486, 488, 736
Broglie, Louis de, 87, 90, 407–9, 412–13, 415–18
Brown, H. Runham, 596
Brown, Robert, 88
Brown Book of the Hitler Terror, The, 600
Brownian motion
Einstein's first paper on, 87–90
other references, 90, 138
Brüning, Heinrich, 543
Brussels, Belgium, 183, 278, 565, 574, 581, 593
Buber, Martin, 37
Buchau, Germany, 20–21
Bucky, Gustav, 34, 243, 576, 630, 632–34, 647, 692, 694, 762
Bucky, Mrs. Gustav, 632–34
Bulletin of the Atomic Scientists, 718
Bund Neues Vaterland, 230, 232, 235, 238, 249, 274, 296, 328
See also German League for Human Rights
Burckhardt, Heinrich, 73
Bureau of Ordnance, U.S. Navy, 692–93
Bush, Vannevar, 667, 684–85, 692, 695
Butler, Arthur, 303
Byland, Hans, 46
Byrnes, James Francis, 707

California Institute of Technology (Pasadena)
Einstein at, 523, 526–27, 539–41
other references, 399–400, 404, 515, 536–37, 544–46, 556, 624
Cambridge Observatory, 513
Cambridge University, Einstein visits, 514, 539
Campbell, W. W., 208, 371–72
"Can Quantum-Mechanical Description of Physical Reality Be Considered Complete?" (Einstein-Podolsky-Rosen), 651–53
Cantor, Georg, 157
Caputh, Germany, 500–3, 549, 563
Carnegie Hall (New York), 688
Carnegie Institute of Technology, 640, 697
Carr, Herbert, 307
"Causal Law and Experience" (Frank), 148
Causality, 148–49, 198, 313, 405–7, 415, 423, 506, 648
Cavendish Laboratory (Cambridge), 157, 172, 195, 202, 211, 302, 323, 393, 619
Central Association of German Citizens of Jewish Faith, 461
Chadwick, Sir James, 664, 670, 696
Chain Reaction, nuclear, 663, 668–69, 675, 679, 681, 696, 708
Chamberlain, Sir Austen, 599, 609, 611

Chamberlain, Houston Stewart, 33
Chaplin, Charles, 474, 522
Chavan, Lucien, 80, 171, 176
Cherwell, 1st Baron, *see* Lindemann, Frederick Alexander, Viscount Cherwell
Chicago, University of, 399, 697, 701
Christ Church, Oxford, *see* Oxford University
Churchill, Sir Winston, 76, 124, 140, 185, 491, 541, 566, 598–600, 682, 699, 729
City College of New York, 358, 473, 687
Clarendon Laboratory (Oxford), 323, 344
Cline, Barbara, 419
Cockroft, Sir John Douglas, 363, 662–63
Cohen, Bernard, 203–4
Cohen, Morris Raphael, 53, 65, 358, 430, 473, 587
Collège de France
  Einstein visits, 354–55
  other references, 172, 279, 351, 574, 665–66, 678–79
Columbia University (New York), 128, 192, 331, 472, 678
Comert, Pierre, 362, 431–32, 434
Committee of Imperial Defense, 666
Complementary principle, 416–17
Comptes Rendus, 408
Compton, Arthur Holly, 399, 416, 559, 682, 683, 696, 698, 707, 719
Compton, Karl, 560, 674
Compton effect, 399–400
Conant, James, 683
"Concerning the Investigation State of Ether in Magnetic Fields" (Einstein), 42
Condon, A. E., 653
Conseil de Physique Solvay, *see* Solvay Congress
Contemporary Jewish Record, 705
Conway, Sir Martin, 299
Copernicus, Nicolaus, 639
Copley Medal, 305
Coq-sur-Mer, Le, Belgium, 567, 581, 590
Corpuscular theory of light, 91, 97, 146, 181, 313–14
Cosmic religion, Einstein's, 38, 516–17
"Cosmological Considerations on the General Theory of Relativity" (Einstein), 266–69
"Cosmological constant," 269–70
"Cosmological Implications" (Einstein), 523
Cosmology, 262, 266–71, 401, 504, 523–25, 651
Cottingham, E. T., 285–86
Coulomb, Charles Augustin de, 55
Crimea eclipse expedition (1914), 206–8, 221–23, 251
Critique of Pure Reason (Kant), 34
Crommelin, A. C. D., 285
Cryogenic Laboratory (Leiden), 288, 312
Cunard, Lady, 338, 340
Cunningham, E., 158, 382
Curie, Marie Sklodowska, 138, 161, 184–86, 189, 191, 195–96, 226, 280, 354, 360–62, 377, 430–32, 436, 439, 551, 660–61

Dafni, Reuven, 760–62
Dahlem (Berlin), 211, 220
Daily Chronicle, 494
Dalton, John, 57, 76
Dampier, Sir William, 56
Dampier-Whetham, Sir William, 661
Darwin, Charles Robert, 34, 102, 337, 524
Davidson, C. R., 289
Davidson, Randall Thomas, Archbishop of Canterbury, 338–40, 502
Davidson, Mrs. Randall Thomas, 340
Davos, Switzerland, 422
Dean, Dr., 762, 764
Debye, Peter Joseph Wilhelm, 147, 189, 279, 319
"Deductions from the Phenomena of Capillarity" (Einstein), 66
Deneke, Margaret, 533
Deneke Lecture (Oxford), 583, 588
Dessauer, Friedrich, 326
Deutsche Allgemeine Zeitung, 372
Deutsche Physik (Lenard), 638
Deutscher Naturforscher und

Aertzte, Versammlung, 157, 160–61, 188, 199, 362
"Development of Our Views on the Nature and Constitution of Radiation, The" (Einstein), 163
Dirac, Paul A. M., 418
Disarmament Conference (Geneva 1932), 446, 449–54, 540
"Dr. Einstein's Mistaken Notions . . . ," (Joffe, Vavilov, et al.), 716
Döppler shift, 182
Douglas, A. Vibert, 752–54
Driesch, Hans, 509
Drummond, Sir Eric, 359, 429–30, 437
Dufour-Feronce, Albert, 449–50, 612
Dukas, Helen, 422, 425, 614, 632–33, 642, 686, 691, 708, 746–47, 749, 761–62
Dukas, Rosa, 425
Dulles, John Foster, 759
Dundas, R. H., 534–35
Dutch Royal Academy, 289
Dyslexic Society, 27
Dyson, Sir Frank, 263–64, 284–86, 289, 299

Eban, Abba, 36, 749, 760
Ebert, Karl, 249–50, 347
Eclipse Committee, Joint Permanent, 284
Eclipse expedition (1914), 205–8, 221–23, 251
Eclipse expeditions (1919), 283–88
Eclipse expeditions (1922), 370–72
École Polytechnique Fédérale (EPF), *see* ETH (Eidgenossische Technische Hochschule)
Eddington, Sir Arthur
early history of, 261–62
eclipse expedition (1919), 263–64, 284–89
Einstein visits at Cambridge, 513
reaction to General Theory of Relativity, 261
other references, 120, 125, 297–99, 301, 304–7, 319, 336–38, 347, 371, 401–2, 430, 493, 496, 525, 527, 640, 753
Ehrat, Jakob, 50, 62, 69, 166
Ehrenfest, Paul
first meeting with Einstein, 193–94
relationship with Einstein, 194, 282, 632
other references, 25, 175, 198, 217, 223, 231, 242, 259, 265, 273–74, 287–89, 313–14, 315, 320, 322, 379, 390, 396–98, 417–18, 475, 558, 572, 606, 722, 727
Ehrenfest, Tatyana Alexeyevna, 398
Ehrenhaft, Felix, 200, 332, 326, 388, 689
Ehrmann, Rudolf, 737, 762
Einstein, Abraham (grandfather), 21
Einstein, Albert
academic affiliations: California Institute of Technology, 510, 523, 526–27, 539–41; Institute for Advanced Study, 544–45, 619–23, 640, 647–53, 687, 692, 711, 735–37, 740–41, 745; Kaiser Wilhelm Institute, 213, 221, 361, 387, 392, 396; Leiden University, 281–83, 312, 396–99; Oxford University, 511, 528–29, 531–32, 534–36, 540–42, 580, 582; Prussian Academy of Sciences, 213–16, 220-21, 567–70
on academic freedom, 724–27
ancestry, 19–22
anti-Germanism of, 20, 32, 47–49, 217, 234–37, 245–46, 273, 281, 557, 570, 597–98, 695
and anti-Semitism, 315–29, 359–62, 373, 456, 458–62, 466, 470, 501, 507–9, 547, 556, 561–62, 565, 570–73, 600, 604
awards: Barnard Medal (Columbia University), 472; Copley Medal (Royal Society), 305; Gold Medal (Royal Astronomical Society), 305; Foreign Fellowship (Royal Society), 311; Foreign Press Association, 718; Max Planck award, 506; Nobel Prize for Physics, 90, 215, 248, 276, 312, 363–64

birth of, 20, 23
births of children, 85, 170
Bohr and, *see* Bohr, Niels
Born and, *see* Born, Max
breakup of first marriage, 223–24, 239
and Bureau of Ordnance (U.S. Navy), 692–94
charisma, 51, 641
childhood, 22–28
Communism and, 590
death, 764
death of mother, 243, 273
death of 2nd wife, 646
degrees: Cambridge University, 513; Geneva, University of, 161; Glasgow, University of, 590; Manchester, University of, 335; Oxford University, 528, 534; Paris, University of, 498; Princeton University, 473; Zurich, University of, 73, 149
divorce, 248, 273, 276
early reading, 34
Eddington and, *see* Eddington, Sir Arthur
education: in Aarau, 45–47; elementary school, 28, 29; ETH, 41–42, 44–45, 49–50, 53–55, 59, 61; Luitpold Gymnasium, 28, 30–32, 39–40
Ehrenfest and, *see* Ehrenfest, Paul
emigrates to U.S., 613–14
fiftieth birthday, 498–500
financial affairs: in Berlin, 213, 217, 227, 246, 381; California Institute of Technology, 536–37; Nobel Prize, 248, 367; at Prague, University of, 175–76; in Princeton, 544; at Swiss Patent Office, 73–74, 85; at Zurich, University of, 168
first original papers, 76–78, 86
during First World War, 223–46, 249, 273–74
Freundlich and, *see* Freundlich, Erwin Finlay-
Haber and, *see* Haber, Fritz
Hahn and, *see* Hahn, Otto
health, 737–38, 761–64; dyslexia, 10; heart trouble, 424–25, 491; nervous collapse, 241–45; stomach trouble, 241–44
Hebrew University and, 370, 472, 475–78, 483–86, 576–79, 584–86
homes: Berlin, 220, 244–48, 377, 379–81, 501–2; Berne, 74–75, 85; Munich, 23–25; Prague, 176–79; Princeton, 621, 642–43, 747; Ulm, 23; Zurich, 49, 169, 195
Infeld and, *see* Infeld, Leopold
and International Committee on Intellectual Cooperation, 359, 425, 429–46; Israel and: offered Presidency, 748–51, 757; proposed Independence Day broadcast, 759–61
Jewishness, 25–28, 47, 178, 455
lecturing ability, 170, 653
Lindemann and, *see* Lindemann, Frederick Alexander, Viscount Cherwell
Lorentz and, *see* Lorentz, Hendrik A.
marriages of: first, 78, 81–82, 85; second, 244, 276
militarism, 228, 590–98, 606–7
music, 29, 140, 379, 425, 746
nationality: Austro-Hungarian, 176, 178; German, 19, 47–49, 212, 217–19, 315, 365–66, 564–65, 627; Swiss, 63–65, 238–39, 364–65, 565; U.S., 626–27, 642, 686
Nernst and, *see* Nernst, Walther Hermann
nuclear weapons and, 19–20, 134, 200, 667–75, 695–701, 704–10, 752; letter to Roosevelt (1939), 666, 672–79, 681; letter to Roosevelt (1945), 705–7; post-war debate, 712–23
Olympia Academy, 78–81, 86, 171
pacifism, 20, 168, 226–35, 238, 247, 272, 274, 308, 350, 378, 405, 421, 427, 540, 559, 657, 695, 709, 724, 752; Disarmament Conference (1932), 446, 450–54; League of Nations, 428–52; Palestine and, 733–34; rejection of, 590–98, 606
parents of, 82
physical appearance, 33, 51–52, 80, 233, 352–53, 469
Planck and, *see* Planck, Max Karl Ernst Ludwig

Plesch and, *see* Plesch, Janos
political affiliations: Bund Neues Vaterland, 230, 249, 274, 296, 328; Republican League, 465
publicity, dislike of, 517–18, 521
religion and, 25, 35–38, 502–4, 516–17, 754
Russell-Einstein declaration, 757–61
sailing, 50, 141, 379, 634–35
at Salzburg meeting (1909), 162–64
Samuel and, *see* Samuel, Herbert Louis, 1st Viscount
scientific work, *see* Brownian motion; Indeterminacy; Photo-electric effect; Quantum mechanics; Quantum theory; Relativity, General Theory of; Relativity, Special Theory of; Statistical mechanics; Unified field theory
seventieth birthday, 739–41
Solovine and, *see* Solovine, Maurice
at Solvay Congress, 183–86, 210
Stern and, *see* Stern, Otto
student days, 49–51
at Swiss Patent Office, 68–76, 144, 166
Szilard and, *see* Szilard, Leo
as teacher: Berne, University of, 149–50; ETH, 194; Prague, University of, 173–77; private tutor, 78–80; in Schaffhausen, 68; Winterthur Technical School, 67; Zurich, University of, 164–72
travels: in Belgium, 511, 562–67, 574, 593; in Britain, 333–46, 513–15, 528–34, 540–42, 582, 588, 597–613; in France, 351–57; in Japan, 367–69; in Palestine, 370, 476–81; in South America, 399, 403; in Spain, 370; in U.S., 330, 333–35, 468–76, 519–28, 539–41, 550–61
U.S.S.R., attitude towards, 548, 713–15
war crimes (German), investigation of, 272, 277–78, 281
Watters and, *see* Watters, Leon
Weizmann and, *see* Weizmann, Chaim
women, way with, 49, 51, 52
world government and, 428, 713–17, 721
Zionism and, 19, 168, 178, 247, 272, 277, 296, 308, 330–31, 334, 350, 373, 455–90

Einstein, Mrs. Albert (1st wife—Mileva)
births of children, 85, 170
breakup of marriage, 223–24, 239
divorce, 248, 273, 275–76
marriage, 78, 82, 85
married life, 82–85
other references, 139, 168–69, 183, 186–87, 194–95, 209, 217, 222, 244–46, 367, 566, 629, 635, 645

Einstein, Mrs. Albert (2nd wife—Elsa)
death of, 646–47
family background of, 243–44
marriage to Einstein, 244, 276
in Palestine, 479–81
relationship with Einstein, 247–48, 645–47
in U.S., 468–69, 519–26, 539–40, 621, 623
other references, 52, 217, 247, 273, 328, 333–34, 340–41, 367, 374–75, 388, 404, 425, 473, 494, 500, 505, 512, 515, 530, 533, 543–44, 546, 549–50, 558, 563, 613–14, 627, 629–36, 641–43, 650, 704, 755, 764

Einstein, Eduard (younger son), 170, 223–24, 239, 246, 254, 276, 582, 629, 636
Einstein, Hans Albert (eldest son), 27, 84–85, 139–41, 152, 170, 187, 195, 223–24, 239, 246, 303, 389, 629, 635–36, 763
Einstein, Hermann (father), 21–24, 27, 29, 39, 47, 64
Einstein, Ilse (stepdaughter), 244, 380, 425, 572, 629, 632, 635
Einstein, Jakob (uncle), 23, 25, 29
Einstein, Maja (sister), 25, 39–40, 50, 82, 209, 636, 658, 748
Einstein, Margot (stepdaughter), 244, 425, 572, 629, 635, 686–87, 748, 761–63

"Einstein, Michelson, and the 'Crucial' Experiment" (Holton), 127–28
Einstein, Pauline (mother), 21–22, 26, 29, 44, 209, 243, 246, 273
Einstein, Robert (cousin), 40
Einstein, Siegbert (distant relative), 21
Einstein Affair, The (Reich), 690
"Einstein and the Eddington, The" (Williams), 401–3
"Einstein House" (Caputh), 499–502
Einstein Institute (Potsdam), 391, 396
Einstein on Peace, 552, 593, 610, 708, 718, 724–25, 761
Einstein the Searcher (Moszkowski), 306
"Einstein shift," 260, 299, 401
Einstein-Szilard heat pump, 396
Einstein Tower (Potsdam), 391–92
Einstein and the Universe: A Popular Exposition of the Famous Theory (Nordmann), 352–53, 354, 383–84
"Einstein world," 268, 269, 401, 524, 525
Eisenhart, Churchill, 622, 653, 747
Eisenhart, Dean, 622, 747
Eisenhart, Mrs., 645
electromagnetism, 55, 56–57, 92–93, 96, 111, 114, 117, 145, 492
"Elektrodynamic bewegter Körper" (Einstein), 691
"Elementary Derivation of the Equivalence of Mass and Energy" (lecture, Einstein), 654
Elizabeth, Queen of the Belgians, 511–12, 513, 526, 546, 555, 593, 595, 626, 642, 643, 657, 659, 668–69, 672
Elliott, John, 695
Ellis, Sir Charles Drummond, 97
Emergency Civil Liberties Committee, 726–27
Emergency Committee for Aid to Displaced German Scholars, 609
Emergency Committee of Atomic Scientists, 716–18
Emma Adelheid Wilhelmine Therese, Queen Mother of the Netherlands, 398
Encyclopedia Americana, 516
Encyklopädie der Mathematischen Wissenschaft, 384
"Entwurf einer Verallgemeinerten Relativitätstheorie und eine Theorie der Gravitation" (Einstein, Grossmann), 198
Epstein, Jacob, 301, 603–4, 717
Epstein, Paul, 526
Equivalence, Principle of, 150–56, 181
Erhardt Brigade, 315–16
ETH (Eidgenossische Technische Hochschule)
  Einstein and: fails entrance exam, 44; graduates from, 62; leaves for Berlin, 215–16; as professor at, 194–95; studies at, 41, 42, 44, 45, 49, 50, 53, 54, 59, 61–62; other references, 40, 41–42, 62, 113, 150, 165, 168, 188–92, 275
Ether of Space, The (Lodge), 298–99
Evolution of Physics, The (Einstein-Infeld), 655–56
Exner, Franz, 88

"Fabric of the Universe, The" (*Times* article), 295–96
Falconer, Bruce, 470
Fant, Bertha, 178, 456
Faraday, Michael, 56, 96, 106, 116–17, 154, 224, 248, 327, 643
Fechner, Gustav, 60
"Fehme," 600
Fermi, Enrico, 664–66, 675, 696, 697
Ficker, H. von, 569
Fifth Column in Our Schools, The, 686
Fifth Washington Conference on Theoretical Physics, 665
Fight Against War, The (Einstein), 561
Fisch, Adolf, 55, 170
Fisher, H. A. L., 299, 458, 529
Fitzgerald, George Francis, 110, 111, 112, 113, 120, 127, 131, 526
Fizeau, Armand Hippolyte Louis, 128
Flammarion, Camille, 122

Flamsteed House (Greenwich), 263, 285
Flattery, Martin, 630, 631–32
Fleming, Arthur, 515, 536–39, 546
Fleming, Donald, 683
Flexner, Abraham, 404, 539–47, 584, 623–24, 625, 684
Flugge, Siegfried, 666
"Folgerungen aus der Kapillaritatserscheinungen" (Einstein), 66
Fondation Universitaire, Brussels, 417, 574, 581–82
Föppl, August, 131, 197
Force and Matter (Buchner), 34
Forster, Aimé, 150
Foucault, Jean, 106
"Foundation of the General Theory of Relativity" (Einstein), 252
Foundations of Einstein's Theory of Gravitation, The (Freundlich), 383
Fowler, Sir Ralph, 202
France, Einstein visits, 351–57
Franck, James, 414, 572, 607, 729
Frank, Philipp, 22, 28, 111, 136, 148, 164, 168, 177–78, 179, 186, 203, 217, 241, 244, 328, 331, 414, 471, 480, 501, 505, 543, 549, 576, 581, 607, 621, 660, 748
Frank memorandum, 708, 712
Frankfurter Zeitung, 316–17
Franz Joseph I, Emperor of Austria, 174
Frauenglass, William, 725
Frederick I, King of Prussia, 213
Fresnel, Augustin Jean, 92
Fresnel centenary celebrations (Paris), 418–19
Freud, Sigmund, 197, 442–46, 571, 690
Freundlich, Erwin Finlay-
 correspondence with Einstein, 206
 eclipse expedition (1914), 221–23
 Einstein Tower and, 391
 first meeting with Einstein, 207–8
 leaves Germany, 640
 relationship with Einstein, 390–92
 other references, 206, 208, 227, 261, 283, 334, 371, 383, 396, 756
Freundlich, Mrs. Erwin Finlay-, 207, 222, 243, 391
Frick, Wilhelm, 627
Fried, Amos A., 551
Friedensbewegung, Die, 428
Friedenswarte, Die, 435
Friedmann, A., 270, 753
Frisch, Otto Robert, 164, 640, 660, 664, 670, 682
Fuchs, Klaus, 672
"Fundamental Concepts of Physics and Their Most Recent Changes" (lecture, Einstein), 423

Galileo, 127, 153, 638–39
Gamow, George, 270, 693
Gandhi, Mohandas Karamchand, 643, 695, 725, 752
Gaseous diffusion process, 667, 684
Gasser, Adolf, 67
Gauss, Karl Friedrich, 157
Gehrcke, Ernst, 317–21
"Generalized Theory of Gravitation, A" (Einstein), 743
Geneva, University of, 161
George Gibson Lecture (Glasgow), 583, 589
German Association of Scientists and Doctors, 320–21, 324–26
German League of Human Rights, 328
 See also Bund Neues Vaterland
German Peace Federation, 358
German Physics Society, 321
Germany, Einstein's views on, 20, 32, 47–49, 217, 234–37, 245–46, 273, 281, 557, 570, 597, 695
Gibbs, Josiah Willard, 78, 754
Glasgow, University of, 589
Glenn, Frank, 762
"God does not play dice with the world" (Einstein saying), 38, 97, 149, 415
"God is subtle, but He is not malicious" (Einstein saying), 38, 473, 513
Goiten, David, 750
Gold Medal, Royal Astronomical Society, 305
Goldstein, Herbert, 38, 502, 503
Göttingen, Germany, 157, 196, 255
Gottinger Nachrichten, 157
Gottschalk, Max, 219, 590

Grammar of Science, The (Pearson), 79
Groodt, A. de, 563
Groodt, Frans G. L. A. de, 563
Grossmann, Herr, 69, 71
Grossmann, Kurt, 317, 427
Grossmann, Marcel, 50, 59, 62, 68, 69, 71, 73, 77, 166, 189–90, 191–92, 198, 199, 219, 254–55
Grossmann, Mrs. Marcel, 62
Groves, R. H., 697, 704, 705
"Grundlage der Allgemeinen Relativitätstheorie" (Einstein), 252
Gruner, Paul, 149
Gumbel, Emil J., 724

Haber, Fritz
  death of, 608
  during First World War, 225
  and Kaiser Wilhelm Institute, 211, 606
  relationship with Einstein, 223, 238, 466, 722
  other references, 25, 180, 207, 212, 251, 316, 365, 380, 388, 393, 460, 463
Habicht, Conrad, 68, 75, 79, 80, 85, 87, 88, 90, 131, 259, 738
Haenisch, Benno Fritz Paul Alexander Konrad, 324, 328
Haganah, the, 733
Hahn, Otto
  and fission of uranium, 164, 660, 664, 665
  visits Einstein at Caputh, 503
  other references, 395, 704, 730
Halban, Hans, 682
Haldane, Elizabeth, 340
Haldane, J. B. S., 26, 389, 531–32
Haldane, John Scott, 531–32
Haldane, Kathleen, 531–32
Haldane, Richard Burdon, Viscount, 211, 299, 336–46, 403, 433, 476, 529, 533
Hale, George Ellery, 208, 263, 299, 404, 536, 557–58
Hall, Asaph, 258
Haller, Friedrich, 69–71, 73, 166
Harden, Maximilian, 359–60
Harding, Warren G., 338, 473
Harrod, Sir Roy, 534, 541
Hartmann, E., 287
Hartog, Sir Philip, 576, 579, 586
Harvey, James, 430, 531
Hasenöhrl, F., 133, 138, 184, 702
Heat pump (Einstein-Szilard), 396
Hebrew University (Jerusalem)
  controversy over running of, 483–87, 576–79, 583–87
  Einstein's inaugural address to, 478–79
  other references, 333–35, 370, 399, 464, 471–72, 475–76, 546, 559, 588, 607, 637, 647, 734
Heidelberg Association of Students of Science, 639
Heidelberg University, 724, 726
Heisenberg, Werner
  and quantum mechanics, 411–12
  and Second World War, 703–4
  other references, 98, 281, 415–18, 492, 506, 651–52, 728
Helmholtz, Hermann Ludwig Ferdinand von, 55, 59
Henderson, Arthur, 451
Herbert Spencer Lecture (Oxford), 583, 588, 613
Herriot, Edouard, 591
Hertz, Heinrich Rudolf, 56, 59, 92, 102, 106, 661
Herzl, Theodore, 456, 479, 488
Hevesy, George de, 202–3, 608
Higgins, Eugene, 307
Hindenburg, Paul von, 379, 542, 556
Hiroshima, Japan, 134, 640, 686, 693, 695, 704, 709, 711, 731
History of the Theories of the Aether and Electricity (Whittaker), 130
Hitler, Adolf, 359, 374, 379, 446, 508, 520, 542–44, 556, 564, 571, 605, 629, 633, 639, 704, 728, 731
Hoffman, Banesh, 649
Holton, Gerald, 127, 526
Hopf, Ludwig, 162, 176, 225, 305
House Un-American Activities Committee, 724
Hoyle, Fred, 753
Hubble, Edwin Powell, 266, 268, 401, 404, 523–26, 556
Hugenholtz, J. B. Th., 451, 592
Humason, Milton La Salle, 523
Hume, David, 79
Hundert Autoren Gegen Einstein, 508–9
Hurwitz, Adolf, 55, 62, 63, 139, 221
Hutchinson, Paul, 427
Huxley, T. H., 137, 169, 325, 481, 503
Huygens, Christiaan, 91, 105–6

Hyades, the, 264, 285
"Hymn to Einstein" (Robb), 302, 303

Illustration, L' (Nordmann), 352
Indeterminacy, 200, 203, 393, 412, 416–17, 420, 424, 492, 507, 648, 662, 738
Infeld, Leopold
  collaboration with Einstein, 655–56
  first meeting with Einstein, 386
  other references, 142, 307, 309, 318, 414, 557, 623, 648, 744
Inge, Dr., 339, 527
Institute for Advanced Study (Princeton)
  Einstein at, 544, 545, 619–23, 640, 647–52, 687, 692, 711, 735, 736, 740, 741, 745
  foundation of, 539, 540
  other references, 128, 404, 642, 684, 741, 745
Institute for Solar Research (Potsdam), 391
Institute of Theoretical Physics (Copenhagen), 312, 665, 670
International Catalogue of Scientific Literature, 382
International Committee on Intellectual Cooperation, 359, 425, 429–45
International Congress of Mathematicians, 59
International Institute of Intellectual Cooperation, 439, 444
International League for Combating Anti-Semitism, 569
Introduction to Maxwell's Theory of Electricity (Föppl), 131
"Introduction to Mechanics" (lecture, Einstein), 170
Israel
  Einstein offered Presidency of, 748–51, 757
  Einstein's proposed Independence Day broadcast to, 759–61
  other reference, 735
  See also Palestine

Jackh, Ernst, 443
Jacobi, Karl, 157, 479
Jahrbuch der Radioaktivität und Elektronik, 143, 151
Japan, Einstein visits, 367–69
Japan Weekly Chronicle, 368, 369
Jaumann, Gustav, 174
Jeans, Sir James Hopwood, 97, 136, 159, 184, 298, 323, 523–24, 527, 609, 611
Jens, Walter, 48, 227
Jewell, L. F., 260
Jewish Telegraph Agency, 559, 578, 585, 601, 606, 627
Jewry and Science, 638
Joffe, A. F., 380, 505–6, 698–99, 716
Johnson, Hewlett, Dean of Canterbury, 590
Joliot-Curie, Frédéric, 664, 665, 675, 678, 679, 758
Joliot-Curie, Irene, 664
Jones, R. V., 704
Josiah Macy Jr. Foundation of New York, 496
Jüdische Rundschau, 482
Julius, W. H., 187, 188, 189–90

Kagi, Frau, 49
Kaiser Wilhelm Foundation for Military Technical Sciences, 227, 237
Kaiser Wilhelm Gesellschaft
  Einstein leads Institute at, 213, 221, 361, 387, 392, 396
  foundation of, 210, 211
  Haber leads Institute at, 211
  other references, 261, 327, 379, 381, 510, 556, 606, 660, 665, 671, 676, 679, 704, 730
Kaizo, 710
Kamerlingh Onnes, Heike, 66, 184, 288, 312
Kant, Immanuel, 34, 543
Kapitza, Peter L., 698
Kapp, Edmond, 332, 514
Kapp, Wolfgang, 317
Karr family, 49
Kauffman, W., 132, 143
Kaufman, B., 744
"Kausalgesetz und Erfahrung" (Frank), 148
Kayser, Rudolf (stepson-in-law), 64, 385, 491, 497, 498, 635, 643
Kayser, Mrs. Rudolf, *see* Einstein, Ilse
Kemper, W. T., Jr., 691–92
Kenney, Congressman, 626, 627
Kepler, Johann, 173, 413, 639
Keren Hayesod, 464, 472

Kerr, Philip, *see* Lothian, Philip Henry Kerr, 11th Marquess of
Kieler Zeitung, 372
Kimball Smith, Alice, 716, 718
King's College, London University, Einstein lectures at, 334, 342–43
Kirchhoff, Gustav Robert, 59, 93, 105
Kisch, Frederick, 477–78, 481
Klein, Martin, 193, 405
Kleiner, Alfred, 73, 149, 164–66, 192, 195
Koch, Cäsar, 30, 41, 43, 140, 243, 511, 636, 642, 647
Koch, Pauline, *see* Einstein, Pauline
Koch family, 21, 39, 62, 689
Kocherthaler, Lina, 733, 736
Kollross, Louis, 50, 55, 62, 220
Koppel, Leopold, 227
Kottler, Friedrich, 199
Kowarski, Lew, 682
Krass, Nathan, 517
Krieck, Ernst, 571
Kuznetsov, Boris, 341

Ladenburg, Rudolf, 161, 669
Laeken, Palace of (Belgium), 512, 546, 593
Laing, Graham, 522
Laing, Mrs. Graham, 522
Lampa, Anton, 174–75
Lampe, John, 614
Lanczos, Cornelius, 393
Landau, Albert, 560
Langevin, Paul, 138, 184, 226, 261, 319, 351–54, 356, 378, 408–9, 442–43, 574
Larmor, Sir Joseph, 192, 299, 302, 319
Laub, Jakob Johann, 141, 145–46, 162, 165–66, 317
Laue, Max Theodor Felix von, 32, 142, 144, 169, 195, 311, 319, 321, 362, 378, 383, 393, 506, 511, 572, 639, 723, 730, 756
Lawson, Robert, 199, 296–97, 383
Le Roux, 509
League of Minds, A, 442
League of Nations, 280, 359, 428–52, 713–14
Lehrbuch der Differentialgeometrie (Meyer), 496
Lehrbuch der ebenen Geometrie (Spieker), 34
Leibnitz, Gottfried Wilhelm, 213
Leibus, Rudolph, 360
Leiden University, 188, 281–83, 312–13, 322, 396–99
Lemaître, Abbé G. E., 523–25, 582, 753
Lenard, Philipp A. E., 91–93, 146, 317, 319–21, 326–28, 360, 364, 383, 466, 509, 573, 638
Lenin, Vladimir Ilych, 44, 469, 548
Lessing, Theodor, 600–1, 660
Letters on Wave Mechanics, 407
Leverrier, Urbain Jean Joseph, 558–59
Levi-Civita, Tullio, 25, 177, 254, 262, 319
Levy, Hyman, 196
Library of Congress, 691
Lick Observatory, 208, 371
Light, corpuscular and wave theories of, 91–93, 98, 146–47, 181–82, 313–14
Lindbergh, Charles A., 641, 667, 674–76
Lindemann, Frederick Alexander, Viscount Cherwell
  and Einstein's election to Studentship, Christ Church, Oxford, 534–36
  and Einstein's visit to Oxford (1931), 528–34
  first meeting with Einstein, 184–86
  visits Einstein in Berlin, 323
  other references, 124, 147, 155, 216, 226, 251, 263, 289, 307, 334, 336, 342, 344–45, 377, 391, 541, 547, 580–81, 598, 600, 613, 628–29, 637, 671, 699
Lloyd George, David, 1st Earl, 275, 338, 566, 599
Local Time, System Time, Zone Time (Adler), 240
Locker-Lampson, Oliver Stillingfleet, 566–67, 598–609, 613, 628
Lodge, Sir Oliver, 288–89, 297–99, 337
Loeb, Jacques, 25
London, Bishop of, 299
London School of Economics, 608
Lorentz, Hendrick A.
  early work of, 111–12, 127–33
  Einstein's evaluation of, 754

first meeting with Einstein, 183–84
and International Committee on Intellectual Cooperation, 430–31, 435, 439, 441
relationship with Einstein, 187–91, 239–40, 312
war crimes investigations and, 277–78, 281
other references, 56, 66, 92, 110, 113, 120, 138, 145, 146, 192, 194, 228, 231, 232, 238, 239, 242, 273, 277, 279, 280, 282, 284, 287, 288–89, 302, 312, 319, 322, 351, 367, 378, 383, 390, 396, 406, 416, 523, 526, 566, 606, 661, 702
Los Alamos, New Mexico, 672, 686, 693, 696
Los Angeles University of International Relations, 540
Lothian, Philip Henry Kerr, 11th Marquess of, 530, 534
Lowell Observatory, 523
Lowenstein, Prince Hubertus of, 516
Lowenthal, Elsa, *see* Einstein, Mrs. Albert (2nd wife—Elsa)
Lucerne, Switzerland, 209, 245, 246–47
Ludendorff, Erich, 374
Ludwig I, King of Bavaria, 23
Luitpold Gymnasium, Munich, 28–33, 37, 39–40, 45, 68, 171, 727, 731
Lumen (Flammarion), 122
Lusitania Medal, 246
Lytton, Victor Alexander George Robert, 2nd Earl of, 299

Maariv, 749
McCarthy, Desmond, 663
McCarthy, Joseph, 734
MacIntyre, Marvin H., 624
Mach, Ernst
influence on Einstein, 59, 60, 61
meeting with Einstein, 203, 204
other references, 57, 76, 79, 89, 90, 105, 138, 152, 173, 177, 197, 205, 222, 266, 271, 355, 411, 751, 755
Madrid, University of, 574
Magnes, Judah, 482–85, 547, 577, 579, 583–87
Mainichi, 368
Making of a Theoretical Physicist, The (Klein), 193
Manchester, University of, Einstein lectures at, 333, 335
Manchester Guardian, 335, 651
Manhattan Project, 640, 667, 680–83, 686, 695–97, 699–704, 705, 708, 709, 719, 721
"Manifesto to the Civilized World," 228, 283, 296
"Manifesto to Europeans" (Nicolai), 228–30, 725
Mann, Heinrich, 556, 565
Mann, Thomas, 556, 571
Man's Place in Nature (Huxley), 137
Marianoff, Dmitri (stepson-in-law), 180, 603, 687
Marianoff, Mrs. Dmitri, *see* Einstein, Margot
Maric, Mileva, *see* Einstein, Mrs. Albert (1st wife—Mileva)
Markwalder, Frau, 49
Markwalder, Fräulein, 50–51, 82–83, 736
Marriage and Morals (Russell), 687
Mass-energy equation, 132–35, 163, 184, 331, 653, 712
Mathematical Theory of Relativity, The (Eddington), 264, 753
Mattersdorf, Leo, 650
Maud Report, 682–83
Max Planck Gesellschaft, 227, 730
Maxwell, James Clerk, 55, 58, 59, 66, 70, 89, 92, 96, 106, 109, 113, 114, 116, 117, 127, 131, 156, 253, 327, 643, 661
Mayer, Walther, 496, 497, 505, 518, 544, 546, 572, 573, 580, 614, 649
May-Johnson Bill, 721
Meaning of Relativity, The (Einstein), 743, 744
"Mécanique Nouvelle 1909–10, La" (lecture, Poincaré), 703
Meier, Gustav, 44, 45
Mein Weltbild (Einstein), 635
Meinhardt, Willy, 380, 388, 423
Meitner, Lise, 25, 164, 393, 660, 664, 665
Memoirs (Chateaubriand), 47
Memorabilia Mathematica, 630
Mendeleyev, Dmitri Ivanovich, 260
Mendelsohn, Erich, 391
Menorah Journal, 430
Mercer Street (Princeton), 642, 643, 747–48

Mercier, André, 48, 53, 493
Mercury, movement of perihelion, General Relativity explains, 257–60, 262–63
Metallurgical Laboratory (University of Chicago), 697, 701, 707
Metropolitan Opera, 521
Michelson, Albert, 57, 107, 108, 109, 127–28, 129, 526
Michelson-Morley experiment, 57, 107, 108, 109, 113, 127–31, 304, 400, 473, 526
Michonis Fund (Collège de France), 351
Mieckiewicz, Adam, 574
Miers, Sir Henry, 333
Milan, Italy, 39, 40–41
Militarism, Einstein and, 228, 591–98, 606
Miller, Dayton, 400, 401, 473
Millikan, Robert Andrews, 89, 98, 399–401, 403, 430, 440, 441, 473, 493, 526, 527, 537–39, 540, 544–47, 550–53, 555, 558–59, 561, 603
Millikan, Mrs. Robert, 473
Milne, E. A., 542, 753
Minkowski, Hermann, 25, 53, 55, 150, 157, 158, 160–61, 162, 214, 302, 383, 754
Mitrany, David, 335, 621, 650–51, 702, 741, 749
Montenach, J. D. de, 450
Montgomery, Sir Bernard Law, 1st Viscount Montgomery of Alamein, 244
Monthly Notices, 262, 263, 264, 338
Moore, Dr., 668–69
Moos, Helene, 21
Morgenthau, Henry, 624, 729
Morley, Edward, 57, 107–9
Moseley, Henry Gwyn Jeffreys, 138
Moszkowski, Alexander, 114, 268–69, 306
Mount Wilson Observatory (Pasadena), 208, 270, 299, 400, 401, 404, 515, 526
Mowrer, Edgar, 543
Muhsam, Hans, 743
Münchner Neuesten Nachrichten, 347
Munich, Germany, 23–24, 25, 701
Munich putsch (1923), 374
Murphy, Patrick, 602
Murray, Gilbert, 429–32, 436–37, 439–42, 450, 532
Music, Einstein and, 29, 140–41, 379, 746
Mussolini, Benito, 627
Muste, A. J., 694
"My Answer to the Antirelativity Theory Company Ltd." (Einstein), 319, 320
"My Credo" (Einstein), 427

Nadolny, Rudolf, 364
Nagasaki, Japan, 134, 640, 711, 712, 731
Nahon, Alfred, 593, 595
Napier, John, 332, 560
Nathan, Otto, 621, 723, 763
Nation, 342, 345
National Academy of Sciences (U.S.), 473, 474, 524, 681
National Association of Science Writers, 659
National Committee on Atomic Information, 716
National Defense Research Committee (NRDC), 681, 682
National German Jewish Union, 519
National Labor Committee for Palestine, 733
National Patriotic Council, 547
Nature, 288, 296–97, 306, 382, 492, 669
Naturforscher Gesellschaft, 321, 325
Naturforscherversammlung, 157, 161, 188, 199, 362
Naturwissenschaften, 296, 666, 702
Nehru, Jawaharlal, 759
Nernst, Walter Hermann
  at 1st Solvay Congress, 184
  during First World War, 225
  invites Einstein to Berlin, 212–13, 214
  other references, 138, 179, 210, 215, 219, 223, 311, 316, 321, 365, 366, 390, 393, 568, 570
Nernst, Mrs. Walther Hermann, 223
New History Society, 521
New Palestine, 586
New Statesman, 352, 605
New World, The, 683
New York Herald Tribune, 495
New York Times, The, 303, 325, 348–50, 381, 440, 473, 474, 494, 496, 516–19, 521, 554,

591, 694, 708, 717, 725, 749, 761
New York Times Magazine, 516
New York World, 349, 350
New York World Telegram, 557, 564
Newcomb, Simon, 259
Newton, Sir Isaac, 56, 58, 61, 81–82, 87, 91, 98, 102–6, 124, 127, 133, 152, 153, 156, 181, 203, 224, 253, 257, 266, 290, 299, 300, 304, 343, 430, 638, 639, 764
Neymann, Ernst, 568
Nicolai, George, 228, 230, 245
Nieuwe Rotterdamsche Courant, 349
Nieuwenhuis, Anton, 397
Nitobe, Inazo, 432
No More War movement, 447
Nobel, Alfred B., 224, 363, 364
Nobel Prize for Physics, Einstein awarded, 90, 215, 248, 276, 312, 363, 364
Nordmann, Charles, 352–54, 356, 357, 383
Northcliffe, Alfred Charles William Harmsworth, 1st Viscount, 347
Nouvelle Gazette de Zurich, 434
Noyes, A. A., 536
Nuclear weapons
  discussion of (1939), 664–67
  Einstein's letter to Roosevelt (1939), 667, 672–79, 682
  Einstein's letter to Roosevelt (1945), 705–7
  post-war debate, 712–24
  wartime work on, 684–86, 692–93, 703–4, 707–8
  other references, 19–20, 134, 164, 168, 200, 639–40, 667–75, 695–701, 704–10, 752
Nuesch, Jakob, 68
Nuremberg trials, 227

Oberlaender Trust of Philadelphia, 550, 555
Obernauer, Rebekka, 21
Observatory, 301
O'Connell, Cardinal William Henry, 502
Official Journal (League of Nations), 437
Olympia Academy, 78–81, 86, 171, 255, 466, 648, 738
"On the Electrodynamics of Moving Bodies" (Einstein), 101, 142
"On German-American Agreement" (broadcast, Einstein), 553–54
"On a Heuristic Viewpoint Concerning the Production and Transformation of Light" (Einstein), 91
On the Hypotheses Which Determine the Foundations of Geometry (Reimann), 255
"On the Method of Theoretical Physics" (lecture, Einstein), 588
"On the Motion of Small Particles Suspended in a Stationary Liquid According to the Molecular Kinetic Theory of Induction" (Einstein), 89
"On the Origins of the Special Theory of Relativity" (Holton), 127
100 Authors Against Einstein, 508
One World or None, 715
"Open Letter to the General Assembly of the United Nations" (Einstein), 715
Oppenheimer, J. Robert
  quoted, 103, 124, 134, 413, 648–49, 719
  other references, 261, 648, 682, 727, 739, 748
Opticks (Newton), 91, 133, 181
Oram, Harold, 716
"Origins of the General Theory of Relativity, The" (lecture, Einstein), 589
ORT, 514–15
Ostwald, Friedrich Wilhelm, 66, 76, 89–90, 161
Out of My Later Years (Einstein), 610
"Outline of a General Theory of Relativity and a Theory of Gravitation" (Einstein-Grossmann), 198
Owasco Club, 470
Oxford Luncheon Club, 531
Oxford University
  Christ Church, 544, 619, 628–29
  Einstein's Studentship of, 511, 534–36, 580
  Einstein gives Rhodes Lectures at, 528–29, 532
  Einstein visits, 344, 540–42, 582, 613

Pacifism, Einstein and, 20, 168,

226–36, 238, 247, 272, 274, 308, 350, 378, 405, 421, 427–54, 541, 559, 590–98, 606–7, 657, 695, 709, 724, 733–34, 752
Painlevé, Paul, 351, 430
Pais, Abraham, 740–41
Paix Mondiale, 451
Palestine
  Einstein visits, 370, 476–81
  other references, 377–78, 711, 720–21, 733–34
  See also Israel
Palestine Restoration Fund, 464
Palestine Weekly, 477
Palestine Zionist Executive, 477
Papen, Fritz von, 543
Paris, University of, 498
Paris Observatory, 352
Paris Prize for mathematics, 157
Pasadena, California, 522, 539–41
Patent Office, *see* Swiss Patent Office (Berne)
Patrie Humaine, La, 596
Pauli, Wolfgang, 163, 252, 384, 405, 418, 492, 756
Pauling, Linus, 672, 717, 752
Pearl Harbor, 683–84
Pearson, Karl, 79
Pegram, George, 192, 666, 683
Peierls, Rudolf, 640, 682
Pelseneer, Jean, 183
Peril and a Hope, A (Smith), 716
Periodic table, 260
Perizweig, M. L., 612
Pernet, Jean, 54, 61
Perrin, Jean B., 89
Pétition du Comité de la Fédération des Peuples, 274
Petrie, Flinders, 258
Philosophiae Naturalis Principia Mathematica (Newton), 103
Photoelectric effect
  Einstein's paper on, 91
  other references, 90, 93, 96, 97, 117, 145, 154, 201, 317, 364, 661
Photons, 138, 144, 155, 181, 405
Physical Review, 652, 670
Physics Review, 679
Physikalische Zeitschrift, 326
Physiology and Pathology of the Heart and Blood Vessels (Plesch), 491
Picard, Émile, 355
Pick, George, 169, 177, 187, 254
Planck, Max Karl Ernst Ludwig
  asks Einstein not to leave Berlin, 282–84, 324, 373, 374
  death of, 732
  develops quantum theory, 93, 94, 95
  early days, 24
  first meeting with Einstein, 162
  invites Einstein to Berlin, 212–13, 214
  reactions to Special Theory of Relativity, 142, 174
  other references, 32, 91, 97, 98, 138, 140, 145, 146, 164, 169, 172, 184, 185, 192, 200–2, 206, 208, 210, 215, 218, 225, 228, 249, 265, 281, 289, 303, 311–13, 319, 327, 361, 366, 378, 383, 387, 390–93, 396, 411, 413, 506, 509, 511, 523, 557, 568, 570, 572, 660, 661, 730
Planck, Mrs. Max Karl Ernst Ludwig, 732
Planck's constant, 95, 97, 411
"Planck's Law and the Hypothesis of Light Quanta" (Bose), 408
"Planck's Theory of Radiation and the Theory of Specific Heat" (Einstein), 147
Plesch, Janos
  relationship with Einstein, 424–25, 491
  other references, 26, 52, 118, 169, 242, 315, 380, 498, 499, 506, 572, 619, 634, 729, 735, 736, 761
Plurality of Inhabited Worlds, The (Flammarion), 122
Podolsky, B., 651
Poincaré, Henri
  influence on Einstein, 59
  and relativity, 103, 112, 113, 130
  other references, 110, 120, 131, 133, 172, 184, 189, 191, 433, 702
Polanyi, Michael, 129
Pollak, L. W., 206
Ponsonby, Arthur A. W. H., 1st Baron, 451, 591, 596
Popular Books on Physical Science (Bernstein), 34
Pour le Mérite order, 730
Prague, University of
  Einstein's appointment to, 173–76
  Einstein's departure from, 191

Einstein's lectures in (1921), 331
Einstein's life at, 176–81, 184
Princeton, New Jersey, 614, 619–23, 642, 643
Princeton University, 331, 473, 544
Principe Island, 285, 286
"Principle of Relativity and the Inferences to Be Drawn From It" (Einstein), 151
Principles of Physical Optics, The (Mach), 204
Proceedings (Prussian Academy of Sciences), 494
Prussian Academy of Sciences
Einstein elected to, 213–16
Einstein's inaugural address to, 220
Einstein's resignation from, 568–70
other references, 218, 259, 361, 409, 494, 544, 546, 556, 580
Prussian Ministry of Education, 214, 215
Pugwash conference, 761
Punch, 301
Pupin, Michael Idvorsky, 473

Quantum mechanics, 281, 394, 407, 411–14, 505, 648, 651, 652, 738, 740, 742
Quantum theory
Bohr utilizes in nuclear atom concept, 200–3
Einstein and, 96, 97, 98
Planck develops, 94, 95
other references, 24, 91, 163, 184, 313, 405, 649, 651, 702

Rabdologiae (Napier), 560
Radcliffe Observatory (Oxford), 542
Radiation
Einstein's paper on (1917), 264–65
other references, 93–95, 145–46
Rankin, John, 713
Rapallo, Treaty of, 360
Rathenau, Walther, 351–52, 359–61, 424, 431
Rayleigh, John William Strutt, 3rd Baron, 94, 107, 341
Red Cross, 439
Redemption of Tycho Brahe, The (Brod), 179, 579
Refugee Assistance Fund, 609
Reich, Wilhelm, 689–90
Reichenbach, Hans, 127, 343
Reichinstein, David, 85, 218, 498
Reign of Relativity, The (Haldane), 337
Reiser, Anton, *see* Kayser, Rudolf
Relativitätsprinzip, Das (Laue), 383
"Relativitätsprinzip und die aus demselben gezogenen Folgerungen" (Einstein), 151
Relativity, General Theory of
attempt to test in Crimea (1914), 251, 261
attitude of Nazi authorities to, 572–73, 637–40
confirmation of, 285–91
and cosmology, 262, 265–71, 651
Einstein's first paper on, 198
Einstein's main paper on, 252–54
genesis of, 150–57
principles of, 253–55
test of during eclipse expeditions (1919), 263–65, 284–88
test of during eclipse expeditions (1922), 370–72
worldwide reaction to, 217, 295–308
other references, 66, 79, 131, 158, 169, 199–200, 203, 206, 216, 223–24, 238, 241, 251–71, 275, 363, 381, 401, 419–20, 492–93, 525, 589, 735, 744, 756–57
Relativity, Special Theory of
background to and genesis of, 41–42, 102–16, 127–32
Einstein's first paper on, 74, 101, 116–17
mass-energy equation, 132–35
Minkowski's contribution to, 157–59
principle of, 116–25
reactions to, 141–43
results of acceptance of, 125–26, 135–37
other references, 30, 32, 54, 60, 84, 101–38, 144, 151–54, 156–58, 197–99, 253, 275, 363, 492, 526, 589, 691, 702, 754, 756
Relativity: The Special and the General Theory (Einstein), 383

Religion
Einstein and, 25, 35–37, 62, 516, 517
relativity and, 502, 503
"Religion and Science" (article, Einstein), 516
Renan, Ernest, 353, 354
Report on the Relativity Theory of Gravitation (Eddington), 264, 383
Reporter, The, 726
Republican League, 328, 465
Reuss, 33
Reuter, Ernst, 231
Reuterdahl, Arvid, 509
"Revolution in Science, The" (*Times* article), 297
Revue des Deux Mondes (Nordmann), 352
Rhodes Lectures (Oxford), 528
Ricci, C. G., 177, 254, 262
Riemann, Georg Friedrich Bernhard, 79, 157, 255
Rikitaio, Fujisawa, 369
Ringer, Fritz, 226
Riverside Church (New York), 520
Robb, A. A., 302
Rolland, Romain, 232, 236–38, 245, 246, 452, 596
Roosevelt, Franklin D., 332, 396, 445, 511, 623–26, 667, 668, 672–74, 677, 678, 680–82, 685, 688, 691, 694, 699, 705, 707, 712, 752, 764
Roosevelt, Mrs. Franklin D., 624, 628, 707
Rosen, Nathan, 649, 651, 655
Rosen, Pinhas, 499
Rosenbach, Abraham S. Wolf, 559
Rosenblueth, Felix, *see* Rosen, Pinhas
Rosenfeld, L., 410, 670
Rosenheim, Johann, 157
Rosenthal-Schneider, Ilse, 287
Roszel, Alberta, 764
Rotblat, J., 761
Rothenburg, Dr. von, 366
Rothenstein, William, 263, 342
Rothschild, Lionel Walter, 2nd Baron, 341, 515
Roughton Heath (Norfolk), 602, 608
Rouse Ball Lecture (Cambridge), 541
Royal Aircraft Establishment (Farnborough), 211, 251
Royal Albert Hall, Einstein speaks at, 601, 608–12
Royal Astronomical Society (London), 261–62, 284–86, 289, 305, 338, 340, 372
Royal Geographical Society, 264
Royal Society, 284, 289, 298, 305, 311, 372
Rubens, Otto, 162, 184, 212, 214, 311, 321
Ruhr, Germany, French occupation of, 280, 436–38
Russell, Bertrand A. W., 3rd Earl
relationship with Einstein, 687
on U.S.S.R., 714–15
other references, 53, 117–18, 124, 152, 347
Russell-Einstein Declaration, 757–61
Rust, Bernard, 562, 570–71
Rutherford, Ernest, 1st Baron Rutherford of Nelson, 38, 58, 135, 138, 157, 172, 184, 185, 196, 200, 201–2, 261, 279, 300, 313, 323, 377, 393–94, 401, 406, 418, 475, 582, 607–11, 619, 652, 655, 660–63, 719, 724
Rutherford-Bohr model, 202–3

Sachs, Alexander, 673–81, 720, 721
Sailing, Einstein and, 50, 141, 379, 633–34, 635
Salaman, Esther, 392
Salzburg, Germany, 162, 163, 164
Sampson, R. A., 345
Samuel, Herbert Louis, 1st Viscount
relationship with Einstein, 476
other references, 20, 35, 107, 222, 415, 479, 514, 576, 579
Sanderson, Thomas Henry, 1st Baron, 339
Sanehiko, Yamamoto, 367
Saranac Lake, 646, 708
Sauter, Joseph, 75, 115
Schaffhausen, Germany, 68
Scheidemann, Philipp, 352, 565
Schemberger, 311
Schenk, J. Heinrich, 70
Schonland, Sir Basil, 94, 95, 118, 412–13
Schrödinger, Erwin, 98, 309, 409–12, 416, 418, 580, 628, 629, 640, 721
Schwarz, Paul, 519, 561–62, 633

Schwarzschild, Karl, 225, 259
Schweitzer, Albert, 753–54
Sciama, D. W., 151–52
Science, 669, 678
Science of Mechanics, The (Mach), 60, 105
Scientific American, 307
Seefeld, Austria, 702
Seeley, Evelyn, 557, 564
Seelig, Carl, 82–83, 115, 129–30, 185, 669, 744–45
Seiff Institute (Palestine), 607
Sengier, Edgar, 666
Shankland, R. S., 114, 128–29
Shapley, Harlow, 560, 641, 688
Shaw, George Bernard, 339, 514
Sheen, Archbishop Fulton, 517
Sherrington, Sir Charles Scott, 333
Shirer, William, 571
Shoemaker, F. H., 626
Silliman Lectures, 95–96
Simon, Hugo, 230–31
Sinclair, Upton, 522, 571
Sirius, 401
Sitter, Willem de, 269–71, 282, 301, 523, 524, 540
Skillings, Edward, 382
Slipher, V. M., 523
Smythe Report, 709, 712
Snow, C. P., 140, 190–91
Sobral (Northern Brazil), 285, 286
Société Française de Physique, 195, 355
Society for Social Responsibility in Science, 759
Solovine, Maurice
  correspondence with Einstein, 446, 481, 502, 574, 580, 648, 743
  first meeting with Einstein, 78–79
  other references, 80, 85, 115, 223, 352, 356, 361, 369
Solvay, Ernest, 161, 183, 278
Solvay Congress
  1st, 183–86, 189, 210, 661
  2nd, 279
  3rd, 279
  4th, 279, 280
  5th, 281, 416–18
  6th, 416, 419
Sommerfeld, Arnold, 89, 162, 169, 216, 252, 280, 311, 319, 321–24, 346, 348, 378, 384, 400, 581, 729
Sorbonne, 355
South America, Einstein visits, 399, 403
South German Monthly, 324
Southern California College Student Body Presidents' Association, 554
"Space and Time" (lecture, Minkowski), 157, 160, 162
Space, Time and Gravitation (Eddington), 301, 383
Spain, Einstein visits, 370
Spencer, Herbert, 337, 481, 757
Spieker, 34
Spinoza, Benedict, 38, 79, 502–3, 726
Spiritism: The Hidden Secret in Einstein's Theory of Relativity, 385
Squire, Sir John, 336
Stamfordham, Lord, 338
Star Shell, 692
Stark, Johannes, 77, 509, 638
Statistical mechanics, 89, 91, 96, 138, 395
Stein, Leonard, 457
Steinig, Leon, 442–44
Steinitz, Martha, 447
Steinmetz, Charles, 210
Stellar Movements and the Structure of the Universe (Eddington), 262
Stern, Alfred, 67
Stern, Otto
  with Einstein in Prague, 177
  during First World War, 225
  leaves Germany for U.S., 639
  and nuclear weapons, 697
  other references, 192, 640, 700, 705
Stockholm, Sweden, 364
Stolper, Gustav, 673
Strassman, Fritz, 664
Strauss, Ernest, 516, 745
Strauss, Lewis, 740
Struck, Hermann, 460
"Study Group of German Natural Philosophers," 317–19, 324–25, 328, 466
Stürgkh, Count Karl, 240, 612
"Suggested Draft Letter to Professor Einstein" (Weizmann), 720
Sun, bending of light rays by
  confirmation of (1919), 283–91
  suggested by Einstein (1911), 181–83, 206
Sunday Express, 602

Svizzera Polytecnica Federale (SPF), *see* ETH
Swing, Raymond Gram, 712
Swiss Federal Institute of Technology (FIT), *see* ETH
Swiss Federal Observatory, 63
Swiss Federal Polytechnic School, *see* ETH
Swiss *Gazette*, 70
Swiss Patent Office, Berne
  Einstein joins, 70–71
  Einstein leaves, 166
  Einstein's work at, 74–76
  other references, 67–69, 72–74, 144
Swiss Society of Natural Sciences, 207
Szilard, Leo
  and Academic Assistance Council, 575–76
  chain reaction, nuclear, 663–64, 667, 668, 679
  and Einstein's letter to Roosevelt (1939), 673–77
  and Einstein's letter to Roosevelt (1945), 705–7
  Einstein-Szilard heat pump, 396
  first contacts with Einstein, 395
  leaves Germany, 640
  other references, 25, 34, 608, 654–55, 665, 666, 672, 682, 696, 701, 714, 716–17, 720, 721, 724, 759

Tablet, The, 137, 686
Tagore, Rabindranath, 503, 504
Talmey, Max, 33, 74, 256
Tanner, Hans, 179
Tarner Lectures, 309
Tassin, M., 279
Taub, A. H., 493
Tel Aviv, Israel, 477, 479, 483
Teller, Edward, 640, 673, 677, 696
"Theory of Radiation, The" (lectures, Einstein), 150
Thermodynamics, 77, 91, 96
"Thermodynamics in Einstein's Thought" (Klein), 77
Thibaud, Jean, 97
Thirring, Hans, 134
Thomas, Norman, 555–56, 715, 726
Thomson, Sir Joseph, J., 57–58, 92, 95–96, 111, 132, 156, 157, 201, 211, 290, 298, 301, 323, 333, 338–39, 406, 523, 619, 660–61, 753
Thurring, Bruno, 639
Times, The (London), 101, 131, 290, 295–98, 344, 356, 370, 371, 496, 507, 591, 614
Times Educational Supplement, 307
Tizard, Sir Henry, 666–68, 671
Tokyo University, 367
Tolman, Richard Chase, 515, 523, 526, 556
Toynbee, Arnold, 532
Trevelyan, George, 608
Tristram Shandy (Sterne), 239
Trotter, Wilfred, 598
Trowbridge, A., 441
Truman, Harry S, 707
Tschernowitz, Chaim, 247, 504
Tschisherrin, Georgÿ, 373
Tübingen University, 311
Tuchschmid, August, 45
"Two percent" (speech, Einstein), 521, 527, 552

Über die Hypotheseen, welche der Geometrie zu Grunde liegen (Reimann), 255
Über Relativitätsprinzip, Aether, Gravitation (Lenard), 383
Uexküll, Margarete, 397–98
Uhlenbeck, G. E., 666
Ulbricht, Walter, 731
Ulm, Germany
  Einstein's birth at, 20, 23
  Einsteinstrasse renamed, 562
  street named after Einstein, 312, 370
Uncertainty principle, 411, 415–18, 652
UNESCO, 264, 429
Unified field theory
  Einstein's first paper on, 493–96
  other references, 381, 393, 400, 491, 497, 505, 573, 650–51, 659, 670, 681, 711, 742–45
Union Minière, 666, 668
Union of Soviet Socialist Republics
  Einstein on, 548, 713–15
  Russell on, 714
United Nations, 429, 713
United Nations World, 715
U.S. Minerals Yearbook, 696
U.S. Navy, Bureau of Ordnance, 692–94
U.S. Office of Scientific Research

and Development, 667, 682, 684, 692
University of California at Los Angeles, 552
Uranium, fission of, 660, 664–65
Urey, Harold, 683–85, 707, 716
Ussishkin, Menachem, 478–79
Utrecht University, 187–90

Vallentin, Antonina, 51–52, 388, 512, 646
Van der Pohl, B., 288
Vanity Fair, 358
Van't Hoff, Jacobus Hendrikus, 213, 224
Vavilov, Sergei, 715
Veblen, Oswald, 513, 560
Vevey, Switzerland, 233, 237
Vienna, Austria
  Einstein lectures in (1913), 199
  Einstein lectures in (1921), 332
Vienna Circle, 177
Voigt, W., 121
Völkischer Beobachter, 518, 556, 573, 599
Volksrecht, 172
Vulcan, 258

Wahrheit, Die, 428
Wallace, Alfred Russell, 102, 524
Walter, Bruno, 562
Walton, Ernest Thomas Sinton, 363, 662, 663
War crimes, German, Einstein's investigation of, 272, 277, 278, 281
War Resisters International, 448, 452, 548, 591, 596
War Resisters League, 528
Warburg, Emil, 212, 214
Watch Hill, Rhode Island, 632–34
Watson, Edwin M., 677, 680
Watt Anniversary Lecture, 663
Watters, Leon
  first meeting with Einstein, 553–54
  relationship with Einstein, 630–33, 657–58
  other references, 219, 620, 625, 634–36, 644–47, 654, 752
Watters, Mrs. Leon, 646
Wave mechanics, 309, 407–10, 411, 418, 419
Weber, Heinrich, 54, 55, 59, 61, 69
Weber, Wilhelm, 638
Weisskopf, Victor, 640, 717–19
Weizmann, Chaim
  correspondence with Einstein, 479, 481, 484–85, 488, 489, 546, 547, 582–85, 631
  death of, 748–49
  early life of, 462
  Hebrew University and, 483–86, 577–79, 584–87
  Jewish Agency and, 488
  post-war plan for inviting Einstein to Palestine, 719–21
  relationship with Einstein, 463–64
  visits U.S. with Einstein, 468–75
  other references, 52, 185, 378, 455, 457, 464–67, 515, 528, 559, 576, 588, 607, 751
Weizmann, Vera, 52, 468, 515
Weizsäcker, C. F. von, 676, 678–79, 704
Wells, H. G., 450, 474, 514, 597
Wertheimer, Max, 250, 271, 466
Westernland (ship), 613, 614
Weyl, Hermann, 169, 275, 358, 383, 493, 496, 544, 607, 743, 753
Weyland, Paul, 317–21
Where Is Science Going? (Planck), 162
White House (Washington, D.C.), 623–26
Whitehead, Alfred North, 289–90, 307, 339, 342, 345
Whittaker, Sir Edmund Taylor, 130, 256
Whittle, Frank, 118
Why War? (Einstein-Freud), 445–46
Whyte, Lancelot Law, 507–8
Wien, Wilhelm, 57, 94, 141, 145, 162, 185
Wigner, Eugene P., 640, 668–69, 671–73, 677, 679, 680–81, 696
Wilhelm II, Emperor of Germany, 218, 231, 234, 236, 249, 496
Wilhelmina, H. M. Queen of the Netherlands, 398
Wilkinson, Ellen, 600–1
Willard Gibbs Lecture, 654
Williams, W. H., 401
Willstatter, Richard, 225
Windt, 188
Wings Over Europe, 663
Winteler, Anna, *see* Besso, Mrs. Michelangelo

Winteler, Jost, 45
Winteler, Paul, 82, 209
Winteler, Mrs. Paul, *see* Einstein, Maja
Winterthur Technical School, 67
Wise, Stephen, 472, 570, 586
Witkowski, 142
Wolf, M., 321
Wolfer, Alfred, 54, 63
Women's International League for Peace and Freedom, 446
Wood, R. W., 94–95
World as I See It, The (Einstein), 430, 587
World Committee for the Victims of German Fascism, 600
World Congress of Intellectuals, 723
World Court, 443
World government, 428, 713–17, 721
World Union of Jewish Students, 612

Yahuda, Abraham Shalom, 579

Zangger, Heinrich, 233, 235, 246
Zeeman, Pieter, 473
Zeitschrift für Physik, 409
Zionism
  birth of, 455, 456
  Einstein and, 19–20, 168, 178–79, 247, 272, 277, 296, 308, 330–31, 334, 350, 373, 377, 378, 455–90
  other references, 177, 518, 519, 549, 751
Zionist Congress, 1st (Basel), 456
Zionist Congress, 7th (Basel), 456
Zionist Congress, 16th (Zurich), 486–88
Zionist Federation of Germany, 562
Zionist Organization of America, 585
Zuoz, Switzerland, 424
Zurich, Switzerland, 41, 44, 49–50, 169, 195
Zurich, University of, 68, 86, 164–72, 188–89, 275–76
Zurich Polytechnic, *see* ETH
Zurich Student Union, 358
Zweig, Arnold, 556